D1612398

OOK OF
CLINICAL
INTERVIEWING
WITH CHILDREN

HANDBOOK OF
CLINICAL
INTERVIEWING
WITH CHILDREN

Edited by

MICHEL HERSEN
Pacific University

JAY C. THOMAS
Pacific University

SAGE Publications
Los Angeles • London • New Delhi • Singapore

For information:

Sage Publications, Inc.
2455 Teller Road
Thousand Oaks, California 91320
E-mail: order@sagepub.com

Sage Publications Ltd.
1 Oliver's Yard
55 City Road
London EC1Y 1SP
United Kingdom

Sage Publications India Pvt. Ltd.
B 1/I 1 Mohan Cooperative Industrial Area
Mathura Road, New Delhi 110 044
India

Sage Publications Asia-Pacific Pte. Ltd.
33 Pekin Street #02-01
Far East Square
Singapore 048763

Printed in the United States of America.

Library of Congress Cataloging-in-Publication Data

Handbook of clinical interviewing with children / editors, Michel Hersen and Jay C. Thomas.
    p. cm.
Includes bibliographical references and index.
ISBN 978-1-4129-1718-6 (cloth : alk. paper)
    1. Interviewing in child psychiatry. 2. Mental illness—Diagnosis. 3. Interviewing in mental health.
I. Hersen, Michel. II. Thomas, Jay C., 1951-
[DNLM: 1. Interview, Psychological—methods. 2. Child. 3. Mental Disorders—diagnosis.
WS 105 H2357 2007]

RJ503.6.H3669 2007
618.92'89—dc22

2007004817

This book is printed on acid-free paper.

07   08   09   10   11   10 9 8 7 6 5 4 3   2 1

Acquisitions Editor:	Cheri Dellelo
Editorial Assistant:	Anna Mesick
Project Editor:	Tracy Alpern
Copy Editor:	Carla Freeman
Typesetter:	C&M Digitals (P) Ltd.
Proofreader:	Sally Jaskold
Cover Designer:	Edgar Abarca
Marketing Associate:	Amberlyn Erzinger

CONTENTS

PREFACE

The *Handbook of Clinical Interviewing With Children* and the companion *Handbook of Clinical Interviewing With Adults* have been designed by the editors to be the most comprehensive work in the area published to date. Indeed, in our review of existing literature on interviewing, we were not able to find any comparable work of this magnitude and scope. Thus, we see these two volumes as a pragmatic resource for interviewers, in general, and as a specific resource to be used by course instructors for teaching clinical interviewing with adults and children.

The *Handbook of Clinical Interviewing With Children* is organized into three parts: Part I: General Issues, Part II: Specific Disorders, and Part III: Special Populations and Issues. The three parts of this volume were specifically selected to deal, respectively, with the general and theoretical, the pragmatic with respect to diagnostic entities, and the more unusual with respect to special populations. Part I, "General Issues," includes nine chapters: Overview of Interviewing Strategies, Unstructured Interviewing, Structured and Semistructured Diagnostic Interviews, Developmental Issues, Mental Status Examination, Multicultural and Diversity Issues, Dealing With School Systems and Teachers, Selecting Treatment Targets and Referrals, and Writing Up the Intake Interview. Part II, "Specific Disorders," includes 10 chapters, with a generally consistent format across chapters to the extent possible, as dictated by the relevant data, including sections on Description of the Disorder or Problem, Interviewing Strategies, Interviewing Obstacles and Solutions, Interviewing Parents and Teachers, Case Illustration, Multicultural and Diversity Issues, Differential Diagnosis and Behavioral Assessment, Selection of Treatment Targets and

Referral, and a Summary. This approach was designed to serve as a pedagogic tool and, we believe, should facilitate the work of both teachers and students, given its pragmatic focus. None of the competing volumes on child interviewing handles the material in this fashion. Finally, in Part III, "Special Populations and Issues," topics given short shrift in all prior books on the topic are presented in five chapters: Neglected, Physically Abused, and Sexually Abused Children; Habit Disorders: Tics, Trichotillomania; Juvenile Firesetting; Enuresis and Encopresis; and Sleep Disorders.

Recognizing that instructors using this handbook may decide to assign selected chapters to their students due to course requirements and time limitations, we have not attempted to remove any minor duplication of material that may occur across chapters. To the contrary, for the specific disorders and problems and special topics, we see each chapter as representing the most up-to-date thinking in the area with respect to interviewing strategies.

Many individuals have contributed to the fruition of this handbook. First, we thank our eminent contributors, who agreed to share their expertise with us. Second, we thank Linda James and Carole Londerée for their invaluable editorial assistance and sense of timing. Third, we thank Cynthia Polance, Heidi Meeke, and Christopher Brown for their assistance with the indices. And finally, we thank the editorial staff at Sage Publications for all of their efforts. In particular, the inestimable contribution of our copy editor, Carla Freeman, has earned our appreciation beyond words.

Michel Hersen
Jay C. Thomas
Portland, Oregon

PART I

GENERAL ISSUES

1

Overview of Interviewing Strategies With Children, Parents, and Teachers

Manuela Villa and David Reitman

The interview is the bedrock of applied clinical psychology and continues to be the most commonly used evaluation method across subspecialty areas, theoretical models, and diagnostic categories (Busse & Rybski Beaver, 2000). A sampling of reviews reveals the multifaceted nature of clinical interviewing. Clinical interviews often serve as the foundation of the information-gathering process leading to the confirmation of diagnosis status (Dawson, 2005). More broadly, clinical interviews have been regarded as "setting the tone" for subsequent interactions between the client and clinician (Hersen, 2004; House, 2002; Sarwer & Sayers, 2004). Others have viewed interviewing as a vehicle for facilitating conceptualization, problem formation, and, ultimately, the delivery of effective treatment (Turner, Hersen, & Heiser, 2003). For example, clinical interviews can assist in the identification of potential barriers to treatment, as well as facilitate rapport building (Boggs, Griffin, & Gross, 2003). Commenting on the challenges facing interviewers, Sharp, Reeves, and Gross (2006) note that therapists must convey empathy and understanding while simultaneously extricating information pertinent to the larger purpose of the interview. Faust (1998) describes the clinical interview as analogous to a tightly choreographed dance in which the therapist guides the interviewee through a series of intricate steps.

In the present chapter, we provide an overview of the major interviewing issues confronting professionals working with children, adolescents, and their families. We first discuss types of clinical interviews as well as the impact of theoretical models on interviewing. The remainder of the chapter concerns itself with general recommendations for child interviewers, as well as illustrating the role of the clinical interview in facilitating a comprehensive multimethod assessment. Finally, we discuss special considerations for conducting child, parent, and teacher interviews, including the consideration of cultural factors and training issues.

Types of Interviews

One of the most enduring methods for distinguishing between interviews has been to focus on the relative flexibility of the interview (i.e., the extent to which questions can be altered or dropped or the sequence of information gathered can be changed) (Bloomquist & Schnell, 2002; Busse & Rybski Beaver, 2000; Greenspan & Thorndike-Greenspan, 2003; McConaughy, 2000; Orvaschel, 2006). At their most structured, diagnostic interviews explore relatively circumscribed topics (e.g., reported symptoms and history related to symptoms) and provide users with a standardized method for eliciting information. Such interviews are often used to assign children or adolescents to categories described in the *Diagnostic and Statistical Manual of Mental Disorders, Fourth Edition, Text Revision (DSM-IV-TR)* (American Psychiatric Association, 2000). Structured interviews are considered very useful for promoting the acquisition of a consistent set of information, specifying the onset and duration of symptoms, as well as providing information about comorbidity. Although structured interviews maximize diagnostic reliability, they often yield only limited information about family, peer, and contextual factors and may compromise rapport (Reitman, Hummel, Franz, & Gross, 1998).

Unstructured interviews allow for maximum flexibility in information gathering, potentially greater focus on problems considered relevant by the child or family, and assessment of a broader range of clinical information (e.g., family functioning, peer relations). The only real constraints on unstructured interviews are imposed by the interviewer's theoretical model and practical considerations, such as obtaining demographic information for clerical functions. Unfortunately, unstructured interviews can lead to inconsistent or incomplete diagnostic formulations with very poor psychometric qualities (e.g., low reliability; see Jensen & Weisz, 2002). For this reason, some reviewers recommend that unstructured interviews be used only in combination with other data (Bloomquist & Schnell, 2002).

Finally, semistructured interviews provide for flexibility within a standard format. Typically, a framework and specific questions are provided, but additional queries may be employed as needed. Interviewers utilizing semistructured interviews should be skilled in the nonspecific, clinical aspects of interviewing (e.g., session management) for both unstructured and semistructured interviews, as the lack of structure may prove overwhelming to novice therapists. Obviously, the various interview formats may be combined to obtain the range and depth of information needed for individualized assessment and treatment. Discussion and review of the most commonly used interviews appear in Chapter 2 (O'Brien & Tabaczynski) and Chapter 3 (Nock, Holmberg, Photos, & Michel). Table 1.1 provides an overview of each interview's advantages and disadvantages.

Busse and Rybski Beaver (2000) propose an alternative interview classification system based on the level of information that the interview is designed to obtain. According to this model, there are three types of interviews: omnibus, behavior specific, and problem solving. *Omnibus interviews* are designed for gathering a wide range of information, with relatively little depth

TABLE 1.1   **Advantages and Disadvantages of the General Interview Formats**

	Advantages	*Disadvantages*
Structured	• Maximizes reliability and validity • Minimizes interviewer bias • Produces consistent data • Specifies symptom onset and duration	• Focus on diagnosis, not intervention • Requires extensive training • Gathers limited information on nondiagnostic factors
Unstructured	• Highly flexible • Allows tailoring to individual needs • Helpful in problem conceptualization and treatment planning	• Minimal structure may lead to problems with reliability and validity • Comparison between unstructured interviews is difficult • Requires high level of interviewing skills
Semistructured	• Allows flexibility while maintaining a standard format • Provides a framework • Allows for follow-up as needed	• Weak reliability and validity

(e.g., developmental histories). Such interviews are helpful in generating hypotheses, because information concerning a functioning across a wide range of domains may be gathered. Omnibus interviews can be time-consuming, however, and may lack the detail needed to design effective interventions. *Behavior-specific interviews* (e.g., teacher interviews for a child's academic problems) provide more comprehensive information about a limited number of problems. The use of narrowly focused, behavior-specific interviews at the time of initial referral, however, may increase the risk of misdiagnosis. Finally, *problem-solving interviews* focus on the development of a range of intervention strategies. Compared with the behavior-specific interviews, problem-solving interviews are more exploratory in nature and emphasize the process of "problem definition." In practical terms, problem-solving interviews employ behavior-specific interviewing techniques as one component of the broader interviewing process (Busse & Rybski Beaver, 2000).

Theoretical Models and Interviewing

"To intervene without an underlying theoretical framework is akin to building a house without a foundation" (Orvaschel, Faust, & Hersen, 2001, p. 6). Conceptual models guide the interviewing process, diagnostic procedures, and progression of treatment. Conceptual models also influence the interviewer's and the client's therapeutic roles as well as the establishment of treatment goals (Sharf, 2000).

Person-centered and psychodynamic approaches have historically been associated with nondirective interviewing styles that place greater emphasis on listening techniques. Within the nondirective approach, interviewers encourage clients to speak freely about their concerns, with minimal structure or direction, although the reasons for this are somewhat different within dynamic and person-centered models (Sommers-Flanagan & Sommers-Flanagan, 2003). For example, client-centered therapists posit that the likelihood of change is maximized when clients are allowed to freely express their thoughts and emotions in an accepting and empathic environment characterized by unconditional positive regard (Bohart, 1995).

Traditional psychodynamic interviews emphasize the importance of free association, allowing unconscious conflicts to emerge into consciousness. An underlying assumption of most dynamic interviewing approaches is that direct assessment of psychological problems is unlikely to be fruitful because clients lack the ability to directly access the unconscious conflicts responsible for their suffering. In addition, when interviews are conducted directly with young children, many dynamically oriented assessors emphasize the use of projective techniques, such as doll play and drawing. When working with children and adolescents, nondirective therapists utilize play as the primary mode of assessment and treatment, since children's ability to verbalize emotions is considered to be limited (Panichelli & Kendall, 1995).

Behavioral and cognitive-behavioral interviewing have typically been regarded as more structured than dynamic and person-centered approaches; however, all approaches emphasize the need for assessors to facilitate a collaborative relationship with the client (Sharp et al., 2006). In addition to obtaining information about the antecedents and consequences of the behaviors targeted for change, clinicians may also seek information about maladaptive thinking and behavioral patterns that may be contributing to the maintenance of psychological problems. In each case, care must be taken to consider the developmental level of the child and unique cultural and socioeconomic factors that affect families (Sharp et al., 2006). Behavioral interviews are sometimes viewed as puzzle-solving exercises, facilitated by the conduct of a functional behavioral assessment of the presenting problem (Boggs et al., 2003; Morganstern, 1976; Sparzo, 1999; Sulzer-Azaroff & Mayer, 1991). Once completed, the behavioral interview should yield a clear definition of the problem behaviors and identify the factors that may be contributing to or maintaining these behaviors (Reitman et al., 1998). Cognitive-behavioral approaches to interviewing, particularly those involving internalizing disorders, place relatively greater emphasis on identifying problematic cognitions that may contribute to the development and maintenance of problem behavior (Woodruff-Borden & Leyfer, 2006).

Family therapy models are extremely diverse, perhaps as diverse theoretically as psychology as a whole. As noted by Kaslow and Celano (1995), "There is not one brand of family therapy"

(p. 354); thus, it is difficult to describe a set of unique interviewing strategies associated with the approach. Generally, however, key areas of concern in family therapies are family interactions and communication strategies, as opposed to the problem behaviors of a specific child (i.e., the identified patient) (Goldenberg & Goldenberg, 2002). Consequently, the interviewing strategies of family therapists tend to focus attention on family processes and relations rather than on the presence or absence of diagnostic signs or indicators of psychopathology (Kaslow & Celano, 1995).

GENERAL INTERVIEWING GUIDELINES

Regardless of theoretical orientation, effective interviewers must develop a broad knowledge of psychopathology, excellent organizational skills, the ability to convey empathy, and a high degree of self-awareness (Turner et al., 2003). Knowledge of psychopathology and the current diagnostic nomenclature is paramount to the proper evaluation of the information obtained in the clinical interview. Social skills and sensitivity are needed to foster cooperation and trust. Good interviewers possess strong communication skills and,

perhaps most important, the ability to listen. Effective listening involves hearing *what* the informant says as well as *how* they say it (e.g., tone of voice, hesitation, emphasis, inconsistencies). Effective listening also requires the interviewer to note what is *not* said by the informant, conveying both empathy and an understanding of the unreported content (Dawson, 2005). Finally, session management skills are needed. Interviewers must estimate how long the interview will take, assess whether or not the interview is proceeding at an appropriate pace, and complete the interview in the allotted time (see Table 1.2).

Although there are few formal "standards" for conducting an initial interview, a consensus is emerging (Sarwer & Sayers, 2004). Most interviews begin with a discussion of the presenting concerns. The initial query is usually open-ended, such as "What brings you here today?" or, if conducted with a child, "What did your parents tell you about coming here?" What happens following the invitation to talk depends a great deal on one's theoretical orientation.

For the purposes of the present overview, we focus on techniques and considerations relevant to behavioral interviewing and note, where appropriate, how interviewing from within other models may diverge. For example, within

TABLE 1.2   Basic Interviewing Skills

Basic Skills	Definition
1. Knowledge	• Comprehensive foundation in psychopathology and diagnostic classification • Understanding of typical versus abnormal development • Awareness of the influence of development on symptom presentation • Awareness of the influence of culture and ethnicity on symptom manifestation and attitudes towards treatment • Knowledge of interview conduction processes
2. Empathy	• The ability to perceive and understand the client's feelings as if the therapist were experiencing them
3. Validation	• The ability to use verbal and nonverbal (e.g., facial expressions, body gestures) strategies to convey the communication of empathy
4. Therapist language	• The ability to formulate questions in a clear and comprehensive manner without the use of clinical jargon and with consideration for the client's education level, life experiences, vocabulary, and language • Therapist language is the tool by which patients are guided in the specificity and clarity of their responses
5. Time management	• The ability to estimate how long the interview will take, assess whether pace is appropriate, and conduct the complete assessment in allotted time period

the behavioral model, problem definition is followed by an effort to elicit detailed information about the frequency of the difficulties, antecedents and consequences, and the context in which the problematic behavior occurs. Behavioral interviews rely heavily on parents and teachers or other significant adults for information about presenting problems (Boggs et al., 2003). Initial questions typically address the duration, frequency, and intensity of the behaviors. Further questioning focuses on determining the context in which the behavior is present (or absent) and the identification of behavior patterns across various settings (Morganstern, 1976; Schloss & Smith, 1998). A history of the presenting problem is also obtained. The session usually closes with a summary of what has been learned, a discussion of any additional information that is needed, and therapist acknowledgment of the family's effort to change. In less directive models, a more focused line of questioning about antecedents and consequences of problem behavior might be avoided in favor of rapport-building strategies described in this chapter and throughout the text. In family therapy, greater emphasis might be placed on obtaining multiple perspectives on "the problem" from each member of the family. As with the treatment, it is common for interviewers to blend techniques associated with different theoretical models.

One practical consideration in interviewing concerns who should be present during the interview (Busse & Rybski Beaver, 2000; Silverman & Saavedra, 2004). Interviewing parents and children together is common in both behavioral and family therapy models and yields important information about the parent-child relationship, in addition to providing an opportunity to explain the purpose of the interview to the child. When parents and children are interviewed jointly, interactions and communication patterns can be readily observed, and the therapist can obtain information about how family members relate to one another. In some cases, parents and children are asked to discuss difficult issues, and important communication patterns can be formally analyzed (Dishion & Kavanagh, 2003). Individual interviews with the child may provide an opportunity for rapport building and the discussion of sensitive topics that children may be unwilling to discuss in the presence of their parents.

Special Considerations When Interviewing Children

Multidimensional Assessment

Gathering information from both indirect and direct sources, as well as from multiple informants, is the cornerstone of effective diagnostic interviewing with children and adolescents, since obtaining information from multiple sources allows the formulation of a more comprehensive conceptualization of the presenting problem (Barkley, 1997; Bloomquist & Schnell, 2002; Morrison & Anders, 2001). Silverman and Saavedra (2004) regard the acquisition of multiple measures from those who know the child well as essential for both arriving at a correct diagnosis and formulating the appropriate treatment. Shapiro and Kratochwill (2000) regard the clinical interview as a form of indirect assessment, in contrast with direct measures that provide information in real time under "naturally occurring" conditions (e.g., self-monitoring). Specifically, indirect assessments consist of measures that provide information at times and places removed from the behavior and include clinical interviews and self/informant reports (including checklists and rating scales).

Child, parent, and teacher interviews are major components of contemporary child behavioral assessment (Boggs et al., 2003; Lentz & Wehmann, 1995; Reitman et al., 1998; Shapiro & Kratochwill, 2000). All sources of information are not created equal, however (Shapiro & Kratochwill, 2000). For example, parents can provide information about child and family history, demographics, family functioning (e.g., cohesion, stress level), behavioral concerns, and home contingencies. They also contribute their unique view of their child's strengths and weaknesses. Parents typically "know the child best"; however, teacher reports provide information about aspects of the child's academic or social behavior (e.g., peer relationships, academic abilities, social behavior) that the parents may be less familiar with (Bloomquist & Schnell, 2002). Furthermore, teacher reports are unique in that they are informed by the respondent's experience with many other children, which may facilitate normative comparisons. Although the agreement between parent and teacher reports tends to be low (Choudhury, Pimentel, & Kendall, 2003), the inconsistencies are thought to reflect the effect of contextual factors on a child's behavior rather than invalid or unreliable reports (Bloomquist & Schnell, 2002).

Child Development

Knowledge of normative developmental processes is vital for the assessment of childhood disorders (Boggs et al., 2003). To become capable of recognizing deviations from typical developmental patterns, child clinicians must familiarize themselves with normal development and the attainment of physical, cognitive, and emotional milestones in children. Knowledge of a child's developmental level is also essential for phrasing questions appropriately during the child interview (Powell & Lancaster, 2003). Another important developmental consideration is that childhood presentations of certain disorders may differ from adult presentations of the same conditions (Boggs et al., 2003). Differences may be apparent even from early childhood to adolescence. For example, infant depression (i.e., failure to thrive) may present in the form of feeding or sleeping problems, while school-age children with mood disorders may be more likely to exhibit irritability.

The Referral Source

Clinical interviewing is inevitably influenced by the referral source and nature of the referral question. Consideration of the role that the referral agent plays in the child's life along with careful specification of the purpose of the examination is an essential first step for interviewers (Faust, 1998). Children are almost always evaluated because of concerns raised by the adults responsible for their welfare (House, 2002). Because children rarely seek treatment voluntarily, it is not surprising that many appear resistant to efforts to interview them concerning their "problem" behavior. Consequently, a child or adolescent's reluctance or refusal to participate in the clinical interview must be dealt with in a way that elicits cooperation and enhances motivation. Many interviewers attempt to facilitate cooperation with the interview by educating the child about the purpose of the interview and by exploring the ways in which the evaluation may benefit the child and his or her family (House, 2002).

The Interview Setting

Interviews are conducted in a variety of settings (i.e., high stress, hospitals, crisis centers, schools, outpatient clinics), and each context requires special consideration. The interview setting may influence client expectations, the content of questioning, and the degree of cooperation that can be expected (Faust, 1998; Turner et al., 2003). For example, when interviews are conducted under high-stress conditions, such as following admission to an emergency shelter, clinicians often limit their interviews to the information needed to gauge the child's mental status or emotional state or to isolate the events leading up to the crisis. In such cases, therapists "settle" for data sufficient to render a provisional diagnosis and facilitate proper disposition of the case. Crisis situations supersede concerns about establishing a precise diagnosis. Instead, the purpose of the interview is to obtain the information needed to protect the child and family and minimize harm (Turner et al., 2003).

When assessing children and adolescents in the hospital or inpatient settings, privacy is likely to be compromised (Faust, 1998). Interviews often take place in the patient's room and may be interrupted by other personnel (e.g., nurses, social workers, physicians, etc.) who require contact with the patient. Under some circumstances, medical patients or their families may not have requested mental health services, and the referral is frequently the decision of the primary treating physician (Turner et al., 2003). Indeed, patients (and their families) who view themselves as being treated solely for medical conditions may find it hard to understand why a mental health professional was referred to them. In such cases, it is imperative for the interviewer to explain the nature of the consultation, state the referral source, and discuss the nature of the therapeutic relationship at the initial contact (Turner et al., 2003).

Despite the challenges associated with conducting sound clinical interviews across settings, several actions have been found to maximize the amount and accuracy of information obtained from children during interviews (Gabarino & Scott, 1989; Powell & Lancaster, 2003). A summary of recommendations for preparing the interview setting is presented in Table 1.3.

TABLE 1.3   Helpful Suggestions for Arranging Child Interview Settings

- Make the interview setting as relaxed and neutral as possible.
- Allow young children to explore the setting prior to beginning questioning.
- Use mats on the floor, to sit at the same level of a preschool child.
- Use child-sized tables and chairs for young children (5- to 6-year-olds) to facilitate drawing.
- Allow children to leave their seats occasionally.
- Sit at a diagonal (to the right or left of the child) instead of on the opposite side of the table. This will reduce the test-like quality of the setting.
- Prepare the room prior to the interview and minimize distractions.
- If possible, remove toys, games, or childlike objects from the room when interviewing adolescents.
- Provide manipulatives (e.g., clay or drawing materials) to ease children who show discomfort when talking.

PARTICULARS OF THE INTERVIEW SOURCE: CHILD, PARENT, AND TEACHER INTERVIEWS

Up until this point, we have focused on general issues related to interviewing. In the next section, we detail issues unique to obtaining clinical information from each of the most common sources of interview data: parents and teachers, and children and adolescents themselves.

Child Interview

Children are complex individuals who reveal information at their own pace and in their own words (Greenspan & Thorndike-Greenspan, 2003). Skilled interviewers must be able to obtain diagnostically relevant information from the child and gain the child's trust to maximize the likelihood of successful treatment outcome (Kratochwill & Shapiro, 2000; McConaughy, 2000). Child interviews permit direct observation of the child's behavior, affect, and interaction style and provide an opportunity to assess the child's perspective on his or her own problems and competencies. Specifically, Hughes and Baker (1990, as cited in McConaughy, 2000) proposed that several domains be assessed in the child interview, including activity level, attention span, impulsivity, distractibility, reactions to frustration and praise, responsiveness to limit setting, communicative competence, nervous mannerisms, range of emotional expression, and thought processes.

During the course of the interview, the clinician can gauge the feasibility of applying various interventions and compare the child's account with information obtained through other sources. For example, in the context of functional assessment (see O'Neill et al., 1997), children may be able to clarify questions concerning parent or

teacher reports of the likely antecedents and consequences of specific problem behaviors. Research has shown that children as young as 4 years old can provide information relevant for assessment and treatment purposes (Irwin & Johnson, 2005), but the accuracy and utility of the information reported by children varies by age, type of information sought, and manner in which the information is obtained (Bloomquist & Schnell, 2002). For instance, children tend to underreport externalizing symptoms, while they are important sources of information regarding covert antisocial behavior and internalizing symptoms.

Confidentiality. Establishing the limits of confidentiality and conditions under which confidentiality agreements must be broken is complex when children and adolescents are involved. First, clinicians must acknowledge that in most circumstances involving children under age 18, parents are "holders of the privilege" and thus have legal right to access the child's file and the information contained therein upon request. Second, obvious developmental differences between parents and children in the ability to comprehend the complex issues raised in discussion of confidentiality often dictate separate discussions of confidentiality. Third, even when adolescents are intellectually mature enough to understand that confidentiality must be violated when the child or others are in "imminent danger" or when therapists are compelled by court orders to produce notes or other information, there may still be reasons to carefully evaluate how confidentiality discussions are conducted. For example, an adolescent may have questions concerning when the therapist must break confidentiality that relates to drug use or sexual activity, where precisely what constitutes imminent danger is uncertain. If parents are present during the discussion of confidentiality, a child may not ask for clarification and instead choose to withhold information that would be essential for case formulation. Finally, the frequent reliance on collateral interviews in clinical work with children and adolescents requires that a more complex series of releases be obtained than is typical in adult therapy. As a result, the task of communicating one's therapeutic role and the complexity of confidentiality agreements can be magnified significantly.

To address the issues raised above, we typically hold separate discussions of confidentiality with children/adolescents and parents and then bring both parties together for a final agreement and clarification of any misunderstandings. With adolescents and their caretakers, we often find ourselves asking for substantial leeway (i.e., trust) in determining what constitutes imminent danger. We try to maximize the likelihood that adolescents will be forthcoming with information about their substance use and sexual activity, while ensuring that high-risk behavior carrying a strong probability of harm is reported to parents and other adults. Where the ethical or legal responsibilities concerning confidentiality are unclear, interviewers should consult the American Psychological Association (2002) ethical principles of psychologists and code of conduct. In many cases, it is also wise to consider obtaining additional supervision or professional consultation (Sommers-Flanagan & Sommers-Flanagan, 2003).

Building Rapport. In a social context where children are increasingly taught to be wary of strangers, building rapport may prove to be a challenge, especially with younger children. Rapport is considered essential to conducting a child interview and is associated with a greater likelihood that the child will produce useful clinical information (Irwin & Johnson, 2005). Child-interviewer rapport can be defined as "present" when the therapist is perceived as supportive, nonjudgmental, and child centered (Powell & Lancaster, 2003). Although many practitioners attempt to build rapport with children by asking them a series of focused questions, research has shown that it is more fruitful to ask nonfocused, open-ended questions (e.g., regarding an enjoyable activity) followed by minimal prompts intended to elicit further information (Powell & Lancaster, 2003). The open-ended nature of the initial query also serves as an opportunity to

assess the child's cognitive and linguistic levels, and it tends to enhance the quality and elaborateness of the child's subsequent responses. During the initial meeting, therapists are encouraged to interact informally with the child and steer away from more sensitive topics that may be addressed at another time or at the end of the session (Sattler, 1992).

According to Irwin and Johnson (2005), discussing children's interaction preferences with their parents prior to the child interview allows clinicians to identify factors that may facilitate children's comfort level in the interview setting. For instance, they caution clinicians about making assumptions regarding common preferences in children for rapport-building activities (e.g., drawing). In fact, communicating the purpose of the interview may be a more effective strategy for eliciting cooperation than drawing or other "ice-breaking" techniques (Siegal, 1991). Sattler (1998) recommends that clinicians clarify their roles and ask children what they know about the reasons for the interview, to ensure that misconceptions are clarified.

Questioning Strategies. Interviewers need to be flexible in their use of questioning strategies when interviewing children and adolescents. It is important that the child's cognitive-developmental level, language capabilities, and social interaction style be taken into account (McConaughy, 2000). In general, interviewers are advised to ask one question at a time and "follow the child's lead." As noted previously, the use of open-ended questions has been proven more effective than multiple specific questions in obtaining accurate, detailed information from children (McConaughy, 2000; Powell & Lancaster, 2003). It is important to note, however, that very young children tend to have difficulty responding to exclusively open-ended questions, and the structure provided by more direct questions and probes may also be beneficial. In general, it is helpful to begin with relatively simple queries to establish rapport and proceed with open-ended questions interspersed with direct questions to clarify responses.

Interviewers of children and adolescents should refrain from asking leading questions that could result in attempts to generate socially desirable or defensive responding. For example, interviewers should avoid "why" questions that may be perceived as accusations, threats, or tests of knowledge (McConaughy, 2000). One way to avoid this common error is to turn "why" questions into "what" questions (Hughes & Baker, 1990). For example, rather than asking a child, "Why did you hit your brother in the waiting room?" one might ask, "What happened between you and your brother in the waiting room?" "What" questions are more likely to yield information about the child's ability to problem solve, and they provide information about the child's ability to understand cause and effect.

Hughes and Baker (1990) also propose the use of multiple-choice options as a means to reduce response complexity. They note that this technique is particularly helpful when children have difficulty responding to open-ended questions regarding abstract concepts (e.g., feelings). Multiple-choice questions may also be used by the interviewer to probe sensitive issues in areas where the interviewer has acquired knowledge by interviewing collateral sources (e.g., parents and teachers).

Last, it is recommended that questions with obvious "right" answers be avoided, that children are given ample time to provide a response, and that the interviewer refrain from following every response by the child with another question (Hughes & Baker, 1990). Toward the end of the interview, it is helpful to readdress confidentiality limitations, in addition to briefly summarizing the content of the interview. Children should also be informed of any plans for additional interviews or scheduled assessments (McConaughy, 2000).

Parent and Teacher Interviews

Effective assessment incorporates multiple methods, individuals, and settings (Busse & Rybski Beaver, 2000). Because of the inherent limitations of interviewing children and adolescents, informant interviews play a crucial role in child assessment. For example, informant interviews provide vital information about the feasibility of potential interventions from the perspective of the adults who are likely to implement them (Lentz & Wehmann, 1995; Luiselli, 2002). When interviewing parents and teachers, the interviewer needs to cultivate a nonjudgmental attitude, being careful about conveying blame during a line of inquiry (Busse & Rybski Beaver, 2000). Interviewers may be able to enhance the interview by focusing questions on positive aspects of the child's behavior or techniques that

adults have found useful when interacting with the child (Boggs et al., 2003). Interviews can also be improved by encouraging adults to describe important events in the most objective and descriptive terms possible.

Interviews with parents and teachers require the basic interviewing skills mentioned earlier (e.g., active listening, observation). During the opening of the interview, it is recommended that the interviewer clearly define his or her role and discuss confidentiality issues. In addition, open-ended questioning tends to elicit more information at this stage (e.g., "Tell me about your concerns"). Drawing from several sources on interviewing skills, Busse and Rybski Beaver (2000) propose the acronym PACERS, a set of basic elements that should form the core of any informant interview: Paraphrasing, Attending, Clarifying, Eliciting, Reflecting, and Summarizing. Similarly, Dawson (2005) recommends that interviewers follow several steps when conducting a parent or teacher interview:

1. Establish rapport.

2. Begin with open-ended questions.

3. Identify the most salient concerns.

4. Develop precise descriptions by translating vague concerns into observable behaviors.

5. Generate hypotheses about what may be causing or maintaining the behavior of concern.

6. Develop an assessment plan.

7. Set a date to review assessment results.

Dawson (2005) notes a number of other considerations when interviewing teachers and parents. First, when speaking to teachers, time is always a concern. For this reason, an emphasis should be placed on identifying and elucidating the specific behaviors of concern, rather than rapport building or exploring broad issues. Instead, rapport is built by communicating awareness of the teacher's time constraints and multiple responsibilities. For instance, rapport may be established by conducting the interview in a convenient setting (e.g., at school or via telephone) and by presenting with a collaborative, colleague-to-colleague approach. Second, it has been shown that teachers tend to describe problem behaviors in terms of student traits (e.g., "lazy"). For this reason, it is important to translate these terms into language that clearly identifies the problematic behavior (e.g., "makes numerous mistakes on homework assignments"). Finally, when interviewing parents, their issues should be addressed first, even if the referral was made by another source (e.g., school teacher). It is recommended that parents be interviewed outside of school team meetings so that they have an opportunity to voice their concerns and increase the likelihood that they will perceive the clinician as the child's advocate.

INTERVIEWING STRATEGIES FOR THE THERAPIST-IN-TRAINING

One of the most salient events in a young clinician's career is the completion of the initial client interview (Hersen & Turner, 2003). Regardless of the degree of the young therapist's preparation, many approach the first interview with considerable anxiety. Fortunately, through exposure and practice, most clinicians-in-training ultimately demonstrate competency in acquiring diagnostic information and in learning the intricacies of building rapport and session management. Nevertheless, the beginning therapist can be distinguished from the more experienced professional in a variety of ways. For example, novice therapists have greater difficulty in limiting their use of jargon and nonfamiliar vocabulary, and they tend to self-disclose more during interviews (Faust, 1998). In addition, novice therapists tend to give more advice, presumably in an effort to "fix" the presenting problem. Novice therapists may also tend to probe superfluous issues too deeply and, conversely, may fail to explore or avoid important or sensitive topics. Although the assessment and intervention process may become manageable once the target behaviors are known and defined, inexperienced therapists may be uncertain about how to determine what the problem is (Morganstern, 1976). Chapter 8 (Soler-Baillo & Marx) in this volume provides guidance for those seeking to enhance their ability to select treatment targets.

Sommers-Flanagan and Sommers-Flanagan (2003) establish some practical guidelines that can alleviate some of the anxiety and increase the likelihood that the interview experience will be satisfactory for both the novice therapist and the interviewee:

1. Know yourself: You are the instrument through which you listen to and respond to clients, so be aware of your biases, style, and physical presence.

2. Know your terrain: Be able to set up an interviewing environment where your clients feel comfortable.

3. Know how to listen: Listen with all of your senses and let your client know (through your responses) that you are listening.

4. Practice: Only through direct interviewing experience will you become an expert in applying the basic interviewing principles.

5. Learn how to prioritize information: Gain the ability to sort through all available (verbal and nonverbal) material to focus on the important clinical issues.

6. Apply your evaluation and interviewing skills in a variety of settings.

7. Know how to troubleshoot: Be familiar with diagnostic symptoms and concepts so that you can determine the needs of your patient.

MULTICULTURAL ISSUES IN INTERVIEWING

Ethnic-minority children constitute the most rapidly growing segment of the U.S. population, and increased awareness regarding the provision of "culturally competent" services has become a goal of mental health practitioners (Quintana, Castillo, & Zamarripa, 2000). Cultural competency is a complex construct consisting of three domains: (1) the attitudes/beliefs domain—awareness of one's own biases, values, and attitudes; (2) the knowledge domain—understanding of the client's worldviews; and (3) the skills domain—the ability to develop and utilize culturally sensitive intervention strategies and techniques (Sue & Sue, 2003).

Fontes (2005) offers an ecosystemic framework as a means for professionals to integrate individual, cultural, and environmental factors into the interviewing process. According to Fontes (2005), children and families who present for treatment are nestled in a social and material context that is highly interconnected. The most intimate domain is occupied by the individual child, followed by the child's home and family, the ethnic culture, the proximal social system (e.g., neighborhood, school, treatment providers, peers), and the wider social system (e.g., state and/or national policies affecting all other domains). All of these contextual variables need to be carefully considered in the initial interview and throughout treatment.

The integration of cultural competency and an ecosystemic focus takes place in a four-phase model of multicultural assessment (Quintana et al., 2000). Within this model, cultural data are identified, interpreted, and incorporated into assessment and treatment decisions via the use of multiple data collection methods (e.g., parents, teachers, children). For example, interviews should integrate the family's cultural background in the assessment process. This can be done by conducting the interview in the client's native language or conducting the interview in more familiar settings (e.g., a local community center). Cultural competence can also be demonstrated by altering the goals of assessment and treatment and the framework used to assess and evaluate the child's behavior. Multicultural interviewing principles and diversity issues are addressed in more detail in Chapter 6 (Tinsley Li & Magneson).

INTEGRATING THE INTERVIEW WITH OTHER DATA

Clinical work with children is more complex than many beginning therapists may recognize. The range of potential assessment methods and numerous possible sources of information can be bewildering even to seasoned professionals. Consequently, proper assessment requires the judicious use and integration of methods and sources of information (Kratochwill & Shapiro, 2000). Standardized behavior assessment measures and direct observations of behaviors can be extremely helpful in assisting clinicians with determining which behavioral problems to target for more in-depth interview (Reitman, 2006).

Direct observation can also serve as an important supplement to the clinical interview. In our work, observations may either proceed or follow child, parent, or teacher interviews. In most cases, we prefer to conduct observations before interviews have been completed (to reduce reactivity). Nonetheless, observations conducted after interviews can serve as important checks on various "hypotheses" developed during the course of interviews. For example, if parents report that they have difficulty following through on discipline practices during the interview, the validity

of the information can be "checked" with a home or analog (in-clinic) observation of parent-child interaction during informal tasks (e.g., play) and/or more formal tasks (e.g., academic work) (Boggs et al., 2003; Sulzer-Azaroff & Mayer, 1991).

The use of standardized rating scales allows the therapist to efficiently gather information from multiple informants regarding specific aspects of the child's behavior. In addition, rating scales allow the clinician to gather information about behaviors that would not be readily observed in a clinic setting (e.g., stealing, fighting) (Reitman et al., 1998); and some children and adults will reveal information on rating scales that they are unable to relate during face-to-face interviews. For example, an adolescent may acknowledge suicidal ideation on the Child Depression Inventory (Kovacs, 1992) but deny such ideation during the clinical interview. Furthermore, the use of standardized self-reports and rating scales facilitates the monitoring of the treatment outcome in a way that is impossible or impractical with clinical interviews (Ey & Hersen, 2004). Discussions of the many options available to those seeking to assess child and adolescent psychopathology using rating scales or self-reports is beyond the scope of this volume but can be accessed in a number of publications on the subject (see Barrett & Ollendick, 2004; Christophersen & Mortweet, 2001; Kelley, Reitman, & Noell, 2003; Reitman et al., 1998).

SUMMARY

Interviewing is the cornerstone of assessment, and gathering information from multiple sources has become standard practice in clinical work with adolescents and children. Because of their flexibility, ease of use, and utility, clinical interviews are likely to continue to play an important role in contemporary clinical practice with children and adolescents. That being said, a recent study by Jensen and Weisz (2002) raises troubling questions about differences in interviewing practices in across-clinic settings. Specifically, clinician-generated chart diagnoses were compared with diagnoses generated from a well-known structured interview. The authors found very poor agreement between diagnoses derived from the structured interview and clinician-generated diagnoses for both individual and broad diagnostic clusters. Indeed, only for attention-deficit/hyperactivity disorder and conduct disorder did agreement exceed chance!

The wide gulf between the results of diagnostic interviews as conducted by practitioners and researchers also has implications for the dissemination of empirically based practice. As noted by Jensen and Weisz (2002),

> Given the importance of shared communication among and between researchers and clinicians, the present findings are a cause for concern. They suggest that the nature of the *DSM*, or the way that it is being used, may lead to wide discrepancies between the diagnoses generated in regular clinical practice and those generated by systematic and standardized procedure. (p. 166)

The authors go on to say that since most empirically supported interventions are delivered to children assessed with formal diagnostic interviews, it is possible that empirically supported interventions intended for relatively homogenous populations of children (e.g., children with depression) may be applied to a much different population in clinical practice. In essence, empirically supported treatments could be delivered to "the wrong children." This chapter, and this volume as a whole, elaborates on many of the considerations that apply when professionals seek to obtain clinical information from parents, teachers, and children. Awareness and adherence to established interviewing guidelines, including those derived from structured clinical interviews, can promote effective assessment practices, even for novice therapists. The reasons for the apparent gap between interviewing practices in research and practice remain poorly understood, and it is uncertain whether the problem will be resolved any time soon.

In summary, although much has been learned about interviewing practices with children and adolescents, much remains to be explored. Contemporary research on assessment has begun to focus interest on the extent to which we can establish empirical support for various forms of assessment and, in particular, has settled on the concept of incremental validity. Briefly, the "incremental validity of assessment" concerns the extent to which any assessment method can be shown to have a positive impact on treatment outcome (see Nelson-Gray, 2003). For example, Miller's (see

Miller & Rollnick, 2002) innovative work on "motivational interviewing" has seen only limited application with children and adolescents, despite the fact that children and adolescents are frequently resistant to participating in clinical interviews and therapy more generally. The limited work that has been done so far has focused on adolescent substance abuse and related high-risk behaviors, such as smoking (see Baer & Peterson, 2002), but more recent work based on the model has been extended to families (Dishion & Kavanagh, 2003). For example, a small ($N = 10$), uncontrolled study by Slavet et al. (2005) suggests that incarcerated adolescents exposed to a motivational-interviewing intervention based on Dishion and Kavanagh's (2003) "Family Check-Up" were more confident in their ability to resist drug use. Parents that participated reported increased confidence in their ability to influence their children's risky behavior.

Although more studies are needed, it is encouraging that assessment practices and, in particular, interviewing, are being subjected to renewed empirical scrutiny. Ultimately, all methods of assessment, including interviews, are likely to require validation in terms of clinical utility (Nelson-Gray, 2003; Reitman, 2006).

REFERENCES

American Psychiatric Association. (2000). *Diagnostic and statistical manual of mental disorders* (4th ed., Text rev.). Washington, DC: Author.

American Psychological Association. (2002). Ethical principles of psychologists and code of conduct. *American Psychologist, 49,* 1597–1611.

Baer, J. S., & Peterson, P. L. (2002). Motivational interviewing with adolescents and young adults. In W. R. Miller & S. Rollnick (Eds.), *Motivational interviewing: Preparing people for change* (2nd ed., pp. 320–332). New York: Guilford Press.

Barkley, R. A. (1997). *Defiant children: A clinician's manual for assessment and parent training* (2nd ed.). New York: Guilford Press.

Barrett, P. M., & Ollendick, T. H. (Eds.). (2004). *Handbook of interventions that work with children and adolescents.* Chichester, UK: John Wiley & Sons.

Bloomquist, M. L., & Schnell, S. V. (2002). *Helping children with aggression and conduct problems: Best practices for intervention.* New York: Guilford Press.

Boggs, K. M., Griffin, R. S., & Gross, A. M. (2003). Children. In M. Hersen & S. M. Turner (Eds.), *Diagnostic interviewing* (pp. 3–20). New York: Kluwer Academic.

Bohart, A. C. (1995). The person-centered therapies. In A. S. Gurman & S. B. Messer (Eds.), *Essential psychotherapies: Theory and practice* (pp. 107–148). New York: Guilford Press.

Busse, R. T., & Rybski Beaver, B. (2000). Informant report: Parent and teacher interviews. In E. S. Shapiro & T. R. Kratochwill (Eds.), *Conducting school-based assessments of child and adolescent behavior* (pp. 235–272). New York: Guilford Press.

Christophersen, E. R., & Mortweet, S. L. (2001). *Treatments that work with children: Empirically supported strategies for managing childhood problems.* Washington, DC: American Psychological Association.

Choudhury, M. S., Pimentel, S. S., & Kendall, P. C. (2003). Childhood anxiety disorders: Parent-child (dis)agreement using a structured interview for the *DSM-IV. Journal of the American Academy of Child & Adolescent Psychiatry, 42,* 957–964.

Dawson, P. (2005). Using interviews to understand different perspectives in school-related problems. In R. Brown-Chidsey (Ed.), *Assessment for intervention: A problem-solving approach* (pp. 155–174). New York: Guilford Press.

Dishion, T. J., & Kavanagh, K. (2003). *Intervening in adolescent problem behavior: A family-centered approach.* New York: Guilford Press.

Ey, S., & Hersen, M. (2004). Pragmatic issues of assessment in clinical practice. In M. Hersen (Ed.), *Psychological assessment in clinical practice: A pragmatic guide* (pp. 3–20). New York: Brunner-Routledge.

Faust, J. (1998). General issues. In M. Hersen & V. B. Van Hasselt (Eds.), *Basic interviewing* (pp. 1–21). Mahwah, NJ: Lawrence Erlbaum.

Fontes, L. A. (2005). *Child abuse and culture: Working with diverse families.* New York: Guilford Press.

Gabarino, J., & Scott, F. M. (1989). *What children can tell us.* San Francisco: Jossey-Bass.

Goldenberg, H., & Goldenberg, I. (2002). *Counseling today's families* (4th ed.). Belmont, CA: Wadsworth.

Greenspan, S. I., & Thorndike-Greenspan, N. (2003). *The clinical interview of the child.* Washington, DC: American Psychiatric Publishing.

Hersen, M. (Ed.). (2004). *Psychological assessment in clinical practice: A pragmatic guide.* New York: Brunner-Routledge.

Hersen, M., & Turner, S. M. (Eds.). (2003). *Diagnostic interviewing.* New York: Kluwer Academic.

House, A. E. (2002). *The first session with children and adolescents: Conducting a comprehensive mental health evaluation.* New York: Guilford Press.

Hughes, J. N., & Baker, D. B. (1990). *The clinical child interview.* New York: Guilford Press.

Irwin L. G., & Johnson, J. (2005). Interviewing young children: Explicating our practices and dilemmas, *Qualitative Health Research, 15,* 821–831.

Jensen, A. L., & Weisz, J. R. (2002). Assessing match and mismatch between practioner-generated and standardized interview-generated diagnoses for clinic-referred children and adolescents. *Journal of Consulting and Clinical Psychology, 70,* 158–168.

Kaslow, N. J., & Celano, M. P. (1995). The family therapies. In A. S. Gurman & S. B. Messer (Eds.), *Essential psychotherapies: Theory and practice* (pp. 343–402). New York: Guilford Press.

Kelley, M. L., Reitman, D., & Noell, G. H. (Eds.). (2003). *Practitioner's guide to empirically based measure of school behavior* (AABT Clinical Assessment Series). New York: Kluwer Academic/Plenum.

Kovacs, M. (1992). *The Children's Depression Inventory (CDI) manual.* North Tonawanda, NY: Multi-Health Systems.

Kratochwill, T. R., & Shapiro, E. S. (2000). Conceptual foundations of behavioral assessment in schools. In E. S. Shapiro & T. R. Kratochwill (Eds.), *Behavioral assessment in schools* (pp. 3–103). New York: Guilford Press.

Lentz, F. E., & Wehmann, B. A. (1995). Best practices in interviewing. In A. Thomas & J. Grimes (Eds.), *Best practices in school psychology* (3rd ed., pp. 637–649). Washington, DC: National Association of School Psychologists.

Luiselli, J. K. (2002). Focus, scope, and practice of behavioral consultation to public schools. In J. K. Luiselli & C. Diament (Eds.), *Behavior psychology in the schools: Innovations in evaluation, support, and consultation* (pp. 5–21). New York: Haworth Press.

McConaughy, S. H. (2000). Self-report: Child clinical interviews. In E. S. Shapiro & T. R. Kratochwill (Eds.), *Conducting school-based assessments of child and adolescent behavior* (pp. 170–202). New York: Guilford Press.

Miller, W. R., & Rollnick, S. (Eds.). (2002). *Motivational interviewing: Preparing people for change* (2nd ed.). New York: Guilford Press.

Morganstern, K. P. (1976). Behavioral interviewing: The initial stages of assessment. In M. Hersen & A. S. Bellack (Eds.), *Behavioral assessment: A practical handbook* (pp. 51–76). New York: Pergamon.

Morrison, J., & Anders, T. F. (2001). *Interviewing children and adolescents: Skills and strategies for effective DSM-IV diagnosis.* New York: Guilford Press.

Nelson-Gray, R. O. (2003). Treatment utility of psychological assessment. *Psychological Assessment, 15,* 521–531.

O'Neill, R. E., Horner, R. H., Albin, R. W., Sprague, J. R., Storey, K., & Newton, J. S. (1997). *Functional assessment and program development for problem behavior: A practical handbook* (2nd ed.). Pacific Grove, CA: Brooks/Cole.

Orvashel, H. (2006). Stuctured and semistructured interviews. In M. Hersen (Ed.), *Clinician's handbook of child behavioral assessment* (pp. 159–180). New York: Academic Press.

Orvaschel, H., Faust, J., & Hersen, M. (2001). General issues in conceptualization and treatment. In H. Orvaschel, J. Faust, & M. Hersen (Eds.), *Handbook of conceptualization and treatment of child psychopathology* (pp. 1–8). Amsterdam: Pergamon.

Panichelli, S. M., & Kendall, P. C. (1995). Therapy with children and adolescents. In B. Bongar & L. E. Beutler (Eds.), *Comprehensive textbook of psychotherapy: Theory and practice* (pp. 356–358). New York: Oxford University Press.

Powell, M. B., & Lancaster, S. (2003). Guidelines for interviewing children during child custody evaluations, *Australian Psychologist, 38,* 46–54.

Quintana, S. M., Castillo, E. M., & Zamarripa, M. X. (2000). Assessment of ethnic and linguistic minority children.

In E. Shapiro & T. R. Kratochwill (Eds.), *Behavioral assessment in schools* (pp. 435–463). New York: Guilford Press.

Reitman, D. (2006). Overview of behavioral assessment with children. In M. Hersen (Ed.), *Clinician's handbook of child behavioral assessment* (pp. 4–24). New York: Academic Press.

Reitman, D., Hummel, R., Franz, D. Z., & Gross, A. M. (1998). A review of methods and instruments for assessing externalizing disorders: Theoretical and practical considerations in rendering a diagnosis. *Clinical Psychology Review, 18*, 555–584.

Sarwer, D. B., & Sayers, S. L. (2004). Behavioral interviewing. In M. Hersen (Ed.), *Psychological assessment in clinical practice: A pragmatic guide* (pp. 63–78). New York: Brunner-Routledge.

Sattler, J. M. (1992). *Assessment of children* (3rd ed.). San Diego, CA: Author.

Sattler, J. M. (1998). *Clinical and forensic interviewing of children and families: Guidelines for the mental health, education, pediatric, and child maltreatment fields.* San Diego, CA: Author.

Schloss, P. J., & Smith, M. A. (1998). *Applied behavioral analysis in the classroom.* Boston: Allyn & Bacon.

Shapiro, E. S., & Kratochwill, T. R. (2000). Conducting a multidimensional behavioral assessment. In E. S. Shapiro & T. R Kratochwill (Eds.), *Conducting school-based assessments of child and adolescent behavior* (pp. 1–19). New York: Guilford Press.

Sharf, R. S. (2000). *Theories of psychotherapy and counseling concepts and cases.* Belmont, CA: Wadsworth.

Sharp, W. G., Reeves, C. B., & Gross, A. M. (2006). Behavioral interviewing of parents. In M. Hersen (Ed.), *Clinician's handbook of child behavioral assessment* (pp. 103–124). New York: Academic Press.

Siegal, M. (1991). Concern for the conversational environment: Questioning children in custody disputes, *Professional Psychology: Research and Practice, 22*, 473–478.

Silverman, W. K., & Saavedra, L. M. (2004). Assessment and diagnosis in evidence-based practice. In P. M. Barrett & T. H. Ollendick (Eds.), *Handbook of interventions that work with children and adolescents: Prevention and treatment* (pp. 49–69). West Sussex, Chichester, UK: John Wiley & Sons.

Slavet, J. D., Stein, L. A. R., Klein, J. L., Kolby, S. M., Barnett, N. P., & Monti, P. M. (2005). Piloting the Family Check-Up with incarcerated adolescents and their parents. *Psychological Services, 2*, 123–132.

Sommers-Flanagan, J., & Sommers-Flanagan, R. (2003). *Clinical interviewing* (3rd ed.). Hoboken, NJ: Wiley.

Sparzo, F. J. (1999). *The ABC's of behavior change.* Bloomington, IN: Phi Delta Kappa Educational Foundation.

Sue, D. W., & Sue, D. (2003). *Counseling the culturally diverse: Theory and practice* (4th ed.). New York: Wiley.

Sulzer-Azaroff, B., & Mayer, G. R. (1991). *Behavior analysis for lasting change.* Chicago: Holt, Rinehart & Winston.

Turner, S. M., Hersen, M., & Heiser, N. (2003). The interviewing process. In M. Hersen & S. M. Turner (Eds.), *Diagnostic interviewing* (pp. 3–20). New York: Kluwer Academic.

Woodruff-Border, J., & Leyfer, O. T. (2006). Anxiety and fear. In M. Hersen (Ed.), *Clinician's handbook of child behavioral assessment* (pp. 267–290). New York: Academic Press.

2

UNSTRUCTURED INTERVIEWING

WILLIAM H. O'BRIEN AND TRACY TABACZYNSKI

Unstructured interviewing is a term used to denote clinical interactions with children that are designed to gather information about the form and function of behavior using verbal exchange strategies that fall between a typical social interaction and a structured interview. Unlike a conventional social interaction, the clinician has predetermined goals and a rough outline of how he or she will proceed with the interview. Unlike structured interviewing, however, there is great flexibility in how the goals of the interview will be realized and very broad topic coverage.

Clinician survey data and reviews of the literature indicate that unstructured interviewing is the most commonly used method for evaluating adults and children in clinical settings. For example, O'Brien, McGrath, and Haynes (2003) surveyed members of the Association for Advancement of Behavior Therapy in order to ascertain the most commonly used assessment methods in clinical settings. The survey contained several items that were used in prior investigations of assessment practices to evaluate whether there were changes across time (Elliot, Miltenberger, Kaster-Bundgaard, & Lumley, 1996; Swan & MacDonald, 1978). A summary of the results is provided in Table 2.1. An examination of the table reveals a striking consistency in the extent to which psychologists reported using

various assessment methods. It is also clear that unstructured interviewing (with the client, a significant other, or another professional) was the most commonly used assessment method reported by a national sample of psychologists.

Although unstructured interviews do not have a predetermined sequence of questions, prompts, and decision trees, they are structured in the sense that the therapist aims to gather information that will permit him or her to better understand what the problems are and why they occur. These two interrelated goals are sometimes referred to as the *topographical analysis of behavior* and the *functional analysis of behavior*. The former goal requires the therapist to inquire about, and subsequently develop, clear operational definitions of the target behaviors and the variables that influence them. The latter goal involves the development of a case conceptualization that summarizes and integrates information about the interrelationships among hypothesized causes, target behaviors, and the effects of the target behaviors on other behaviors.

In addition to gathering information about the topography and function of behavior, which can be thought of as the *content* of the interview, the therapist needs to manage the interview process. Important *process* elements include establishing rapport and conducting careful observations of child behavior in relation to variation in interview

TABLE 2.1   Results of Survey Investigating Assessment Methods Used by Members of the Association for the Advancement of Behavior Therapy

Assessment Method	Percentage of Clients Assessed With This Method	
	O'Brien et al. (2003)	Elliot et al. (1996)
Interview with client	92	93–94
Direct behavioral observation	55	52
Behavior rating scales and questionnaires	49	44–67
Self-monitoring	44	44–48
Interview with significant others	42	42–46
Interview other professionals	37	38–42
Mental status exam	32	27–36
Structured diagnostic interview	31	23–29
Personality inventory	16	15–20
Role play	15	19–25
Intellectual assessment	11	16–20
Analog functional analysis	10	10–16
Projective testing	3	3–5

context, such as the presence or absence of a parent, the topic of questions, and the level of abstraction needed to answer questions.

In this chapter, we present an overview of the content and process of interviewing. First, we present the conceptual foundations that underlie our approach to interviewing. These conceptual foundations are rooted in a contemporary cognitive-behavioral approach to assessment and therapy. Second, we summarize the primary goals and content areas that are evaluated in an unstructured interview. Finally, we present strategies that can be used to integrate interviewing information with other assessment methods in order to generate an integrated case conceptualization.

CONCEPTUAL FOUNDATIONS

Several fundamental assumptions about problematic behavior underlie a cognitive-behavioral approach to child interviewing. The first assumption is *environmental determinism:* the philosophical position that problem behaviors are produced by the child in response to changing environmental contexts. Thus, the interviewer strives to gain an understanding of how even the most seemingly random or uncontrollable problem behaviors function as coherent and

meaningful responses to environmental events that precede, co-occur, and/or follow them. This assumption underlies a key aspect of interviewing: Be alert to and critical of improbable and unwarranted beliefs by others (e.g., parent, teacher) asserting that the child's behavior is random or that it primarily arises from presumed (and typically unevaluated) internal experiences. In the former instance, these problematic beliefs are found in statements such as "Nothing works" to change behavior. These sorts of statements stand in direct opposition to the environmental-deterministic assumption. If a life form as simple as a planeria responds predictably to changes in the environment (see Carew & Sahley, 1986), then it is highly likely that a human child, even a human child for whom "Nothing works," will respond to them as well.

In the latter instance, these problematic beliefs are revealed in statements that the child "has a chemical imbalance" or is "oppositional" or is "manipulative." Similarly, the interviewer may hear the child's problems described in diagnostic language (e.g., attention-deficit disorder, oppositional defiant disorder, separation anxiety disorder). These beliefs are incompatible with environmental determinism and often conform to the fundamental attribution bias (Green, Lightfoot, Bandy, & Buchanan, 1985). Specifically, the parent or teacher is attributing the causes of the child's problems to stable and internal characteristics rather than contextual factors. While there may be important internal and/or dispositional factors influencing target behavior, they do not negate the critical importance of identifying how environmental factors act to intensify or ameliorate them. This principle is particularly important in child interviewing because the intervention ultimately created for the child will frequently target modification of the child's environment (parent behavior, contingencies of reinforcement in the classroom) rather than the presumed internal determinants of behavior.

A second assumption is that the child's behavior can be most effectively understood when an *empirical approach* is used in assessment. Thus, the interviewer strives to obtain information that will allow him or her to develop unambiguous and measurable operational definitions of problem behaviors, contextual factors, and the relationships among them (Haynes & O'Brien, 2000).

In child interviewing, the importance of an empirical approach cannot be overstated. As noted above, there is a tendency for parents and significant others to misattribute the causes of child behavior to internal dispositional factors. Importantly, these hypothesized and typically presumed internal factors cannot be directly observed. Instead, they must be inferred from observed behavior. Thus, there is the very real problem of circular reasoning emerging in the causal explanations offered by parents, teachers, and significant others. To better understand this difficulty, one can imagine posing two types of questions to determine whether an explanation is potentially tautological. The first question elicits the causal explanation offered by the parent or significant other (e.g., "What do you see as the cause of your child's tantruming?"). The second question is designed to obtain evidence that is used by the parent or significant other to support the causal assertion (e.g., "What experiences have led you to the conclusion that this is the cause of your child's problems?"). An example follows:

Interviewer: What are some possible reasons for her crying and tantruming?

Parent: She's manipulative. [The presumed cause is described as an internal, dispositional, and nonobservable characteristic of the child.]

Interviewer: How is it that you know she is manipulative? [A question designed to elicit evidence supporting the causal inference.]

Parent: Because she tantrums when she doesn't get her way. When we give in and let her have what she wants, she stops.

In this example, the parent initially offered a tautological and nonempirical explanation for the child's behavior: occurrence of tantruming is used to support the presence of manipulativeness. In turn, manipulativeness is used to explain why tantruming occurs. From an empirical perspective, the only potentially observable causal sequence provided in this description is the relationship between tantruming behavior and parent response. Thus, manipulativeness has not been demonstrated, but potential parental reinforcement of tantruming has. By adopting an empirical approach, the interviewer will seek to articulate relationships between the observable parent response and observable child behavior. This focus on empirical strategies, in turn, will permit the interviewer to generate potentially testable hypotheses about behavior and collect data that can plausibly confirm or disconfirm their verity.

A third assumption about problematic behavior is that a *hypothetico-deductive* approach should be used to evaluate the potential causes and correlates of the behavior. Consistent with this assumption, the interviewer will develop hypotheses about variables that may be influencing the target behaviors and then test the plausibility of the hypotheses via careful questioning about causation, in-session observation, testing, and data collection in natural environments.

A fourth assumption is contextualism. *Contextualism* refers to the position that the relationships among target behaviors and causal events are bounded by internal and external contexts. Thus, the interviewer aims to gather information not only on hypothesized causal variables that reside in the environment but also on those that reside within the client and function as important individual difference mediators (e.g., appraisals, beliefs, developmental level).

A fifth assumption, *multivariate multidimensionalism,* presupposes that problem behaviors and contextual variables are constructs that often comprise many specific and qualitatively distinct dimensions by which they can be measured. Consequently, the interviewer must carefully consider the many ways that a given target behavior or contextual variable can be experienced and described by the client and his or her family members.

A sixth assumption, *reciprocal causation,* underlies the position that target behaviors and contextual variables can exert bidirectional influences on each other. An example of reciprocal causation can be found in patterns of behavior observed among children with somatic complaints. Specifically, a child may verbalize complaints about stomach pain when he or she is distressed. The verbal complaints may also be accompanied by dramatic and overt behavioral expressions of pain. These somatic complaint behaviors may then evoke supportive or helping responses from a parent or caregiver. In turn, the supportive behavior can then function as a reinforcer and thereby increase the likelihood that the somatic complaints will be expressed in the future. Hence, the somatic complaint behaviors may trigger reinforcing consequences, and the reinforcing consequences may then act as important determinants of future somatic complaint behavior (O'Brien & Haynes, 1995).

The aforementioned assumptions have implications for child interviewing. First, interviewers should be familiar with contemporary principles of learning and psychopathology and how they apply to behavior problems observed in clinical settings. Familiarity with these principles, in turn, will allow the interviewer to better understand complex behavior-context interactions. Second, in addition to being well versed in learning theory, interviewers should also strive to carefully construct questions so that unambiguous descriptions of problem behavior can be obtained. Third, interviewers must know how to organize the information so that they can gain a reasonable understanding of the complex relationships that exist among behaviors and contextual variables.

In the following section, we review procedures used by therapists to operationalize, measure, and evaluate problem behavior and contextual variables in the unstructured interview.

GOALS AND APPLICATIONS OF UNSTRUCTURED CHILD INTERVIEWING

A primary goal of the initial child interview is to obtain reliable and valid information about the nature of problem behavior and the factors that influence it. In turn, this information can be used to help with treatment planning. This primary goal is realized through two types of questions that are used by interviewers: (a) those directed at obtaining clear descriptions of behavior and (b) those directed at identifying and evaluating relationships among problem behaviors and contextual factors. The first area of inquiry is the *topographical analysis,* while the second area of inquiry is the *functional analysis.*

Topographical Analysis: The Operationalization and Quantification of Target Behaviors and Contextual Variables

Target Behavior Operationalization: Modes of Responding. A critical initial goal of interviewing is to obtain unambiguous and potentially measurable operational definitions of problem behaviors. To accomplish this, the therapist must initially inquire about the many possible behaviors that are creating difficulty for the client and then select the target behaviors that will typically be the focus of the intervention.

Once a target behavior has been identified, the therapist must determine its essential characteristics via the development of an operational definition. Complex target behaviors can be partitioned into at least three interrelated modes of responding: cognitive-verbal behaviors, physiological-affective behaviors, and overt-motor behaviors. The *cognitive-verbal mode* subsumes cognitive experiences such as self-statements, images, irrational beliefs, attitudes, and the like. The *physiological-affective mode* subsumes physiological responses and felt emotional states. Finally, the *overt-motor* mode subsumes observable actions.

The process of operationally defining a target behavior requires careful interviewing. For example, a child who is described as having separation anxiety may be presenting with many cognitive, emotional, and overt-motor behaviors, including overestimations of risk for harm, catastrophic beliefs about outcomes, negative expectancies for the future, social withdrawal, separation avoidance, checking on parents, and expressed distress upon separation. However, another child who is described as having separation anxiety may present with a very different configuration of verbal-cognitive, physiological-affective, and overt-motor behaviors. Thus, if the interviewer investigates only a restricted number of response modes (e.g., focusing only on what the child is feeling), the case conceptualization and the effectiveness of the intervention may be adversely affected.

There are several ways to frame questions to gather information about modes of responding. For example, to learn about verbal-cognitive experiences, the therapist can ask the child questions such as the following: "If I had a video recorder that could make a movie of the thoughts and images you experience when you are frightened, what would I hear and see in the movie?" or "Tell me about the things you say to yourself when you are frightened." Similarly, the affective-physiological mode can be investigated with questions such as these: "When you feel frightened, what does it feel like?" or "When you feel frightened, how does your body feel different?" or "What kinds of changes do you feel coming from your body?" Finally, the overt-motor mode can be accessed by asking questions such as these: "If I could take a movie of you when you are frightened and also when you are not frightened, how would you look and act differently?" or "What do you do differently when you are frightened?"

Each of the aforementioned question examples is phrased using an open-ended structure, which can lead to more accurate accounts of experience (see Roberts, Lamb, & Sternberg, 2004). Note, however, that they are also focused enough to direct the child to provide information about a specific mode of target behavior responding. Of course, each question will have to be followed up with additional open-ended questions that can provide enhanced information about each mode of responding (e.g., "When you say you imagine something bad happening when you leave for school, please tell me more about what you mean by that. What is the bad thing that you imagine?").

Target Behavior Operationalization: Parameters of Responding. Once a target behavior has been operationalized in terms of modes, it is beneficial to determine its parameters. The most commonly used parameters are frequency, duration, and intensity. *Frequency* refers to how often the behavior occurs across a relevant time interval (e.g., number per day, per hour, per minute). *Duration* refers to the time that elapses between the onset and termination of a response. *Intensity* refers to the "force" or salience of the behavior. Oftentimes, intensity can be gauged by using a rating scale (e.g., a 0–10 scale, grades) or

a visual analog scale (e.g., "Fear Thermometer"). Sample interview questions follow:

> *Frequency:* "How many times each day do you notice that you feel very frightened?" "How often do you feel frightened?"

> *Duration:* "When you feel frightened, how long does the feeling usually last?" "When you feel frightened, how long does it take before the fear goes away?"

> *Intensity:* "When you feel frightened, how scary does it get?" "When you have the thought that something bad might happen, how much do you believe it to be true?"

In summary, one of the initial goals of the interview is to learn about the three modes of target behavior responding and the parameters of responding. This preliminary operationalization of the target behavior allows the child, significant others, and the interviewer to gain a reasonably precise and consensual understanding of the difficulties that the child is experiencing. In essence, during this initial phase of the interview, the interviewer will have translated what are often colloquial and dispositionally biased descriptions of target behaviors into terms that are (a) consistent with contemporary psychological phraseology, (b) observable, and (c) quantifiable.

Contextual Variable Operationalization: Classes of Contextual Variables. Subsequent to obtaining an operational definition of target behaviors, the therapist will need to acquire operational definitions of important contextual variables. Contextual variables are internal and external events that precede, co-occur with, and/or follow the target behavior and exert important causal influences upon it. Contextual factors can be sorted into two broad classes: environmental/contextual factors and intrapersonal/contextual factors (O'Brien et al., 2003). Environmental/contextual factors can be further divided into social context (e.g., interactions with others) and physical context (e.g., interactions with built environment, temperature, noise levels, lighting levels, etc.). Intrapersonal contextual factors include verbal-cognitive, affective-physiological, and overt-motor behaviors that may exert significant causal effects on the target behavior.

The contextual factor measurement parameters are similar to those used with target behaviors.

That is, frequency, duration, and intensity of occurrence are most often assessed. For example, the intensity and duration of exposure to adult attention and demanding tasks can be reliably measured and has been shown to have a significant impact on the frequency and magnitude of problem behavior in children (Derby et al., 1992; Durand & Crimmins, 1988; McConaughy, 2005; Taylor & Carr, 1992).

Questions that can be used to assess contextual factors are worded in a fashion similar to those used for target behavior operationalization. For example, to assess social contextual factors, the therapist may ask, "How is your fear different depending upon who you are with?" or "What sorts of changes happen with your fear when you are with a friend or someone in your family?" Similarly, to assess nonsocial contextual factors, the therapist might ask, "How does the time of day affect your fear?" or "What effect does location have on your fear? How does it change depending on where you are?" or "In what ways does your fear differ depending on the time of day?" Finally, to assess the intrapersonal context, one can ask, "In what ways does your fear change depending on your mood (or any other potentially relevant internal state or experience)?"

In summary, careful operationalization of behavior and potential contextual variables is one of the primary goals of child interviewing. Target behaviors can be partitioned into three modes, and within each mode, several dimensions of measurement may be used. Similarly, contextual variables can be partitioned into classes and measured along specific dimensions. This interaction between target behavior components and contextual factor variables is illustrated in Table 2.2.

TABLE 2.2   Interactions Among Target Behavior Modes and Contextual Variable Types

| Contextual Variable Class | Target Behavior Modes | | |
	Cognitive-Verbal	Affective-Physiological	Overt-Motor
Social/Environmental			
Nonsocial/Environmental			
Intrapersonal/ Cognitive-Verbal			
Intrapersonal/ Affective-Physiological			
Intrapersonal/ Overt-Motor			

Applications of the Topographical Analysis of Behavior and Contexts. The operationalization and quantification of target behavior and contextual factors serve important functions in child interviewing. First, a clear operational definition can help the child, his or her parents, and the therapist think carefully and objectively about the nature of the target behaviors and the contexts within which they occur. This can help guard against oversimplified, biased, and nonscientific descriptions of target behaviors and settings. Returning to our earlier example, a parent may initially state that his or her child is having "tantrums." This initial description, of course, is incomplete and not sufficient for measurement, diagnosis, or treatment design. By articulating the topography of "tantrums" and how they vary according to context, the interviewer and the parents may agree that a "tantrum" means screaming loudly and falling down on the floor with crying about three times per week, with each episode lasting about 10 minutes. At the same time, the child repeatedly yells, "I want it," which seems to indicate that she is experiencing thoughts that are associated with denial of access to a preferred activity or item. From an affective-physiological perspective, the child appears to be experiencing both sadness (as evidenced by crying and wailing) and anger (as evidenced by yelling and periodic attempts to hit others or throw objects). Contextually, the tantrums appear most likely to occur in public settings, especially grocery stores, after the parents refuse to allow the child to take an item from the shelves. Alternatively, refusal to provide preferred items in nonpublic settings seems produce to a less intense and shorter period of distress.

Second, operational definitions permit the therapist to assess the social significance of the target behavior. Thus, he or she can evaluate the magnitude of the problem relative to peers and thereby make determinations of the need for an intervention. Finally, operationalization of target behaviors makes it possible to assign a psychiatric diagnosis using the American Psychiatric Association *Diagnostic and Statistical Manual of Mental Disorders, Fourth Edition* (*DSM-IV,* 1994) or the ninth edition of the American Medical Association *International Classification of Diseases* (*ICD-9-CM,* 2005). Although diagnosis of childhood disorders remains controversial, it can help with the selection of an empirically supported treatment protocol if one is available for a specific disorder.

Functional Analysis: The Identification of Functional Relationships and Development of a Case Conceptualization

Once target behaviors and contextual factors have been operationally defined, the therapist will need to develop a case conceptualization. The case conceptualization is also referred to as the "functional analysis" in the cognitive-behavioral literature. The term *functional analysis* has appeared in many texts and research publications, and experts have argued that the functional analysis is the core outcome of a clinical interview and associated assessment methods (see Nelson-Gray, 2003). The functional analysis has been identified as a core outcome because if it is incorrect or incomplete, the therapist is apt to design or select less effective interventions (e.g., Haynes & O'Brien, 2000; Iwata, Kahng, Wallace, & Lindberg, 2000).

Even though the functional analysis is considered to be a critical component of assessment, the term has been used to characterize a diverse set of assessment methods, including (a) the operationalization of target behaviors, (b) the operationalization of situational factors, (c) single-subject experimental procedures

where hypothesized causal variables are systematically manipulated while measures of target behavior are collected, and (d) an overall integration of operationalized target behaviors and contextual variables (see O'Brien et al., 2003). Because of the ambiguity surrounding the term, we have proposed that the functional analysis be defined as "the identification of important, controllable, causal functional relationships applicable to a specified set of target behaviors for an individual client" (Haynes & O'Brien, 1990, p. 654). Sugai et al. (2000) offered a compatible definition of the functional analysis as "a systematic process of identifying problem behaviors and the events that (a) reliably predict occurrences and nonoccurrences of those behaviors and (b) maintain the behaviors across time" (p. 137).

These definitions of functional analysis have several important features that are relevant for interviewing. First, it is important to note that taken alone, a functional relationship implies only that two variables covary. In child interviewing, the presence of a functional relationship is typically supported by the child or parent reporting that there is covariation among one or more target behaviors and one or more contextual variables. Alternatively, the interviewer may directly observe a functional relationship between one or more target behaviors and one or more contextual variables during the interview. Some of these reported and observed functional relationships represent a causal process, while others do not. Because information about causality is most relevant to treatment design (where the goal is to understand what variables exert a direct influence on the target behavior), the functional analysis and interviewing questions pertaining to its derivation emphasize the selection and integration of causal functional relationships.

Many variables can exert causal effects on target behaviors. Because of this, the interviewer must decide which causal functional relationships should be emphasized in the functional analysis. Two criteria can be used to help with this determination. The first is the notion of importance. Specifically, causal functional relationships that exert the greatest impact on the target behavior should be emphasized relative to variables that exert less significant impact. Further, it is important to emphasize causal functional relationships that are not only important but also controllable. The notion here is treatment utility; the interviewer will ultimately want to develop a case conceptualization that provides information about how to modify the target behavior via modification of important causal variables (see Nelson-Gray, 2003).

Another important characteristic of the functional analysis is its focus on the individual child in specific circumstances. Thus, the interviewer will structure his or her inquiry so that information about specific target behaviors for an individual child is highlighted. This idiographic focus is consistent with a cognitive-behavioral approach to interviewing where the goal is to maximize the understanding of how an individual child's behavior varies in relation to changes in context. Along these lines, the interviewer's questions will emphasize an understanding of behavior-context interactions.

Interviewing Methods Used to Generate a Functional Analysis. To generate a functional analysis, the interviewer must attempt to identify and then integrate the many causal functional relationships among target behaviors and contextual variables. Reliable covariation between a target behavior and a contextual variable is the most essential requirement for identifying a causal functional relationship. However, covariation alone does not imply causality. To differentiate causal functional relationships from noncausal functional relationships, the interviewer should attempt to demonstrate (a) temporal order (the changes in the hypothesized causal variable precede effects on the target behavior), (b) a logical basis or research-supported explanation for the relationship, and (c) the exclusion of plausible alternative explanations.

The primary method used by interviewers to identify causal relationships is to ask the child and/or parents to provide an explanation as to "why" the target behavior is occurring. For example, the interviewer may ask, "What do you think causes you to be more frightened at school compared to being at home?" The child's or parent's response to this question is then treated as an index of the presence of a possible causal functional relationship.

The major advantage to this informal questioning strategy for causal variable identification is ease of use. An interviewer can identify many potential causal functional relationships within a single interview. However, interview-based causal assertions are very limited in terms of validity. Specifically, the interviewer cannot determine how well the client's reports of causation mirror causal relationships in criterion (i.e., real-world) settings. Factors that influence the validity of client-reported marker variables include developmental capacity to recognize and understand casual relationships, social desirability, capacity to adequately express the nature of causal relationships to the interviewer, and a host of commonly occurring judgment errors (e.g., illusory correlation, anchoring effects, recency effects, representativeness heuristic, and confirmatory biases) (De Los Reyes & Kazdin, 2005; Johnston & Murray, 2003). In addition, the interviewer's own cognitive limitations and biases influence how questions are posed (which leads to variability in client reporting) and what information is encoded and recalled (Garb, 1996).

To enhance the validity of client reports of causal relationships, the interviewer should carefully and systematically inquire about covariation, temporal order, and the logical basis for the causal assertion. To accomplish this, the interviewer can envision a 2 × 2 table, as shown in Table 2.3, and ask a series of questions that will provide information relevant to each cell (see Table 2.4).

In addition to simply inquiring about causal relationships, the interviewer can collect informal observational data during the interview itself. Most commonly, observations are made

TABLE 2.3   A 2 × 2 Table Illustrating Essential Conditions for Causal Assertion

	Causal Variable Present	Causal Variable Absent
Target Behavior Present	Evidence Supporting Causation (Necessary Condition)	Evidence Against Causation
Target Behavior Absent	Evidence Against Causation	Evidence Supporting Causation (Sufficient Condition)

TABLE 2.4   Prototypical Questions That Pertain to Each Causal Assertion Condition

	Causal Variable Present	*Causal Variable Absent*
Target Behavior Absent	*Conditional probability of occurrence questions:* General format: "When the causal event occurs, what is the likelihood that the target behavior will occur?"	*Base rate of occurrence questions:* General format: "When the causal event does not occur, what is the likelihood that the target behavior will occur?"
	Example: "On a school day, how likely is it that you will get a bad stomachache in the morning?"	Example: "On a weekend, how likely is it that you will get a bad stomachache in the morning?"
Target Behavior Present	*Conditional probability of nonoccurrence:* General format: "When the causal event occurs, what is the likelihood that the target behavior will not occur?"	*Base rate of nonoccurrence:* General format: "When the causal event does not occur, what is the likelihood that the target behavior will not occur?"
	Example: "On a school day, how likely is it that you will feel fine in the morning?"	Example: "On a weekend, how likely is it that you will feel fine in the morning?"

about how the client reacts to certain types of interview questions (e.g., those focusing on the problem areas versus other nonsensitive topics) and the behavior of another person who is participating in the interview (e.g., a parent or significant other). In both cases, the interviewer can note the presence of covariation between target behaviors and possible causal variables and then form an intuitive judgment about the strength of association. In addition, the interviewer can, if he or she is quite adept, estimate the extent to which the relationships conform to the 2 × 2 table illustrated in Table 2.3.

The utility of an informal observation strategy was made clear in a case where a 9-year-old boy was referred by a neurologist for treatment of a "hysterical paralysis." The boy was initially treated for a persistent psychogenic cough at a regional hospital. After 2 days of hospitalization and tests, the cough resolved, but the boy reported that he could no longer move his legs. Medical tests indicated that there appeared to be no neurological damage. The paralysis persisted; the boy was discharged; and he began using a wheelchair to ambulate. Upon interview, the boy presented as a worried, soft-spoken, articulate, and friendly child. He reported that his legs simply did not work no matter how hard he tried to walk. As the child was describing his difficulties, we noted that he would shift his feet and legs in his wheelchair. We then removed the foot supports from the wheelchair so his legs could swing freely. This tendency to move his legs was enhanced with the increased freedom of movement. We further

noted that leg movement covaried with symptom awareness. That is, when we asked him to describe his difficulties walking, he would look at his feet and describe various physical sensations. As he did so, his feet would be nearly immobile. When we asked him to talk with us about other topics, however, he would look up and become engaged in the conversation, and his feet would begin to swing.

These observations allowed us to hypothesize that (a) there was a capacity for leg movement and ambulation and (b) attentional focus intensified symptoms whereas distraction reduced them. This hypothesis was tested further in subsequent sessions using EMG feedback as an objective measure of leg movement. Once we provided the child with information about our observations of leg movement and how his thinking influenced it, he articulated a metaphor that we used in treatment. Specifically, he described his experiences as something analogous to the "leap of faith" depicted in the "Indiana Jones" movie *Temple of Doom.* In the scene, Indiana Jones must cross a chasm. He learns that the only way to cross is to step out into the air and believe that he will not fall. Any hesitation or doubt must be avoided. When he does take the "leap of faith," his feet land on an invisible bridge. The child noted that his fears were similar to those of Indiana Jones—the notion of stepping out of his chair and placing weight on his legs created an intense, albeit irrational, fear of falling and breaking his legs. He came to acknowledge that his legs worked, but he feared that they were not strong enough to support his weight. We thus were able to design a graded-exposure intervention wherein he would place increasing levels of weight on his legs until he was able to stand and then ambulate without support.

Functional-analytic experimentation and observation can also be used to enhance client self-reports of causation. This strategy involves systematically modifying some aspect of the interview context and observing consequent changes in the target behavior. This hypothesis-testing approach has been extensively developed and validated by Kohlenberg (e.g., Kohlenberg et al., 2004) and Iwata and colleagues (e.g., Iwata, Smith, & Michael, 2000). For example, a child was referred for evaluation of disruptive behavior. To assess the possible impact of social attention, tangible reward, and escape on the behavior, we asked the child's parent to sit with the child and engage in one of three activities for 5 minutes. The social attention condition involved having the parent read a magazine while the child had access to play items. Whenever the child interrupted the parent with a disruptive behavior, the parent was instructed to provide attention as she might normally do in the home (e.g., put aside the magazine, talk with the child for a moment to ascertain the concern, and then redirect the child to a play activity). Once the child was engaged in play, she would then resume reading.

The tangible reward condition was similar to the social attention condition, except in this case, the parent provided the child with a tangible item whenever a disruption occurred (e.g., a piece of gum, a pencil, or a different toy). In the escape condition, the child was instructed to clean up the toys independently, with the parent supervising and providing attention but not actively participating in the cleanup. We counted the number of disruptions that occurred in each condition and compared it with behavior observed prior to the formal assessment (baseline condition). The results indicated that the child had the highest rates of disruptive behavior in the social attention condition. Consequently, an intervention was designed that provided social attention for non-occurrence of disruptive behavior in the home.

A number of single-subject experimental designs have been developed that can help interviewers confirm or disconfirm hypotheses using this strategy. Although most have been used to evaluate the outcomes of an intervention, they are readily applicable to the interview and

assessment setting. As illustrated in the aforementioned case example, we used an A–B–C–D design (where A = baseline, B = social attention, C = tangible reward, D = escape) to evaluate the extent to which disruptive behavior was functionally related to key reinforcers.

Functional-analytic experiments have gained renewed interest in recent years because (a) they are particularly well suited for establishing causal relationships between target behaviors and causal variables, (b) they have been extensively evaluated as a tool for generating functional analyses and interventions, and (c) they can be readily incorporated into interviews and clinical settings. Excellent examples of protocols that can be used to determine the function of behavior have been developed by Iwata and colleagues (e.g., Iwata, et al., 1994) and Durand and colleagues (e.g., Durand, 1990).

Iwata et al. (1994) summarized data from 152 case studies that used the aforementioned assessment/observation protocol to design treatments. For example, if a client displayed higher rates of problem behavior in the social attention or tangible reinforcement conditions, a matching intervention would use procedures such as noncontingent attention, differential reinforcement of other behavior (e.g., providing attention or access to preferred materials/activities when self-injurious behavior was not observed), or time-out. If a client exhibited higher rates of problem behavior during the negative-reinforcement condition, a matching treatment would use procedures that capitalized on negative-reinforcement principles, such as noncontingent negative reinforcement (providing breaks from aversive tasks independent of problem behavior) or differential reinforcement of other behavior (providing breaks from the aversive task contingent upon performance of nonproblem behavior). Results from Iwata et al.'s (1994) study indicated that 80% of the treatments based on functional-analytic experiments were successful (operationally defined as achieving problem behavior rates that were at or below 10% of those observed during baseline). Alternatively, interventions not based on the functional-analytic experiment results were described as having minimal effects.

Other researchers supported the general findings reported by Iwata et al. (1994). For example, Carr, Robinson, and Palumbo (1990) summarized the results of a literature review of 96 case studies that evaluated the outcomes of interventions for self-injurious behavior that used functional-analytic experiments to identify the function of the target behavior. They concluded that the success rate (defined as 90% or more suppression in the level of behavior problems relative to baseline) was "much lower for procedures not based on functional analysis than it was for procedures based on such an analysis" (p. 365).

Similar to Iwata et al. (1994) and Carr et al. (1990), Derby and colleagues (1992) evaluated the treatment utility of functional-analytic experimentation on 83 outpatient cases. They reported that the goal of their project was to adapt this technique and use it in a standard clinic setting. Clients were assessed using single-subject designs in which different stimulus conditions were presented, while target behavior occurrence was recorded. An emphasis was placed on evaluating variation in target behavior under conditions of contingent social attention, contingent tangible reward, contingent negative reinforcement, and intrinsic-reinforcement conditions. Each stimulus condition was presented for 10 minutes, and two independent observers recorded the number of times the target behaviors occurred. Data were then plotted on a graph and visually inspected. Results indicated that a specific reinforcement condition elicited higher rates of problematic behavior in 74% of the cases. The authors concluded that the functional-analytic experiment was an effective strategy for identifying specific contextual factors that may reinforce problematic behavior. They also demonstrated that functional-analytic experiments can be effectively used in a standard clinical setting. Finally, they noted that the results of the functional-analytic experiments yielded information that was very helpful in intervention design.

Robert Horner (1994) reviewed a number of functional-analytic experimental studies and generated a commentary about the efficacy and future directions of this methodology. First, he noted that it is important to consider analog observation in general and functional-analytic experiments in particular as ongoing assessment procedures that do not need to be restricted to the initial consultation. Second, he suggested that the procedures be extended so that antecedent variables and conditions can be more fully evaluated. Third, he argued that the ultimate clinical utility of these procedures will be based on their ability to contribute meaningful clinical information while simultaneously balancing the increment in knowledge against the costs involved. Finally, Horner suggested that procedures and decisional strategies for evaluating analog observational data and translating them into intervention design need to be more fully developed.

Integrating Interview Information Using Causal Modeling

Often, the information yielded by an unstructured interview is complex and difficult to communicate with the child, parents, and significant others. Causal modeling is one strategy that can be used to aid in the explanation of a case conceptualization. Clinical case models summarize the functional analysis using vector diagrams. Variables included in the clinical case model include target behaviors, contextual variables, and the relationships among them. An example of a clinical case model for an adolescent child is provided in the following section.

There are several potential advantages for using clinical case modeling. First, it can aid in the clinical decision-making process by encouraging the clinician to attend to the complexity of the case, the functional properties of target behaviors, and whether sufficient information has been collected and analyzed to support the hypothesized presence of the various functional relationships. Second, it promotes greater integration of assessment data and treatment design. Third, it can provide a parsimonious and more accessible explanation of the many factors influencing target behaviors.

Case Example: An Adolescent Client Presenting With a Hemiparesis Exacerbated by Stressful Situations and Negative Self-Statements. Figure 2.1 is an example of a functional-analytic causal model developed for an adolescent who was referred for treatment of a hemiparesis (partial paralysis of an arm that was caused by central nervous system trauma) that he and his parents felt was exacerbated by "stress." The hypothesized causal relationships contained in this model were initially identified using unstructured interviewing and observation of target behavior-context interactions that occurred during the interview. Specifically, it was observed that when the client discussed "stressful" topics (e.g., recalling situations in which his hemiparesis resulted in social rejection), his face flushed, his talking became more tangential, and the muscles in the hemiparetic arm became visibly tensed (i.e., his hand formed a tight fist and his arm curled up toward his chest). The client also stated that when he became "stressed," he tended to "lose track" of his thinking and "forget" to monitor his affected hand and arm.

FIGURE 2.1   A Clinical Case Model for a Client With Arm Hemiparesis

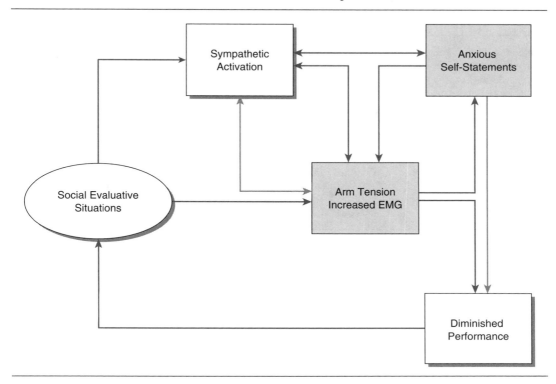

After the clinical interview was completed, the client was asked to self-monitor arm tension, stress levels, and pleasant feelings on a 0-to-10 scale four times per day (where 0 = *no tension* and 10 = *maximum tension*). The client also recorded the occurrence of potential causal variables (both situational and intraindividual events) that preceded, co-occurred with, and followed periods of elevated arm tension.

At the end of 2 weeks, the self-monitoring information was evaluated (see Table 2.5). Results indicated that arm tension was significantly associated with self-reported stress levels. The self-monitoring information also indicated that difficult academic tasks, social interactions, and negative self-statements (e.g., anticipating failure) appeared to be associated with the greatest levels of stress and arm tension/dysfunction.

An experimental manipulation was subsequently designed to evaluate the extent to which stressful situations (e.g., difficult tasks, social interactions) and negative self-statements brought about (a) increased physiological activation and (b) increased muscle tension levels (EMG) in the affected arm. Measures of general physiological activation (heart rate, skin conductance, blood volume pulse amplitude) and EMG levels were obtained in a psychophysiological laboratory under the following conditions: a resting baseline, balloon blowing (a physical stressor), balloon popping (startle), serial subtraction (stressful task), and guided imagery of stressful social interactions.

Visual analysis of the psychophysiological data indicated that the EMG levels obtained from the client's hemiparetic arm were significantly higher and more variable during the serial subtraction and guided-imagery conditions. A conditional-probability analysis of the data confirmed the presence of statistically significant relationships between laboratory stressor presentations and

TABLE 2.5   Two-Way Contingency Table Between Stress Level and Hemiparetic Symptoms

		Arm Tension Levels		
		High	Low	
Stress Levels	High	23	3	26
	Low	6	6	12

Conditional Probabilities:
Probability of high arm dysfunction given high stress: 23/26 = .88
Probability of high arm dysfunction given low stress: 6/12 = .50
Probability of low arm dysfunction given high stress: 3/26 = .12
Probability of low arm dysfunction given low stress: 6/12 = .50

Chi-Square Analysis:

Chi-Square	D.F.	Significance
4.76027	1	.03

increased levels of general physiological activation and EMG.

The treatment designed for the client described in this case targeted three sets of causal relationships. First, we provided the client with biofeedback to increase his awareness of arm tension levels. Second, we provided relaxation training to help him gain better control of sympathetic nervous system activation. Third, we provided self-instructional training to help the client learn to identify and then replace anxious thoughts with more adaptive ways of thinking. Finally, the client was guided though a number of graded-exposure experiences to provide him with opportunities to use his self-management skills in criterion (e.g., social interaction) situations.

SUMMARY

In summary, unstructured interviewing is one of the most commonly used assessment strategies in clinical settings. We have argued that one approach to unstructured interviewing incorporates a series of decisions and assessment activities. First, the clinician will enter into the interviewing session carrying several assumptions about the nature of problem behaviors. Second, he or she will interview the child,

parents, and significant others, with an emphasis on obtaining information on the topography and function of the problem behavior and contextual factors. Third, because causal statements are often inaccurate, the clinician should augment interviewing information with systematic observation. Fourth, the information yielded by the interview and observation can be integrated using a clinical case model. Finally, the clinical case model can help the clinician design interventions that will emphasize the modification of important target behavior-context interactions.

Several important questions about the unstructured interviewing, the functional analysis, and clinical case modeling remain unanswered. First, to what extent does unstructured interviewing yield reliable and valid clinical case conceptualizations? Second, to what extent does the use of clinical case models based on functional analyses lead to more effective interventions? Third, how generalizable are the functional analyses and functional-analytic causal models across clients, behaviors, and settings? And, fourth, can single-subject statistical methods be extended for the purposes of testing functional-analytic causal models? Systematic research of these questions is certainly warranted given that one of the most commonly used assessment methods has no clear empirical validation.

REFERENCES

American Medical Association. (2005). *International classification of diseases, ninth revision, clinical modification.* Chicago: Author.

American Psychiatric Association. (1994). *Diagnostic and statistical manual of mental disorders* (4th ed.). Washington, DC: Author.

Carew, T. J., & Sahley, C. L. (1986). Invertebrate learning and memory: From behavior to molecules. *Annual Review of Neuroscience, 9,* 435–487.

Carr, E. G., Robinson, S., & Palumbo, L. R. (1990). The wrong issue: Aversive versus nonaversive treatment; the right issue: Functional versus nonfunctional treatment. In A. C. Repp, & S. Nirbhay (Eds.), *Perspectives on the use of nonaversive and aversive interventions for persons with developmental disabilities* (pp. 361–379). Sycamore, IL: Sycamore Publishing.

De Los Reyes, A., & Kazdin, A. E. (2005). Informant discrepancies in the assessment of childhood psychopathology: A critical review, theoretical framework, and recommendations for further study. *Psychological Bulletin, 131,* 483–509.

Derby, K. M., Wacker, D. P., Sasso, G., Steege, M., Northrup, J., Cigrand, K., & Asmus, J. (1992). Brief functional analysis techniques to evaluate aberrant behavior in an outpatient setting: A summary of 79 cases. *Journal of Applied Behavior Analysis, 25,* 713–721.

Durand, V. M. (1990). *Severe behavior problems: A functional communication training approach.* New York: Guilford Press.

Durand, V. M., & Crimmins, D. (1988). Identifying the variables maintaining self-injurious behavior. *Journal of Autism and Developmental Disorders, 18,* 99–117.

Elliot, A. J., Miltenberger, R. G., Kaster-Bundgaard, J., & Lumley, V. (1996). A national survey of assessment and therapy techniques used by behavior therapists. *Cognitive and Behavior Practice, 3,* 107–125.

Garb, H. N. (1996). *Studying the clinician: Judgment research and psychological assessment.* Washington, DC: American Psychological Association.

Green, S. K., Lightfoot, M. A., Bandy, C., & Buchanan, D. (1985). A general model of the attribution process. *Basic and Applied Social Psychology, 6,* 159–179.

Haynes, S. N., & O'Brien, W. H. (1990). The functional analysis in behavior therapy. *Clinical Psychology Review, 10,* 649–668.

Haynes, S. N., & O'Brien, W. H. (2000). *Principles and practice of behavioral assessment.* New York: Plenum Press.

Horner, R. (1994). Functional assessment: Contributions and future directions. *Journal of Applied Behavior Analysis, 27,* 215–240.

Iwata, B. A., Kahng, S., Wallace, M., & Lindberg, J. (2000). The functional analysis model of behavioral assessment. In J. Austin & J. E. Carr (Eds.), *Handbook of applied behavior analysis* (pp. 61–89). Reno, NV: Context Press.

Iwata, B. A., Pace, G. M., Dorsey, M. F., Zarcone, J. R., Vollmer, B., & Smith, J. (1994). The function of self-injurious behavior: An experimental-epidemiological analysis. *Journal of Applied Behavior Analysis, 27,* 215–240.

Iwata, B. A., Smith, R. G., & Michael, J. (2000). Current research on the influence of establishing operations on behavior in applied settings. *Journal of Applied Behavior Analysis, 33,* 411–418.

Johnston, C., & Murray, C. (2003). Incremental validity in the psychological assessment of children and adolescents. *Psychological Assessment, 15,* 496–507.

Kohlenberg, R. J., Kanter, J. W., Bolling, M., Wexner, R., Parker, C., & Tsai, M. (2004). *Mindfulness and acceptance: Expanding the cognitive-behavioral tradition.* New York: Guilford Press.

McConaughy, S. H. (2005). *Clinical interviews for children and adolescents: Assessment to intervention.* New York: Guilford Press.

Nelson-Gray, R. (2003). Treatment utility of psychological assessment. *Psychological Assessment, 15,* 521–531.

O'Brien, W. H., & Haynes, S. N. (1995). A functional analytic approach to the assessment and treatment of a child with frequent migraine headaches. *In Session: Psychotherapy in Practice, 1,* 65–80.

O'Brien, W. H., McGrath, J. J., & Haynes, S. N. (2003). Assessment of psychopathology: Behavioral approaches. In J. Graham & J. Naglieri (Eds.), *Handbook of psychological assessment* (pp. 509–529). New York: Wiley.

Roberts, K. P., Lamb, M. E., Sternberg, K. J. (2004). The effects of rapport building style on children's reports of a staged event. *Applied Cognitive Psychology, 18,* 189–202.

Swan, G. E., & MacDonald, M. L. (1978). Behavior therapy in practice. A national survey of behavior therapists. *Behavior Therapy, 9,* 799–807.

Sugai, G., Horner, R., Dunlap, G., Heineman, M., Lewis, T., Nelson, C., et al. (2000). Applying positive behavioral support and functional behavioral assessment in schools. *Journal of Positive Behavior Intervention, 2,* 131–143.

Taylor, J. C., & Carr, E. G. (1992). Severe problem behaviors related to social interaction. 1: Attention seeking and social avoidance. *Behavior Modification, 16,* 305–335.

3

STRUCTURED AND SEMISTRUCTURED DIAGNOSTIC INTERVIEWS

MATTHEW K. NOCK, ELIZABETH B. HOLMBERG,
VALERIE I. PHOTOS, AND BETHANY D. MICHEL

Methods of classifying and assessing psychopathology have changed substantially over the years. In many early civilizations, such as those of the Greeks, Egyptians, and Chinese, behavioral problems were believed to be caused by demonic possession, and those responsible for diagnosis and treatment did not carefully evaluate and distinguish among the different behavioral problems observed. Around the fifth century BCE, Hippocrates brought the responsibility for classifying, assessing, and treating psychopathology into the purview of health care professionals and delineated three main categories of psychopathology: melancholia, mania, and phrenitis (i.e., fever of the brain). Since that time, various methods have been used to classify and assess psychopathology, ranging from dunking individuals in water to determine whether they would confess to being witches to showing them a series of cards with blots of ink on them and interpreting their responses as evidence of different forms of mental disorder.

As scientific understanding of the etiology and form of different mental disorders has slowly evolved, so have the methods for assessing and classifying them. Perhaps most significantly, the creation of the *Diagnostic and Statistical Manual of Mental Disorders (DSM)* (American Psychiatric Association [APA], 1994) and the *International Classification of Diseases (ICD)* (World Health Organization [WHO], 2003) brought a fundamental change to the classification of mental disorders. The third and fourth editions of the *DSM* (*DSM-III* and *DSM-IV*) outlined specific symptoms of each disorder that can be readily observed and assessed by clinicians so that diagnosis of mental disorders can be made with much greater reliability, aiding in the legitimatization of diagnostic practices themselves and clinical psychiatry and psychology more generally.

The publication of the *DSM-III* (APA, 1980) and *DSM-IV* (APA, 1994) was followed by the development of structured and semistructured clinical interviews that greatly enhanced the ability of clinicians to reliably assess the signs and symptoms of each mental disorder by asking a series of questions drawn directly from the *DSM* symptoms. *Structured diagnostic interviews* (also called "respondent-based interviews") are those in which the interviewer follows a specific script, reading questions verbatim, and it is thus largely up to the respondent (i.e., the interviewee) to interpret the question and formulate a response. In contrast, *semistructured diagnostic interviews* (also called "interviewer-based interviews") are those in which the interviewer is provided with a set list of questions but has flexibility in the wording and ordering of items and is permitted to give or request additional information in an effort to ensure clarity and comprehensiveness in diagnosis.

Fully structured interviews generally are considered to be more *reliable* because they provide little variability in the wording of questions. They also are easier to administer and require less training, since the interviewer reads the items precisely as they are written. While perhaps less reliable than structured interviews, semistructured interviews are considered to be more *valid,* as they allow for follow-up questions and clinical judgment to ensure that the information obtained truly matches the threshold for symptom endorsement.[1] Semistructured interviews, however, are intended to be administered by a clinician rather than a layperson and often require extensive training in the administration of the interview. All of these factors should be considered in making decisions about whether to use structured versus semistructured interviews (referred to jointly as "structured diagnostic interviews" in this chapter unless otherwise noted).

In both types of interviews, clinicians record which symptoms are present and synthesize this information to diagnose a wide range of mental disorders. Although the earliest structured diagnostic interviews were developed for adults, interviews for child and adolescent mental disorders soon followed. The number and sophistication of these structured diagnostic interviews has increased significantly over the past several decades.

The purpose of this chapter is to provide an introduction to the use of structured and semistructured diagnostic interviews currently available for generating *DSM-IV* diagnoses for children and adolescents.[2] We begin with a brief review of the strengths and limitations associated with the use of such interviews in both research and clinical settings and highlight several factors known to limit the validity and reliability of these instruments, as well as several key considerations for selecting an interview for use in one's research or clinical work. Next, we outline and describe eight of the most well-researched

interviews and provide information about each, including the format, training required, reliability, and validity. Notably, this review does not provide coverage of interviews that assess only specific types of mental disorders or behavior problems, those that focus on personality disorders, or dimensional measures that are not designed to generate *DSM* diagnoses.

STRENGTHS OF STRUCTURED AND SEMISTRUCTURED DIAGNOSTIC INTERVIEWS

There are currently no biological assays or behavioral tests for the diagnosis of mental disorders as in other areas of clinical science. Instead, clinical scientists and practitioners make diagnoses largely based on individuals' self-reports of their current and past experiences and on clinical observation of individuals' presenting behavior. Although this is far from ideal and significant research efforts are currently aimed at improving the validity and reliability of diagnostic classification and assessment procedures, the use of structured diagnostic interviews provides several advantages over the use of unstructured clinical interviews in both research and clinical contexts.

First, structured interviews greatly facilitate research by providing a method for precisely quantifying psychological symptoms and diagnoses, which is necessary in the study of mental disorders and their treatment. For instance, if we decided to conduct a study of the effectiveness of a new treatment for major depressive disorder, how would we know who is depressed and who is not? And how would we know whether the number and severity of depressive symptoms change over the course of treatment? Structured interviews provide systematic information needed to make both within- and between-group comparisons and to test the relations between mental disorders and other constructs of interest (e.g., hopelessness, activity in different brain regions). It is for this reason that structured interviews are used very frequently in research settings, such as epidemiologic studies, experimental psychopathology, and clinical trials.

Second, structured interviews facilitate the comprehensive and efficient assessment of a broad range of symptoms and diagnoses. Most structured diagnostic interviews include each symptom of all of the disorders assessed, and most interviews assess more than 30 different disorders. This coverage conveys important advantages in both research and clinical settings. In addition to providing a mechanism for thoroughly examining the disorder believed to be the presenting problem in clinical settings or the one of most interest to the researcher, structured diagnostic interviews identify and quantify symptom-level and diagnostic information that might not otherwise have been considered. Indeed, it is doubtful that clinicians using open-ended, unstructured interviews assess as many diagnoses and as many symptoms within each diagnosis as is possible using structured diagnostic interviews. As a result, it is likely that many important symptoms are missed. For example, a recent study by Prinstein, Nock, Spirito, and Grapentine (2001) assessed the presence of recent suicidal thoughts and suicide attempts among a sample of adolescent psychiatric inpatients, using several methods, including both structured diagnostic interviews and unstructured clinical interviews (i.e., child psychiatrists' standard initial interview for children and adolescents admitted to the inpatient unit). Interestingly, use of structured diagnostic interviews detected a significantly higher rate of recent suicide attempts (34.6%) than did unstructured interviews (24.2%). This difference is likely due to the fact that in the structured diagnostic interviews, the interviewer must ask each interviewee about each item, whereas in an unstructured interview, the clinician may decide which questions he or she thinks are most relevant, and this reliance on clinical judgment is often not as accurate as we believe it to be (e.g., Dawes, Faust, & Meehl, 1989).

Although the breadth provided by structured interviews is beneficial, occasionally researchers and clinicians are interested only in a single disorder or lack the time or resources to assess the full range of diagnoses in a given interview. A third advantage to using structured interviews is that most are extremely flexible given their modular format. For instance, while many researchers are interested in examining whether a particular manipulation or intervention holds for people of various diagnostic makeups, others may be interested only in whether participants meet criteria for a specific disorder. Most interviews offer maximum flexibility and increased efficiency by allowing the researcher or clinician to use only the module or modules of interest to them.

Fourth, the organization and precision of items included in structured interviews makes them much more reliable than unstructured interviews. This reliability is demonstrated by research showing that results from structured interviews are consistent across different interviewers (interrater reliability), over time (test-retest reliability), and among items within specific modules or sections of the interviews (internal-consistency reliability). Reliability is important in all areas of scientific and clinical work because it increases our confidence in the validity of our findings (i.e., although reliability does not ensure validity, the absence of reliability suggests that results lack validity) and improves our ability to accurately understand, predict, and treat different conditions.

LIMITATIONS OF STRUCTURED AND SEMISTRUCTURED DIAGNOSTIC INTERVIEWS

Although structured diagnostic interviews have numerous strengths, several notable limitations should be considered when making decisions about the appropriateness of using a structured diagnostic interview. Perhaps most important, despite the impressive reliability of structured diagnostic interviews, the extent to which they provide valid information about the diagnoses being assessed remains a source of debate. *Validity* refers to the extent to which an assessment or classification system accurately measures the intended construct or condition. In using structured diagnostic interviews, we assume that the information collected provides a valid measurement of the cognitive, emotional, and behavioral functioning of the individual being assessed. Several aspects of such interviews, however, introduce potential threats to the validity of the information they provide.

First, both structured and semistructured diagnostic interviews rely almost exclusively on participant self-report. Children and adolescents are likely the best reporters of a great deal of information, such as their experiences of depressed or anxious mood. However, for multiple reasons they are undoubtedly limited in their ability to provide completely valid diagnostic information about aberrant perceptual experiences, such as hallucinations and the occurrence of private behaviors, such as self-injury. Children and adolescents may not know which cognitive, emotional, and behavioral experiences are abnormal or are impairing their functioning. For instance, if adolescents have always been socially anxious or have always engaged in compulsive behaviors, they may have not yet learned that this is irregular or excessive relative to their peers. In cases where children and adolescents have insight into the nature of their problem behaviors, they may be unwilling to report them to the interviewer or even to their parents due to embarrassment or fear of expected consequences. For example, children may conceal enuresis or encopresis due to shame or may deny firesetting or stealing for fear of punishment. Further still, children and adolescents may lack the cognitive skills, memory, or vocabulary needed to communicate cognitive, emotional, or behavioral experiences. All of these factors can limit the validity of the information obtained in structured diagnostic interviews, and, unfortunately, the interviewer is often unaware of whether and to what extent each has influenced the data collected.

Second, although they are quite comprehensive and their structure ensures strong reliability, this structure introduces limits on the range of constructs that may be assessed and the amount of detail that can be obtained in any one area. Because there are so many diagnoses to assess, the interviewer may not have time to add detailed questions about any particular disorder. To address this point, most interviews include a period of open-ended questions at the beginning of the interview in order to gather information about developmental and social history, and many interviewers follow up structured diagnostic interviews with a less structured clinical interview aimed at obtaining greater detail about any clinical issues that may have arisen during the structured interview (although this is usually done more frequently in clinical rather than research settings).

Third, structured diagnostic interviews provide dichotomous results of the presence or absence of particular diagnoses; however, prior research suggests that many forms of psychopathology are best conceptualized as dimensional (Achenbach & Edelbrock, 1984; Beauchaine, 2003). For instance, previous studies have suggested that child and adolescent depression is a continuous rather than categorical construct, whether using a child or parent report, as well as when examining different age groups and genders (Hankin, Fraley, Lahey, & Waldman, 2005). These findings also challenge the validity of classifying individuals strictly as "depressed" versus "nondepressed." A related concern is that while structured diagnostic interviews examine the form of psychopathology, they do not take into account the function of different behaviors. Such information may be especially useful for both assessment and treatment purposes (Hayes, Wilson, Gifford, Follette, & Strosahl, 1996; Nock & Prinstein, 2004). Of course, the debate about whether the dimensionality and function of psychopathology should be included in the classification of mental disorder is not specific to structured diagnostic interviews, but is perhaps best addressed in future editions of the *DSM*. Nevertheless, since structured diagnostic interviews are derived directly from the *DSM*, they contain many of the limitations therein.

A fourth limitation of structured diagnostic interviews is that although most structured diagnostic interviews assessing child and adolescent psychopathology include information from a separate interview with the parent(s), overall, parent-child agreement is consistently poor. This weak interinformant reliability raises questions about the validity of the assessments. For instance, if a child repeatedly denies disobeying his parents but the parents report that he does so, how is this information to be synthesized, and how are we to know whether we are accurately measuring the symptom of interest? Is the child downplaying his behavior, do the parents have a particularly low threshold for what constitutes disobeying parental commands, or both? Although the methods for integrating parent and child reports vary across the different interviews reviewed below, poor parent-child agreement is observed across them all. It is likely that this poor agreement will persist until additional assessment methods (e.g., biological tests, performance-based tests, behavioral observations) are included as part of the diagnostic process. Some factors known to influence the level of agreement between child and parent responses on structured clinical interviews are outlined below and represent important areas of consideration for future research and clinical utilization of these instruments.

FACTORS THAT INFLUENCE PARENT-CHILD AGREEMENT ON STRUCTURED INTERVIEWS

Structured clinical interviews incorporate reports from both the child and a parent to make a diagnosis. Because of the prevalence of discordant reports, researchers have worked on identifying the areas in which clinicians should be careful of misinformation and what the implications of the differing reports may be for the final endorsing of a symptom (De Los Reyes & Kazdin, 2005). Some of the most common factors that influence the reliability between parent and child report are outlined below.

Type and Severity of Disorder

The most stable finding in the parent-child concordance literature is that agreement is quite poor across informants (De Los Reyes & Kazdin, 2005). In most cases, parents and children have better agreement on the presence or absence of externalizing behaviors compared with that of internalizing behaviors (Kolko & Kazdin, 1993; Silverman & Eisen, 1992). This is not always the case, however, and in some instances, agreement for internalizing symptoms is comparable to or better than agreement for externalizing symptoms (Briggs-Gowan, Carter, & Schwab-Stone, 1996; DiBartolo, Albano, Barlow, & Heimberg, 1998). These latter findings might be explained by instances of children attempting to conceal some behavior problems from parents in order to prevent negative consequences. Specifically, this explanation has been suggested to account for discrepancies between parents and children regarding conduct disorder or substance use symptoms (Jensen et al., 1995). Likewise, researchers have suggested careful interpretation of reports by individuals with conduct behavior problems, since lying is one of the symptoms associated with this disorder (Crowley, Mikulich, Ehlers, Whitmore, & MacDonald, 2001; Perez, Ezpeleta, Domenech, & de la Osa, 1998). Thus, it would seem pertinent to explore these possibilities when poor agreement is found for externalizing symptoms, particularly conduct disorder. Severity of disorder may also be a factor in low parent-child reliability.

Age of Child

As children get older, they become more reliable reporters in terms of test-retest reliability, arguably due to increased cognitive capacity to understand the questions in the interview. In one specific example, children from age 6 to 9 interviewed with the Diagnostic Interview Schedule for Children (DISC) were less reliable than those aged 10 to 13 and 14 to 18; this increase in reliability for child report was matched, however, with a decrease in reliability of parents' reports for older children. Parents were more reliable reporters of a child's symptoms if the child was between 6 and 9 than if he or she was between 10 and 13 or 14 and 18 (Edelbrock, Costello, Dulcan, Kalas, & Conover, 1985). Though clinicians should always carefully weigh the information provided by both informants, the skepticism with which answers are received is different for younger and older children and their parents.

Gender of Child

There are mixed results of studies that investigate the influence of gender on the reliability of children reporters and agreement with parents, though there is some evidence that girls tend to be more consistent in terms of test-retest reliability (Fallon & Schwab-Stone, 1994), especially in terms of affective disorders (Jensen et al., 1995) and substance abuse disorders (Roberts, Solovitz, Chen, & Casat, 1996). However, boys are generally more concordant with their parents (Rapee, Barrett, & Dadds, 1994). This could possibly be explained by a gender differential in the presence of externalizing versus internalizing symptoms; since reliability is better between informants for externalizing symptoms than it is for internalizing symptoms, boys may be more concordant with parents because boys tend to have more externalizing symptoms than girls do.

Parent Characteristics

Parents may underreport a child's symptoms because they fear being stigmatized if the child is diagnosed with a mental illness. Another reason for underreporting a child's symptoms may be to avoid raising any suspicions about other aspects of family life, such as abuse or divorce. Parents who are multiply stressed are less likely to notice changes in the behavior of children due to being overwhelmed with other matters, and thus underreport problem behavior or worrisome symptoms. Overreporting by parents can also result from a desire to secure services from mental health professionals that the parents think they may not receive if their child is not "sick" enough. Overreporting could also result from an unconscious primacy effect: The parent simply remembers the recent bad behavior more vividly because it happened more recently.

Parent Psychopathology

Results from research are unclear regarding whether parental psychopathology may also influence discrepant reports between parents and children (Breslau, Davis, & Prabucki, 1988; Rapee et al., 1994). Some believe that parents who are themselves mentally ill may more accurately report their children's symptoms because they are more sensitive to the warning signs and are able to better interpret the experiences of their children (e.g., Breslau et al., 1988). Other researchers have found that mentally ill parents overreport their children's symptoms, possibly due to a projection of their own symptoms onto their children or a lower threshold for inappropriate behavior (e.g., Briggs-Gowan et al., 1996). While interviewing children with behavior problems, it is important to remember that the mechanism underlying the familial transmission of externalizing disorders is primarily a highly heritable general vulnerability (Hicks, Krueger, Iacono, McGue, & Patrick, 2004). Therefore, the possibility of the parent having a previous diagnosis of an externalizing disorder (such as conduct disorder) is present. Parents with a previous (or current) diagnosis of antisocial, conduct, or substance abuse disorder may be more likely to be uncooperative in an interview or to minimize the effects of their children's dangerous behavior (Miles et al., 1998).

Interviewer Characteristics

If the same clinician interviews both child and parent, there is a danger for information from the first interview to cause the clinician to interpret information from the second informant with bias. One mechanism for this occurs through an alteration in the style of probing based on knowledge from the first informant, possibly leading to the engagement of leading questions by the clinician. Still, the method of using the same interviewer seems preferable to having two clinicians interview the parent and child separately, since

clarifying questions can be asked of either informant before diagnoses are made. The skill and experience of a clinician can, of course, influence the discrepancy between parent and child answers, since more skilled clinicians are aware of more accurate methods of probe questions. This is not as much of a problem in fully structured (i.e., respondent-based) interviews.

SELECTING AN INTERVIEW FOR RESEARCH OR CLINICAL WORK

Though all structured clinical interviews provide researchers and clinicians with Axis I diagnoses, they differ in the diagnostic criteria used, number of disorders assessed, developmental level of the questions asked, time required for each interview, and amount of training required. All of these factors can and should be considered when selecting an interview for use in one's research or clinical work. Below, we raise several important questions to consider in deciding between the many interviews currently available.

What Diagnostic Criteria Are Used?

All of the structured clinical interviews reviewed in this chapter include scoring systems that generate diagnoses using *DSM* criteria, though they differ regarding which versions of the *DSM* diagnostic criteria are included in the scoring sections. If diagnoses are required that include both *DSM-IV* criteria and those of older versions of the *DSM* (e.g., if comparing current results with those from studies conducted prior to the publication of the *DSM-IV*), this requirement will limit the choice of interview. Moreover, some research may require *ICD* diagnostic criteria in addition to *DSM-IV* criteria (e.g., cross-cultural studies).

Which Disorders Will Be Assessed?

Interviews vary in the number of disorders assessed as well as the time frame for those disorders. Most interviews examine at least 20 different Axis I disorders, but some include well over 30. Perhaps more important, some provide only current diagnoses, while others offer current, past-year, and lifetime histories of each disorder. Generally, interviews assessing a broader range of diagnoses and time frame will require more administration time, and this is a trade-off that should be considered very seriously when selecting an interview.

Who Will Be Administering the Interviews?

In general, fully structured interviews can be administered by laypersons with no specific training in psychology. In contrast, semistructured interviews require interviewers with a master's or doctoral degree in psychology, social work, or related fields, though people with a bachelor's degree in these fields can be trained to administer the interviews in well-supervised circumstances. Thus, for research projects in which research assistants will be administering the diagnostic interviews, fully structured interviews are a more appropriate choice.

What Resources Are Available for Training?

Structured and semistructured interviews vary greatly in the amount of time required to train staff and clinicians to administer them in a valid and reliable manner. When choosing an interview for your clinic or research project, you must weigh the cost of an expensive training program or time-intensive practice against having a more sophisticated and thorough interview.

Structured diagnostic interviews have multiple strengths that make them invaluable tools for researchers and clinicians. Although limitations exist, most of which challenge the validity of such interviews, we believe the strengths far outweigh these limitations, particularly given the current lack of alternative methods of classification and diagnosis. There is currently a fairly wide selection of structured and semistructured interviews from which to choose. In the next two sections, we review several of the most well-researched diagnostic interviews currently available. A summary of the characteristics of each interview is presented in Table 3.1.

REVIEW OF STRUCTURED DIAGNOSTIC INTERVIEWS

NIMH Diagnostic Interview Schedule for Children-IV (NIMH DISC-IV)

Description and Format. The National Institute of Mental Health Diagnostic Interview Schedule for Children, Version IV (NIMH DISC-IV) (Shaffer, Fisher, Lucas, Dulcan, & Schwab-Stone, 2000) is a comprehensive, structured diagnostic instrument that assesses over 30 psychiatric diagnoses in children aged 6 to 17 years, using both *DSM-IV* (APA, 1994) and *ICD* (WHO, 1993) criteria. This is the oldest and most well-studied structured diagnostic interview for children. The original DISC-1 (Costello, Edelbrock, Dulcan, Kalas, & Klaric, 1984) was modeled after the Diagnostic Interview Schedule (DIS) used with adults (Robins, Helzer, & Croughan, 1981; Robins, Cottler, Bucholz, & Compton, 1996) and was developed in response to a request by the National Institute of Mental Health (NIMH) for a measure that could be used in epidemiologic studies to examine the prevalence and correlates of child mental disorders in the United States. Revisions have since been made to improve the performance of the measure and correspond to changes to the *DSM*, including the DISC-2.1 (Jensen et al., 1995) and DISC-2.3 (Shaffer et al., 1996), the latter of which was also translated into Spanish (Bravo, Woodbury-Farina, Canino, & Rubio-Stipec, 1993). The current version, the DISC-IV (Shaffer et al., 2000), includes new items in both the schizophrenia and substance use sections, allowing for greater comparison to other adult and youth diagnostic interview schedules. It is also offered as a computerized program, the C-DISC-4.0, which facilitates its administration in a variety of settings. Moreover, the recently developed DISC Predictive Scales provide an efficient and effective means of accurately screening for a wide range of mental disorders in a relatively short amount of time (Lucas et al., 2001).

This instrument has been used in research and clinical settings, in addition to the large-scale epidemiological surveys for which it was designed. The DISC-IV includes separate modules for the child and parent/caretaker, as do most of the interviews reviewed below. The information from these interviews can be considered separately or synthesized to generate a single, best-estimate diagnosis. The complete DISC-IV consists of approximately 3,000 questions, to be read verbatim. The interview begins with an introductory module that includes demographic questions and is followed by six modules assessing different diagnoses (anxiety, mood, disruptive, substance use, schizophrenia, and miscellaneous disorders), each of which is structured to be self-contained. Endorsements

TABLE 3.1   Summary of Structured and Semistructured Interviews for Children and Adolescents

Interview	Version	Diagnostic Criteria	No. of Disorders Assessed	Time Frame Assessed	Intended Age Range	Interview Time in Minutes	Training Time
Structured							
NIMH DISC	DISC-IV	DSM-IV DSM-III-R ICD-10	30	Current/Past 4 weeks Past year Lifetime	6–17 years	Community = 70 Clinical = 105	C-DISC = 2–3 days DISC-IV = 4–6 days
ChIPS	ChIPS	DSM-IV	20	Current	6–18 years	Community = 20 Outpatient = 30–40 Inpatient = 50	2–6 days
MINI	MINI-Kid	DSM-IV ICD-10	28	Current	6–18 years	15–30 per informant	1–3 hours
CIDI	CIDI-A	DSM-IV ICD-10	25	Current/Past year Lifetime	13–17 years	120	40-hour self-study CD-ROM and 3-day in-person training
Semistructured							
K-SADS	K-SADS-P K-SADS-E K-SADS-P/L	DSM-IV DSM-III-R	33	Current Past year Lifetime	6–18 years	120–180	2–4 weeks
DICA	DICA	DSM-IV DSM-III-R ICD-10	26	Current Lifetime	6–17 years	60–120	2–4 weeks
CAPA	CAPA YAPA PAPA	DSM-IV DSM-III-R ICD-10	>30	Current/ Past 3 months	3–6 years 9–17 years 18+ years	60–120	2–4 weeks
ISCA	ISCA-C&L ISC-C&I FISA	DSM-IV	>30	Current/Lifetime Current/Interim	8–17 years 18+ years	Children = 45–90 Parent = 120–150	2–4 weeks

NOTE: All interview abbreviations are spelled out in the text.

37

of "stem" questions are followed by additional questions more specific to that symptom. A minor drawback of this approach is that symptoms associated with more than one disorder, such as irritability, restlessness, and concentration problems, may be queried more than once. Time frames assessed are the past 4 weeks and the past 12 months, with an optional lifetime module. Administration of the DISC-IV youth interview requires approximately 70 minutes per informant in community samples and 105 minutes per informant in clinical samples (Shaffer, Fisher, & Lucas, 1999).

Training Required. Given the highly structured format of the DISC-IV and the limited clinical decision making required, training in the use of this measure is relatively brief, taking 2 to 3 days for the computer-assisted version and an additional 2 to 3 days for the paper format (Shaffer et al., 2000).

Reliability and Validity. The DISC-2.1, DISC-2.3, and DISC-IV all show acceptable test-retest reliability in both community and clinical samples (Jensen et al., 1995; Schwab-Stone et al., 1996; Shaffer et al., 2000). Although the validity of the DISC-IV has not yet been formally tested, the validity of the DISC-2.3 has been demonstrated by showing moderate to good agreement on the presence versus absence of each disorder when using the DISC-2.3 relative to a clinical follow-up interview, with an average kappa of 0.59, ranging from 0.40 for separation anxiety disorder to 0.80 for conduct disorder (Schwab-Stone et al., 1996).

Comments on the NIMH-DISC-IV. The primary advantage of the DISC-IV is that the highly structured format is designed for optimal reliability for trained laypersons and clinical interviewers alike. In addition, the computer-assisted version is both inexpensive and easy to use and allows for maximum standardization and reduced error. Overall, the DISC-IV is a cost-efficient and adaptive instrument for assessing a comprehensive range of child and adolescent diagnoses.

Children's Interview
for Psychiatric Syndromes (ChIPS)

Description and Format. The Children's Interview for Psychiatric Syndromes (ChIPS) (Teare, Fristad, Weller, Weller, & Salmon, 1998a) is a fully

structured interview administered to children aged 6 to 18 years that assesses 20 different Axis I disorders using *DSM-IV* criteria, as well as a range of psychosocial stressors, such as child abuse and neglect. The ChIPS was developed with the aim of providing a briefer, more simply worded structured diagnostic interview than was previously available (Weller, Weller, Fristad, Teare, & Schechter, 2000). The wording of this interview was initially intended for children aged 6 to 12 years but is appropriate for adolescents as well. A benefit of the simpler wording and shorter interview items is greater brevity and comprehension. Given the focus on brevity and on providing *DSM-IV* diagnoses, each section of the ChIPS begins by querying several of the cardinal symptoms needed to meet diagnostic criteria, and if these are absent, remaining questions in that section are skipped. While designed for use in epidemiologic studies, the ChIPS may also be utilized in clinical research settings, as an assessment tool in mental health clinics, and in nonclinical arenas, such as schools.

The 20 Axis I disorders assessed by the ChIPS include attention-deficit/hyperactivity disorder, oppositional defiant disorder, conduct disorder, substance abuse, specific phobia, social phobia, separation anxiety, generalized anxiety, obsessive-compulsive disorder, acute stress disorder, posttraumatic stress disorder, anorexia, bulimia, depression, dysthymia, mania, hypomania, enuresis, encopresis, and schizophrenia/psychosis. Completion of the ChIPS is indeed quite brief, requiring approximately 50 minutes for those from inpatient samples, 30 minutes for outpatients, and 21 minutes for those from community-based samples (Weller et al., 2000).

Training Required. Like the DISC interviews, the ChIPS is designed to be administered by lay interviewers with at least a bachelor's degree in a mental-health-related field and good familiarity with psychopathology. A training manual and preferred training format have been developed, which includes a review of the disorders covered and the ChIPS interview itself, observation of a training video, and supervised practice of repeated administrations. It is estimated that training on the administration of the ChIPS takes less than 1 week to complete.

Reliability and Validity. The ChIPS has demonstrated strong interrater reliability, with agreement for all trained interviewers ≥.90 (Teare et al., 1998a). Multiple studies have consistently supported the validity of ChIPS diagnoses when compared with semistructured interviews and clinician interviews (e.g., Herjanic & Reich, 1982). Moderate to strong correspondence between the ChIPS and the Diagnostic Interview for Children and Adolescents (described below) has been demonstrated across settings, including inpatient (Fristad, Glickman et al., 1998; Teare et al., 1998a, 1998b), outpatient (Teare et al., 1998b), and community (Fristad, Cummins et al., 1998) samples. Fristad and colleagues (Fristad, Teare, Weller, Weller, & Salmon, 1998) also demonstrated moderate agreement (average kappa = 0.41) between the parent version of the ChIPS (P-ChIPS) and the child version, and between the P-ChIPS and clinician diagnosis (average kappa = 0.49).

Comments on the ChIPS. The primary advantages of the ChIPS compared with other diagnostic instruments are that it (a) contains simple, developmentally appropriate language and short sentence structure, to facilitate respondent cooperation and comprehension; (b) is quite brief; (c) has good reliability and validity; and (d) has high sensitivity as a screening instrument, meaning that it identifies a high percentage of true-positive cases. Several drawbacks to the ChIPS are that it (a) does not cover as many diagnoses as some other instruments; (b) has been examined primarily by only one research team; (c) has not been as widely used and evaluated as some other measures; and (d) has a trade-off to its high sensitivity—a less impressive specificity, meaning that it tends to overidentify cases. The ChIPS may be best used as a screening instrument for major forms of psychopathology, where there is an interest in brevity and case identification, and when working with younger children or those with potential cognitive limitations.

MINI International Neuropsychiatric Interview (MINI-Kid)

Description and Format. The MINI International Neuropsychiatric Interview for Children and Adolescents (MINI-Kid) (Sheehan, Shytle, & Milo, 2004) is a fully structured interview designed for children and parents that assesses 28 Axis I diagnoses using *DSM-IV* criteria. Parent and child are interviewed separately for children over 13 years of age and together for

those less than 13, with questions directed at the child. The MINI-Kid generates current diagnoses, with the time frame addressed varying depending on the *DSM-IV* diagnosis in question. For instance, for major depressive disorder, questions focus on the past 2 weeks, whereas for oppositional defiant disorder, they focus on the past 6 months. The presence of lifetime diagnosis is examined only for some diagnoses (panic disorder, psychotic disorders, and mood disorder with psychotic features). The MINI-Kid is modeled after adult interviews from the MINI series of instruments, which include the MINI (16 disorders assessed in an approximately 15-minute interview), the MINI-Plus (23 disorders assessed in an approximately 45- to 60-minute interview), and the MINI-Tracking (each symptom from 16 disorders assessed on a 0–4 scale) (see Sheehan et al., 1998).

Like the original MINI, the MINI-Kid begins with a screening interview that includes between one and four summary questions from each diagnosis in order to determine which modules from the main body of the MINI-Kid should be administered. This significantly reduces the number of questions asked of each child, and thus the amount of time required to administer the MINI-Kid, but may limit the sensitivity of this measure. Once in the body of the MINI-Kid, each module begins with one or more cardinal symptoms that must be endorsed in order to continue with the rest of that module. Considering these are the symptoms required to make a given *DSM-IV* diagnosis, skipping the rest of the items in the module following a "no" response here will have no effect on the diagnoses generated. If one is interested in collecting symptom-level data, however, one may choose to ignore these skip rules or select a measure without such rules.

Training Required. The MINI family of instruments was designed to be easily administered by research or clinical staff with at least a bachelor's degree in a health-related field. The authors recommend training and using professional interviewers or "health information technicians" to administer the interviews (Sheehan et al., 1998). Training is available from the test developer and can be completed in approximately 1 to 3 hours.

Reliability and Validity. The reliability and validity of the MINI-Kid are currently being evaluated, and data on this measure were not yet available at the time this chapter was completed. Notably, prior studies have demonstrated the reliability and validity of the adult versions of the MINI (Sheehan et al., 1997; Sheehan et al., 1998).

Comments on the MINI-Kid. The MINI-Kid is a brief yet comprehensive instrument that is easy to follow and administer and is a good choice for both research and clinical settings. It is administered in less than half the time of most semistructured interviews, is much shorter than many structured interviews, and generates a fairly wide range of *DSM-IV* diagnoses. One caveat is that data on the reliability and validity of the MINI-Kid are not yet available. Given the strong performance of the adult MINI and the close correspondence between the MINI and the MINI-Kid in terms of structure, it is likely that evidence of the reliability and validity of the MINI-Kid will soon be available.

Composite International Diagnostic Interview-Adolescent Version (CIDI-A)

Description and Format. The Composite International Diagnostic Interview-Adolescent Version (CIDI-A) is a fully structured diagnostic interview that assesses child and adolescent mental disorders and is part of the CIDI series of instruments. The World Health Organization CIDI (WHO, 1990) was initially developed as an expansion of the DIS (Robins et al., 1981; Robins et al., 1996) undertaken because although the DIS provides *DSM* diagnoses, it does not generate diagnoses based on the *ICD* and thus is of limited usefulness in countries that follow the *ICD* system. The CIDI was subsequently expanded by the WHO World Mental Health (WMH) Survey Initiative to include an assessment of risk factors and consequences of mental disorders as well as characteristics and patterns of treatment received, to form the WMH-CIDI (Kessler, Abelson, et al., 2004; Kessler & Ustun, 2004).

The CIDI-A was modeled after the WMH-CIDI, with modifications to make it more appropriate for interviewing youth aged 13 to 17 years. For instance, the CIDI-A includes a greater focus on disorders of childhood and adolescence and differences in some of the risk factors and social consequences examined. In addition, the CIDI-A incorporates several recent technological advances of the WMH-CIDI, including the use of computer-assisted administration and direct data entry

scoring software, which greatly facilitate large-scale research projects (see Kessler & Ustun, 2004). Given the interviewees are adolescents and not children, there is a greater emphasis on adolescent report than on parent report of symptoms. Nevertheless, although the CIDI-A interview is conducted with the adolescent only, parents complete a self-administered questionnaire that assesses parent report of adolescent symptoms, functioning, risk factors, consequences, treatment, and other related domains.

Training Required. Training in the use and administration of the CIDI family of instruments is available in 25 different languages from the WMH-CIDI Training and Research Center (see http://www3.who.int/cidi). Training consists of completion of a 40-hour self-study CD-ROM module, followed by a 3-day, face-to-face training session at one of the WMH-CIDI training sites.

Reliability and Validity. The CIDI-A is currently undergoing evaluation in the NCS-A, a project conducted as part of the National Comorbidity Survey Replication (NCS-R) (Kessler & Merikangas, 2004) that involves interviewing a nationally representative sample of 10,000 adolescents in the United States carried out from 2001 to 2002. Data have been collected and are undergoing analysis at the time this chapter was written, and so data on the reliability and validity of the CIDI-A are not yet available. Notably, as in the NCS and NCS-R adult surveys (Kessler, Berglund, et al., 2004; Kessler et al., 1994), clinical reappraisal interviews are being carried out among a subsample of respondents in the NCS-A to examine the validity of the CIDI diagnoses. In the NCS-A, a clinical interviewer assesses the adolescent and a parent via telephone, using a semistructured clinical interview (K-SADS, described in the next section) in order to determine the level of agreement between CIDI-A diagnoses and those generated from the semistructured clinical interview. The adult version of the WMH-CIDI has demonstrated strong reliability and validity (Kessler, Abelson, et al., 2004), and it is expected that the CIDI-A will demonstrate strong reliability and validity as well.

Comments on the CIDI-A. The CIDI interviews are an excellent choice if conducting a large-scale study ($N > 1,000$) of the presence, correlates, and consequences of mental disorders and other areas of health-related functioning. Notable strengths include the availability of computer-assisted administration and scoring, strong psychometric properties, and availability of training and assessment materials in 25 different languages. One disadvantage of using the CIDI series is the comparative cost and time required for training, making it a less desirable option for smaller studies in which the conduction of more clinically informed semistructured interviews is feasible.

REVIEW OF SEMISTRUCTURED DIAGNOSTIC INTERVIEWS

Schedule for Affective Disorders and Schizophrenia for School-Age Children (K-SADS)

Description and Format. The Schedule for Affective Disorders and Schizophrenia for School-Age Children, Present State (K-SADS-P) (Chambers et al., 1985) was originally developed from the Schedule for Affective Disorders and Schizophrenia (Endicott & Spitzer, 1978) as a combined parent and child semistructured interview for assessing child and adolescent psychopathology, both in the past week and past 12 months. The parent and child versions of the interviews are identical in content. Subsequently, an epidemiologic version (K-SADS-E) (Puig-Antich, Orvaschel, Tabrizi, & Chambers, 1980) was designed to include the most severe past-episode and lifetime diagnoses. The K-SADS-E also introduced screening questions that if not endorsed allowed for subsequent questions to be skipped.

The K-SADS-P has undergone four iterations to keep it up-to-date with the current *DSM* and Research Diagnostic Criteria (RDC) (Spitzer, Endicott, & Robins, 1978) systems. Currently, it provides diagnostic criteria for both the *DSM-III-R* and *DSM-IV,* and it includes the addition of the Clinical Global Impressions Scale, measuring both severity and improvement. A duration question was also added following each symptomatic assessment to determine the date of onset and offset for each disorder.

The K-SADS-E is in its fourth version and is applicable to *DSM-III, DSM-III-R, DSM-IV,* and RDC systems. Past episodes are coded as *present* or *absent,* while current episodes are rated as

mild, moderate, or *severe.* The most significant change from previous versions is the addition of generalized anxiety and posttraumatic stress disorder symptoms and criteria.

In addition to the K-SADS-P and K-SADS-E, Kaufman and colleagues (1997) developed the K-SADS-P/L (Present and Lifetime), reflecting both *DSM-III-R* and *DSM-IV* criteria. The K-SADS-P/L assesses both current (prior 2 months) and lifetime diagnoses. The format of the interview was modified slightly to an 82-symptom screen interview, which queries key symptoms in 20 diagnostic areas, and 5 supplemental score sheets (affective, psychotic, anxiety, behavioral, and substance abuse/other disorders) to be completed when items from the corresponding key symptoms sections are endorsed. Approximately 2 to 3 hours is required to complete a combined parent/child K-SADS-P/L interview (Ambrosini, 2000).

Training Required. Because the K-SADS is a semistructured interview, more extensive training is required to administer it than for the previously described structured interviews. Interviewers typically have a bachelor's or master's degree in psychology, social work, or a related field. Comprehensive K-SADS training entails gaining familiarity with a version of the K-SADS, didactic and interviewer-observer training to develop the flow for the interview and explain scoring nuances, and several joint interviews with other interviewers for rater-reliability training in probing and scoring. This process often takes anywhere from a few days to several weeks.

Reliability and Validity. The K-SADS displayed strong psychometric properties (Ambrosini, 2000). Specifically, the test-retest reliability for the K-SADS-P/L demonstrated an average kappa statistic of 0.74 for current diagnoses, with kappa coefficients ranging from 0.63 for attention-deficit/hyperactivity disorder to 0.90 for major depression. For the K-SADS-E, the average kappa statistic for current diagnoses was 0.69, ranging from 0.51 for oppositional disorder to 0.77 for attention-deficit/hyperactivity disorder.

The K-SADS has proven to be a sensitive and effective instrument for assessing psychiatric diagnoses. It has been shown to have good criterion validity compared with a number of measures of depressive symptoms, including the Beck Depression Inventory (BDI) (Beck, Ward,

Mendelson, Mock, & Erbaugh, 1961), the Children's Depression Inventory (CDI) (Kovacs, 1985), and the Hamilton Rating Scale for Depression (HRSD) (Hamilton, 1960; McConville, Ambrosini, Somoza, Bianchi, & Minnery, 1995; McLaughlin, Ambrosini, Fallon, Bianchi, & Metz, 1997). The K-SADS has been shown to effectively distinguish (a) nondepressed psychiatric controls from depressed psychiatric subjects and (b) those with major depressive disorder from those with minor depression/dysthymic disorder (McConville et al., 1995; McLaughlin et al., 1997). Furthermore, criterion validity has been established for current diagnoses from the K-SADS-P/L using the Internalizing and Externalizing subscales of the Child Behavior Checklist (Achenbach & Edelbrock, 1983); the Conners' Parent Rating Scale (Conners, Sitarenios, Parker, & Epstein, 1998) for attention-deficit/hyperactivity disorder; the Screen for Child Anxiety-Related Emotional Disorders (Birmaher et al., 1997) for anxiety disorders; and the CDI and BDI for depressive disorders (Kaufman et al., 1997).

Comments on the K-SADS. The K-SADS is a widely used diagnostic tool that generates current, past, and lifetime psychopathology in children and adolescents. A primary advantage of the K-SADS is its comprehensiveness and flexibility. The K-SADS also scores each symptom using a graded-severity scale (i.e., 0–2 rather than no/yes), thus providing a more nuanced psychopathological profile for each respondent. The structure of the K-SADS-P/L as a series of screening questions, with supplements to assess endorsed symptoms further, allows the length of the interview to be proportional to severity of the clinical presentation.

Diagnostic Interview for Children and Adolescents (DICA)

Description and Format. The Diagnostic Interview for Children and Adolescents (DICA) (Herjanic & Campbell, 1977), like the NIMH-DISC and CIDI, was modeled after the Diagnostic Interview Schedule (DIS) (Robins et al., 1981; Robins et al., 1996), to be administered by nonclinicians in epidemiologic studies. In subsequent versions, the DICA has evolved from a structured to a semistructured interview, retaining structured wording but allowing the interviewer to deviate from the script and probe for information

using their own clinical decision making (Reich, 2000). To elicit the most accurate information, some questions also require examples of the behaviors and feelings endorsed by respondents. The DICA generates diagnoses based on criteria from the *DSM-III-R, DSM-IV,* and *ICD-10.* In addition to formal diagnoses, the DICA assesses psychosocial risk and protective factors, such as parental arguing or drug use, with an added section on respondents' appearance and demeanor. The DICA assesses lifetime disorders as well as current diagnoses.

The DICA is available in three versions: child (DICA-C), adolescent (DICA-A), and parent (DICA-P) (Reich, Herjanic, Welner, & Gandhi, 1982). The DICA-C and DICA-A differ only in the developmental level of the wording; however, the DICA-P also includes a perinatal module with questions about the mother's pregnancy and an early development section about the child's temperament, behavior disorders, medical history, physical disabilities, and developmental milestones. All versions are also offered as computerized interviews, such that the DICA may be self-administered, with respondents receiving instructions and answering questions on a computer screen. The psychometric properties of the computerized versus the interviewer-administered DICA demonstrates kappa coefficients that are slightly lower for the computerized version (Reich, Cottler, & McCallum, 1995), which may suggest that it is best used as a screening tool to be consulted during face-to-face interviews.

Training Required. Training for the DICA, as with most semistructured interviews, takes more time and requires a higher level of clinical training than structured interviews. Training for the DICA requires approximately 2 to 4 weeks of instruction and practice.

Reliability and Validity. The DICA-C and DICA-A have demonstrated good test-retest reliability in both clinical and community samples, as well as adequate validity when compared with information obtained from other clinical sources, including clinical interview and ratings scales (Boyle et al., 1993; De la Osa, Ezpeleta, Domenech, Navarro, & Losilla, 1997; Reich, 2000; Welner, Reich, Herjanic, Jung, & Amado, 1987).

Comments on the DICA. The DICA is a fairly straightforward and easy-to-use semistructured interview that is likely to be beneficial to those working with children and adolescents in both research and clinical settings. It assesses a broad range of diagnoses, psychosocial stressors, and developmental constructs and has been shown to have strong psychometric properties. Moreover, newer, computerized versions make it a viable prescreening tool for clinical research.

Child and Adolescent Psychiatric Assessment (CAPA)

Description and Format. The Child and Adolescent Psychiatric Assessment (CAPA) (Angold et al., 1995) assesses psychopathology in those aged 9 to 17 years, using a semistructured, modular format such that sections may be administered independent of the complete interview schedule (Angold & Costello, 1995, 2000). The CAPA provides symptom profiles and diagnostic criteria for *DSM-III-R, DSM-IV,* and *ICD-10* systems. Mandatory, structured questions are followed by suggested supplemental questions for further clarity or detail. The CAPA manual functions primarily as a glossary, with detailed descriptions of symptoms to assist the interviewer in determining appropriate probes. The CAPA is also available in computer-assisted format.

The CAPA assesses symptoms occurring in the past three months, termed the *primary period,* due to concerns about problems with the accuracy of recall beyond three months. Symptoms are assessed on three levels: intensity, time-related severity ratings, and psychosocial impairment related to the presence of the symptom. Intensity relates to symptom strength and is rated on a 3- or 4-point scale. Time-related severity ratings refer to either the duration of symptomatic episodes or the quantity of episodes, and psychosocial impairment refers to incapacity in 19 different domains, such as home or school. Both the parent version (CAPA-P) and the child version (CAPA-C) require approximately 1 hour for administration.

Three kinds of probe questions are used in the CAPA. First, screening questions assess key phenomena, such as depression, and are typically asked verbatim. If a screening question is endorsed, two more levels of probing are used. Mandatory probes are asked of everyone, unless the information has been provided previously, and discretionary probes are asked only when information is specifically needed for clinical or research purposes. The CAPA ends with interviewer ratings of 67 observable behaviors, including ratings for motor behavior, mood state, quality of social interaction, and psychotic behavior.

Several alternate versions of the CAPA have been developed for those above and below the developmental level addressed by the CAPA. The Young Adult Psychiatric Assessment (YAPA) (Simonoff et al., 1997) is an adapted CAPA interview schedule administered to those 18 years old and above, with age-appropriate questions regarding areas of functioning, including living situations and relationships. Information is not obtained from the parent on the YAPA. Alternatively, the Preschool-Age Psychiatric Assessment (PAPA) (Egger, Ascher, & Angold, 1999) is a parent report interview for diagnosing psychiatric disorders in preschool children aged 2 through 5 years. A computerized version of the original CAPA is also currently in development.

Reliability and Validity. The adolescent interview has shown strong test-retest reliability, with an average kappa value of 0.81 across diagnoses, ranging from 0.55 for conduct disorder and 1.00 for substance abuse/dependence (see Angold & Costello, 2000). The CAPA has also shown good construct validity along 10 criteria: diagnostic rates across age and gender, diagnostic comorbidity, symptom correlation with psychosocial impairment, agreement of parent/child reports with parent/teacher reports, use of mental health services, family history of psychopathology, divergence in genetic profiles associated with specific diagnoses, consistency over time, prediction of negative life outcome, and correlation of interviewer observation with diagnoses and treatment.

Comments on the CAPA. A useful, unique feature of the CAPA is the glossary, which is used in matching the symptoms described by the interviewee in response to questions to determine the presence, absence, or quality of the symptom. Moreover, unlike most other semistructured interviews, the CAPA has formal rules about the use of probe and screening questions. The development of the different versions of the CAPA is a great benefit, as it will increase its use in more diverse populations across multiple domains. Limitations primarily involve the high cost and time required for training.

Interview Schedule
for Children and Adolescents (ISCA)

Description and Format. The Interview Schedule for Children and Adolescents (ISCA) (Kovacs, 1997) is a semistructured diagnostic interview originally designed to assess childhood-onset mood disorders in children aged 8 to 17 years. Consequently, two versions were developed: an intake version for use as a first assessment and a follow-up version to track symptom change over time. These are currently the ISCA-Current and Lifetime (ISCA-C&L) and the ISCA-Current and Interim (ISCA-C&I), respectively (Kovacs, 1997). The ISCA has been formatted for both *DSM-III-R* and *DSM-IV* systems; items have been added to more extensively assess dysthymic, manic, and hypomanic symptoms; and a version was developed for use with young adults. To evaluate respondents who are young adults at first administration (i.e., 18+ years), the Follow-up Interview Schedule for Adults (FISA) has also been developed (Kovacs, 1995).

Each version of the ISCA examines signs and symptoms of over 30 different Axis I disorders (Sherrill & Kovacs, 2000). The ISCA also assesses the respondents' mental status and includes sections for the interviewers' behavioral observations, clinical impressions, and information about the respondents' developmental milestones, followed by one additional item about global functioning. Multiple phrasings are offered for each item to provide standardized administration while also ensuring respondent comprehension. The ISCA is a relatively extensive diagnostic interview, with parent interviews lasting approximately 120 to 150 minutes and child interviews taking 45 to 90 minutes. ISCA administration begins with the parent interview, then the child, and afterward the interviewer determines summary ratings for the symptoms and makes diagnostic determinations. Unlike other interviews reviewed here, the ISCA does not include skip logic, which means that all questions are administered to all respondents. This provides comprehensive information for each respondent but increases the time required for assessment.

Training Required. As with all semistructured diagnostic interviews, evaluators should be clinicians familiar with the *DSM* system, and administrators should receive comprehensive training in the use of this measure before conducting clinical interviews.

Reliability and Validity. The ISCA has undergone extensive psychometric testing and has demonstrated strong reliability and validity across multiple studies (see Sherrill & Kovacs, 2000, for a review). More specifically, prior studies have demonstrated the strong interrater reliability (Kovacs, Feinberg, Crouse-Novak, Paulauskas, & Finkelstein, 1984; Kovacs, Obrosky, Goldston, & Drash, 1997) and test-retest reliability (Last, Hersen, Kazdin, Finkelstein, & Strauss, 1987) of the ISCA. Moreover, studies evaluating the psychosocial correlates of ISCA-assessed diagnoses have demonstrated the construct validity of this measure. For instance, children diagnosed with current depressive and/or conduct disorders scored lower on social competence as measured by the Child Behavior Checklist (Achenbach & Edelbrock, 1983). In addition, researchers have found that for children with early-onset affective disorders, family members were five times more likely to have lifetime depressive disorders and two times more likely to have recurrent unipolar depressive disorders compared with psychiatric controls (Kovacs, Devlin, Pollock, Richards, & Mukerji, 1997). Mothers of children with ISCA-diagnosed separation anxiety disorder and/or overanxious disorder exhibited higher rates of lifetime and current anxiety disorders than those for psychiatric controls (Last, Hersen, Kazdin, Francis, & Grubb, 1987).

Comments on the ISCA. The ISCA has several notable strengths. First, severity ratings are more sensitive than for other diagnostic instruments, providing valuable information for symptom analysis. Also, because all symptoms for each diagnosis are assessed in the core instrument, the symptom profiles for the ISCA are more comprehensive than for most other interview schedules. The ISCA has been used widely and successfully for a number of longitudinal studies, and the development of the FISA ensures that subjects may be readministered the instrument well into adulthood. Limitations of the ISCA are that due to its comprehensive structure, interview administration is generally long.

NEW DEVELOPMENTS IN DIAGNOSTIC INTERVIEWING WITH YOUNGER CHILDREN

Given that there are so many factors that influence poor parent-child agreement, as mentioned above, it would be useful to have a structured interview that requires only one informant but yields accurate diagnostic information. One attempt at this is the "Dominic" (Smolla, Valla, Bergeron, Berthiaume, & St-Georges, 2004; Valla, Bergeron, & Smolla, 2000), a structured computerized assessment consisting of symptom descriptions accompanied by cartoons, which is specifically designed to assess mental disorders in children aged 6 to 11.

"Dominic" is a child placed in daily situations illustrating emotions and behaviors. The voice-over describes the pictures and asks the child whether he or she would react like Dominic—a nonjudgmental approach. Children click on *Yes* or *No*. Because of the known difficulty that children have in understanding frequency, duration, and onset questions, those types of questions have been omitted. This instrument provides assessment of the seven most frequent difficulties in primary-school children: attention-deficit/hyperactivity, opposition, conduct, depression, separation anxiety, generalized anxiety, and specific phobias. Support for use of the Dominic in combination with structured interviews has been recently derived from a study that compared DICA questions (usual administration) with the same questions matched with the Dominic cartoons. Kappa values were found to be high for these two administrations, and, importantly, children commonly reported better understanding of the questions paired with the Dominic cartoons (Reich, 2000). Thus, it seems that adapting structured interviews in this manner may help improve younger children's comprehension of the questions, and, subsequently, the reliability of their reports.

Another measure aimed at increasing child understanding of symptom domains and thus improving the reliability and validity of responses is the Berkeley Puppet Interview (BPI) (Measelle, Ablow, Cowan, & Cowan, 1998). The BPI is an interview developed for young children 4 to 8 years of age, in which the interviewer queries the child on multiple domains using puppets that present bipolar response options for each item, in an attempt to increase understanding of each item and decrease social desirability. Children can respond to each item verbally or nonverbally, thus increasing responding among socially anxious or inhibited children.

The BPI assesses children's self-perceptions regarding academic competence, achievement motivation, social competence, and peer acceptance. The BPI also includes domains related to mental disorders, such as depression-anxiety and aggression-hostility. Although the BPI does not generate the wide range of clinical diagnoses provided by other interviews reviewed here, it does generate ratings on children's self-perceptions that correspond with ratings from other informants (Measelle et al., 1998), and the depression anxiety and aggression hostility subscales have moderate to strong internal consistency and test-retest reliability in clinical samples, as well as evidence for their validity via significant relations with other measures of psychopathology (Ablow et al., 1999; Luby et al., 2002). Although the Dominic and BPI are newer methods with less empirical support than most of the instruments reviewed here, they have received strong support in early studies and represent useful and innovative means of examining the presence of mental disorders among younger children.

Summary

The most reliable and valid method of diagnosing mental disorders among children and adolescents currently available is the use of structured and semistructured diagnostic interviews. Although there are factors that can limit the reliability and validity of the results of these interviews, they offer many advantages over the use of unstructured clinical interviews and represent the current gold standard in the diagnosis of mental disorders. A wide range of structured and semistructured interviews are available for use in both research and clinical settings, and we have reviewed the characteristics of eight of the most commonly used and well-researched instruments, as well as factors to consider when selecting from among these interviews, in an effort to guide those interested in incorporating these methods into their scientific or clinical work.

In addition to continuing to examine the usefulness of existing interview methods, recent and future work on the assessment of child and adolescent mental disorders is incorporating novel, developmentally appropriate methods of obtaining information from younger children, such as the use of cartoons and puppets. In addition, future work in this area will undoubtedly incorporate changes in diagnostic procedures required after the release of the fifth edition of the *DSM* in the coming years, and it may increasingly be combined with other assessment methods, such as biological, behavioral, and neurocognitive tests, in the diagnosis of child and adolescent mental disorders. Regardless of the specific nature of these changes, for years to come, the use of structured and semistructured diagnostic interviews will continue to represent an important method of identifying, assessing, and tracking the treatment course of children and adolescents suffering from a wide range of mental disorders.

Notes

1. This distinction is perhaps clearest in modules assessing psychotic disorders. It is not entirely uncommon for nonpsychotic interviewees to endorse items about delusions or hallucinations (e.g., "Have you ever believed that people are plotting against you?") based on normal, nonpsychotic experiences. The ability to ask for specific examples and to ask clarifying follow-up questions can limit the occurrence of false-positive diagnoses that can result from such instances.

2. We use the term *children* to refer to both children and adolescents unless specifically noted.

References

Ablow, J. C., Measelle, J. R., Kraemer, H. C., Harrington, R., Luby, J., Smider, N., et al. (1999). The MacArthur Three-City Outcome Study: Evaluating multi-informant measures of young children's symptomatology. *Journal of the American Academy of Child & Adolescent Psychiatry, 38,* 1580–1590.

Achenbach, T. M., & Edelbrock, C. (1983). *Manual for the Child Behavior Checklist and Revised Child Behavior Profile.* Burlington: University of Vermont Department of Psychiatry.

Achenbach, T. M., & Edelbrock, C. S. (1984). Psychopathology of childhood. *Annual Review of Psychology, 35,* 227–256.

Ambrosini, P. J. (2000). Historical development and present status of the Schedule for Affective Disorders and Schizophrenia for School-Age Children (K-SADS). *Journal of the American Academy of Child & Adolescent Psychiatry, 39,* 49–58.

American Psychiatric Association. (1980). *Diagnostic and statistical manual of mental disorders* (3rd ed.). Washington, DC: Author.

American Psychiatric Association. (1994). *Diagnostic and statistical manual of mental disorders* (4th ed.). Washington, DC: Author.

Angold, A., & Costello, E. J. (1995). A test-retest reliability study of child-reported psychiatric symptoms and diagnoses using the Child and Adolescent Psychiatric Assessment (CAPA-C). *Psychological Medicine, 25,* 755–762.

Angold, A., & Costello, E. J. (2000). The Child and Adolescent Psychiatric Assessment (CAPA). *Journal of the American Academy of Child & Adolescent Psychiatry, 39,* 39–48.

Angold, A., Prendergast, M., Cox, A., Harrington, R., Simonoff, E., & Rutter, M. (1995). The Child and Adolescent Psychiatric Assessment (CAPA). *Psychological Medicine, 25,* 739–753.

Beauchaine, T. P. (2003). Taxometrics and developmental psychopathology. *Development and Psychopathology, 15,* 501–527.

Beck, A. T., Ward, C. H., Mendelson, M., Mock, J., & Erbaugh, J. (1961). An inventory for measuring depression. *Archives of General Psychiatry, 4,* 561–571.

Birmaher, B., Khetarpal, S., Brent, D., Cully, M., Balach, L., Kaufman, J., et al. (1997). The Screen for Child Anxiety Related Emotional Disorders (SCARED): Scale construction and psychometric characteristics. *Journal of the American Academy of Child & Adolescent Psychiatry, 36,* 545–553.

Boyle, M. H., Offord, D. R., Racine, Y., Sanford, M., Szatmari, P., Fleming, J. E., et al. (1993). Evaluations of the Diagnostic Interview for Children and Adolescents for use in general population samples. *Journal of Abnormal Child Psychology, 21,* 663–681.

Bravo, M., Woodbury-Farina, M., Canino, G. J., & Rubio-Stipec, M. (1993). The Spanish translation and cultural adaptation of the Diagnostic Interview Schedule for Children (DISC) in Puerto Rico. *Culture, Medicine, and Psychiatry, 17,* 329–344.

Breslau, N., Davis, G. C., & Prabucki, K. (1988). Depressed mothers as informants in family history research: Are they accurate? *Psychiatry Research, 24,* 345–359.

Briggs-Gowan, M. J., Carter, A. S., & Schwab-Stone, M. (1996). Discrepancies among mother, child, and teacher reports: Examining the contributions of maternal depression and anxiety. *Journal of Abnormal Child Psychology, 24,* 749–765.

Chambers, W. J., Puig-Antich, J., Hirsch, M., Paez, P., Ambrosini, P. J., Tabrizi, M. A., et al. (1985). The assessment of affective disorders in children and adolescents by semi-structured interview: Test-retest reliability of the schedule for affective disorders and schizophrenia for school-age children, present episode version. *Archives of General Psychiatry, 42,* 696–702.

Conners, C. K., Sitarenios, G., Parker, J. D. A., & Epstein, J. N. (1998). The revised Conners' Parent Rating Scale. *Journal of Abnormal Child Psychology, 26,* 257–268.

Costello, A. J., Edelbrock, C. S., Dulcan, M. D., Kalas, R., & Klaric, S. H. (1984). *Report of the NIMH Diagnostic Interview Schedule for Children (DISC).* Washington, DC: National Institute of Mental Health.

Crowley, T. J., Mikulich, S. K., Ehlers, K. M., Whitmore, E. A., & MacDonald, M. J. (2001). Validity of structured clinical evaluations in adolescents with conduct and substance problems. *Journal of the American Academy of Child & Adolescent Psychiatry, 40,* 265–273.

Dawes, R. M., Faust, D., & Meehl, P. E. (1989). Clinical versus actuarial judgment. *Science, 243,* 1668–1674.

De la Osa, N., Ezpeleta, L., Domenech, J. M., Navarro, J. B., & Losilla, J. M. (1997). Convergent and discriminate validity of the structured diagnostic interview for children and adolescents (DICA-R). *Psychology in Spain, 1*, 37–44.

De Los Reyes, A., & Kazdin, A. E. (2005). Informant discrepancies in the assessment of childhood psychopathology: A critical review, theoretical framework, and recommendations for further study. *Psychological Bulletin, 131*, 483–509.

DiBartolo, P. M., Albano, A. M., Barlow, D. H., & Heimberg, R. G. (1998). Cross-informant agreement in the assessment of social phobia in youth. *Journal of Abnormal Child Psychology, 26*, 213–220.

Edelbrock, C., Costello, A. J., Dulcan, M. K., Kalas, R., & Conover, N. C. (1985). Age differences in the reliability of the psychiatric interview of the child. *Child Development, 56*, 265–275.

Egger, H. L., Ascher, B. H., & Angold, A. (1999). *The Preschool Age Psychiatric Assessment: Version 1.1.* Durham, NC: Center for Developmental Epidemiology, Department of Psychiatry and Behavioral Sciences, Duke University Medical Center.

Endicott, J., & Spitzer, R. L. (1978). A diagnostic interview: The Schedule for Affective Disorders and Schizophrenia. *Archives of General Psychiatry, 35*, 837–844.

Fallon, T., & Schwab-Stone, M. (1994). Determinants of reliability in psychiatric surveys of children aged 6–12. *Journal of Child Psychology and Psychiatry, 35*, 1391–1408.

Fristad, M. A., Cummins, J., Verducci, J. S., Teare, M., Weller, E. B., & Weller, R. A. (1998). Study IV: Concurrent validity of the *DSM-IV* Revised Children's Interview for Psychiatric Syndromes (ChIPS). *Journal of Child and Adolescent Psychopharmacology, 8*, 227–236.

Fristad, M. A., Glickman, A. R., Verducci, J. S., Teare, M., Weller, E. B., & Weller, R. A. (1998). Study V: Children's Interview for Psychiatric Syndromes (ChIPS): Psychometrics in two community samples. *Journal of Child and Adolescent Psychopharmacology, 8*, 237–245.

Fristad, M. A., Teare, M., Weller, E. B., Weller, R. A., & Salmon, P. (1998). Study III: Development and concurrent validity of the Children's Interview for Psychiatric Syndromes-Parent Version (P-ChIPS). *Journal of Child and Adolescent Psychopharmacology,* 221–226.

Hamilton, M. (1960). A rating scale for depression. *Journal of Neurology, Neurosurgery, and Psychiatry, 23*, 56–62.

Hankin, B. L., Fraley, R. C., Lahey, B. B., & Waldman, I. D. (2005). Is depression best viewed as a continuum or discrete category? A taxometric analysis of childhood and adolescent depression in a population-based sample. *Journal of Abnormal Psychology, 114*, 96–110.

Hayes, S. C., Wilson, K. G., Gifford, E. V., Follette, V. M., & Strosahl, K. (1996). Experimental avoidance and behavioral disorders: A functional dimensional approach to diagnosis and treatment. *Journal of Consulting and Clinical Psychology, 64*, 1152–1168.

Herjanic, B., & Campbell, W. (1977). Differentiating psychiatrically disturbed children on the basis of a structured interview. *Journal of Abnormal Child Psychology, 5*, 127–134.

Herjanic, B., & Reich, W. (1982). Development of a structured psychiatric interview for children: Agreement between child and parent on individual symptoms. *Journal of Abnormal Child Psychology, 10*, 307–324.

Hicks, B. M., Krueger, R. F., Iacono, W. G., McGue, M., & Patrick, C. J. (2004). Family transmission and heritability of externalizing disorders: A twin-family study. *Archives of General Psychiatry, 61*, 922–928.

Jensen, P., Roper, M., Fisher, P., Piacentini, J., Canino, G., Richters, J., et al. (1995). Test-retest reliability of the Diagnostic Interview Schedule for Children (DISC 2.1): Parent, child, and combined algorithms. *Archives of General Psychiatry, 52*, 61–71.

Kaufman, J., Birmaher, B., Brent, D., Rao, U., Flynn, C., Moreci, P., et al. (1997). Schedule for Affective Disorders and Schizophrenia for School-Age Children-Present and Lifetime Version (K-SADS-PL): Initial reliability and validity data. *Journal of the American Academy of Child & Adolescent Psychiatry, 36*, 554–565.

Kessler, R. C., Abelson, J., Demler, O., Escobar, J. I., Gibbon, M., Guyer, M. E., et al. (2004). Clinical calibration of *DSM-IV* diagnoses in the World Mental Health (WMH) version of the World Health Organization (WHO) Composite International Diagnostic Interview (WMHCIDI). *International Journal of Methods in Psychiatric Research, 13*, 122–139.

Kessler, R. C., Berglund, P., Chiu, W. T., Demler, O., Heeringa, S., Hiripi, E., et al. (2004). The U.S. National Comorbidity Survey Replication (NCS-R): Design and field procedures. *International Journal of Methods in Psychiatric Research, 13*, 69–92.

Kessler, R. C., McGonagle, K. A., Zhao, S., Nelson, C. B., Hughes, M., Eshleman, S., et al. (1994). Lifetime and 12-month prevalence of *DSM-III-R* psychiatric disorders in the United States. Results from the National Comorbidity Survey. *Archives of General Psychiatry, 51*, 8–19.

Kessler, R. C., & Merikangas, K. R. (2004). The National Comorbidity Survey Replication (NCS-R): Background and aims. *International Journal of Methods in Psychiatric Research, 13*, 60–68.

Kessler, R. C., & Ustun, T. B. (2004). The World Mental Health (WMH) Survey Initiative Version of the World Health Organization (WHO) Composite International Diagnostic Interview (CIDI). *International Journal of Methods in Psychiatric Research, 13*, 93–121.

Kolko, D. J., & Kazdin, A. E. (1993). Emotional/behavioral problems in clinic and nonclinic children: Correspondence among child, parent, and teacher reports. *Journal of Child Psychology and Psychiatry, 34*, 991–1006.

Kovacs, M. (1985). The Children's Depression Inventory (CDI). *Psychopharmacology Bulletin, 21*, 995–998.

Kovacs, M. (1995). *Follow-Up Interview Schedule for Adults (FISA).* Pittsburgh: Western Psychiatric Institute and Clinic.

Kovacs, M. (1997). *The Interview Schedule for Children and Adolescents (ISCA): Current and Lifetime (ISCA-C &*

L) and Current and Interim (ISCA-C & I) Versions. Pittsburgh, PA: Western Psychiatric Institute and Clinic.

Kovacs, M., Devlin, B., Pollock, M., Richards, C., & Mukerji, P. (1997). A controlled family history study of childhood-onset depressive disorder. *Archives of General Psychiatry, 54,* 613–623.

Kovacs, M., Feinberg, T. L., Crouse-Novak, M. A., Paulauskas, S. L., & Finkelstein, R. (1984). Depressive disorders in childhood, I: A longitudinal prospective study of characteristics and recovery. *Archives of General Psychiatry, 41,* 229–237.

Kovacs, M., Obrosky, D. S., Goldston, D., & Drash, A. (1997). Major depressive disorder in youths with insulin-dependent diabetes mellitus: A controlled study of course and outcome. *Diabetes Care, 20,* 45–51.

Last, C. G., Hersen, M., Kazdin, A. E., Finkelstein, R., & Strauss, C. C. (1987). Comparison of *DSM-III* separation anxiety and overanxious disorders: Demographic characteristics and patterns of comorbidity. *Journal of the American Academy of Child & Adolescent Psychiatry, 26,* 527–531.

Last, C. G., Hersen, M., Kazdin, A. E., Francis, G., & Grubb, H. J. (1987). Psychiatric illness in the mothers of anxious children. *American Journal of Psychiatry, 144,* 1580–1515.

Luby, J. L., Heffelfinger, A., Measelle, J. R., Ablow, J. C., Essex, M. J., Dierker, L., et al. (2002). Differential performance of the MaCarthur HBQ and DISC-IV in identifying *DSM-IV* internalizing psychopathology in young children. *Journal of the American Academy of Child & Adolescent Psychiatry, 41,* 458–466.

Lucas, C. P., Zhang, H., Fisher, P. W., Shaffer, D., Regier, D. A., Narrow, W. E., et al. (2001). The DISC Predictive Scales (DPS): Efficiently screening for diagnoses. *Journal of the American Academy of Child & Adolescent Psychiatry, 40,* 443–449.

McConville, B. J., Ambrosini, P. J., Somoza, G., Bianchi, M. D., & Minnery, K. (1995). Optimal cut-off points for depression rating scales in adolescent depression. *Proceedings of the American Academy of Child & Adolescent Psychiatry, XI,* 126.

McLaughlin, J., Ambrosini, P. J., Fallon, T., Bianchi, M., & Metz, C. (1997). Validity parameters of the Children's Depression Inventory in preadolescent outpatients. *Proceedings of the American Academy of Child & Adolescent Psychiatry, XIII,* 139.

Measelle, J. R., Ablow, J. C., Cowan, P. A., & Cowan, C. P. (1998). Assessing young children's views of their academic, social, and emotional lives: An evaluation of the self-perception scales of the Berkeley Puppet Interview. *Child Development, 69,* 1556–1576.

Miles, D. R., Stallings, M. C., Young, S. E., Hewitt, J. K., Crowley, T. J., & Fulker, D. W. (1998). A family history and direct interview study of the familial aggregation of substance abuse: The adolescent substance abuse study. *Drug and Alcohol Dependence, 49,* 105–114.

Nock, M. K., & Prinstein, M. J. (2004). A functional approach to the assessment of self-mutilative behavior. *Journal of Consulting and Clinical Psychology, 72,* 885–890.

Perez, R. G., Ezpeleta, L. A., Domenech, J. M., & de la Osa, N. C. (1998). Characteristics of the subject and interview influencing the test-retest reliability of the diagnostic interview for children and adolescents-revised. *Journal of Child Psychology and Psychiatry, 39,* 963–972.

Prinstein, M. J., Nock, M. K., Spirito, A., & Grapentine, W. L. (2001). Multimethod assessment of suicidality in adolescent psychiatric inpatients: Preliminary results. *Journal of the American Academy of Child & Adolescent Psychiatry, 40,* 1053–1061.

Puig-Antich, J., Orvaschel, H., Tabrizi, M. A., & Chambers, W. (1980). *Schedule for affective disorders and schizophrenia for school-age children: Epidemiologic version.* New York: New York State Psychiatric Institution.

Rapee, R. M., Barrett, P. M., & Dadds, M. R. (1994). Reliability of the *DSM-III-R* childhood anxiety disorders using structured interview: Interrater and parent-child agreement. *Journal of the American Academy of Child & Adolescent Psychiatry, 33,* 984–992.

Reich, W. (2000). Diagnostic Interview for Children and Adolescents (DICA). *Journal of the American Academy of Child & Adolescent Psychiatry, 39,* 59–66.

Reich, W., Cottler, L., & McCallum, K. (1995). Computerized interviews as a method of assessing psychopathology in children. *Comprehensive Psychiatry, 36,* 40–45.

Reich, W., Herjanic, B., Welner, Z., & Gandhi, P. R. (1982). Development of a structured psychiatric interview for children: Agreement on diagnosis comparing child and parent interviews. *Journal of Abnormal Child Psychology, 10,* 325–336.

Roberts, R. E., Solovitz, B. L., Chen, Y. W., & Casat, C. (1996). Retest stability of *DSM-III-R* diagnoses among adolescents using the Diagnostic Interview Schedule for Children (DISC-2.1C). *Journal of Abnormal Child Psychology, 24,* 349–362.

Robins, L., Cottler, L., Bucholz, K., & Compton, W. (1996). *The Diagnostic Interview Schedule, Version 4.* St. Louis, MO: Washington University.

Robins, L. N., Helzer, J. E., & Croughan, J. L. (1981). National Institute of Mental Health Diagnostic Interview Schedule: Its history, characteristics, and validity. *Archives of General Psychiatry, 38,* 381–389.

Schwab-Stone, M. E., Shaffer, D., Dulcan, M. K., Jensen, P. S., Fisher, P., Bird, H. R., et al. (1996). Criterion validity of the NIMH Diagnostic Interview Schedule for Children Version 2.3 (DISC-2.3). *Journal of the American Academy of Child & Adolescent Psychiatry, 35,* 878–888.

Shaffer, D., Fisher, P., Dulcan, M. K., Davies M., Piacentini J., Schwab-Stone, M. E., et al. (1996). The NIMH Diagnostic Interview Schedule for Children-Version 2.3 (DISC-2.3): Description, acceptability, prevalence rates, and performance in the MECA study. *Journal of the American Academy of Child & Adolescent Psychiatry, 35,* 865–877.

Shaffer, D., Fisher, P. W., & Lucas, C. P. (1999). Respondent-based interviews. In D. Shaffer, C. P. Lucas & J. E. Richters (Eds.), *Diagnostic assessment in child and adolescent psychopathology* (pp. 3–33). New York: Guilford Press.

Shaffer, D., Fisher, P., Lucas, C. P., Dulcan, M. K., & Schwab-Stone, M. E. (2000). NIMH Diagnostic Interview Schedule for Children-Version IV (NIMH DISC-IV): Description, differences from previous versions, and reliability of some common diagnoses. *Journal of the American Academy of Child & Adolescent Psychiatry, 39,* 28–38.

Sheehan, D. V., Lecrubier, Y., Sheehan, K. H., Amorim, P., Janavs, J., Weiller, E., et al. (1998). The Mini-International Neuropsychiatric Interview (M.I.N.I.): The development and validation of a structured diagnostic psychiatric interview for *DSM-IV* and *ICD-10. Journal of Clinical Psychiatry, 59*(Suppl. 20), 22–33.

Sheehan, D. V., Lecrubier, Y., Sheehan, K. H., Janavs, J., Weiller E., Keskiner, A., et al. (1997). The validity of the MINI according to the SCID-P and its reliability. *European Psychiatry, 12,* 232–241.

Sheehan, D. V., Shytle, D., & Milo, K. (2004). *MINI International Neuropsychiatric Interview for Children and Adolescents-M.I.N.I.-Kid.* Tampa, FL: Author.

Sherrill, J. T., & Kovacs, M. (2000). Interview schedule for children and adolescents (ISCA). *Journal of the American Academy of Child & Adolescent Psychiatry, 27,* 268–277.

Silverman, W. K., & Eisen, A. R. (1992). Age differences in the reliability of parent and child reports of child anxious symptomatology using a structured interview. *Journal of the American Academy of Child & Adolescent Psychiatry, 31,* 117–124.

Simonoff, E., Pickles, A., Meyer, J. M., Silberg, J. L., Maes, H. H., Loeber, R., et al. (1997). The Virginia Twin Study of adolescent behavioral development: Influences of age, sex and impairment on rates of disorder. *Archives of General Psychiatry, 54,* 801–808.

Smolla, N., Valla, J. P., Bergeron, L., Berthiaume, C., & St-Georges, M. (2004). Development and reliability of a pictorial mental disorders screen for young adolescents. *Canadian Journal of Psychiatry, 49,* 828–837.

Spitzer, R. L., Endicott, J., & Robins, E. (1978). Research diagnostic criteria: Rationale and reliability. *Archives of General Psychiatry, 35,* 773–782.

Teare, M., Fristad, M. A., Weller, E. B., Weller, R. A., & Salmon, P. (1998a). Study I: Development and criterion validity of the Children's Interview for Psychiatric Syndromes (ChIPS). *Journal of Child and Adolescent Psychopharmacology, 8,* 205–211.

Teare, M., Fristad, M. A., Weller, E. B., Weller, R. A., & Salmon, P. (1998b). Study II: Concurrent validity of the *DSM-III-R* Children's Interview for Psychiatric Syndromes (ChIPS). *Journal of Child and Adolescent Psychopharmacology, 8,* 213–219.

Valla, J. P., Bergeron, L., & Smolla, N. (2000). The Dominic-R: A pictorial interview for 6- to 11-year-old children. *Journal of the American Academy of Child & Adolescent Psychiatry, 39,* 85–93.

Weller, E. B., Weller, R. A., Fristad, M. A., Teare, R. M., & Schechter, J. (2000). Children's Interview for Psychiatric Syndromes (ChIPS). *Journal of the American Academy of Child & Adolescent Psychiatry, 39,* 76–84.

Welner, Z., Reich, W., Herjanic, B., Jung, K. G., & Amado, H. (1987). Reliability, validity and parent-child agreement studies of the Diagnostic Interview for Children and Adolescents (DICA). *Journal of the American Academy of Child & Adolescent Psychiatry, 5,* 649–653.

World Health Organization. (1990). *Composite International Diagnostic Interview.* Geneva, Switzerland: Author.

World Health Organization. (1993). *The ICD-10 classification of mental and behavioral disorders: Diagnostic criteria for research.* Geneva, Switzerland: Author.

World Health Organization. (2003). *International classification of diseases and related health problems* (10th ed.). Geneva, Switzerland: Author.

4

DEVELOPMENTAL ISSUES

CHRISTY JAYNE, SCOTT BETHAY, AND ALAN M. GROSS

This chapter examines developmental issues in the interviewing of children. *Development* refers to maturational and growth factors that influence child behavior. Understanding and interpreting these influences is challenging, since the course of development varies across individuals. That is, two children of the same age may be at different points in each area of their developmental progress (Holmbeck, Greenley, & Franks, 2003). As such, recognition of developmental factors when interviewing children and their families is critical for successful diagnostic and treatment efforts.

The interview is one of the primary elements of the assessment process. In addition to being a relatively straightforward way of gathering information, the interview affords the clinician opportunities to make diagnostic hypotheses, to build rapport with clients and their families, to develop and evaluate treatments, and to conduct behavioral observations, while probing for environmental variables that may be maintaining a problem behavior (Sharp, Reeves, & Gross, 2006).

Although there are many parallels between the process of interviewing adults and that of interviewing children, there are important differences. Children are usually presented for treatment rather than seeking it on their own. As such, they may not be aware that a problem exists, or they may disagree with their caregivers about the nature of the problem. While adult referrals may require conducting a diagnostic interview with only the target individual, clinical work with children routinely involves interviewing not only the youngster but also significant adults in the child's life (e.g., parents, siblings, teachers). Age and developmental level influence not only the types of problems children display but also their ability to observe and report their experiences. Interviewing relevant adults is necessary in order to provide defining contextual information. Finally, and perhaps most important, developmental processes influence both the practical aspects of interviewing children and the determination as to whether the youngster's behavior is a source of concern.

The purpose of this chapter is to present an overview of the developmental issues associated with interviewing children and their families. Following a brief examination of the evolution of the *Diagnostic and Statistical Manual of Mental Disorders (DSM)* with regard to childhood disorders, an overview of child-focused clinical interviewing is presented. This is followed by a discussion of major developmental factors relevant to interviewing and diagnosis with children. It is hoped that this discussion will begin to provide a contextual backdrop illustrating how developmental factors may affect the process and content of interviews with children. In short, we attempt to enhance awareness of developmental factors important to the process of describing and obtaining reliable and valid information from children and their caregivers and how to use this information in assessing the nature and severity of childhood disorders.

Evolution of the *DSM*

While efforts to classify and define human behavior can be traced back as far as 450 BCE (e.g., Hippocrates), the foundation of modern methods of classifying psychopathology is primarily based on the work of Emil Kraeplin. Kraeplin's sixth edition of his *Textbook of Psychiatry*, published in 1899, listed 16 major categories of psychopathology and served as the basis for the current diagnostic system (Leahey, 2004).

The American Psychiatric Association's (APA, 1933) first diagnostic system contained 24 categories of adult psychopathology. The initial system developed as a means of collecting statistical information through the U.S. census. This information was used to develop an appropriate nomenclature for diagnosing inpatients with severe psychiatric and neurological disorders. The nomenclature was developed after World War II to incorporate outpatient servicemen and veterans (APA, 2000). This system eventually evolved into our current system of diagnosis and classification.

The APA *Diagnostic and Statistical Manual of Mental Disorders (DSM)* is the most widely adopted classification system of mental disorders. It contains standard terms and definitions used by mental health professionals. The first edition (APA, 1952) contained three major classes of psychopathology: organic brain syndromes, functional disorders, and mental deficiency; and it described 108 separate diagnoses. Aside from the diagnosis of adjustment reaction of childhood and adolescence, disorders occurring in children and adolescents were not included.

Not only did the second edition, *DSM-II*, increase the number of categories of mental illness and diagnoses, it included a section devoted to diagnosing children, titled, "Behavior Disorders of Childhood-Adolescence" (APA, 1968). This section contained diagnoses such as unsocialized reaction, withdrawing reaction, group delinquent reaction, aggressive reaction, runaway reaction, and hyperkinetic reaction. As in the first edition, science had relatively little to do with the development of this manual, and there were no guidelines as to how to diagnose each disorder. For instance, *DSM-II* did not specify how many characteristics of a disorder must be present for a diagnosis to be relevant (Schwartz & Johnson, 1985).

The third edition, *DSM-III* (APA, 1980), revealed a major overhaul from the vague and unreliable diagnostic criteria found in prior editions. Unsupported theoretical references were eliminated and replaced by a multiaxial categorical classification system, which included specific diagnostic criteria for each disorder. This system allowed for diagnosis and assessment of functioning in a broad and more meaningful sense by presenting a description of the diagnosis along with some information concerning the influence of individual, family, and community contexts on behavior.

The revision of the *DSM-III* to the *DSM-III-R* (APA, 1987) continued efforts to increase diagnostic specificity and emphasized the relevance of empirical findings. Also included in the *DSM-III-R* was a section of disorders related specifically to children and adolescents, called "Disorders First Evident in Childhood and Adolescence." Categories of childhood problems listed in this section included developmental disorders, disruptive behavior disorders, anxiety disorders of childhood or adolescence, eating disorders, gender identity disorders, tic disorders, elimination disorders, and a section for other disorders of infancy, childhood, and adolescence.

The latest editions of the *DSM* (*DSM-IV*, APA, 1994; *DSM-IV-TR*, APA, 2000) incorporate several changes (e.g., the addition of several new diagnoses), while continuing with the *DSM-III-R*'s utilization of operationally defined criteria and empirical findings outlining diagnoses. The major change seen in reference to children was the acceptability of applying to children diagnoses formerly generally reserved for adults. Consistent with this change, several child-specific diagnoses were incorporated into traditional adult diagnostic categories (e.g., avoidant disorder of childhood has been incorporated within social phobia).

Children can now be diagnosed with most disorders that were once considered to be limited to adults. However, children and adults may differ somewhat in their presentation of the same disorders. For example, an adult with depression is likely to exhibit symptoms including depressed mood, diminished interest in activities, significant weight loss or gain, and sleep disturbance. Age and developmental level of a child significantly influence symptom presentation. Depressed infants may present with disturbances in sleep or appetite, sad affect, and decreased exploratory behavior or attentiveness. Preschoolers may complain of physical symptoms, experience separation anxiety, or show irritability in the form of temper tantrums. Older children may experience sadness, pessimism, decreased self-esteem, or academic difficulties. Depressed adolescents may exhibit symptoms such as suicidal ideation, social withdrawal, or disordered eating habits (Schwartz, Gladstone, & Kaslow, 1998). The *DSM-IV-TR* provides useful information designed to help clinicians recognize developmental differences in symptom presentation.

The *DSM-IV-TR* is widely recognized as the gold standard in psychiatric classification. Although it is routinely used in practice and research settings, a number of problematic issues remain. Concerns have been expressed regarding the overlap of symptoms across diagnostic categories. High comorbidity rates among disorders raise questions relevant to issues of diagnostic validity. The *DSM-IV-TR* also fails to provide a clear definition of normality (Faul & Gross, 2006). Finally, the *DSM-IV-TR* has been criticized for its failure to include more emphasis on situational and contextual factors associated with problematic behavior (Faul & Gross, 2006). This latter issue is particularly important in work with children and adolescents because of the necessity of interpreting child behavior against the backdrop of variability in responding associated with the course of normal development.

INTERVIEWING STRATEGIES

Interviewing Parents

When parents seek assistance for their children's behavior problems, the assessment process generally begins with interviewing the parents. The goals of this interview generally involve gathering diagnostic information, assessing environmental contingencies, and formulating treatment strategies (Sharp et al., 2006). Initially, the focus of questioning may be directed toward an attempt to categorize the child's behavior problems. Familiarity with the various childhood syndromes is essential, as this information influences the nature and content of interview questions (Allen & Gross, 1994). This

process often consists of requesting parents to describe the primary features of the suspected disorder.

In the process of defining the disorder, questions are also directed toward determining the environmental contingencies that may be contributing to the child's difficulties. This information is particularly useful in treatment development as antecedent and consequent stimuli maintaining problem behavior are delineated. Parents should also be asked to discuss the youngster's developmental and family history. For instance, the clinician should ask about pregnancy and delivery complications and when the child achieved significant milestones (e.g., sitting up, talking, potty training). Moreover, efforts to understand the child's social environment should also occur. Considerable data suggest that factors such as marital discord, divorce, parental psychopathology, and peer relationships have significant impact on child functioning (e.g., Lamb, Hwang, Ketterlinus, & Fracasso, 1999; Rubin, Coplan, Nelson, Cheah, & Lagace-Seguin, 1999; Weersing & Brent, 2003).

Following the determination of problem behavior and the variables associated with its occurrence, the focus of the interview shifts to treatment development. Questioning is now guided by an attempt to determine alternative behaviors parents would like to see their child display, identifying behavioral assets, and discovering potential stimuli that are rewarding and aversive to the child. Developing an understanding of the child's individual strengths and how they may affect the treatment process is also important. The clinician should also look at the parents' roles in maintaining the problem behavior.

Parent expectations and general knowledge of child development should be addressed as well. Oftentimes, parent expectations may be unreasonable for the child's developmental level, and one of two things may happen. Either the parents are overly concerned about a behavior that is well within the realm of normal development or the parents are not concerned about their child's deviant behavior. Identifying unreasonable parent expectations is one element of the interview that will aid the clinician in understanding the presenting problem. Parents' knowledge of child development is a significant influence on their interpretation of the child's behavior. For instance, the clinician may need to soothe parents' concerns over whether their child's behavior is "normal" if milestones are not met within a certain time frame.

Interviewing Children

The objectives of interviewing the child parallel those of parent interviews. The clinician attempts to learn the child's definition of the problem, determine the youngster's behavioral strengths, and identify potential antecedent and consequent stimuli that contribute to maintaining problem responding. While practical information can be obtained in the child interview, a primary goal of this part of assessment is to inform the child that the family, not the youngster, is the focus of treatment. It is important that children recognize that their thoughts and feelings will be considered during treatment development (Gross, 1985).

The information gathered during parent and child interviews is designed to inform diagnosis and treatment development. As stated above, the *DSM–IV-TR* provides some guidelines to help clinicians recognize developmental differences in symptom presentation. Clearly, clinicians need to be familiar with the course and covariates of behavioral disorders. While lists of potential age-related differences in symptom presentation are useful, they represent only one factor to be considered in the process of determining how to obtain and interpret clinical data related to child functioning. Successful interviewing requires a developmental point of view. That is, clinicians must display an appreciation of the influence of cognitive, social/emotional, behavioral, and physical development on child behavior. Development provides the necessary contextual data for understanding the nature of child functioning. Sattler (2001) provided a thorough review of maturational considerations, as well as potential markers of abnormal development for birth to 18 years of age.

THE IMPACT OF DEVELOPMENTAL FACTORS

Cognitive Factors

Awareness of cognitive development is essential to determining what a child is capable of understanding, as well as his or her ability to respond meaningfully to various environmental demands. Recognition of a child's level of cognitive functioning is important because it influences the kinds of information children can provide about their functioning and determines the manner in which clinicians seek information from a youngster. Moreover, cognitive developmental level also provides necessary contextual information to assist clinicians in determining whether the child's behavior is normatively deviant.

Advances in cognitive development are readily observable as children mature. Preschool, for instance, is a time of rapid growth in many domains. Preschoolers' emerging conceptual abilities allow them to describe themselves and others in terms of observable behaviors and physical characteristics. When asked to describe others, they may apply labels such as "She has black hair" or "He tells us to be quiet at school." As these abilities develop, preschoolers show an increased ability to self-regulate and to interact successfully with others.

Despite these impressive competencies, preschoolers possess some cognitive limitations with which clinicians should be familiar. Because they rely on concrete thought processes to interpret the social environment, preschoolers' conceptions of social roles may be somewhat inflexible. For example, preschoolers may believe that only boys play basketball and that only girls are cheerleaders. Also, they are usually unable to understand that one can experience conflicting emotions simultaneously. Because of these limitations, preschoolers have a hard time understanding the complex motivational factors that underlie problematic situations such as divorce and familial conflict (Welsh & Bierman, 2003).

Middle childhood is marked by continued progress in language and cognition, and these emerging abilities provide children in middle childhood with many capabilities not found in preschool children. These allow children to formulate more complex descriptions of themselves and others, moving beyond the mere description of physical characteristics and overt behavior toward a more sophisticated use of dispositional constructs (e.g., "mean," "nice," "friendly," etc.). For example, some research suggests that around 6 years of age, children begin to use psychological constructs (e.g., emotions) to predict the behavior of others, as well as to make inferences about others' mental states (Yuill & Pearson, 1998). Consequently, grade school children are more skilled at understanding logical cause-and-effect sequences and making inferences based on internal (e.g., emotions, dispositions) and external (e.g., norms, standards) factors that influence their behavior as well as the behavior of others. In addition, at this developmental level, they are better able to anticipate interpersonal events and to comment on the behaviors and motives of others (Welsh & Bierman, 2003).

During adolescence, the continued development of thinking and language abilities affords capabilities not typically seen in earlier stages of development. Adolescents are able to consider many different explanations and vantage points for problems they encounter, and their language skills and sense of self have matured so that they provide clearer descriptions of themselves and make clearer distinctions between themselves and other people. Further, adolescents become better at perceiving thoughts and feelings, both in themselves and others, and can make more accurate appraisals of others' intentions and interests (Sattler, 2001). Because of their increased sensitivity and perspective-taking abilities, adolescents may become acutely aware of how they are viewed by others and may be overly sensitive to criticism (Welsh & Bierman, 2003).

Cognitive developmental level has many implications for the interview process (Underwood & Gross, 1989). For instance, the language and style of the interview should be adapted depending on the age and developmental level of the child (Stone & Lemanek, 1990) to ensure adequate reliability (Parker, 1984). It is essential to use vocabulary and language at or just above the child's cognitive level (e.g., Monaco, Rayfield, & Geffken, 1997). Properly phrasing questions appropriate to the developmental level of the child is not an easy task, because children are no more a homogenous group than are adults. That is why it is important to spend adequate time building rapport with children. This interaction will give the clinician a chance to adapt to the child's language abilities.

The types of questions used during an interview will also depend on the age and level of cognitive development of the child. Moreover, preschool children's answers can be easily swayed by the question type (e.g., Edelbrock, Costello, Dulcan, Kalas, & Conover, 1985; Goodman & Schaaf, 1997; White, Leichtman, & Ceci, 1997). Open-ended questions should be used whenever possible, because they broaden the amount of information that the child can give and allow the child freedom to respond.

Research suggests that children under the age of 7 may be better able to describe the behavior of others than they are able to explain it (Stone & Lemanek, 1990). They are likely to respond to questioning with concrete responses based on observable variables, such as physical appearance and specific behaviors. At this stage of development, children are likely to consider only the immediate context in their responses. Thus, it may be useful for clinicians to give the child a hypothetical situation and have the youngster describe what is going on and what he or she would have done in the situation. Others suggest that the child should be asked what other children the same age would do in a given situation, so that questions are not misinterpreted as accusations (Parker, 1984). For instance, rather than asking the child, "What would you do if someone took your toy?" it might prove more productive to ask, "What would your friends do if someone took their toys?"

At 7 or 8 years of age, children are better able to understand others' perspectives as well as why others behave the way they do, and their expanding vocabularies allow them to label more complex emotional states, such as pride, guilt, envy, and remorse. These emerging abilities allow grade school children to respond to assessment tasks involving more complex aspects of social cognition, such as identifying social goals and expectations and formulating solutions to interpersonal conflicts (Welsh & Bierman, 2003).

By adolescence, children can finally move beyond the immediate situation and see dispositional causes of behavior. Thus, clinicians should expect that adolescents' responses will be much more complex than those obtained from younger children (Stone & Lemanek, 1990). Adolescents are capable of providing detailed descriptions of complex interpersonal events that require the processing of multiple vantage points, as well as an understanding that conflicting emotional states can coexist. As such, adolescents are better equipped to process and comment on complex social situations, such as divorce, problematic peer relations, and familial conflict.

Finally, the clinician needs to be aware of general intellectual ability as a contextual factor in interpreting behavior. At one end of the spectrum, children who are intellectually gifted may display inattentive or disruptive behaviors when the school environment is not sufficiently stimulating. If these environmental deficits are not addressed, the resulting behavioral disturbance may cause problems in relationships with peers and teachers. Conversely, children with intellectual deficits may display high levels of off-task and disruptive behaviors if they are unable to keep up academically. At a more fundamental level, low general cognitive ability may be predictive of prosocial skills deficits that lead to problematic peer relations, particularly when the cognitive deficits are accompanied by symptoms of inattention (Bellanti & Bierman, 2000).

Social Factors

Children's social interactions provide a context for learning relationship skills that cannot be obtained elsewhere (Underwood & Gross, 1989), and research has consistently demonstrated that problematic peer relations are associated with a number of negative outcomes, including school dropout, delinquency, and psychopathology (e.g., Bierman, 2004; Coie & Cillesen, 1993; Ladd, 2005). As such, children's social interactions and patterns of relationships are crucial content areas in the assessment of child behavior problems. Clinicians should have a familiarity with the developmental trajectories of children's social behaviors in order to appraise the appropriateness of a child's social interactions and to determine areas for possible intervention.

There are important developmental trajectories in the nature of children's social interactions. In the earliest stages of development, parents are primary sources of social and emotional support; however, as children mature, peer relationships become increasingly important. First friendships typically emerge during preschool, when children's budding cognitive skills allow for cooperative play behaviors, leading to an increase in time spent interacting with others (Ladd, 2005). During the grade school years, children are exposed to more structured social contexts, and more stable friendships emerge as they negotiate the demands of competition, conformity, and achievement (Bierman, 2004). As these more stable relationships develop, children experience increased social support and are provided with an opportunity to experience the rewards and demands of sustaining close personal relationships. By adolescence, young people begin to affiliate with different social groups that are distinguished by different interaction styles, values, and behavioral norms. In experimenting with these different social groups, adolescents become more aware of their personal values and standards,

and a more stable sense of self emerges. These adolescent peer relationships also provide an important source of social support, which eases the transition into young adulthood (Bierman, 2004).

As can be seen from the foregoing review, peer relationships form an important context for the experiences that shape appropriate social skills. Although many children experience transient difficulties in getting along with others, a small but significant number of children experience chronic peer rejection, which interferes with these important developmental processes. Some of these children exhibit deficits in the skills necessary to enter into play interactions, leading to social anxiety and avoidance (Crick & Ladd, 1993). Such socially withdrawn children may be particularly vulnerable to teasing, bullying, and other forms of peer victimization. By contrast, a significant number of rejected children exhibit high levels of aggression (Coie & Cillesen, 1993). Such children tend to be intrusive and domineering in their interactions with others; thus, they are avoided and disliked by their peers.

Problematic peer relations can result in a negative cycle of social difficulties that perpetuates itself over time (Sandstrom & Coie, 1999). For instance, in one landmark study, Coie and Dodge (1983) found that nearly half the children rejected by peers in fifth grade remained so when followed over a 5-year period. More recently, Ladd and Troop-Gordon (2003) found that aggressive behaviors first exhibited in kindergarten were directly related to maladjustment and relational stressors in fourth grade. A history of such adverse relationships has a deleterious effect on children's self-concepts, as well as the beliefs they form about their peers. Particularly during middle childhood, children's emerging capabilities for acquiring accurate self-knowledge set the stage for a period in which relational problems are likely to have a profound impact on their beliefs about their social competence. Subsequently, negative beliefs about social competence may lead to anxiety, helplessness, or other internalizing behaviors. For example, Ladd and Troop-Gordon (2003) found that the relationship between peer difficulties and internalizing problems was partially mediated by self and peer beliefs. It is also probable that aversive peer experiences lead children to have negative beliefs about their peers' social goals and intentions— that is, chronically rejected children may come to view their peers as hostile or capricious. Such attributional biases are likely to encourage children to continue to behave in ways that foster peer rejection (e.g., aggression or anxiety and withdrawal), even when they are exposed to different peer groups. Further, recent research (Rieffe, Villaneuva, & Terwogt, 2005) has suggested that in addition to the aforementioned hostile attributional biases, rejected children may show a general delay in the development of social cognition.

The assessment of children's social difficulties should be founded on our current understanding of the developmental issues that affect peer relationships. This means that clinicians need to assess for behavioral dispositions (e.g., aggression, anxious or withdrawn behavior, inattention) that predispose children toward peer difficulties. It is also important to assess children's beliefs about their social competence as well as their beliefs and expectancies regarding their peers. With younger children, videos or vignettes portraying common interpersonal situations can be used to assess many facets of social cognition. For example, a clinician might show or tell a child a story about a youngster who is trying to enter a new peer group and then ask the child to come up with ways that the protagonist might successfully negotiate the task (Welsh & Bierman, 2003).

It is also essential to gather information about children's actual peer relations. In addition to helping to determine whether the child is following a normal social developmental pathway, understanding this area of development also contributes to the identification of specific social behavioral deficits. Although peer sociometric methods have proven very useful for gathering such information in research settings, such methods are often impractical and unethical in clinical practice (Underwood & Gross, 1989). Bierman (2004) suggested that teachers are the preferred adult informants because they are in a position to observe children's social interactions in a normative context over time. Teachers, however, may be privy only to interactions that occur in the classroom; thus, they may overestimate the peer acceptance of children who perform well in class but have difficulties in less structured settings (Bierman, 2004). Parents are usually able to provide some information about their children's social behaviors, but they aren't often in a position to observe children's interactions in a normative peer group context. For these reasons, it is essential that clinicians gather information from multiple informants in order to get a more accurate appraisal of a child's functioning among peers.

Behavioral Factors

Understanding behavioral development is a prerequisite for determining whether child behavior reflects adjustment difficulties or normal behavioral variation associated with development. Interpreting child behavior can be difficult because behavior varies across ages, and behavior that is acceptable at one age would be considered problematic at another age. Moreover, the appropriateness of a given child behavior is also determined by its relative frequency, intensity, and duration (Underwood & Gross, 1989).

Research clearly demonstrates age-related differences in impulsive conduct (e.g., Whalen & Henker, 1998) and oppositional behaviors (e.g., Frick, 1998). The challenge is to determine whether problem responding reflects transient behavior that is part of normal variability associated with age. Further complicating this issue are multiple pathways to problem behavior development (Holmbeck et al., 2003). Children displaying the same disorder may have experienced very different developmental trajectories. In addition, behaviors considered normal at one developmental level can be considered problematic at another level.

The above issue is most easily illustrated by the problem of nocturnal enuresis. Bed-wetting, or nocturnal enuresis, is a relatively common problem in 2- to 3-year-old children, occurring in approximately 40% of children (Pruitt, 1998). At 2, 3, and even 4 years of age, wetting the bed occasionally is not considered a problem. However, approximately 10% of school-age children (5 to 16 years) continue to wet the bed (Houts, 2003). In this age group, wetting the bed is considered problematic. It can contribute to stress for the child and may cause significant impairment in other areas of functioning. For instance, enuretic behavior may result in the child limiting his or her social activities for fear of social embarrassment (e.g., not wanting to spend the night away from home). Enuresis may contribute to problems in self-esteem as well. Difficulties may also result for the youngster whose parents respond to the problem with punishment strategies (e.g., APA, 2000; Houts, 2003; Mellon & McGrath, 2000). Although it is generally held that in the absence of treatment, the majority of children will outgrow this problem, clinicians should be sensitive to assessing the impact of this problem on child functioning and consider variations in development when addressing the issue.

As illustrated by the above example, determining whether a child's behavior is problematic or simply reflects normal behavioral variation requires recognition of the influence of age and developmental level. Although developmental stages are essentially constructs imposed on the processes of maturation, they provide a necessary frame of reference around which to organize typical behavioral variation in children. Use of these stages requires the establishment of normative baselines for various behaviors. Familiarity with norms aids in understanding the impact of development on the presenting behavior, thus affecting diagnosis and treatment development (Coie & Jacobs, 1993). Research in the areas of childhood fears and anxieties is an example of the usefulness of these data.

Experiencing fears and anxiety is a normal part of development and is reflected in children commonly displaying different fears across developmental stages. For instance, infants generally exhibit fear in response to immediate and concrete events (e.g., strangers, loud noises, separation from caretakers), while older children and adolescents experience fears that are more abstract and global in nature (e.g., poor grades, peer rejection) (Gullone, 2000). In addition, a number of childhood fears appear to correspond to the social, emotional, and cognitive tasks associated with normal development. For example, the developmental tasks for school-age children involve developing social and academic competence. It is relatively common for children of this age to display anxieties related to school performance and social acceptance (Davies, 2004).

Normative data suggest that infants' fears relate to the immediate environment (Berger, 2000). This is followed closely by an emerging fear of strangers, unknown objects, and heights. Preschool children tend to have fears of being alone and in the dark, along with fears of animals. Fears relating to supernatural phenomena, bodily injury, and failure and criticism are common during middle childhood. Adolescents tend to experience fears relating to more global concerns, such as economics and political events (Gullone, 2000). Research reveals relationships between age and number of fears children display,

and age and intensity of children's fears, as well as insight into the long-term consequences of childhood fears (Gullone, 2000). Numerous studies attest to the idea that normative fears are relatively short-lived and generally do not continue into adulthood (Gullone, 2000).

Examination of childhood fears indicates that children commonly exhibit a number of fears that are both age specific and transitory in nature (e.g., Barrios & O'Dell, 1998; Underwood & Gross, 1989). Considerable normative data exist regarding this domain of childhood emotional functioning. Evaluating the severity and age appropriateness of a child's fears requires being familiar with behavioral development factors.

Normative data for a number of common childhood problem behaviors are available. For example, the work of Thomas Achenbach has resulted in an extensive database in this area. The Child Behavior Checklist (CBCL) is an empirically based, dimensional classification system covering a wide range of problems and has been shown to have solid psychometric properties (Achenbach, 1991; Achenbach & Edelbrock, 1981; Edelbrock & Costello, 1988). Achenbach analyzed over 600 clinical case histories of children to identify easily observed symptoms. Further research and consultation resulted in the items that make up the behavior problems on the CBCL. The Child Behavior Checklist-4–18 and 1991 Profile (CBCL-4–18) combine a seven-part social competency checklist with a 113-item behavior problems checklist. Parent responses to the CBCL result in comprehensive descriptions of child behavior. The clinician can use the results to distinguish between typical developing children and those suffering from significant behavioral problems. The scoring profile for the CBCL-4–18 includes (a) three component scales (Activities, School, and Social); (b) a total competence scale score; (c) eight syndrome scales (Aggressive Behavior, Anxious-Depressed, Attention Problems, Delinquent Behavior, Social Behavior, Somatic Complaints, Thought Problems, and Withdrawn); (d) an internalizing-problem scale score; (e) an externalizing-problem scale score; and (f) a total-problem scale score.

The Behavioral Assessment System for Children (BASC), developed by Reynolds and Kamphaus (1992), also uses a dimensional approach to define childhood behavior. The BASC collects information from multiple informants with a parent form, self-report form, and teacher form. The different forms are used to gather different viewpoints about a child's behavior in multiple environments. The combined responses from multiple informants result in the identification of symptom clusters organized across broad dimensional syndromes (e.g., externalizing problems, internalizing problems, school problems, adaptive skills, behavioral symptoms index, and others). Narrow problematic behavior clusters exist within the broad syndromes (e.g., aggression, hyperactivity, conduct problems, anxiety, and depression) (Reynolds & Kamphaus, 1992). The CBCL and BASC, along with other classification systems, are useful supplementary sources of diagnostic information. Such measures can be administered at the beginning of diagnosis and treatment, as well as at the end of treatment to document progress.

As has been noted throughout this chapter, children are in a constant state of behavioral flux. They commonly display problematic behaviors that vary in frequency, intensity, and duration. The task of the clinician is to determine whether reported problems reflect a transient fluctuation in a child's behavior versus a significant and severe disruption in functioning requiring clinical intervention. Knowledge of typical child development, along with the use of available behavioral norms, is essential to this process. Sensitivity to typical behavioral development not only facilitates interpretation of assessment data but also provides a useful framework for determining the focus of interview questions for children and their parents.

Physical Factors

Child behavior can be profoundly affected by a youngster's physical characteristics. While there are age- and gender-related variabilities in children's physical development, youngsters who deviate significantly from the mean in height and weight are at risk for psychosocial problems (Davies, 2004). Behavior problems may result from children being treated differently by peers and adults as a result of their physical stature (Lewis, 1990).

Children who are unusually short or tall for their age may be treated according to their size rather than age. For example, parents, family members, and teachers may view the short stature child as "cute." As such, parents may provide

age-inappropriate clothing or discourage the child from engaging in age-appropriate activities (e.g., sports) due to concerns about the child's ability to compete with larger peers. It is also not uncommon to see adults hold lower performance expectations (e.g., chores, academic achievement, decision-making responsibility) for children of short stature (Lewis, 1990). The consequences of these kinds of contingencies may be the encouragement of dependent behaviors and the failure for children to receive the encouragement needed to achieve their full potential.

Children who are unusually tall for their age may also experience reactions from their environment that contribute to behavioral difficulties. Adults often mistake taller children as being older than they are and treat them accordingly. As such, expectations regarding performance may be developmentally inappropriate. For example, research has shown that mothers of preschoolers expect more advanced cognitive and social behavior from taller children (Eisenberg, 1984). As a result of heightened parental expectations, children can experience frustration, stress, and a sense of failure. These experiences can make the child less venturesome and more dependent on his or her family and, ultimately, can result in an increased likelihood of social isolation (Dietz, 1998).

Differences in rates of sexual maturation can cause problems as well. Children who reach puberty at an age consistent with normative development report experiencing this area of maturation more positively than do those who develop either early or late (Berger, 2000). Early-maturing girls and late-maturing boys report significant social problems. For instance, girls who are taller and more developed than their peers can suffer from teasing and poor body image (Berger, 2000). A number of studies suggest that early-maturing girls may lack self-confidence, suffer from anxiety, and be at risk for being socially withdrawn (e.g., Ge, Conger, & Elder, 1996; Graber, Lewinsohn, Seeley, & Brooks-Gunn, 1997). They are also more likely to engage in risky behaviors, such as smoking, drinking, and sexual activity (e.g., Brooks-Gunn, 1991; Dick, Rose, Viken, & Kaprio, 2000).

In contrast to girls, it appears that boys reaching puberty later than same-sex peers are at risk for problem behaviors. These boys have been shown to have lower self-esteem and behavior problems, such as being disruptive in class. Late-maturing boys may have a higher likelihood of behavior problems as a result of the cultural emphasis that is placed on male size and strength (Berger, 2000).

Because adolescents are likely to feel most at ease with peers who are at similar levels of biological maturity, being at the extremes in physical development may set the stage for the development of social and emotional difficulties (Stattin & Magnusson, 1990). In addition, it may be that early maturation results in both boys and girls associating with older peer groups, who may promote activities (e.g., drug and alcohol use, sexual activity) that youngsters are not emotionally equipped to manage (Ge, Brody, Conger, Simons, & Murray, 2002).

Along with deviations in height, problems associated with extreme weight can also occur. The rapidly increasing incidence of childhood obesity is a significant problem in the United States. Rates of obesity in children are up 50% since 1991, with no signs of decreasing (Borra, Kelly, Shirreffs, Neville, & Geiger, 2003). Socially, overweight children are subject to social discrimination and teasing from peers (Dietz, 1998). For instance, they are viewed as more passive than their peers and are often given insulting nicknames. These children may turn to food as a way to compensate for the social isolation and rejection. Eating to deal with problems can become a vicious cycle, as it is likely to lead to additional weight gain and further rejection (e.g., Berger, 2000; Sheiman & Slonim, 1988).

Being overweight can be a significant problem for development because of the value that children place on how they are viewed by their peers (Morgan, Tanofsky-Kraff, Wilfley, & Yanovski, 2002). Teasing may cause the child to withdraw from social interactions. If the child is not engaged in active social situations (e.g., sports), this can serve to further exacerbate the problem of social isolation. Overweight children tend to pick friends who are younger than they are and who are less likely to discriminate against them, again limiting age-appropriate interactions with others (Dietz, 1998). Regardless of the reason, failing to interact consistently with peers limits the opportunity for social growth and development. Numerous studies attest to the developmental significance of peer relationships (e.g., Rubin et al., 1999).

The potential impact of physical development on behavior indicates the importance of considering this variable during the interview process. Traditionally, physical growth patterns can be assessed using age- and gender-specified weight-for-height growth charts (WHP). The Centers for Disease Control charts were most recently revised in 2000 and are simple enough for clinicians to use (Centers for Disease Control, 2000). Other procedures (e.g., predicting growth) can be done by medical specialists. More important, the above review suggests the relevance of understanding the potential contribution of physical factors in the examination of child behavior problems. Recognizing the potential impact physical stature holds for how children are treated by adults and peers in their environment provides important clues concerning information to be gathered during interviews. Attention to this aspect of development also enhances the likelihood of successfully tailoring treatment to the needs of the child.

SUMMARY

An appreciation of the variability displayed in cognitive, social/emotional, behavioral, and physical maturation is critical to successful clinical work with children and their families. Clinicians need to be aware of the issues that are likely to be salient for a child at a given developmental stage. Being sensitive to these variables is important for many reasons. These developmental factors significantly influence the content and form of child, and to a lesser degree, parent interviews. The role of the child in the assessment and treatment process is greatly influenced by the youngster's level of cognitive development. Knowledge of norms for social and behavioral development allows clinicians to calibrate whether a child's responding requires clinical intervention or merely reflects age-related developmental variation. Understanding the impact of physical development on the behavioral and psychological functioning of children results in important clues regarding the determination of relevant environmental variables contributing to a child's behavioral difficulties. Moreover, an understanding of these complex developmental processes is vital to effective treatment development. Highlighting these issues is designed to raise awareness of the significance of a developmental perspective for clinical interviewing of children and their families.

REFERENCES

Achenbach, T. M. (1991). *Manual for the Child Behavior Checklist/4–18 and 1991 Profile.* Burlington: University of Vermont, Department of Psychiatry.

Achenbach, T. M., & Edelbrock, C. S. (1981). Behavioral problems and competencies reported by parents of normal and disturbed children ages four through sixteen. *Monographs of the Society for Research in Child Development, 46*(1, Serial No. 188), 1–82.

Allen, J., & Gross, A. M. (1994). Children. In M. Hersen & S. Turner (Eds.), *Diagnostic Interviewing* (pp. 305–326). New York: Plenum Press.

American Psychiatric Association. (1933). *Standard classified nomenclature of diseases.* Washington, DC: Author.

American Psychiatric Association. (1952). *Diagnostic and statistical manual of mental disorders.* Washington, DC: Author.

American Psychiatric Association. (1968). *Diagnostic and statistical manual of mental disorders* (2nd ed.). Washington, DC: Author.

American Psychiatric Association. (1980). *Diagnostic and statistical manual of mental disorders* (3rd ed.). Washington, DC: Author.

American Psychiatric Association. (1987). *Diagnostic and statistical manual of mental disorders* (3rd ed., Rev.). Washington, DC: Author.

American Psychiatric Association. (1994). *Diagnostic and statistical manual of mental disorders* (4th ed.). Washington, DC: Author.

American Psychiatric Association. (2000). *Diagnostic and statistical manual of mental disorders* (4th ed., Text rev.). Washington, DC: Author.

Barrios, B. A., & O'Dell, S. L. (1998). Fears and anxieties. In E. J. Mash & R. A. Barkley (Eds.), *Treatment of childhood disorders* (2nd ed., pp. 249–337). New York: Guilford Press.

Bellanti, C. J., & Bierman, K. L. (2000). Disentangling the impact of low cognitive ability and inattention on social behavior and peer relationships. *Journal of Clinical Child Psychology, 29*, 66–75.

Berger, K. S. (2000). *The developing person: Through childhood and adolescence* (5th ed.). New York: Worth.

Bierman, K. L. (2004). *Peer rejection.* New York: Guilford Press.

Borra, S. T., Kelly, L., Shirreffs, M. B., Neville, K., & Geiger, C. J. (2003). Developing health messages: Qualitative studies with children, parents, and teachers help identify communications opportunities for healthful lifestyles and the prevention of obesity. *Journal of the American Dietetic Association, 103*, 721–728.

Brooks-Gunn, J. (1991). How stressful is the transition to adolescence for girls? In M. E. Colten & S. Gore (Eds.), *Adolescent stress: Causes and consequences* (pp. 131–149). New York: Aldine de Gruyter.

Centers for Disease Control and Prevention. (2000). *2000 CDC growth charts: United States.* Atlanta, GA: U.S. Department of Health and Human Services, Centers for Disease Control and Prevention.

Coie, J. D., & Cillesen, A. H. N. (1993). Peer rejection: Origins and effects on children's development. *Current Directions in Psychological Science, 2*, 89–92.

Coie, J. D., & Dodge, K. A. (1983). Continuities and changes in children's social status: A five-year longitudinal study. *Merrill-Palmer Quarterly, 29*, 261–282.

Coie, J. D., & Jacobs, M. R. (1993). The role of social context in the prevention of conduct disorder. *Development and Psychopathology, 5*, 263–275.

Crick, N. R., & Ladd, G. W. (1993). Children's perceptions of their peer experiences: Attributions, loneliness, social anxiety, and social avoidance. *Developmental Psychology, 29*, 244–254.

Davies, D. (2004). *Child development: A practitioner's guide.* New York: Guilford Press.

Dick, D. M., Rose, R. J., Viken, R. J., & Kaprio, J. (2000). Pubertal timing and substance use: Associations between and within families across late adolescence. *Developmental Psychology, 36*, 180–189.

Dietz, W. H. (1998). Health consequences of obesity in youth: Childhood predictors of adult disease. *Pediatrics, 101*, 518–526.

Edelbrock, C., & Costello, A. J. (1988). Convergence between statistically derived behavior problem syndromes and child psychiatric diagnoses. *Journal of Abnormal Child Psychology, 16*, 219–231.

Edelbrock, C., Costello, A. J., Dulcan, M. K., Kalas, R., & Conover, N. C. (1985). Age differences in the reliability of the psychiatric interview of the child. *Child Development, 56*, 265–275.

Eisenberg, N. (1984). Sex differences in the relationship of height to children's actual and attributed social and cognitive competencies. *Sex Roles, 11*, 719–734.

Faul, L. A., & Gross, A. M. (2006). Diagnoses and classification. In M. Hersen & J. C. Thomas (Eds.), *Comprehensive handbook of personality and psychopathology* (pp. 3–15). New York: Wiley.

Frick, P. (1998). Conduct disorders. In T. H. Ollendick & M. Hersen (Eds.), *Handbook of child psychopathology* (3rd ed., pp. 213–237). New York: Plenum Press.

Ge, X., Brody, G. H., Conger, R. D., Simons, R. L., & Murray, V. (2002). Contextual amplification of the effects of pubertal transition on African-American children's deviant peer affiliation and externalized behavioral problems. *Developmental Psychology, 38*, 42–54.

Ge, X., Conger, R. D., & Elder, G. H., Jr. (1996). Coming of age too early: Pubertal influences on girls' vulnerability to psychological distress. *Child Development, 67*, 3386–3400.

Goodman, G. S., & Schaaf, J. M. (1997). Over a decade of research on children's eyewitness testimony: What have we learned? Where do we go from here? *Applied Cognitive Psychology, 11*, S5–S20.

Graber, J. A., Lewinsohn, P. M., Seeley, J. R., & Brooks-Gunn, J. (1997). Is psychopathology associated with timing of pubertal development? *Journal of the American Academy of Child & Adolescent Psychiatry, 36*, 1768–1776.

Gross, A. M. (1985). Children. In M. Hersen & S. M. Turner (Eds.), *Diagnostic Interviewing* (pp. 309–335). New York: Plenum Press.

Gullone, E. (2000). The development of normal fear: A century of research. *Clinical Psychology Review, 20*, 429–451.

Holmbeck, G. R., Greenley, R. N., & Franks, E. A. (2003). Developmental issues and considerations in research and practice. In A. E. Kazdin & J. R. Weisz (Eds.), *Evidenced-based psychotherapies for children and adolescents* (pp. 21–41). New York: Guilford Press.

Houts, A. C. (2003). Behavioral treatment for enuresis. In A. E. Kazdin & J. R. Weisz (Eds.), *Evidenced-based psychotherapies for children and adolescents* (pp. 389–406). New York: Guilford Press.

Ladd, G. W. (2005). *Children's peer relations and social competence.* New Haven, CT: Yale University Press.

Ladd, G. W., & Troop-Gordon, W. (2003). The role of chronic peer difficulties in the development of children's psychological adjustment problems. *Child Development, 74,* 1344–1367.

Lamb, M. E., Hwang, C. P., Ketterlinus, R. D., & Fracasso, M. P. (1999). Parent-child relationships: Development in the context of the family. In M. H. Bornstein & M. E. Lamb (Eds.), *Developmental psychology: An advanced textbook* (4th ed., pp. 411–450). Mahwah, NJ: Lawrence Erlbaum.

Leahey, T. H. (2004). *A history of psychology: Main currents in psychological thought* (6th ed.). Upper Saddle River, NJ: Pearson/Prentice Hall.

Lewis, C. (1990). Short stature: The special case of growth hormone deficiency. In A. M. Gross & R. S. Drabman (Eds.), *Handbook of clinical behavioral pediatrics* (pp. 337–348). New York: Plenum Press.

Mellon, M. W., & McGrath, M. L. (2000). Empirically supported treatments in pediatric psychology: Nocturnal enuresis. *Journal of Pediatric Psychology, 25,* 193–214.

Monaco, L., Rayfield, A., & Geffken, G. R. (1997). A practical guide for interviewing the young client. *Journal of Psychological Practice, 3,* 160–173.

Morgan, C. M., Tanofsky-Kraff, M., Wilfley, D. E., & Yanovski, J. A. (2002). Childhood obesity. *Psychiatric Clinics of North America, 11,* 257–278.

Parker, W. C. (1984). Interviewing children: Problems and promise. *Journal of Negro Education, 53,* 18–28.

Pruitt, D. B. (1998). *Your child: What every parent needs to know about childhood development from birth to adolescence.* New York: HarperCollins.

Reynolds, C. R., & Kamphaus, R. W. (1992). *Behavioral Assessment System for Children.* Circle Pines, MN: American Guidance Service.

Rieffe, C., Villanueva, L., & Terwogt, M. (2005). Use of trait information in the attribution of intentions by popular, average, and rejected children. *Infant and Child Development, 14,* 1–10.

Rubin, K. H., Coplan, R. J., Nelson, L. J., Cheah, C. S. L., & Lagace-Seguin, D. G. (1999). Peer relationships in childhood. In M. H. Bornstein & M. E. Lamb (Eds.), *Developmental psychology: An advanced textbook* (4th ed., pp. 451–501). Mahwah, NJ: Lawrence Erlbaum.

Sandstrom, M. J., & Coie, J. D. (1999). A developmental perspective on peer rejection: Mechanisms of stability and change. *Child Development, 70,* 955–966.

Sattler, J. M. (2001). *Clinical and forensic interviewing of children and families: Guidelines for the mental health, education, pediatric, and child maltreatment fields.* San Diego, CA: Author.

Schwartz, J. A., Gladstone, T. R. G., & Kaslow, N. J. (1998). Depressive disorders. In T. H. Ollendick & M. Hersen (Eds.), *Handbook of child psychopathology* (pp. 269–289). New York: Plenum Press.

Schwartz, S., & Johnson, J. H. (1985). *Psychopathology of childhood: A clinical-experimental approach* (2nd ed.). New York: Pergamon Press.

Sharp, W., Reeves, C., & Gross, A. M. (2006). Behavioral interviewing of parents. In M. Hersen (Ed.), *Comprehensive handbook of behavioral assessment* (pp. 103–124). New York: Elsevier.

Sheiman, D. L., & Slonim, M. (1988). *Resources for middle childhood: A source book.* New York: Garland.

Stattin, H., & Magnusson, D. (1990). *Pubertal maturation in female development.* Mahwah, NJ: Lawrence Erlbaum.

Stone, W. L., & Lemanek, K. L. (1990). Developmental issues in children's self-reports. In A. M. La Greca (Eds.), *Through the eyes of the child: Obtaining self-reports from children and adolescents* (pp. 18–56). Boston: Allyn & Bacon.

Underwood S. L., & Gross, A. M. (1989). Developmental factors in child behavioral assessment. In M. Hersen (Ed.), *Innovations in child behavior therapy* (pp. 57–77). New York: Springer.

Weersing, V. R., & Brent, D. A. (2003). Cognitive-behavioral therapy for adolescent depression: Comparative efficacy, mediation, moderation, and effectiveness. In A. E. Kazdin & J. R. Weisz (Eds.), *Evidenced-based psychotherapies for children and adolescents* (pp. 135–147). New York: Guilford Press.

Welsh, J. A., & Bierman, K. L. (2003). Using the clinical interview to assess children's interpersonal reasoning and emotional functioning. In C. R. Reynolds & R. W. Kamphaus (Eds.), *Handbook of psychological and educational assessment of children* (pp. 219–234). New York: Guilford Press.

Whalen, C. K., & Henker, B. (1998). Attention-deficit/hyperactivity disorders. In T. H. Ollendick & M. Hersen. (Eds.), *Handbook of child psychopathology* (3rd ed., pp. 181–211). New York: Plenum Press.

White, T. L., Leichtman, M. D., & Ceci, S. J. (1997). The good, the bad, and the ugly: Accuracy, inaccuracy, and elaboration in preschooler's reports about a past event. *Applied Cognitive Psychology, 11,* S37–S54.

Yuill, N., & Pearson, A. (1998). The development of biases for trait attribution: Children's understanding of traits as causal mechanisms based on desire. *Developmental Psychology, 34,* 574–586.

5

MENTAL STATUS EXAMINATION

A Comprehensive Multicultural, Developmental Approach

LAURA PALMER, MELISSA FIORITO, AND LAURA TAGLIARENI

The mental status exam (MSE) uniquely stands out as the hallmark of a psychological or psychiatric intake with a patient of any age. Adult MSE procedures are well documented and detailed and straightforward for the most part. By comparison, conducting a pediatric MSE is more complex, requiring triangulation of multiple sources of information and conceptualizing the findings within the dynamic process of psychosocial development. This chapter provides a historical overview of the MSE and includes the specific areas to be assessed when working with children. Moreover, a brief review of major developmental tasks is provided, along with special considerations for conducting the MSE with children. The outcome of a thorough pediatric MSE should provide sufficient information to develop a detailed, multicultural, and developmentally sensitive treatment plan, which will facilitate assisting children to achieve their optimal potential.

HISTORICAL OVERVIEW OF THE MENTAL STATUS EXAM

The MSE remains a standard component of the psychiatric, psychological, and neurological exam (Morrison, 1995). During the early 20th century, Adolf Meyer, psychiatrist and professor of psychiatry, modeled the MSE after the physical medical exam in order to assess various elements of psychological functioning (Groth-Marnat, 2003). The initial application of the MSE was used almost exclusively with adults.

While pediatric psychology and psychiatry have emerged as significant areas of focus in the literature, this was not always the case. During the formative years of psychology, child mental health was not as significant a concern as that of adults. In fact, prior to 1900, there was a dearth of literature regarding the importance of child psychiatry in America, with the term *child psychiatry* being introduced in 1933 (Mash & Barkley, 2003). While it was eventually determined that a designation of a child's mental health was important, directly observing and interviewing the child would not be part of the process for some time to come. In fact, up until the 1950s and 1960s, children's mental health was typically assessed through interviews with parents (Groth-Marnat, 2003). Minimal psychological assessments were conducted with children before this period, and direct observations were generally limited to observing children during play therapy sessions (Goodman & Sours, 1998;

Groth-Marnat 2003). Moreover, diagnosis was not a central component of mental health with children. Rather, diagnosis was thought to be resultant of therapy (Goodman & Sours, 1998).

Several other factors delayed the utilization of MSEs with children. Until recently, a significant proportion of findings with children have been extrapolated from theory and research with adults (Mash & Barkley, 2003). MSEs were considered inappropriate due to children's developmental limitations. Specifically, children were thought to be ill-equipped and too developmentally immature to handle the techniques of an MSE, due to limited verbal skills and cognitive processes. Integrating a developmental component in corroboration with age-appropriate techniques with the MSE was not foreseeable in the early to mid-20th century (Goodman & Sours, 1998).

Post–World War II marked the beginning of a modern era of child development research (Kail, 2007). As views on childhood disorders and child psychology changed, the field of child psychology began making significant advances. As structured interviews became more prevalent with adults during the 1970s, psychologists began to change the focus from adults' reports of their children to children's reports of their experiences (Groth-Marnat, 2003). Structured interviews became an integral component of examinations for both parents and child patients, and direct contact and questioning became inclusive in child interviews. While a preponderance of literature has emerged within the past few decades, the majority of the contributions regarding the MSE originate with adults. Thus, there is an ongoing need for more developmentally informed assessments grounded in scientific theory for children.

CURRENT PRACTICE
WITH THE MENTAL STATUS EXAM

Present-day MSEs are utilized by psychiatrists, psychologists, and neurologists to determine a patient's level of cognitive, emotional, and behavioral functioning. More specifically, the MSE is often utilized most comprehensively by psychiatrists during the clinical interview (Koocher, Norcross, & Hill, 2005), or it may be a component of a psychological or neurological assessment. In pediatric populations, the MSE is utilized to obtain a comprehensive understanding of the child's psychological status, determine the most

appropriate diagnosis, and formulate a treatment plan (Robinson, 2005).

The MSE findings are most completely understood within the context of developmental history along with social and family functioning. The first component of this matrix of information requires an interview with the parent or guardian accompanying the child. The child's prenatal, perinatal, and developmental history should be carefully reviewed and documented. Familial history should also be obtained, including mental health, educational, and medical backgrounds for each parent and sibling(s). The parent or guardian is typically the principal informant regarding the child's present behavior and significant history. In addition to the parent's perception of the child's functioning, observation and understanding of the parent-child dyad will provide a better understanding of this primary relationship and attachment capacity for each member of the dyad (Goodman & Sours, 1998). In addition, if the child has siblings or other extended-family members in the home, the quality of these relationships should be explored to be able to more fully understand the environmental and relationship variables that are affecting the child.

The primary focus of the MSE is the child's current cognitive functioning in conjunction with affect, behavior, and any symptomatology. The MSE can easily be adjusted to address various assessment objectives, and professionals vary widely with their utilization of this tool. For example, the MSE may be part of a formal, standardized assessment, or it may be included as part of a standard intake. For psychologists, most of the information needed for MSE can be obtained during the course of clinical interviewing and testing (Maruish, 2002). The exam may be a screening tool for problematic behaviors or symptomatology or may alert professionals to signs or symptoms of psychiatric conditions (Hannay, Fischer, Loring, & Howieson, 2004). Information gathered during the MSE may also provide baseline data for future follow-up studies and remind the examiner of the child's initial functioning (Goodman & Sours, 1998). Professionals tend to administer variations of the MSE according to the patient's needs.

A common, yet less comprehensive evaluation process is the mini–mental status exam (MMSE) (Folstein, Folstein, & McHugh, 1975). The MMSE is most widely utilized as a screening tool for cognitive impairment. While practitioners may use the MMSE in lieu of the more comprehensive

MSE, it is understood to yield less diagnostic information. Further, diagnostic impressions must be carefully considered, and the MMSE should not be the sole criterion for arriving at a diagnosis.

When obtaining information from a MSE, information should also be gathered through direct questioning and observation. For example, observing children during play will provide relevant information for the MSE: A child may demonstrate aggressive themes in the play, choose developmentally inappropriate toys, or become more verbally expressive when engaged in puppet play. When imaginative play is completely absent or very limited, concrete, and noninteractive, it may suggest pervasive developmental disorder (Sadock & Sadock, 2003).

Our outline is a collaborative framework derived from our clinical experience with a pediatric population as well as numerous references. We have compiled our list based on what we feel should be included in each examination. While examiners have flexibility when choosing a format and administering the MSE, it is recommended that most MSEs address the aspects of a child's functioning listed below.

ELEMENTS OF THE CHILD MENTAL STATUS EXAM

Child MSEs assess the child's current cognitive functioning through observation and specific questioning of the child and parent/guardian. Although most child MSEs have been based upon adult exams, the approach to the child exam is clearly distinguishable from that of the adult exam. This is obviously necessary, as children's mental health disorders differ from those of adults. For example, in the *Diagnostic and Statistical Manual of Mental Disorders, Fourth Edition, Text Revision (DSM-IV-TR)* (American Psychiatric Association, 2000), psychological disorders for children differ from adult diagnoses. Symptom presentation, duration, and age of onset of symptoms required for diagnoses are often different for children compared with requirements for adults. A child may present with a symptom similar to that of an adult; however, it may manifest itself differently. As one example, a child may present with hallucinations, which may result from fevers, infections, or acute brain syndromes; however, the child's functioning may not be regressive with regard to thought processes, as in adult disorders such as delirium or dementia (Goodman & Sours, 1998). Furthermore, true hallucinations in childhood psychiatric disorders are uncommon.

Facilitating the MSE with children is distinct from the process used with adults. Specifically, gaining the trust of children requires a clear understanding of developmental processes and cultural and power dynamics. A successful interview requires a skillful clinician capable of utilizing various means of communication, including developmentally appropriate play techniques, art, music, and the capacity to use developmentally appropriate language. Specific developmental considerations will be discussed in later sections of this chapter. The following critical features of the MSE with children are delineated in preexisting literature, including appearance, attitude and behavior, emotional state, social relatedness, motor behavior, speech and language, cognition, thought process and content, and insight and judgment (Goodman & Sours, 1998).

Appearance

The child's appearance, particularly dress, can provide a significant amount of information, including but not limited to gender identity, sex role assignment, social status, level of parental supervision and care, religious background in some cases, peer group identification, attention to detail, and self-esteem. Physical appearance provides the examiner with an immediate sense of any obvious disabilities, height and weight that may fall outside of normal range, racial- or ethnic-group identity, gross motor abilities, and cleanliness. The examiner should be alert to obvious signs of trauma or injury, such as extensive bruising, burns, or cuts. In addition, unkemptness and odorous signs may indicate some form of neglect or lack of services. Concerns about abuse or neglect should be carefully explored with the child and caregiver. If a clinician suspects abuse or neglect, a report will need to be provided to child protective services.

Attitude and Behavior

The child's attitude should be assessed early on, including attitude toward the clinician and the accompanying adults. Observe the ease of separation between the child and adults as the child accompanies the examiner and note the reunion with the adult following the interview. Extreme reluctance to leave the caregiver may indicate a separation or attachment issue. The child's approach to the examiner is also significant. Does the child "cling" to the examiner immediately? Overly friendly or eager behavior may be indicative of attachment or interpersonal issues. Note whether the child appears anxious, withdrawn, inhibited, distracted, or apathetic.

Emotional State

Evaluation of emotional state includes a survey of the child's mood and affect. *Mood* refers to the child's subjective experience of emotion. For example, a child may be feeling angry, euthymic (happy), euphoric, anxious, irritable, happy, content, guilty, disgusted, or surprised. If a child does not indicate how he or she is feeling, the examiner may ask the child to draw a picture of this. Young children do not typically have an extensive vocabulary to express their feeling states. The use of "feeling posters" that include photographs expressing various emotions can be helpful in facilitating the child's identification of present mood state. Examining nonverbal behaviors also provides insight into the child's feelings. For example, is the child picking at his or her cuticles, suggestive of anxiety? Does the child appear sluggish, with moistened eyes, suggestive of sadness?

Affect refers to how a person expresses his or her feelings. Does the child's range of emotional expressivity appear to be flat, blunted, restricted, normal or broad, or appropriate? Determine whether the child's mood is congruent with his or her affect. For example, does the child laugh without apparent reason while calmly sitting and drawing? Does the child appear to be labile, that is, suddenly changing emotions? Is this lability seen at home but not in other environments? Is it related to specific types of provocation or seen in the absence of any identifiable stressors? The assessment of affect and affect regulation is a critical part of the examination with children. Poor affect and behavioral regulation is frequently the precipitant of a child's referral to therapy. The examiner will want to understand the child's awareness of various emotional states, recall of angry outbursts, ability to identify sources of provocation, and

willingness to gain control of emotional outbursts. If lability is primarily seen at home, you may want to explore how the child understands or explains this discrepancy in his or her behavior. If the emotional lability has resulted in aggression or destruction of property, determine whether the child experiences remorse and has attempted to apologize or make restitution.

Social Relatedness

Evaluate the child's social skills and eye contact. Does the child relate to the examiner? Alternatively, does the child demonstrate poor social skills, such as adamant avoidance of eye contact or verbal interaction? What are the child's modes of communication? Does the child communicate during play, drawing, or speaking? Discern through discussion, drawings, or play who is most important to the child. For example, who does the child turn to when she wakes from a bad dream? Who is the child's best friend? What does the child do during recess? Has the child ever had a friend that only he could see? How did things change when baby sister was born? When an older sibling left for college? Does the child maintain contact with her best friend who moved during the school year? Questions like these and others can provide the examiner with an understanding of the child's capacity for attachment, sense of connection, age-appropriate social relatedness, and adjustment to changes in relationships.

Motor Behavior

Assess the child's functioning with regard to gross motor and fine motor skills, activity level, ability to pay attention, coordination, and cerebral dominance. In addition, observations of involuntary movements, tremors, and the presence of tics or stereotypes are included here. With regard to coordination, note the child's posture, balance, and gait throughout the interview. Note whether one side of a child dominates the other. At 12 months old, for example, a child should be using both hands interchangeably. Note whether gross motor and fine motor skills have been attained at the 1-year mark. Is a 1-year-old able to hold a crayon (fine motor) and sit up without support (gross motor)? Assess whether the child is unable to sit still, maintain eye contact, or focus, which may be indicative of hyperactivity. If there is excessive motor movement, does it interfere with or assist concentration and interaction? If motor or stretch breaks are provided, does the child seem more organized and attentive when he or she returns to the interview?

Determining whether the child's gross motor skills are developmentally appropriate can be achieved through the child interview. For example, ask the child whether he or she is riding a bike independent of training wheels, skating, swimming, or horseback riding. If so, does the child enjoy the sport or activity? These are all individual activities that generally emerge for children during their early latency age years. Active involvement and enjoyment of team sports often gives you other types of information, such as comfort in social groups, capacity for receiving and utilizing large amounts of sensory information, and ability to take direction from an authority figure.

Speech and Language

The examiner should assess the child's expressive and receptive language and language acquisition. Receptive language includes the child's ability to hear the examiner, recognize the words, and comprehend what he or she has heard (Goodman & Sours, 1998). Expressive language includes the child's rate of speech, rhythm, spontaneity, intonation, articulation, and prosody. For example, note whether a child speaks incessantly or has articulation difficulties. Is the child's language age appropriate? Speaking, reading, writing, and spelling should be noted if the child is of the age at which these skills should be emerging or are proficient. Are the child's phrases or sentences coherent and organized? Does the child engage in reciprocal exchange across conversation? If the child uses minimal verbal language, is he or she proficient in signing or gesturing? What is the level of sophistication of the language used? If bilingual, how proficient is the child in the first and second language? What is required of the examiner to foster verbal interaction?

Cognition

Examiners may choose to administer an MMSE, which will tap into orientation, attention and concentration, language, and memory. A well-known example of a MMSE was established by Folstein et al. (1975). The MMSE is most widely utilized as a screening tool for cognitive impairment. The MMSE can be modified to incorporate age-appropriate tasks. Assessment of cognition should include attention, concentration, intellectual functioning, orientation, memory, and registration. Formal or informal assessment can be used to document cognitive abilities. While it is very difficult to estimate IQ without standardized testing, you will quickly have a sense of a child's relative cognitive maturity.

Attention is the ability of a child to direct mental energy when fully alert to the examiner or to the task. *Digit span* is an appropriate task to measure attention in school-age children. Informally, you can observe how quickly children map out your office, remembering where specific toys or objects are. Have them look carefully around your office for 10 seconds, then close their eyes and name as many items as they can remember. If children are oriented and alert, it should be relatively easy for them to recall 5 to 10 items after a quick scan around the room. This engaging, fun game can give you a sense of general attentional capacity. It does not generalize, however, to attentional capacity in routine or highly stimulating environments.

Concentration is the child's ability to maintain sustained attention for a period of time. Concentration is frequently tested with *serial sevens task*. In this task, school-age children are asked to start at the number 100 and subtract 7 from 100, then repeat subtractions of the number 7. Older children may be asked to calculate arithmetic problems without counting on their fingers.

Assessment of *orientation* to person, place, and time varies significantly with younger and older children. Awareness and understanding of time is a temporal skill that emerges around 4 years of age. Children are typically 7 or 8 years of age when they learn to read an analog clock. In general, when assessing for orientation, remember that time includes time of day, day of the week, date, month, and season. *Place* includes the site of the interview, such as the hospital, office, floor level, city, and state. *Person* is the identity of the examiner and the accompanying family member. Younger children are not expected to know the date; however, older children should recognize the date and time. Impairments in orientation may suggest low intelligence, organic damage, or a thought disorder (Sadock & Sadock, 2003). In addition, it is the unusual child that can remember the examiner's name after one introduction. If children are expected to remember your name, make sure you have them repeat it a couple of times, or shorten it; for example, instead of "Dr. Michael van Swearingen," you could introduce yourself to younger children as "Dr. Mike."

Memory functioning is assessed across immediate recall, short-term memory, and long-term recall. Short-term memory or recent memory can be assessed by asking a child to name three unrelated objects present in the room, such as a pen, a clock, and a button. Five minutes later, ask the child to recall the items. Registration, or immediate memory, is the recall of new information, such as recalling a short list of digits or letters (Robinson, 2005). To assess long-term recall, for example, you might ask a child to name a favorite gift from his or her last birthday, to retell his or her favorite story or movie (assuming you know it), or to describe something he or she did last summer vacation or some other activity that would give you a sense of the child's ability to recall significant events or learned material.

Deficits in memory may reflect anxiety, brain injury, trauma, or learning disabilities (Sadock & Sadock, 2003). History and further evaluation would be necessary to determine etiology of significant memory deficits.

Thought content and process are assessed with consideration for what is expected and inappropriate for a child according to age. *Thought content* includes interests, fears, wishes, obsessions, delusions, suicidal ideation, homicidal ideation, excessive magical thinking, paranoia, and phobias. If this does not become apparent across the interview, the examiner can ask the child to make three wishes. Direct inquiry about worries, concerns, fears, or suicidal or homicidal feelings or intent is appropriate. If the child is old enough to read and write, he or she could complete a self-report measure, such as the Behavior Assessment System for Children, Second Edition, or complete one of the sentence completion tests available for children.

Thought process includes production of thought and continuity of thought. For example, how is the child's flow of thought, meaning rate, rhythm, and association? Does the child exhibit a flight of ideas, loose associations, tangentiality, rumination, perseveration, thought blocking, or echolalia?

Insight and judgment refer to the child's capacity to reflect upon his or her own thoughts, behaviors, and feelings and consider why and when they occur. Does the child ever consider how others react toward him? If the child experiences negative reactions from other children, does he or she have a sense of responsibility in the interaction? Is it realistic? Does the child appear to have an understanding of the purpose or potential outcome of the evaluation? Does the child understand the role of the clinician? If the child reportedly engages in high-risk behaviors, does he or she have a sense of vulnerability or some intent for self-harm, or simply miscalculate the risks involved?

The aforementioned features of an MSE are meaningful only if assessed within a developmental framework that attends to cultural considerations, attachment, and psychosocial factors. These are reviewed below, with special consideration given to the impact of a history of abuse and/or neglect, acculturation, and disability.

CULTURAL CONSIDERATIONS

All behaviors, relationships, thought processes, and emotional experiences of children occur within the context of multiple factors and are best understood within a cultural framework. You will want to know how the family understands the child's presenting issues as well as how mental health practitioners are viewed within their cultures. In addition, you will want to know what cultural values are most salient to the child. It is not unusual for a child to embrace the values of the dominant American culture, seemingly turning away from his or her family's cultural values. This is often the cause of both intrapsychic as well as intrafamilial conflict. You may be working with a child from a bicultural family, and which cultural norms are most salient and how these factors interface with your own and current practice guidelines will have to be explored. If you are unfamiliar with the child's cultural background, seek consultation and guidance from a colleague who is more knowledgeable in this area. Understanding the relevance of culture for a particular client is pivotal in an accurate assessment, diagnosis, and intervention. Equally pivotal in a child's life are his or her primary and secondary attachments.

Attachment/Relationships

Attachment is an enduring emotional connection between people that produces a desire for continual contact as well as feelings of distress during separation (Berger, 2001). This experience is among the most important interactions in the early lives of infants and may be a preview of a child's social and personality development in the years to come (Lefrancois, 1995). According to Greenspan and Lieberman (1989), infants have two principal tasks during this early period of their development. The first task is to achieve a balance between their physical and emotional needs, a balance termed *homeostasis*. In this regard, homeostasis is maintained when the infant is not too hungry, thirsty, cold, or hot. The second task, which is required to maintain homeostasis, involves forming an attachment.

Since an infant cannot describe to us the process of forming an affectional tie with his or her caregiver, measurements of an infant's attachment are always indirect. Investigators must observe an infant's reactions toward a person, a thing, or a situation in order to make inferences about the process of attachment (Lefrancois, 1995). Attachment theorists describe four phases in the development of an infant's attachment, beginning with the first phase, described as *preattachment*. It appears that from the very beginning, infants are predisposed to identify and respond to stimulation from other people, especially from their mothers. At this stage, infants position their bodies in synchrony with adult human speech and are able to discriminate the mother's voice from that of other women (DeCasper & Fifer, 1980).

The second phase (into second half of the first year), *attachment in the making*, bears some similarity to the aforementioned concept of homeostasis, and the infant focuses on behaviors that promote contact with adults, such as crying, smiling, and sucking. At this stage, the infant produces the "selective social smile"—regarded as the smile that occurs in recognition of familiar faces—whereas smiling in response to unfamiliar faces becomes uncommon. The third phase (second half of the first year), *clear-cut attachment*, becomes apparent with infants' development of locomotor abilities. Now they can do much more than cry or laugh to gain the attention of caregivers; they begin to use their motor abilities by crawling, climbing, or clinging

on to their caregivers. Some time in the second year, infants enter the fourth phase, *goal-corrected attachment*, in which they begin to understand something of the points of view of others, as well as developing notions of *self* and *others* as being separate and permanent. The idea of cause-and-effect relationships becomes more salient to infants, and they begin to make inferences about the effects of their behaviors and of their caregivers' behaviors as well.

Depending on the quality of the relationship and interactions between the child and the primary caregiver(s), the infant can form a secure, avoidant, or ambivalent attachment. *Securely attached infants* use their caregivers as a base for exploration. They go about freely and play in a room, but often reestablish contact by looking at, speaking to, or returning to the caregiver. These infants are usually distressed when the caregiver leaves, but greet the caregiver upon his or her return. In contrast, *avoidant infants* either ignore the caregiver's return or actively avoid contact with him or her, sometimes by looking away or perhaps pushing the caregiver away. Similar to the securely attached infant, the *ambivalent infant* is often very upset when his or her caregiver leaves; however, the infant often displays anger toward the caregiver upon his or her return (Ainsworth, Blehar, Waters, & Wall, 1978).

Although we experience different forms of attachment throughout the lifespan, an infant's attachment pattern may be a preview of the child's social and personality development in the years to come. For example, securely attached infants tend to become children who interact with teachers in friendly and appropriate ways and who are competent in a wide array of social and cognitive skills (Lefrancois, 1995). Although salient, developing a secure or insecure attachment during infancy does not inherently determine whether a child will thrive; rather, attachment is a sign, a symptom, and sometimes a predictor of the direction a child's development will take (Berger, 2001). The idea that early relationships do not inevitably determine later social relationships is important. A sensitive caregiver who fosters a secure attachment is likely to continue this approach as the child matures, thus encouraging the development of curiosity and independence. Similarly, insensitive care that contributes to insecure attachment is also likely to be maintained. Shifts in family circumstances due to divorce, a new baby, or better child care, however, can often alter patterns of family interaction and attachment. As the attachment pattern changes, so do the long-term effects, thus suggesting that a child who is insecurely attached at age 1 might become securely attached at age 2. It is also important to consider additional factors. Research implies that although responsive parenting and frequent synchrony are likely to lead to secure attachment, it is not always the parents' fault when the attachment is insecure. Rather, the child's temperament seems to affect the parent-child connection (Rosen & Burke, 1999).

In conclusion, tremendous physical, cognitive, linguistic, emotional, and social growth occurs in the first 2 years of life. This process may be hampered or encouraged by both the immediate family and the culture to which they belong. What we can be certain about, however, is that the ability to thrive demands a nurturing context (Berger, 2001). Therefore, the MSE should include observations of the child with the primary caregiver to determine the level of attachment. In addition to observations of the parent/child interactions, the evaluator can use drawings, puppet play, and sand tray techniques to provide the child with mechanisms to represent his or her primary attachments symbolically. The sense of secure attachment can be inferred by asking a child to identify who they go to with a worry and who understands them best. In addition to primary attachments, friendships and relationships with siblings, classmates, teachers, neighbors, and others should be explored as well.

Sense of Self

One of the pivotal accomplishments in the psychosocial development of children and adolescents is the process of self-awareness. *Self- awareness,* a term used interchangeably with *self-perception,* is the highest level described in consciousness: the ability to be aware of oneself and the relation of the self to the environment (Stuss, 1992). Self-awareness is multifaceted, as it includes physical awareness, awareness of self, awareness of others, and social awareness (Strauss & Goethals, 1991). A mature self-awareness requires an integrated appreciation of one's physical status and ongoing relationship with the immediate external environment: in other words, an appreciation of being a distinctive person in a world that mainly exists outside of one's immediate awareness and is inhabited by many other distinctive individuals, and an appreciation of oneself as an interactive part of the network of social relationships (Lezak, 1995).

According to Shapka and Keating (2005), with each developmental milestone, children's perceptions of themselves become increasingly differentiated and comprehensive. It appears as though very young infants have no sense of self. To them, for example, their arms and hands are interesting because they appear and disappear. By the age of 1 year, however, most infants begin to discover themselves. They begin to realize that they are distinct from other people (Harter, 1996). By the age of 2, most children are aware of the "do's and don'ts." They begin to develop self-awareness, which allows toddlers to be self-critical and to have emotional responses, such as guilt (Lefrancois, 1995). This relationship between self-awareness and emotions permits children to react in an entirely new way to their misdeeds. At this stage of emotional development, for example, it is typical for a child to spill juice on the carpet with pride, with the intention of making his or her mother or father angry. Although this stage is often challenging for parents, the child's taking obvious pride to act counter to convention is possible only when self-awareness is firmly established.

Research has found that between ages 1 and 6, children progress from an emergence of awareness that they are independent individuals to a firm understanding of their identities regarding who they are, how they see themselves as individuals within a social construct, and what they like (Harter, 1983). According to Erikson's psychosocial theory (Berger, 2001), between the ages of 3 and 6, young children's self-esteem is dependent upon the skills and competencies that demonstrate their independence and initiative. Preschoolers often reflect positively upon themselves by regularly overestimating their abilities. At this stage, they enjoy undertaking tasks that will allow them the opportunity to show off their great talents to sing, dance, and count. Yet even though self-confidence is tied to competency and competency demands repeated demonstration of mastery, children at this age are also sensitive to the judgments and criticisms of others. As they begin developing a sense of self and others, they will inevitably feel guilty when their efforts result in failure or criticism (Berger, 2001).

Whereas preschoolers are preoccupied with overestimating their competencies and showing them off, middle childhood (7 to 11 years) is a period in which children begin to learn their areas of strengths and weakness. During Erikson's (Berger, 2001) "crisis of industry versus inferiority stage," children effortlessly try to master whatever their culture values. Unlike a 3-year-old, however, during this stage of development, the child judges himself or herself as either competent or incompetent. Cognitive advances afford children the ability to understand that human behavior is not simply a response to specific thoughts or desires. Rather, they understand the etiology of various behaviors and begin to analyze the implications of whatever action a person may take. As in every stage of development, they will encounter adversity and challenges, but they learn how to manage their emotions more effectively. Unlike preschoolers, in middle childhood, children become more concerned with the judgment of their peer groups (Pipher, 1994). They must learn how to negotiate, compromise, share, and defend themselves, which is often an arduous and challenging task during this stage of development (Hartup, 1996).

By adolescence, psychosocial development is best understood in terms of answering the question "Who am I?" The physical, social, and emotional changes challenge the adolescent to find his or her identity (Kroger, 2000). Erikson (Berger, 2001) referred to the challenges of this stage as "identity versus role confusion." The search for identity is an ongoing challenge that can be approached in several ways. The ultimate goal is referred to as *identity achievement,* which is reached when adolescents establish their own identities by accepting and rejecting the goals and values set by their parents and cultures (Berger, 2001). Some adolescents may never examine these goals and values. Rather, they choose to accept them without hesitation and foreclose on the process of exploration. It is also possible that some adolescents feel as though they cannot live up to their parents' expectations. This may result in a *negative identity,* whereby the adolescent does the exact opposite of what is expected of him or her. Other young people experience a period of *identity diffusion.* This is characterized by having few commitments or goals and perhaps being indifferent about trying to take on any role. This may be seen as sedentary behavior or lack of motivation. Last, some young adults choose to experiment with a variety of identities. This is referred to as *identity moratorium*

and is a period of exploration. Research suggests that many adolescents go through many of these stages before they reach a mature identity. This process of identification can be one of the most difficult to achieve, and it sometimes takes 10 years or more (Marcia, Waterman, Matteson, Archer, & Orlofsky, 1993).

Although we have minimally reviewed the challenges of psychosocial development throughout childhood, each stage is a progressive step toward attaining an accurate, healthy, and developed sense of self. The MSE should comprehensively evaluate the child's sense of self. This can be achieved through projective drawings, sentence completion tasks, and structured interviewing, with queries such as the following: "What would your best friend say is the best thing about you?" "What do you like best about yourself?" "If you could change one thing about yourself, what would it be?" This developing sense of self is so very critical in understanding all other findings from the MSE.

COGNITIVE DEVELOPMENT

Cognitive development refers to the changes that occur in an individual's cognitive structures, abilities, and processes (Driscoll, 1994). More specifically, cognition involves mental processes such as thinking, knowing, and remembering (Berger, 2001). Cognitive development is best understood as a successive progression throughout the lifespan, beginning in early infancy, when fundamental skills and acute sensory abilities (sight, smell, touch, and hearing) are mastered. In the years following infancy, there is a dramatic transformation of the child's undifferentiated, unspecialized cognitive abilities into an adult's conceptual competence and problem-solving skills (Driscoll, 1994).

Infants were once thought of as passive and unknowing. It was commonly believed that until they mastered language, young children were incapable of thinking or forming complex ideas. Today, we know otherwise. From the very start, young children are aware of their surroundings and interested in exploring them. Scientists from several fields have shown that from the first weeks of life, babies are active learners. They are busy gathering and organizing knowledge about their world. These milestones highlight young children's progress in developing perceptual and thinking skills.

Jean Piaget was the first major theorist to stress that infants are active learners and that early learning is based on sensory abilities (Berger, 2001). Piaget (Berger, 2001) believed that children's *schemes,* or logical mental structures, change with age and are initially action based (sensorimotor) and later move to a mental (operational) level (Driscoll, 1994). Piaget proposed four major periods of cognitive development, which are guided by the human need for *cognitive equilibrium,* that is, a state of mental balance (Flavell, 1999). Simply stated, this means that the ability of individuals to make sense of new experiences depends largely upon their existing understanding. From birth to 2 years of age, during the *sensorimotor period,* infants use their senses and motor abilities to understand the world. At this stage, their cognitive capacity does not afford them the ability to reflect or conceptualize. Rather, this sensorimotor period is marked by a chain of mental and physical actions.

Between the ages of 2 and 6, during the *preoperational thought* period, preschool children acquire representational skills in the area of mental imagery and especially language. According to Piaget (1970), one apparent difference between cognition during infancy and cognition during the preschool years is symbolic thinking. *Symbolic thinking* can be described as the ability to use symbols, such as words or objects, to signify other objects, behaviors, or experiences. Children at this stage, however, have not yet learned to use logical principles in their conceptualization of their experiences. For example, at this stage, a child has a tendency to focus on one aspect of a situation. It is challenging for the child to acknowledge alternatives. This bears some similarity to the concept of *egocentrism,* characterized by a child who contemplates the world exclusively from his or her personal perspective.

In Piaget's (Berger, 2001) view, the most important cognitive milestone of middle childhood is the attainment of *concrete operational thought* between the ages of 7 and 11 (Flavell, 1999). Achieving this milestone suggests that children can reason logically about the things and events they perceive. Whereas a preschooler uses subjective insights to understand the process by which a caterpillar becomes a butterfly, a school-age child seeks a rational explanation for the transformation (Berger, 2001). A school-age child is not satisfied with the explanation that the caterpillar felt like becoming a butterfly, whereas a preschooler would be. During this stage, the child strives to understand by applying logical operations or principles to help interpret experiences objectively and rationally, rather than intuitively.

Another cognitive milestone during this stage is the child's ability to take into account another person's point of view and consider more than one perspective simultaneously. With their thought processes being more logical, flexible, and organized than in early childhood, they are able to consider alternatives. Although they can understand concrete problems, however, according to Piaget (Berger, 2001), they have not mastered the ability to contemplate or solve abstract problems.

By 12 years of age through adulthood, adolescents gain a tremendous amount of knowledge and are more sophisticated in their use of analysis, logic, and reason (Piaget, 1970). Although they appear to be advanced, this stage of development can also be challenging. As their thinking becomes more abstract and hypothetical, they also become vulnerable to ideas and insights that may be troubling or dangerous (Berger, 2001). Piaget thought that during this stage of cognitive development, adolescents begin to reach *formal operational thought,* which is the fourth and final stage. Adolescents demonstrate the capacity to approach experience from a theoretical perspective. They have the capacity for hypothetical thought, involving reasoning about propositions that may or many not reflect reality. For example, an adolescent may not believe in implementing a longer school day but could nevertheless provide a convincing argument of why it is important, despite his or her personal beliefs. On the contrary, a younger child would have tremendous difficulty arguing against his or her personal beliefs.

A child's cognitive development is best described as the emergence of progressively more logical forms of thought. As cognitive development progresses in children, allowing them to use powerful symbol systems to understand and manipulate the environment, they gain a sense of independence and self-awareness (Lefrancois, 1995).

RACIAL/MULTICULTURAL IDENTITY

Racial or multicultural identity can be considered an element of ethnicity. Biological traits such as hair and skin color, which distinguish one race from another, are much less significant to development than are the attitudes and experiences that may arise from ethnic or racial consciousness (Templeton, 1998). Although two people may "look related," they may have had different upbringings, heritages, and experiences. In this respect, ethnicity is synonymous with culture in that it provides people with beliefs, values, and traditions that will affect their development and the ways in which they conceptualize their experiences.

In terms of identity development, Erikson has been one of the most prominent theorists contributing to the understanding of establishing a stable sense of self. According to Erickson (1968), the formation of ego identity and self-identity results in positive psychological outcomes. As noted previously, by adolescence, psychosocial development is best understood in terms of answering the question "Who am I?" It is a period marked by physical, social, and emotional changes, which challenge the adolescent to explore his or her identity (Kroger, 2000). The process of establishing an identity is confounded by forces outside the individual, however, including the surrounding culture (Grotevant & Cooper, 1998, as cited in Berger, 2001). Throughout development, the surrounding culture contributes to identity formation in that it defines values as well as social structures and customs, which ease the transition from childhood to adulthood. This may be significant for a child or adolescent who is a part of a culture in which everyone holds similar general moral, political, religious, and sexual values. In modern industrial societies, by contrast, this idea of cultural consensus is rare. Although it varies for each individual, the search for identity is an ongoing challenge that can be approached in several ways. Yet, ultimately, the person's objective is identity achievement (Berger, 2001).

It appears as though racial- and ethnic-identity formation is a salient developmental task for children from preschool through adolescence. The developmental literature suggests that the preschool period marks the beginning of children's understanding of racial and ethnic differences. A particularly controversial set of studies conducted over the last half century has examined racial identity and self-esteem among preschool children (Spencer & Markstrom-Adams, 1990). In particular, these studies suggest that minority

preschool children have internalized societal perceptions of the lower status of their own and other racial minority groups, yet they maintain feelings of high self-esteem. Other research emphasizes the value and influence of parental racial socialization in promoting positive racial identity in preschool children (Caughy, O'Campo, Randolph, & Nickerson, 2002). In middle childhood, children tend to struggle with racial and ethnic differences through questions and inquiries regarding ethnic/racial groups, particularly their own reference groups. During this period, they also begin to show a preference for the group with which they belong (Murray & Mandara, 2002). They are capable of choosing and distinguishing these differences because of their cognitive advancement. At this point, they have achieved a tremendous amount of knowledge and are more sophisticated in their use of analysis, logic, and reason (Piaget, 1970). Furthermore, research also indicates that racial discrimination and lack of community ethnic identification may potentially negatively impact developmental outcomes for minority school-age children (Johnson, 2001).

During adolescence, the process of identity formation is a significant developmental task. At this age, children demonstrate the capacity to approach experience from a theoretical perspective and the ability for hypothetical thought involving reasoning about propositions that may or many not reflect reality. For the most part, this exploration period requires thorough examination that is often pursued through same-race friendships and overt references to racial and ethnic pride (Phinney & Tarver, 1988). Those with a strong sense of ethnic identity display positive perceptions of and connections to their ethnic groups. Some research suggests that ethnic identity is a "protective" factor for these adolescents that may positively influence their psychological well-being (Phinney, 1990).

Despite the rewards and challenges presented at each stage of development, racial and ethnic formation plays a critical role in helping a child develop a healthy sense of self and collective belonging. This is true not only for minority children, but for all children. Therefore, it is safe to say that we are all influenced by the cultures in which we belong.

The practice of reviewing children's sense of racial and ethnic identity as part of the MSE is recent. Inquiry into this area of self-awareness yields a great deal of knowledge about how children are localized within their cultures—how they mediate the difference between dominant and personal cultural values, potential conflict they may experience with their families over ethnic or cultural identification, negative- or positive-encounter experiences with children whose backgrounds differ from their own, and any internalized negative racial or ethnic stereotypes. This type of exploration will require the examiner to be competent in multicultural counseling, aware of his or her own background and privilege and how this might be experienced by the client. For additional reading in this area, see Carter (2005), *Handbook of Racial-Cultural Psychology and Counseling: Practice and Training.* Gibbs and Huang (2003) provided specific multicultural considerations for children and adolescents in *Children of Color: Psychological Interventions With Culturally Diverse Youth.*

CORROBORATING INFORMATION

In completing a child MSE, it is imperative to include collateral interviews, minimally with parents or a primary caregiver. On the day of the MSE, it is generally more productive to have the parents give the child permission to talk with the examiner, discussing any topic with candor and without reservation. While this does not guarantee the child will actually talk with the examiner openly, it does increase the child's comfort level. In addition to securing parental permission for the child to meet with you, the parents will provide the primary information for the following: developmental and medical history; history of the presenting problem; what interventions have been tried, successful or not; description of family dynamics and school performance; pertinent cultural information; history of trauma or stressors; and specific goals for the evaluation. Parents can also complete various measures, such as the BASC2 or the Child Behavior Checklist for Ages 6–18, Conners' Checklist, that provide norm-referenced scores across a number of clinical and adaptive scales based on the parent's observations.

It is often helpful to have both parents complete separate forms, when possible, as this can yield information about how the child responds to each caregiver. A significant difference between the caregiver reports can reflect different parenting expectations, styles, emotional resource of one or the other parent, and many other possible reasons that would become more evident across the parent intake or parent/child observations. In addition to an understanding of the nature of the presenting problems, parents should be able to identify the child's various strengths and interests, important assets for treatment planning.

In addition to parent report, teachers of school-age children can provide other types of information, including the most obvious: academic potential and academic performance. In addition, the teacher typically is able to comment on how the child compares with his or her classmates on a number of variables, including but not limited to behavioral and emotional regulation, attentional capacity, social interaction, executive functions (initiation, inhibition, organization, self-monitoring), arousal, atypical features of behavior, and areas of strength.

Other caregivers, such as family members and au pairs, can provide additional perspective. While a parent might find the child reluctant to engage easily in the morning routine, the grandmother may have success. It is important to determine whether this difference is localized in a relationship issue or simple behavioral antecedents and rewards.

If the siblings are available for an intake session, a play session can be very revealing about these relationships. It should be determined whether there is any ongoing sibling violence, intense sibling rivalry, or parental preferential treatment occurring that might also lead to a better understanding of forces affecting the child's behavior. Alternative to siblings as a source of stress, the clinician might identify a sibling as a source of support, mentoring, or role model.

Clinicians who are currently working or have previously worked with the child and his or her family can provide additional information regarding response to therapy or specific interventions. In addition, the clinician referring the child for an evaluation can serve as a consultant to the examiner on history and other factors known to be related to the presenting problem. This information can often accelerate the process, providing focus and detail that would have otherwise gone undetected or required significant time to uncover.

LIMITATIONS AND CONSIDERATIONS OF THE MENTAL STATUS EXAM

Several limitations of both the adult and child MSE must be considered. First, interviews are generally a source of bias (Groth-Marnat, 2003). Reliability and validity of exams pose a threat to validity when no formal assessment is provided. Adding structure helps control for bias and increases the interrater reliability and validity of the assessment (Groth-Marnat, 2003). Other common limitations include interviewer bias. Commonly known as the *halo effect,* when an examiner perceives a client to be pleasant or attractive in some way, he or she may "rate" the person more favorably on specific tasks. Interviewees may also distort their responses. While this may not be feasible during tasks, such as digit span, which result in a concrete response, a child may falsify information to impress the interviewer. Data are not quantifiable; therefore, normative comparisons can be made only qualitatively.

Children have more limited attention compared with adults. The length of the exam may cause discomfort (Maruish, 2002). Adding breaks often facilitates the adjustment to the length of the exam. Attention span improves gradually throughout preschool years; therefore, older children should be able to work through the entire exam with less difficulty than younger children (Kail, 2007).

A structured format is recommended; however, examiners must be capable of modifying their questions based on a child's behavior and functioning. Of consideration is that highly structured interviews may impede the examiner's ability to make astute observations of the child (Maruish, 2002).

Clinicians must consider the child from a developmental perspective throughout the exam. Specifically, they must be adept at using language suitable for the child and relating to the child through play. Child MSEs require that clinicians understand the vicissitudes of normal and abnormal behavior.

Last, during the interview, the examiner should consider the child's mental status, which can be influenced, for example, by anxiety or amount of sleep. Considering the child within a contextual approach will help provide a more accurate picture of the child's functioning. Groth-Marnat

(2003) provided a detailed outline of the MSE in the *Handbook of Psychological Assessment.* Trzepacz and Baker (1993) provided a very detailed description of the process, including in-depth discussions of each area of functioning to be explored, along with useful definitions of various behavioral and psychological presentations. While each of these references are helpful, there is no attention given to the developmental considerations involved in conducting the MSE with children.

SPECIAL CONSIDERATIONS IN THE PEDIATRIC MENTAL STATUS EXAM

Being a multiculturally competent clinical interviewer involves both knowing what is possible to know about the backgrounds and cultures of clients and being sensitive to areas beyond one's knowledge that might be influenced by culture. Therefore, this section briefly discusses special considerations when conducting a pediatric MSE.

Some children, depending on developmental level, may not be able to articulate answers to sophisticated questions during a MSE. Therefore, examiners must be knowledgeable regarding age-appropriate cognitive, social, and emotional functioning. For example, among other variables, a clinician may encounter a child who has a developmental disability. This is defined as a severe, chronic impairment that creates substantial functional limitations in three or more of the following areas of major life activity: self-care, language, learning, mobility, self-direction, potential for independent living, and potential for economic self-sufficiency as an adult (U.S. Department of Health and Human Services, 2004). Since effective interviewing will not come naturally to all professionals, it is the responsibility of clinicians to be more aware of their clients' limitations.

Regardless of age and capability, the clinician must be willing to engage in conversation about the child's experiences, including his or her expectations for the interview itself. This component of interviewing can become complicated, however, when the child is developmentally delayed or when a second language is involved. In cross-cultural work, informants such as parents, teachers, and family relatives may be able to provide additional information that cannot be communicated by the child. In this way, informants could potentially explain and describe their experiences in a way that becomes helpful for the clinician and, ultimately, the child (Sommers-Flanagan & Sommers-Flanagan, 1999).

In addition to disabilities and acculturation status, child abuse and neglect is another area for exploration when working with children. First, reporting suspected or known child abuse is required by law and by professional ethical guidelines and codes of conduct. Although ethical dilemmas may arise when reporting cases of suspected child abuse or neglect, the law is explicit. We must also be knowledgeable regarding the prevalence and rate of child abuse and neglect, as well as the signs and symptoms associated with this type of circumstance.

According to the National Child Abuse and Neglect Data System (2005), which was developed by the Children's Bureau of the U.S. Department of Health and Human Services, an estimated 906,000 children were determined to be victims of child abuse or neglect in 2003. Furthermore, more than 60% of child victims experienced neglect. Almost 19% were physically abused; 10% were sexually abused; and 5% were emotionally maltreated. In addition, 17% were associated with "other" types of maltreatment, based on specific state laws and policies. Children from birth to 3 years of age had the highest rates of victimization, at 16.4 per 1,000 children of the same age group. Girls were slightly more likely to be victims than were boys. Concerning culture, Pacific Islander, American Indian or Alaska Native, and African American children had the highest rates of victimization compared with their national populations. While the rate of White victims of child abuse or neglect was 11.0 per 1,000 children of the same race, the rate for Pacific Islanders was 21.4 per 1,000 children, the rate for American Indian or Alaska Natives was 21.3 per 1,000 children, and the rate for African Americans was 20.4 per 1,000 children.

Reports of child abuse and neglect stated that in 2003, an estimated 2.9 million referrals concerning the welfare of approximately 5.5 million children were made to child protective service agencies throughout the United States (National Child Abuse and Neglect Data System, 2005). Of these children, approximately two thirds (an estimated 1.9 million) were accepted for investigation or assessment; one third were not accepted.

More than one half (57%) of all reports that alleged child abuse or neglect were made by professionals such as educators, law enforcement and legal personnel, social services personnel, medical personnel, mental health personnel, child day care providers, and foster care providers. Nonprofessionals such as friends, neighbors, and relatives submitted approximately 43% of reports. Approximately 30% of the reports that were investigated included at least one child who was found to be a victim of abuse or neglect. Fifty-eight percent of the reports were found to be unsubstantiated (including those that were intentionally false); the remaining reports were closed for additional reasons (National Child Abuse and Neglect Data System, 2005). In an effort to assess for child abuse and neglect, as clinicians, we must also consider who the potential perpetrators are. Approximately 80% of the perpetrators were parents. Therefore, although we may depend on parents in assisting during interviewing, it may be helpful to spend time working individually with the child. Other relatives accounted for 6% of perpetrators, and unmarried partners of parents accounted for 4%. The remaining perpetrators included persons with other (camp counselor, school employee, etc.) or unknown relationships to the child victims (National Child Abuse and Neglect Data System, 2005).

In conclusion, the aforementioned strategies, key developmental and multicultural factors, and special considerations can serve the pediatric MSE process by fostering a comprehensive matrix of information to not only help better understand the presenting problems but also identify contributing stressors as well as strengths and resources—yielding a more specific diagnosis and treatment plan.

REFERENCES

Ainsworth, M. D. S., Blehar, M. C., Waters, E., & Wall, S. (1978). *Patterns of attachment*. Hillsdale, NJ: Lawrence Erlbaum.

American Psychiatric Association. (2000). *Diagnostic and statistical manual of mental disorders* (4th ed., Text rev.). Washington, DC: Author.

Berger, K. S. (2001). *The developing person through the lifespan*. New York: Worth.

Carter, R. T. (2005). *Handbook of racial-cultural psychology and counseling: Practice and training*. New York: Wiley.

Caughy, M., O'Campo, P., Randolph, S., & Nickerson, K. (2002). The influence of racial socialization practices on the cognitive and behavioral competence of

African-American preschoolers. *Child Development 73*, 1611–1625.

DeCasper, A. J., & Fifer, W. P. (1980). Of human bonding: Newborns prefer their mother's voices. *Science, 208*, 1174–1175.

Driscoll, M. P. (1994). *Psychology of learning for instruction.* Needham Heights, MA: Allyn & Bacon.

Erickson, E. H. (1968). *Identity: Youth and crisis.* New York: Norton.

Flavell, J. H. (1999). Cognitive development: Children's knowledge about the mind. *Annual Review of Psychology, 16*, 21.

Folstein, M., Folstein, S., & McHugh, P. R. (1975). Mini–mental state: A practical method for grading the cognitive state of patients for the clinician. *Journal of Psychiatric Research, 12*, 189–198.

Gibbs, J. T., & Huang, L. N. (2003). *Children of color: Psychological interventions with culturally diverse youth.* San Francisco: Jossey-Bass.

Goodman, J. D., & Sours, J. A. (1998). *The Child Mental Status Examination* (Expanded ed.). Northvale, NJ: Jason Aronson.

Greenspan, S. I., & Lieberman, A. F. (1989). A quantitative approach to the clinical assessment of representational elaboration and differentiation in children two to four. In S. I. Greenspan & G. H. Pollock (Eds.), *The course of life: Vol. II. Early childhood* (pp. 3–32). Madison, CT: International Universities Press.

Grotevant, H., & Cooper, C. R. (1998). Individuality and connectedness in adolescent development. In E. Skoe & A. von der Lippe (Eds.), *Personality development in adolescence: A cross-national and life span perspective* (pp. 3–37). London: Routledge.

Groth-Marnat, G. (2003). *Handbook of psychological assessment* (4th ed.). Hoboken, NJ: Wiley.

Hannay, H. J., Fischer, J. S., Loring, D. W., & Howieson, D. B. (2004). Observational methods, rating scales, and inventories. In M. D. Lezak, D. B. Howieson, & D. W. Loring (Eds.), *Neuropsychological assessment* (4th ed., pp. 698–737). New York: Oxford University Press.

Harter, S. (1983). Developmental perspectives on the self-esteem. In P. H. Mussen (Ed.), *Handbook of child psychology: Vol. IV. Socialization, personality, and social development* (pp. 275–385). New York: Wiley.

Harter, S. (1996). Teacher and classmate influences on scholastic motivation, self-esteem, and level of voice in adolescents. In J. Juvonen & K. R. Wentzel (Eds.), *Social motivation: Understanding children's school adjustment* (pp. 11–42). New York: Cambridge University Press.

Hartup, W. W. (1996). The company they keep: Friendships and their developmental significance. *Child Development, 35*, 445–459.

Johnson, D. (2001). Parental characteristics, racial stress, and racial socialization processes as predictors of racial coping in middle childhood. In A. Neal-Barnett, J. Contreras, & K. Kerns (Eds.), *Forging links: African American children clinical developmental perspectives* (pp. 57–74). Westport, CT: Praeger.

Kail, R. V. (2007). *Children and their development.* Upper Saddle River, NJ: Pearson/Prentice Hall.

Koocher, G. P., Norcross, J. C., & Hill, III, S. S. (2005). *Psychologists' desk reference* (2nd ed.). Oxford, NY: Oxford University Press.

Kroger, J. (2000). *Identity development: Adolescence through adulthood.* Thousand Oaks, CA: Sage.

Lefrancois, G. R. (1995). *Of children: An introduction to child development.* Belmont, CA: Wadsworth.

Lezak, M. D. (1995). *Neuropsychological assessment* (3rd ed.). New York: Oxford University Press.

Marcia, J. E., Waterman, A. S., Matteson, D. R., Archer, S. L., & Orlofsky, J. L. (1993). *Ego identity: A handbook for psychosocial research.* New York: Springer-Verlag.

Maruish, M. E. (2002). *Essentials of treatment planning.* New York: Wiley.

Mash, E. J., & Barkley, R. A. (2003). *Child psychopathology* (2nd ed.). New York: Guilford Press.

Morrison, J. (1995). *The first interview revised for DSM-IV.* New York: Guilford Press.

Murray, C., & Mandara, J. (2002). Racial identity development in African American children: Cognitive and experiential antecedents. In H. McAdoo (Eds.), *Black children: Social, educational, and parental environments* (pp. 73–96). Thousand Oaks, CA: Sage.

National Child Abuse and Neglect Data System. (2005). *Child maltreatment 2004: Summary of key findings.* Retrieved May 31, 2006, from http://www.nccan ch.acf.hhs.gov /pubs/factsheets/canstats.cfm

Phinney, J. (1990). Ethnic identity in adolescents and adults: Review and integration. *Psychological Bulletin, 108*, 499–514.

Phinney, J., & Tarver, S. (1988). Ethnic identity search and commitment in Black and White eight graders. *Journal of Early Adolescence, 8*, 265–277.

Piaget, J. (1970). *The child's conception of time* (A. J. Pomerans, Trans.). New York: Basic Books.

Pipher, M. (1994). *Reviving Ophelia: Saving the selves of adolescent girls.* New York: Ballantine Books.

Robinson, D. J. (2005). *The Mental Status Exam explained* (2nd ed.). Port Huron, MI: Rapid Psycher Press.

Rosen, K. S., & Burke, P. B. (1999). Multiple attachment relationships within families: Mothers and fathers with two young children. *Developmental Psychology, 35*, 436–441.

Sadock, B. J., & Sadock, V. A. (2003). *Synopsis of psychiatry, behavioral sciences/clinical psychiatry.* Philadelphia: Lippincott Williams & Wilkins.

Shapka, J. D., & Keating, D. P. (2005). Structure and change in self-concept during adolescents. *Canadian Journal of Behavioral Science, 37*, 83–96.

Sommers-Flanagan, R., & Sommers-Flanagan, J. (1999). *Clinical interviewing* (2nd ed.). New York: Wiley.

Spencer, M., & Markstrom-Adams, C. (1990). Identity processes among racial and ethnic minority children in America. *Child Development, 61*, 290–310.

Strauss, J., & Goethals, G. R. (1991). *The self: Interdisciplinary approaches.* New York: Springer-Verlag.

Stuss, T. D. (1992). Biological and psychological development of executive functions. *Brain and Cognition, 20*, 8–23.

Templeton, A. R. (1998). Human aces: A genetic and evolutionary perspective. *American Anthropologist, 100*, 632–650.

Trzepacz, P. T., & Baker, R. W. (1993). *The psychiatric mental status examination.* New York: Oxford Press.

U.S. Department of Health and Human Services. (2004). Retrieved May 31, 2006, from http://www.naic.acf.hhs .gov/admin/glossaryd.cfm

6

MULTICULTURAL AND DIVERSITY ISSUES

SUSAN TINSLEY LI AND JENNIFER MAGNESON

Children represent an untapped resource in understanding multicultural and diversity issues. Unlike adults, children's conceptualizations of race, ethnicity, and culture are fluid, developing over time, and affecting their perceptions of the world both directly and indirectly. Multicultural and diversity issues are significant considerations when interviewing children and primary caregivers, but the fluidity makes them different than when interviewing adults. In this chapter, we attempt to address some of the ways in which diversity considerations impact the interviewing process, by attending to recommendations from the multicultural interviewing literature, addressing unique concerns that differentially affect diverse youth, and presenting tools to aid the cross-cultural interview.

THE FRAMEWORK

In this chapter, we adopt a broad definition of *diversity* that includes constructs such as ethnicity, social class, religion, and sexual orientation (Hays, 2001). Although the majority of the information we present and review comes from literature focused on racial and ethnic diversity, other aspects of diversity are still considered to be important and influential. An ecosystemic framework (Bronfenbrenner & Morris, 1998) has been particularly helpful when applied to identify myriad factors that affect children's behaviors and responses. In the realm of clinical interviewing, an ecosystemic model allows the interviewer to identify the important sources of information that need to be accessed to gain a complete picture of the child's current concerns. Culture is just one of the contexts that influences children, in addition to families, peers, and schools. Having a complete picture of the cultural context allows information to be viewed in a different light, and thus a comprehensive and systematic evaluation of the child's cultural context is warranted. For example, in diverse children, the way in which symptoms may be defined, expressed, and understood may be linked to the cultural context. Furthermore, children from diverse backgrounds have unique concerns that are not represented in children from the dominant-culture group. In the next several sections, we review the multicultural interviewing literature for adults and extend this work to child/adolescent populations.

Multicultural Interviewing

There is a modest but informative literature on multicultural interviewing developed for clinical work with diverse adult populations. In general, writings in this area emphasize recommendations for effective interviewing when dealing with individuals from culturally diverse backgrounds.

Takushi and Uomoto (2001) have recommended that before conducting the multicultural interview, the clinician has an understanding of constructs such as worldview, cultural and ethnic identity, and the acculturation level of the interviewee. They also recommend attending to emic-etic distinctions (i.e., intracultural versus universal dimensions) in clinical conceptualization. Martinez (2000) has emphasized that the cross-cultural interview requires attending to the reasons that motivated the patient to initiate help-seeking behavior and the differences in symptom presentation across individuals. Many diverse individuals use nonspecific terms for expressing problems or distress that may be idiosyncratic to the individual or family. Unfamiliar terms or expressions may also be culturosyncratic (i.e., unique to the culture) and therefore unknown to the inexperienced interviewer. In addition, misidentification of the causal sources of the client's distress is a common problem, as diverse individuals may not attribute difficulties to the same sources as do dominant-culture individuals.

To aid clinicians in conducting interviews with diverse individuals, Berg-Cross and Takushi-Chinen (1995) developed the Person-in-Culture Interview (PICI) as a model of multicultural interviewing. As part of this model, these authors recommend knowing the client's culture-specific definitions of deviant behaviors and knowing accepted norms of behavior. Clinicians are encouraged to be familiar with culturally acceptable methods of social influence and know what community resources are available to the client as well as which services the client is likely to access (Berg-Cross & Takushi-Chinen, 1995).

Several writers have noted the importance of attending to the language of the interview, communication, and verbal and nonverbal behavior of diverse individuals during the interview process (Takushi & Uomoto, 2001). Turner, Hersen, and Heiser (2003) have discussed some of the communication problems that can result from sociocultural differences and the misinterpretation of verbal and nonverbal behavior. Due to variations in experience and normative bias, clinicians are likely to rate individuals with the same symptoms from various ethnic groups differently, such that clinical judgments are likely to depend on characteristics of the individual being interviewed. Cultural expertise of the interviewer and ethnic matching may reduce the potential for bias and misunderstanding and increase positive perceptions of the clinician (Want, Parham, Baker, & Sherman, 2004). Whether ethnic matching produces a significantly better treatment outcome for child and adolescent clients, however, is a subject of debate (Gamst, Dana, Der-Karabetian, & Kramer, 2004).

Clinician bias in the interview is a significant concern and has been noted as a problem in effective and accurate diagnosis of diverse individuals (Li, Jenkins, & Sundsmo, in press). Almost every author who writes on the topic of multicultural interviewing begins with a caution regarding the need for researchers and practitioners to attend to personal biases that may affect clinical judgment and the collection of information in the clinical interview (e.g., Ridley, Li, & Hill, 1998).

To facilitate the multicultural interview, Santiago-Rivera, Arredondo, and Gallardo-Cooper (2002) developed the Culture-Centered Clinical Interview (CCI). Unlike general models of multicultural interviewing that tend to lack specificity, the CCI is formatted as a clinical interviewing tool that provides a direct reminder to the clinician of important areas to evaluate in the interview. As such, it differs significantly from the PICI (Berg-Cross & Takushi-Chinen, 1995) in both structure and content. For example, the CCI form contains areas in which to rate the individual's language dimensions, acculturation, and use of indigenous healers. When used in the same way as a semistructured clinical interview, the CCI provides important and unique information for the conceptualization of the client.

While informative and useful, the multicultural interviewing literature primarily focuses on adult populations. The available literature on child or adolescent multicultural interviewing is limited in comparison and has lagged behind the adult literature. Although recommendations from the adult literature can be applied to children, children also have unique considerations that preclude the direct downward extension of adult models. For example, one of the key distinctions of child-focused research and practice is the emphasis on development as a context for child behavior. When applied to the interviewing literature, it is clear that a developmental perspective is critical.

In the general child interviewing literature, authors such as Greenspan and Greenspan (2003) and Boggs, Griffin, and Gross (2003) have identified developmental phase as an important influence on symptom presentation in children and adolescents. For example, common symptoms of depression vary from infancy to adolescence (Stark, Ballatore, Hamff, Valdez, & Selvig, 2001). Other concerns when interviewing children and adolescents include the frequency with which they fail to meet diagnostic criteria and greater rates of comorbidity in this population. It is well known that with the exception of the diagnoses first developed for infancy and childhood (American Psychiatric Association, 2000), the majority of diagnoses applied to children and adolescents (e.g., mood and anxiety) were developed primarily for adults. In terms of comorbidity, symptomatology in children is often less well-differentiated, resulting in complex profiles. How these considerations may be similar or different in nondominant diverse children, however, is unknown.

In the child multicultural interviewing literature, Canino and Spurlock (2000) have echoed the need to attend to developmental process while also attending to cultural considerations. They have provided a number of recommendations for interviewing culturally diverse children and adolescents, such as taking into account cultural expectations of child development and behavior and cultural attitudes toward health practices. Attending to cultural influences on child-rearing practices is informative for the interviewing process with both children and primary caregivers. In particular, with regard to symptomatology, culturally diverse children and adolescents may present with variations in mental status and symptom expression. However, there is relatively little literature that discusses culture-specific syndromes in youth and how to view symptom profiles differently in diverse children and adolescents (Canino & Spurlock, 2000).

Another source of recommendations in the child multicultural interviewing literature are Garcia Coll and Szalacha (2004). Garcia Coll and Szalacha have utilized a systemic approach to emphasize that although all children are engaged in multiple contexts, these contexts differ for diverse children. Specifically, the authors have identified three aspects of social stratification (social position, racism, and segregation) that differentially impact the development of diverse children relative to dominant-culture peers. Thus, the development of children of color and immigrant children is a function of primarily negative social variables along with general child and family constructs, adaptive cultural elements, and the degree to which children are embedded in promoting or inhibiting environments. When applied to symptomatology and problem behaviors, it is recommended that deficits be viewed in light of the adaptive processes children and families have developed to cope with negative aspects of social stratification, rather than invoking a purely maladaptive and negative perspective. Garcia Coll and Szalacha defined adaptive processes as "manifestations of adaptive cultures as families develop goals, values, attitudes, and behaviors that set them apart from the dominant culture" (p. 81). They have suggested that beginning in middle childhood, clinicians need to identify racism as a possible interpretation for negative social interactions with peers, teachers, and authority figures when evaluating diverse children.

CASE APPLICATION

As interesting and compelling as Garcia Coll and Szalacha's (2004) recommendations seem, it is helpful to illustrate these points with a case example:

> Pablo, a 6-year-old boy, was the only minority in his private school class. As his teachers, family, and peers were acutely aware, Pablo was able to attend this school only through private donations designed to help underprivileged children receive a better education. Pablo was discouraged and frustrated. He had been held back a grade due to "not being able to read" and was in danger of being held back again. Rating scales from the teacher and parent were contradictory with the teacher's report indicating problems with disruptive behavior and oppositionality. In contrast, his mother's report showed no significant clinical elevations with the exception of mild symptoms of withdrawn behaviors.

The clinician was left to determine the true nature of the child's problems. After a comprehensive evaluation, the child was diagnosed with attention-deficit/hyperactivity disorder, and the clinician proceeded to establish a behavioral plan at school to improve the child's performance. It quickly became clear that in this school environment, Pablo had been stereotyped as the "poor, bad Mexican boy," without much hope for change. Switching his school environment to one that had a positive view of Mexican children was essential in establishing a context for therapeutic change. The culture of the child and surrounding environment were key in his treatment and allowed for information collected during the evaluation process to be viewed differently in diagnosis. Had the clinician not assessed the cultural context during the interviewing process, social stratification variables may have sabotaged effective treatment and diagnosis.

Although most child clinicians and researchers recognize the need to attend to culture, there are still those who underestimate its impact and importance. From our review of the literature and our work with diverse youth, we provide the following additional thoughts. When viewed in a positive light, multicultural interviewing enhances the child professional's ability to perform essential tasks. Germaine to competent interviewing of diverse children is remembering to ask about cultural sources of strength and protection, resiliency, and resources to counteract negative social processes, such as discrimination. Professionals who can determine the supportiveness of environments and whether school, peer, and neighborhood contexts are promoting or inhibiting will have greater diagnostic accuracy and intervention success.

Child clinicians are in the business of understanding child behavior. At a basic level, the functional analysis of behavior requires cultural understanding and knowledge of diversity elements. The behaviorally oriented clinician must be able to determine how a behavior is being maintained and reinforced, with the understanding that the same behavior may be maladaptive in one context but adaptive in another. Maintenance factors differ for nondominant, culturally diverse children and adolescents and need to be considered. Finally, the ability to interpret the function of a behavior across cultures is essential when working with diverse children. In summary,

without knowledge of multicultural and diversity issues and with a lack of experience in multicultural interviewing, clinicians may miss critical pieces of information that become the missing link in a complex conceptualization.

SPECIAL CONSIDERATIONS FOR DIVERSE YOUTH

As Garcia Coll and Szalacha (2004) noted, diverse youth present with unique concerns and special considerations that set them apart from dominant-culture children. For example, diversity has significant effects on the shaping of interpersonal relationships with family and peers. Ethnic minorities report greater family interdependence, differences in autonomy, and variability in the likelihood of complying with parental requests (Phinney, Kim-Jo, Osorio, & Vilhjalmsdottir, 2005). In peer relationships, race and ethnicity affect the composition of friendships and the likelihood of having interracial friends (Kao & Joyner, 2004). Best friends are more likely to be of the same ethnicity and to engage in more shared activities. Of particular relevance to diverse youth are the constructs of ethnic identity and acculturative stress. Among adults, acculturative hassles, discrimination, and ethnic identity have been linked to adjustment (Gaudet, Clement, & Deuzeman, 2005), with high-ethnic-identity individuals showing more positive outcomes (St. Louis & Liem, 2005). Among adolescents, higher ethnic identity is related to higher levels of self-esteem (Bracey, Bamaca, & Umana-Taylor, 2004) and may be an important factor in developing treatment interventions (DeCarlo, 2005). In the next two sections, we explore cultural differences by highlighting ethnic-identity development and stress and acculturative stress processes as important unique considerations for diverse youth.

Ethnic Self-Understanding and the Development of Ethnic Identity

A key component to assess in multicultural interviewing is the *self* or *identity*. How the child or adolescent construes the self and the mental representation of the self are important in the clinician's conceptualization. Children can have multiple identities (Rattansi & Phoenix, 2005), and thus it is important to evaluate all aspects of the child's self. Particularly for nondominant-culture individuals, it is essential to investigate the ethnic self or the ethnic identity of the child.

In children, ethnic identity has been a topic of research in terms of its conceptualization, formation, and developmental change over time. Bernal and Knight (1993) have defined *ethnic identity* as a set of self statements about one's ethnic-group membership that involves five components: ethnic self-identification, ethnic constancy, ethnic-role behaviors, ethnic knowledge, and ethnic preferences and feelings. Parents and the cultural group are the primary socializers of ethnic identity, and parents' own ethnic backgrounds and teachings affect children's ethnic behavior and identity (Davey, Fish, Askew, & Robila, 2003; Knight, Bernal, Cota, Garza, & Ocampo, 1993).

The development of ethnic identity parallels other similar components, such as gender, in that awareness precedes self-identification, which precedes constancy. However, ethnic identity appears to occur at later ages than either gender or racial identity and awareness (Ocampo, Bernal, & Knight, 1993; Ocampo, Knight, & Bernal, 1997). In the process of developing an ethnic identity, children first acquire an ethnic self-label or self-identification that they learn is stable over time (i.e., ethnic constancy). Younger children may engage in ethnic role behaviors but may not know the relevance of those behaviors for their ethnic groups. Older children, in contrast, can provide complex traitlike reasons for ethnic-group membership and in later stages may have ethnic feelings and preferences that guide their behavior (Bernal, Knight, Ocampo, Garza, & Cota, 1993).

The theoretical conceptualization of adolescent ethnic identity is unique compared with the models of ethnic identity postulated for adults (e.g., Cross's stages of Nigrescence; Cross & Vandiver, 2001) and the general developmental models of how children's self-understanding emerges. Phinney (1993) provided a conceptualization of ethnic-identity development for adolescents based on Erickson and Marcia's models of ego identity development. For American-born ethnic-minority adolescents, Phinney found three stages of ethnic-identity development: unexamined ethnic identity, ethnic-identity search (i.e., moratorium), and achieved identity. In the unexamined stage, adolescents gave a variety of responses to questions about their ethnicity. Some showed a preference for dominant-culture values, while others had a clear lack of interest in topics related to ethnicity. Another set of adolescents was guided by their families' teachings and had adopted their values and conceptualization of their ethnicity without question.

Unlike adolescents in the unexamined stage, adolescents in the stage of ethnic-identity search were currently experiencing an identity crisis and reported dissonance regarding dominant- and ethnic-group values. These adolescents were actively seeking experiences of culture, thinking about the ethnic self, and attempting to learn more about their backgrounds and cultures. However, they had not yet made a commitment to an integrated ethnic identity. The adolescents with an achieved identity had a "clear, confident sense" (Phinney, 1993, p. 71) of their ethnicity, which was reflected in high self-esteem and positive peer and family relationships. Achieved adolescents had made a commitment to an ethnic identity and were no longer experiencing crisis in regard to this aspect of the self.

The stage of ethnic-identity development of children or adolescents can affect their responses to questions regarding cultural behaviors and values and the way in which they respond to clinical interviewing. Adolescents in various stages of ethnic-identity development would be expected to respond very differently to psychological interviewing and questions about culture and values. Adolescents in the unexamined stage are likely to respond with indifference, may fail to provide a coherent answer, or may question why the examiner is asking them questions about this irrelevant topic. Adolescents currently in crisis may be acutely interested in their own responses to the questions and may potentially provide conflicting answers across the interview that reflect different components of the self that are being examined but are not yet integrated. Finally, achieved-identity adolescents will have a coherent ethnic identity that comes across in the interview and can be challenged to think about how cultural values and ethnicity may affect their experience of daily stress, their symptoms, and their attitudes toward mental health treatment. Therefore, it is important for the clinician to understand the general trajectory of ethnic-identity development in order to have a conceptualization of how to view the child's responses and how the child's reports are influenced by developmental level. Variability in child and adolescent responses or inconsistency between caregiver statements and the child's conceptualization may be reflective of normative developmental processes.

Stress and Acculturative Stress

Stress, in the form of both major life events and daily hassles, is a well-known risk factor for psychopathology in children and adolescents (Compas, 1987; Quamma & Greenberg, 1994). A comprehensive assessment of stressful experiences in the lives of youth can provide important information as to the precipitating factors that have led to changes in behavior. Clinical interviewing that systematically addresses sources of stress for children and adolescents will likely produce better evidence- and theory-based conceptualizations of their problems. As part of the probing to determine relevant stressors for the child, it is important to establish a framework for evaluating stress. Most interviewers are attuned to the need to ask about major life events such as death, divorce, and school transitions; however, research since the 1990s has emphasized the role that "hassles" (i.e., daily or chronic, mild negative experiences) play in the development of symptoms (Deater-Deckard, Dodge, Bates, & Pettit, 1998; Gore, Aseltine, & Colton, 1992). For most children and adolescents, these daily stressors occur in predictable domains, such as family, school, and friends. As the literature in this area advanced, however, it became apparent that existing stress scales were primarily developed for middle-class Caucasian youth and failed to capture the unique experiences of diverse, urban, and low-income youth (Seidman et al., 1995). A number of researchers subsequently developed scales to assess the types of stress experienced by Asian (Kim-Bae, 2000), urban African American (Miller, Webster, & MacIntosh, 2002), and Latino youth (Gonzales, Gunnoe, Samaniego, & Jackson, 1995). New domains of stress emerged from these measures, such as perceived discrimination, exposure to violence, and acculturative stress.

Youth from diverse backgrounds are not unique in being affected by stressful experiences (Deardorff, Gonzales, & Sandler, 2003; Guerra, Huesmann, Tolan, Van Acker, & Eron, 1995; Li, Nussbaum, & Richards, in press; Wu & Lam, 1993); however, it is apparent that they experience stress that significantly differs from that of dominant-culture peers. In addition to areas mentioned above, immigrant children and adolescents may experience stress due to the context of the immigration experience, language use and proficiency, cultural values, and acculturation (Cuellar, 2000; Fuglini, 1998). Of considerable attention has been the role of acculturative stress in the lives of diverse and immigrant youth (Szapocznik & Kurtines, 1993). *Acculturative stress* is best understood as stress and strain resulting from the intersection of two cultures that is inherently tied to acculturation processes (Gil, Vega, & Dimas, 1994; Roysircar-Sodowsky & Maestas, 2000). Children and adolescents have been conceptualized as especially vulnerable to family-based acculturative stress due to differential rates of acculturation between adults and children (Portes, 1997). Children are thought to acculturate more quickly because they acquire new languages more easily, are socialized in the dominant culture through the educational system, and are heavily exposed to dominant-culture media influences. The rapid acculturation of children can lead to intergenerational differences in values (Phinney, Ong, & Madden, 2000), variation in perceptions of family roles and responsibilities, and multiple allegiances to cultural elements of home and the dominant-culture society.

In sum, culturally diverse youth are a population with a high likelihood of experiencing acculturative stress that may be either risk promoting or growth producing. Given the unique considerations faced by diverse youth, how can professionals effectively address these issues in the interviewing process? We recommend the use of a cultural interviewing tool to enhance the collection of culturally relevant information.

THE INTERVIEW

Development of the CASI

Having a complete understanding of a child's sociocultural history has significant clinical utility. At present, we know of no interviewing tools available to make the collection and recording of sociocultural information relatively straightforward. This is in contrast to the multitude of child interviewing forms that are currently available for assessing history and background, basic developmental information, and symptomatology. Thus, we endeavored to develop a form that would enable the clinician to assess sociocultural factors in the same manner as other interviewing variables of interest. This led to the development of the CASI: the Child/Adolescent Sociocultural Interview. Much of the basic form of the CASI came from the Culture-Centered Clinical Interview (CCI) developed by Santiago-Rivera et al. (2002). The CCI, however, was developed for adults and for use with Latino populations. As such, it was not developmentally sensitive to the contexts in which children are most often embedded. The CCI was also limited in its conceptualization of diversity and therefore did not include the broadest range of diversity domains available. We adhere to a model of diversity popularized by Hays (2001), which includes multiple aspects of diversity (e.g., socioeconomic status, sexual orientation, and disability) in addition to ethnic differences.

When used as intended, the CASI is a supplement to a traditional psychosocial history. It is designed to provide an addendum to a traditional clinical interview, not to replace it. Therefore, detailed information about topics such as symptomatology, family functioning, peer relationships, school performance, involvement in deviant behaviors, and sexual risk taking are not addressed, but should be part of a basic preliminary clinical interview. In contrast, this supplemental interview addresses the impact of diversity on these topics in ways that are often excluded in traditional interviews.

Description of the Interview. Several domains of sociocultural experience are assessed through the CASI. These include child and family strengths, language dimensions, family structure/home environment, social functioning and relationships, school environment and educational history, cultural dimensions, economic status, spiritual dimensions, and disabilities. The full form is presented in Table 6.1. The interview begins with child and family strengths, in order to focus on positive child traits, identify potential protective factors (Luthar, 2003), decrease the child's perceived threat involved in interviewing, and combat the tendency to focus on negative factors when dealing with diverse disadvantaged children.

Format. The CASI provides the inexperienced clinician with sentence stems for questions

regarding sociocultural information. It includes both clinician ratings and child self-reported responses that are recorded by the interviewer. Experienced clinicians may use the form as a guide or reminder for important domains to address during the interview. Clinicians who have significant child interviewing experience may choose to ignore the particular wording of items provided, in favor of their own styles.

Item Development, Revisions, and the Pilot Study. Initially, issues that were thought to be important in understanding a child within his or her sociocultural context items were developed by the authors. Items were reviewed and revised and then piloted with a group of beginning clinicians. The first version of the CASI was administered by a group of first-year master's-in-counseling psychology students. Students were at the end of their first year of training and thus had practiced interviewing with adult pseudoclients. Many of them, however, had limited experience interviewing child clients. Students were instructed to complete the form with a child of any age. Given time constraints and subject burden, students were asked to complete at least three sections of the form, to carefully track the time for each interview section, and to make suggestions for revision.

The interview was administered to 30 children between the ages of 3 and 16. The majority of children were early to middle adolescents (age 12 to 16; $n = 20$). Seven children were school age (age 6 to 11), and 3 were preschoolers (age 3 to 4). Roughly 60% of the children were Caucasian, and 40% were from nondominant ethnic groups. This reflects the emphasis on diversity as applicable to both dominant- and nondominant-culture members of society rather than being exclusively applied to ethnic minorities. Approximately 63% of the youth were females, and 35% were males, allowing for a diversity of gender-related responses.

Students were asked to track the time they took to complete the interview. This varied greatly for the whole form, from 30 minutes as a low estimate to 1½ hours. Some factors related to length of interview were the number of sections administered, the age of the child, and the diversity of his or her background.

Overall, comments on the interview suggested the following strengths. Students found the form easy to understand and use. They liked

Table 6.1   Child/Adolescent Sociocultural Interview (CASI)

Name_____Date of Interview_____

Date of Birth_____Age_____Grade_____Gender: M   F

Language spoken during interview_____Preferred_____

Use of Mixture Language (e.g., ☐ "Spanglish")? ☐ Yes ☐ No
Clinician Rating of Language: ☐ Monolingual ☐ Partial Bi/Multilingual ☐ Fully Bi/Multilingual

Child Strengths/Interests:

Tell me about some of the things you are really good at.
What kinds of things do you like to do for fun?
When people ask you to tell them about yourself, what do you say?

Family Strengths/Family Structure/Home Environment:

What kinds of things does your family do together when they want to have a good time?
What are the "best" things about your family?
How do you celebrate special occasions?

    What is the most important holiday for your family?

Tell me about your home.

    What is it like where you live?

    Do you have your own room, or do you share with someone?

Tell me about who is in your family. *Check all that apply. (Circle individuals living with child. If child has more than one home, indicate below.)*

    ☐ *Mother:* ☐ *Biological* ☐ *Step* ☐ *Adoptive* ☐ *Foster*

    ☐ *Father:* ☐ *Biological* ☐ *Step* ☐ *Adoptive* ☐ *Foster*

    ☐ *Siblings:* ☐ *Biological* ☐ *Step* ☐ *Adoptive* ☐ *Foster*

    ☐ *Extended Family:* ☐ *Grandparent* ☐ *Other Relative*

    ☐ *Other:* ☐ *Parent Partner* ☐ *Friend*

    Has this changed recently? ☐ Yes ☐ No

    In what way?

Who is "the boss" in your family (i.e., who makes the decisions in your family)?
Do you have brothers and sisters? ☐ Yes ☐ No

    Number of siblings

    Are you oldest, middle, youngest, only child, etc.?

    How do you feel about being (oldest, middle, youngest, only child, etc.)?

    Do you receive any privileges or special things that your brothers/sisters do not have?

    Do you have any chores/responsibilities that they do not have?

    If you could choose to be the (oldest, middle, youngest, only child, etc.), which would you want/not want to be?

    Why?

Are boys and girls treated the same in your family?
Do you ever get in trouble?

    What kinds of things do you get in trouble for?

    If/when you get into trouble, who punishes you?

    How are you punished?

NOTE: Designed as a supplemental interview for school-aged children and young adolescents

Tell me about bedtime in your family.

    What time do you have to go to bed?

    Who helps you get ready for bed, or do you get ready by yourself?

    Who sleeps with you, or do you sleep by yourself?

    [Clinician-rated assessment of structure and presence or absence of a bedtime routine]

Language Dimensions: *[This section is primarily clinician rated]*

*First Language*_____ ☐ *Read and Write*_____

*Second Language*_____ ☐ *Read and Write*_____

    At what age introduced?

    How?

Language spoken at home?

    At school?

    With friends?

    With grandparents?

When you talk to yourself, what language do you use [*language of self-talk?*]

    Language of emotions (e.g., when the child gets upset, what language is used)?

Social Functioning and Relationships:

Who are your friends?

    What do you like to do when you are with your friends?

    Do your parents like (approve)/dislike (disapprove) of your friends? Why?

    Are your friends the ☐ same ethnicity, ☐ mixed ethnicity, ☐ other ethnicity as you?

    For younger children substitute with:
        Are your friends the same as you or different from you?
        How are they different from you?
        Do they look like you?
        Why or why not?

    How does your family feel about this?

Additional Social Functioning and Relationship Questions for Adolescents:

What do your parent(s) think about dating?

    What do you think about dating?

    Does your family have "rules" about dating (age, groups only, chaperones, etc.)?

When was the first time you knew that you "liked" someone?

    What was that like?

    Do you have a boyfriend/girlfriend/romantic interest? ☐ Yes ☐ No

    Tell me a little about this person. What is he/she like?

    Is he/she the same (age, ethnicity, gender) as you?

    [For older children with indicators of homosexual attraction or when clinician judgment indicates, note the following]:
        Age of awareness of same-sex attraction?
        Level of engagement in same- and opposite-sex activities?
        Need for further assessment? ☐ Yes ☐ No

School Environment/Educational History: *[Questions meant to be supplemental only]*

Where do you go to school?

    If child is homeschooled, how long/how structured?

(Continued)

Table 6.1 (Continued)

What is your school like?

>   Are the kids at your school similar to or different from you?

>   How so?

Have you always gone to school, or were there times when you didn't go?

>   *[Clinician-rated assessment of inconsistent schooling]*

How does your school differ from schools you have gone to in the past?

>   *[Probe for schooling differences pre/postmigration.]*

Cultural Dimensions:

Where were you born? (Place of nativity)
Have you lived anywhere before living here?

>   Tell me about those places.

>   Do you like living here more or less than the last place you lived? Why?

Clinician-Rated Generation Status:

>   ☐ *1st (Born in _____)*

>   ☐ *2nd (Born in U.S./at least one parent born outside U.S.)*

>   ☐ *3rd (Born in U.S./Both parents born in U.S.)*

Clinician-Rated Acculturation Level:

>   *Integrated/Bicultural (combines traditional and majority cultures)*

>   *Assimilated (has abandoned traditional culture and adopted majority culture)*

>   *Marginalized (rejects both traditional and majority cultures)*

>   *Traditionalist (rejects majority culture ideas and values)*

>   *Ambivalent about cultural background, ideas, and values*

Clinician-Rated Native Culture Contacts: ☐ *High*   ☐ *Moderate*   ☐ *Low*

Immigration History: *[If child moved to the United States from another country]*

>   Tell me what it was like when you lived in (name of country). (i.e., premigration history)

>   Do you know why your family decided to move here? (i.e., precipitating events)

>   What was it like getting here? (i.e., migration experience)

>   What was it like when you first moved to this country? (i.e., postmigration experience)

Clinician-Rated Ethnicity/Ethnic Identity:

What is your ethnicity? Culture?
When people ask you to tell them about your background, what do you say?
What does it mean to be a/an (ethnic/cultural group identity) . . . ?

>   *[Suggestions for younger children who don't understand the above questions]*

>   Are you . . . ? *[Clinician gives a list of ethnic/cultural groups and evaluates the child's response]*

>   Which one looks like you? *[Clinician provides the child with a picture of diverse faces and allows the child to choose among the pictures]*

Stress: Do you ever experience stress due to differences between you and your family because of your values, traditions, acceptance of American culture, etc.? (i.e., acculturative stress)

>   *Clinician-Rated Sources of Stress:*

> | ☐ *Residency* | ☐ *Immigration* | ☐ *Educational* | ☐ *Language* |
> | ☐ *Discrimination* | ☐ *Ability* | ☐ *Familial* | ☐ *Economic* |
> | ☐ *Gender* | ☐ *Sexuality* | ☐ *Weight/Height* | ☐ *Peers* |
> | ☐ *Other* | | | |

Economic Status:

What does your father do?

What does your mother do?

Do you think you have the SAME amount of money as your friends, LESS money than your friends, or MORE money than your friends

> *If different,*

> Does this bother you?

Would you say you are:

☐ Upper Class   ☐ Upper-Middle Class   ☐ Middle Class

☐ Lower-Middle Class   ☐ Lower Class   ☐ Poor

Is where you live similar to or different from where your friends live?

> Compared with people in your school?

Have you ever:

☐ Gone to bed hungry?

☐ Known that your family could not pay some of the bills?

☐ Worried about your family's money situation?

When you want something that costs money, do you usually get it?

> How do you try to get something if you really want it?

Spiritual Dimensions:

Do you attend a place of worship (church, mosque, temple, synagogue, etc.)?

> How often do you attend?

> ☐ Practicing   ☐ Nonpracticing

> Who do you go with?

> How are the people at your church similar to or different from you (church context)?

What is the name of your religion/church?

> Same religion as family of origin?

> Converted?

> At what age?

What kinds of special religious occasions (i.e., traditional religious milestones, such as baptism, bar mitzvah, quincinera, etc.) are celebrated?

Is there a special (elder, minister, priest, rabbi, imam, shaman, spiritual guide, etc.) you know and talk to?

Do you "talk" to God?

> Does your family pray together/encourage you to pray?

How important is (religion, spirituality, ethnic/cultural identity)to you?

Disabilities:

Do you have any physical problems?

> Problems with your body?

> Trouble hearing or seeing?

> Difficulty talking or speaking?

> Trouble doing your schoolwork?

What is it like for you to have difficulty with (name disability)?

Conclusion: Do you have any questions that you would like to ask me?

the emphasis on child and family strengths and the in-depth nature of the questions. Weaknesses and suggestions reflected several consistent themes. Students uniformly noted the need to develop separate forms for school-age children and adolescents. This was particularly suggested in regard to questions about romantic and sexual relationships. Another area of difficulty that students noted was the wording of the cultural questions for both younger and older youth. Students found it challenging to ask younger children the cultural-identity questions. Format suggestions included adding more space on the interview form for comments and allowing for the possibility that children may not know the answers to the interviewer's questions. Students were also sensitive to the need to expand questions regarding family composition, to allow for greater detail and diversity of both family constellation and variability in whom the child lives with from week to week. Given that the pilot interviewers were beginning student clinicians, they also recommended adding more general instructions at the beginning of the interview to (a) provide a rationale for the questions; (b) remind the user of the purpose of the interview (i.e., meant to be supplemental); (c) encourage the interviewer to be flexible in the use of the form, allowing for the user to choose relevant sections to administer rather than the entire form; and (d) remind the interviewer to attend to his or her own behavior when interviewing, by looking interested, adding clarification where needed, using examples, and not trying to read the entire form verbatim. Excerpts from the student interviews, including child participant comments, are presented in Table 6.2. These examples are used in the next section to illustrate the content of the CASI and how children might respond to these questions.

Explanation of the Interview

Content of the CASI. As noted previously, the interview begins with child and family strengths. An evaluation of strengths is also clinically useful to obtain from the child's perspective for later use in treatment. In this section, as recommended by Canino and Spurlock (2000), the child also reports various special occasions and holidays celebrated in the child's family. This set of questions provides the clinician with information on how the family celebrates and with whom, and

indirect information on the diversity domains with which the family identifies based on the particular holidays the family chooses to recognize.

As noted earlier, language is a key aspect of interviewing diverse children. Assuming the interviewer and child have a common language with which to communicate, there are a number of aspects of the child's language development that require evaluation. The traditional model of a monolingual speaker who learned his or her first language at home, is educated in that language, and speaks that language across peer, school, and family contexts will more likely be the exception than the norm in the 21st century. Thus, where and when languages are learned, why and when they are used, and personal preferences for language use will become more important to ascertain.

The next area of the interview focuses on the family context, including family structure and the home environment. At a most basic level, diversity impacts the family constellation and whom a child defines as family, including nuclear, extended, adoptive, and absorbed (i.e., nonfamily members who are treated as family). Cultural norms impact parenting behaviors, attitudes toward gender socialization, and family organization and routines. The questions in this section are designed to illuminate these constructs by having children provide information about bedtime and evening routines, sleeping arrangements, and privileges and responsibilities associated with birth order and gender. These questions allow the clinician to recognize that the experiences of first-born sons may be very different from those of younger female siblings and that sleeping arrangements may differ in culturally diverse families from the Western standard of a single bedroom for each child.

The fourth and fifth sections of the interview focus on social functioning, peer relationships, and the school environment. Given the clear consensus among child professionals regarding the importance of social relationships and school functioning for healthy development, it is expected that general questions regarding these topics will have been addressed. Thus, we focus this section on supplemental questions that are less likely to be evaluated, such as the fit between the child and his or her context. As Pablo's circumstances illustrated in the vignette presented earlier, culturally diverse youth may be part of the majority in their school or peer group or may

TABLE 6.2   Illustrative Responses to the CASI Questions for Six Child/Adolescent Participants

Illustrative Responses

Participant 1. 8-year-old African American female living in a domestic violence shelter.

Are boys and girls are treated differently in your family? "Boys are treated bad, and girls are treated better." "Boys are punished more." What ethnicity are your friends at the shelter and at school? My friends are "White." Do you choose White friends over other kinds of friends? "Yes." Why? "Because they are nice." How does your mom feel about this? "She likes it."

Participant 2. 16-year-old half-Japanese and half-Caucasian male born in the United States.

Do you see yourself as more Caucasian, Japanese, or both (in between)? "More as Caucasian." Why? "Most of my friends are Caucasian" and "I don't look Japanese that much."

Participant 3. 12-year-old Costa Rican/Italian male from intact middle-class family.

Tell me about your background/ethnicity? "Mexican, Italian, Portuguese, Costa Rican, and American—that's the most important." Have you ever experienced discrimination or felt like you were being treated differently than other kids at school or in your neighborhood? [He had a problem when taking a standardized test at school, because he checked the box for "Hispanic." The teacher corrected him by checking "Caucasian." He tried to explain he was Hispanic, but she called his parents to discuss the matter.] How did that make you feel? [child laughed] "I guess that my skin is pretty light, but I know I am Hispanic because I asked my parents the night before."

Participant 4. 14-year-old African American male from middle-class background.

Do you ever get in trouble? "I've never been in big trouble or been grounded, but when my parents catch me swearing I have to put money in the family jar." [This rule applies for everyone in the family, and the money in the jar is used to help pay for family activities such as camping.] What is it like where you live? "My parents love the neighborhood we live in because it's safe, but they don't think it's very diverse." "Most of our neighborhood is White." Why do your parents stay in the neighborhood? "My parents said if we moved to an area with more Black people it probably wouldn't be a safe neighborhood." Have you ever experienced discrimination? "My grandparents used to tell me stories about discrimination." "Yes, I think some people are scared of me or think I am a criminal because I'm Black or expect me to be really good at sports."

Participant 5. 14-year-old half-Jewish male from upper-class background.

Do you think you have the *same* amount of money as your friends, *less* money than your friends, or *more* money than your friends? "Less money than one friend but about the same as most." "One friend lives in a mansion, but the rest are fairly similar, some live in the country though." Have you ever worried about your family's money situation? "Once when dad went to a different dealership that paid less." When you want something that costs money, do you usually get it? "Under fifteen dollars I usually get it, but if it's more expensive, I have to save my allowance." How are the people at your synagogue similar to or different from you [church context]? "At synagogue, people look similar, but they know Hebrew and I don't." How important is religion to you? "Kinda' neutral, not a 'have to,' but it's okay, something I do with my dad. He's happy."

Participant 6. 16-year-old bisexual Caucasian female born in the Philippines and raised in Guam. [Interviewer noted the following stressors: change in residency to the United States, some issues related to her gender and sexuality, familial and interpersonal dynamics, and economic difficulties.]

When was the first time you knew that you "liked" someone? "14." What was that like? "Nerve-wracking." Do you have boyfriend/girlfriend/romantic interest? "Yes, he's younger." Age of awareness of same-sex attraction? [She first felt an attraction toward a male at age 14. At 16, she felt her first attraction toward and experimented with a female, a girl that later became her first girlfriend. Currently, she is involved with a male whom she reported wanting to marry.]

be "flying solo" in all contexts except the home environment. Given that diversity affects the composition of friendships, parental attitudes toward the child's friends, and peer acceptance, these are areas in need of assessment (Kao & Joyner, 2004; see responses from Participant 1 in Table 6.2). Questions regarding dating are separated in an indented section but primarily address child and parental attitudes toward dating and same- or opposite-sex attraction. Items regarding parental attitudes are included due to evidence in the literature of large heterogeneity across groups in attitudes and rules about dating and the acceptance of dating outside of one's group. Dating has been shown to be a significant source of stress between parents and older youth, with heightened conflict for adolescents and young adults who date outside of their parents' preferences (Chung, 2001). In regard to schooling experiences, it is not uncommon for diverse youth to have had disruptions in schooling due to immigration or to change schools frequently due to migrant or economic conditions. The interviewer who focuses only on the current school situation may miss a significant educational history that is relevant for the presenting concerns.

Cultural dimensions are assessed in the next section of the CASI and address expected areas, such as migration history, acculturation level and ethnicity/ethnic identity, and cultural stress, such as discrimination. Given the importance of evaluating stress among diverse youth, there is a specific section of the interview in which the clinician can indicate the categories of stress that the child may be experiencing and can note individual stressors (see responses for Participant 6 in Table 6.2). This section also attends to the importance of evaluating acculturative stress for immigrant youth and culturally diverse children and adolescents (Canino & Spurlock, 2000). Of greatest difficulty in this section is obtaining the child's view of these constructs. For example, the 3-year-old biracial child who picks out a picture of a Black child on a poster of racially diverse children and says, "That one's me," or can tell his mother that he is "Black" but she is "vanigla" (interpret as "vanilla"), like ice cream, obviously has a racial and ethnic self-understanding. Getting the same child to spontaneously provide this information in response to interviewing questions, however, can be quite challenging. Furthermore, what the interviewer believes to be a common or currently acceptable term may be unfamiliar, not the preferred term, or idiosyncratically defined. This is illustrated by the case of the biracial Eurasian adolescent who staunchly rejected the term *biracial* since that referred only to "kids who are Black and White—and that's not me." Sample comments from Participants 2, 3, and 4 in Table 6.2 provide examples of responses to questions regarding perceived discrimination and ethnic self-understanding. Each youth's response is unique, reflecting his or her experiences, social influences, developmental level, and conceptualization of ethnicity (Brown & Bigler, 2005).

The last three sections of the CASI address economic status, spiritual or religious diversity, and disability. Children in poverty, homeless children, and children who experience rapid changes in economic status due to natural disaster, divorce, or death may be acutely aware of their economic circumstances. Of interest is the match or mismatch between the family's resources and those of peers or classmates and the child's perceptions of this situation. For youth who haven't experienced economic disruption or disadvantage, parental attitudes toward spending, saving, or buying for the child may be informative (see responses from Participant 5 in Table 6.2). Rarely do general child history forms evaluate children's spirituality and religious diversity; however, concerns faced by religious youth (e.g., Jewish orthodox) highlight the need to evaluate the role of religious orientation in mental health and adjustment of children and families (Fukuyama & Sevig, 1999; Margolese, 1998; see Participant 5 in Table 6.2). Last, we evaluate the child's awareness of any physical limitations and how this affects perceptions and self-views.

Usage. As with any interview, the skills of the clinician are essential in the successful completion of the CASI. Many of the child subjects indicated that they would lose interest in a lot of questions if "they had to sit in a chair and answer them." The nonverbal behavior of the interviewer is just as important as the questions asked. As one child aptly stated, "Some of it sounds like a report, but you look like you really want to know," highlighting the importance of the clinician's interactions with the child. Given the length of the measure, it is appropriate to choose various sections that might be more relevant to a particular child rather than trying to attempt to complete all aspects of the form. For some individuals, socioeconomic level and religion may be the primary areas of diversity, in contrast to emphases on culture, language, and ethnicity for other children.

Developmental Considerations. The CASI has been designed for use with school-age children and early adolescents based on the need to consider the child's developmental context when conducting a cultural interview. Clearly, the developmental level of the child dictates the length of the interview and the content. As illustrated previously, children's understanding of their ethnicity varies with age and will impact their ability to be interviewed about the effect of ethnicity on the family and school contexts. Advances in cognitive understanding and metacognition are tied to the ability to reflect on one's experience and to be aware of differences between self and other (Li & Rogers, 2006). Self-conscious emotions that may result from experiences of prejudice or being different are a hallmark of middle childhood and are less easily accessed in the reports of young children. Adolescents who have developed the ability to reflect on their own experiences may respond better to open-ended questions. They may spontaneously elaborate and can easily discern the nature of clinicians' questions. Younger children may not know the answers to examiners' questions and may respond by looking confused or remaining quiet; for example, a child may not know the name of his family's place of worship or religion. In contrast, an adolescent may not only know the name of the religion but also be able to discuss aspects of doctrinal beliefs with which she agrees or disagrees and to what extent she identifies with the religious label of her family of origin. In summary, cognitive and emotional development cannot be separated from child and adolescent responses to a cultural interviewing experience. Development must be taken into consideration in the framing and content of the questions.

In the CASI, clinicians are required to use their judgment in deciding age-appropriateness of various questions. In the initial pilot of the measure, child- and adolescent-oriented questions were combined, and the age range was not restricted. Based on comments from the pilot, the following guidelines are presented. We do not recommend using the CASI with young children (i.e., below age 4), because they do not have the necessary cognitive skills to complete the interview. Isolated questions such as bedtime routines and the best things about one's family, however, are likely to be appropriate for young children. In a similar vein, older adolescents will probably find the questions too specific and may prefer broad questions about their cultural backgrounds and how their worldviews have been shaped by cultural influences. Although there are

areas where questions for adolescents have been placed in a subsection, this is not the norm. In particular, questions regarding sexuality, same-sex attraction, and engagement in sexual relationships have been removed from the main body of questions in response to feedback regarding the interview form.

SUMMARY

In this chapter on multicultural and diversity issues when interviewing children and adolescents, our goals were threefold. We wanted to provide the reader with a current overview of the state of the multicultural interviewing literature for adults and youth, along with a summary of some of the suggestions and recommendations from that literature. A second goal was to highlight a few of the unique issues confronted by multicultural youth that set them apart from dominant-culture individuals. We recognize that the average interviewer may not have an in-depth understanding of the development of ethnic identity or be aware of cultural stress in the lives of diverse youth. We hope that we have not only described these constructs and processes as they pertain to this population but have also given interviewers a clearer rationale for why addressing these issues in interviews is important and useful for conceptualizing and understanding mental health in diverse individuals.

Last, we believe that suggestions and recommendations are best followed when concrete models are provided. Thus, we embedded in this chapter a sociocultural interviewing tool. We described the design and purpose of this interview and included preliminary feedback on naive interviewers' use of the interview. We augmented the interviewer's perspective with sample responses obtained from a nonclinical population of children and adolescents. Although much work and revisions remain, we believe we have not only operationalized what it means to conduct a multicultural/sociocultural interview with children and adolescents, but have also provided specific questions and modeled a procedure that can be used to accomplish this goal. In our opinion, knowledge, recommendations, and suggestions are not sufficient to advance the field. Individual interviewers must feel comfortable implementing techniques and translating guidelines into action in order to enhance actual interviewing behavior with diverse youth. Adoption of techniques and tools, even in preliminary stages, can lead to sophisticated skills as interviewers take steps to make multicultural interviewing a reality and standard practice in most research, clinical, and community settings.

REFERENCES

American Psychiatric Association. (2000). *Diagnostic and statistical manual of mental disorders.* (4th ed., Text rev.). Washington, DC: Author.

Berg-Cross, L., & Takushi-Chinen, R. (1995). Multicultural training models and the Person-in-Culture Interview. In J. G. Ponterotto, J. M. Casas, L. A. Suzuki, & C. M. Alexander (Eds.), *Handbook of multicultural counseling* (pp. 333–356). Thousand Oaks, CA: Sage.

Bernal, M. E., & Knight, G. P. (1993). *Ethnic identity: Formation and transmission among Hispanics and other minorities.* Albany: State University of New York Press.

Bernal, M. E., Knight, G. P., Ocampo, K. A., Garza, C. A., & Cota, M. K. (1993). Development of Mexican American identity. In M. E. Bernal & G. P. Knight (Eds.), *Ethnic identity: Formation and transmission among Hispanics and other minorities* (pp. 31–46). Albany: State University of New York Press.

Boggs, K., Griffin, R., & Gross, A. (2003). Children. In M. Hersen & S. Turner (Eds.), *Diagnostic interviewing* (2nd ed., pp. 393–413). New York: Kluwer Academic/Plenum.

Bracey, J. R., Bamaca, M. Y., & Umana-Taylor, A. J. (2004). Examining ethnic identity and self-esteem among biracial and monoracial adolescents. *Journal of Youth and Adolescence, 33,* 123–132.

Bronfenbrenner, U., & Morris, P. A. (1998). The ecology of developmental processes. In. W. Damon & R. M. Lerner (Eds.), *Handbook of child psychology: Vol. 1. Theoretical models of human development* (5th ed., pp. 993–1028). New York: Wiley.

Brown, C. S., & Bigler, R. S. (2005). Children's perceptions of discrimination: A developmental model. *Child Development, 76,* 533–553.

Canino, I., & Spurlock, J. (2000). History taking. In *culturally diverse children and adolescents: Assessment, diagnosis, and treatment* (2nd ed., pp. 47–83). New York: Guilford Press.

Chung, R. H. G. (2001). Gender, ethnicity, and acculturation in intergenerational conflict of Asian American college students. *Cultural Diversity & Ethnic Minority Psychology, 7,* 376–386.

Compas, B. E. (1987). Stress and life events during childhood and adolescence. *Clinical Psychology Review, 7,* 275–302.

Cross, W. E., & Vandiver, B. J. (2001). Nigrescence theory and measurement: Introducing the Cross Racial Identity Scale (CRIS). In J. G. Ponterotto, J. M. Casas, L. A. Suzuki, & C. M. Alexander (Eds.), *Handbook of*

multicultural counseling (2nd ed., pp. 333–356). Thousand Oaks, CA: Sage.

Cuellar, I. (2000). Acculturation and mental health: Ecological transactional relations of adjustment. In I. Cueller & F. Paniagua (Eds.), *Handbook of multicultural mental health: Assessment and treatment of diverse populations* (pp. 45–62). San Diego, CA: Academic Press.

Davey, M., Fish, L. S., Askew, J., & Robila, M. (2003). Parenting practices and the transmission of ethnic identity. *Journal of Marital and Family Therapy, 29,* 195–208.

Deardorff, J., Gonzales, N., & Sandler, I. (2003). Control beliefs as a mediator of the relation between stress and depressive symptoms among inner-city adolescents. *Journal of Abnormal Child Psychology, 31,* 205–217.

Deater-Deckard, K., Dodge, K. A., Bates, J. E., & Pettit, G. S. (1998). Multiple risk factors in the development of externalizing behavior problems: Group and individual differences. *Development and Psychopathology, 10,* 469–493.

DeCarlo, A. (2005). Identity matters: A new intervention threshold for social work practitioners working with African American adolescents. *Child and Adolescent Social Work Journal, 22,* 35–55.

Fuglini, A. J. (1998). Adolescents from immigrant families. In V. C. McLoyd & L. Steinberg (Eds.), *Studying minority adolescents: Conceptual, methodological and theoretical issues* (pp. 127–143). Mahwah, NJ: Lawrence Erlbaum.

Fukuyama, M. A., & Sevig, T.D. (1999). *Integrating spirituality into multicultural counseling* (pp. 83–103). Thousand Oaks, CA: Sage.

Gamst, G., Dana, R. H., Der-Karabetian, A., & Kramer, T. (2004). Ethnic matching and treatment outcomes for child and adolescent mental health center clients. *Journal of Counseling and Development, 82,* 457–465.

Garcia Coll, C., & Szalacha, L. (2004). The multiple contexts of middle childhood. *Future of Children, 14,* 81–97.

Gaudet, S., Clement, R., & Deuzeman, K. (2005). Daily hassles, ethnic identity, and psychological adjustment among Lebanese-Canadians. *International Journal of Psychology, 40,* 157–168.

Gil, A. G., Vega, W. A., & Dimas, J. M. (1994). Acculturative stress and personal adjustment among Hispanic adolescent boys. *Journal of Community Psychology, 22,* 43–54.

Gonzales, N. A., Gunnoe, M. L., Samaniego, R., & Jackson, K. (1995). *Validation of a multicultural event schedule for adolescents.* Paper presented at the Biennial Conference of the Society for Community Research and Action, Chicago, IL.

Gore, S., Aseltine, R. H., & Colton, M. E. (1992). Social structure, life stress, and depressive symptoms in a high school-aged population. *Journal of Health and Social Behavior, 33,* 97–113.

Greenspan, S. I., & Greenspan, N. T. (2003). *The clinical interview of the child* (3rd ed.). Washington, DC: American Psychiatric Publishing.

Guerra, N. G., Huesmann, L. R., Tolan, P. H., Van Acker, R., & Eron, L. D. (1995). Stressful events and individual beliefs as correlates of economic disadvantage and aggression among urban children. *Journal of Consulting and Clinical Psychology, 63,* 518–528.

Hays, P. A. (2001). *Addressing cultural complexities in practice: A framework for clinicians and counselors.* Washington, DC: American Psychological Association.

Kao, G., & Joyner, K. (2004). Do race and ethnicity matter among friends? Activities among interracial, interethnic, and intraethnic adolescent friends. *Sociological Quarterly, 45,* 557–573.

Kim-Bae, L. (2000). *Cultural identity as a mediator of acculturative stress and psychological adjustment in Vietnamese American adolescents* (Doctoral dissertation, Arizona State University). *Dissertation Abstracts International, 60*(7-B), 3570.

Knight, G. P., Bernal, M. E., Cota, M. K., Garza, C. A., & Ocampo, K. A. (1993). Family socialization and Mexican American identity and behavior. In M. E. Bernal & G. P. Knight (Eds.), *Ethnic identity: Formation and transmission among Hispanics and other minorities* (pp. 31–46). Albany: State University of New York Press.

Li, S. T., Jenkins, S., & Sundsmo, A. (in press). Impact of race and ethnicity on the expression, assessment, and diagnosis of psychopathology. In M. Hersen, S. Turner, & D. Beidel (Eds.), *Adult psychopathology and diagnosis* (5th ed.). New York: Wiley.

Li, S., Nussbaum, K., & Richards, M. H. (in press). Risk and protective factors for urban inner-city African-American youth. *American Journal of Community Psychology.*

Li, S. T., & Rogers, S. L. (2006). Developmental considerations. In M. Hersen (Ed.), *Clinician's handbook of child behavioral assessment* (pp. 25–62). New York: Elsevier.

Luthar, S. (2003). *Resilience and vulnerability: Adaptation in the context of childhood adversities.* New York: Cambridge University Press.

Margolese, H. (1998). Engaging in psychotherapy with the Orthodox Jews: A critical review. *American Journal of Psychotherapy, 52,* 37–53.

Martinez, C. (2000). Conducting the cross-cultural clinical interview. In I. Cueller & F. Paniagua (Eds.), *Handbook of multicultural mental health: Assessment and treatment of diverse populations* (pp. 311–323). San Diego, CA: Academic Press.

Miller, D. B., Webster, S. E., & MacIntosh, R. (2002). What's there and what's not: Measuring daily hassles in urban African American adolescents. *Research on Social Work Practice, 12,* 375–388.

Ocampo, K. A., Bernal, M. E., & Knight, G. P. (1993). Gender, race, and the ethnicity: The sequencing of social constancies. In M. E. Bernal & G. P. Knight (Eds.), *Ethnic identity: Formation and transmission among Hispanics and other minorities* (pp. 11–30). Albany, NY: State University of New York Press.

Ocampo, K. A., Knight, G. P., & Bernal, M. E. (1997). The development of cognitive abilities and social identities in children: The case of ethnic identity. *International Journal of Behavioral Development, 21,* 479–500.

Phinney, J. S. (1993). A three-stage model of ethnic identity development in adolescence. In M. E. Bernal & G. P. Knight (Eds.), *Ethnic identity: Formation and transmission among Hispanics and other minorities* (pp. 31–46). Albany: State University of New York Press.

Phinney, J. S., Kim-Jo, T., Osorio, S., Vilhjalmsdottir, P. (2005). Autonomy and relatedness in adolescent-parent disagreements: Ethnic and developmental factors. *Journal of Adolescent Research, 20,* 8–39.

Phinney, J. S., Ong, A., & Madden, T. (2000). Cultural values and intergenerational value discrepancies in immigrant and non-immigrant families. *Child Development, 71,* 528–539.

Portes, A. (1997). Immigration theory for a new century: Some problems and opportunities. *International Migration Review, 31,* 799–825.

Quamma, J. P., & Greenberg, M. T. (1994). Children's experience of life stress: The role of family social support and social problem-solving skills as protective factors. *Journal of Clinical Child Psychology, 23,* 295–305.

Rattansi, A., & Phoenix, A. (2005). Rethinking youth identities: Modernist and postmodernist frameworks. *Identity, 5,* 97–123.

Ridley, C. R., Li, L. C., & Hill, C. L. (1998). Multicultural assessment: Reexamination, reconceptualization, and practical application. *Counseling Psychologist, 26,* 827–910.

Roysircar-Sodowsky, G., & Maestas, M. V. (2000). Acculturation, ethnic identity, and acculturative stress: Evidence and measurement. In R. H. Dana (Ed.), *Handbook of cross-cultural and multicultural personality assessment* (pp. 131–172). Mahwah, NJ: Lawrence Erlbaum.

Santiago-Rivera, A. L., Arredondo, P., & Gallardo-Cooper, M. (2002). *Counseling Latinos and la familia: A practical guide.* Thousand Oaks, CA: Sage.

Seidman, E., Allen, L., Aber, J. L., Mitchell, C., Feinman, J., Yoshikawa, H., et al. (1995). Development and validation of adolescent-perceived microsystem scales: Social support, daily hassles, and involvement. *American Journal of Community Psychology, 23,* 355–388.

Stark, K. D., Ballatore, M., Hamff, A., Valdez, C., & Selvig, L. (2001). Childhood depression. In H. Orvaschel, J. Faust, & M. Hersen (Eds.), *Handbook of conceptualization and treatment of child psychopathology* (pp. 107–132). Amsterdam: Pergamon/Elsevier.

St. Louis, G., & Liem, J. (2005). Ego identity, ethnic identity, and the psychosocial well-being of ethnic minority and majority college students. *Identity: An International Journal of Theory and Research, 5,* 227–246.

Szapocznik, J., & Kurtines, W. (1993). Family psychology and cultural diversity. *American Psychologist, 48,* 400–407.

Takushi, R., & Uomoto, J. (2001). The clinical interview from a multicultural perspective. In L. Suzuki,

J. Ponterotto, & P. Meller (Eds.), *Handbook of multicultural assessment: Clinical, psychological, and educational applications* (2nd ed., pp. 47–66). San Francisco: Jossey-Bass.

Turner, S., Hersen, M., & Heiser, N. (2003). The interviewing process. In M. Hersen & S. Turner (Eds.), *Diagnostic interviewing* (2nd ed., pp. 3–20). New York: Kluwer Academic/Plenum.

Want, V., Parham, T. A., Baker, R. C., & Sherman, M. (2004). African American students' ratings of Caucasian and African American counselors varying in racial consciousness. *Cultural Diversity and Ethnic Minority Psychology, 10,* 123–136.

Wu, K. K., & Lam, D. J. (1993). The relationship between daily stress and health: Replicating and extending previous findings. *Psychology and Health, 8,* 329–344.

7

DEALING WITH SCHOOL SYSTEMS AND TEACHERS

JASON T. HURWITZ, ELIZABETH R. GAEBLER,
AND THOMAS R. KRATOCHWILL

The primary purpose of this chapter is to describe a popular and empirically supported interviewing process used in school settings. Problem-solving consultation provides a vehicle for this three-phase interviewing process and delivery of psychological and educational services in school settings. We further discuss the technical adequacy of this interviewing process, drawing upon evidence from more than three decades of research. Finally, we describe some general considerations involved in interviewing in schools, including logistical issues (e.g., demands of physical space and time), whom to interview, and legal and ethical responsibilities of interviewers working from within or outside the school.

PROBLEM-SOLVING INTERVIEWS

Two of the most popular interviewing formats include those conceptually based on traditional or behavioral orientations. Traditional interviews tend to focus on historical information, assume problems reside within the person, and yield information for classification purposes, such as determining special education diagnoses.

In contrast, behavioral interviews focus on identifying current problem behaviors, consider environmental and temporal variables that contribute to and maintain the behaviors, and provide information for selecting additional assessment procedures and designing interventions.

Busse and Beaver (2000) distinguished the content and purposes of behavioral interviews further, between *behavior-specific* and *problem-solving* interviews. Behavior-specific interviews focus on only a few problems, possibly only one, related to the specific behaviors of concern (Kratochwill, Elliott, & Stoiber, 2002) and are particularly useful when the presenting concerns are vague or numerous. When the focus is too specific, however, practitioners may misidentify the initial referral issue, resulting in lost time and ineffective outcomes (Busse & Beaver, 2000). In contrast, problem-solving interviews are simply an extension of behavior-specific interviews, broadening the focus to assessing the problem in context rather than assessing only specific behaviors (Busse & Beaver, 2000). The central defining feature of problem-solving interviews, however, is that they occur within the context of and provide the structure for problem-solving consultation. Thus, problem-solving interviews occur between a consultant and consultee (e.g., teacher or parent) at multiple times, rather than between a therapist and client (e.g., child) on a single occasion (Gresham & Davis, 1988). Although various models of consultation are available (see Bergan & Kratochwill, 1990; Brown, Pryzwansky, & Schulte, 2001; Erchul & Martens, 2002), the problem-solving, or behavioral, model of consultation developed by Bergan (1977) and his associates remains the most popular and widely researched model for use in school settings.

Problem-Solving Consultation and Interviews

Behavioral consultation provides a framework for the problem-solving interview process. Although a variety of behavioral interviewing formats are available for consultation in school settings (e.g., Gutkin & Curtis, 1999; Lentz & Wehmann, 1995; Witt & Elliot, 1983), the behavioral, or problem-solving, consultation model described by Bergan (1977), Bergan and Kratochwill (1990), and Kratochwill and Bergan (1990) dominates the behavioral consultation literature (Shapiro, 1999). Shapiro concluded from his review of the literature that consultants can be trained to use these behavioral consultation interviewing procedures reliably (e.g., Bergan, 1977; Erchul, Covington, Hughes, & Meyers, 1995; Gresham, 1984; Kratochwill, Elliott, & Busse, 1995), and scripts for the interviews have been developed (e.g., Gresham, 1984; Witt, 1990; Witt, Erchul, McKee, Pardue, & Wickstrom, 1991).

Based originally on the tenets of behavioral therapy and modification, a major characteristic of behavioral consultation is its focus on overt behaviors (Kratochwill & Bergan, 1990). Another major characteristic, however, is a strong emphasis on the empirical evaluation of treatment procedures (Kazdin & Hersen, 1980) that may stem from diverse theoretical orientations and approaches. Kratochwill et al. (2002) therefore suggested replacing the term *behavioral* with *problem-solving* to accurately identify the contemporary understanding and application of this consultation model. Indeed, Kratochwill and Bergan (1990) noted that the problem-solving approach of behavioral consultation is one of its unique advantages, wherein,

The difficulties that clients bring to the attention of a consultant are defined and solved within the context of a problem or a set of problems . . . [with] an emphasis on determining what can be done about a given circumstance to improve existing conditions. (p. 27)

Gutkin and Curtis (1999) further combined the descriptions of problem-solving and behavioral approaches under the term *ecobehavioral consultation*, extending the original focus on proximal environmental variables to distal environmental variables (see Gutkin, 1993).

The primary goals of any problem-solving consultation, consistent with best practices and behavioral theory, are to reduce problem behaviors and increase socially appropriate behaviors or competencies of the clients and/or consultees. This principle extends from individual to systems-level consultation focused on improving a program or functioning of an organization. Another goal, or rather condition, of successful behavioral consultation is the development of a collegial relationship, wherein the consultant and the consultee each contribute and apply his or her own special expertise to facilitate problem resolutions (Kratochwill & Bergan, 1990). That is, the consultee possesses specific knowledge about the problem, client characteristics, and available resources, while the consultant contributes expertise on the consultation process and the psychoeducational practice and principles necessary to effect positive client outcomes.

Problem Identification Interview (PII). Problem-solving consultation is a four-stage process accomplished through standardized interviews in three stages.[1] Table 7.1 provides a brief outline of three problem-solving interviews. In the first stage, Problem Identification, consultants use the Problem Identification Interview (PII) to help consultees specify, in observable and objectively measurable terms, and prioritize the problem(s) of concern. An operational definition of the problem behaviors (i.e., estimated magnitude, latency, duration, and frequency) and conditions (antecedent, consequent, sequential) helps (a) promote mutual understanding of the problem, (b) determine the methods for gathering additional baseline data, and (c) improve consistency of data often collected by the consultees or others who spend time with the target child. Successful completion of this stage is especially important to the efficacy of the consultation process and outcomes (Bergan & Tombari, 1976).

TABLE 7.1   Behavioral Consultation Interview Phases, Objectives, Steps, and Examples of Script

Interview Phase	General Objectives	Specific Objectives	Examples of Script
Problem Identification Interview (PII)	To specify the problem and prioritize concerns	1. Specify the goal In developmental consultation: • Establish general and subordinate performance objectives In problem-centered consultation: • Obtain precise description of behaviors, the conditions in which they occur, and the strength of the behavior 2. Assess the concern • Agree on type of measure • Specify what will be recorded • Specify how data will be recorded, how much, by whom, and the recording schedule 3. Consider procedural details • Agree on detail (e.g., date and time) of next interview • Arrange to contact consultee during baseline data collection	• What are your general concerns? • As far as _____ is concerned, what are some of the things you are talking about? • Give some examples of _____ • What would _____ have to do to demonstrate that? • The first thing we need to do is collect baseline data . . . Let's discuss those details.
Problem Analysis Interview (PAI)	To determine whether a problem exists, set goals, and measure progress	1. Validate the problem • Evaluate baseline data to determine whether adequate • Decide whether discrepancy exists by comparing baseline data to goals for client • Come to an agreement about the nature of the problem and its existence 2. Analyze the problem • Share assessment results • Obtain information about performance enhancement techniques used during baseline • Ask about antecedent, consequent, and sequential conditions during baseline 3. Design a plan to address the problem • Devise planning strategies for treatment implementation • Establish tactics for treatment plan • Determine how performance will be assessed during treatment implementation 4. Consider procedural details • Agree on details (e.g,. date, time) for the problem evaluation interview • Devise a plan to monitor implementation process, including follow-up with consultee • Arrange consultee training, if necessary	• Let's look at the baseline data you collected. • Do you agree that a problem exists? • What happens before the behavior? During? After? • What else may affect the behavior? • What we need to do is make up a plan. . . . • Can you continue to collect the same kind of data? • When can we meet to evaluate the plan?

(Continued)

TABLE 7.1 (Continued)

Interview Phase	General Objectives	Specific Objectives	Examples of Script
Treatment Evaluation Interview (TEI)	To evaluate goal achievement, intervention effectiveness and acceptability, and discuss consultation termination	1. Analyze level of goal attainment In developmental consultation: • Analyze and summarize data collected during baseline • Analyze and summarize data from treatment implementation • Ask consultee's opinion about goal attainment • Continue process for each performance objective, then move on to subordinate objectives In problem-centered consultation: • Select one of the behavioral goals to analyze (if more than one) • Analyze the baseline data and summarize the behavioral goal • Analyze and summarize plan implementation data • Compare baseline data to implementation data and ask consultee's opinion about client goal attainment • Continue process for all behavioral goals 2. Provide guidance • Indicate need to either progress to next stage or move back to an earlier stage 3. Evaluate effectiveness of treatment plan • Determine whether plan was effective and acceptable 4. Plan for postimplementation • Decide whether to keep implemented plan, remove it, or design a new plan • Establish recording procedures for plan • Establish procedures for possibility of problem recurrence 5. Consider procedural details • Agree on details (e.g., date, time) for next interview if goal(s) not achieved • End consultation relationship if goal(s) attained	• Do you think the goals were attained? • Let's analyze the progress so far. . . . Perhaps we should move back to an earlier stage. • Let's consider what would happen if we kept the plan in effect? Removed it? Devised a new plan? • How will progress be recorded for the postimplementation plan? • Since the goal was not met, let's schedule another interview. . . . • The goal was attained, so consultation can now be terminated.

SOURCE: Adapted from Kratochwill, T. R., & Bergan, J. R. (1990). *Behavioral consultation in applied settings: An individual guide.* New York: Plenum Press.

Problem Analysis Interview (PAI). The consultant and consultee then evaluate the baseline data, generally collected over at least 1 week, for adequacy during the second interview stage, the Problem Analysis Interview (PAI). They evaluate these data to (a) determine consensus on whether a discrepancy between current and desired behavior exists and constitutes a problem, (b) develop achievable, mutually agreed-upon, and socially valid goals, and (c) measure progress toward those goals. Progress through the PAI relies on the specialized knowledge that the consultant and consultee each possess and contribute to (a) develop testable hypotheses for potential variables that influence (i.e., increase or maintain) the behaviors of concern (i.e., environmental/temporal conditions, client skill deficits and assets), (b) develop a mutually acceptable plan for altering those influences upon the behavior, translating into the achievement of previously determined goals, and (c) determine the resources required to achieve the plan.

During the treatment implementation phase, data collection continues as the client and consultee implement the intervention plan for a few weeks. Although no formal interview is conducted during this phase, the consultant frequently monitors treatment progress and integrity through brief dialogue with consultees or direct observation. Consultants are also responsible for helping the consultee or client develop the skills necessary to implement the treatment. Frequent follow-ups allow for prompt and, many times, minor adjustments or revisions made to the intervention procedures or implementation.

Treatment Evaluation Interview (TEI). The consultant and consultee later review and evaluate the data during the final stage, the Treatment Evaluation Interview (TEI). Specifically, they evaluate achievement of the short-term goals they established, the effectiveness and acceptability of the intervention implemented to achieve those goals, and whether and how to terminate consultation. The ultimate success of any intervention, however, is characterized by the maintenance and generalizability of behavior change across time and settings. If the evidence suggests no progress toward the goals, the consultant and consultee must determine whether the treatment was implemented as planned (i.e., treatment integrity) and return to earlier stages

to reassess the goals and hypotheses and possibly develop a new intervention plan. Otherwise, they could simply decide to terminate consultation and seek alternative services.

PSYCHOMETRIC PROPERTIES

School-based consultation is an effective and increasingly popular means of service delivery (Kratochwill et al., 1995; Medway & Updyke, 1985; Sheridan, Welch, & Orme, 1996). School psychologists' expertise in assessment and intervention is a necessary prerequisite as a consultant but is not sufficient, however, to achieve beneficial outcomes of consultation (Gutkin & Curtis, 1999). Rather, school psychologists must focus their attention and expertise on adults in order to effectively serve children (Gutkin & Conoley, 1990). A defining feature of consultation, after all, is the *indirect approach* to service delivery, whereby the consultant influences client change through work with the consultee. Recommending the most effective interventions with the strongest of empirical support and based on evaluation of comprehensive assessment data will not result in beneficial client outcomes unless they are accepted and implemented by the consultee (e.g., parent, teacher). Gutkin and Curtis (1982) noted that consultation is an "interpersonal exchange," in which "the consultant's success is going to hinge largely on his or her communication . . . skills" (p. 599). The collection and evaluation of relevant data and establishment of an effective relationship necessary for successful outcomes begin during the interview.

Consultants and consultees gather and integrate information from a variety of sources, environments, and methods (e.g., behavioral observations, questionnaires/checklists/rating scales, reviews of permanent products) on which they base their treatment-planning and evaluation decisions. The single most important assessment method and information source that defines consultation is the interview. As such, Gresham and Davis (1988) pointed out that many researchers argue that behavioral assessment techniques, including interviews, should be held to the same psychometric standards as more traditional assessment techniques (e.g., tests; Cone, 1977, 1978, 1979; Goldfried & Linehan, 1977; Linehan, 1980), whereas others contend that traditional concepts of reliability and validity contradict the assumptions and purposes of behavioral assessment (e.g., Johnston & Pennypacker, 1980; Nelson, 1983). The purpose of psychometric information is to guide professionals' decisions about selection and use of appropriate assessment and intervention practices and thus lead to improved outcomes (Barnett, Lentz, & Macmann, 2000). Standards of professional practice require that psychologists evaluate the technical adequacy of the services they provide. Psychometric data influence decisions about which measures to use for a particular purpose. Barnett et al. (2000) urged that useful data should reflect the consequences of an accumulation of assessment decisions that ultimately result in beneficial outcomes for the client (i.e., student).

Traditional assessment techniques, with the purpose of classification, rarely include psychometric data concerning the outcomes of decisions based on the test scores (Barnett et al., 2000; Gresham & Davis, 1988). The purposes of behavioral assessment techniques, however, are treatment planning and evaluation (e.g., problem identification, selection and ongoing evaluation of treatment process and outcomes) and a focus on environmental variables, rather than an internal construct, that maintain behaviors (Barnett et al., 2000; Gresham & Davis, 1988). Validity and reliability properties of behavioral assessment techniques should therefore evaluate whether the assessment data consistently achieve clear purposes and positive consequences (Barnett et al., 2000). The following discussion on the reliability and validity of problem-solving interviews describes a sampling, not an exhaustive review, of the relevant research. In addition to the evidence available in the literature, the problem-solving consultation process itself inherently involves evaluating the quality and consequences of assessment data.

Reliability

Reliability refers to the consistency of data obtained by a measure or assessment method over time and across settings and examiners. All measures contain some degree of random or unpredictable error that causes variability in their results. The range of error associated with a measure is quantifiable (e.g., correlation coefficient, r), allowing professionals to judge the quality of both a potential measure and uncertainties in interpretation of the resultant data (Barnett et al., 2000). Interviews traditionally contain measurement error that stem from four sources that can have a cumulative effect: (1) interviewee (e.g., attitudes, memory, interpretation of events, and reason for interviewing); (2) interviewer (e.g., technique and style, recording of data, interview administration, perceptions and expectancies, and training); (3) interview setting (e.g., location, physical environment, and time of day); and (4) the interview itself (e.g., method, subjectivity in interpretation of directions, items, and scoring) (American Educational Research Association [AERA] American Psychological Association [APA], & National Council on Measurement in Education [NCME], 1999; Barnett et al., 2000; Sattler, 2001).[2] Variability of assessment results due to treatment effects, learning, or maturation and systematic errors, such as the difficulty of a test form, however, are not considered measurement error (AERA, APA, & NCME, 1999). Most research supporting the reliability of problem-solving interviews focuses primarily on the consistency of administration and agreement among raters on classifying features of the interview dialogue.

Internal Consistency. Internal consistency allows evaluation of the extent to which interviewers consistently complete the objectives of each of the three problem-solving interviews. Consultant-training studies collect internal-consistency data both to check the integrity of consultation interviews and to evaluate improvement of consultants' interviewing skills during training and generalization to field-based practice (e.g., Kratochwill et al., 1995; Kratochwill, VanSomeren, & Sheridan, 1989; Lepage, Kratochwill, & Elliott, 2004; Sheridan, Eagle, Cowan, & Mickleson, 2001). For example, Lepage and colleagues (2004) found that the immediate increase in consultants' skills in attaining the interview objectives following training maintained at a high level during the casework phase. All 21 consultants who participated in the casework interviewing phase attained at least 80% of the expected objectives in all interviews, including 7 consultants who attained at least 90% and 10 who attained 100% of the objectives. In another example, Sheridan and colleagues (2001) observed a generalization of training to field-based casework on attainment of the interviewing objectives coded from 230 interviews with teachers and parents in 57 conjoint consultation cases conducted by 30 consultants. Consultants collectively met 82%, 83%, and 80% of objectives for the conjoint PII, PAI, and TEI, respectively. Although the research focus may not be upon consultant training, virtually all investigations into problem-solving consultation include a consultant-training component. Beavers, Kratochwill, and Braden (2004), for example, investigated the effects of two related problem-solving interview and assessment techniques (i.e., functional and empiric) on consultation outcomes. After scoring audiotaped recordings of interviews using a checklist that assesses completion of interview objectives, they found that consultants achieved 100% accuracy in their adherence to the consultation protocols. The greater the integrity of the interview, the less likely that sources of error, such as deviation from the interview protocol traditionally known as "therapist drift" in the intervention literature (Peterson, Homer, & Wonderlich, 1982), will bias results that can ultimately influence treatment outcomes. Consultant training and use of a procedural manual or checklist improves interview integrity (e.g., Kratochwill et al., 1995; Kratochwill et al., 1989).

Interrater Agreement. Evidence for the reliability of problem-solving interviews comes largely from research involving interrater agreement in classifying types of verbalizations. Bergan and Tombari (1975) first introduced a coding system for classifying verbal interchange between consultants and consultees in problem-solving interviews to facilitate research and training. Although other coding systems have since become available (see Martens et al., 1992), the Consultation Analysis Record (CAR) developed by Bergan and Tombari (1975) is a popular measure for analyzing verbalizations in consultation research and remains virtually unchanged (see Bergan & Kratochwill, 1990).

Using interview transcripts or audio/video recordings, the CAR enables researchers to classify verbalizations according to four categories: (1) source, (2) content, (3) process, and (4) control. *Source* refers to the person speaking (i.e., consultant or consultee). *Content* refers to the topic of discussion, which includes several subcategories (e.g., behavior setting, behavior,

observation, and plan). The *process* category describes the purpose of the content, which includes five subcategories (i.e., specification, evaluation, inference, summarization, and evaluation). *Control* identifies the type of utterance as either (a) an elicitor for a response from the other person (e.g., request for information) or (b) an emitter (e.g., declarative statement or exclamatory remark). Figure 7.1 displays an example of the CAR.

Bergan and Tombari (1975, 1976) achieved interrater reliability between two coders who independently analyzed 50 statements from problem identification and problem analysis interviews. They observed Scott's (1955) coefficients of .88, .87, and 1.00 for control, content, and process categories on the PII, and .92, .90, and 1.00 in the respective categories on the PAI. Further studies have reported similar findings of relatively high interrater agreement in coding consultant and consultee verbalizations in problem-solving interviews, using other indices of interrater agreement, including percentage agreement and kappa (e.g., Anderson, Kratochwill, & Bergan, 1986; Bergan, Byrnes, & Kratochwill, 1979; Bergan & Neumann, 1980; Brown, Kratochwill, & Bergan, 1982; Busse, Kratochwill, & Elliott, 1999; Curtis & Watson, 1980; Erchul et al., 1995; Hughes & DeForest, 1993; Kratochwill et al., 1989; Martens et al., 1992; Martens, Lewandowski, & Houk, 1989; McDougall, Reschly, & Corkery, 1988; Tombari & Bergan, 1978; Witt et al., 1991).

Test-Retest. The test-retest reliability of problem-solving interviews refers to the extent that a consultant may reinterview the same consultees within a brief time period and consistently identify the same number and nature of problems (Barnett et al., 2000; Gresham, 1984; Gresham & Davis, 1988). The call for published research examining test-retest reliability, however, remains unanswered (Beaver & Busse, 2000; Bergan & Kratochwill, 1990; Gresham, 1984; Gresham & Davis, 1988). Although potential for problems inherent to a retesting study requires consideration (e.g., recency effects, change in target behaviors and settings), Beaver and Busse (2000) suggested that behavioral assessment methods should evidence high levels of test-retest reliability for those behaviors that persist across time, particularly within 2 weeks, or months.

FIGURE 7.1   Example of a Consultation Analysis Record (CAR)

Consultation-Analysis Record

Consultant: _____

Consultee: _____

Case Number: _____

Interview Type: _____

Page: _____

Message		Verbalizations																							
		1	2	3	4	5	6	7	8	9	10	11	12	13	14	15	16	17	18	19	20	21	22	23	24	25
Message Source	Consultee																									
	Consultant																									
Message Content	Background Environment																									
	Behavior Setting																									
	Behavior																									
	Individual Characteristics																									
	Observation																									
	Plan																									
	Other																									
Message Process	Negative Evaluation																									
	Positive Evaluation																									
	Inference																									
	Specification																									
	Summarization																									
	Negative Validation																									
	Positive Validation																									
Message Source	Elicitor																									
	Emitter																									

SOURCE: Reprinted from Bergan, J. R., & Tombari, M. L. (1975). The analysis of verbal interactions occurring during consultation. *Journal of School Psychology, 13*(3), 209–226, with permission of Elsevier.

Validity

Validity refers to the extent that an assessment technique or method actually measures what it purports to measure. Theory and accumulated evidence must provide a sound scientific basis for the interpretation and use of the assessment data for specific and meaningful purposes (AERA, APA, & NCME, 1999). Thus, validity refers to use and interpretation of assessment results, not the assessment method itself. Reliability is a necessary but insufficient component of validity. The multiple purposes of a given assessment method dictate the multiple types of additional and corresponding validity evidence.

Construct Validity. Construct validity concerns the extent to which a test or assessment technique measures a particular psychological construct or trait (Sattler, 2001). In other words, a measure is one indicator of a given construct and should therefore reflect, or account for, changes in other variables related to the construct (Haynes & Jensen, 1979; Messick, 1989). Viewed broadly, Messik (1995) argued that "any evidence that bears on the interpretation or meaning of the test scores—including content- and criterion-related validity—are subsumed as part of construct validity" (p. 742). Researchers evaluate the construct validity of problem-solving interviews by investigating the relationships between the interview items and the general features, or constructs, that the interview is designed to assess (Bergan & Kratochwill, 1990). Specifically, researchers examine four different types of validity data that differentiate these relationships: (1) content validity; (2) criterion validity; (3) congruent, or convergent, validity; and (4) divergent, or discriminant, validity.

Content validity refers to the extent to which test or interview items (i.e., content) represent the domains they are intended to measure (Sattler, 2001). In other words, this type of validity relies on expert judgments of whether the interview content is relevant to, and representative of, the content of a particular behavioral domain of interest (Messick, 1989). Specific research on the content validity of problem-solving interviews, including use of expert panels, remains absent from the literature (Beaver & Busse, 2000). Many early investigations of problem-solving interviews and use of the CAR and similar coding methods (e.g., Bergan, 1977; Bergan et al., 1979; Bergan & Neumann,

1980; Bergan & Tombari, 1975, 1976; Brown et al., 1982; Curtis & Watson, 1980; Tombari & Bergan, 1978), however, indicate general consensus in the field that "behavioral interviews appear to be relevant to the purposes of measurement, make a reliable sample [of] the domains of interest, and yield information that has generally accepted meanings" (Gresham & Davis, 1988, p. 486).

Criterion validity refers to the relationship between the interview data and some other type of assessment criteria or outcomes against which the data can be judged (Beaver & Busse, 2000; Sattler, 2001). There are two types of criterion validity: (1) predictive and (2) concurrent. *Concurrent validity* compares interview data with criteria or outcomes that are currently available, whereas *predictive validity* compares interview data with criteria that will be available in the future. An early study by Bergan and Tombari (1975, 1976) provided a classic and widely cited example of predictive validity, despite some criticisms of the statistical analysis they used (see Beaver & Busse, 2000). In this study, 11 psychologists received training in problem-solving consultation and worked with teachers (consultees) in providing services to 806 children (Grades K–3), to whom the consultees referred for various academic and behavioral concerns. Analysis and coding of the interview transcripts indicated that problem identification was the best predictor of plan implementation ($R = .776$; i.e., 60% of variance accounted for) and that plan implementation was the best predictor of problem solution ($R = .977$; i.e., 95% of variance accounted for). That is, the better the consultant's skills in problem identification, the more likely consultation will result in successful resolution of the problem.

Beaver and Busse (2000) cited findings from numerous studies that provided further evidence of the predictive validity, such as significantly high correlations between (a) consultants' less frequent use of behavior and plan specification verbalizations and positive child outcomes (Busse et al., 1999), (b) consultant skill and quality and quantity of information provided by teachers (Curtis & Watson, 1980), (c) personal support and causal hypotheses provided by consultants during initial interviews and teachers' perceptions of higher consultant effectiveness (Hughes & Deforest, 1993), and (d) consultants' validation statements and teacher satisfaction (Martens et al., 1989).

No published research has directly examined the concurrent validity of problem-solving interviews. Future research in this area must investigate the relationship between consultees' descriptions of behaviors solicited in the interview (e.g., rate, duration, frequency, intensity) and actual behaviors assessed through observations, rating scales, self-reports, or measures of interviewer effectiveness (Beaver & Busse, 2000; Bergan & Kratochwill, 1990; Gresham & Davis, 1988). Although consultants in many studies independently assess the target behavior following the PII, researchers do not examine the extent of congruence between the teacher reports and direct assessment of the problem behaviors. Some studies, however, find little, if any, correlation between teacher reports and direct assessments of treatment integrity and outcomes (e.g., Lepage et al., 2004; Noell et al., 2005). Teachers' perceptions are necessary but not sufficient criteria for evaluating the effectiveness of consultation, particularly student outcomes (Fuchs & Fuchs, 1989; Hughes & DeForest, 1993; Schwartz & Baer, 1991; Watson, Sterling, & McDade, 1997). Beaver and Busse (2000) suggested two alternative approaches to examining concurrent validity by comparing verbalizations in problem-solving interviews to (a) the criterion of Bergan and Tombari's (1975) guidelines for the effective quantity and quality of verbalizations and (b) the criterion of interviewee outcomes. For example, Busse and colleagues (1999) found that consultant verbalizations followed the guidelines hypothesized for effective problem-solving consultation, and Tombari and Bergan (1978) found that teachers who responded to behavioral cues were more optimistic about problem solving than were teachers who responded to medical model cues.

The third type of validity is based on a high correlation between different measures of variables that are theoretically related to the same (i.e., *convergent*) or similar (i.e., *congruent*) construct. Beavers et al. (2004) compared the effects on treatment selection and outcomes stemming from two different problem-solving assessment techniques: (1) functional assessment and (2) empiric approach. Consultants ($N = 3$) used the same problem-solving interview process (i.e., PII, PAI, TEI) and similar content in both conditions. Researchers modified the PII content in the functional assessment condition, however, to include questions about environmental conditions (e.g., antecedents, sequences, consequences) surrounding the academic behavior, which the consultants later analyzed and presented to the teachers during the PAI as the rationale for the treatment plan. Consultants in the empiric approach omitted questions about environmental conditions during the PII and problem analysis and instead used an intervention manual to identify and suggest several strategies to teachers that conceptually matched to the reading problem. The only significant differences in outcomes between the two assessment conditions were the costs of time (mean of 7.70 hours [$SD = 1.51$] and 10.10 hours [$SD = 9.80$] for the empiric and functional conditions) and money ($99.10 per empiric case and $129.99 per functional case). Results indicated no significant differences between conditions regarding treatment selection, consultation and treatment integrity, consultee satisfaction, or teacher reports and direct assessments of student outcomes.

Discriminant validity, however, is where different measures of variables theoretically related to *different* constructs evidence *low* correlation. Findings from an early study by Tombari and Bergan (1978) indicated evidence for both discriminant and concurrent validity. They investigated the effects of "medical model" and behavioral cues and summary statements during interviews on teachers' verbalizations and perceptions regarding student concerns and expectations for effective solutions. Medical model interviews often involve open-ended questions concerning individual characteristics and possible remote environmental and internal causes of problems. Behavioral cues, the primary theoretical basis of problem-solving interviews, involve narrower questions about specific student behaviors and immediate environmental conditions surrounding them. Interview scripts contained six questions reflecting the orientation of each condition (e.g., "Tell me about ____'s behavior in your class" versus "Tell me something, anything, you would like about ____"), which they administered to 60 student teachers in analogue conditions. Two raters, blind to the interview conditions, coded teachers' responses using a CAR. Results indicated that medical and behavioral model cues elicited responses that were congruent with the theoretical assumptions of the respective model and that teachers who responded to behavioral cues were more optimistic about solving problems in their classrooms.

Social Validity. Social validity, a term originally coined by Wolf (1978), refers to the value of treatments as judged by stakeholders who participate in their implementation or benefit from their outcomes. Wolf described three levels of evaluating social validity: (1) significance or meaningfulness of the selected treatment goals, (2) appropriateness of the procedures specified to achieve those goals, and (3) importance of and satisfaction with all resulting outcomes. Assessment of social validity in problem-solving consultation research relies primarily on teachers' and parents' (i.e., consultees') judgments, solicited through various rating scales following consultation (e.g., Kratochwill et al., 2002). One widely used measure, the Treatment Evaluation Inventory-Short Form (TEI-SF) (Kelley, Heffer, Gresham, & Elliott, 1989), for example, includes nine items rated on a 5-point Likert scale (1 = *strongly disagree*; 5 = *strongly agree*) that assesses consumers' acceptability of the treatment procedures and their perceived effectiveness. Readers may refer to Finn and Sladeczek (2001) for a review of the development and technical adequacy of TEI-SF and other popular measures of treatment acceptability. Treatment acceptability, one level of social validity and the primary focus of social validity research (Finn & Sladeczek, 2001), specifically refers to "judgments of lay persons, clients, and others of whether the procedures proposed for treatment are appropriate, fair, and reasonable for the problem or client" (Kazdin, 1981, p. 493). Interviewers also obtain a qualitative and ongoing assessment of consultees' judgments concerning the treatment goals, procedures, and outcomes while accomplishing the objectives in each phase of the problem-solving interview.

Although much of the social validity and treatment acceptability research evaluates intervention programs independent of or stemming from consultation, little research has examined the social validity and "assessment" acceptability of the problem-solving interview itself. Some recent problem-solving consultation studies, however, assessed consultees' judgments concerning the effectiveness of the consultant. Noell and his colleagues (2005), for example, administered the Consultant Rating Profile (CRP), which contains 10 items on a 7-point Likert scale, which they developed specifically for use in their study. Seven items rated by teachers (consultees; $n = 45$) assessed the degree of helpfulness of the consultant ($n = 7$) with whom they worked and consultation as an effective use of their time, while the other 3 items assessed integrity of treatment implementation, treatment effectiveness, and satisfaction with the outcomes. Internal consistency of the first 7 items was high (Cronbach's $\alpha = .89$). Results indicated that teachers rated consultants positively, with a mean rating of 6.5 on the 7-point scale.

Similarly, in a training study on problem-solving consultation conducted by Lepage and colleagues (2004), teacher and parent consultees rated their attitudes toward the consultant and consultation services on the Consultant Evaluation Form (CEF) (Erchul, 1987; Erchul & Chewning, 1990), which contains a 12-item, 7-point Likert scale, with higher scores indicating greater satisfaction. Teachers ($n = 26$) and parents ($n = 4$) indicated satisfaction with the consultant and services (i.e., ratings above 4), with mean ratings at or above 5 on all items. In addition, consultants also rated their attitudes toward consultation on a scale of 1 to 5, with higher ratings indicating more positive attitudes. Consultants completed an average of 4.53 ($SD = 4.48$) cases each, ranging from 0 to 14. Consultant respondents ($n = 19$) rated all 15 items of the survey positively. The highest of the mean ratings indicated that consultation was an effective means of service delivery for school psychologists ($M = 4.63$; $SD = 0.50$) that allowed provision of more services to clients ($M = 4.26$; $SD = 0.81$), as well as having positive effects on clients ($M = 4.26$; $SD = 0.56$) and consultees ($M = 4.21$; $SD = 0.63$).

Neither of these two studies, however, specifically assessed consumer satisfaction with the problem-solving interviews nor compared consumer satisfaction among problem-solving consultation and other consultation models. Several studies provided evidence indicating a relationship between (a) interviewers' statements and behaviors and (b) teachers' (i.e., consultees') positive attitudes toward the interviewer and consultation outcomes (Busse et al., 1999; Erchul, 1987; Erchul et al., 1995; Hughes & DeForest, 1993). Beaver and Busse (2000) argued for further research into the variables related to interviewees' judgments concerning the social validity of the content and process of behavioral interviews.

Treatment Validity. Treatment validity refers to the extent to which the assessment data contributes to the effectiveness of treatment outcomes or, specifically, the consequences of the databased decisions that ultimately result in socially significant and beneficial outcomes for the stakeholders (e.g., target child, parent, and teachers). Several studies described earlier in this chapter support the treatment validity of problem-solving interviews in improving the skills and perceptions of interviewers and interviewees. In a review of empirically based research on consultation outcomes, Sheridan and her colleagues (1996) identified 21 studies published between 1985 and 1995 that specifically investigated problem-solving consultation, of which 95% reported positive results. Conclusions about the "effectiveness" of this service delivery model made by many of the studies were based primarily upon teacher (i.e., consultee) reports of treatment acceptability, treatment integrity, and student outcomes. Recent studies, however, find little, if any, correlation between teacher reports and direct assessments of integrity and outcomes (e.g., Lepage et al., 2004; Noell et al., 2005). Teachers' perceptions are necessary but not sufficient criteria for evaluating the effectiveness of consultation, particularly student outcomes (Fuchs & Fuchs, 1989; Hughes & DeForest, 1993; Schwartz & Baer, 1991; Watson et al., 1997).

In addition to teachers' perceptions of a student's overall improvement, best practices requires direct and frequent measures of student progress across baseline and treatment phases to evaluate outcomes and control for extraneous effects. Research that has used such rigorous designs often reports wide variance in overall effect sizes within and across studies. For example, overall effect sizes (mean differences divided by baseline standard deviation) across all cases reported in three recent studies ranged from (a) −0.36 to 7.08 with a mean of 1.10 ($SD = 1.07$; $n = 66$ cases and 30 consultants; Sheridan et al., 2001); to (b) −2.44 to 2.83 with a mean of 0.51 ($SD = 1.04$; $n = 35$ cases and 21 consultants; Lepage et al., 2004); to (c) 0.39 to 1.86 with a mean of 0.55 ($SD = 0.55$; $n = 32$ cases and 3 consultants; Beavers et al., 2004). Additional research that involves the direct assessment of student outcomes resulting from problem-solving consultation and interviews is needed.

CHALLENGES AND CONSIDERATIONS TO INTERVIEWING IN SCHOOLS

Setting

A wide variety of interviewing challenges are specific to the school setting. One common challenge is the limited availability of time. The length and nature of the school day limits teachers' time to meet and discuss student concerns. Planning time and other free periods when interviews must be scheduled are often short, limiting the potential scope of any given interview. Therefore, it is essential that an interview be pared down to only the most essential questions necessary for understanding the particular student's behavior of concern and related impacting variables. This task is often difficult to do without moving too quickly through the interview, which can cause resistance (Cormier & Nurius, 2003).

In addition to teachers' schedules, students also have limited time to participate in the interviewing process. This concern is often particularly evident in secondary school settings, where there are few breaks between classes and a number of different teachers involved in educating a particular student.

A variety of supplemental assessment instruments can make efficient use of the available interviewing time. Specifically, many rating scales, checklists, and questionnaires are commercially available and often come in student, teacher, and parent versions. For example, Beaver and Busse (2000) recommend using the parent Structured Developmental History of the Behavior Assessment System for Children (BASC) (Reynolds & Kamphaus, 2004) to collect information about a child's bio-psycho-social history. These instruments allow the interviewees to provide background information and clarification on the issues of concern. They can provide detailed information on a variety of topics (e.g., frequency and intensity of specific concerns, normative comparisons) for a number of specific types of concerns (e.g., anxiety, depression, and attention). In addition to these instruments, it is also often helpful to prepare questionnaires for use with a specific interviewee. Direct observations of the interviewee in the environment before the interview is conducted may provide helpful information. When completed in advance of and reviewed before the interview, assessment instruments of all types can help to reduce interview time. They help direct questions during the interview to specific areas of concern already identified, thus further promoting efficient use of limited interviewing time.

Another common challenge faced in schools is the limited availability of private space for interviewing. Interviews generate confidential information and thus require a private setting where confidentiality can be ensured. Cormier and Nurius (2003) discussed the importance of various aspects of the environment and the interviewee's perceptions of it, including the arrangement of the physical environment. Private interview areas are often limited in school settings where additional space often does not exist. This concern is particularly true for interviews involving students or parents. A young child may not mind meeting over lunch in a quiet area of the cafeteria or on the playground during class time. This is often not the case, though, for older children and adolescents, who may have more significant concerns with social stigmas attached to mental health services. Finding space to interview teachers may be relatively easier, and discussing matters behind a closed classroom door protects confidentiality.

Resistance from parents and teachers can also be a challenge in the school setting. Teacher resistance can be caused by a host of variables, including feelings of being blamed, controlled, or overwhelmed with other concerns in the classroom. To help prevent resistance, explicit discussion of the roles prior to establishing the interviewing or consultation relationship can help. Interviewees must be assured that the interviewing relationship is based on compromise and is necessary to support the best interests of the child and his or her functioning in the school setting. Campbell (1993) suggested that sitting in a conference room, for example, having the counselor (or interviewer) sit around a table with the parents (or interviewees), instead of behind a desk or at the head of the table, can help parents understand their equality in the relationship. Contracting procedures that clearly define the roles of the interviewer and interviewee can also be helpful in preventing or overcoming resistance. This type of contract will be discussed in more detail in the last section.

A shared responsibility for students among a number of different school professionals presents both a unique benefit and a challenge specific to school settings. In schools, the psychologist is not the only professional involved in the design or implementation of a student's intervention. A number of different individuals are involved, often including a building intervention assistance team. This team of teachers and other school staff can often make interviewing easier, because several teachers can be interviewed simultaneously regarding a single student. This forum-style approach can assist in understanding a child's situation, including different influencing factors present in different environments and among teaching styles. The team can also provide opportunities to enhance teacher commitment to the solution process by encouraging public agreement to try strategies that may influence the environmental variables they recognize as within their own control (e.g., instructional practices).

Despite all of these benefits, the team model can be challenging because of the nature of shared responsibility. Each member of the building team comes to the situation with a unique perspective and guiding theory. The result is that it can sometimes be difficult to come to a group consensus on the origin of the problem and plans for remedying the issue of concern. The focus of any interview used in the consultation process can therefore be difficult to formulate because of the wide variety of contributing opinions about the cause of the referral concern.

Teacher and Parent Interviewees

Separate Parent Interviews. In separate parent interviews, a wealth of information can be gathered about a child's unique situation. This assessment can include detailed information about the child's medical/birth history, family background, peer relationships, social functioning, community involvement, academic functioning, and perceptions of the child's strengths and weaknesses. Some information provided in separate parent interviews, such as insight into the child's daily routines and habits at home, can be provided only by parents or other caregivers. Information about contributing environmental factors at home, such as marital and financial difficulties, available resources, and potential roadblocks to treatment and recovery, may also be obtained (Sattler, 2001). Although some of this information can be gathered through other means (e.g., observation, record review, and interviews with school personnel), it is important to gain insight about the parents' concerns about the presenting issue and their child's functioning at school.

Separate Teacher Interviews. Separate teacher interviews often provide important information about the child's behavior in the classroom and other school settings. A wide variety of information can be gathered, including information about the functional aspects of the child's behaviors in structured and unstructured settings, peer relationships, and the child's functioning compared with peers in the classroom. Sattler (2001) stated that interviewers can also gather information about (a) the child's behaviors, including severity and frequency, affect on the child's functioning, situations when the behaviors do and do not occur, and potential factors that maintain or exacerbate the behaviors; (b) academic performance; (c) social skills and peer relationships; and (d) attendance record. Teachers can also provide information about other pupil services professionals who are involved in students' academic lives (e.g., administrators, librarians, bus drivers) and who may be helpful to interview. The ease of availability of teachers in the school setting also makes them a frequent choice for consultation and interview work (Kratochwill & Pittman, 2002).

Although it is also important to directly observe the child in the classroom, a teacher's perspective gained through an interview is essential to gain a better understanding of some of the specific issues of concern for the teacher. In a recent qualitative study of four psychologist-teacher consultation relationships, it was found that the teachers and school psychologists often had different perspectives about causal attributions and "different yardsticks for measuring intervention success" (Athanasiou, Geil, Hazel, & Copeland, 2002, p. 293). Because improving the child's functioning in the classroom and academic performance is often the goal of intervention in schools, it is essential to consider the perspective of the teacher who is most directly involved in supporting the child. Separate interviews with teachers provide a time to voice individual opinions about the situation and can

provide information about acceptability of future interventions.

In both types of separate interviews, it is important to remember that parents and teachers may often feel anxious before and during the interview. This anxiety may be the result of feeling blamed for the issue of concern or feeling uncomfortable with discussing private matters with an unfamiliar person. Other teachers may feel that their skills as a teacher are being questioned because they need to ask for assistance. The reasons for negative feelings toward the interview process vary among interviewees and interviewers (e.g., an interviewer who is an outside consultant may elicit different feelings from an interviewee than from someone who regularly works in the school). Regardless of the specific situation, communication of genuineness, positive regard, and empathy can help to alleviate some potential negative opinions about the interviewing relationship. The interviewer should remember that the interviewer-interviewee, or consultant-consultee, relationship is nonhierarchical and that the interviewee or consultee always has the right to disagree with any recommendations made (Jacob & Hartshorne, 2003). Keeping a nonjudgmental problem-solving focus to the interview can greatly help to ensure a positive interviewing experience for all involved parties.

Conjoint Parent-Teacher Interviews. When used appropriately, conjoint parent-teacher interviews provide a unique opportunity for both parties to share information about the child's situation. Sheridan and Kratochwill (1992) recommended that in general, conjoint behavioral consultation (CBC) should be avoided if animosity will prevent parties from working cooperatively. If the relationship between the parent(s) and teacher/school personnel is not positive, then a conjoint interview may prevent one or both parties from speaking freely and honestly.

When appropriate, however, CBC offers clear advantages over interviewing parents and teachers separately. Among the general benefits of behavioral consultation, CBC fosters (a) collaboration between teachers and parents, (b) shared responsibility and decision making for developing and implementing problem solutions across settings, (c) learning of strategies for coordinating across home-school systems, and (d) focus on mutually constructed and socially valid goals, rather than perceived problems within the systems (Sheridan et al., 2001; Sheridan et al., 2004). In addition, the consultant is able to gather information across settings in an efficient manner. Separate interviews, however, allow the consultant to determine differences in primary concerns and goals between parents and teachers. These individual interviews with parents or teachers may also help the consultant to identify differences between the teacher and parent(s) in their willingness to change and invest time in rectifying the problem. Good clinical judgment is necessary to make a decision about which type of interview is most appropriate for the particular situation.

Legal and Ethical Considerations

A wide variety of legal and ethical issues must be taken into consideration when interviewing and consulting in a school setting. In general, an interviewer in a school setting must abide by all applicable federal and state laws, professional ethical codes, and school policies that govern interviewing and related services. Similar to those followed in other clinical environments, these include rules regarding informed consent, client welfare and autonomy, self-determination, and nondiscrimination (Jacob & Hartshorne, 2003). In addition, special consideration must be made for rules and laws concerning confidentiality. To use the field of school psychology as an example, the National Association of School Psychologists' *Principles for Professional Ethics* (2000) states that "school psychologists inform children and other clients of the limits of confidentiality at the outset of establishing a professional relationship" (p. 20). In many states, school professionals serve as mandated reporters and thus have limitations to their confidentiality that are important to express before a client or interviewee provides information that the interviewer cannot keep confidential. Specific ethical and legal obligations such as this example are important to consider when interviewing in a school setting. Table 7.2 lists some examples of applicable ethical guidelines and legal regulations related to interviewing in school settings.

The changing nature of the school system also presents a challenge. Over the years, schools and associated policies have changed and continue to change. New legislation, regulations, and professional ethical guidelines are regularly passed that affect interviewing in school settings. These changes present a challenge to the training and preparation of professionals working in school settings. Swerdlik and French (2000) described a number of these changes that affect training of school psychologists in particular, including changing population trends and increases in diversity, poverty, types of family structures, and children educated in schools with special needs. Because these changes occur throughout a professional's career, it is essential that professionals working in schools continue their education throughout their careers. This education is important to remain current with changes that may affect interviewing and the provision of other services in the school setting and the ethical and legal regulations related to these changes.

The issue of holding more than one professional role should also be considered in a school setting. Interviewers may hold different roles in the school setting, depending on the situation. For example, school psychologists can function as interviewers, consultants, therapists to various individuals, and in-service trainers. They may also work directly for the school or indirectly as a consultant from an outside organization. Because the legal and ethical requirements for each of these roles are different, it is important to be aware of the current helping role and the specific regulations regarding it. Hughes (1986), for example, discusses the differences in ethical obligations when a school psychologist works as an internal versus an external consultant. When working as a school psychologist in a school, the primary ethical obligation is to the child, in comparison to an external consultant, whose primary obligation may be to the hiring administrator, presenting a potentially incompatible combination of responsibilities. Similar ethical and legal requirements arise in other situations; and thus, it is the practitioner's responsibility to be knowledgeable about the requirements of any role undertaken.

Regardless of the position held in the school setting, the interviewer must be clear about the responsibilities and limitations of all parties involved. Jacob and Hartshorne (2003) noted that it is the responsibility of the consultant to clearly define and communicate the roles of parents, students, and school personnel. This principle also applies to interviewing. This information can help to alleviate any anxiety experienced by those involved and clarify the

TABLE 7.2   Examples of Professional Ethical Standards and Legal Regulations Related to School
Interviewing and Consultation

Description	Legal/Ethical Responsibilities
Provide services within areas of competency	NASP-PPE, II, A, #1 APA-ES 2.01
Provide services in a nondiscriminatory and culturally sensitive manner	NASP-PPE, III A, #2 APA-ES 3.01; GP E
Avoid any potential harm to the client	NASP-PPE, I Intro APA-ES 3.04; GP A
Avoid multiple relationships with clients	NASP-PPE, III A, #7 APA-ES 3.05
Refrain when interests may impair judgment or the professional relationship	NASP-PPE, III A, #5 APA-ES 3.06
Provide parents with other applicable resources if a conflict of interest exists	NASP-PPE, III C, #4
Clarify the professional relationship and notify parents before beginning services	NASP-PPE, III, A, #3, C, #2 APA-ES 3.07, 3.11
Work with other professionals in a cooperative and respectful manner	NASP-PPE, III E, #1 APA-ES 3.09
Report suspected child abuse or neglect	Child Protective Services (CPS) (legal requirements vary by state)
Obtain parental consent in writing before beginning an evaluation	IDEA
Ensure that all confidential and privileged information is protected (e.g., student records)	NASP-PPE, III A, #9, C, #6; IV, D, #5 APA-ES 4.01 FERPA Applicable state statutes
Be knowledgeable of the school's guiding philosophy and goals for working with clients	NASP-PPE, IV B, #1, #2
Advocate for and safeguard the dignity and rights of the client	NASP-PPE, III A, #1; IV A, #2 APA, GP E
Respect a parent's choice to object and remember that consent is voluntary	NASP-PPE, III C, #4 IDEA
Clearly explain services to parents	NASP-PPE, III A, #3; III, C, #1
Ensure client understands how information will be used, the purpose for its collection, and limitations to confidentiality	NASP-PPE, III A, #11; III, B, #2 APA-ES, 4.02

NOTE: NASP-PPE = *Principles for Professional Ethics,* by the National Association of School Psychologists (2000); APA-ES = *Ethical Standards of Psychologists,* by the American Psychological Association (2002); APA-GP = "General Principles," by the American Psychological Association (2002); FERPA = Family Educational Rights and Privacy Act of 1974, P.L. 94-142, 20 U.S.C. and 34 C.F.R. § 99; IDEA = Individuals with Disabilities Education Act of 1997, P.L. 105-17, 20 U.S.C. § 1400 *et seq.,* and Individuals with Disabilities Education Improvement Act of 2004, P.L. 108-446.

boundaries of the working relationship. Conoley and Conoley (1982) advocated the use of a verbal or written agreement (e.g., contract) to help with role clarification. A written contract, in particular, can be helpful to use as a reference if questions arise in the future about roles and responsibilities. These contracts, often used in consulting relationships, can include a wide variety of information but often include the following components: (a) general goals and discussion of setting future specific goals, (b) time frame for the consultation relationship, (c) general and specific responsibilities of the consultant, (d) general consultee responsibilities, and (e) the parameters of confidentiality (Gallessich, 1982, as cited in Jacob & Hartshorne, 2003). The contract should be formulated and agreed upon prior to beginning the consulting relationship.

SUMMARY

In this chapter, we provided an overview of how various interview assessment technologies can be used to assess children through parents and teachers in educational and applied settings. We introduced the concept of problem solving and, specifically, problem-solving consultation as a framework for conducting interview assessment technology. One of the major compelling reasons for introducing this model is that it is conceptualized as a series of problem-solving phases along with well-developed interview protocols that an assessor or therapist/consultant can use in implementing the process. In this regard, it is linked to the implementation of prevention and intervention programs in applied settings.

A review of interviews also focused on specific psychometric criteria that need to be invoked when these approaches are used in applied and clinical settings. Most of the standard psychometric characteristics apply to interviews and interview technology. As noted in the chapter, considerable work still needs to be done to develop the foundations for high-quality interviewing around traditional psychometric criteria. Nevertheless, among the more important criteria that might be invoked are those that are referred to as treatment validity or treatment utility of the interview process. Currently, conceptual models that embrace a problem-solving process that extends through the intervention process, including selection, implementation,

and evaluation of the prevention and intervention program, are likely to have the most treatment utility, at least at the conceptual level. Nevertheless, this issue awaits empirical investigation and support in what will likely be the next generation of studies in this area.

Finally, we discussed a variety of challenges that are likely to emerge in the context of conducting interviews within applied settings. Some of these issues are contextual variables that are likely to impact most of the assessment technology applied in developing, implementing, and evaluating interventions. Among the more salient were setting variables, which are related to who is interviewed, including the option of conjoint processes for soliciting information for intervention development and implementation. A number of legal and ethical issues were also highlighted as part of the process of considering this assessment technology in applied settings.

Interviews provide a useful and important technology for developing, implementing, and evaluating interventions in applied settings. The problem-solving consultation framework of Bergan and Kratochwill (1990) provides a technology for this problem-solving process that can be linked to a variety of conceptual frameworks in applied settings.

NOTES

1. The following descriptions are based on Kratochwill and Bergan (1990).

2. Sattler (2001) described these sources of error and strategies for minimizing some of them. See Chapter 4 (Jayne, Bethay, & Gross) and Chapter 6 (Li & Magneson) in this volume, concerning developmental issues and multicultural and diversity issues, respectively.

REFERENCES

American Educational Research Association, American Psychological Association, & National Council on Measurement in Education. (1999). *Standards for educational and psychological testing.* Washington, DC: Author.

American Psychological Association. (2002). *Ethical standards of psychologists.* Washington, DC: American Psychological Association.

Anderson, T. K., Kratochwill, T. R., & Bergan, J. R. (1986). Training teachers in behavioral consultation and therapy: An analysis of verbal behaviors. *Journal of School Psychology, 24,* 229–241.

Athanasiou, M. S., Geil, M., Hazel, C. E., & Copeland, E. P. (2002). A look inside school-based consultation: A qualitative study of the beliefs and practices of school psychologists and teachers. *School Psychology Quarterly, 17,* 258–298.

Barnett, D. W., Lentz, F. E. J., & Macmann, G. (2000). Psychometric qualities of professional practice. In E. S. Shapiro & T. R. Kratochwill (Eds.), *Behavioral assessment in schools: Theory, research, and clinical foundations* (2nd ed., pp. 355–386): Guilford Press.

Beaver, B. R., & Busse, R. T. (2000). Informant reports: Conceptual and research bases of interviews with parents and teachers. In E. S. Shapiro & T. R. Kratochwill (Eds.), *Behavioral assessment in schools: Theory, research, and clinical foundations* (2nd ed., pp. 257–287): Guilford Press.

Beavers, K. F., Kratochwill, T. R., & Braden, J. P. (2004). Treatment utility of functional versus empiric assessment within consultation for reading problems. *School Psychology Quarterly, 19,* 29–49.

Bergan, J. R. (1977). *Behavioral consultation.* Columbus, OH: Charles E. Merrill.

Bergan, J. R., Byrnes, I. M., & Kratochwill, T. R. (1979). Effects of behavioral and medical models of consultation on teacher expectancies and instruction of a hypothetical child. *Journal of School Psychology, 17,* 307–316.

Bergan, J. R., & Kratochwill, T. R. (1990). *Behavioral consultation and therapy.* New York: Plenum Press.

Bergan, J. R., & Neumann, A. J. (1980). The identification of resources and constraints influencing plan design in consultation. *Journal of School Psychology, 18,* 317–323.

Bergan, J. R., & Tombari, M. L. (1975). The analysis of verbal interactions occurring during consultation. *Journal of School Psychology, 13,* 209–226.

Bergan, J. R., & Tombari, M. L. (1976). Consultant skill and efficiency and the implementation and outcomes of consultation. *Journal of School Psychology, 14,* 3–14.

Brown, D. K., Kratochwill, T. R., & Bergan, J. R. (1982). Teaching interview skills for problem identification: An analogue study. *Behavioral Assessment, 4,* 63–73.

Brown, D., Pryzwansky, W. B., & Schulte, A. C. (2001). *Psychological consultation* (5th ed.). Boston: Allyn & Bacon.

Busse, R. T., & Beaver, B. R. (2000). Informant report: Parent and teacher interviews. In E. S. Shapiro & T. R. Kratochwill (Eds.), *Conducting school-based assessments of child and adolescent behavior* (pp. 235–273): Guilford Press.

Busse, R. T., Kratochwill, T. R., & Elliott, S. N. (1999). Influences of verbal interactions during behavioral consultations on treatment outcomes. *Journal of School Psychology, 37,* 117–143.

Campbell, C. (1993). Strategies for reducing parent resistance to consultation in the schools. *Elementary School Guidance & Counseling, 28,* 83–91.

Cone, J. D. (1977). The relevance of reliability and validity for behavioral assessment. *Behavior Therapy, 8,* 411–426.

Cone, J. D. (1978). The behavioral assessment grid (BAC): A conceptual framework and a taxonomy. *Behavior Therapy, 9,* 882–888.

Cone, J. D. (1979). Confounded comparisons in triple response mode assessment research. *Behavioral Assessment, 1,* 85–95.

Conoley, J. C., & Conoley, C. W. (1982). *School consultation: A guide to practice and training.* New York: Pergamon Press.

Cormier, W. H., & Nurius, P. S. (2003). *Interviewing strategies for helpers* (5th ed.). Pacific Grove, CA: Brooks/Cole.

Curtis, M. J., & Watson, K. L. (1980). Changes in consultee problem clarification skills following consultation. *Journal of School Psychology, 18,* 210–221.

Erchul, W. P. (1987). A relational communication analysis of control in school consultation. *Professional School Psychology, 2,* 113–124.

Erchul, W. P., & Chewning, T. G. (1990). Behavioral consultation from a request-centered relational communication perspective. *School Psychology Quarterly, 5,* 1–20.

Erchul, W. P., Covington, C. G., Hughes, J. N., & Meyers, J. (1995). Further explorations of request-centered relational communication within school consultation. *School Psychology Review, 24,* 621–632.

Erchul, W. P., & Martens, B. K. (2002). *School consultation: Conceptual and empirical bases of practice* (2nd ed.). New York: Kluwer Academic/Plenum.

Finn, C. A., & Sladeczek, I. E. (2001). Assessing the social validity of behavioral interventions: A review of treatment acceptability measures. *School Psychology Quarterly, 16,* 176–206.

Fuchs, D., & Fuchs, L. S. (1989). Exploring effective and efficient prereferral interventions: A component analysis of behavioral consultation. *School Psychology Review, 18,* 261–279.

Goldfried, M. R., & Linehan, M. M. (1977). Basic issues in behavioral assessment. In A. Ciminero, K. Calhoun, & H. Adams (Eds.), *Handbook of behavioral assessment* (pp. 15–46). New York: Wiley Interscience.

Gresham, F. M. (1984). Behavioral interviews in school psychology: Issues in psychometric adequacy and research. *School Psychology Review, 13,* 17–25.

Gresham, F. M., & Davis, C. J. (1988). Behavioral interviews with teachers and parents. In E. S. Shapiro & T. R. Kratochwill (Eds.), *Behavioral assessment in schools: Conceptual foundations and practical applications* (pp. 455–493). New York: Guilford Press.

Gutkin, T. B. (1993). Moving from behavioral to ecobehavioral consultation: What's in a name. *Journal of Educational and Psychological Consultation, 4,* 95–99.

Gutkin, T. B., & Conoley, J. C. (1990). Reconceptualizing school psychology from a service delivery perspective: Implications for practice, training, and research. *Journal of School Psychology, 28,* 203–223.

Gutkin, T. B., & Curtis, M. J. (1982). School-based consultation: Theory and techniques. In C. R. Reynolds & T. B. Gutkin (Eds.), *The handbook of school psychology* (pp. 796–828). New York: Wiley.

Gutkin, T. B., & Curtis, M. J. (1999). School-based consultation theory and practice: The art and science of indirect service delivery. In C. R. Reynolds & T. B. Gutkin (Eds.), *The handbook of school psychology* (3rd ed., pp. 598–637). New York: Wiley.

Haynes, S., & Jensen, B. (1979). The interview as a behavioral assessment instrument. *Behavioral Assessment, 1,* 97–106.

Hughes, J. N. (1986). Ethical issues in school consultation. *School Psychology Review, 15,* 489–499.

Hughes, J. N., & DeForest, P. A. (1993). Consultant directiveness and support as predictors of consultation outcomes. *Journal of School Psychology, 31,* 355–373.

Jacob, S., & Hartshorne, T. S. (2003). *Ethics and law for school psychology* (4th ed.). Hoboken, NJ: Wiley.

Johnston, J. M., & Pennypacker, H. S. (1980). *Strategies and tactics of human behavioral research.* Hillsdale, NJ: Lawrence Erlbaum.

Kazdin, A. E. (1981). Acceptability of child treatment techniques: The influence of treatment efficacy and adverse side effects. *Behavior Therapy, 12,* 493–506.

Kazdin, A. E., & Hersen, M. (1980). The current status of behavior therapy. *Behavior Modification, 4,* 283–302.

Kelley, M. L., Heffer, R. W., Gresham, F. M., & Elliott, S. N. (1989). Development of a modified Treatment Evaluation Inventory. *Journal of Psychopathology & Behavioral Assessment, 11,* 235–247.

Kratochwill, T. R., & Bergan, J. R. (1990). *Behavioral consultation in applied settings: An individual guide.* New York: Plenum Press.

Kratochwill, T. R., Elliott, S. N., & Busse, R. T. (1995). Behavior consultation: A five-year evaluation of consultant and client outcomes. *School Psychology Quarterly, 10,* 87–117.

Kratochwill, T. R., Elliott, S. N., & Stoiber, K. C. (2002). Best practices in school-based problem-solving consultation. In A. Thomas & J. Grimes (Eds.), *Best practices in school psychology* (4th ed., Vol. 1, pp. 583–608). Bethesda, MD: National Association of School Psychologists.

Kratochwill, T. R., & Pittman, P. H. (2002). Expanding problem-solving consultation training: Prospects and frameworks. *Journal of Educational and Psychological Consultation, 13,* 69–95.

Kratochwill, T. R., VanSomeren, K. R., & Sheridan, S. M. (1989). Training behavioral consultants: A competency-based model to teach interview skills. *Professional School Psychology, 4,* 41–58.

Lentz, F. E. J., & Wehmann, B. A. (1995). Interviewing. In A. Thomas & J. Grimes (Eds.), *Best practices in school psychology* (3rd ed., pp. 637–650). Washington, DC: National Association of School Psychologists.

Lepage, K., Kratochwill, T. R., & Elliott, S. N. (2004). Competency-based behavior consultation training: An evaluation of consultant outcomes, treatment effects, and consumer satisfaction. *School Psychology Quarterly, 19,* 1–28.

Linehan, M. M. (1980). Content validity: Its relevance to behavioral assessment. *Behavioral Assessment, 2,* 147–159.

Martens, B. K., Erchul, W. P., & Witt, J. C. (1992). Quantifying verbal interactions in school-based consultation: A comparison of four coding schemes. *School Psychology Review, 21,* 109–124.

Martens, B. K., Lewandowski, L. J., & Houk, J. L. (1989). The effects of entry information on the consultation process. *School Psychology Review, 18,* 225–234.

McDougall, L. M., Reschly, D. J., & Corkery, J. M. (1988). Changes in referral interviews with teachers after behavioral consultation training. *Journal of School Psychology, 26,* 225–232.

Medway, F. J., & Updyke, J. F. (1985). Meta-analysis of consultation outcome studies. *American Journal of Community Psychology, 13,* 489–505.

Messick, S. (1989). Validity. In R. L. Linn (Ed.), *Educational measurement* (3rd ed., pp. 13–103). New York: American Council on Education, and Macmillan.

Messick, S. E. T. S. (1995). Validity of psychological assessment: Validation of inferences from persons' responses and performances as scientific inquiry into score meaning. *American Psychologist, 50,* 741–749.

National Association of School Psychologists. (2000). Principles for professional ethics. *School Psychology Review, 29,* 621–630.

Nelson, R. O. (1983). Behavioral assessment: Past, present, and future. *Behavioral Assessment, 5,* 195–206.

Noell, G. H., Witt, J. C., Slider, N. J., Connell, J. E., Gatti, S. L., Williams, K. L., et al. (2005). Treatment implementation following behavioral consultation in schools: A Comparison of three follow-up strategies. *School Psychology Review, 34,* 87–106.

Peterson, L., Homer, A. L., & Wonderlich, S. A. (1982). The integrity of independent variables in behavior analysis. *Journal of Applied Behavior Analysis, 15,* 477–492.

Reynolds, C. R., & Kamphaus, R. W. (2004). *Behavior assessment system for children* (2nd ed.). Circle Pines, MN: American Guidance Service.

Sattler, J. M. (2001). *Assessment of children: Cognitive applications.* San Diego, CA: Author.

Schwartz, I. S., & Baer, D. M. (1991). Social validity assessments: Is current practice state of the art? *Journal of Applied Behavior Analysis, 24,* 189–204.

Scott, W. A. (1955). Reliability of content analysis: The case of nominal scale coding. *Public Opinion Quarterly, 19,* 321–325.

Shapiro, E. S. (1999). *Academic skills problems: Direct assessment and intervention* (2nd ed.). New York: Guilford Press.

Sheridan, S. M., Eagle, J. W., Cowan, R. J., & Mickelson, W. (2001). The effects of conjoint behavioral consultation results of a 4-year investigation. *Journal of School Psychology, 39,* 361–385.

Sheridan, S. M., Erchul, W. P., Brown, M. S., Dowd, S. E., Warnes, E. D., & Marti, D. C. (2004). Perceptions of helpfulness in conjoint behavioral consultation: Congruence and agreement between teachers and parents. *School Psychology Quarterly, 19,* 121–140.

Sheridan, S. M., & Kratochwill, T. R. (1992). Behavioral parent-teacher consultation: Conceptual and research considerations. *Journal of School Psychology, 30,* 117–139.

Sheridan, S. M., Welch, M., & Orme, S. F. (1996). Is consultation effective? A review of outcome research. *Remedial and Special Education, 17,* 341–354.

Swerdlik, M., & French, J. (2000). School psychology training for the 21st century: Challenges and opportunities. *School Psychology Review, 39,* 361–385.

Tombari, M. L., & Bergan, J. R. (1978). Consultant cues and teacher verbalizations, judgments, and expectancies concerning children's adjustment problems. *Journal of School Psychology, 16,* 212–219.

Watson, T. S., Sterling, H. E., & McDade, A. (1997). Demythifying behavioral consultation. *School Psychology Review, 26,* 467–474.

Witt, J. C. (1990). Face-to-face verbal interaction in school-based consultation: A review of the literature. *School Psychology Quarterly, 5,* 199–210.

Witt, J. C., & Elliott, S. N. (1983). Assessment in behavioral consultation: The initial interview. *School Psychology Review, 12,* 42–49.

Witt, J. C., Erchul, W. P., McKee, W. T., Pardue, M. M., & Wickstrom, K. F. (1991). Conversational control in school-based consultation: The relationship between consultant and consultee topic determination and consultation outcome. *Journal of Educational and Psychological Consultation, 2,* 101–116.

Wolf, M. M. (1978). Social validity: The case for subjective measurement or how applied behavior analysis is finding its heart. *Journal of Applied Behavior Analysis, 11,* 203–214.

8

SELECTING TREATMENT TARGETS AND REFERRALS

JOSE M. SOLER-BAILLO AND BRIAN P. MARX

The methods by which a clinician selects the behavior(s) that are targeted for a client's treatment are a critical part of the assessment process. How well a psychologist operationalizes, identifies, and prioritizes a client's problems can ultimately determine whether or not an intervention proves successful. This process, however, is a complex one that, unfortunately, is often overlooked, simplified, or deemphasized by both clinicians and researchers. How treatment targets are selected has traditionally been an idiographic process that is usually based on the clinician's expertise, intuition, and theoretical orientation, as well as the client's presenting problem(s). Although it is difficult to argue against an individualized approach to identifying a client's problems, this tradition has made the process of selecting treatment targets one that is fraught with variability and bias. Furthermore, clinicians seeking guidance from the assessment literatures are unlikely to find a consensus on what the best strategies are to define, select, and assess treatment targets for most clinical syndromes as they are currently conceptualized.

This chapter explores the methods associated with the selection of treatment targets in psychological assessment. The first section examines traditional and behavioral approaches to selecting treatment targets. This is followed by an exploration of the theoretical and conceptual issues that are important for clinicians to consider when attempting to define and identify the most important targets for intervention. Specific issues pertaining to the complexities of child and adolescent assessment are addressed in the next section. Finally, we discuss the referral issues that arise when identified treatment targets fall outside the scope of the clinician's expertise.

MODELS FOR SELECTING TREATMENT TARGETS

When determining which behaviors to target in treatment, it is necessary to have a strong theoretical foundation that informs the clinical decision process. Selecting treatment targets can be a daunting process for clinicians, and not having an organized approach can lead clinicians to make poor decisions at this critical stage of clinical intervention. The models described subsequently help provide an organized framework for the identification and assessment of clinically relevant target behaviors. Although these models are not mutually exclusive, they are discussed separately to highlight the relative strengths and weaknesses of each approach.

The Traditional (Classification) Model

Traditional diagnostic and classification models assume that individuals can be categorized on the basis of symptoms that are shared with others who also exhibit those features. Because the underlying mechanisms that lead to pathology are presumed to be shared across individuals in a given diagnostic category, treatment targets are often selected on the basis of diagnosis rather than a specific individual complaint (Kanfer, 1985). Thus, a clinical assessment based on this model will focus on identifying the behaviors that will lead to a differential diagnosis. The strength of using classification systems such as the *Diagnostic and Statistical Manual of Mental Disorders, Fourth Edition (DSM-IV)* (American Psychiatric Association, 1994) is that interventions that target symptom clusters that commonly occur together are implied. The strong heuristic value of these systems further facilitates the development of assessment tools (e.g., Diagnostic Interview Schedule for Children) and interventions that can be studied empirically and readily disseminated.

The *DSM,* however, fails to adequately explain the high co-occurrence of what are considered to be different response classes. It has been well established that anxiety and depression often co-occur in the same individual (e.g., Klein, Dougherty, & Olino, 2005), as do attention-deficit/hyperactivity disorder (ADHD) and disorders related to aggression (e.g., Pelham, Fabiano, & Massetti, 2005). The heterogeneity of commonly occurring problems is traditionally explained in terms of comorbidity, but this explanation has received considerable dispute (e.g., Beutler & Malik, 2002). Achenbach (2005) argued that the boundaries between different childhood disorders have not been well validated empirically. He noted that common diagnostic assessment practices fail to accurately determine whether a child's behavior problems may reflect two or more separate disorders or whether they are broad and nonspecific behaviors common to many disorders. Given these arguments, the *DSM* can be criticized for being limited in its ability to help define treatment targets for individuals that experience unique combinations of symptoms or for those that do not fall neatly into any diagnostic category.

The Functional-Analytic (Behavioral) Model

Behavioral assessment focuses on identifying the causal variables and causal relations that affect clients' behavior (e.g., Haynes, Nelson, Thacher, & Keaweaimoku, 2002). *Causal variables* refers to the factors (i.e., antecedents) that affect or change some aspect of a subsequent behavior of interest, while *causal relations* refers to the form, strength, magnitude, and direction of the change that occurs when Variable a affects Variable b. Traditionally, behavioral assessment has defined treatment targets in terms of their causal relation to the problem behavior. The complexity of human behavior, however, dictates that for any given behavior problem, there are likely to be multiple causal variables that change the form, strength, magnitude, and direction of the problem behavior in a number of ways. Identifying the causal variables that lead to the greatest desired change in the problem behavior is the most important challenge in behavioral assessment.

Although many heuristics have been developed to determine the causal variables that would make the most effective treatment targets, Haynes and colleagues (Haynes et al., 2002; Haynes & O'Brien, 1990;) emphasized a functional-analytic approach to target selection. The term *functional analysis* refers to an idiographic approach to behavioral assessment and has been defined as "the identification of important, controllable, causal functional relationships applicable to a specified set of target behaviors for an individual client" (Haynes & O'Brien, 1990, p. 656). Haynes and colleagues have suggested that this approach should focus on identifying causal variables that are important (that account for a large and clinically significant amount of variance in the problem behavior), contemporaneous (i.e., currently related to the problem behavior), and modifiable (can be changed). Selecting targets that have a causal but small or clinically insignificant relationship with the problem behavior may not be cost-effective and would yield only small gains, if any. Selecting target variables that are historically but not currently related to the problem behavior may also be clinically inappropriate. For example, peer influences may be historically related to the onset of an individual's smoking habit but may be unrelated to the contingencies that maintain his or her current addiction. Some variables may have strong causal relations to the behavior problem but are generally unmodifiable (e.g., family income, traumatic past experiences, genetics). The functional-analytic approach has been lauded for helping to create individualized treatment plans that can be assessed and modified over the course of treatment. Some critics have argued, however, that this approach is not cost-effective and can be overly complex. Nevertheless, this approach is most closely associated with the concept of selecting treatment targets, and, as such, we will subsequently focus on it here.

The Behavioral Interview

A multifaceted interview is a critical source of information in the child clinical assessment process for determining relevant causal variables for the behavior of interest. While there are many interview formats and strategies available to the clinician (e.g., diagnostic vs. functional analytic, structured vs. unstructured), one of the initial decisions a clinician will make is the extent to which they involve the child in the interview process. This decision will usually be made on the basis of the developmental capabilities of the child and the extent to which he or she is able to communicate about the problem. Regardless of developmental level, the child can provide a unique and important perspective, and at least some time should be spent in creating an environment in which he or she is an active participant. This may not only contribute valuable information to the assessment but also help establish rapport for the treatment phase.

Whether or not the child is an active participant, there are several goals that should be accomplished over the course of the interview. First and foremost, the interview should lead to a broad understanding of the client's overall functioning. This includes assessing the overall intensity, frequency, and severity of the problem and developing a list of the client's goals for treatment. An assessment of the child's academic, social, family, and medical functioning will help determine the areas of greatest impairment and may determine which problems require primary attention. The client's presenting complaint will not always be the primary focus of treatment if it is determined that other problems or concerns take priority. A child presenting to the clinic for bed-wetting, for example, should have that issue placed on hold if it is determined that he or she is also being physically abused in the home.

A second goal of the behavioral interview is to begin the process of identifying and defining the behaviors that may be related to the client's problem. Though the selection of target behaviors is a dynamic process that extends into the treatment phase, the clinician should leave the interview with an understanding of the behaviors, cognitions, affects, and interpersonal relationships that are associated with the client's problem. Questions such as "What does the child do when he feels anxious?" "What is he afraid might happen?" and "How do you respond when he demonstrates this anxiety?" will lead not only to a greater understanding of the problem but also to a framework of possible intervention strategies.

A good behavioral interview should also gather information regarding the conditions and situations under which the problem is likely and unlikely to be observed. Behavior is contextual, and clients' problems are more or less likely to occur at certain times of the day, in certain environments, and in the presence of certain individuals.

IMPORTANT CONSIDERATIONS IN THE TARGET SELECTION PROCESS

It is important to keep in mind additional guidelines for determining which behaviors to target in treatment (Mash & Terdal, 1981). For example, behaviors that are dangerous to the child or others (e.g., suicidality, pyromania) should be the primary focus of any clinical intervention. Targeting behaviors that tend to be reinforced by the child's natural environment, such as increasing prosocial behaviors, has also been thought to improve clinical outcome and maintain therapeutic gains. In addition, including treatment targets that are desirable and healthy can help keep clients from being overly pathologized and help children focus on what they can do in certain situations, not only on what they should not do. In treating children, there should also be an emphasis on selecting behaviors that are necessary for maximizing a normal course of development. Language and cognitive development, as well as motor skills and proper school behavior, are considered necessary not just to improve the child's overall functioning, but are also fundamental in the hierarchy of development. A child with poor language skills, for example, is unlikely to learn appropriate verbal responses to perceived threats in his or her social environment. Ignoring these essential elements of development is likely to lead to subsequent behavioral impairment. An emphasis has also been placed on targeting behaviors that improve the child's flexibility in adapting to subsequent foci in treatment. In treating children with anxiety, for example, coping skills are often taught prior to the implementation of exposures in order to maximize the effectiveness of the exposures and to encourage the children to remain in the feared situation long enough for habituation to occur (e.g., Kendall, 1994). Another common conceptual strategy for selecting treatment targets focuses on choosing behaviors that are likely to change existing contingency systems in the child's environment. Children's problem behaviors may be part of a vicious cycle fueled by maladaptive response chains in the child's social environment. Parents and teachers may have learned to respond to the child in ways that increase the likelihood of the problem behavior occurring. Selecting behaviors in children that are likely to break that cycle are thought to contribute to long-term treatment gains.

The preceding list of conceptual criteria developed to aid in the selection of treatment targets focuses on behaviors specific to the child, but arguments can be made that effective treatment programs should also focus on modifying behaviors related to the child's social context. Some theorists have argued that intervening at a social rather than an individual level may be a more effective approach for improving child treatment outcome (e.g., Barrett, 2000). An important likely target of environmental change is the child's familial relationships. Parental psychopathology, for example, has been shown to be a poor prognostic indicator of treatment success in children with anxiety disorders (Berman, Weems, Silverman, & Kurtines, 2000), and addressing parents' psychopathology in the context of the child's behavior may lead to increased therapeutic gains. Some research has shown that including parents as active participants in the treatment of children with externalizing disorders can help improve outcome (Woolfenden, Williams, & Peat, 2002), though similar studies with children with internalizing disorders have been less conclusive (Barmish & Kendall, 2005). While research on the effects of active parent

participation in treatment is ongoing, addressing the modifiable environmental and social factors that influence child behavior is a necessary step in developing effective intervention strategies.

Although the explicit guidelines presented here can be of utility to clinicians, empirical evidence supporting which targets may have greatest clinical impact for certain types of behavior problems is not always specified. Additional research is necessary to determine which behavioral targets are necessary to successful treatment outcome and which ones might be counterindicative or superfluous when treating certain problem behaviors. In addition, it is necessary to have an organized approach that informs the treatment target selection process. The following section discusses some of the more commonly cited models of assessing and selecting the behaviors that are to be the focus of clinical intervention.

OPERATIONALIZING TARGET BEHAVIORS

Most target behaviors (e.g., aggression, anxiety, self-esteem) can be operationalized in countless ways and countless situations. Thus, for the purposes of effective treatment, the target behaviors and the contexts in which they occur need to be defined precisely and consistently across all assessors. The strategies and issues associated with operationalizing treatment targets are further discussed in the following sections.

Determination of Targeted Behaviors

Defining the behavior of interest is at the core of the assessment process. This process, as important as it may be, is often considered mere fodder for undergraduate research methods courses and is rarely examined in scientific, peer-reviewed journals. The ways in which psychologists operationalize behaviors vary by the complexity of the behavior in question. Broader, more complex behavioral constructs (e.g., openness, self-esteem) can be defined in countless ways, while narrower, more specific behaviors (e.g., purging) often have a smaller range of possible operationalizations. Sturmey (1996) noted that even problem behaviors that are ostensibly simple, such as nocturnal enuresis, can be operationalized and measured a number of different ways. He offered these options, each potentially being valid under different circumstances:

- Number of bed wets per night

- Number of nights during which an accident occurs

- Time lapsed between wetting incidents

- Size of wet patch

- Number of dry nights

- Number of times that correct voiding occurs

- Weight of wet linens

- Amount of fluid a child can drink prior to sleeping, without voiding

While we will not discuss the validity of these possible operationalizations here, this example demonstrates that even simple behaviors can be operationalized and measured a number of different ways, and it is important for psychologists to determine the most appropriate ways to define and measure a client's behavior. For example, a client a may present with depression that is marked by symptoms of anhedonia but shows few markers of sadness or low mood. The targeted behaviors in this case should be operationalized using measures that are sensitive to the expression of positive emotion (e.g., observed laughter) rather than those that may be less relevant to the client's complaint (e.g., crying spells). Because these two independent behaviors (anhedonia and sadness) frequently co-occur, however, clinicians may be tempted to operationalize this particular client's difficulties in ways that are not meaningful.

The Context in Which Behaviors Are Assessed

Central to the issue of how behaviors are operationalized is the context or situation in which behaviors are assessed. Problem behaviors occur in a variety of different situations and often operate under different contingencies in different environments. Aggressive behavior, for example, can be operationalized many different ways (e.g., arguing, hitting, bragging, bullying, throwing things) and can be assessed in a number of different contexts (e.g., home, school, and therapy environments), by a number of different raters (e.g., child, peers, parents, teachers, clinician), and through different modalities (e.g., naturalistic observation, rating scales, self-report). The

"best" way to operationalize aggression and the proper methods to assess these behaviors remain highly idiographic decisions that are often based on clinical judgment. It is critically important, however, that the defined target behaviors, along with the setting in which they are assessed and the methods by which they are observed, relate directly to the client's presenting problem. For example, for a child who presents to treatment for exhibiting relational but nonphysical aggression toward peers, targets that reflect the relational nature of his or her aggression should be assessed (e.g., teasing, arguing, bullying). In addition, these behaviors should be assessed in particular situations (e.g., school) to the extent that they are problematic in these contexts and by raters who have greater knowledge of and access to these behaviors (e.g., teachers). In this example, the parents' report of the child's aggression at home may provide an inaccurate, incomplete, or irrelevant depiction of the nature of the problem. Also, certain assessment procedures, such as behavioral role plays in the clinic, may not accurately represent the true nature of the clinical problem as it plays out in the real world (Kazdin, 1985).

When operationalizing potential targets for treatment, it is important to consider assessing multiple channels of behavior that are associated with the presenting problem. For example, anxiety is traditionally thought of as being characterized by behavioral avoidance, self-reported distress in the presence of the feared stimulus, maladaptive cognitions, and physiological arousal (Barlow, 2002). Any one of these measurement channels may represent certain aspects of the behavior of interest, but no individual channel may accurately reflect the full scope of the problem (monomethod bias). For these reasons, assessing multiple channels of behavior can be useful in providing both overlapping and unique information about the nature of the problem. There are caveats, however, to using a multiple-channel approach to assess a client's problem. First, the relations among these channels are likely to vary between individuals who present with similar problems. Some children, for example, may show behavioral manifestations of separation anxiety (e.g., clinginess, refusing school) without reporting distress (Jensen, 1999). These two assessment channels, therefore, may not be correlated. In addition, for the same child, certain environments and situations are likely to lead to different effects on the expression of certain classes of behavior. The same child with separation anxiety may be more likely to verbally express distress in the absence of his or her parents than in their presence. These different contexts (parents present or not present), therefore, will have systematic effects on separate behavioral channels. For these reasons, caution needs to be used when integrating information gathered through different behavioral channels.

Using Multiple Informants in Child Assessment

Identifying the problems to target in child assessment is a collaborative process that typically involves gathering information from at least two sources: children and parents. Making matters even more complicated is that when necessary, teacher report is also frequently obtained. One of the important challenges that clinicians face is how to integrate information acquired from these multiple sources. High agreement between informants may increase the clinician's confidence in deciding which behaviors to target in treatment. If these informants do not agree, however, clinicians are faced with the dilemma of having to decide whose report is more or less valid. Because parents usually make the referrals and because they typically decide whether or how long to keep children in treatment, many clinicians might choose to rely exclusively or more heavily on their reports of the problem than the children's (Adelman, Kaser-Boyd, & Taylor, 1984). In addition, as a result of developmental limitations, children may have limited insight into the nature of the problem or may not have the ability to verbally express themselves (Shirk & Saiz, 1992). Some clinicians, on the other hand, may choose to give greater weight to the child's report of the clinical problem. This may be truer when the clinical problem appears to be more systemic or when the behaviors that adults bring to the equation are thought to be more problematic. Clinicians may also want to increase children's motivation to remain involved in treatment by addressing the behaviors that they perceive to be a problem (Hawley & Weisz, 2003). A third option may be for clinicians to create a more collaborative therapeutic environment by selecting targets that both parents and children agree to be problematic. This may ensure that both parents and children remain motivated to participate in treatment.

This approach, however, may not be plausible when children and parents have goals that are not compatible.

The issue of how to integrate information gathered from multiple sources has come under close scrutiny in light of recent evidence that has shown high rates of disagreement between children's and parents' reports in clinical assessment (De Los Reyes & Kazdin, 2005; Hawley & Weisz, 2003; Yeh & Weisz, 2001). Yeh & Weisz (2001) found that at the onset of treatment, as many as 63% of parent-child dyads failed to agree on even one identified problem behavior, and an additional 25% agreed on only one behavior they felt was an issue. Even when expanding the definition of a successful match from specific behaviors (e.g., stealing) to broader categories (e.g., delinquent behavior), agreement remained low, with 34% failing to match on any categories and 45% agreeing on only one. Extending this work, Hawley and Weisz (2003) compared the extent to which parents, children, and therapists agreed on specific problem behaviors and found that as many as 76% of these triads failed to agree on even a single target problem. They also examined the behaviors that parents and children identified as a problem and found that parents were more likely to endorse targets that were internal to the child (e.g., anxious/depressed), while children were more likely to identify family and environmental problems (e.g., divorce, abuse). These findings highlight the dilemma that therapists face in trying to plan treatment strategies in the face of such widespread disagreement between informants. Unfortunately, however, these descriptive studies provide little insight as to the reasons why disagreement occurs and no guidance on how therapists should proceed with target selection when disagreement occurs.

The only framework developed so far to help explain the high disagreement between informants is the attribution bias context (ABC) model developed by De Los Reyes and Kazdin (2005). Borrowing from sociocognitive theories, the ABC model proposes that informants bring systematic biases into the clinical assessment process that frequently lead to divergent views regarding the causes of problem behavior. Drawing from research on the actor-observer phenomenon, De Los Reyes and Kazdin posited that in assessing children's behavior, observers (parent, teacher, therapist) will be more likely to attribute problem behaviors to the child's disposition, while the child (actor) will be more likely to attribute problems to contextual and situational variables. For example, a child referred to treatment for aggression problems may attribute the causes of his or her behavior to constant teasing received in school (i.e., for self-protection), while parents and teachers may attribute this behavior to an aggressive temperament. Given these attribution biases, children and observers are more likely to draw information from memory that is consistent with their perspectives. In addition, the ABC model also posits that the goals of the clinical assessment process, which are mainly to assess negative aspects of the child's behavior that may require treatment, activate these biases and exacerbate the discrepancies in informants' reports. Following from this model, the authors recommended that because informants are discrepant in the extent to which they attribute problems to dispositional or environmental variables, clinicians need to make a concerted effort to balance the types of questions such that both dispositional and contextual/environmental factors are considered. In addition, the authors cautioned that no single report should be used as the "gold standard" by which to measure a child's behavior problems. Relying too heavily on either children's or parents'/teachers' reports when selecting treatment targets may lead to an under- or overidentification of certain problems that could lead to treatment failure.

KAZDIN'S VALIDATIONAL ASSESSMENT MODEL

The difficulty with defining and operationalizing target behaviors has been further addressed by Kazdin (1985) using what he called a *validational assessment model*. Adopting principles from psychometric theory, Kazdin emphasized the need for researchers to find empirical relationships between selected target behaviors and current and future functioning. Specifically highlighted were the relevance of concurrent validity (the correlation between a measure and other measures of a related construct, such as current psychological functioning, which are assessed at the same time) and predictive validity (association between a measure and a related construct assessed at a future point in time). Kazdin (1985) identified three types of concurrent validity that should be addressed by the

assessment process. First, selected target behaviors should correlate with other measures of the client's clinical problem. A child diagnosed with ADHD, for example, may be determined to have social skills deficits (e.g., poor eye contact, aggressiveness) that contribute to or are associated with the problem. It is important, however, that these targeted social skills correlate with other measures of the client's social complaints, which might include parent and teacher evaluations along with behavioral observations. It is also important to determine whether these target behaviors correlate with other aspects of the clinical syndrome, which in ADHD may include impulsivity, inattention, and hyperactivity. Perhaps more important, selected treatment targets should be associated with more global measures of everyday functioning. In ADHD children, these more commonly include family functioning, peer relationships, and academic functioning (e.g., Angold, Costello, Farmer, Burns, & Erkanli, 1999; Pelham et al., 2005). Treatment targets that are weakly related to or unassociated with functional impairment are also unlikely to be associated with clinically significant improvements.

Finding a relationship between treatment targets and other measures of related constructs or functional impairment, however, is insufficient. It must also be demonstrated that a change in the targeted behavior leads to a desired change in the related measures. An intervention designed to increase eye contact in ADHD children, for example, needs to demonstrate that a change in this behavior is also related to a desired change in related behaviors, such as attention and compliance with parents. Although these behaviors might correlate during an initial assessment, it is possible that a change in one might not lead to concurrent changes in the other, more clinically meaningful behavior (recent evidence, however, suggests that in this example, it does; Kapalka, 2004). There is no evidence, however, to suggest that improved eye contact in ADHD children might lead to changes in other important areas of functioning, such as impulsivity and aggression toward peers. This behavior, while perhaps a justifiable target for certain ADHD-related impairments, might be limited in its scope to treat a wider constellation of behaviors. It is important, then, to have clear empirical support for the breadth and scope of functional changes that might be expected given a change in a certain behavioral target.

While demonstrating that behavioral targets show that concurrent validity to other related behaviors is a necessary endeavor, it is also important that the targets demonstrate predictive validity with respect to future outcomes. That is, changes in identified targets need to predict long-term gains. It is frequently the case that changes in targeted behaviors might be functionally related to therapeutic improvement during the course of treatment, but these same changes may not be related to the maintenance and stability of long-term improvement. For example, weight gain might be a targeted behavior during the course of therapy with an eating-disordered adolescent. This change, while perhaps necessary to ensure the client's safety, may not in itself be predictive of therapeutic success. A more effective target might be the underlying maladaptive cognitions regarding body shape and weight (Fairburn, Marcus, & Wilson, 1993). In this case, both weight gain and maladaptive cognitions might be appropriate treatment targets over the course of treatment, but while weight gain may demonstrate concurrent validity with other important measures of functioning, addressing the maladaptive cognitions may be more predictive of long-term therapeutic improvement.

REFERRALS

The process of making referral decisions, including knowing the boundaries of one's expertise, managing client transfers, deciding when and how to terminate, and considering the legal and ethical parameters of these decisions, can pose a unique challenge to clinicians. Clinicians are regularly faced with making important referral decisions without strong empirical or theoretical support. Complicating this endeavor, established guidelines created to aid this process (e.g., the American Psychological Association's [APA] *Ethical Principles of Psychologists and Code of Conduct,* 2002) can at times be vague or inadequately defined. Nonetheless, an understanding and implementation of effective referral practices is a necessary facet of professional clinical practice.

Recognizing the Need for Referral

Clinicians who work with children and their families know very well of the need to establish extensive referral networks. At a basic level, clinicians will regularly be presented with children who exhibit complex behavioral, social, family, academic, and medical problems that may extend well beyond the limits of their expertise. As a result, child clinical psychologists should understand the boundaries of their competence as well as the scope of practice of other professionals, who may be more qualified referrals or may be an integral part of a multidisciplinary effort to treat the problem. These professionals may include other psychologists, psychiatrists and physicians, occupational therapists, legal advocates, social workers, and speech and language therapists, who may each contribute unique professional expertise that may contribute to the overall improvement of the client's functioning.

Perhaps the first step in successfully managing referrals is for clinicians to clearly define the boundaries of their own competence. These boundaries should be determined "based on education, training, supervised experience, consultation, study, or professional experience" (APA, 2002, p. 1063). Clients who present with problems or display characteristics (e.g., age, multicultural) that fall outside the clinician's scope of competence should be referred to professionals who are more qualified to treat the client. In many cases, clinicians may feel competent to work with some aspects of the clients' presenting problems, but not others. In these situations, clinicians should clearly specify as early as possible the problems that will be addressed in treatment as well as those that may be more adequately treated by other professionals. A psychologist, for example, may feel competent addressing some of the behavioral difficulties associated with autism but may not have the expertise to effectively address some of the language and sensory concerns frequently associated with the disorder. Being clear about the limits of treatment will help the client understand what he or she should and should not expect out of treatment and will help the client take the necessary steps to address other aspects of the child's functioning, which in this case might include making referrals to a speech and/or occupational therapist.

Although the need for developing referral networks is clearly important, there are few established guidelines with respects to the most ethical and effective ways to address the referral of clients. The APA's most recent ethics code does not give explicit guidance on the criteria that should be used in determining how and to whom clients should be referred. The 2002 version of the code removed vague language from the previous version that stated that "psychologists arrange for appropriate consultation and referrals based principally on the best interest of their patients (APA, 1992, p. 1602), but it does not offer more explicit guidelines. As a result, clinicians may be left unsure of the most effective way to handle client referrals or how the best interests of the client might be defined. Wood and Wood (1990) have suggested that clients should be referred to other service providers on the basis of professional competency, which should include the experience and reputation of the professional. Other factors that are important to consider are cultural characteristics and competencies (e.g., bilingual) that may make a possible referral source uniquely qualified to treat the client. Although the extent to which psychologists should assess the competency of referral sources is also not explicitly stated in the APA ethics code, psychologists should make efforts to know the background of the professionals in their referral network as well as the problems that they may be uniquely qualified to treat.

In situations in which a client is being treated by multiple professionals, it becomes necessary for each member of the team, whether it is defined as a team or not, to clearly establish his or her role in the treatment effort. Failing to do so can create confusion for the client, or even between the professionals, about the expectations, goals, and boundaries of treatment. It is also important for the providers working on the case to establish a responsible line of communication to aid the progress of treatment. This is reflected in Standard 3.09 of the ethics code, which states, "When indicated and professionally appropriate, psychologists cooperate with other professionals in order to serve their clients/ patients effectively and appropriately" (APA, 2002, p. 1065). This standard should not be treated perfunctorily, as open cooperation between professionals working on a case can help ensure that goals developed are complementary and consistent with each other. In addition, professionals such as teachers, social workers, and school advocates can be valuable assets in the implementation of behavioral change programs that psychologists implement, and they should be actively involved when appropriate.

In cases in which multiple professionals may be enlisted to treat a client, it is usually beneficial for the referring clinician to serve as case manager, whose role it is to coordinate the treatment effort between the different providers and to facilitate communication between them. A case manager typically takes the lead on the case and can provide a central figure who is accountable for the outcome of the treatment and to whom the client can address any significant concerns about the treatment.

Accepting Referrals

In deciding to accept referrals, there are a number of important considerations for clinicians to make. Initially, one must decide whether the case has the potential of being appropriate given the clinician's expertise. While oftentimes this will not be clear until a full assessment is completed, an initial phone screen or conversation will reveal that the clinician may not be a good fit given the client's goals or characteristics.

It is also important very early on for there to be a clear understanding between all parties involved of who the client is. In cases in which the referral originates from an outside agency (e.g., the court system), clinicians need to ensure that all parties are aware of who the defined client is, and, in addition, the limits to confidentiality that may exist. If a court orders an evaluation, for example, clients need to be made aware that the information provided will be shared with the court.

SUMMARY

This chapter reviews and discusses two of the more important decisions that clinicians face over the course of treatment with children and adolescents: how to determine which behaviors to target in treatment and what the best strategies are for making referral decisions. While both areas are critically important endeavors of clinical psychologists, they are also relatively understudied compared with other tasks psychologists perform.

In the discussion of treatment target selection, we described the primary strategies that clinicians have at their disposal, including both nomothetic and idiographic approaches. We also emphasized the importance of reliably and objectively defining the behaviors of interest and highlighted the unique challenges of selecting treatment targets in child and adolescent populations—most notably, the importance, and the caveats, of incorporating multiple raters in the assessment process. Ultimately, an effective clinical assessment should consider the history of the client's problem, the context in which the problem behaviors do and do not occur, the contingencies that cause and maintain the behaviors, and the dynamic nature of client's problems. Furthermore, this chapter should be used only as a general guide to aid the treatment target selection process. To select effective targets of intervention for specific behavior problems or disorders, knowledge of the available empirical data is an indispensable asset to any clinician and should be used to inform the process.

Once the client's problem has been identified, psychologists may be faced with important legal, ethical, and moral decisions regarding referral decisions that may need to be made. Unfortunately, well-defined and specific guidelines on adopting effective referral practices in psychotherapy remain elusive. To date, psychologists are most often left to rely on their intuition when making decisions such as to whom to refer a case, what this process should entail, what the role should be of each therapist involved in the case, and who should have primary responsibility for the case. Despite the lack of guidance from the field, therapists need to be aware of the ethical, legal, moral, and practical issues that are involved with the referral process. Clinicians should understand the limits of their expertise and develop strong referral networks to ensure that clients are being served by the individuals that may be most likely to help them.

References

Achenbach, T. M. (2005). Advancing assessment of children and adolescents: Commentary on evidence-based assessment of child and adolescent disorders. *Journal of Clinical Child and Adolescent Psychology, 34,* 541–547.

Adelman, H. S., Kaser-Boyd, N., & Taylor, L. (1984). Children's participation in consent for psychotherapy and their subsequent response to treatment. *Journal of Clinical Child Psychology, 13,* 170–178.

American Psychiatric Association. (1994). *Diagnostic and statistical manual of mental disorders* (4th ed.). Washington, DC: Author.

American Psychological Association. (1992). Ethical principles of psychologists and code of conduct. *American Psychologist, 47,* 1597–1611.

American Psychological Association. (2002). Ethical principles of psychologists and code of conduct. *American Psychologist, 57,* 1060–1073.

Angold, A., Costello, E. J., Farmer, E. M. Z., Burns, B. J., & Erkanli, A. (1999). Impaired but undiagnosed. *Journal of the American Academy of Child & Adolescent Psychiatry, 38,* 39–48.

Barlow, D. H. (2002). *Anxiety and its disorders: The nature and treatment of anxiety and panic* (2nd ed.). New York: Guilford Press.

Barmish, A. J., & Kendall, P. C. (2005). Should parents be co-clients in cognitive-behavioral therapy for anxious youth? *Journal of Clinical Child and Adolescent Abnormal Psychology, 34,* 569–581.

Barrett, P. M. (2000). Treatment of childhood anxiety: Developmental aspects. *Clinical Psychology Review, 20,* 479–494.

Berman, S. L., Weems, C. F., Silverman, W. K., & Kurtines, W. M. (2000). Predictors of outcome in exposure-based cognitive and behavioral treatments for anxiety disorders in children. *Behavior Therapy, 31,* 713–731.

Beutler, L. E., & Malik, M. (Eds.). (2002). *Rethinking the DSM: Psychological perspectives.* Washington, DC: American Psychological Association.

De Los Reyes, A., & Kazdin, A. E. (2005). Informant discrepancies in the assessment of childhood psychopathology: A critical review, theoretical framework, and recommendations for further study. *Psychological Bulletin, 131,* 483–509.

Fairburn, C. G., Marcus, M. D., & Wilson, G. T. (1993). Cognitive behavior therapy for binge eating and bulimia nervosa: A treatment manual. In C. G. Fairburn & G. T. Wilson (Eds.), *Binge eating: Nature, assessment, and treatment* (pp. 361–404). New York: Guilford Press.

Hawley, K. M., & Weisz, J. R. (2003). Child, parent, and therapist (dis)agreement on target problems in outpatient therapy: The therapist's dilemma and its implications. *Journal of Consulting and Clinical Psychology, 71,* 62–70.

Haynes, S. N., Nelson, K. G., Thacher, I., & Keaweaimoku, J. (2002). Outpatient behavioral assessment and treatment target selection. In M. Hersen & L. K. Porzelius (Eds.), *Diagnosis, conceptualization, and treatment planning for adults* (pp. 35–70). Mahwah, NJ: Lawrence Erlbaum.

Haynes, S. N., & O'Brien, W. H. (1990). Functional analysis in behavior therapy. *Clinical Psychology Review, 10,* 649–668.

Jensen, P. S. (1999). Parent and child contributions to diagnosis of mental disorders: Are both informants always necessary? *Journal of the American Academy of Child & Adolescent Psychiatry, 38,* 1569–1579.

Kanfer, F. H. (1985). Target selection for clinical change programs. *Behavioral Assessment, 7,* 7–20.

Kapalka, G. M. (2004). Longer eye contact improves ADHD children's compliance with parent's commands. *Journal of Attention Disorders, 8,* 17–23.

Kazdin, A. E. (1985). Selection of target behaviors: The relationship of the treatment focus to clinical dysfunction. *Behavioral Assessment, 7,* 33–47.

Kendall, P. K. (1994). Treating anxiety disorders in children: Results of a randomized clinical trial. *Journal of Consulting and Clinical Psychology, 62,* 100–110.

Klein, D. N., Dougherty, L. R., & Olino, T. M. (2005). Towards guidelines for evidence-based assessment of depression in children and adolescents. *Journal of Clinical Child and Adolescent Psychology, 34,* 412–432.

Mash, E. J., & Terdal, L. G. (Eds.). (1981). *Behavioral assessment of childhood disorders.* New York: Guilford Press.

Pelham, W. E., Fabiano, G. A., & Massetti, G. M. (2005). Evidence-based assessment of attention deficit hyperactivity disorder in children and adolescents. *Journal of Clinical Child and Adolescent Psychology, 34,* 449–476.

Shirk, S. R., & Saiz, C. C. (1992). Clinical, empirical, and developmental perspectives on the therapeutic relationship in child psychotherapy. *Development & Psychopathology, 4,* 713–728.

Sturmey, P. (1996). *Functional analysis in clinical psychology.* Chichester, UK: John Wiley & Sons.

Wood, E. C., & Wood, C. D. (1990). Referral issues in psychotherapy and psychoanalysis. *American Journal of Psychotherapy, XLIV,* 85–94.

Woolfenden, S. R., Williams, K., & Peat, J. K. (2002). Family and parenting interventions for conduct disorder and delinquency: A meta-analysis of randomized controlled trials. *Archives of Disease in Childhood, 86,* 251–256.

Yeh, M., & Weisz, J. R. (2001). Why are we here at the clinic? Parent-child (dis)agreement on referral problems at ourpatient treatment entry. *Journal of Consulting and Clinical Psychology, 69,* 1018–1025.

9

WRITING UP THE INTAKE INTERVIEW

CATHERINE MILLER AND SEAN DODGE

A written intake report should accomplish two main goals. First, it should tie together discrepant sources of information and data points into a thorough, accurate description of the client and his or her functioning. This description may include hypotheses about etiology and maintenance of behaviors, as well as differential diagnostic considerations (Wolber & Carne, 1993). Second, a report should provide specific recommendations for individualized interventions and ongoing assessment of progress based on client presentation (Harvey, 1997; Wolber & Carne, 1993). In summary, a good intake report is one that is detailed yet concise, comprehensive yet comprehensible. It should also provide clear direction for future assessment and treatment.

This chapter will address two main issues in writing an intake report: (1) tips on writing a professional, grammatically correct report and (2) ethical issues in report writing. In addition, a suggested template for report formatting will be presented, along with a sample intake report.

PROFESSIONAL WRITING STYLE

It is imperative that clinicians consider their audiences when writing intake reports (Wolber & Carne, 1993). Although such reports will be read primarily by the clinician(s) treating the child, parents will likely have access to the reports (Harvey, 1997). In addition, teachers and other caregivers may have access to the reports, as long as parental permission is obtained. Therefore, intake reports must be written in a clear format, so that they can be easily understood by someone without formal training in psychology (Segal, 1998). Otherwise, clinicians risk "being misunderstood and having important recommendations ignored" (Harvey, 1997, p. 274). To increase the likelihood that information and recommendations contained in intake reports will be utilized, clinicians should strive to apply the following nine guidelines when writing intake reports.

Include Specific Details

Clinicians should be as specific as possible about details (Segal, 1998). For example, rather than stating that the client was born in the South, the report should indicate that the client was born, for example, in Galliano, Louisiana. Rather than stating, "The client moved to Oregon several years ago," the report should state, "The client moved to Oregon in July 1999." Throughout the report, clinicians should strive to provide specific examples of behaviors rather than relying solely on general terms. For example, rather than saying, "Mary appeared tired," a better sentence might be "Mary appeared tired, as evidenced by yawning repeatedly, stretching, and falling asleep in the waiting room."

Use Objective Statements

Clinicians should use clear, precise language and strictly avoid personal opinions or self-disclosures in the intake report (Segal, 1998). Clients, particularly child clients, may make vague statements and provide indirect answers to intake questions. It is the clinician's job to translate these indistinct client statements into "objective, behaviorally specific terms" (Segal, 1998, p. 133). In addition, when a client uses slang or colloquialisms, it is the clinician's job to explain these terms (Segal, 1998). To accomplish this, the clinician may choose to include the exact client statement in quotes and then describe the meaning in more objective, clinical terms (Morrison, 1995). For example, if the child's mother states that the child has been "cranky lately," the clinician should query the mother further so as to be able to include more objective information in the report (e.g., "Mother reported that the child has been irritable for the past 3 weeks, as evidenced by crying several times per day each day and refusing to comply with requests"). Clinicians must be careful, however, not to excessively quote from the client, but instead use specific quotations to illustrate examples of client statements, always remembering to objectively describe the facts (Segal, 1998; Segal & Hutchings, 2007).

Avoid Jargon

Clinicians should carefully review each report to reduce instances of jargon or technical terms. Examples of jargon include the following terms: *boundary issues, codependency,* and *transference.* Any terms that are used should be fully explained (Harvey, 1997). In addition, any acronym that is used (e.g., NOS, ADHD), should be spelled out and explained the first time it is used (Harvey, 1997). For example, rather than saying, "This client has been diagnosed with ADHD," a better statement would be "This client has been diagnosed with attention-deficit/hyperactivity

disorder (ADHD), due to his tendency to fidget frequently, daydream during class time, and respond impulsively." Finally, clinicians should avoid their own slang terms or colloquialisms, such as "worrywart" or "bad attitude" (Segal, 1998).

Cite Sources of Information

Clinicians would do well to remember that any information presented during an intake session "is not necessarily factual, but rather is only the client's view of the situation" (Segal, 1998, p. 132). Therefore, clinicians should regularly cite the source of any information presented in the report, rather than stating such information as fact. For example, rather than stating, "The child's father is an alcoholic," a better statement is "The child's mother called the child's father 'an alcoholic,' reporting that he regularly drinks to intoxication and has received treatment for his drinking in the past." When writing the report, clinicians may want to avoid using the terms *allege* or *claim,* as these carry negative connotations, and instead use the terms *report* or *state.*

Remain Respectful of the Client

Throughout the intake report, adults should be addressed as *Mr.* or *Ms.* (or other preferred title), while children or adolescents under the age of 18 may be addressed by their first names. Clinicians should avoid writing "the client" throughout the report and should never refer to a client by a diagnostic category (e.g., "this borderline patient").

Ensure That Correct Grammar Is Used

Clinicians must proofread all reports to ensure correct grammar usage. Common mistakes made in intake reports include the excessive use of the passive voice, inconsistent verb tense, inconsistent pronoun use, inconsistent use of apostrophes, and neglecting to use semicolons when necessary (Harvey, 1997; Segal, 1998).

First, as much as possible, sentences should be written in the active rather than passive voice. For example, rather than saying, "The door was slammed by Timmy," a better statement is "Timmy slammed the door." Second, verb tense should be consistent within each section of the report. Present tense (e.g., "Mary states that she is in fifth grade") or past tense (e.g., "Mary stated that she is in fifth grade") may be used, as long as it is used consistently throughout the report (Segal, 1998). Third, pronouns must be consistent with the subject they are replacing. For example, it is incorrect to state, "A child often forgets their friends' birthdays." Instead, that statement may be correctly reworded in either of the following ways: "A child often forgets his/her friends' birthdays," or "Children often forget their friends' birthdays."

Fourth, apostrophes must be used correctly. Apostrophes should not be used in the plural forms of words (e.g., one book plus one book equals "two books," not "two "book's"); instead, they should be used to indicate possession (e.g., "It is Mary's book"). If the item is possessed by one person, place the apostrophe before the "s" (e.g., "That is the girl's book," indicating that the book is owned by one girl). If the item is possessed by more than one person, however, place the apostrophe after the "s" (e.g., "That is the girls' book," indicating that the book is owned by two or more girls).

Finally, semicolons must be used to separate two separate sentences joined by the word "however." For example, it is incorrect to state, "Mary's mother stated that she is a talkative child, however she was very quiet during the intake." Instead, the sentence may be correctly rewritten as follows: "Mary's mother stated that she is a talkative child; however, she was very quiet during the intake."

Ensure That the Report Is Readable

Research has found that most psychological reports are written at a 12th-grade reading level or higher (Harvey, 1997). For example, Wedig (1984) found that school psychological reports typically are written at the Grade 14 level, while Harvey (1997) found that psychological reports are written at the Grade 13 level. According to the National Assessments of Adult Literacy Survey (2003), however, the average reading level in the United States is somewhere between eighth and ninth grades. This suggests that most psychological reports are written in language that is likely to be misunderstood. Instead, clinicians should rely on simple, declarative sentences throughout their reports. Other suggestions for ensuring readability of reports are to utilize short sentences (Harvey, 1997) and to increase the use of subheadings (Wolber & Carne, 1993). Finally,

for maximum readability, authors should write reports that are no longer than three to four single-spaced pages (Wolber & Carne, 1993).

Ensure Professional Presentation of the Report

Reports should be printed out on letterhead and presented in a neat and uniform manner (Wolber & Carne, 1993). All reports should be written from the third-person point of view (e.g., "he," "she," or "they") rather than the first person (e.g., "I" or "we") (Wolber & Carne, 1993). Finally, to decrease the likelihood of reports being read by others than the intended audience, all reports should be stamped "Confidential" in red, eye-catching letters.

Ensure Timeliness of the Report

Because "timeliness is vital to the professional image of clinical psychology," Wolber and Carne (1993, p. 7) strongly cautioned clinicians to write reports as soon as possible after the intake date, with no more than 2 to 3 days passing between intake and report completion.

ETHICAL ISSUES WHEN WRITING INTAKE REPORTS

Throughout their training, clinicians are taught to behave in an ethical manner during all phases of therapy, including intake, assessment, intervention, and termination sessions. However, clinicians may not stop to consider ethical issues when writing up the intake report. Child intake reports may be read by parents or other caregivers; in addition, these reports form the basis of treatment decisions. Therefore, it is imperative that clinicians consider the issues of competence, confidentiality, and informed consent when writing up an intake report.

Competence

In its ethics code, the American Psychological Association (APA, 2002) emphasized the importance of competence in Standard 2.01, stating that psychologists provide services only within the boundaries of their competence, based on their education, training, supervised experience, consultation, study, or professional experience.

Competence in writing up an intake implies that the clinician has a sufficient level of knowledge and training to determine appropriate assessment instruments and how to administer/score them. Competence also implies that the clinician understands how to integrate results from discrepant informants (e.g., children, parents, teachers). Finally, it implies that the clinician has adequate writing skills to communicate findings in a written format. While in training, intake clinicians should have each intake report reviewed by a supervisor until such time as the supervisor approves the report. Periodically, clinicians should have intake reports reviewed by a consultant, to maintain competence in writing reports.

Informed Consent

Each person undergoing an intake assessment (or his or her legal guardian) must agree to be evaluated prior to the intake and after being given relevant information about the intake (APA Committee on Psychological Tests and Assessment, 1996). Such information should include the reasons for administration of different assessment devices, intended uses of data, possible consequences (including risks and benefits), what information will be released (if any), and to whom the information will be released (APA Committee on Psychological Tests and Assessment, 1996). The importance of providing such information prior to intake is reviewed in Standard 3.10 (Informed Consent) in the 2002 version of the APA ethics code.

Because children generally are not presumed to be competent to provide consent in most cases, substitute consent typically must be obtained from parents or legal guardians (Pryzwansky & Bersoff, 1978). Nevertheless, clinicians are encouraged to provide information to children in developmentally appropriate language about the particular intake procedures employed (Keith-Spiegel, 1983; Miller & Evans, 2004). Everstine and colleagues (1980) recommended that clinicians document in the intake report that they have obtained both of the following: (a) consent from the parent and (b) assent from the child. The term *assent* suggests that the child agrees to participate in the intake but may not completely understand the nature and purpose of assessment or his or her involvement in it (Keith-Spiegel, 1983).

Confidentiality

Koocher and Keith-Spiegel (1998) defined *confidentiality* as "a general standard of professional conduct that obliges a professional not to discuss information about a client with anyone" (p. 116). APA (2002) emphasized the importance of confidentiality primarily in Standards 4.01 and 4.02 of its ethics code; these standards require psychologists to inform test takers, prior to assessment, of any mandatory, as well as any likely, releases of information. Wolber and Carne (1993) cautioned clinicians to respect each client's confidentiality by avoiding "reporting of findings [in the intake report] which are not relevant to the intake and which would unduly invade the private lives of those individuals evaluated" (p. 9). They also cautioned clinicians to respect other persons' confidentiality, stating that "the inclusion of names and information about individuals other than the subject of the report should be undertaken with caution or clearly omitted" (Wolber & Carne, 1993, p. 9).

SECTIONS OF THE WRITTEN REPORT

There are many possible ways to format an intake report, and clinicians must be familiar with agency or supervisor formatting requirements when writing an intake report (Segal & Hutchings, 2007). The following sections should be used as a model or template from which child intake reports may be generated (see Table 9.1 for suggested sections of the report and Appendix 9.A for a sample report).

Title

The title of the report should appear first. Typically, the report will be labeled "Intake Report" or "Intake Evaluation," centered on the page, and typed in capital letters or bold font. The client's full name and date of birth are often included in the title section. In addition, including the name of the evaluator, dates of evaluation, and date of report generation in the title aids future readers of the report. The report should be written on letterhead and should include notification (written or stamped) that the contents are confidential, as intake reports are often requested by outside agencies or professionals (Segal, 1998).

Demographic Information

To help readers of the report place test results, diagnoses, and treatment recommendations in context, it is important to begin the report with basic demographic information about the client. Gender, ethnicity, nationality, primary language, religion, current age, and school grade are important pieces of information to include in this section (Morrison, 1995; Morrison & Anders, 1999; Segal, 1998). The following is an example of a good opening paragraph:

> Timmy Rogers, born on August 29, 1998, presented to the clinic as a 7-year-old male attending second-grade classes. He is a native-born citizen of the United States from an Anglo-Saxon ethnic background, and he is a native English speaker.

As children do not typically attend intake interviews alone, information on who accompanied the child to the interview (e.g., parents,

social worker) should be included in this section. Specific names of the accompanying adult(s) should be stated, as well as information on who has legal authority to consent for treatment.

Finally, the referral source and reasons for referral should be included in this section, as this may provide useful information for therapeutic purposes. Although adult clients may be self-referred (meaning that they took their own initiative to attend therapy), children typically do not seek treatment on their own and may not be old enough to legally consent to treatment. Instead, an intake report stating that the child was self-referred suggests that the parents are seeking treatment. Other common referral sources for child clients include primary care physicians, insurance companies, mental health professionals, teachers, school counselors, clergy, psychotherapists, family members, and friends (Segal, 1998). An example of referral information follows: "Timmy's primary care physician, Dr. Sam Walsh, referred him for treatment after Timmy reported symptoms of depression, including trouble sleeping and eating, and lack of interest in prior activities."

List of Assessment Measures Employed

There are several different methods of assessment, including interviews, self-report, self-monitoring, direct observation, and reports by others (Cone, 1978). Multiple methods of assessment should be used during intakes (McMahon & Estes, 1997), and all methods included in the intake should be stated in this section. Interviews are considered the most common type of assessment method employed (Sattler, 1992; Sharp, Reeves, & Gross, 2006). Intake reports should indicate which type of interview format (i.e., unstructured, semistructured, or structured) was employed (Rogers, 2001). If self-report measures, such as the Children's Depression Inventory (Kovacs, 1992), Minnesota Multiphasic Personality Inventory-Adolescent Version (Butcher et al., 1992), or self-monitoring forms (e.g., daily food diaries, thought records), are utilized during the intake, these should be listed in this section. Direct observations, which may be formal, such as the Interpersonal Process Code (Rubsy, Estes, & Dishion, 1991, as cited in Freeman & Hogansen, 2006) or informal (e.g., subjective impressions of the assessor), should be noted as well.

Gathering collateral information from multiple informants is crucial when working with children and adolescents, for two reasons. First, children may exhibit different behaviors across different settings and caregivers (Freeman & Hogansen, 2006). Second, children, particularly under the age of 11, generally are not considered reliable informants of their own overt behavior (Schwab-Stone, Fallon, Briggs, & Crowther, 1994). Possible informants include parents and other family members, teachers, school counselors, prior therapists, and case workers. Collateral information may be gathered via three methods. First, significant others, such as parents or teachers, may be interviewed. Second, significant others may complete rating forms to provide information on how this particular child client compares with a normative sample (e.g., Child Behavior Checklist: Achenbach & Edelbrock, 1986; Conners' Parent Rating Scales: Conners, Sitarenios, Parker, & Epstein, 1998). Finally, a review of records, such as school records or prior therapy notes, is essential in any child intake. It is important in this section to list everyone who was interviewed, including dates of the interviews and how these interviews were conducted (e.g., in person, on the phone), as well as all records that were reviewed. Because sources of information should be cited throughout the body of the report, a thorough listing of all information sources at the beginning of the report should aid in clarifying later sections.

Presenting Problems

Presenting problems are the difficulties the child is currently experiencing. These difficulties should be reported by both the child and collateral sources, such as parents and teachers. The amount of collateral information gathered will depend largely on the specific nature of the client's problem and age. With younger children, the clinician will likely need to gather a greater amount of information from other sources, while adolescents may be able to provide more information directly pertaining to their symptom presentation (Morrison & Anders, 1999).

The presenting problems section should cover the following four areas: (1) description of symptoms, (2) contextual variables, (3) impact of symptoms, and (4) reasons for seeking treatment. First, detailed and specific descriptions of symptoms must be presented, rather than solely relying

on vague labels (Segal, 1998). It is not helpful to merely say that the parents reported that the child is "depressed." Rather, it is more useful to state that "the parents reported that the child is depressed, as evidenced by difficulty attending to tasks, frequent incidences of irritability, and loss of interest in previously enjoyed activities." To increase specificity of the report, description of the presenting problems should always include information on the intensity, duration, and frequency of the symptoms.

Second, context of the presenting problem should also be discussed in this section. Particularly with children, behavior may vary dramatically in different contexts. It is important to include any differences or inconsistencies in the child's symptoms in various contexts. For example, rather than stating that "Timmy reported feeling anxious," it is better to state the following: "Timmy reported that he feels very anxious while at school, as evidenced by difficulty concentrating, rapid heartbeat, and feelings of dizziness. However, Timmy reported that he does not experience these symptoms in other settings."

Third, the impact of the child's current difficulties on the client and others should be presented. For example, it would be informative to state that "Timmy's anxiety symptoms are reported by parents to have a negative impact on his performance at school, as he has received C's and D's on his school assignments this term, whereas he was previously receiving all A's and B's." In addition, any strategies that have already been used to deal with the current difficulties and what, if any, effectiveness those strategies have had should be presented in this section.

Finally, many clinicians include a brief statement as to why the child or caregiver chose to seek treatment at this particular time (Segal, 1998). In most cases, the current difficulties will have been present for some time. Knowing why the client is coming to treatment now may give the reader a better understanding of the current difficulties (e.g., the child was recently suspended from school).

History

Historical information is important for diagnosing and conceptualizing the case, as well as aiding in treatment planning. Many beginning clinicians fail to include the absence of certain things. For example, if a client denied experiencing any abuse, it is important to include this information (Morrison, 1995).

Clinicians may organize the history section in different manners. Some may choose to write the history in one chronological section, while others may separate the history into different sections (as in this chapter). Regardless of how the information is presented, the following seven areas should be addressed:

Family History. Family history is particularly important when working with children and adolescents. The report should include basic information, such as where the family lives, the number of siblings and their ages, birth order, parental separations or divorces, adoptions, information on noncustodial parents, and general living arrangements (Morrison, 1995; Morrison & Anders, 1999; Segal, 1998). It is also important to include any pertinent information about family members, including any family history of mental illness, suicide, substance abuse, legal problems, employment or income difficulties, physical disorders or illnesses (including learning disorders and mental retardation), and any major traumas (Morrison, 1995; Morrison & Anders, 1999; Segal, 1998). Finally, information should be included on family dynamics. This includes the quality of interpersonal relationships within the family and any noteworthy personality traits or characteristics of the family members. It is of utmost importance that clinicians include information on the presence or absence of any physical, emotional, or sexual abuse or neglect.

Developmental History. Information about the child's birth, such as any pregnancy complications or being born early or late, may be useful for diagnoses and treatment purposes (Morrison, 1995). This section should also include information on all noteworthy developmental milestones, such as first words or first steps (see Morrison & Anders, 1999, for a list of important developmental milestones).

Medical History and Current Medications. All of the child's relevant medical history should be recorded in this section, including information on any major operations, illnesses, immunizations, allergies, and non-mental health-related hospitalizations (Morrison & Anders, 1999). Also, any medications that the child is taking, either prescribed or over-the-counter, should be noted. If possible, the name and dosage of all medications, as well as the name of the prescribing physician, should be noted (Segal, 1998).

Psychological History. In this section, any previous therapy the child has received should be included: names of service providers, number of sessions, reasons for treatment, and reasons for termination (Segal, 1998). Any previous mental-health-related hospitalizations should also be noted. It is crucial that clinicians report the presence or absence of any previous suicide attempts.

Educational History. This section refers to the child's academic performance. Information should be included regarding grades, areas of strengths or interests, areas of difficulty, school suspensions or expulsions, peer relations, and relationships with teachers and school counselors (Morrison & Anders, 1999).

Drug/Alcohol History. In addition to illicit substances, clinicians should include information on the child's use of alcohol and tobacco. Use of caffeine, including soft drinks, "energy" drinks, and caffeine pills, should also be noted, as these substances may affect symptom presentation.

Legal History. In this section, any arrests, warrants, or truancy citations should be noted. In addition, the clinician should discuss any involvement the child has had with the legal system (e.g., the child was a victim of physical abuse and testified in legal proceedings; the child was involved in a custody evaluation).

Assessment Results

Any self-report measure, rating by others, or other testing form that can be scored should be presented in this section. It is important that this section contain specific scores rather than global statements of findings in order to aid in diagnosing and treating the client.

Mental Status Examination (MSE) and Behavioral Observations

In writing the observations section, clinicians should always report the child's physical appearance, including attire, grooming, and hygiene (Segal, 1998). Anything about the individual that appears unusual or strange (e.g., wearing a winter coat in the middle of summer, strong odor) should be discussed in this section. Also, the following areas should be noted: (a) behavior during the interview (e.g., attentive, distracted, avoided eye contact); (b) psychomotor activity (e.g., restlessness, agitation, retardation); (c) attitude toward the clinician (e.g., cooperative, hostile, suspicious, defensive); (d) speech patterns (e.g., volume, pace); (e) thought processes (e.g., circumstantiality, tangentiality, looseness of associations); (f) memory; and (g) orientation to time, place, person, and situation (Zuckerman, 2000). Finally, this section should include a discussion of the child's strengths (e.g., strong family network, high IQ).

Diagnosis and Diagnostic Justification

In this section, provide any applicable diagnoses using the *Diagnostic and Statistical Manual of Mental Disorders, Fourth Edition, Text Revision (DSM-IV-TR)* of the American Psychiatric Association (2000). The *DSM-IV-TR* has a five-axes system, and all axes should be included in an intake report. It is important that full diagnoses are employed, including all specifiers and severity indicators, as this degree of specificity will greatly aid in treatment planning. In addition, clinicians should be careful to note which diagnosis is primary. If not specifically stated, the first diagnosis listed under Axis I will be read as the primary or main diagnosis. Child clinicians must remember that personality disorders have a minimum age requirement of 18; therefore, children and adolescents should never be diagnosed with a personality disorder.

Following the presentation of the five axes, clinicians should specifically outline how the client met criteria for each of the diagnoses. A diagnostic justification may also include information on provisional diagnoses or explain why other diagnoses should be ruled out.

Case Conceptualization

This section may be brief, as clinicians typically formulate a tentative conceptualization only following the intake; conceptualization is more thoroughly developed following several assessment sessions. Nevertheless, a working conceptualization should be proposed in this section and should address the following three main areas: (1) the clinician's guiding orientation, (2) hypotheses about causal factors, and (3) hypotheses about factors that may be maintaining the current symptom presentation.

Treatment Recommendations

In this section, the clinician must first indicate whether treatment is necessary, based on the diagnostic picture. Second, the clinician should suggest recommended treatment modalities (e.g., individual therapy, family therapy, group therapy). Third, the clinician should make initial referral recommendations (e.g., referral to the family physician to rule out a physical cause for the symptoms presented during the intake). Finally, the clinician should begin to outline early treatment goals that were noted by the child or the family during the intake session(s).

Summary

A summary section is optional. If it is utilized, it should only briefly summarize the earlier sections of the report and should not add any new information.

Signatures

All final intake reports must be signed and dated by the intake clinician and any appropriate supervisor.

Summary

Written intake reports are useful for two main reasons: consolidating information into a case conceptualization and planning treatment. Clinicians should write a timely, professional report for each intake and should strive to clearly communicate intake results and future goals. Although there is no one single correct report format, clinicians should utilize a template like the one included in this chapter to ensure that a thorough report is written.

References

Achenbach, T. M., & Edelbrock, C. S. (1986). *Child Behavior Checklist and Youth Self-Report*. Burlington, VT: Author.

American Psychiatric Association. (2000). *Diagnostic and statistical manual of mental disorders* (4th ed., Text rev.). Washington, DC: Author.

American Psychological Association. (2002). Ethical principles of psychologists and code of conduct. *American Psychologist, 57,* 1060–1073.

American Psychological Association Committee on Psychological Tests and Assessment. (1996). Statement on the disclosure of test data. *American Psychologist, 51,* 644–648.

Butcher, J. N., Williams, C. L., Graham, J. R., Archer, R., Tellegen, A., Ben-Porath, Y. S., et al. (1992). *MMPI: A manual for administration, scoring, and interpretation.* Minneapolis: University of Minnesota Press.

Cone, J. D. (1978). The Behavioral Assessment Grid (BAG): A conceptual framework and a taxonomy. *Behavior Therapy, 9,* 882–888.

Conners, C. K., Sitarenios, G., Parker, J. D. A., & Epstein, J. N. (1998). Revision and restandardization of the Conners' Parent Rating Scale (CPRS-R): Factor structure, reliability, and criterion validity. *Journal of Abnormal Child Psychology, 26,* 257–268.

Everstine, L., Everstine, D. S., Heymann, G. M., True, R. H., Frey, D. H., Johnson, H. G. et al. (1980). Privacy and confidentiality in psychotherapy. *American Psychologist, 35,* 828–840.

Freeman, K. A., & Hogansen, J. M. (2006). Conduct disorders. In M. Hersen (Ed.), *Clinician's handbook of child behavioral assessment* (pp. 477–501). San Diego, CA: Elsevier.

Harvey, V. S. (1997). Improving readability of psychological reports. *Professional Psychology: Research and Practice, 28,* 271–274.

Keith-Spiegel, P. (1983). Children and consent to participate in research. In G. B. Melton, G. P. Koocher, & M. J. Saks (Eds.), *Children's' competence to consent* (pp. 179–211). New York: Plenum Press.

Koocher, G. P., & Keith-Spiegel, P. (1998). *Ethics in psychology: Professional standards and cases* (2nd ed.). New York: Oxford University Press.

Kovacs, M. (1992). *Children's Depression Inventory manual.* North Tonawanda, NY: Multi-Health Systems.

McMahon, R. J., & Estes, A. M. (1997). Conduct problems. In E. J. Mash & L. G. Terdel (Eds.), *Assessment of childhood disorders* (3rd ed., pp. 130–193). New York: Guilford Press.

Miller, C. A., & Evans, B. (2004). Ethical issues in assessment. In M. Hersen (Ed.), *Psychological assessment in clinical practice: A pragmatic guide* (pp. 21–32). New York: Brunner-Routledge.

Morrison, J. (1995). *The first interview: Revised for the DSM-IV.* New York: Guilford Press.

Morrison, J., & Anders, T. F. (1999). *Interviewing children and adolescents: Skills and strategies for effective DSM-IV diagnosis.* New York: Guilford Press.

National Assessments of Adult Literacy. (2003). *NAAL: 2003 overview.* Retrieved October 17, 2005, from http://www.nces.ed.gov/naal/

Pryzwansky, W. B., & Bersoff, D. N. (1978). Parental consent for psychological evaluations: Legal, ethical, and practical considerations. *Journal of School Psychology, 16,* 274–281.

Rogers, R. (2001). *Handbook of diagnostic and structured interviewing.* New York: Guilford Press.

Sattler, J. M. (1992). *Assessment of children* (Rev. & updated 3rd ed.). San Diego, CA: Author.

Schwab-Stone, M., Fallon, T., Briggs, M., & Crowther, B. (1994). Reliability of diagnostic reporting for children aged 6–11 years: A test-retest study of the Diagnostic Interview Schedule for Children-Revised. *American Journal of Psychiatry, 151,* 1048–1054.

Segal, D. L. (1998). Writing up the intake interview. In M. Hersen & V. Van Hasselt (Eds.), *Basic interviewing: A practical guide for counselors and clinicians* (pp. 129–143). Mahwah, NJ: Lawrence Erlbaum.

Segal, D. L., & Hutchings, P. (2007). Writing up the intake interview: A primer for clinicians. In M. Hersen & J. Thomas (Eds.), *Handbook of clinical interviewing with adults.* Thousand Oaks, CA: Sage.

Sharp, W. G., Reeves, C. B., & Gross, A. M. (2006). Behavioral interviewing of parents. In M. Hersen (Ed.), *Clinician's handbook of child behavioral assessment* (pp. 103–124). San Diego, CA: Elsevier.

Wedig, R. R. (1984). Parental interpretation of psychoeducational reports. *Psychology in the Schools, 21,* 477–481.

Wolber, G. J., & Carne, W. F. (1993). *Writing psychological reports: A guide for clinicians.* Sarasota, FL: Professional Resource Press.

Zuckerman, E. L. (2000). *Clinician's thesaurus: The guidebook for writing psychological reports* (5th ed.). New York: Guilford Press.

APPENDIX 9.A   SAMPLE CHILD INTAKE REPORT

CHILD INTAKE REPORT

Name: Maya Bertuccelli
Date of Birth: 10/16/93 (12 years of age)
Name of Evaluator: Catherine Miller, PhD
Dates of Evaluation: 12/15/05, 12/16/05
Date of Report: 12/18/05

Demographic Information

Maya Bertuccelli, a 12-year-old U.S. citizen of Italian descent, presented to the clinic with her biological parents, Roberto and Johnna Bertuccelli. The Bertuccellis consented for Maya to participate in the intake and to receive psychological services. Although English is her primary language, Maya reported speaking both English and Italian in the home. She has been raised as a Catholic, and her parents reported that the family attends church on a weekly basis.

List of Assessment Measures Employed

Interviews
Semistructured interviews with Maya on 12/15/05 and 12/16/05
Semistructured interviews with Mr. and Mrs. Bertuccelli on 12/15/05 and 12/16/05
Unstructured phone interview with Mrs. Mary Pawlowski, Maya's teacher, on 12/15/05
Mental Status Examination on 12/15/05
Informal observations of parent-child interactions on 12/16/05
Self-Reports
Youth Self-Report on 12/16/05
Children's Depression Inventory on 12/16/05

Ratings by Others
Child Behavior Checklist completed by mother on 12/15/05
Child Behavior Checklist completed by father on 12/15/05
Teacher Report Form completed by teacher on 12/16/05

Presenting Problems

Mr. and Mrs. Bertuccelli reported that Maya has appeared depressed, as evidenced by sad affect, withdrawal from peers and parents, and lack of interest in previously enjoyable activities (e.g., school band, reading). Maya reported feeling sad and "down" most of the day for the past 2 to 3 months. She also reported that she is having trouble sleeping through the night and that she doesn't want to talk to any of her friends from school. She reported that she quit the school band in early December 2005, after 4 years of playing the clarinet, as she was "not interested" in pursing this interest any longer. She reported feeling hopeless and as if "nothing" could cheer her up again. The Bertuccellis reported that they decided to seek treatment at the present time, as Maya had recently informed them that she was quitting the school band.

Mr. and Mrs. Bertuccelli explained Maya's current presentation as being due to several recent changes in her life (e.g., she transitioned from elementary to middle school in September 2005; her 18-year-old brother went to college in Wyoming in September 2005; and her best friend of 6 years moved out of state in October 2005).

History

Family History: Mr. and Mrs. Bertuccelli reported that Maya is the only child still living in their home in Beaverton, Oregon, as Maya's 18-year-old brother is currently attending college in Wyoming. The Bertuccellis reported that they have been married since 1980 and that both pregnancies were planned. They moved to Oregon in 1987, following the birth of their first child. The Bertuccellis denied any family history of violence. Both parents are employed (Mr. Bertuccelli works as an accountant, while Mrs. Bertuccelli works as a salesperson at Pottery Barn).

Developmental History: Mrs. Bertuccelli reported that her pregnancies were both normal and that she received prenatal care. Maya was born 2 days prior to her scheduled due date and the delivery presented no complications. The Bertuccellis reported that Maya began walking at 10 months and talking at 12 months. No developmental problems were noted.

Medical History: The Bertuccellis denied that Maya has had any significant medical problems. She had her tonsils removed at age 6 and has received all immunizations. She was hospitalized for 2 days at the age of 26 months due to a mild case of pneumonia. The Bertuccellis denied that Maya is currently taking any prescribed medications. She reportedly last saw her pediatrician approximately 3 months prior to this intake, and no physical concerns were noted.

Psychological History: The Bertuccellis denied any family history of mental illness or hospitalizations. They denied any prior treatment for Maya.

Educational History: Maya reported that she is in the 6th grade at Walker Middle School. The Bertuccellis denied that Maya has ever had to repeat a grade; instead, they reported that Maya has always received grades of A's and B's on her report cards. No suspensions or expulsions from school were noted.

Drug/Alcohol History: The Bertuccellis denied any family history of drug or alcohol problems. Mr. and Mrs. Bertuccelli reported that they each drink one to two glasses of wine with dinner each night. They admitted that Maya has tasted wine during dinner on several occasions, but they denied any problems with alcohol. Maya denied drinking alcohol on any other occasions. She also denied using any illicit substances. She admitted that she consumes one to two soft drinks per day for the past 2 years. She denied ever even experimenting with cigarettes.

Legal History: The Bertuccellis reported no involvement with the legal system currently or in the past.

Assessment Results

Mr. and Mrs. Bertuccelli each completed the Child Behavior Checklist (CBCL). The resulting profiles were remarkably similar with each other and with their verbal reports during the interview portions of the intake. The Depressed scale was elevated on both parents' profiles; all other scales fell within the normal range. Similarly, on the TRF completed by Mrs. Pawlowski, the Depressed scale was the only scale that was elevated. The results from Maya's self-report forms, however, were inconsistent with the reports of adults in her life. She completed two self-report inventories, the Youth Self-Report (YSR) and the Children's Depression Inventory (CDI). No problems were noted on either the YSR or the CDI, as all scales fell within the normal range.

Mental Status Examination (MSE) and Behavioral Observations

Maya was oriented ×4, meaning that she knew who she is, her location, time and date, and situation. Her behavior toward the clinician appeared to be open and trusting, as evidenced by her making frequent eye contact and answering all questions. She described her mood as "sad and worried." Her speech and thought processes appeared to be within normal range. Maya's affect appeared depressed, as evidenced by crying at times when discussing recent changes in her life (e.g., her brother and friend moving out of town).

Diagnosis and Justification

Axis I: Adjustment Disorder with Depressed Mood, Acute
Axis II: No diagnosis
Axis III: None
Axis IV: Social Environment
Axis V: GAF Current: 75

Maya has met criteria for Adjustment Disorder with Depressed Mood, Acute, due to her reaction to changes in her life within the last 3 to 4 months (i.e., transitioning to a new school, her brother and best friend moving out of town). Major Depressive Disorder Single Episode was considered but ruled out, as Maya's symptoms appear to be better explained by Adjustment Disorder and there is no family history of depression.

Case Conceptualization

From a behavioral orientation, behavior is maintained if (a) it is followed by something the person values (e.g., attention) or (b) it prevents the occurrence of something the person doesn't enjoy (e.g., it allows escape from homework). Maya's depressed and withdrawn behavior first evidenced after several recent changes in her life. It is likely that Maya's depressed behaviors were reinforced by attention from her parents, her teachers, and perhaps even some of her peers. It is also possible that her withdrawn behavior was reinforced, as it allowed her to avoid confronting any uncomfortable feelings regarding making new friends once her best friend had moved out of town. Maya's prognosis is good, due to the short duration of her symptoms, her strong family support, and good premorbid functioning.

Treatment Recommendations

Based on her symptom presentation, Maya and her parents were informed that short-term family therapy is indicated. Specifically, based on the case conceptualization, family therapy should focus on teaching Maya's parents to reinforce more adaptive behaviors exhibited by Maya. Because Maya appeared to have adequate social skills, treatment should focus on exposing Maya to any anxiety or uncomfortable feelings she has when attempting to meet new friends.

Summary

Maya Bertuccelli presented to the clinic with her biological parents due to depressive symptoms secondary to recent life events (i.e., school transition, brother and best friend moving out of town). Maya's prognosis is good, due to the short duration of her symptoms, her strong family support, and good premorbid functioning. Brief, focused family therapy targeting parental reaction to Maya's behaviors and exposure to anxiety-provoking situations is recommended to alleviate Maya's symptom presentation.

Signature: _____

Date: _____

PART II

SPECIFIC DISORDERS

10

DEPRESSIVE DISORDERS

LISA ROBERTS CHRISTIANSEN AND JESSICA BOLTON

DESCRIPTION OF THE DISORDERS

Despite the significant developmental changes in cognitive, emotional, and interpersonal functioning that occur throughout childhood and adolescence, the clinical presentation of depression in this population is quite similar to that of adults, and, in large part, the same diagnostic criteria applies. The current edition of the *Diagnostic and Statistical Manual of Mental Disorders (DSM-IV-TR)* (APA, 2000) delineates a *major depressive episode* as comprising at least five of the following symptoms present for at least 2 weeks and representing a change from previous functioning: depressed mood, anhedonia, significant changes in weight or appetite, changes in sleep pattern, psychomotor agitation or retardation, lack of energy, feelings of worthlessness, lack of concentration, and suicidal ideation. For children, irritable mood is allowed as an equivalent to dysphoria, and failure to make developmentally expected growth and weight gains is considered to meet appetite and weight disruption criteria. The criteria for major depressive disorder are otherwise identical for children, adolescents, and adults. An additional exception exists in the criteria for dysthymic disorder, a chronic mild depressive state, in that symptom duration may be 1 year for children rather than the 2 years required for adults.

Although diagnostic criteria and the general clinical picture remain the same, subtle differences in the manifestation of depression may be seen based on developmental stage. Preschoolers may appear apathetic, uninterested in play, and uncooperative (Grabill, Griffith, & Kaslow, 2001). Elementary school children may exhibit social withdrawal, somatic complaints, agitation, separation anxiety, and, in some severe cases, auditory hallucinations (Grabill et al., 2001; Ryan et al., 1987). Adolescents may experience mood swings, excessive irritability, inattention to personal appearance and hygiene, sensitivity to interpersonal rejection, rebellious behaviors, and parasuicidal or suicidal behavior (Kutcher & Marton, 1989; Lewinsohn, Rohde, & Seeley, 1993). Changes in sleep and appetite, as well as low self-esteem and guilt, tend to be more apparent in adolescents than in children, who may instead express symptoms through somatic complaints (Park & Goodyer, 2000). Differences may also be seen based on gender. Adolescent girls report internalized depressive symptoms, such as low self-esteem and negative body image (Gjerde, Block, & Block, 1988). Boys often deny feeling sad and instead present as moody, irritable, or bored, along with exhibiting externalizing characteristics such as disagreeableness, antagonistic behavior, fights or other trouble at school, and disruptions in social relationships (Park & Goodyer, 2000).

Prevalence estimates of depression among children and adolescents vary widely based on methodology (see reviews by Fleming & Offord, 1990; Waslick, Shoenholz, & Pizarro, 2003). Studies have differed in setting, diagnostic categories considered, and age ranges included in calculation of estimates. Prevalence studies have also varied in whether the diagnosis is obtained through self-report, parent report, or a combination of the two. This pervasive lack of uniform sampling and research methodology, coupled with variations in assessment instruments and shifting diagnostic criteria, results in frequent incongruency and a wide range of prevalence estimates: from 0.4% to 4% for prepubertal children and 0.4% to 8.3% for adolescents (Angold & Costello, 1995; Birmaher et al., 1996; Fleming & Offord, 1990). Some general trends may be observed, however. First, higher rates of depression are found in adolescents than in children. Explanations proposed for this increase include biological and hormonal effects of puberty, increased self-awareness associated with development, and a decrease in emotional and behavioral protective factors, such as spending time with family (Harrington, 1993). Second, while depression occurs at the same rate in girls and boys during childhood, it is diagnosed twice as often in females during adolescence and adulthood. Sex differences after puberty are thought to be associated with biological, hormonal, and psychosocial changes that affect girls differently and at an earlier age than boys (Angold, Costello, & Worthman, 1998; Nolen-Hoeksema & Girgus, 1994).

The prevalence of depressive disorders also varies among different ethnic and cultural groups. Unfortunately, few studies have been published that specifically address epidemiology among minority groups. Roberts (2000) conducted a review of depression rates in African American youth and found mixed results, with some studies demonstrating lower scores on depression measures for African American children and adolescents than for European American youth, other studies showing equal rates of depression between the two groups, and yet other studies reporting higher scores on depression measures for African American youth than for European Americans. Asian American children have been found to be generally less likely to be diagnosed with depression or dysthymia than European Americans

(Nguyen et al., 2004). Specific prevalence estimates have been found for Chinese American youth, ranging from 1.9% to 2.9%, somewhat lower than rates reported for European American children and adolescents (Roberts, Roberts, & Chen, 1997). Latino youth have consistently been found to have the highest rates of depression of all studied cultural groups. For example, Mexican American youth were reported by one study to have a prevalence rate of 12% (Choi, 2002). We found no information about Native American child and adolescent depression rates; however, American Indians and Alaskan Natives have reported suicide rates 50% higher than the overall suicide mortality rate in the United States, making them the ethnic group at highest risk for suicide (Moscicki, 1997). Finally, sexual minority youth have been reported to be at higher risk than heterosexual youth for depression and suicide (Fergusson, Horwood, & Beautrais, 1999).

The data suggest the average duration of most childhood major depressive episodes is 6 to 9 months, with recovery rates of over 90% within 1 to 2 years (Kovacs, Obrosky, Gatsonis, & Richards, 1997; Park & Goodyer, 2000; Ryan et al., 1987). Estimates from various studies indicate a recurrence rate of 54% to 72% within 3 to 8 years, however, suggesting the majority of childhood depression is recurrent and likely to continue into adulthood (Emslie & Mayes, 1999; Weissman et al., 1999). Predictors of recurrent depression include earlier age at onset, number of episodes, severity of episodes, psychosocial stressors, family history of depression or other mood disorder, and comorbid dysthymia (Kovacs, 1992; Kovacs et al., 1997). Dysthymia tends to resolve within 3 to 4 years in both clinical and community samples, but approximately 70% of children and adolescents with dysthymia will experience a major depressive episode within 5 years (Kovacs et al., 1997).

Children and adolescents experiencing depression are generally not self-referred for treatment. Rather, parents are usually the ones to seek evaluation due to indications of impaired functioning, such as decline in school grades; somatic complaints; oppositional behavior; antisocial behavior; family conflict; or substance abuse (Emslie & Mayes, 1999; Wagner, 2003; Waslick, Kandel, & Kakouros, 2002). Accurate diagnosis and treatment of pediatric depression is vital. Waslick et al. (2003) noted that in the year 2000, suicide was the third leading cause of death for individuals aged 15 to 24 and the sixth leading cause of death for children aged 5 to 14. Equally alarming, at least one research study found that 7.7% of adolescents diagnosed with major depression commit suicide by early adulthood (Weissman et al., 1999). Assessing for the presence of mood disorder is therefore an essential component of any evaluation of a child or adolescent.

INTERVIEWING STRATEGIES

Accurate diagnosis of pediatric depression depends on utilizing a multimodal, multiinformant model of assessment, in which information is gathered from the child or adolescent, his or her parent(s), teacher(s), and other concerned and knowledgeable parties using a variety of methods. In this section, we focus on obtaining information from the child or adolescent.

Clinical Interviews

It is essential to conduct the interview assessment within a developmental context, as the expression of depressive symptoms can vary significantly depending on the child's or adolescent's age and whether a behavior falls within the parameters of normal development for that age (Schwartz, Gladstone, & Kaslow, 1998). For example, tearfulness at school may be interpreted differently in an elementary student than in a high school student, depending both on developmental appropriateness and context of the behavior. It is therefore crucial that the interviewer acquire a solid foundation in childhood and adolescent development to be able to accurately distinguish normative behavior from psychopathology.

At the beginning of the clinical interview, it is advisable to first concentrate on the presenting concern and areas of greatest distress to the interviewee. This serves the purpose of establishing rapport and allows the child to understand that his or her perspective is being listened to and that the interviewer cares about what is important to him or her. The interviewer can then proceed with questions that address all pertinent domains of functioning and can gather more detail about diagnostic criteria as appropriate. A combination of closed-ended questions and open-ended questions is likely to result in the most complete picture of the youth's current psychological functioning. Closed-ended questions

allow for detailed examination of specific diagnostic criteria and minimize ambiguity, while open-ended questions allow the child or adolescent the freedom to express personal concerns in a manner in which he or she feels comfortable. Asking a general open-ended question about each domain of functioning, such as school, home, family relationships, and peer relationships, may ensure that no important information is missed due to a failure by the interviewer to ask. In addition to a general psychosocial history and direct questions about specific depressive symptoms, the interviewer should probe for manifestations of depression in the behavioral, cognitive, and affective domains.

Behavior. Depressed youth may display impairments in adaptive behaviors, including daily living skills, communication, and socialization (Grabill et al., 2001). The interview should include questions regarding the child's or adolescent's ability to prepare for school in a timely fashion, to complete schoolwork and household chores, and to participate in normal activities. The interviewer may also observe inadequate hygiene and personal care behaviors in depressed youth. Significant impairment in interpersonal and social functioning has been documented by several researchers as being connected to childhood depression (e.g., Goodyer, 1996; Monroe, Rohde, Seeley, & Lewinsohn, 1999). Specifically, negative life events, such as the breakup of a romantic relationship, failure to meet academic or social goals, or death of a family member or close friend, have been demonstrated to be precipitating factors in the onset of depression in children and adolescents and should be carefully assessed. The interview should also include a discussion of friendship patterns, as poor peer relationships and social skills may predate the onset of a depressive episode and can serve as a maintaining factor of the disorder.

Cognition. In general, children with depression tend to have a negative self-image, feelings of helplessness, and perceptions of incompetence. They lack motivation to complete tasks accurately and efficiently, associated with the decreased concentration and psychomotor retardation symptoms of the disorder. Grabill et al. (2001) cited specific cognitive errors common to depressed youth. Children and adolescents with depression often subscribe to an external locus of control, believing that their behavior cannot impact environmental events and that they cannot influence outcomes for good or ill. Depressed youth do not feel they act upon their environments; rather, events happen to them and are perceived as out of their control. Further, children with depression often employ a maladaptive attributional style, believing that they are to blame for negative events and that the causes of these events are stable and global in applicability. A depressed child who experiences a social rejection will think, "I am unlovable; I will never be accepted; everyone will reject me no matter what I do." In contrast, positive events are seen as the doing of others or of circumstances out of the child's control and are viewed as unstable and specific to the situation. A depressed child who receives an invitation to a social gathering of peers will think, "Her parents made her invite me; she doesn't really want me to go; no one will invite me to anything again." The interviewer can probe for cognitive distortions by asking about positive and negative events in the child's recent past and attending to the manner in which the child explains the events.

Affect. In addition to expressing negative emotions consistent with depression, such as sadness, shame, anger, and self-directed hostility, the interviewer may also observe outward manifestations of depressive affect, including tearfulness, restricted range of facial expression, and flat speech intonation. Children and adolescents who are depressed may also exhibit impaired emotion regulation abilities that result in mood swings, sudden displays of aggression, or unexplained and inconsistent withdrawal from normal activities and interactions.

When interviewing children and adolescents who are members of minority groups, it is important to distinguish symptoms indicative of a depressive disorder from expected and typical mood disturbance related to identity development, acculturation, and discrimination. Reported behaviors and affects that may meet criteria as depressive symptoms should be evaluated from within the youth's cultural context. Asking the question "Is this behavior considered normative or unusual within the child's culture?" or "Do other children of similar backgrounds also exhibit this behavior?" can be helpful in avoiding underdiagnosis or overdiagnosis of depression in minority groups. Similarly, many models of racial minority identity development and sexual minority identity development (see Pedersen, 1997) involve a stage in which the minority individual becomes acutely aware of his or her differences from the majority culture and of the negative experiences of being a minority. Feelings of sadness or alienation that result from identity exploration or adjustment to a new culture should not be diagnosed as depression. Finally, it is common for minority youth to experience psychological distress as the result of being the target of discrimination. The interviewer would do a disservice to mislabel such distress as clinical depression.

When ending the clinical interview, it is important to briefly review the youth's responses and to resolve any ambiguities by asking clarifying questions. The interviewer may also wish to consider making sure he or she has not missed any important information by asking a question such as "Is there anything else you would like to tell me or that would be important for me to know that I didn't ask about?"

Semistructured Interviews

A variety of structured and semistructured interviews have been developed to aid in the diagnosis of pediatric depression. Essau, Hakim-Larson, Crocker, and Petermann (1999) discussed the primary differences between the two types of diagnostic interviews. Structured interviews are primarily used in research settings and can be administered by trained lay interviewers. They contain exact wording of questions, specific sequencing of questions, and rules for recording and rating the respondent's answers that allow for a diagnosis to be made with no clinical judgment on the part of the interviewer. Semistructured interviews, on the other hand, are often used in clinical settings and should be administered by a trained clinician. They allow for greater flexibility in wording of questions and clarification of ambiguous responses than do highly structured interviews, while still specifying the topics to be investigated, offering a consistent definition of symptoms and terminology, and providing methods of rating the presence and severity of each diagnostic criterion.

Incorporating a semistructured interview into the clinical assessment process offers several advantages. First, it preserves the interviewer's ability to probe more deeply with follow-up questions and to clarify that the child understands the meaning of the questions being asked, while also ensuring that all diagnostic criteria are evaluated. Second, utilizing a consistent set of questions allows for clear comparison of symptoms across multiple informants. Third, information about the reliability and validity of published semistructured interviews should be available in the psychological literature and in the instrument's manual, allowing the evaluator to select an interview with robust psychometric properties. A list of well-researched semistructured diagnostic interviews appears in Table 10.1.

Self-Report Measures

While researchers generally regard self-report measures as useful screening tools to ascertain the presence and subjective intensity of depressive symptoms, they are also viewed as lacking adequate specificity to be used as reliable diagnostic instruments without corroborating information from other sources (Emslie & Mayes, 1999; Park & Goodyer, 2000). Further, self-report inventories should not be used with children below the age of 8, as young children lack the developmental skills needed to reliably reflect on their own cognitive processes and to accurately respond to questionnaires about how

often and how intensely they experience various symptoms (Kaminer, Feinstein, & Seifer, 1995). Children may, however, offer information on a self-report measure that they do not disclose in an interview. In this manner, self-report data can be utilized to identify areas to probe further in a follow-up interview with the child and with informants. Self-report data may also prove useful in tracking symptom improvement throughout the course of treatment. A list of self-report measures commonly used in the assessment of pediatric depression appears in Table 10.2.

Interviewing Obstacles and Solutions

Accurate diagnosis of depression depends on either the parent or the child being able to report about the child's internal affect state. This presents particular problems when assessing very young children due to developmental limitations in cognitive and verbal abilities. Young children may not recognize or understand the meaning of some depressive symptoms and may not be able to adequately communicate their inner emotional experience to others (Waslick et al., 2002). Any parental attempt to extrapolate internal affect state from observation of a child's external behaviors will be inherently fraught with speculation. One method used to overcome this

TABLE 10.1   **Semistructured Diagnostic Interviews for Pediatric Depression**

Instrument	Appropriate Ages	Informant(s)
Child and Adolescent Psychopathology Scale (CAPS; Lahey et al., 2004)	4–17	Child and Parent
Schedule for Affective Disorders and Schizophrenia for School-Age Children (K-SADS-PL; Kaufman et al., 1997)	7–18	Child and Parent
Interview Schedule for Children and Adolescents (ISCA; Sherrill & Kovacs, 2000)	8–17	Child
Child Assessment Schedule (CAS; Hodges et al., 1982)	5–18	Child and Parent
Structured Clinical Interview for *DSM-IV*, Child Edition (KID-SCID; Matzner, Silva, Silvan, Chowdhury, & Nastasi, 1997)	8–18	Child and Parent
Children's Depression Rating Scale (CDRS-R; Poznanski & Mokros, 1996)	6–12	Child and Parent
Child and Adolescent Psychiatric Assessment (CAPA; Angold & Costello, 2000)	9–17	Child and Parent

TABLE 10.2   **Self-Report Measures of Pediatric Depression**

Instrument	Appropriate Ages
Children's Depression Inventory (CDI; Kovacs, 1992)	7–17
Reynolds Child Depression Scale (RCDS; Reynolds, 1989)	8–12
Reynolds Adolescent Depression Scale (RADS; Reynolds & Mazza, 1998)	12–17
Beck Depression Inventory (BDI-II; Beck, Steer, & Brown, 1996)	12–18
Mood and Feelings Questionnaire (MFQ; Angold et al., 1987)	8–18

difficulty involves asking a child to examine a series of visual representations of emotional states, such as cartoon faces or pictures of other children, and pointing to the picture that he or she is "most like" (Ryan, 2001). Ablow and Measelle (1993) developed the Berkeley Puppet Interview (BPI) for children aged 4.5 to 7.5 years old specifically to address the problem of inadequate self-report of cognitions and emotions in this age group. As described by Garber and Kaminski (2000) in their review, during the interview, children are presented with two puppets that make opposing statements (e.g., "Kids don't like me" and "Kids like me"), followed by one of the puppets asking the child, "How about you?" While the depression subscale of the BPI has thus far not been demonstrated to possess strong psychometric properties, the instrument offers ideas about how to obtain information from young children about their self-perceptions in a creative way. Play therapy can also offer useful strategies, in that a child may be able to express his or her feelings through imaginative play with a doll or through the course of a game. It is important to note, however, that projective assessment methods have in general been found to possess inadequate psychometric properties and should not be used as diagnostic instruments in the absence of additional information (La Greca, 1990).

Interview questions that are often difficult even for older children include those related to internal emotional state and time concepts (Perez, Ascaso, Domenech Massons, & de la Osa Chaparro, 1998). The evaluator can offer the child greater opportunity to describe his or her emotional state in concrete terms by asking a series of simple questions, rather than a compound question; using child-specific terms; and using multiple synonyms for the same affect state (Ryan, 2002). The interviewer can also assist the child in accurately answering questions that involve time concepts by anchoring symptom onset and duration in a concrete manner using school years and life events. For example, a child could be asked whether he has been having trouble sleeping "since school started this year" or whether he remembered starting to feel sad "before or after his birthday." Establishing a general timeline through parental questioning will often provide concrete events that can be used to better structure time questions for the child. Creating a chart in which events and stressors are recorded alongside depressive symptoms may help the child establish temporal links and identify events that serve as causal or maintaining factors in his depression, as well as assist the interviewer in identifying any seasonal or cyclical patterns (Park & Goodyer, 2000).

Some depressed youth may be unwilling to disclose personal information due to fears of negative evaluation by others or simple noncompliance (Garber & Kaminski, 2000). Allowing the child to express these feelings and empathizing with them may be effective in establishing rapport and securing cooperation. Further, asking children and adolescents about those they confide in and what that person thinks or knows may be useful in opening a discussion of sensitive topics (Park & Goodyer, 2000).

Parent-child discrepancies in the report of depressive symptoms are well documented in the pediatric mood disorder literature, with agreement that generally, children tend to give more accurate descriptions of their internal affect states, while parents give more reliable descriptions of behaviors (Angold, Weissman, John, & Merikangas, 1987; Ryan, 2001). As both affective and behavioral domains are important in arriving at an accurate diagnosis, the standard clinical practice is to use multiple informants, especially for children and younger adolescents (Kazdin, 1994). Grabill et al. (2001) emphasized that discrepancies do not necessarily indicate that one informant is "right" and the other "wrong," but rather the differing reports may reflect the fact that children may present differently depending on the situation and the person they are interacting with. There is presently no clear consensus about resolving discrepancies or determining which report is most reliable. Some researchers favor using an "or" approach, in which a diagnostic criterion is assumed to be present if either the parent or the child endorses it (Bird, Gould, & Staghezza, 1992). Others have debated the merits of an "and" approach, in which a diagnostic criterion would be considered to be met only if both the parent and the child endorse it (Waslick et al., 2002). One can readily see how each strategy may result in errors of underdiagnosis or overdiagnosis. Ryan (2002) advocated asking the parent and child about discrepancies together, as the resulting discussion can often assist the interviewer in judging whether a diagnostic criteria should be viewed as present or not. The best clinical solution is to utilize a multimodal method of assessment, collecting information from interviews and rating scales completed by the child, parents, and teachers, as well as incorporating data from available medical, educational, or social service records, formal psychological testing, and direct behavioral observations. This minimizes the chance of one data source being ascribed undue weight in determining diagnosis.

Interviewing Parents and Teachers

Interviewing Parents

It is often advisable to interview parents and children separately, so that both will be more likely to offer honest reports of symptoms and concerns. It is usually also more effective to interview the parent before the child, in that the information provided by the parent can identify periods of time, events, and areas of concern that are important to include in the interview with the child and will prevent the interviewer from missing information about episodes and symptoms the child may neglect to volunteer without prompting (Ryan, 2002).

A good strategy for opening the parent interview is to ask a broad question, such as "Tell me what concerns you have about (child's name)." This open-ended question allows the parent to express concerns or problems that are perceived as most pressing first and builds rapport by helping the parent to feel that his or her concerns are being listened to by the interviewer. The interviewer also gains valuable information from the parent's

answer to this question by attending to what symptoms and functional impairments the parent stresses. Such information can provide insight into the child's behavior at home and may shorten the number of specific depressive symptoms the interviewer needs to ask about in follow-up questions. Attending to the language of the parent's report can also help the interviewer to formulate interventions in a manner that will be easily understood by the parent. For example, if a parent stresses the child's uncooperativeness and oppositional behavior as the largest areas of concern, the interviewer can explain how treating the child's depression may have a positive impact on those behaviors.

The two main goals of the parental interview are, first, to gain a qualitative perspective of the child's behavior at home and in family and social relationships and, second, to obtain concrete information about the onset and duration of current depressive symptoms and previous episodes. Utilizing a semistructured interview with the parent as informant is a useful tool for meeting the latter goal and also allows direct comparison between the parent's report and the child's report. Important additional areas to include in a parental interview are the presence and timeline of psychosocial stressors, such as family dissolution or divorce and friendship conflicts, rejections, or losses, as these are common precipitants of depression (Goodyer, 1996). Long-term stressors and environmental risk factors should also be assessed, including child abuse, neglect, marital dysfunction, family history of psychopathology, suicidality, substance abuse, and impulsivity (American Association of Child and Adolescent Psychiatry, 1998). The child's potential strengths and achievements should also be considered to encourage a balanced view of the child (Park & Goodyer, 2000).

Parents of depressed children are at relatively high risk for experiencing depression themselves (Ferro, Verdeli, Pierre, & Weissman, 2000). Depressed parents may unintentionally exacerbate depressive symptoms in a child by modeling negative thinking patterns, assuming a critical parenting style, and being less able to monitor and attend to the child's needs (Waslick et al., 2002). Therefore, a brief assessment of psychopathology is a valuable addition to a parent interview and may offer insights that inform intervention strategies. Further, the accuracy of parents' reports can often be influenced by their own psychopathology. For example, depressed mothers often overreport symptoms of depression in their children (Ryan, 2001). The interviewer should interpret such reports with caution.

Interviewing Teachers

Once children begin attending school full-time, they often spend more hours of the day in the company of their teachers than they do with their parents. Therefore, teachers are in an important position to be able to observe a child's behavior outside the home and to offer information about behavioral manifestations of depression and other forms of psychopathology. With parental consent and proper authorization, the evaluator should gather information from a child's teacher(s) whenever possible. While an ideal discussion would take place in person following a direct observation of the child in the classroom by the interviewer, practical considerations may necessitate a phone interview. In such cases, the interviewer should be well prepared in advance with questions designed to elicit the greatest amount of specific information in a short period of time. However, this guideline does not suppose a rapid-firing of closed-ended questions. Rather, the interview should open with an introduction to the purpose and a few open-ended questions before proceeding to query of diagnostic criteria.

Depressed children often present as difficult students in the classroom and are often referred for evaluation due to poor academic performance (Park & Goodyer, 2000). For this reason, it is often advisable to begin the interview with the child's teacher in a way that encourages a balanced view of the student, by asking a question such as "Let's start with (child's name)'s strengths. What does she do well?" The youth's areas of strength then give a context from which to examine behavior problems and can provide a contrast to assess the severity of weaknesses. Exploration of difficulties can begin with an open-ended query of problems the teacher has observed, followed by questions directly addressing diagnostic criteria. Phrasing internal criteria in behavioral terms may provide more useful information. For example, when asking about sadness, the interviewer could ask the teacher whether he or she has observed the student becoming tearful in class, whether the student seems to smile or to be as emotionally responsive as typical students, and

whether the student has verbally expressed feelings of sadness. In addition to gaining a perspective about the student's general functioning outside the home and specific depressive symptoms, a goal of the teacher interview is to obtain information about onset and duration of symptoms in order to better construct a timeline in corroboration with parent and child reports. It is also possible the child evidences differing levels of functional impairment in different settings, which can offer potential directions for intervention.

Behavior Checklists

In addition to a clinical interview and a semi-structured interview, a behavioral checklist completed by one or both parents and by a child's teacher is a useful tool for gathering additional information about the child in a quantitative manner and can also counterbalance any lack of objectivity observed in the interview. A broad-band checklist, such as the Child Behavior Checklist for parents (CBCL) (Achenbach, 2001) and the corresponding Teacher Report Form (TRF) (Achenbach, 2001), provides a comprehensive assessment of competencies and a wide range of internalizing and externalizing symptoms. The interviewer can examine the resultant clinical scales profile to determine whether the parent or teacher has rated the child as falling above the cut-off score for clinical significance in areas reflective of depressive symptoms. Parent and teacher ratings can be compared with each other and can also be compared with child ratings on the corresponding Youth Self-Report for children 11 years of age and older (YSR) (Achenbach, 2001). Finally, use of a broad-band measure can serve as a screening tool for comorbid diagnoses and impairments in other domains that may not have been included in the interview.

Puura et al. (1998) examined parent and teacher ratings of depressed children on a behavioral checklist and found that both parents and teachers endorsed problem behaviors in the domains of conduct problems and social behavior more frequently for depressed children than for nondepressed children. Depressed boys were also identified by both parents and teachers as having more difficulty in the antisocial behavior domain than their nondepressed peers. Teachers noted problems with anxious behavior for depressed children, while parents noted problems with somatic symptoms for depressed children. The items that discriminated best between depressed and nondepressed groups on parent ratings were oppositional behaviors, somatic complaints, subjective depressed mood, and social problems, such as not being liked by peers, tending to be on one's own, and being bullied. The items that discriminated best between depressed and nondepressed groups on teacher ratings were unresponsiveness, squirming/restlessness, somatic complaints, being bullied, and poor school performance. These findings indicate that parents and teachers are likely to identify depressed children on behavioral checklists as evidencing impairment in social functioning, expressing somatic complaints, and demonstrating oppositional behaviors at home and academic difficulties at school. Such domains should be carefully examined when behavioral checklists are available and may benefit from further exploration during a follow-up interview.

CASE ILLUSTRATION WITH DIALOGUE

Paul is a 7-year-old boy who recently began attending the first grade. He is from a middle-class family and always appears to be dressed and groomed appropriately for school. At the first parent-teacher conference, Paul's parents ask his teacher whether she has noticed any strange behaviors at school, because they are noticing some at home. They state that Paul has been waking up one or two times throughout the night and has been getting up early in the morning to watch cartoons on television but that he does not seem to enjoy watching the cartoons when asked about it. They also note Paul has appeared apathetic and lethargic at home and that he completes household chores only with a great deal of prompting. Although the teacher has nothing to report at this time, she notices more abnormality as the year progresses.

Paul appears to be sleepy most days in the classroom. Often, when asked to complete a relatively simple task, such as writing the alphabet, he refuses to pick up his pencil and, instead, hangs his head. Paul's teacher offers to help him get started, but he does not respond. Upon no response, Paul's teacher moves him to a quiet corner of the classroom where there are minimal distractions so he can attend solely to his assignment. The teacher informs Paul that if he does not finish his work, he will not be allowed to

participate in playtime later that day. At that time, Paul sometimes finishes his work, but it is done carelessly and obviously does not reflect his best effort.

At playtime, Paul tends to withdraw, preferring to play by himself. His favorite activity is to make structures out of building blocks. If another student tries to join Paul, he tends to get irritated and sometimes suddenly knocks the other child's blocks over. When other students report Paul's behavior to the teacher, she notices he appears frustrated, upset, and occasionally in tears. When asked to explain why he knocked the other child's blocks over, he is unable to make appropriate eye contact with his teacher or to explain his actions.

Paul's teacher shares her observations with his parents during the second parent-teacher conference. His parents report that his oppositional behaviors have worsened at home and that he expresses no interest in playing with other children in the neighborhood when invited. They state he is easily frustrated and occasionally bursts into tears. At this point, Paul's parents and his teacher together determine he would benefit from a mental health evaluation and potential counseling.

Prior to meeting with the family, the interviewer obtains the necessary permission to speak with the teacher and obtains the above information in a phone interview. When asked, "What are Paul's strengths?" his teacher reports that he is able to build quite elaborate structures with the blocks during playtime and that when cooperative with classroom activities, he demonstrates reading and drawing skills that are above average. The interviewer notes from the above information that the teacher endorses the following symptoms of depression for Paul: tearfulness and irritable mood, suspected sleep disturbance due to sleepiness in class, fatigue, and difficulty concentrating.

When the family arrives for their appointment, the interviewer first meets with Paul's parents. The interviewer notes that Paul fails to make eye contact when she introduces herself to the family, that his facial affect appears flat, and that he appears thin for his age. She opens the interview with a discussion of his parents' concerns: "Tell me what your most pressing concerns are about Paul." His parents report that Paul seems "different" since beginning school. They state he is usually an active child who laughs and enjoys interacting with family and friends but that he has become increasingly withdrawn and inactive. They note a change in disciplinary actions as well, observing that Paul used to get in trouble by pushing limits and doing things that are against the rules but that now he is disciplined for refusing to do anything. His parents also discuss the sleep disturbance noted above and, when prompted by the interviewer, note that during his last physical exam, Paul was documented to have lost some weight. From the information provided in the parental interview, the interviewer concludes that Paul's parents view him as meeting the following criteria for a depressive episode: tearfulness, lack of interest in formerly pleasurable activities, sleep disturbance, failure to make developmentally expected weight gains, and psychomotor retardation.

Interviewing Paul's parents and teachers before meeting with Paul provided the interviewer with some helpful information. She learned that Paul's current behavior was a change from his previous functioning and that this was his first suspected episode of depression. Knowing his depressive symptoms seem to have appeared around the time he began school also gave the interviewer a timeline to work from in asking Paul questions about his symptoms. Importantly, she also learned about Paul's enduring interest and strength in building blocks and was therefore able to bring blocks to her office as a means of engaging Paul in conversation. Paul again does not make eye contact or exhibit emotional responsiveness when he enters the interviewer's office, but he readily agrees to play with the building blocks. The interviewer slowly engages Paul in conversation by asking him questions about what he is doing with the blocks. Once he appears reasonably comfortable answering her questions, the interviewer begins the assessment:

Interviewer: You seem to be pretty good at this. Do you like building things with blocks?

Paul: Yeah, I guess.

I: What else do you like to do?

P: [Pause] I dunno.

I: Can't think of anything?

P: Uh-uh.

I: What about baseball? Your parents told me you enjoyed going to the park and playing with some of the kids in your neighborhood this summer. Is that something you liked?

P: Oh. Yeah, I guess that was fun.

I: Have they invited you to go play baseball since school started?

P: Yeah, but I don't go.

I: Why not?

P: Just don't feel like it.

I: It sounds like that's something that's different from summer to now. You used to like playing baseball, but now you don't. Is that true?

P: Yeah.

I: Are there other things that are different now from the summer? Other things you used to like to do that you don't now, or other things you did that you don't do anymore?

P: Well, I guess I used to go do a lot of stuff with friends. And now I pretty much stay home. I don't have any friends.

I: Don't have any friends? What about the kids who asked you to play baseball, but you didn't want to go?

P: They don't really like me.

I: Did something happen to make you think they don't really like you?

P: I heard Mom saying she was worried about me not doing anything, and then one of them came over and asked me to go to the park and play, so they don't really want to play with me, they were just doing it because Mom asked them to.

I: How about at school?

P: Nope. Nobody likes me there, either. I'm always getting in trouble.

I: What kind of trouble?

P: I just don't feel like doing anything, and the teacher gets mad at me.

I: What about when you try to do stuff at school? What happens then?

P: Sometimes I can do it, but it's hard for me to try. My head feels tired and it's hard to do anything.

I: Tired . . . Are you sleeping okay?

P: I guess, but I wake up a lot and in the morning I feel tired.

I: Is that different from this summer?

P: [Pause] Yeah, I guess I didn't watch the early cartoons then like I do now.

I: Do you like watching the early cartoons?

P: Not really. They just give me something to do.

Although the above dialogue is a truncated sample of a clinical interview, already one can gather a sense of Paul's depressive symptoms based on self-report, including anhedonia, diminished self-worth, inability to concentrate, fatigue, and sleep changes. Based on the interview data obtained from Paul, his parents, and his teacher, the interviewer diagnosed Paul with major depressive disorder and referred him for treatment.

DIFFERENTIAL DIAGNOSIS AND BEHAVIORAL ASSESSMENT

Accurate identification of pediatric depression is hampered by common comorbidity of depressive symptoms with other psychiatric conditions, including anxiety disorders, disruptive behavior disorders, eating disorders, substance abuse or dependence, and learning or attention-deficit disorders (Waslick et al., 2002). While these various conditions often occur together, it is important to identify the symptoms that distinguish these disorders from one another to avoid inappropriately mislabeling depression. Further, several culture-bound syndromes exist that may mimic a depressive disorder, and these will also be discussed.

Anxiety disorders and depressive disorders are often difficult to discriminate between due to shared symptoms, such as poor concentration, indecisiveness, insomnia, fatigue, and irritability. One study found approximately that one third of children and adolescents diagnosed with major depressive disorder also met criteria for an anxiety disorder (Kovacs, Gatsonis, Paulauskas, & Richards, 1989). To assist in distinguishing between these two classifications of disorders, Clark and Watson (1991) proposed a tripartite model of depression and anxiety, in which both clinical conditions were thought to be related to general negative affect, while depression was characterized specifically by anhedonia or low positive affect and anxiety was characterized specifically by physiological hyperarousal. Joiner and Lonigan (2000), among others, have extended the tripartite model to children and adolescents, confirming that a combination of low positive affect and high negative affect is specific to depression and may discriminate it from anxiety and externalizing diagnoses. The interviewer should therefore not rely solely upon the presence of negative affect, such as sadness and irritability, when considering a diagnosis of depression, but should carefully assess the absence of positive affect by probing for symptoms of anhedonia, or the loss of interest or pleasure in activities that are normally enjoyable.

Disruptive behavior disorders are commonly misdiagnosed in depressed youth, especially in boys, who may tend to manifest externalizing symptoms of depression, such as irritable mood, interpersonal conflict, and apathy or defiance. For example, between 15% and 30% of depressed children and adolescents are diagnosed with conduct disorder (Angold & Costello, 1993). Careful identification of symptom onset and duration is helpful in distinguishing between a depressive disorder and a disruptive behavior disorder, in that the conditions should be diagnosed together only when a child meets criteria for a disruptive behavior disorder when mood symptoms are not present, and vice versa. If the child or adolescent evidences disturbances in behavior only when depressed, depression should be the sole diagnosis. Similarly, when a child or adolescent exhibits a disturbance in mood characterized by irritability rather than by sadness or loss of interest and pleasure, the interviewer must be cautious not to misdiagnose depression when a disruptive behavior disorder would better account for the mood symptoms noted.

Eating disorders, such as anorexia, share several symptoms with depression, such as irritability, weight loss, sleep disturbance, social withdrawal, diminished interest, and concentration difficulties (Grabill et al., 2001). When evaluating a child or adolescent who has experienced significant weight loss or who has failed to make expected developmental weight gains, the interviewer must conduct a meticulous assessment of the child's cognitions to ascertain whether the individual has a desire for excessive weight loss or has an excessive fear of gaining weight. If so, a diagnosis of anorexia should be considered as opposed to, or in addition to, a diagnosis of depressive disorder.

As with adults, it is not uncommon for depressed youth to attempt to impact their mood with drugs and alcohol or to use substances as a maladaptive coping mechanism. In such cases, the most appropriate course of action is to diagnose both conditions and to treat the substance abuse or dependence concurrently with the depressive disorder. Certain substances may cause depressive symptoms, however, meriting a diagnosis of substance-induced mood disorder. A careful construction of the timeline of symptom presentation, a detailed inventory of current and past drug use, and information from corroborating sources can assist in identifying potential depressive effects or interactions of substances. When the veracity or completeness of the youth's self-report is in doubt and no reliable informant is available, a urinary analysis may provide the critical data needed to make an accurate diagnosis.

Learning and attention-deficit disorders in children with depression present a challenge to the evaluator, in that it is sometimes difficult to determine whether the child is experiencing difficulty at school due to depressive symptoms or whether the child is experiencing depression related to struggling at school. In their study, Biederman et al. (1987) found that 32% of children with attention-deficit/hyperactivity disorder met criteria for major depressive disorder. These two conditions may be easily confused, in that impairment in concentration is a common symptom of depression and children who are later diagnosed with depression are often initially referred for evaluation due to declining academic performance (Wagner, 2003). Construction of a timeline through careful interviewing can help to determine whether depressive symptoms began before or after difficulty in school was noted. When primacy of symptoms is in question, referral for a comprehensive psychoeducational evaluation may be appropriate to determine whether a learning disorder or attention-deficit disorder is present.

The interviewer should also be aware of a variety of culture-bound syndromes that may mimic depression. The *DSM-IV-TR* (APA, 2000) discusses several such syndromes in which depressive-like symptoms are combined with somatic complaints, anxiety, psychotic states, and behavioral disturbances. In certain African cultures, high school and college students at times experience a condition known as "brain fag," or "brain tiredness," in which symptoms consistent with depression, such as difficulty concentrating and fatigue, appear alongside a variety of somatic complaints. Members of many American Indian tribes experience a condition known as "ghost sickness," which includes the depression-like symptoms of lack of appetite, sleep disturbance, preoccupation with death and the deceased, weakness, and feelings of futility, alongside other symptoms such as loss of consciousness, dizziness, fear and feelings of danger, confusion, and hallucinations. *Shenjing shuairuo,* or neurasthenia, is a condition within Chinese culture characterized by somatic complaints, concentration difficulties, memory loss, sleep disturbance, physical and mental fatigue, sexual dysfunction, and irritability or excitability. A condition within Mediterranean cultures that is thought to especially affect children is *mal de ojo,* or "evil eye," which includes symptoms of sleep disturbance, unexplainable crying, diarrhea, vomiting, and fever. Members of Latin American cultures may experience *susto,* or "soul loss," which is attributed to a frightening event and includes symptoms of appetite and sleep disturbance, sadness, lack of motivation, low self-worth, and feelings of dirtiness, along with somatic symptoms. Finally, the idea of *nervios,* or "nerves," appears in many cultures as a vulnerability to stress and reaction to stressful life events and incorporates a wide range of emotional, somatic, and functional disturbance, including some symptoms that may appear consistent with depression, such as sleep difficulties, tearfulness, and poor concentration.

A final area of concern in considering differential diagnosis is the potential for children with depression to later develop a bipolar mood disorder. Researchers have found that approximately 13% of children and adolescents diagnosed with dysthymic disorder and 20% of those diagnosed with major depressive disorder will later develop a bipolar disorder (Waslick et al., 2003). A detailed psychosocial history may be the interviewer's best tool in identifying children who are at risk for later manic or hypomanic episodes, in that family history of bipolar disorders and assessment of current or past manic episodes are the two main clues in differentiating between a depressive disorder and a bipolar disorder. Family history of bipolar disorder may also inform psychopharmacological treatment options.

SELECTION OF TREATMENT TARGETS AND REFERRAL

Treatment of pediatric depression should be conceptualized as a multimodal effort, involving the child, the family, and the school. The primary goal of treatment is to resolve the current depressive episode as quickly as possible, to prevent recurrence, and to minimize the negative consequences of depressive symptoms (Emslie & Mayes, 1999). Interventions to consider include individual psychotherapy, group psychotherapy, family therapy, psychoeducation, and psychopharmacology.

Individual Psychotherapy

Both cognitive-behavioral and interpersonal approaches to individual psychotherapy have been documented to be efficacious in treating pediatric depression. Cognitive-behavioral psychotherapy is usually time limited and focuses on identifying thought patterns and behaviors that precipitate feelings of depression and serve to maintain the disorder. Behavioral interventions play an important role in teaching the child coping skills for feelings of depression and may help to prevent worsening of symptoms. For example, assisting the child in structuring the day to spend as much time as possible functioning normally may prevent further social withdrawal and negative rumination, two factors that have been shown to compound depression and hamper recovery (Emslie & Mayes, 1999). Common cognitive-behavioral themes and interventions include emotional education to help the child distinguish between different kinds of emotions and to link emotions and events;

self-monitoring of emotions, thoughts, and events; self-reinforcement, where the child learns to reward himself or herself for desired behavior; and cognitive reframing, or challenging of maladaptive thinking patterns. Cognitive-behavioral therapy has been found to be more effective than supportive therapy (Brent et al., 1998). Researchers have also compared cognitive-behavioral therapy with various other modalities and interventions and have found higher rates of remission from depression in the cognitive-behavioral group than in the other treatment groups (Brent et al., 1997; Harrington, Whittaker, Shoebridge, & Campbell, 1998).

Interpersonal therapy has been adapted for use with adolescents and focuses on the manner in which interpersonal relationships can serve a role in the maintenance of depression. Researchers have found not only that poor interpersonal relationships are associated with the onset and maintenance of depression, but social skills deficits also tend to persist even after depressive symptoms remit (Puig-Antich et al., 1993). Like cognitive-behavioral therapy, interpersonal therapy is usually time limited. The therapist and adolescent work collaboratively to select one problem area on which to focus throughout the course of treatment. Themes and interventions include psychoeducation about common developmental issues and the role of social relationships in depression, the development of problem-solving strategies to address a specific area, and the encouragement of the client as he or she implements the problem-solving strategies. Interpersonal therapy has been found to have positive results in treating depressed adolescents, with gains maintained 1 year after the completion of treatment (Mufson & Fairbanks, 1995). Recovery rates have been found to be higher for adolescents who received interpersonal therapy than for a control group (Mufson, Weissman, Moreau, & Garfinkel, 1999).

Group Psychotherapy

Group cognitive-behavioral therapy has been found to be effective in treating depressed and at-risk adolescents (e.g., Clarke et al., 1995), though it is often not recommended for younger children, due to their developmentally limited verbal skills. One study conducted by Clarke, Rohde, Lewinsohn, Hops, and Seeley (1999) found higher rates of recovery for adolescents who participated in cognitive-behavioral therapy groups, both with and without a corresponding parent group, compared with a wait list control group.

Family Therapy

Often, the functioning of the child's family has been severely impacted by the child's depression. Assessing the changes in the family resulting from the child's illness, as well as the family's attempts to manage the disorder, can point to adaptive or maladaptive family coping strategies that can, in turn, be either reinforced or changed. While no research currently supports family therapy as a sole treatment for child and adolescent depression, factors in the family environment such as parental criticism, poor parent-child relationships, and family conflict may impact the onset and course of pediatric depression. Addressing these factors through family therapy as an adjunct to individual psychotherapy may have a positive impact on recovery. Also, up to 50% of depressed youth have a parent who qualifies for a mood disorder diagnosis at the time the child is being treated (Emslie & Mayes, 1999). Family therapy may provide an avenue for assessing all family members' current mental health, educating family members about depression, and offering referrals for treatment as appropriate.

Psychoeducation

One important focus of treatment is to educate parents and teachers about the child's diagnosis in terms of probable symptom manifestation and ways in which they can facilitate recovery from the disorder. Parents of depressed children and adolescents often report high levels of parenting stress and perceive their children as "difficult" (Tan & Rey, 2005). Educating parents about how to manage a child's irritability, defiance, or social withdrawal can reduce stress at home and create a less hostile environment for all family members. As Emslie and Mayes (1999) stated, "Parents also need to know that mood disorders are biological conditions and not personality flaws. Rather than punishment for unacceptable behaviour, the child needs reassurance and support" (p. 184). Encouraging parents to attend to the positive

aspects of an adolescent's behavior is often a simple intervention that reduces critical comments and creates an atmosphere more conducive to increases in positive behavior and recovery from depression (Park & Goodyer, 2000). Incorporating an educational component into treatment has also been shown to decrease the likelihood of early withdrawal from the treatment process (American Association of Child and Adolescent Psychiatry, 1998).

Further, educating teachers about developmental manifestations of depression can influence how the child is treated by the educational system and can prevent inappropriate punishment or reprimand for poor performance (Park & Goodyer, 2000). At times, treatment may involve changes to the child's educational setting to reduce stress, such as shortening the school day, limiting the amount of schoolwork, and developing checklists for assignment completion (Weinberg, Harper, & Emslie, 1994).

Psychopharmacology

Emslie and Mayes (1999) list several factors to consider when determining whether or not to refer depressed children and adolescents for treatment with medication. These factors include the severity of the depressive symptoms, depression that is recurrent, unresponsiveness to psychotherapy, other family members' histories of treatment with medication and their response to medication, and the presence of psychosocial stressors that may be expected to hinder efforts to reduce depression via behavioral methods. Park and Goodyer (2000) offer treatment guidelines according to severity of depressive symptoms, with severe depression warranting treatment with a combination of psychotherapy and medication, moderate depression indicating treatment with psychotherapy and the addition of medication if symptoms are unresponsive, and mild depression signifying treatment with psychotherapy alone.

If a referral to a psychiatrist for a medication evaluation is made, it is likely the treating physician will prescribe an antidepressant from the selective serotonin reuptake inhibitor (SSRI) family of drugs, as these medications have been found to be effective in treating pediatric depression (e.g., Emslie et al., 1997). The use of tricyclic antidepressants (TCAs) in children and adolescents has not been documented to be effective (Hazell, O'Connell, Heathcote, Robertson, & Henry, 1995). The efficacy of monoamine oxidase inhibitors (MAOIs) has not yet been satisfactorily evaluated in children and adolescents (Park & Goodyer, 2000).

One concern that may arise in treating pediatric depression with medication is the potential for the development of manic symptoms. Approximately 3% to 6% of children with severe depression can switch to manic symptoms, and bipolar disorder often presents initially as major depression (Emslie & Mayes, 1999). The treating therapist should carefully monitor any emerging manic symptoms and should communicate such information to the prescribing psychiatrist.

SUMMARY

As is evident from the above discussion, many treatment options exist for pediatric depression. If children and adolescents are given access to appropriate interventions, the prognosis can be a positive one. Appropriate treatment begins with accurate diagnosis, however, and accurate diagnosis relies upon a complete and comprehensive clinical interview and diligent gathering of corroborating information from parents and teachers. Therefore, the interviewing strategies presented in this text provide a vital foundation for assisting children and adolescents along the path to recovery from depression.

REFERENCES

Ablow, J. C., & Measelle, J. R. (1993). *Berkeley Puppet Interview: Administration and scoring system manuals.* Berkeley: University of California.

Achenbach, T. M. (2001). *Manual for the ASEBA school-age forms and profiles.* Burlington: University of Vermont Department of Psychiatry.

American Association of Child and Adolescent Psychiatry. (1998). Practice parameters for the assessment and treatment of children and adolescents with depressive disorders. *Journal of Child Psychology and Psychiatry, 37,* 63S–83S.

American Psychiatric Association. (2000). *Diagnostic and statistical manual of mental disorders* (4th ed., Text rev.). Washington, DC: Author.

Angold, A., & Costello, E. J. (1993). Depressive comorbidity in children and adolescents: Empirical, theoretical, and methodological issues. *American Journal of Psychiatry, 150,* 1779–1791.

Angold, A., & Costello, E. J. (1995). The epidemiology of depression in children and adolescents. In I. M. Goodyer (Ed.), *Depressed child and adolescent: Developmental and clinical perspectives* (pp. 143–178). Cambridge, UK: Cambridge University Press.

Angold, A., & Costello, E. J. (2000). The Child and Adolescent Psychiatric Assessment (CAPA). *Journal of the American Academy of Child & Adolescent Psychiatry, 39,* 39–48.

Angold, A., Costello, E. J., & Worthman, C. M. (1998). Puberty and depression: The roles of age, pubertal status, and pubertal timing. *Psychological Medicine, 28,* 51–61.

Angold, A., Weissman, M. M., John, K., & Merikangas, K. R. (1987). Parent and child reports of depressive symptoms in children at low and high risk of depression. *Journal of Child Psychology and Psychiatry, 28,* 901–915.

Beck, A. T., Steer, R. A., & Brown, G. K. (1996). *Beck Depression Inventory-II.* San Antonio, TX: Psychological Corporation.

Biederman, J., Munir, K., Knee, D., Armentano, M., Autor, S., Waternaux, D., et al. (1987). High rate of affective disorders in probands with attention deficit disorder and in their relatives: A controlled family study. *American Journal of Psychiatry, 144,* 330–333.

Bird, H. R., Gould, M. S., & Staghezza, B. (1992). Aggregating data from multiple informants in child psychiatry epidemiological research. *Journal of the American Academy of Child & Adolescent Psychiatry, 31,* 78–85.

Birmaher, B., Ryan, N. D., Williamson, D. E., Brent, D. A., Kaufman, J., Dahl, et al. (1996). Childhood and adolescent depression: A review of the past ten years. Part I. *Journal of the American Academy of Child & Adolescent Psychiatry, 35,* 1427–1439.

Brent, D. A., Holder, D., Kolko, D., Birmaher, B., Baugher, M., Roth, C., et al. (1997). A clinical psychotherapy trial for adolescent depression comparing cognitive, family, and supportive therapy. *Archives of General Psychiatry, 54,* 877–885.

Brent, D. A., Kolko, D., Birmaher, B., Baugher, M., Bridge, J., Roth, C., et al. (1998). Predictors of treatment efficacy in a clinical trial of three psychosocial treatments for adolescent depression. *Journal of the American Academy of Child & Adolescent Psychiatry, 37,* 906–914.

Choi, H. (2002). Understanding adolescent depression in ethnocultural context. *Advances in Nursing Science, 25,* 71–85.

Clark, L. A., & Watson, D. (1991). Tripartite model of anxiety and depression: Psychometric evidence and taxonomic implications. *Journal of Abnormal Psychology, 100,* 316–336.

Clarke, G. N., Hawkins, W., Murphy, M., Sheeber, L. B., Lewinsohn, P. M., & Seeley, J. R. (1995). Targeted prevention of unipolar depressive disorder in an at-risk sample of high school adolescents: A randomized trial of a group cognitive intervention. *Journal of the American Academy of Child & Adolescent Psychiatry, 34,* 312–321.

Clarke, G. N., Rohde, P., Lewinsohn, P. M., Hops, H., & Seeley, J. R. (1999). Cognitive-behavioral treatment of adolescent depression: Efficacy of acute group treatment and booster sessions. *Journal of the American Academy of Child & Adolescent Psychiatry, 38,* 272–279.

Emslie, G. J., & Mayes, T. L. (1999). Depression in children and adolescents: A guide to diagnosis and treatment. *CNS Drugs, 11,* 181–189.

Emslie, G. J., Rush, A. J., Weinberg, W. A., Kowatch, R. A., Hughes, C. W., Carmody, T., et al. (1997). Recurrence of major depressive disorder in hospitalized children and adolescents. *Journal of the American Academy of Child & Adolescent Psychiatry, 36,* 785–792.

Essau, C. A., Hakim-Larson, J., Crocker, A., & Petermann, F. (1999). Assessment of depressive disorders in children and adolescents. In C. A. Essau & F. Petermann (Eds.), *Depressive disorders in children and adolescents: Epidemiology, risk factors, and treatment* (pp. 27–67). Northvale, NJ: Jason Aronson.

Fergusson, D. M., Horwood, L. J., & Beautrais, A. L. (1999). Is sexual orientation related to mental health problems and suicidality in young people? *Archives of General Psychiatry, 56,* 876–880.

Ferro, T., Verdeli, H., Pierre, F., & Weissman, M. M. (2000). Screening for depression in mothers bringing their offspring for evaluation or treatment of depression. *American Journal of Psychiatry, 157,* 375–379.

Fleming, J. E., & Offord, D. R. (1990). Epidemiology of childhood depressive disorders: A critical review. *Journal of the American Academy of Child & Adolescent Psychiatry, 29,* 571–580.

Garber, J., & Kaminski, K. M. (2000). Laboratory and performance-based measures of depression in children and adolescents. *Journal of Clinical Child Psychology, 29,* 509–525.

Gjerde, P. F., Block, J., & Block, J. H. (1988). Depressive symptoms and personality during late adolescence: Gender differences in the externalization-internalization of symptom expression. *Journal of Abnormal Psychology, 97,* 475–486.

Goodyer, I. M. (1996). Recent undesirable life events: Their influence on subsequent psychopathology. *European Child and Adolescent Psychiatry, 5,* 33–37.

Grabill, C. M., Griffith, J. R., & Kaslow, N. J. (2001). Depression. In M. Hersen & V. B. Van Hasselt (Eds.), *Advanced abnormal psychology* (2nd ed., pp. 243–260). New York: Kluwer Academic/Plenum.

Harrington, R. (1993). *Depressive disorder in childhood and adolescence.* Chichester, UK: John Wiley & Sons.

Harrington, R., Whittaker, J., Shoebridge, P., & Campbell, F. (1998). Systematic review of efficacy of cognitive behaviour therapies in childhood and adolescent depressive disorder. *British Medical Journal, 316,* 1559–1563.

Hazell, P., O'Connell, D., Heathcote, D., Robertson, J., & Henry, D. (1995). Efficacy of tricyclic drugs in treating child and adolescent depression: A meta-analysis. *British Medical Journal, 310,* 897–901.

Hodges, K., McKnew, D., Cytryn, L. Stern, L., & Kline, J. (1982). The Child Assessment Schedule (CAS) diagnostic interview: A report on reliability and validity. *Journal of the American Academy of Child & Adolescent Psychiatry, 21,* 468–473.

Joiner, T. E., & Lonigan, C. J. (2000). Tripartite model of depression and anxiety in youth psychiatric inpatients: Relations with diagnostic status and future symptoms. *Journal of Clinical Child Psychology, 29,* 372–382.

Kaminer, Y., Feinstein, C., & Seifer, R. (1995). Is there a need for observationally based assessment of affective symptomatology in child and adolescent psychiatry? *Adolescence, 30,* 483–489.

Kaufman, J., Birmaher, B., Brent, D., Rao, U., Flynn, C., Moreci, P., et al. (1997). Schedule for Affective Disorders and Schizophrenia for School-Age Children-Present and Lifetime Version (K-SADS-PL): Initial reliability and validity data. *Journal of the American Academy of Child & Adolescent Psychiatry, 36,* 980–988.

Kazdin, A. E. (1994). Informant variability in the assessment of childhood depression. In W. M. Reynolds & H. F. Johnston (Eds.), *Handbook of depression in children and adolescents* (pp. 249–271). New York: Plenum Press.

Kovacs, M. (1992). *Children's Depression Inventory (CDI) manual.* North Tonowanda, NY: Multihealth Systems.

Kovacs, M., Gatsonis, C., Paulauskas, S. L., & Richards, C. (1989). Depressive disorders in childhood: IV. A longitudinal study of comorbidity with and risk for anxiety disorders. *Archives of General Psychiatry, 46,* 776–782.

Kovacs, M., Obrosky, D. S., Gatsonis, C., & Richards, C. (1997). First-episode major depressive and dysthymic disorder in childhood: Clinical and sociodemographic factors in recovery. *Journal of the American Academy of Child & Adolescent Psychiatry, 36,* 777–784.

Kutcher, S. P., & Marton, P. (1989). Parameters of adolescent depression: A review. *Psychiatric Clinics of North America, 12,* 895–918.

La Greca, A. M. (1990). Issues and perspectives on the child assessment process. In A. M. LaGreca (Ed.), *Through the eyes of the child: Obtaining self-reports from children and adolescents* (pp. 3–17). Boston: Allyn & Bacon.

Lahey, B. B., Applegate, B., Waldman, I. D., Loft, J. D., Hankin, B. L., & Rick, J. (2004). The structure of child and adolescent psychopathology: Generating new hypotheses. *Journal of Abnormal Psychology, 113,* 358–385.

Lewinsohn, P. M., Rohde, P., & Seeley, J. R. (1993). Psychosocial characteristics of adolescents with a history of suicide attempt. *Journal of the American Academy of Child & Adolescent Psychiatry, 32,* 60–68.

Matzner, F., Silva, R., Silvan, M., Chowdhury, M., & Nastasi, L. (1997). Preliminary test-retest reliability of the KID-SCID. In *1997 Annual meeting, new research program and abstracts* (pp. 1127–1123). Washington, DC: American Psychiatric Association.

Monroe, S. M., Rohde, P., Seeley, J. R., & Lewinsohn, P. M. (1999). Life events and depression in adolescence: Relationship loss as a prospective risk factor for first onset of major depressive disorder. *Journal of Abnormal Psychology, 108,* 606–614.

Moscicki, E. K. (1997). Identification of suicide risk factors using epidemiologic studies. *Psychiatric Clinics of North America, 20,* 499–517.

Mufson, L., & Fairbanks, J. (1995). Interpersonal psychotherapy for depressed adolescents: A one-year naturalistic follow-up study. *Journal of the American Academy of Child & Adolescent Psychiatry, 35,* 1145–1155.

Mufson, L., Weissman, M. M., Moreau, D., & Garfinkel, R. (1999). Efficacy of interpersonal psychotherapy for depressed adolescents. *Archives of General Psychiatry, 56,* 573–579.

Nguyen, L., Arganza, G. F., Huang, L. N., Liao, Q., Nguyen, H. T., & Santiago, R. (2004). Psychiatric diagnoses and clinical considerations of Asian American youth in children's services. *Journal of Child and Family Studies, 13,* 483–495.

Nolen-Hoeksema, S., & Girgus, J. (1994). The emergence of gender differences in depression during adolescence. *Psychological Bulletin, 115,* 424–443.

Park, R. J., & Goodyer, I. M. (2000). Clinical guidelines for depressive disorders in childhood and adolescence. *European Child and Adolescent Psychiatry, 9,* 147–161.

Pedersen, P. B. (1997). *Culture-centered counseling interventions: Striving for accuracy.* Thousand Oaks, CA: Sage.

Perez, R., Ascaso, L., Domenech Massons, J., & de la Osa Chaparro, N. (1998). Characteristics of the subjects and interview influencing the test-retest reliability of the Diagnostic Interview for Children and Adolescents–Revised. *Journal of Child Psychology and Psychiatry, 39,* 963–972.

Poznanski, E. O., & Mokros, H. B. (1996). *Children's depression rating scale-revised manual.* Los Angeles: Western Psychological Services.

Puig-Antich, J., Kaufman, J., Ryan, N. D., Williamson, D., Dahl, R. E., Lukens, E., et al. (1993). The psychosocial functioning and family environment of depressed adolescents. *Journal of the American Academy of Child & Adolescent Psychiatry, 32,* 244–253.

Puura, K., Almqvist, F., Tamminen, T., Piha, J., Kumpulainen, K., Rasanen, E., et al. (1998). Children with symptoms of depression: What do the adults see? *Journal of Child Psychology and Psychiatry, 39,* 577–585.

Reynolds, W. M. (1989). *Reynolds Child Depression Scale: Professional manual.* Odessa, FL: Psychological Assessment Resources.

Reynolds, W. M., & Mazza, J. J. (1998). Reliability and validity of the Reynolds Adolescent Depression Scale with young adolescents. *Journal of School Psychology, 36,* 353–76.

Roberts, R. E. (2000). Depression and suicidal behaviors among adolescents: The role of ethnicity. In I. Cuellar & F. A. Paniagua (Eds.), *Handbook of multicultural mental health* (pp. 359–388). San Diego, CA: Academic Press.

Roberts, R. E., Roberts, C. R., & Chen, Y. R. (1997). Ethnocultural differences in prevalence of adolescent depression. *American Journal of Community Psychology, 25,* 95–110.

Ryan, N. D. (2001). Diagnosing pediatric depression. *Biological Psychiatry, 49,* 1050–1054.

Ryan, N. D. (2002). Depression. In S. Kutcher (Ed.), *Practical child and adolescent psychopharmacology* (pp. 91–105). New York: Cambridge University Press.

Ryan, N. D., Puig-Antich, J., Ambrosini, P., Rabinovich, H., Robinson, D., Nelson, B., et al. (1987). The clinical picture of major depression in children and adolescents. *Archives of General Psychiatry, 44,* 854–861.

Schwartz, J. A. J., Gladstone, T. R. G., & Kaslow, N. J. (1998). Depressive disorders. In T. H. Ollendick & M. Hersen (Eds.), *Handbook of child psychopathology* (3rd ed., pp. 269–289). New York: Plenum Press.

Sherrill, J. T., & Kovacs, M. (2000). Interview Schedule of Children and Adolescents (ISCA). *Journal of the American Academy of Child & Adolescent Psychiatry, 39,* 67–75.

Tan, S., & Rey, J. (2005). Depression in the young, parental depression, and parenting stress. *Australian Psychiatry, 13,* 76–79.

Wagner, K. D. (2003). Major depression in children and adolescents. *Psychiatric Annals, 33,* 266–270.

Waslick, B. D., Kandel, R., & Kakouros, A. (2002). Depression in children and adolescents: An overview. In D. Shaffer & B. D. Waslick (Eds.), *The many faces of depression in children and adolescents* (pp. 1–36). Washington, DC: American Psychiatric Publishing.

Waslick, B., Shoenholz, D., & Pizarro, R. (2003). Diagnosis and treatment of chronic depression in children and adolescents. *Journal of Psychiatric Practice, 9,* 354–366.

Weinberg, W. A., Harper, C. R., & Emslie, G. J. (1994). The effect of depression and learning disabilities on school behavior problems. *Directory of Clinical Psychology, 4,* 1–21.

Weissman, M. M., Wolk, S., Goldstein, R. B., Moreau, D., Adams, P., Greenwald, S., et al. (1999). Depressed adolescents grown up. *Journal of the American Medical Association, 281,* 1707–1713.

11

ANXIETY DISORDERS

WENDY K. SILVERMAN AND YASMIN REY

DESCRIPTION OF THE DISORDERS

According to Barlow (2002),

Anxiety seems best characterized as a future-oriented emotion, characterized by perceptions of uncontrollability and unpredictability over potentially aversive events and a rapid shift in attention to the focus of potentially dangerous events or one's own affective response to these events. (p. 104)

Barlow noted two main consequences when anxiety becomes a clinical condition: avoidance and worry. Both avoidance and worry, when they become pervasive, intense, or uncontrollable, represent maladaptive ways in which individuals attempt to handle their aversive anxious states. As individuals are confronted with anxiety-provoking situations, elevated physiological arousal arises. As such, Barlow endorsed the three-response system to anxiety formulated earlier by Lang (1968). Fear is similar to anxiety at a response level, in that fear is also characterized by cognitive, behavioral, and physiological reactions, but fear is "the unadulterated, ancient, possibly innate alarm system" (Barlow, 2002, p. 104).

Although anxiety and fear are common in children and adolescents, young people should

be evaluated for possible phobic and/or anxiety disorders when the fear, anxiety, or both are (a) beyond that expected for the youth's developmental level, (b) irrational, and (c) lead to significant interference or impairment in one or more areas of daily functioning (e.g., school, friends, family) and/or internal subjective distress.

The *Diagnostic and Statistical Manual of Mental Disorders, Fourth Edition (DSM-IV)* (American Psychiatric Association [APA], 1994) delineates the diagnostic criteria for the different subtypes of anxiety disorders. Of these subtypes, separation anxiety disorder (SAD) is the only anxiety disorder subtype specific to children and adolescents. The remainder of the anxiety disorder subtypes can be applied to both adults and youth. These include generalized anxiety disorder (GAD), obsessive-compulsive disorder (OCD), panic disorder (PD), posttraumatic stress disorder (PTSD), social phobia (SOP), and specific phobia (SP). Each anxiety disorder subtype is generally characterized by apprehension and avoidance of situations or objects (Barlow, 2002; Silverman & Kurtines, 1996). The main difference among the subtypes is in the content of the apprehension and avoidance (e.g., a dog for a child with SP; separation experiences for a child with SAD; speaking to others for a child with SOP; Silverman & Kurtines, 1996).

INTERVIEWING STRATEGIES

The clinical interview is the most common strategy used to assess problems in children and adolescents, including anxiety disorders (Ollendick & Hersen, 1993; Silverman, 1994). Clinical interviews are characterized as either unstructured or structured (Richardson, Dohrenwend, & Klein, 1965). Unstructured clinical interviews are nonstandardized, in that there are no specific questions the interviewer must ask, no designated format, and no specific method to record responses. Semistructured and structured interviews, in contrast, are standardized, in that identical questions are asked of all informants and there are specified methods to capture the data and record responses.

Unstructured Interviewing Strategies

Because of the nonstandardized nature of the unstructured clinical interview, interviewers have considerable leeway. Despite the absence of definitive rules, there are important pieces of information that are useful to obtain from the youth and parent(s) to attain a comprehensive assessment of the youth's potential difficulties with excessive fear and anxiety (American Academy of Child and Adolescent Psychiatry, 1997).

One important piece of information is the history and development of the youth's anxiety symptoms. Specifically, once the youth and parents have described the presenting problem, the interviewer should further inquire about the onset, frequency, and intensity of the anxiety symptoms. The interviewer should also inquire about the presence of avoidant behaviors (e.g., refusal to go to school) and the pervasiveness of the avoidance. Information about the antecedents and consequences of the youth's anxious and avoidant behaviors should also be obtained. To solicit this information, the interviewer might ask the youth and parents to relay the details about what occurs before, during, and after the youth's display of anxious/avoidant behaviors, focusing particularly on factors that may be maintaining the behaviors, including inadvertent parental reinforcement (e.g., attention). Of additional importance is to inquire about how the youth's anxious/avoidant behaviors interfere in school or with academic tasks, with family members, and with friends. If the goal of the interview is to formulate a *DSM-IV* anxiety disorder diagnosis, the

interviewer should systematically inquire about the presence or absence of symptoms that make up each anxiety disorder. In addition, the interviewer should screen for other disorders that are highly comorbid with anxiety disorders (e.g., attention-deficit/hyperactivity disorder [ADHD], depression).

Other important areas of inquiry are the youth's developmental, medical, academic, social, and family histories. A developmental history is taken to gather information regarding the youth's age at meeting developmental milestones, his or her temperament during early development, prior delays or present behavioral deficits or excesses, response to separation, and early fears. A medical history of the youth also includes the number of medical visits relating to the anxious symptoms, any medications taken that may produce anxious symptoms (e.g., antihistamines, selective serotonin reuptake inhibitors, cold medications), and the presence of medical disorders that may mimic anxiety (e.g., hypoglycemia, hyperthyroidism, cardiac arrhythmias, seizure disorders, and migraines). Information on how the youth generally functions at school and with friends is also important to obtain to help determine whether additional difficulties, such as learning disabilities, may be present. Information to obtain about family history should include presence of stressful life events (e.g., loss, separation, exposure to abuse, violence, death), resources, parental coping styles, and family psychiatric history (American Academy of Child and Adolescent Psychiatry, 1997).

Structured Interviewing Strategies

Although unstructured interviews are flexible, they produce considerable variance to the extent that interviewers differ in the specific questions they ask of youth and parents, as well as their interview styles and handling of diagnostic criteria (Silverman, 1994). Unstructured interviews may also lead the interviewer to inadvertently omit some key questions that might be needed to assess the broad spectrum of the youth's problems, especially in light of the high rates of comorbidity that exist among disorders of childhood and adolescence (Anderson, Williams, McGee, & Silva, 1987; Bird, Gould, & Staghezza, 1992; Kashani & Orvaschel, 1988; McGee et al., 1990). Partly in response to the limits of unstructured interviews, semistructured and structured diagnostic interview schedules were developed for use with children and adolescents, including those with fear and anxiety problems (Silverman & Ollendick, 2005).

Structured and semistructured interviews can reliably and accurately determine the presence or absence of specific anxiety disorder diagnoses and other disorders. To the extent that an interviewer implements a treatment with the most research support for reducing anxious symptoms (i.e., exposure-based cognitive-behavior therapy [CBT]; Ollendick & King, 1998; Silverman & Berman, 2001), it would seem important to use structured and semistructured interviews to determine accurate diagnoses, so that the appropriate exposure tasks can be assigned (e.g., a youth with SP of dogs would be exposed to dogs; a youth with SOP would be exposed to evaluative situations; Silverman & Ollendick, 2005).

Table 11.1 presents a short description of the most commonly used structured and semistructured interview schedules, which contain sections for each *DSM-IV* anxiety disorder, and the reliability estimates obtained when the interviews were used to diagnose some of the anxiety disorders. The studies listed in Table 11.1 reported reliability estimates for anxiety disorders that were diagnosed in sufficient numbers within the study's samples; thus, some of the anxiety disorders have reliability estimates, and others do not. As Table 11.1 shows, with the exception of the Child and Adolescent Psychiatric Assessment (CAPA) (Angold & Costello, 2000), all the interview schedules have respective youth and parent versions. The interview schedules can be used across a wide age range (6 to 18 years old) and require minimal responses (i.e., yes, no), which can be especially helpful when working with young children as well as children with limited verbal expression. Many of the interview schedules contain rating scales to assist in prioritizing the range of disorders of the youth. Many also contain additional questions that assess the medical and developmental histories of youth and academic and social functioning.

Most of the interview schedules listed on Table 11.1 rely on comparable interviewing strategies. Specifically, the schedules begin with an introductory section designed to help build rapport with the informants, including queries about school and free-time activities and questions about the youth's presenting problems. Symptoms are then presented within specified sections or modules within the interviews. Usually, a few screening questions are asked of the youth and parent, which require either a "yes" or "no" response. If a "yes" response is received to any screening question from the youth, parent, or both, the entire module is typically administered, including obtaining frequency, intensity, and interference ratings. If a "no" response is received, the module is usually skipped and the interviewer moves on to the subsequent module. Diagnoses are generated upon completion of both the youth and parent interviews and are determined either by rules derived by the interview developers or by computerized algorithms, depending on the specifications of the interview schedule.

The interview schedule that provides the most comprehensive coverage of the *DSM-IV* anxiety disorders is the Anxiety Disorders Interview Schedule for Children for *DSM-IV*: Child and Parent Versions (ADIS-IV: C/P) (Silverman & Albano, 1996). The ADIS-IV: C/P contains questions that allow for the diagnoses of all the anxiety disorders as well as questions about the history of the youth's anxious difficulties and contextual factors that may be maintaining these difficulties. In addition, modules are included for all the major *DSM* disorders displayed by children and adolescents (e.g., ADHD, conduct disorder, oppositional defiant disorder [ODD], depression), as well as screening questions for other disorders (e.g., enuresis, schizophrenia; Silverman & Ollendick, 2005). Questions about the youth's medical, developmental, and psychiatric history, as well as family history of psychiatric disorders, are also included.

The ADIS-IV: C/P provides a pictorial rating scale (i.e., "Feelings Thermometer") that allows interviewers to obtain ratings from the youth and parents on the youth's fear and/or avoidance of specific situations for those anxiety disorders diagnoses in which fear and/or avoidance occurs (e.g., SOP, SP). The Feelings Thermometer also allows the interviewer to obtain ratings from the youth and parents on the youth's level of distress and/or interference in functioning related to each disorder on a 0- *(none)* to 8- *(very much)* point scale (Silverman & Ollendick, 2005). A rating of 4 *(some)* or higher from either the youth or parents is considered a clinically significant diagnosis. The most severe and interfering disorder is considered the primary diagnosis, the one that would be targeted using exposure-based CBT (Albano & Silverman, 1996).

TABLE 11.1 Structured and Semistructured Interview Schedules for Diagnosing *DSM-IV* Anxiety Disorders in Youth

Diagnostic Interview Schedule	Structured or Semistructured	Versions	Age (Years)	Diagnoses	Kappa Coefficients of Reliability			
					Child	Adolescent	Parent	Combined
Anxiety Disorders Interview Schedule for *DSM-IV*: Child and Parent Versions (ADIS for *DSM-IV*: C/P; Silverman & Albano, 1996; Silverman, Saavedra, & Pina, 2001)	Semistructured	C/P	6 to 18	GAD SAD SOP SP	.63 .78 .71 .80		.72 .88 .86 .65	.80 .84 .92 .81
Child and Adolescent Psychiatric Assessment (CAPA; Angold & Costello, 2000)	Structured	C	9 to 13	GAD OAD	.79 .74			
Diagnostic Interview for Children and Adolescents (DICA; Herjanic & Reich, 1982; Reich, 2000)	Semistructured	C/P/A	6 to 17	OAD SAD SP	.55 .60 .65	.72 .75 (past)		
NIMH Diagnostic Interview Schedule for Children Version IV (NIMH DISC-IV; Shaffer, Fisher, Lucas, Dulcan, & Schwab-Stone, 2000)	Structured	C/P	9 to 17	GAD SAD SOP SP	.46 .25 .68		.65 .58 .54 .96	.58 .51 .48 .86
Schedule for Affective Disorders and Schizophrenia for School-Age Children (K-SADS; Ambrosini, 2000)	Semistructured	C/P	6 to 18	OAD SP				.78 .80

NOTE: *DSM-IV* = *Diagnostic and Statistical Manual of Mental Disorders* (4th ed.), C = child, P = parent, A = adolescent, SAD = separation anxiety disorder, SOP = social phobia, SP = specific phobia, GAD = generalized anxiety disorder, and OAD = overanxious disorder.

Interviewing Obstacles and Solutions

A number of obstacles may be encountered when using unstructured, semistructured, and structured interview schedules, which may affect the quantity and quality of the information obtained. This section provides an overview of the most common obstacles the authors have encountered when working with children and adolescents who present with anxiety disorders. Although not all the obstacles covered in this section are necessarily unique to anxious children, attention is focused on those obstacles that largely occur due to key clinical features of anxiety disorders.

Not Separating From Parents

Obstacle. One obstacle frequently encountered is the child's difficulty in separating from parents and being alone with the interviewer, especially among SAD cases. In some cases, the child's refusal can be as extreme as refusing to leave the car. It has not been unusual for the parent to enter the clinic in exasperation and seek assistance in coaxing the child from the car. On several occasions, the authors have actually walked with the parent to the car and have explained to the child what he or she will be experiencing during the interview procedures. This information can often be helpful in alleviating children's concerns, especially because many parents do not inform their children ahead of time what they will be experiencing at the clinic. If the provision of this type of information is helpful, the child may agree to accompany us to the clinic but still refuse to participate in the interviewing procedure. The child may cry, throw temper tantrums, or cling to his or her parents when asked to accompany the interviewer for the interview. The child may display similar signs of distress when the parents need to be interviewed without the child present.

Solution. The child and his or her parents may not be fully aware of the details of the intake procedures, and the parents may not inform the child about the procedures. Being unaware of the interview procedures may cause apprehension in any child, but this apprehension is likely to be exacerbated for the child who is suffering from an anxiety disorder. It is important to provide the child or adolescent with the necessary information to help allay any concerns he or she may have about the interview process. For example, it is usually helpful if the interviewer informs the child that they are going to talk only about the youth's thoughts, feelings, and behaviors. It also is helpful if the interviewer informs the child that no medicines or shots will be given. For the child with SAD, it can be further reassuring if the interviewer can show the child where his or her parents will be during the interview and allow the child to check in on the parents if necessary.

Not Acknowledging Difficulties

Obstacle. Another interview obstacle, especially when working with a youth with SOP, is that the youth may have high self-presentational concerns (Kendall & Chansky, 1991; Silverman & Rabian, 1995) and may thereby express socially desirable answers (Dadds, Perrin, & Yule, 1998). For example, the youth may not acknowledge that he or she is actually experiencing difficulties related to anxiety, due to concerns about being evaluated by the interviewer. Youth expression of social desirability has been found to be influenced by both age and ethnicity (Dadds et al., 1998; Pina, Silverman, Saavedra, & Weems, 2001). Younger children score significantly higher than adolescents on the "Lie Scale" of the Children's Manifest Anxiety Scale-Revised (RCMAS) (Reynolds & Richmond, 1985; Dadds et al., 1998; Pina et al., 2001); African Americans score significantly higher than European Americans (Dadds et al., 1998), and Hispanic/ Latinos also score significantly higher than European Americans (Pina et al., 2001). Interviewers, therefore, need to be aware of the presence of social desirability in certain segments of youth because of the potential influence that social desirability may have on the validity of youth reports.

Solution. In working with the child or adolescent who may express socially desirable answers due to high self-presentational concerns, the authors have found it useful to universalize the youth's experiences. This can be done by informing the youth that there is unlikely to be anything that he or she will say that will surprise the interviewer, because most of the youth's feelings or behaviors are more common than the youth probably realizes. The interviewer can inform the youth from the onset of the interview that there are "no right or wrong answers" and that answering the interview questions "as honestly as possible" would be most helpful during this process. It is important to underscore that the youth is not being evaluated based on his or her responses to the interview questions.

Not Responding to Interview Questions

Obstacle. Another obstacle frequently encountered is the child or adolescent who shows reluctance or refusal to speak during the clinical interview. This occurs most among children or adolescents who are suffering from either severe SOP or selective mutism (SM). In such cases, parents' reports are particularly valuable. Nevertheless, even when the youth is not verbally communicating during the interview, the interview context provides a valuable opportunity for the interviewer to directly observe the nature and severity of the youth's social anxiety difficulties. For example, the interviewer can observe the youth's eye contact, whether the youth at least responds "yes" or "no" to questions, whispers the responses, or merely nods and whether the youth displays positive emotional reactions, such as smiles and laughter. The interview can also help in determining whether the youth's social anxiety difficulties are compounded by either social skills deficits (e.g., does not ask questions) or inappropriate social skills (e.g., asks rude questions).

Solution. In working with the child or adolescent who shows reluctance or refusal to speak during the clinical interview due to severe SOP or SM, the authors have found it useful to use forms of nonverbal communication to assess the youth's anxiety. Thus, interviewers can advise the youth to respond to the interview questions either by pointing to the words "yes" or "no" written on a board or sheet of paper or by nodding or shaking his or her head. As noted earlier, interview schedules may be particularly useful in gathering information from youth with severe SOP or SM because interview schedules require minimal responses from youth. As also noted, some interview schedules such as the ADIS-IV: C/P contain pictorial rating scales (i.e., Feelings Thermometer), which assist in the process of obtaining ratings of fear and/or interference from such youth.

Not Deciding on Responses

Obstacle. Another obstacle the authors have frequently encountered is youth indecision about how to respond to the interview questions. Youth indecision may be related in part to high levels of social desirability, discussed above. Youth indecision about how to respond may also be related to the clinical features that characterize some of the specific anxiety disorders. Generalized anxiety disorder (GAD), for example, is characterized by perfectionism. As a consequence, the youth with GAD may be "searching" for the correct answer to the interview question to ensure that he or she is doing a "good job" or, even better, a "perfect job" during the interview process. Another example is the youth with panic disorder (PD), which is characterized by symptoms, such as derealization and fear of going crazy, which are generally abstract. As such, youth may have difficulty in deciding how to respond to interview questions that focus on these types of abstract symptoms, as the answers to these questions can rarely be fully verified as "perfectly" correct.

When a youth is indecisive during the interview, the interviewer will likely observe that the youth has difficulty in answering simple "yes" or "no" answers to the interview questions. Rather, the youth may respond with "It depends" and proceed to explain the diverse set of circumstances regarding why sometimes the answer is affirmative and other times the answer is negative. In some cases, the youth may ask the interviewer to return to an interview module already completed because the youth has reconsidered his or her initial responses to the previous questions.

Solution. In the authors' experience in working with youth indecision during the interview, it has been useful to instruct the youth to answer the interview questions according to how true each question is for him or her. It also has been useful to further explain to the youth that answering "yes" would mean the anxious symptoms occur "more often than not" or "more yes than no" and answering "no" would mean the anxious symptoms hardly or never occur. If the youth answers "sometimes," the interviewer may further ask, "Is it more yes or more no?" so that a definitive answer to the question is obtained. If the youth has difficulty answering questions relating to the duration of anxious symptoms, the authors have found it helpful to inform the youth that the duration of anxious symptoms can be "about" or "approximately" and not necessarily an exact number. Several interview schedules, such as the ADIS-IV: C/P, include calendars to assist the youth in determining symptom duration.

Not Concentrating/Cooperating

Obstacle. Difficulties with concentration, cooperation, or both are additional obstacles that the authors have frequently encountered when interviewing children and adolescents with anxiety disorders. Such difficulties occur particularly among youth with the most common externalizing disorders that co-occur with anxiety disorders, such as ADHD and ODD (e.g., Last, Hersen, Kazdin, Finkelstein, & Strauss, 1987). Anxious youth with comorbid ADHD, for example, may not only have difficulty in concentrating on the interview questions and staying seated during the interview but may also be distracted easily, be overly talkative, answer questions before the interviewer has finished asking them, and steer away from the focus of the interview questions. Anxious youth with comorbid ODD may not cooperate with the interviewer during the interview. The youth may be reluctant or refuse to answer certain interview questions, and, in some cases, may even make efforts to discontinue the interview. In cases where anxious youth display behaviors during the interview that are associated with other clinical disorders (e.g., ADHD or ODD), it is important to determine whether these other disorders should be assigned as diagnoses to the youth. As noted, structured and semistructured interview schedules contain questions that allow for the diagnoses of anxiety disorders as well as other comorbid disorders in youth.

Solution. Although rapport building is always an essential component of the interview process, the authors have found that adequate rapport between the interviewer and the youth is perhaps even more critical when working with children or adolescents who display difficulties in concentration, cooperation, or both. Thus, with an adolescent, it can be helpful for the interviewer to initially ask general, nonthreatening questions in a rather unstructured manner as a way to enhance the adolescent's trust and cooperation. With children, it can be helpful to begin by first asking similar nonthreatening questions and suggesting that they play several rounds of some game, such as "hangman." For some children, however, initiating a semistructured or structured interview is often a way to focus their attention, as the structure is precisely what some children need.

It can also be helpful with some youth to arrange an agreement that they will be able to receive intermittent "breaks" from the interview and play a round or two of the game during the break. Relatedly, if the interviewer observes during the course of the interview that the youth is becoming increasingly restless, the interviewer might suggest a brief break and resume the interview after the break. It can also be helpful to repeat back the question just asked of the youth as a way to redirect his or her attention. Alternatively, the interviewer can ask the youth to repeat back the question.

INTERVIEWING PARENTS OR TEACHERS

Interviewing Parents

Parents are important and necessary informants in the interview process of children and adolescents with anxiety disorders. Parents can provide rich information based on their daily observations of their children's behaviors. Parents usually can also provide more accurate information than their children regarding the history of their anxiety problems, including onset, duration, frequency, and severity (Schniering, Hudson, & Rapee, 2000). Parents usually can also provide more accurate and detailed information about their children's developmental and medical histories. Interviewing parents also creates an opportunity to build trust and rapport, which is essential for subsequent treatment implementation. Parents and their children are frequently discordant in their responses, however, especially regarding anxiety problems (Choudhury, Pimentel, & Kendall, 2003; Comer & Kendall, 2004; Grills & Ollendick, 2003), and so obtaining information from parents takes on even greater import to derive as full and complete a picture of the child's functioning as possible.

Factors Affecting Youth-Parent Agreement on Anxiety Disorders and Symptoms

As just noted, although a few studies have found moderate to good youth-parent agreement for some anxiety disorders subtypes found in youth (SOP: Rapee, Barrett, Dadds, & Evans, 1994; SAD and SOP: Safford, Kendall, Flannery-Schroeder, Webb, & Sommer, 2005), the majority of studies have found low levels of youth-parent agreement on anxiety disorders (Choudhury et al., 2003; Grills & Ollendick, 2003) and anxiety symptoms (Comer & Kendall, 2004; Edelbrock, Costello, Dulcan, Conover, & Kalas, 1986; Herjanic & Reich, 1982) when assessed via structured and semistructured interview schedules. Some factors may contribute to the low levels of agreement found among youth and parent reports on the youth's anxiety. These are briefly summarized next.

Youth Age. Several researchers have hypothesized that youth-parent agreement would be lower for children (approximately 6 to 9 years) than adolescents (approximately 10 to 16 years) because younger children lack the cognitive sophistication to fully understand and describe their emotions and behaviors (Brenton et al., 1995; Edelbrock, Costello, Dulcan, Kalas, & Conover, 1985; Rapee et al., 1994; Schwab-Stone, Fallon, Briggs, & Crowther, 1994). In support of this hypothesis, some studies have found higher youth-parent agreement for older than younger children on some anxiety symptoms and disorders (Edelbrock et al., 1986; Rapee et al., 1994). Other studies, however, have found higher youth-parent agreement for younger than older children (Choudhury et al., 2003), and other studies have found no age differences in agreement (Grills & Ollendick, 2003; Safford et al., 2005). These discrepant findings would therefore suggest that whether parents and their children agree or disagree in their reports is not solely determined by the youth's age.

Parental Psychopathology. The presence of psychopathology in the parent is another factor that has been shown to be related to low levels of youth-parent agreement on anxiety disorders

and symptoms (e.g., Engel, Rodrigue, & Geffken, 1994; Frick, Silverthorn, & Evans, 1994; Krain & Kendall, 2000). Some studies have found that anxious and depressed parents significantly over-report their children's anxiety symptoms (Frick et al., 1994; Krain & Kendall, 2000). Thus, it may be important for the interviewer to be aware of parental anxiety and/or depression when interviewing parents about their children's anxious symptoms. This can be done by administering an anxiety and/or depression rating scale to the parent(s), such as the Hamilton Anxiety Scale (Hamilton, 1959) or the Beck Depression Inventory (Beck, Ward, Mendelson, Mock, & Erbaugh, 1961). Parents can also be asked about their past psychiatric histories and current medication status to further ascertain whether anxiety, depression, or both have been a "problem" for them. In cases where anxiety and depression are present in parents, it may be important to determine the role the parents' pathology may be playing in maintaining the child's anxiety. In some cases, it may be helpful to recommend that the parents seek services for themselves.

Parental Unawareness of Children's Internal Distress. Another factor that may contribute to low levels of youth-parent agreement on anxiety disorders and anxiety symptoms is parental unawareness of the extent of their children's internal distress (Kendall & Flannery-Schroeder, 1998). Some studies that have evaluated youth-parent agreement on a number of psychiatric symptoms showed that youth endorsed more symptoms of anxiety and also rated those symptoms as more severe than did their parents, perhaps due to parents' limited awareness of their children's internal distress (Edelbrock et al., 1986; Herjanic & Reich, 1982).

Although parents may be valuable informants regarding their child's observable symptoms of anxiety (e.g., refusal to sleep without an attachment figure in SAD or avoidant behaviors related to SP), parents may not be aware of the unobservable symptoms of anxiety (e.g., excessive and uncontrollable worry in GAD, worry about harm befalling attachment figures in SAD) that may be distressing to their child. Thus, it is important to include the youth as an informant in the assessment of his or her anxiety symptoms, particularly when assessing the presence of anxious symptoms that are manifested primarily through subjective or cognitive reactions.

In sum, although parents are important and necessary informants in the interview process of children and adolescents with anxiety disorders, youth and parents are frequently discordant in their reporting of anxiety problems (Choudhury et al., 2003; Comer & Kendall, 2004; Grills & Ollendick, 2003). Furthermore, some evidence exists that certain factors (e.g., parental psychopathology, youth age) may affect youth-parent agreement. As such, it is important to obtain information from the parents as well as the child to derive as full and complete a picture of the youth's functioning as possible.

Interviewing Teachers

Teachers may not be as useful for assessing child and adolescent internalizing problems, such as anxiety disorders, as they are for assessing externalizing problems (Loeber, Green, & Lahey, 1990). This is because teachers are more likely to notice when a student is calling out of turn (an externalizing problem) than when a student is experiencing subjective distress because he or she is about to be called on (an internalizing problem). Nevertheless, interviewing teachers can be helpful in cases where the youth's anxious symptoms and avoidant behaviors are displayed in the classroom setting.

In gathering information from the teacher regarding the youth's anxiety, it is more feasible to use less structured interviewing procedures and not necessarily rely on face-to-face encounters, but arrange instead to speak with the teacher over the telephone. The interviewer might begin by first asking whether the teacher has any concerns about the youth's performance in the classroom, whether academic, behavioral, or peer related. The interviewer should then focus on behaviors described by the teacher that would appear to be related to anxiety. For example, the teacher might describe to the interviewer that whenever the class is required to read aloud and it is the child's turn to read, he or she begins to cry and refuses to read aloud. The interviewer might then ask the teacher questions regarding how often and how long this behavior occurs and if there are other situations in the classroom in which the youth might also cry and refuse to perform. The interviewer might also ask the teacher how much this behavior interferes with the youth's functioning in the classroom.

Gathering information from the teacher about the youth's anxious behaviors, albeit informal, is useful especially if the youth's anxious behaviors are displayed in the classroom. An informal interview with the teacher also provides the interviewer with an opportunity to establish rapport, which is important if the teacher might be an active participant in the youth's anxiety treatment (e.g., assisting with the execution of out-of-session exposure tasks, administering rewards).

CASE ILLUSTRATION WITH DIALOGUE

Case Description

Jessica was a 10-year-old Hispanic girl referred to an anxiety disorders specialty clinic for children and adolescents by her school counselor. Jessica was referred due to difficulties related to separating from her parents at school. Jessica's parents reported that she was afraid of going to school and cried almost every night before school and almost every morning when preparing to leave for school. Jessica told her parents that she was afraid they would not come back to pick her up once the school day was over. Jessica's parents also reported that she was afraid of sleeping alone and needed her mom to lie down with her until she fell asleep. Jessica had been experiencing these difficulties for 2 years; however, they had recently intensified, for reasons that were unclear.

Clinical Interview

Jessica and her mother were individually administered the ADIS-IV: C/P. Although the full interview schedules are lengthy to administer (approximately 60–90 minutes with the youth and parent, respectively), interviewers have the flexibility of using the interview schedules as templates that can guide their questioning, rather than as scripts that must be precisely followed (Silverman & Kurtines, 1996). By using the interview schedule in this way, the interviewer has available a full range of *DSM*-oriented questions to which he or she can refer if necessary.

The interviewer began the assessment by interviewing Jessica first, using the ADIS: C. The first portion of the interview requests that the child give a brief description of the presenting problem. Once Jessica described the presenting problem, the interviewer explained to Jessica how to use the Feelings Thermometer to provide ratings on the fear or avoidance of certain objects and/or situations and on the interference of anxious symptoms on a 0- *(none)* to 8- *(very much)* point scale. Once the interviewer explained how to use the Feelings Thermometer and ensured that Jessica understood by practicing with some examples, the interviewer proceeded to ask Jessica questions contained in the SAD module. The following is an excerpt of Jessica's interview.

Interviewer: Some children worry a lot about being away from their parents or from home. Do you feel really scared or worried when you are away from your mom or dad, and do you do whatever you can to be with them?

Jessica: Yes.

I: Can you tell me a little more about that?

J: When I am in the classroom, I ask my teacher to let me call my parents so that I could go home.

I: Do you get very upset, cry, or beg your parents to stay home when they plan to go somewhere without you?

J: My parents never go out without me.

I: Is it because you get upset when they plan to go somewhere without you?

J: No.

I: When your parents leave you, do you cry or feel very bad because you miss them a lot?

J: Yes. I miss my parents a lot.

I: Can you tell me more about that?

J: When my mom drops me off at school, I cry because I don't want her to leave me.

I: When you know that you are going to be away from home or your parents, do you get very upset and worry ahead of time?

J: Yes.

I: Can you tell me more about that?

J: I worry about having to go to school every morning because then I have to be away from my mom.

I: When you are not with your parents, do you worry a lot that something bad might happen to them, like they might get sick or hurt and die?

J: Yes.

I: What do you think might happen to them?

J: They might get into a car accident and have to go to the hospital.

I: When you are not with your parents, do you worry that they might leave and never come back?

J: Yes.

I: Can you tell me more about that?

J: Well, I am afraid that when I get dropped off at school, my parents will not come back to pick me up because they got into an accident.

I: Do you worry a lot that something bad might happen to you, like someone might take you or you might get lost, so you couldn't see your parents again?

J: Yes.

I: What do you think might happen to you?

J: I can get kidnapped or I could get lost, and then my parents wouldn't be able to find me.

I: Some children find some places hard to go to, like over to a friend's house, because they are afraid to be away from their parents. Are there any places that you won't go, because you are afraid to be away from your parents?

J: Yes.

I: What places won't you go to?

J: I try not to go to school, but my parents make me.

I: What other places won't you go to?

J: I don't go to my friends' houses if my parents don't stay. I like when my friends come and play with me in my house.

I: Do you try as hard as you can to always be near your mom or dad, or someone else that you love?

J: Yes.

I: Can you tell me more about that?

J: I like being with my mom all the time.

I: Do you try as hard as you can to never be at home alone?

J: No. I am never home alone.

I: When you are at home with your parents, are you scared of being alone in your room or any other place in the house? For example, if your parents are on one side of the house, like in the kitchen, and you are on the other side of the house, like in your bedroom, do you go to the kitchen so you can be with your parents?

J: Yes.

I: Can you tell me more about that?

J: I don't like being alone in my room because I am scared that something will come out of my closet.

I: Do you often want to have your mother or dad stay close to you when it's time to go to sleep at night? For example, do you like to have someone, like your mother or father, lie down next to you when it's time to go to bed?

J: Yes.

I: Do you sleep alone?

J: Yes, but my mom likes to tuck me in at night.

I: How long does she stay with you?

J: Until I fall asleep.

I: How long do you think that takes?

J: I don't know; like an hour?

I: Is it hard for you to sleep over other kids' houses because you are afraid to be away from your parents?

J: No. My parents don't let me sleep over at other kids' houses.

I: Do you have bad dreams about being away from your parents?

J: No.

I: When you have to leave home to go to school or someplace else, do you usually feel sick? For example, do you get stomachaches or headaches or feel like you are going to throw up?

J: Yes; like when I go to school in the morning, I have a stomachache.

I: Are there any other places that you have to go to that make you feel sick?

J: Sometimes when I get dropped off at a friend's house because my mom has to go somewhere, I feel sick and my heart beats really fast.

I: Has this feeling of being scared or worried when you are not with your parents been going on for at least 4 weeks?

J: Yes.

I: Okay, I want to know how much you feel this problem has messed things up in your life. That is, how much has it messed things up for you with friends, in school, or at home? How much does it stop you from doing things you would like to do? Tell me how much by using the Feelings Thermometer we discussed earlier, okay?

J: A lot, a 6.

I: Well, how do you think it messes things up for you at school?

J: Well, I cry every morning before going, and I try really hard not to go.

I: So you get very upset about having to go to school?

J: Yes.

I: Do you miss school or get bad grades because you are afraid to be away from your parents?

J: No. I don't miss school because my parents won't let me.

I: How does it mess things up with your friends?

J: Well, my friends are starting to get annoyed about always coming to my house to play. They really want me to go to their house.

I: How does it mess things up for you with your parents?

J: Well, they get upset with me every morning when I put up a fight about having to go to school.

Differential Diagnosis and Behavioral Assessment

Differential Diagnosis

There is considerable symptom overlap among the various subtypes of anxiety disorders as well as among anxiety disorders and other disorders (Labellarte, Ginsburg, Walkup, & Riddle, 1999). Structured and semistructured interview schedules are designed to allow for the differential diagnosis of the anxiety disorders subtypes and other disorders. If unstructured interviewing strategies are employed to assess the presence of an anxiety disorder, the interviewer should be aware of similarities across the anxiety disorders, as well as similarities among anxiety disorders and other disorders, and ask questions aimed at deriving the most accurate diagnosis. The following are some of the issues involved in the differential diagnosis of the *DSM-IV* anxiety disorders subtypes.

To accurately diagnose GAD, it is important to ensure that the excessive worrying is not focused solely on social situations (i.e., SOP), specific objects (i.e., SP), and separation from attachment figures (i.e., SAD) and that the worries do not occur only during the course of posttraumatic events (i.e., PTSD). GAD should also be distinguished from excessive worrying about having a panic attack (i.e., PD) and worrying in the form of obsessions (i.e., OCD). Restlessness or difficulty concentrating may be symptoms associated with GAD and ADHD. ADHD, however, does not have the added component of excessive worrying. It also is important that the symptoms of GAD are not due to the direct physiological effects of a substance or a general medical condition and does not occur only during a mood, psychotic, or pervasive developmental disorder.

OCD should be distinguished from the preoccupation associated with a fear-provoking object (i.e., SP) or the preoccupation associated with social situations (i.e., SOP). OCD should also be distinguished from excessive worrying associated with GAD (e.g., excessive worrying about real life). In OCD, the content of the obsessions does not typically involve real-life problems, and the obsessions are experienced as inappropriate by the individual. Tics (i.e., tic disorder) and stereotyped movements (i.e., stereotypic movement disorder) must be distinguished from compulsions. In contrast to compulsions, tics and stereotyped movements are not aimed at neutralizing an obsession. It is also important that the worrying and associated symptoms of OCD are not due to the direct physiological effects of a substance or a general medical condition and do not occur only during a mood or psychotic disorder.

To accurately diagnose PD, it is important to ensure that the panic attacks are not cued by a specific object (i.e., SP), an evaluative situation (i.e., SOP), separation from attachment figures (i.e., SAD), a traumatic event (i.e., PTSD), excessive worrying (i.e., GAD), and thoughts about exposure to the object or situation related to an obsession (i.e., OCD). A panic attack should be distinguished from certain medical conditions (e.g., asthma, arrhythmias, myocardial infarction, seizures) and substances (e.g., caffeine, cold medications) that may also produce symptoms that mimic panic attacks.

PTSD is the only anxiety disorder that requires the presence of a traumatic event to meet diagnostic criteria. In PTSD, the event must be of an extreme (i.e., life-threatening) nature. If a youth is experiencing symptoms of PTSD due to a stressor that is not extreme (e.g., parental divorce), the diagnosis of adjustment disorder is more appropriate. The presence of recurrent intrusive thoughts occurs in PTSD and OCD; however, in OCD, the thoughts are experienced as inappropriate and are unrelated to a traumatic event. Flashbacks in PTSD need to be distinguished from hallucinations that may occur in psychotic disorders, substance-induced disorders, and psychotic disorders due to a general medical condition.

SAD is distinguished from GAD in that the excessive worry is predominantly related to separation from home and attachment figures. In children with SAD, threats of separation may lead to having a panic attack, but the panic attack is not uncued or "out of the blue" as with PD. Symptoms of separation anxiety can be related to pervasive developmental disorder and psychotic disorders (APA, 1994). If the symptoms of SAD occur only during the course of one of these disorders, a separate diagnosis of SAD is not given.

SOP in children and adolescents is frequently confused with GAD. In SOP, the worry about social and academic tasks stems from the fear of negative evaluation by others. In contrast, the worry about social and academic tasks in GAD typically involves a fear of failing oneself by not reaching some self-generated standard (i.e., fear of receiving less than adequate grades). The social avoidance associated with SOP should be distinguished from the social avoidance due to having an unexpected panic attack (i.e., PD with agoraphobia) or the social avoidance due to concerns about being separated from attachment figures (i.e., SAD). In pervasive developmental disorder, social situations are avoided because of a lack of interest in social relationships. In contrast, youth with SOP have the capacity for and interest in social relationships.

SP should be distinguished from fear that is related to separation from attachment figures (i.e., SAD), social evaluation or embarrassment (i.e., SOP), and dirt or contamination (i.e., OCD). SP should be further distinguished from avoidance due to a traumatic event, as in PTSD. In youth with SP, exposure to the feared object or situation may lead to a panic attack. In contrast to PD, the panic attack is cued by exposure to the feared object or situation, rather than being unexpected.

Behavioral Assessment

The *DSM-IV* delineates the symptoms that make up diagnostic criteria for each anxiety disorder subtype; however, it does not cover myriad anxious behaviors that youth might exhibit as well as the functions of these behaviors. Thus, in addition to administering a structured or semistructured interview schedule to derive an anxiety disorder diagnosis, it is also important to conduct a behavioral assessment of the youth's specific anxious behaviors. Behavioral assessments are useful for obtaining descriptive information about the youth's specific anxious behaviors and the factors maintaining those behaviors (Ollendick & Hersen, 1984). Once the youth's specific anxious behaviors have been identified, those behaviors can be targeted in an exposure-based cognitive-behavioral treatment.

One way to conduct a behavioral assessment is to assess the youth's specific anxious behaviors and the factors maintaining them during the administration of the clinical interview. The interviewer might ask the youth and parents to provide detailed descriptions of the youth's anxious behaviors, including the frequency, intensity, and duration of those behaviors. Once the behaviors have been identified, the interviewer may begin to probe in greater depth about the antecedents and consequences of those behaviors. For example, the

interviewer might ask the youth and parents to describe the situations in which the anxious behaviors occur (i.e., antecedents). The interviewer might also ask the parents about their own behaviors when their child is displaying those anxious behaviors (i.e., consequences).

Another way to conduct a behavioral assessment is via self-monitoring. In the area of youth anxiety disorders, self-monitoring has been used to identify and quantify the youth's anxious behaviors and the factors maintaining those behaviors (see Silverman & Kurtines, 1996). One approach to self-monitoring is the daily diary (Silverman & Serafini, 1998). Daily diaries require the youth to keep a record of the feared situations, any avoidant behaviors displayed in those situations, any thoughts associated with the feared situations, and a severity rating. Daily diaries have been shown to be clinically useful for providing information on the youth's anxious behaviors and thoughts, as well as the antecedents and consequences of the behaviors (Beidel, Neal, & Lederer, 1991). Daily diaries are also clinically useful in that they provide information on important aspects of the youth's anxiety that can be addressed in treatment.

A more direct way of conducting a behavioral assessment relative to the methods described above is by direct behavioral observations of the youth's anxious symptoms and behaviors (Silverman & Ollendick, 2005). In the youth anxiety disorders research area, behavioral observations consist of behavioral avoidance tasks, social evaluative tasks, and youth-parent observation tasks (e.g., Beidel, Turner, & Morris, 2000; Hamilton & King, 1991; Hudson & Rapee, 2002; Kendall, 1994; Woodruff-Borden, Morrow, Bourland, & Cambron, 2002). In the behavioral avoidance task (Hamilton & King, 1991; Ost, Svensson, Hellstrom, & Lindwall, 2001), the youth is asked to approach a fear-provoking stimulus or participate in the fear-provoking situation, and how closely the youth can approach the fear-provoking stimulus or the amount of time that the youth can participate in the anxiety-provoking situation is measured.

In social evaluative tasks (Beidel et al., 2000; Ferrell, Beidel, & Turner, 2004; Kendall, 1994), youth are informed of the evaluative nature of the task and are given standard behavioral assertiveness instructions. In Kendall (1994), for example, youth were asked to talk about themselves for 5 minutes in front of a video camera. Observers rated the youth on overall anxiety levels, fearful facial expressions, and performance.

Parent-youth observation tasks assess for any factors related to the parent-youth relationship that may be controlling or maintaining the youth's anxiety. Typically, in parent-youth observation tasks, parents and youth are observed while engaging in problem-solving situations or having conversations (Barrett, Dadds, & Rapee, 1996; Hudson & Rapee, 2002; Woodruff-Borden et al., 2002). For example, Woodruff-Borden et al. (2002) conducted parent-youth observation tasks using a sample of anxious youth and their parents (25 anxious, 32 nonanxious). Parent-youth dyads were videotaped during two 10-minute tasks: (1) working on unsolvable anagrams and (2) preparation for a speech, followed by delivering the speech in front of a video camera. Of interest was the degree of parental involvement during the youth's task, such as the degree to which the parent exerted control over the task.

SELECTION OF TREATMENT TARGETS AND REFERRAL

After conducting the clinical interview with the youth and his or her parents and a behavioral assessment has been conducted, the next step is selecting the specific symptoms and behaviors that will be targeted in the youth's treatment. Given that anxiety disorders are frequently comorbid with other anxiety disorders as well as other internalizing disorders (depression) and externalizing disorders (ADHD) (e.g., Brady & Kendall, 1992; Last, Perrin, Hersen, & Kazdin, 1992; Zoccolillo, 1992), a key issue involves prioritizing the various difficulties reported by the youth and his or her parents. In cases where a youth has been diagnosed with more than one disorder, it is important to determine how much the symptoms related to each of the disorders interfere in the youth's functioning at school, home, or with peers. One way to prioritize the youth's difficulties is by obtaining youth and parent ratings of interference during the clinical interview. As previously mentioned, the ADIS-IV: C/P (Silverman & Albano, 1996) assists with this by containing a pictorial rating scale (i.e., Feelings Thermometer). The anxiety disorder or other disorder that is determined to be the most interfering would be the disorder targeted in treatment.

To the extent that the youth's primary diagnosis is determined to be something other than an anxiety disorder diagnosis, such as depression or ADHD, it becomes necessary to determine which of these symptoms, if any, may interfere with an anxiety treatment program. The symptoms that are deemed as interfering may deserve primary attention, using modified methods of treatment or referral to an alternative agency that is more appropriate for the youth's needs.

To the extent that the primary diagnosis is an anxiety disorder, the treatment option with the most research evidence is exposure-based CBT (Ollendick & King, 1998; Silverman & Berman, 2001). The components of CBT include psychoeducation, relaxation training, identification and modification of anxious thoughts (cognitive restructuring), contingency management, exposure to anxiety-provoking situations, and techniques focused on generalization of gains and relapse prevention (e.g., Silverman & Kurtines, 1996).

The specific anxiety disorder diagnosis assigned to the youth plays an important role in selecting the most appropriate and effective exposures. Despite the common reactions across the various anxiety disorder subtypes (behavioral, cognitive, and physiological reactions) and the common change-producing procedure (exposure), what varies across the subtypes is the content of the reactions. Thus, the content of the anxiety disorder diagnosis will help guide the selection of exposure tasks (Silverman & Kurtines, 1996). In other words, knowing that a youth has been diagnosed with SOP or SAD simplifies the selection of appropriate and effective exposure tasks. For example, the exposure tasks for youth diagnosed with SOP would be focused on situations that involve social evaluation and performance. Exposure tasks for a youth that has been diagnosed with SAD, for example, would be focused on situations that involve separation from attachment figures.

Because most anxious youth display a wide range of symptoms and behaviors related to a specific anxiety disorder diagnosis, exposure tasks should be focused on the specific symptoms and behaviors that interfere most with the youth's daily functioning. For example, a youth diagnosed with SAD may be unable to sleep alone, have difficulty staying in school, and be unable to be alone around the home. What may be interfering most with the youth's functioning is the youth's difficulty staying in school. Thus, the exposure tasks should be focused on the youth gradually staying in school for the duration of the day.

A comprehensive assessment of the youth's anxiety may provide information about whether other adjunctive treatment strategies might be needed in addition to CBT. For example, research studies have shown that the ways in which parents manage their children is associated with anxious behaviors in youth (e.g., Bush, Melamed, Sheras, & Greenbaum, 1986; Zabin & Melamed, 1980). Thus, parenting behaviors may also be targeted in the youth's anxiety treatment. Research studies have shown that some youth, especially those with SOP, may possess significantly poorer social skills than those without psychiatric disorders (Beidel, Turner, & Morris, 1999; Spence, Donovan, & Brechman-Toussaint, 2000). Problematic peer relationships (stemming from poor social skills) may further contribute to anxiety disorders in youth (Ginsburg, La Greca, & Silverman, 1998). Thus, in cases where an anxious youth also exhibits poor social skills and problematic peer relationships, an adjunctive strategy of social skills training might be included in the youth's anxiety treatment.

REFERENCES

Albano, A. M., & Silverman, W. K. (1996). *Guide to the Anxiety Disorders Interview Schedule for Children-IV (Child and Parent Versions)*. San Antonio, TX: Psychological Corporation.

Ambrosini, P. J. (2000). Historical development and present status of the Schedule for Affective Disorders and Schizophrenia for School-Age Children (K-SADS). *Journal of the American Academy of Child & Adolescent Psychiatry, 39*, 49–58.

American Academy of Child and Adolescent Psychiatry. (1997). Summary of the practice parameters for the assessment and treatment of children and adolescents with anxiety disorders. *Journal of the American Academy of Child & Adolescent Psychiatry, 36*, 1639–1642.

American Psychiatric Association. (1994). *Diagnostic and statistical manual of mental disorders* (4th ed.). Washington, DC: Author.

Anderson, J. C., Williams, S. M., McGee, R., & Silva, P. A. (1987). DSM-III disorders in preadolescent children: Prevalence in a large sample from the general population. *Archives of General Psychiatry, 44*, 69–76.

Angold, A., & Costello, E. J. (2000). The Child and Adolescent Psychiatric Assessment (CAPA). *Journal of the American Academy of Child & Adolescent Psychiatry, 39*, 39–48.

Barlow, D. H. (2002). *Anxiety and its disorders: The nature and treatment of anxiety and panic* (2nd ed.). New York: Guilford Press.

Barrett, P. M., Dadds, M. R., & Rapee, R. M. (1996). Family treatment of childhood anxiety: A controlled trial. *Journal of Consulting and Clinical Psychology, 64*, 333–342.

Beck, A. T., Ward, C. H., Mendelson, M., Mock, J. E., & Erbaugh, J. K. (1961). An inventory for measuring depression. *Archives of General Psychiatry, 4*, 561–571.

Beidel, D. C., Neal, A. M., & Lederer, A. S. (1991). The feasibility and validity of a daily diary for the assessment of anxiety in children, *Behavior Therapy, 22*, 505–517.

Beidel, D. C., Turner, S. M., & Morris, T. L. (1999). Psychopathology of childhood social phobia. *Journal of the American Academy of Child & Adolescent Psychiatry, 38*, 643–650.

Beidel, D. C., Turner, S. M., & Morris, T. L. (2000). Behavioral treatment of childhood social phobia. *Journal of Consulting and Clinical Psychology, 68*, 1072–1080.

Bird, H. R., Gould, M. S., & Staghezza, B. (1992). Aggregating data from multiple informants in child psychiatry epidemiological research. *Journal of the American Academy of Child & Adolescent Psychiatry, 31*, 78–85.

Brady, E. U., & Kendall, P. C. (1992). Comorbidity of anxiety and depression in children and adolescents. *Psychological Bulletin, 111*, 244–255.

Brenton, J., Bergeron, L., Valla, J., Lepine, S., Houde, L., & Gaudet, N. (1995). Do children aged 9 through 11 years understand the DISC version 2.25 questions? *Journal of the American Academy of Child & Adolescent Psychiatry, 34*, 946–956.

Bush, J. P., Melamed, B. G., Sheras, P. L., & Greenbaum, P. E. (1986). Mother-child patterns of coping with anticipatory medical stress. *Health Psychology, 5*, 137–157.

Choudhury, M. S., Pimentel, S. S., & Kendall, P. C. (2003). Childhood anxiety disorders: Parent-child (dis)agreement using a structured interview for the DSM-IV. *Journal of the American Academy of Child & Adolescent Psychiatry, 42*, 957–964.

Comer, J. S., & Kendall, P. C. (2004). A symptom-level examination of parent-child agreement in the diagnosis of anxious youths. *Journal of the American Academy of Child & Adolescent Psychiatry, 43*, 878–886.

Dadds, M. R., Perrin, S., & Yule, W. (1998). Social desirability and self-reported anxiety in children: An analysis of the RCMAS Lie Scale. *Journal of Abnormal Child Psychology, 26*, 311–317.

Edelbrock, E., Costello, A. J., Dulcan, M. K., Conover, N., & Kalas, R. (1986). Parent-child agreement on child psychiatric symptoms assessed via structured interview. *Journal of Child Psychology & Psychiatry, 27*, 181–190.

Edelbrock, C., Costello, A. J., Dulcan, M. K., Kalas, R., & Conover, N. C. (1985). Age differences in the reliability of the psychiatric interview of the child. *Child Development, 56*, 265–275.

Engel, N. A., Rodrigue, J. R., & Geffken, G. R. (1994). Parent-child agreement on ratings of anxiety in children. *Psychological Reports, 75*, 1251–1260.

Ferrell, C., Beidel, D., & Turner, S. (2004). Assessment and treatment of socially phobic children: A cross cultural comparison. *Journal of Clinical Child & Adolescent Psychology, 33*, 260–268.

Frick, P. J., Silverthorn, P., & Evans, C. (1994). Assessment of childhood anxiety using structured interviews: Patterns of agreement among informants and association with maternal anxiety. *Psychological Assessment, 6*, 372–379.

Ginsburg, G. S., La Greca, A. M., & Silverman, W. K. (1998). Social anxiety in children with anxiety disorders: Relation with social and emotional functioning. *Journal of Abnormal Child Psychology, 26*, 175–185.

Grills, A. E., & Ollendick, T. H. (2003). Multiple informant agreement and the Anxiety Disorders Interview Schedule for Parents and Children. *Journal of the American Academy of Child & Adolescent Psychiatry, 42*, 30–40.

Hamilton, D. I., & King, N. J. (1991). Reliability of a behavioral avoidance test for the assessment of dog phobic children. *Psychological Reports, 69*, 18.

Hamilton, M. (1959). The assessment of anxiety states by rating. *British Journal of Medical Psychology, 32*, 50–55.

Herjanic, B., & Reich, W. (1982). Development of a structured psychiatric interview for children: Agreement between child and parent on individual symptoms. *Journal of Abnormal Child Psychology, 10*, 307–324.

Hudson. J. L., & Rapee, R. M. (2002). Parent-child interactions in clinically anxious children and their siblings. *Journal of Clinical Child &Adolescent Psychology, 31*, 548–555.

Kashani, J. H., & Orvaschel, H. (1988). Anxiety disorders in mid-adolescence: A community sample. *American Journal of Psychiatry, 145*, 960–964.

Kendall, P. C. (1994). Treating anxiety disorders in youth: Results of a randomized clinical trial. *Journal of Consulting and Clinical Psychology, 62*, 100–110.

Kendall, P. C., & Chansky, T. E. (1991). Considering cognition in anxiety disordered children. *Journal of Anxiety Disorders, 5*, 167–185.

Kendall, P. C., & Flannery-Schroeder, E. C. (1998). Methodological issues in treatment research for anxiety disorders in youth. *Journal of Abnormal Child Psychology, 26*, 27–38.

Krain, A. L., & Kendall, P. C. (2000). The role of parental emotional distress in parent report of child anxiety. *Journal of Clinical Child Psychology, 29*, 328–335.

Labellarte, M. J., Ginsburg, G. S., Walkup, J. T., & Riddle, M. A. (1999). The treatment of anxiety disorders in children and adolescents. *Biological Psychiatry, 46*, 1567–1578.

Lang, P. J. (1968). Fear reduction and fear behavior. In J. Schlein (Ed.), *Research in psychotherapy* (pp. 85–103). Washington, DC: American Psychological Association.

Last, C. G., Hersen, M., Kazdin, A. E., Finkelstein, R., & Strauss, C. (1987). Comparison of *DSM-III* separation anxiety and overanxious disorders: Demographic characteristics and patterns of comorbidity. *Journal of the American Academy of Child & Adolescent Psychiatry, 26*, 527–531.

Last, C. G., Perrin, S., Hersen, M., & Kazdin, A. E. (1992). *DSM-III-R* anxiety disorders in children: Sociodemographic and clinical characteristics. *Journal of the American Academy of Child & Adolescent Psychiatry, 31*, 1070–1076.

Loeber, R., Green, S. M., & Lahey, B. B. (1990). Mental health professionals' perception of the utility of children, mothers, and teachers as informant on child psychopathology. *Journal of Clinical Child Psychology, 19*, 136–143.

McGee, R., Feehan, M., Williams, S., Partridge, F., Silva, P. A., & Kelly, J. (1990). *DSM-III* disorders in a large sample of adolescents. *Journal of the American Academy of Child & Adolescent Psychiatry, 29*, 611–619.

Ollendick, T. H., & Hersen, M. (1984). *Child behavioral assessment: Principles and procedures.* New York: Pergamon Press.

Ollendick, T. H., & Hersen, M. (1993). Child and adolescent behavioral assessment. In T. H. Ollendick & M. Hersen (Eds.), *Handbook of child and adolescent assessment* (pp. 3–14). New York: Pergamon Press.

Ollendick, T. H., & King, N. J. (1998). Empirically supported treatments for children with phobic and anxiety disorders. *Journal of Clinical Child Psychology, 27*, 156–167.

Ost, L. G., Svensson, L., Hellstrom. K., & Lindwall, R. (2001). One-session treatment of specific phobias in youths: A randomized clinical trial. *Journal of Consulting and Clinical Psychology, 69*, 814–824.

Pina, A. A., Silverman, W. K., Saavedra, L. M., & Weems, C. F. (2001). An analysis of the RCMAS lie scale in a clinic sample of anxious children. *Journal of Anxiety Disorders, 15*, 443–457.

Rapee, R. M., Barrett, P. M., Dadds, M. R., & Evans, L. (1994). Reliability of the *DSM-III-R* childhood anxiety disorders using structured interview: Interrater and parent-child agreement. *Journal of the American Academy of Child & Adolescent Psychiatry, 33*, 984–992.

Reich, W. (2000). Diagnostic Interview for Children and Adolescents (DICA). *Journal of the American Academy of Child & Adolescent Psychiatry, 39*, 59–66.

Reynolds, C. R., & Richmond, B. O. (1985). *Revised Children's Manifest Anxiety Scale: Manual.* Los Angeles: Western Psychological Services.

Richardson, S. A., Dohrenwend, B. S., & Klein, D. (1965). *Interviewing: Its forms and functions.* New York: Basic Books.

Safford, S. M., Kendall, P. C., Flannery-Schroeder, E., Webb, A., & Sommer, H. (2005). A longitudinal look at parent-child diagnostic agreement in youth treated for anxiety disorders. *Journal of Clinical Child & Adolescent Psychology, 34*, 747–757.

Schniering, C. A., Hudson, J. L., & Rapee, R. M. (2000). Issues in the diagnosis and assessment of anxiety disorders in children and adolescents. *Clinical Psychology Review, 20*, 453–478.

Schwab-Stone, M. E., Fallon, T., Briggs, M., & Crowther, B. (1994). Reliability of diagnostic reporting for children aged 6–11 years: A test-retest study of the Diagnostic Interview Schedule for Children-Revised. *American Journal of Psychiatry, 151,* 1048–1054.

Shaffer, D., Fisher, P., Lucas, C., Dulcan, M. K., & Schwab-Stone, M. E. (2000). NIMH Diagnostic Interview Schedule for Children-Version IV (NIMH DISC-IV): Description, differences from previous versions, and reliability of some common diagnoses. *Journal of the American Academy of Child & Adolescent Psychiatry, 39,* 28–38.

Silverman, W. K. (1994). Structured diagnostic interviews. In T. H. Ollendick, N. J. King, & W. Yule (Eds.), *International handbook of phobic and anxiety disorders in children and adolescents* (pp. 293–315). New York: Plenum Press.

Silverman, W. K., & Albano, A. M. (1996). *Anxiety Disorders Interview Schedule for Children for DSM-IV: Child and Parent Versions.* San Antonio, TX: Psychological Corporation/Graywind.

Silverman, W. K., & Berman, S. L. (2001). Psychosocial interventions for anxiety disorders in children: Status and future directions. In W. K. Silverman & P. D. A. Treffers (Eds.), *Anxiety disorders in children and adolescents: Research, assessment, and intervention* (pp. 313–334). Cambridge, UK: Cambridge University Press.

Silverman, W. K., & Kurtines, W. M. (1996). *Anxiety and phobic disorders: A pragmatic approach.* New York: Plenum Press.

Silverman, W. K., & Ollendick, T. H. (2005). Evidence-based assessment of anxiety and its disorders in children and adolescents. *Journal of Clinical Child & Adolescent Psychology, 34,* 380–411.

Silverman, W. K., & Rabian, B. (1995). Test-retest reliability of the *DSM-III-R* childhood anxiety disorders symptoms using the Anxiety Disorders Interview Schedule for Children. *Journal of Anxiety Disorders, 9,* 1–12.

Silverman, W. K., Saavedra, L. M., & Pina, A. A. (2001). Test-retest reliability of anxiety symptoms and diagnoses using the Anxiety Disorders Interview Schedule for *DSM-IV:* Child and Parent Versions. *Journal of the American Academy of Child & Adolescent Psychiatry, 40,* 937–944.

Silverman, W. K., & Serafini, L. T. (1998). Assessment of child behavior problems: Internalizing disorders. In A. S. Bellack & M. Hersen (Eds.), *Behavioral assessment: A practical handbook* (4th ed., pp. 342–260). Needham Heights, MA: Allyn & Bacon.

Spence, S. H., Donovan, C., & Brechman-Toussaint, M. (2000). The treatment of childhood social phobia: The effectiveness of a social skills training-based, cognitive-behavioural intervention, with and without parental involvement. *Journal of Child Psychology & Psychiatry, 41,* 713–726.

Woodruff-Borden, J., Morrow, C., Bourland, S., & Cambron, S. (2002). The behavior of anxious parents: Examining mechanisms of transmission of anxiety from parent to child. *Journal of Clinical Child and Adolescent Psychology. 31,* 364–374.

Zabin, M. A., & Melamed, B. G. (1980). Relationship between parental discipline and children's ability to cope with stress. *Journal of Behavioral Assessment, 2,* 17–38.

Zoccolillo, M. (1992). Co-occurrence of conduct disorder and its adult outcomes with depressive and anxiety disorders: A review. *Journal of the American Academy of Child & Adolescent Psychiatry, 31,* 547–556.

12

Posttraumatic Stress Disorder

Debora Bell and Maureen Allwood

An unfortunate part of the lives of many youth is exposure to traumatic events. Estimates indicate that as many as one half of youth have experienced trauma, such as witnessing or being the victim of life-threatening injuries (e.g., in motor vehicle accidents), natural or industrial disasters (e.g., hurricanes, toxic-chemical leaks), physical violence (e.g., beating, stabbing, shooting), and war or terrorist activities (e.g., World Trade Center collapse) (Giaconia et al., 1995; Jenkins & Bell, 1994). For approximately one third of these youth, their trauma exposure will lead to posttraumatic stress disorder (PTSD) (Fletcher, 2003). In this chapter, we briefly describe PTSD and review strategies and instruments for interviewing children about their trauma exposure and responses.

Assessment of PTSD offers challenges, due in part to difficulties inherent in evaluating child experiences, especially those with an internal component, and also due to the fact that the literature on assessment of PTSD in children is less well developed than the literature on other child disorders (e.g., attention-deficit/hyperactivity disorder [ADHD]). Throughout the chapter, we address these challenges by discussing strengths and gaps in the literature, obstacles and potential solutions to conducting psychometrically and clinically valid interviews with children from diverse backgrounds, ways to incorporate important adults into the interview

process, and how to complement interviews with other forms of assessment. Finally, we discuss how the interview process and outcome can be used to guide treatment planning. For more detailed discussion of PTSD and its treatment, interested readers are referred to the American Academy of Child and Adolescent Psychiatry (1998), Eth and Pynoos (1985), Fletcher (2003), and Saigh and Bremner (1999).

Description of the Disorder

PTSD involves a range of significantly distressing and impairing reactions to a traumatic event. Reactions occur in three symptom clusters: reexperiencing, avoidance and numbing, and hyperarousal. Symptoms are more than just immediate and transient stress responses, lasting a minimum of 1 month, and can be classified as acute (less than 3 months) or chronic (more than 3 months). Although many children show signs of trauma response soon after exposure, delayed-onset PTSD can be diagnosed if symptoms emerge 6 months or more after exposure (American Psychiatric Association [APA], 2000).

Trauma Exposure

The requirement of exposure to a traumatic event (Criterion A of the *DSM-IV* diagnosis) makes PTSD fairly unique among the disorders described in the *DSM-IV* (APA, 2000), with acute stress disorder and adjustment disorder being the only other *DSM* disorders to specify a cause of the child's symptoms. For PTSD, the causal event is a severe trauma, involving actual or threatened death or serious injury or threat to physical integrity (e.g., physical violations involved in kidnapping or rape) to which the child is exposed through either direct experience or witnessing. To qualify as a traumatic event (versus, for example, a merely stressful event), the person's response must involve intense fear, helplessness, or horror, although this might be expressed in children as agitated or disorganized behavior (APA, 2000). The literature provides several examples of child trauma exposure that vary with regard to their causes (e.g., natural disaster versus human-made event; La Greca, Silverman, & Wasserstein, 1998; March, Amaya-Jackson, Terry, & Costanzo, 1997; McFarlane, Policansky, & Irwin, 1987), intentionality (e.g., unintended nuclear accident versus intentional kidnapping or rape), whether the target is an individual (e.g., sexual abuse; Wolfe, Gentile, & Wolfe, 1989) or a group (e.g., war; Allwood, Bell-Dolan, & Husain, 2002), and whether the experience is impersonal (e.g., hurricane; La Greca et al., 1998) or personal (e.g., targeted school shooting; Pynoos et al., 1987). Although all of these types of trauma can result in PTSD, the literature suggests that trauma responses tend to be more pronounced when the trauma exposure is more proximal (i.e., the child is physically nearer to the event, typically seeing/hearing more of the experience), more chronic or ongoing, and more personal to the child, particularly if the child is victimized due to a characteristic that is stigmatized by others (e.g., because of his or her ethnicity, gender, or perceived fault) (Pynoos et al., 1987; Terr, 1991).

Trauma Symptoms

Reexperiencing

This symptom cluster (*DSM-IV* Criterion B) includes recollections or experiences that remind the person of being in the traumatic situation. Reexperiencing can take the form of intrusive and distressing memories, talking or daydreaming about the event, having dreams or nightmares, or feeling that the event is recurring (e.g., flashbacks). Especially for younger children, recollections and dreams may be nonspecific (e.g., nightmares or fears with more general themes of danger, monsters). Flashbacks and other classic "reliving" symptoms seem uncommon in children, although children may reenact the traumatic event or engage in posttraumatic play (Terr, 1990). In contrast to developmentally typical play, which functions to enable children to practice and master social roles and tasks and is usually experienced as enjoyable, posttraumatic play involves repeated dramatization of trauma or violence, with negative outcomes in the play (e.g., people are hurt or killed versus saved) and often with distress or negative affect experienced by the participants. Because of the negative themes and activities involved in posttraumatic play, it can be dangerous, particularly if it involves potentially lethal "props," such as knives or guns.

Reexperiencing symptoms can be triggered by either external or internal cues, although the cues may be so subtle or idiosyncratic that they are not readily identified by the child or others. For example, the child's memories may be triggered by cues like men with beards (e.g., if the perpetrator was a bearded man), a "whooshing" sound (e.g., that reminds the child of wind associated with a hurricane), or even a particular activity that the child was engaged in when the event occurred (e.g., brushing her hair). In addition to triggering reexperiencing, these cues can also lead to intense psychological distress or physical symptoms, such as nausea or shaking.

Avoidance and Numbing

Criterion C involves avoidance symptoms. A child with PTSD persistently avoids situations, events, or experiences associated with the trauma. This can include avoidance of things associated directly with the trauma, such as anniversary dates or locations similar to where the event took place. It can also include avoidance of recollections or of stimuli that trigger recollections; for instance, the child who was brushing her hair when the trauma occurred might begin avoiding hairbrushing or other grooming activities. In essence, the avoidance seems to serve the purpose of keeping the child "safe," both from a life-threatening or horrific traumatic event and from the psychological distress of remembering or thinking about the event. Children may avoid reminders of the trauma or may try to forget or refuse to talk about the event.

In addition to active avoidance, children may also engage in more passive (i.e., less effortful or intentional) avoidance symptoms. They may forget important details of the trauma experience (Moradi, Doost, Taghavi, Yule, & Dalgleish, 1999), withdraw from or stop enjoying daily activities, or be unable to imagine or expect a "normal" future (e.g., career, family, normal lifespan). They may also experience emotional "numbing," experiencing restricted or flat affect and feeling emotionally detached from people and from the world (Allwood, 2000). Adolescents in particular may engage in self-mutilating behavior in response to emotional numbing (Cohen & Mannarino, 2004).

Hyperarousal

Increased arousal symptoms (Criterion D) are also persistent for youth experiencing PTSD. They may have difficulties with sleep, concentration, irritability, hypervigilance, and exaggerated startle response. Children in a hyperaroused state are physiologically "on alert" and so may appear watchful, suspicious, and jumpy. They may be more likely than other children to want to sit with their backs to the wall, so that they cannot be approached from behind, or to jump at being touched. This heightened arousal and attention to potential danger can also predispose youth to interpret others' behavior as threatening or hostile and to respond with irritability or aggression (Yule & Canterbury, 1994). Arousal and hypervigilance make it difficult to concentrate on normal daily activities and, indeed, concentration difficulty is the most common hyperarousal symptom reported for school-age children (Fletcher, 2003). Sleep problems can be compounded by nightmares, and sleep deprivation can then further impact concentration and irritability.

Comorbidity and Differential Diagnosis

Assessment and diagnosis of PTSD requires consideration of alternative and comorbid diagnoses. In particular, PTSD symptoms overlap with symptoms of several other disorders that may be more common and thus considered more quickly than PTSD. For example, ADHD is associated with irritability, difficulty concentrating,

and difficulty remembering details of some events, and youth with ADHD may also display disorganized/agitated behavior. Anxiety disorders include symptoms of arousal, avoidance, and distress associated with exposure to a feared stimulus, and depressive disorders include anhedonia, withdrawal/avoidance, self-injury (potentially associated with numbing), and problems with physiological arousal. Behaviors associated with irritability and aggressive or violent posttraumatic play are similar to symptoms of oppositional and conduct disorders. PTSD symptoms also overlap with less common disorders, such as dissociative disorders and schizophrenia, both of which include disorganized behavior and emotional detachment. Thus, the presence of any of these symptoms could indicate several potential diagnoses: PTSD, ADHD, a depressive or anxiety disorder, an externalizing disorder, or a dissociative or thought disorder.

Beyond symptom overlap, PTSD exists comorbidly with several of these other disorders. For example, comorbidity rates of 30% to 40% have been found for PTSD and other internalizing disorders, including generalized anxiety disorder, separation anxiety disorder, major depressive disorder, and dysthymic disorder (Brent et al., 1995; Giaconia et al., 1995; McCloskey & Walker, 2000). Interestingly, research suggests that while preexisting anxiety may increase the risk for youth developing PTSD when exposed to trauma, depressive disorders seem more likely to appear later, possibly resulting from PTSD (Cohen & Mannarino, 2004; La Greca et al., 1998). Comorbidity has also been reported between PTSD and externalizing conditions, such as ADHD, oppositional and conduct disorders, and substance use disorders (Allwood, 2003; Brent et al., 1995; Ford et al., 2000; McCloskey & Walker, 2000).

Although some have speculated that impulsive or disruptive behaviors might place youth at risk for trauma exposure, due to increased risk taking or to behaviors that provoke others and elicit victimization, research generally has not supported this notion (Ford et al., 2000; Wozniak et al., 1999). On the other hand, some research suggests that PTSD may lead to an exacerbation of acting-out behaviors (Allwood, 2005; Ford et al., 2000; Steiner, Garcia, & Matthews, 1997). In particular, early substance abuse seems most likely to result from PTSD, perhaps as a means of self-medication of the distressing symptoms (Chilcoat & Breslau, 1998). Finally, especially in the case of young children with PTSD, developmental regressions may be seen (Scheeringa, Zeanah, Drell, & Larrieu, 1995; Wekerle & Wolfe, 2003). Children may lose language, toileting, or self-care skills. They may become more socially withdrawn or clingy with adults. Although developmental regressions are often thought of as symptoms of sexual abuse, they are, in fact, more general indices of trauma exposure.

Given the multiple ways in which PTSD may overlap with other disorders, it is important to determine whether the child's symptom picture is most consistent with PTSD, with one or more alternative disorders, or with truly comorbid conditions. First, in the face of symptoms that suggest reexperiencing, avoidance, and hyperarousal, one should assess the child's trauma history. Of course, absence of documented trauma does not mean that it did not occur; for reasons discussed later (see "Obstacles" section), youth may not disclose trauma exposure. Likewise, presence of documented trauma does not mean that PTSD is the only or most appropriate diagnosis, as PTSD is simply one potential outcome of trauma exposure. However, identifying a trauma experience can help focus assessment in terms of symptoms (e.g., whether avoidance seems limited to trauma situations or represents a more general anxious or depressive behavior pattern) and time course (e.g., whether symptoms emerged posttrauma). The following sections outline methods that can be used to examine trauma history and PTSD symptoms. For the most comprehensive diagnosis and treatment planning, this assessment should be embedded within a broader assessment of the child's functioning regarding potential comorbid conditions and general adjustment in important life areas.

INTERVIEWING STRATEGIES

General Issues in Selecting and Conducting Child Interviews

When interviewing youth about PTSD, several issues should be considered. First, the interview should weigh the relative benefits of assessing PTSD within the context of broader diagnostic or psychological assessment versus focusing on PTSD specifically. PTSD in childhood is often associated with complex developmental histories, and comprehensive assessment must organize and clarify multiple life events (traumatic as well as normative, e.g., birth of siblings, school changes), symptom presentation across a range of diagnostic categories, and previous diagnoses and treatments. These complexities may be best addressed in a broad interview. On the other hand, interviews designed specifically to assess for PTSD place the traumatic events at the focal point of the interview, which might feel more validating to the youth than a broad range of questions. Moreover, PTSD-specific interviews frequently provide more in-depth assessment of contextual factors and life events (e.g., exposure to war, sexual victimization) that may be important to the youth's trauma experience.

Although comprehensive assessment will likely encompass both broad and focused interview components, the interviewer's decision about how to balance and order these components should depend on the specific purpose of the interview (e.g., research interviews are more likely to be conducted in a standardized order) and individual factors regarding the youth and the nature of the referral (e.g., children referred specifically for an acute trauma may be very focused on the trauma and need to talk about it prior to moving to assessment of other issues).

A second point to consider is which of the available instruments is best suited to the interviewer's purpose. We review interviews of youth trauma exposure and response that are designed in accordance with the *DSM-IV*, describing the interviews and their psychometric properties. Of note is that there are relatively few instruments that assess child and adolescent PTSD, and most available instruments have been developed through several iterations, yielding multiple versions, often with the same or similar names or acronyms. The duplicate assessment protocols sometimes lead to confusion among researchers and clinicians seeking the most recent measures and scoring and interpretation guidelines. Interviewers should check carefully to ensure that they are using the same, and preferably the most recent, version of the instrument and its scoring/interpretation manual. Many of the following interviews also have corresponding parent-report versions; their use with parents is addressed in a later section of this chapter.

Interviewing About Trauma History

In keeping with the structure of *DSM-IV* diagnostic criteria, PTSD interviews generally begin by assessing trauma exposure, with interview strategies varying from open-ended questions about life experiences to closed-ended questions eliciting dichotomous "yes" or "no" responses. Several structured and semistructured interviews assess for trauma exposure by asking whether the youth has experienced a "scary," "threatening," "bad," or "upsetting" event (*DSM-IV* Criterion A1). An affirmative response regarding exposure to a potentially traumatic event (Criterion A1) is required for assessment of peritraumatic responses (i.e., immediate responses during the trauma) (Criterion A2) and posttraumatic response (Criteria B, C, D). For both clinical and research purposes, however, some interviews continue to query responses to events that are not likely to meet Criterion A1 and A2. Despite the importance of establishing lifetime presence or absence of potentially traumatic experiences, many broad diagnostic interviews (e.g., DISC-IV, K-SADS, DICA-R-C, KID-SCID) limit the query of trauma exposure to just a few types of traumas or rely on youth to provide narrative information regarding their experiences (e.g., ChIPS, CPTSDI). Trauma exposure assessment that is embedded within diagnostic interviews is discussed further in the next section.

For more in-depth assessment of exposure to traumatic events, using one of several trauma exposure interviews may be indicated. The Traumatic Events Screening Inventory for Children (TESI-C) (Ribbe, 1996) and the Children's Trauma Questionnaire (CTQ) (Bernstein et al., 1994) have been developed to elicit trauma information from youth. Several inventories also focus on specific types of trauma. For example, the Screen for Adolescent Violence Exposure (SAVE) (Hastings & Kelley, 1997) and the Children's Report of Exposure to Violence (CREV) (Cooley, Turner, & Beidel, 1995) are limited to the assessment of violence exposure.

The TESI-C provides a good example of the type and format of items included in exposure measures. Available in both child report and parent report versions (as well as questionnaire format), the TESI-C consists of 19 questions that are asked verbatim. Endorsed items are followed by both closed- and open-ended probes to gather additional detail about the nature of the event and when it occurred, risks associated with the event (e.g., death, injury), and the youth's response to and appraisal of the event. TESI-C questions are ordered hierarchically, with more intimate types of trauma experiences (e.g., sexual abuse) reserved for later in the interview. Questions are scored as "Yes," "No," "Not Sure," "Refused," or "Questionable Validity," based on clinician assessment of the occurrence of the event in question. Unfortunately, published psychometric data are not available. Further details on other trauma exposure measures are available from the references cited throughout this section.

Interviewing About Trauma Symptoms With Comprehensive Diagnostic Interviews

Structured Interviews

Structured interviews are fashioned after standardized tests and are generally subjected to a lengthy design process, with the wording of each question and probe being carefully selected. As such, each portion of the interview is administered as written or as guided by the instructions.

National Institute of Mental Health Diagnostic Interview Schedule for Children Version IV. The NIMH DISC-IV (Shaffer & Fisher, 1997) is a highly structured interview designed to assess more than 30 psychiatric disorders known to occur in childhood. The DISC was designed for community-based epidemiological studies, but it has been used in both outpatient and inpatient clinical settings. The current DISC-IV evolved from several earlier versions (e.g., DISC-1, DISC-2, DISC 2.1, DISC 2.3, DISC-R), which were reviewed by a panel of expert advisors organized by NIMH. The DISC-IV version coincides with the diagnostic criteria of the *DSM-IV* and the *ICD-10* (World Health Organization, 1993) and is intended for use with youth aged 9 to 17 years old. The DISC-IV contains more than 2,900 questions, with each interview requiring administration of a minimum of 358 "stem" questions (Shaffer, Fisher, Lucas, Dulcan, & Schwab-Stone, 2000). Responses to broader diagnostic questions help determine which subsequent queries and probes are asked. Each question is read exactly as written, and almost all questions require a "yes" or "no" response. The structure of the DISC-IV limits the need for clinical judgment, so the interview can be administered by trained lay interviewers. The interview is extremely time-intensive, however, requiring up to 2 hours for administration (Shaffer et al., 2000).

The PTSD subsection of the DISC was initially introduced as a supplemental module to the DISC 2.1 and 2.3 (P. Fisher, personal communication, January 13, 2006) and was subsequently included as a standard module in the DISC-IV. The current DISC-IV PTSD scale assesses exposure and response to eight trauma experiences (i.e., disasters, risk of being killed, physically attacked/beaten, unwanted sexual contact, threatened with a weapon, bad accident, witness to killing, seeing a dead body). Endorsement of one or more trauma experience leads to queries about frequency of the events and whether the youth thought about them in the past year. The youth then provides a brief description of the "most thought about" event, which becomes the identified event for further response and symptom questions. A total of 25 questions address peritraumatic (Criterion A2) and posttraumatic response (Criteria B, C, D) and symptom duration (Criterion E); 6 questions address functional impairment (Criterion F).

Although all PTSD criteria are addressed in the DISC-IV PTSD module, use of a supplemental trauma exposure measure would enable youth to provide information regarding a broader range of trauma experiences. In addition, because many traumatized youth have multiple exposures, the interviewer may want to query about more than one trauma experience (e.g., the first trauma experience or the worst trauma experience), regardless of whether the experience was thought about most in the past year. Of course, these additional questions will lengthen the interview, which may be challenging for youth to complete.

Published psychometric properties of the DISC interview are based largely on data gathered in conjunction with the Methodology for Epidemiology in Children and Adolescents (MECA), a NIMH four-site study utilizing the DISC 2.3 (Lahey, Flagg, Bird, & Schwab-Stone, 1996). The PTSD subsection of the DISC was not available during that study, and currently there are no known publications that address the psychometrics of the DISC-IV PTSD scale.

Children's Interview for Psychiatric Syndromes. The ChIPS (Weller, Weller, Rooney, & Fristad, 1999) is a structured diagnostic screen of 20 psychiatric symptoms and syndromes in youth aged 6 to 18, including acute stress disorder (ASD) and PTSD. The ChIPS uses very simple language and a "yes/no" response format, making it easy for trained interviewers to complete. Administration of the entire interview averages 20 to 30 minutes for community and outpatient samples, with slightly longer times (approximately 50 minutes) for psychiatric inpatient samples (Weller, Weller, Fristad, Rooney, & Schecter, 2000). The ASD/PTSD portion of the ChIPS is presented in seven separate sections. The first section queries whether the respondent has experienced or witnessed something "very bad," the child's response to the experience, and when the experience occurred. The second section examines dissociative responses relevant for a diagnosis of ASD. The 5 remaining sections address the three symptom clusters, symptom duration, and impairment associated with the potentially traumatic experience. As with the DISC-IV PTSD scale, a trauma exposure measure might be a beneficial supplement to the ChIPS.

In studies with community and clinical samples, the ChIPS PTSD scale has demonstrated good inter-interviewer agreement (Hsu, Chong, Yang, & Yen, 2002), good agreement with other diagnostic interviews (DICA-R) (Fristad. Glickman, et al., 1998), and ability to discriminate youth with PTSD diagnoses after sexual abuse from youth with other psychiatric disorders (Evans, Spirito, Celio, Dyl, & Hunt, in press).

Child and Adolescent Psychiatric Assessment. The highly structured CAPA (Angold & Costello, 1995) requires extensive interviewer training and assesses more than 40 symptoms and syndromes in youth aged 9 to 17 in accordance with the *DSM-IV, DSM-III-R,* and the *ICD-10.* The CAPA focuses primarily on symptom presentation within the 3 months prior to the interview and also assesses family and peer functioning and exposure to negative life events (Angold & Costello, 2000). The CAPA is administered in a modular fashion, with administration time averaging from 1 to 2.5 hours, depending on the number of modules administered (Angold & Costello, 2000).

The Life Events/PTSD module (Costello, Angold, March, & Fairbank, 1998) of the CAPA is perhaps the most thorough and well-studied PTSD assessment embedded within a comprehensive interview. The module consists of three subsections: (1) The CAPA Life Events subsection assesses both extreme or "high-magnitude" stressors that are generally defined as traumas (e.g., fire, serious accident) as well as "low-magnitude" stressors (e.g., breakup with boyfriend or girlfriend); (2) three questions screen for trauma-related distress in all three *DSM-IV* symptom clusters; and (3) symptoms that the youth subjectively links to a trauma event are explored further (Criteria B, C, D) (Costello et al., 1998). Although thorough, the CAPA PTSD module might require more administration time than other structured interviews. In addition, the requirement that youth independently link their symptoms to a substantial trauma event increases the risk of false negatives and might account for some of the variability seen in the psychometric properties.

Psychometric properties of the CAPA PTSD module, evaluated for both clinic and community samples, are variable. Although intraclass correlation of the PTSD symptom data was excellent, test-retest reliability varied widely across symptoms (reports of accidents were least stable across time; reports of sexual and physical abuse were most stable), and agreement with independently established diagnoses was fair to good. As expected, the number of potentially traumatic events reported and the proportion of affirmative responses to the three screening questions were significantly greater for the clinic sample than for the community sample (Costello et al., 1998).

Semistructured Interviews

Like structured interviews, semistructured interviews provide specific questions, probes, and guidelines for diagnostic assessment. In contrast to structured interviews, interviewers are able to add additional probes as needed to clarify and to promote accuracy.

Diagnostic Interview for Children and Adolescents–Revised. The DICA-R (Reich, 1998; Reich, Leacock, & Shanfield, 1994) is a comprehensive structured interview that has undergone several revisions and is currently administered in a semistructured format (Reich, 2000). The DICA-R, including its computerized version, DICA-IV, assesses current and lifetime presence of more than 20 of the most frequent *DSM-III-R* and *DSM-IV* psychiatric symptoms and syndromes found in childhood (Reich, 2000). The DICA-R consists of child (DICA-R-C, 6–12 years) and adolescent (DICA-R-A, 13–17 years) versions, each having an administration time of 1 to 2 hours for the entire interview. The DICA PTSD module was included in the 1988 version of the DICA and was one of the first child PTSD interviews. The PTSD module includes one open-ended question regarding exposure to a "terrible" or "really frightening" experience, followed by 21 peritraumatic and posttraumatic symptom questions. Psychometric properties for the ASD/PTSD module include acceptable internal consistency, interrater reliability, and agreement with clinician diagnosis and ChIPS interview diagnosis (Ahmad, Sundelin-Wahlsten, Sofi, Qahar, & von Knorring, 2000; Keppel-Benson, Ollendick, & Benson, 2002; Reebye, Moretti, Wiebe, & Lessard, 2000; Saigh, 2004). It has also been shown to be sensitive to specific aspects of child sexual abuse, such as severity (Chaffin & Shultz, 2001).

Schedule for Affective Disorders and Schizophrenia for School-Age Children. Like many child interviews, the K-SADS (Puig-Antich & Chambers, 1978) is an extension and modification of an adult version, SADS (Endicott & Spitzer, 1978). Multiple versions of the K-SADS are available for assessment of more than 30 *DSM-IV* childhood psychiatric disorders, including PTSD. The K-SADS-P (see Ambrosini, 2000) assesses current disorders. The K-SADS-PL (Kaufman, Birmaher, Brent, Roa, & Ryan, 1997) assesses both lifetime and current disorders. And the K-SADS-E (Orvaschel, 1995) was developed for epidemiological studies and assesses current and lifetime disorders without regard for severity or impairment. PTSD is one of the more recent additions to the interview, being added to both the K-SADS-E and K-SADS-PL in 1995 (Ambrosini, 2000; Kaufman et al., 1997). Each version of the K-SADS targets youth ages 6 to 18 years old and assesses Axis I disorders within the context of five broad diagnostic areas (i.e., affective disorders, physical disorders, psychoses, behavioral disorders, anxiety disorders). The entire interview takes an average of a half hour for community sample youth and 1.25 to 4 hours for clinical samples (Kaufman et al., 1997; Shemesh et al., 2005).

The PTSD scale is administered as part of the anxiety disorder section and begins with queries regarding exposure to nine different types of events (car accidents, other accidents, disaster, witness to violent crime, victim of violent crime, traumatic news of death or loss, witness to domestic violence, physical and sexual abuse) and other "really bad" or "really scary" events. Although the K-SADS PTSD scale is comprehensive in its queries regarding PTSD symptoms, the measure provides little direction for determining whether youth responses are adequate for Criteria A1 or A2. To administer the K-SADS PTSD scale effectively, the interviewer must be well versed in what constitutes a traumatic event, as well as the necessary peritraumatic response of fear, helplessness, or horror. After establishing past exposure to a potentially traumatic event, the K-SADS PTSD scale asks five screening questions regarding response to a specific event. Unlike much of the K-SADS, which seeks to establish whether symptoms are threshold, sub-threshold, or not present, the PTSD symptom scale is dichotomous ("yes" or "no"). If a "yes" response for any screening item is obtained, the remaining 13 PTSD symptoms are assessed for presence and duration and questions related to functional impairment are administered. The K-SADS-PL PTSD scale has shown good test-retest reliability for both current and lifetime diagnosis and fair to good concordance with clinician-derived diagnosis (Kaufman et al., 1997; Shemesh et al., 2005). It has also been shown to be sensitive to treatment effects (Cohen, Deblinger, Mannarino, & Steer, 2004).

Structured Clinical Interview for DSM-IV Childhood Diagnoses. The KID-SCID (Matzner, Silva, Silvan, Chowdhury, & Nastasi, 1997), adapted from the adult SCID (Spitzer, Williams, Gibbon, & First, 1990), assesses more than 20 *DSM-IV* Axis I disorders seen in childhood. The PTSD subsection assesses trauma exposure with an open-ended question about events that are "scary and upsetting." Ten specific trauma probes (physical abuse or physical assault, sexual molestation/assault by a stranger or someone familiar, familial/parental violence, news of injury of a loved one, loss of parents or sibling,

disaster, fire, serious accident, homelessness, witness to mutilation or murder) guide the narrative report. The youth's report is used to determine whether Criteria A1 and A2 are met and whether questions about symptoms (Criteria B, C, D), duration (Criterion E), and impairment (Criterion F) should be asked. Information on psychometric properties of the KID-SCID is limited, but available evidence indicates fair test-retest reliability for the PTSD module (Matzner et al., 1997) and fair to good interrater reliability for anxiety disorders (including PTSD; Timbremont, Braet, & Dreessen, 2004).

Anxiety Disorders Interview Schedule for Children. The ADIS-C (Silverman & Albano, 1996) represents a midpoint between broad diagnostic interviews that assess the range of childhood disorders and PTSD-specific interviews. The ADIS-C was developed to provide focused assessment and diagnosis of childhood anxiety disorders, including PTSD, but also includes other childhood disorders that may co-occur with anxiety (e.g., eating disorders, ADHD, oppositional defiant disorder). This instrument is arguably the premier interview for diagnosing youth anxiety disorders, with excellent psychometric properties and wide utility in both clinical and research settings (Silverman, Saavedra, & Pina, 2001).

The ADIS-C has been described as one of the more child-friendly semistructured diagnostic interviews, because it begins with questions about the child's school functioning, an area youth are often accustomed to discussing with adults (Beidel & Turner, 1998). After this introduction, youth are asked to report on the presence or absence of symptoms for each disorder included in the ADIS-C. If the child endorses a sufficient number of symptoms to meet the criteria for diagnosis, follow-up questions assess impairment and interference in important areas of functioning, such as school, family, peer, and personal adjustment. The ADIS-C takes approximately 1.5 hours to administer and yields total symptom scores and diagnosis for each assessed disorder. Although the ADIS-C focuses primarily on youth anxiety disorders, it is not widely cited or used for assessment of PTSD; rather, published reports of PTSD tend to use either broader diagnostic interviews or PTSD-specific measures. However, interviewers may find the ADIS-C useful in cases where they want to concentrate on anxiety but also want broader diagnostic coverage.

Overall, the literature provides support for good to excellent interrater reliability and test-retest reliability for ADIS-C symptom scores and diagnoses, good correspondence to other anxiety disorder measures, and sensitivity to treatment effects (Kendall et al., 1997; Rapee, Barrett, Dadds, & Evans, 1994; Silverman et al., 2001; Wood, Piacentini, Bergman, McCracken, & Barrios, 2002). Recent published reports, however, omitted the PTSD module from evaluation and instead focused on modules for which youth answered every symptom question (Silverman et al., 2001). Thus, the reliability and validity of the PTSD module are unknown.

Interviewing About Trauma Symptoms With PTSD-Specific Interviews

Structured Interviews

Clinician-Administered PTSD Scale for Children and Adolescents. The CAPS-C (Nader, Kriegler, Blake, & Pynoos, 1994; Nader et al., 1998), adapted from the adult CAPS (Blake et al., 1990), assesses current and lifetime *DSM-IV* PTSD criteria in youth aged 8 to 18. A unique strength of the CAPS-C is its attention to rapport building with traumatized youth. The interview begins with prebriefing statements explaining the types of questions that will be asked and the purpose of the questions, "So I can learn more about the things that have happened to you . . ." To establish the presence of a Criterion A event, the CAPS-C utilizes a child version of the 17-item Life Events Checklist (see Gray, Litz, Hsu, & Lombardo, 2004) that asks whether the child has been exposed to potentially traumatic events and whether the child heard of, saw, or was directly involved in the event. After completing the Life Events Checklist, the interviewer inquires further, about up to three events. When there are more than three potentially traumatic events, the events are selected based on the "worst" events, the earliest or most recent events, or interest in particular types of events (e.g., sexual abuse, auto accident). Selecting the first traumatic event experienced can provide information regarding lifetime onset of PTSD symptoms and the impact of clinical or subclinical symptoms on development. On the other hand, selecting events that are subjectively the worst events for the child might provide the most accurate estimate of symptom frequency and severity. Thus,

clinician discretion remains an important factor in clinical assessments utilizing the CAPS-C.

After establishing exposure to a traumatic event, the interviewer asks a series of questions to determine the youth's response to the event and the risk of life threat, serious injury, and threat to physical integrity. The CAPS-C then measures 17 symptoms, utilizing 5-point scales with pictorial anchors (i.e., calendar, facial expressions) to measure symptom frequency and intensity. The impact of each traumatic event on social and developmental functioning is also assessed. Administration time is estimated at 45 minutes (Ohan, Myers, & Collett, 2002) but is highly dependent on the number of traumas experienced and queried. The CAPS-C interview yields scores for each of the three symptom clusters as well as categorical information regarding the presence of PTSD.

Although more than 200 studies contribute to the validation of the adult CAPS (Weathers, Keane, & Davidson, 2001), information on psychometric properties of the CAPS-C is scarce. Available evidence, however, suggests that the measure demonstrates excellent interrater reliability and significant correlations with the total score of the Children's PTSD Reaction Index (Nader, Pynoos, Fairbanks, Al-Ajeel, & Al-Asfour, 1993), a self-report questionnaire (Carrion, Weems, Ray, & Reiss, 2002; Cortes et al., 2005).

Semistructured Interviews

Children's PTSD Inventory. The CPTSDI (Saigh, 1998) includes five sections that correspond to each of the *DSM-IV* exposure and symptom criteria. The current CPTSDI was developed for use with 7- to 18-year-old youth and was adapted from an earlier *DSM-III* version (Saigh, 1989). Administration time is approximately 20 minutes, and each item and subtest is scored dichotomously based on the presence or absence of the symptom or symptom cluster. The first section of the interview aims to identify exposure to potentially traumatic events by providing several examples and then asking whether the youth has been exposed to any "very scary things." If the youth endorses exposure, the CPTSDI interviewer then asks open-ended questions about exposure to each event and records the disclosures as stated. The child then responds to three questions regarding his or her response at the time of the event and a question about when the event occurred. Sections 2 through 4 query the presence of PTSD symptoms, including child-specific symptoms such as reenacting the event through play and artwork. Section 5 assesses onset and duration of symptoms to differentiate between acute, chronic, and delayed-onset PTSD. Psychometric properties of the CPTSDI have been evaluated in two studies with overlapping samples of primarily Hispanic youth. The measure demonstrated adequate internal consistency for the symptom composite and three separate symptoms clusters and excellent interrater agreement and test-retest reliability for the overall diagnosis (Saigh et al., 2000).

Adaptation of Self-Administered Questionnaires

Although diagnostic interviews are preferred, particularly in the clinical assessment of youth with complex diagnostic profiles, the time needed to conduct thorough structured or semistructured interviews is not always available. For example, fast-paced inner-city clinics that provide service for countless patients are unlikely to allot time for lengthy, possibly multisession interviews. In recent years, several screening and extended self-report measures have been developed (see Nader, 2004; Saigh, 2004). Measures such as the Child PTSD Symptom Scale (CPSS) (Foa, Johnson, Feeny, & Treadwell, 2001), the UCLA PTSD Index (Pynoos, Rodriquez, Steinberg, Stuber, & Fredrick, 1998; Steinberg, Brymer, Decker, & Pynoos, 2004), Child's Reaction to Traumatic Events Scale (CRTES) (Jones, Fletcher, & Ribbe, 2002), When Bad Things Happen Scale (WBTH) (Fletcher, 1996), and the Pediatric Evaluation of Distress Scale (PEDS) (Saylor, Swenson, Reynolds. & Taylor, 1999) are easily administered during clinical sessions and might be more feasible for large-scale research studies. Similarly, questionnaires that focus primarily on child sexual abuse, the Traumatic Stress Scale for Children (TSSC) (Briere, 1996) and the Children's Impact of Traumatic Events Scale-Revised (CITES-R) (Wolfe, Gentile, Michienzi, Sas, & Wolfe, 1991) are adaptable for interviews addressing symptoms in youth who have been sexually victimized. Of note, the CITES-R also examines cognitions related to victimization. When considering the use of questionnaire measures, it is important to balance the time-efficiency of self-administration with the benefits of rapport building that adapting to interview format can offer. One should also consider, however, that psychometric properties of such adaptations are unknown.

Review of questionnaire measures of PTSD is beyond the scope of this chapter, but one such measure is described briefly here to illustrate the similarities across interview and questionnaire assessments. The UCLA PTSD Index (Pynoos et al., 1998) is a three-part, 49-item, self-administered measure of trauma exposure and response that is easily adapted for clinical interviews. The measure is utilized as a diagnostic screen for PTSD in a multisite study conducted by the National Child Traumatic Stress Network (NCTSN) and was also utilized in the Child and Adolescent Trauma Treatment Service Program, which provided services for youth affected by the terrorist attacks of September 11, 2001 (Steinberg et al., 2004). In Part I, 13 items ask about a variety of traumatic experiences (e.g., accidents, disasters, medical treatments), and Item 14 asks respondents to select the experience that bothers them most. Part II asks 13 questions that assess acute response at the time of the traumatic event. Finally, 22 questions assess *DSM-IV* symptoms and other clinically derived symptoms known to be associated with trauma response in children (e.g., physical fights, guilt).

Early evaluation of the UCLA PTSD Index showed the greatest sensitivity and specificity for detecting PTSD at a cutoff score of 38 or greater (Steinberg et al., 2004). Complete psychometric properties are not yet available, but excellent internal consistency has been reported (Allwood, 2005).

INTERVIEWING OBSTACLES AND SOLUTIONS

General Interviewing Obstacles

Interviewing children about any aspect of their behavior and adjustment involves obstacles that must be recognized and addressed. As described in Part I of this volume and in other sources (e.g., Mash & Terdal, 1997), child interviews are affected by developmental and contextual factors in ways that differ from adult interviews. For example, the child's developmental level influences the way the child participates in the interview and the information that he or she provides. Young children typically do not have the attention span required to complete anything but the most basic interview, and even older children and adolescents can become bored fairly quickly. Children have limited life experience and may not understand even developmentally appropriate questions if they have not directly experienced the event or symptom in question. In addition, developmentally immature memory and verbal expression abilities may limit the youth's ability to describe experiences. For example, especially for younger children, any physical distress "between the nose and the knees" may be described as a stomachache. Similarly, negative affective experiences may be described fairly generically as "bad," rather than more specifically as sad, hopeless, guilty, frightened, or worried, or, worse yet, these terms might be applied interchangeably so that the interviewer has little idea what the child's internal experience is.

What youngsters consider important, and thus what they think to share in an interview, may also be limited by their developmental levels. Children are typically more concrete and present focused than adults and so may be poorer judges of time course and less able than adults to report on duration of symptoms. Similarly, their memories for historic events tend to be both poorer than those of adults and influenced by the details that are important for their developmental levels (e.g., what a 5-year-old child remembers most about a traumatic event may be the impact it had on the bedtime routine or other daily parent–child activities). Even if youth attend to and understand interviewers' questions, they may be unmotivated to fully participate in the interview process. Reasons for this may range from a general wariness about sharing personal details with adults to a wish to protect themselves or others (e.g., parents) from perceived negative outcomes associated with disclosure.

Obstacles Specific to PTSD Interviews

The issues described above are amplified when interviewing youth about PTSD. Not only do several aspects of the PTSD interview itself make it challenging to conduct with children, but the experience of PTSD makes it challenging

for youth with the disorder to participate in interviews. Interviews that focus on trauma exposure and PTSD can be uncomfortable because of the sensitive nature of topics assessed. Even youth who have not been exposed to traumatic events typically do not enjoy talking or thinking about such events, and some may have been socialized to believe that talking about things such as physical violence or sexual abuse is not acceptable. A child who has been traumatized may be unwilling to share details about the event because the interview itself serves as a reexperiencing occasion of the sort that the child is trying to avoid. This may be particularly likely if the child is experiencing guilt or shame about either experiencing or surviving the trauma (e.g., survivor guilt). If the trauma experience involves victimization by a known perpetrator or is ongoing (e.g., sexual or physical abuse, domestic violence, psychological torture), the youngster may also be reluctant to share details due to fear of negative outcomes such as removal of a parent from the home or retaliation from the perpetrator (Wolfe & McEachran, 1997).

In addition, to be comprehensive, PTSD interviews can be quite time-intensive and beyond the capability of youth who are experiencing PTSD-related problems with concentration. As noted earlier, children may not spontaneously report potentially important trauma history or response information, and so the interviewer may need to ask explicitly about a range of potential events. Even children who are referred for a specific traumatic event should be questioned about a full range of possible trauma, because many of them have had multiple trauma experiences (Allwood et al., 2002; Cohen & Mannarino, 2004). Potential comorbid conditions should also be assessed, lengthening the interview process further.

Cognitive limitations that affect child interviews in general may be of particular concern when interviewing youth with PTSD. Because so many PTSD symptoms involve internal experiences that may not be readily observable to others, interviewers must rely heavily on child self-reports. As Scheeringa et al. (1995) noted, however, over one half of the diagnostic criteria involve internal experiences that young children are unlikely to be able to report. Even older youth frequently give interviewers a blank look when questioned about their sense of foreshortened future. In addition, if the child is "successful" with his or her avoidance, it may be natural enough that the child is not aware of (or able to report on) efforts to avoid and also may not be actively reexperiencing the traumatic event.

Memory limitations may also affect the ability of youth to report on their PTSD. Indeed, because difficulty remembering aspects of the trauma is one symptom of the disorder, interviewers may not be able to rely on youth to provide full details about their experiences. Ironically, these memory gaps may not be readily apparent unless the interviewer notices gaps in the child's narrative or has knowledge of the event from other sources. Unfortunately, incomplete memory of the event may mean that potentially important triggers of the child's reexperiencing or other distress go unreported. Memories that the child does report may be distorted, with aspects that the child considers particularly salient magnified in his or her memory. For youth exposed to physical or sexual abuse, suggestibility has also been noted as a concern (Wolfe & Birt, 1997).

Fortunately, two issues minimize the impact of memory distortions and suggestibility on clinical interviews of PTSD. First, research suggests that children are typically resistant to suggestion from others, and, second, while forensic interviews may have the absolute truth as the goal of assessment, this is less important in clinical interviews, where it is beneficial to understand how the child remembers and conceptualizes the trauma even if that memory is somewhat different from others' memories (Cohen & Mannarino, 2004; Wolfe & Birt, 1997).

Potential Solutions to Interviewing Obstacles

Interviews with children must balance the interviewer's desire for comprehensive and detailed information with the reality that there will be limits to the child's willingness and ability to attend to and understand interview questions and to report accurately and completely on his or her trauma experiences. How this balance is achieved depends on the purposes of the interview, the abilities of the individual child, and other available resources, such as parents, teachers, or others who can add to the diagnostic picture. Thus, one of the first tasks of the interviewer is to evaluate these issues and then to formulate an interview/assessment plan.

Typically, the interviewer will know the purpose of the interview at the outset of assessment. Interview strategies and instruments selected for research purposes will likely differ from those selected for clinical assessment; research interviews will typically be more structured, with protocols set prior to contact with research participants and interview obstacles handled in systematic ways that can apply to all participants. For example, researchers interested in children's responses to a recent natural disaster would focus the interview on that specific trauma versus asking children to identify their own events; would select an interview with demonstrated psychometric properties; and would set an interview protocol that was consistent with the age and likely ability level of their sample (e.g., duration of interview period, wording of probe questions). For interviews used clinically, decisions about interview instruments and process can be tailored to the individual child on the basis of an initial assessment of the child and his or her situation. The interviewer may do a preinterview screen with the referral agent or someone who knows the child well to gather initial information on (a) the child's symptoms; (b) the child's general cognitive and verbal ability, attention span, and so on and whether these abilities are compromised by the child's symptoms; (c) the child's willingness to disclose personal information (e.g., about symptoms, experiences) to an adult interviewer/therapist; and (d) who else in the child's environment can supply useful information. The interviewer can use this preliminary information on the child's strengths, resources, and challenges to identify and plan for likely obstacles.

To address anticipated child reluctance to engage in a trauma-focused interview and disclose important personal information, building good rapport and creating a safe environment are key. The prebriefing statements included in the CAPS-C or a similar introduction explaining the importance of understanding the challenging and stressful experiences that children face can help the child and interviewer develop shared expectations about the interview. The interviewer should clearly convey a nonjudgmental and nonblaming attitude: Many youth feel embarrassment or shame after traumatic experiences because they feel responsible for their victimization (e.g., that it was somehow their fault that abuse occurred); they feel guilty for having survived a trauma that others did not; or they think that their symptoms reflect weakness (Fletcher, 2003). Conveying to children that the trauma was not their fault and that PTSD responses are a perfectly understandable reaction to abnormal and horrible life events is crucial to helping children feel comfortable sharing their stories.

Clarifying the uses to which the information will be put, with whom it will be shared, and any limits to confidentiality is also important for establishing trust. Youth need to understand that information leaves the interview/therapy room only on a "need to know" basis; for example, the child's teachers or peers will not learn details of his or her trauma experience, although teachers may be given enough information so that they can help keep the child physically and emotionally safe (e.g., for a child whose reexperiencing symptoms are triggered by crowded places, teachers may be informed of this so that they can help rearrange the child's schedule to omit school assemblies until the child's treatment has progressed to a point that crowds can be managed effectively). Children need to know that identifying abuse perpetrators will not put them in danger, even though this information must be shared with appropriate authorities. For youth with PTSD, the costs of sharing their experiences are likely to be high. Talking about their experiences goes against their efforts to avoid memories and reexperiencing and may lead to additional disruptions to their environment if the trauma is ongoing. Thus, the perceived benefits of the interview must be even higher: The youth must trust that sharing his or her story will ultimately have a positive outcome.

To deal with difficulties with concentration, attention span, and memory, the interviewer can use approaches similar to those often used with younger children. Frequent breaks can help minimize fatigue or distraction. Anchoring time-based questions with events (e.g., the child's birthday or major holidays) can help the child provide information on trauma occurrence or symptom onset or duration. Activities or memory retrieval props (e.g., dolls or toys) can also focus the interview and help youth provide more detailed information (Gee & Pipe, 1995). Finally, recognizing that children may not be able to provide the full picture of their trauma experiences themselves, incorporating other assessment methods is usually necessary. The following sections discuss interviewing important adults in the child's life, namely, parents and teachers, and conducting behavioral assessments. In addition,

because the most useful assessment will be one that is culturally competent, multicultural and diversity issues are addressed.

INTERVIEWING PARENTS AND TEACHERS

Parent and teacher reports can be useful in addressing some of the limitations of child-reported PTSD symptoms. For example, parents may be better able to provide information regarding the historical picture of PTSD, including the child's developmental history, life experiences, and symptom progression. Because PTSD is one of the few disorders requiring a precipitating event, historical information is crucial to the diagnosis, and thus parent participation in the interview process is particularly important. Similarly, both parents and teachers can provide information on impairment in the youth's functioning within school and family contexts. Finally, it is typically adults who refer youth for treatment of psychological problems, and parents are often the primary informants in the assessment of child and adolescent disorders (Mash & Terdal, 1997). To address the need for parental reports, corresponding parent versions of several comprehensive and PTSD-specific child interviews have been developed (e.g., CAPA-P, P-ChIPS, DICA-R-P, DISC-P, ADIS-P, UCLA PTSD Index). Other interviews do not have parent versions (e.g., K-SADS), but are nonetheless sometimes used with parents.

Despite the benefits of adult interviews, the literature suggests that child self-reports of internalizing symptoms might be "the gold standard" compared with adult reports of such symptoms. In most cases, researchers have found low to moderate rates of agreement in adult and youth reports of youth internalizing symptoms (Achenbach, McConaughy, & Howell, 1987; Cantwell, Lewinsohn, Rohde, & Seeley, 1997; Grills & Ollendick, 2002; Mesman & Koot, 2000), and some data indicate that youth and parents show almost no correspondence in their reports of anxiety (Bell-Dolan, Luebbe, Allwood, & Swenson, 2002; Comer & Kendall, 2004).

Parent Reports of
Trauma Exposure and PTSD

There are several reasons to believe that the discordance in parent-child reports of internalizing symptoms might be magnified for youth exposed to traumatic events. For example, after exposure to a traumatic event, parents might be reluctant to share trauma and symptom information due to feelings of guilt or an effort to be "protective" of their traumatized children. Despite the type or context of trauma exposure, parents often experience feelings of guilt or inadequacy if they are not able to protect their children from negative experiences or negative outcomes (Esquilin, 1987). This is especially true for parents who do not trust mental health services to be helpful to their children, as well as parents who believe disclosure regarding trauma or symptoms could potentially lead to undesired consequences, such as protective service referrals. In addition, many parents of trauma-exposed youth have themselves been traumatized (Graham-Bermann & Levendosky, 1998; Levendosky, Huth-Bocks, Semel, & Shapiro, 2002), and gathering information from these parents is associated with many of the same challenges as those in interviewing traumatized youth. Anecdotally, some parents who present for trauma-related interviews report rescheduling several appointments before feeling prepared to undergo the demands of recalling and sharing information about "tragic" events.

To date, both the challenges and advantages of conducting PTSD interviews with parents are understudied. Although parent-child and parent-clinician agreements of PTSD subscales are not available, agreement between parents and other reports for other anxiety disorders tends to be poor to fair (Fristad, Teare, Weller, Weller, & Salmon, 1998; Grills & Ollendick, 2003). In a study of sexually abused youth and their abuse-corroborating, nonoffending caregivers, Chaffin & Shultz (2001) commented, "The lack of even minimal correlations between parents and children in this study is remarkable" (p. 408). Empirical findings also show that compared with children in their reports, mothers are likely to underreport child trauma exposure (Hill & Jones, 1997; Richters & Martinez, 1993). Such discrepancies in exposure report would be expected to lead to discrepancies in the report of PTSD symptoms.

Teachers as Informants of Trauma Exposure and Response

The rates of discordance between parents and other reporters indicate that although parents are expected to be the more accurate historians of children's life events and distress across multiple settings, supplemental information might be necessary. At least one study suggests that compared with parents, teachers may serve as better informants of child internalizing symptoms (Mesman & Koot, 2000). There are several reasons teachers might show greater awareness than parents of child anxiety symptoms. For instance, teachers are able to observe children's social interactions with a variety of peers in one-on-one and group settings, and they may have more educational and experiential background upon which to base judgments of typical versus problematic behavior.

To date, empirical examinations of teacher reports of trauma exposure and PTSD symptoms are rare. Teacher reports of child trauma response have been examined largely through associations between child-reported symptoms and teacher reports on more general measures, such as the Teacher Report Form (Achenbach, 1991). There are no known teacher interviews of child PTSD symptoms, but parent interviews can be adapted for this purpose. Even if teachers are not aware of traumatic experiences of youth, they might be well aware of trauma response and reenactments (e.g., traumatic play, aggression, sexualized behavior) and trauma "triggers" (e.g., response of opposite-sex school personnel, bullying, loud noises, etc.). Of note, field-testing of the Teacher DISC (T-DISC), developed by Lahey and Zahner (Shaffer et al., 2000), is currently under way. However, the T-DISC is limited to behavioral disorders that are likely to be observable by teachers, and it might take several years before PTSD is included.

CASE ILLUSTRATION WITH DIALOGUE

Rita, an 11-year-old Latina girl, was referred to the Psychological Center by her school counselor due to a recent outburst in school, during which she remarked that she wanted to die. Two months prior to that, the teacher had suggested that Rita might have ADHD and should be seen for evaluation. Based on Rita's past school performance, her mother disagreed with the teacher and did not follow up on the suggestion. After this recent outburst, however, Rita's mother sought evaluation and treatment.

Because relatively little information was provided upon referral, a brief, unstructured intake interview was used to assess safety concerns (e.g., suicidality), identify potential problem areas, and direct more structured assessment. During intake, both Rita and her mother reported that Rita had been more moody lately, sometimes refusing to do her chores or follow other household rules. Her mother also reported that Rita had always been an excellent student but that recently she had been receiving calls from the teacher with reports that Rita was sleeping in class and, when awake, she seemed to daydream and to have trouble concentrating. Rita reported having trouble sleeping at night and spending less time with her friends, although she was reluctant to discuss these issues in more detail. Her mother denied knowing of any precipitating factors for Rita's behavior change but noted that Rita and her best friend seemed to have had a "falling out."

Based on the initial information, further assessment of possible trauma exposure was indicated. Because of Rita's reluctance to disclose during intake and the lack of information about (but suspicion of) potential trauma exposure, the interviewer selected an interview that would allow focus on rapport building and would assess a range of potential trauma experiences (e.g., the CAPS-C, the CAPA PTSD module, or the CPTSDI). On the trauma exposure portion of the interview, Rita admitted that at age 9, she had been in a car accident in which no one was injured or required medical attention, and she also reported that more recently, she had been made to "touch someone's body" when she did not want to. Subsequent questions elicited a more complete description of this recent event, including the risks of death, injury, or threat to physical integrity, as well as Rita's peritraumatic response:

Therapist: Rita, I am now going to ask you a few more questions about the time when you touched someone else's body but did not want to. Tell me more about what happened, like where you were and who was there at the time.

Rita reported that her friend's older brother had entered the bathroom while she was visiting their home and "bothered her." Her friend was unaware of what had happened. Rita denied being verbally threatened by the brother but stated that because he was in high school and much bigger than she was, she thought he might harm or even kill her if she did not do what he said. She reported feeling very scared from the moment he entered the bathroom and remaining fearful since that time. Further questions assessed each symptom domain, using rating scales to assess frequency and intensity:

Therapist: Did you think about what happened even when you didn't want to? For example, did you see pictures in your mind or hear sounds in your head from what happened?

Rita: [with tears welling up] I can't stop thinking about it. I should've told him "no." I keep thinking that I'm hearing his voice and thinking about what I should've said.

T: [showing a frequency calendar] How much of the time do you hear his voice or have other thoughts about it?

R: This one [pointing], I think about it all the time. I even have dreams about it.

T: Can you tell me about the dreams?

R: Well, they wake me up at night, or sometimes I stay awake on purpose so I won't have them. They happen a bunch of times every week.

T: [showing a calendar] About how many nights in a usual week would you have dreams like this?

R: [pointing to 4 days on a weeklong calendar] Maybe 4 times, or 5. Not every night.

T: And what happens in the dreams?

This interview began the process of the comprehensive assessment of Rita's trauma history and response that would guide treatment. Additional interview time was scheduled to address other aspects of Rita's adjustment, especially to assess for comorbid conditions such as mood or anxiety disorders or substance use. As assessment continued, it was important for the interviewer to pay careful attention to reports of additional trauma experiences or symptoms that Rita might share as she became more trusting or remembered more details. Plans were also made to help Rita disclose the trauma to her mother, in order to incorporate the mother more fully into assessment and treatment, as well as to begin the process of Rita's healing. Although Rita disclosed relatively freely in the privacy of an individual interview, she initially became quite distressed when discussing whether/what to tell her mother. Thus, it was important to discuss issues of confidentiality and to begin corrective experiences to dispel cognitive distortions about stigma or guilt. As this case illustrates, interviews of PTSD often unfold gradually as youth reveal information that suggests trauma history. In addition, the assessment and intervention aspects of the interview are frequently intertwined as the youth and interviewer explore the nature and meaning of the youth's experience.

MULTICULTURAL AND DIVERSITY ISSUES

Culturally competent interviews of youth PTSD must consider the ways in which culture, ethnicity, or nationality may influence trauma exposure, reactions, and reporting. For mental health professionals in the United States, understanding how these issues might vary across cultures is particularly important for two reasons. First, evidence suggests that minority youth may be at elevated risk for PTSD relative to majority-culture youth. In the United States, minority children are at greater risk for trauma exposure (Fitzpatrick, 1993; Switzer et al., 1999; U.S. Department of Justice, 2001) and are also less likely to have access to mental health services (U.S. Public Health Service, 2000) than their majority-culture youth counterparts. According to data collected from 1993 to 1998 for the National Crime Victimization Survey (NCVS) (U.S. Department of Justice, 2001), African American youth aged 12 and older experienced sexual assault, aggravated assault, and simple assault at 2 to 3 times the rates of other ethnic groups. In addition, in 2002, Hispanics/Latinos, the largest minority pan-ethnic group in the United States, also experienced violent crimes (primarily assaults) at a rate that was higher than that of non-Hispanics, and African American youth were 6 times more likely to be victims of homicide than European Americans (U.S. Department of Justice, 2003).

Second, the changing demographics of the United States suggest that trauma exposure may become even more of an issue for the country's youth in the future. The United States is currently experiencing the largest arrival of immigrants in

history. As of 2003, 12% of the U.S. population were foreign-born, and another 11% were second-generation Americans (U.S. Census Bureau, 2004). In addition, many of the "newcomers" are emigrating from war-torn regions around the world. Between 1990 and 2000, for example, more than 1 million people who immigrated to the United States were refugees. Many of these youth have been exposed to traumatic experiences that will require attention, and trauma-related services (e.g., assessment, treatment) must be structured to meet the diverse needs of these youth from other nations and cultures.

Although PTSD exists among traumatized individuals regardless of ethnicity and nationality (Ellis, Lhewa, Charney, & Cabral, in press; Nader et al., 1993; Sack, Seeley, & Clarke, 1997), there are several reasons to suspect that the disorder may not be experienced or described in the same manner across diverse cultures. For example, it is not clear that the PTSD criteria specified by the *DSM* fully capture all aspects of the posttrauma sequelae as expressed across cultures. According to Friedman (2001), "Each culture or ethnic group has its own unique expression of symptoms, stressors, and strengths, which need to be understood to develop a thorough plan for assessment and treatment" (p. 40). Cross-cultural variations in symptoms of other disorders may also be relevant to PTSD. Studies have found differences in the expression of pathological symptoms across ethnicity and environment (e.g., urban, rural). For example, Fabrega, Mezzich, and Ulrich (1988) found that African Americans from urban settings who were diagnosed with anxiety disorders were more likely to exhibit symptoms related to aggression and suspiciousness than were European Americans diagnosed with anxiety disorders. Similarly, many non-Western cultures do not make distinctions between bodily, psychological, and spiritual complaints. People in these cultures are more likely than Westerners to express distress through somatic symptoms and are more likely to seek medical intervention than mental health intervention (Sue, 1998).

Despite the uncertainty of how cultural factors affect the expression of PTSD symptoms, most studies of PTSD in youth, both nationally and internationally, rely almost exclusively on the symptom expression forwarded by the *DSM*. In fact, all PTSD interviews reviewed in this chapter maintain a fairly strict adherence to the

DSM-IV nosology without consideration for other cultural expressions.

Reporting of trauma exposure and reactions may also vary across diverse cultures. For many cultures, victimization is considered to bring shame upon a person or family, and so youth and their families may be reluctant to admit to being victimized. For example, the spiritual beliefs of some Southeast Asian cultures deem it inappropriate and potentially detrimental to discuss negative aspects of life, such as traumatic experiences (Kinzie, 1993). For others, the experience may be considered private and not something to be discussed with mental health researchers or service providers (Ho, 1992). Even if families aren't reluctant to report symptoms, they may have different thresholds for noticing them or considering them problematic. Assessment of youth trauma response is highly reliant on adult (e.g., parent, teacher) reports (Yule, 2001), yet adult thresholds for defining children's behavior as problematic are culturally regulated. Studies have found that based on cultural expectations of childhood behaviors, adults from different cultures may respond differently to the same child behaviors (Lambert et al., 2001).

To date, limited strides have been made toward addressing ethnocultural aspects of defining and assessing PTSD in youth, and recommendations about conducting more culturally competent interviews are preliminary. Nevertheless, we present some ideas for incorporating diversity issues into PTSD interviews. At the most obvious level, conducting interviews in the language with which youth and their families are most comfortable is preferred. Because many PTSD symptoms reflect emotions or experiences that may be difficult to express in a newly learned language, a child may be able to provide more information in his or her primary language. Several interviews have been or are being translated into Spanish (e.g., DICA: Ezpetela, de la Osa, Domenech, Navarro, & Losilla, 1997; DISC: Bravo et al., 2001), and some have been translated into various other languages (Chinese: DISC, Ho et al., 2005, and ChIPS, Hsu et al., 2002; Dutch: DICA, Kroes et al., 2001). Of course, if the interviewer is not fluent in the child's language, an interpreter will be required, and the presence of an additional person could affect the child's disclosure (Miller, Martell,

Pazdirek, Caruth, & Lopez, 2005). Also, the descriptors for some affective, cognitive, physiological, or psychological experiences are not easily translated, and further research is needed to examine the extent to which translated measures can manage these issues effectively.

To address differences in adults' and children's thresholds for noticing symptoms and defining them as problems, interviewers may want to separate questions about the presence and characteristics of various behaviors from questions about importance. Structured interviews may be a better choice for this than unstructured or semistructured interviews. For example, rather than asking open-ended questions about the child's experience, interviewers might ask whether the child has experienced each one of a list of common symptoms, assess the nature of experiences (e.g., duration, intensity, frequency), and then ask whether that particular symptom was a problem (i.e., distressing or impairing). To minimize value judgments or thresholds influencing reports of symptom characteristics, interviewers can use objective rating scale anchors. Rather than using subjective ratings such as "a little" or "a lot," the interviewer can use a calendar to assess frequency (i.e., number of days in a week or month) or a thermometer to assess percentage of time (e.g., in a day) that a particular symptom occurs. An added benefit of these assessment tools is that their visual nature may enhance communication if spoken language presents a challenge.

The choice of an appropriate interviewer may also need to be considered. Understanding the youth's cultural background can affect selection of an interviewer who is male rather than female, who is older (and thus more respected) rather than younger, or who is perhaps from the clergy or other profession that may be trusted more than mental health (Ho, 1992). Finally, because individual variations within cultures, ethnicities, and nationalities are often greater than they are across these groups (Atkinson, Morten, & Sue, 1998), it is important to understand the individual contextual background of the youth. Letting the youth and his or her family inform the interviewer about what is important in terms of symptoms, information-sharing styles, and so on, will likely yield the most fruitful interview process.

DIFFERENTIAL DIAGNOSIS AND BEHAVIORAL ASSESSMENT

Although direct questioning through interviews or questionnaires are the most commonly used methods of assessing PTSD and associated problems, these methods may be supplemented with other behavioral assessment strategies (see Barrios & Hartmann, 1997, for a review of behavioral assessment strategies that may be applicable to PTSD). Concerns regarding differential diagnosis were presented earlier. When interviewing strategies alone do not resolve differential-diagnosis questions, behavioral assessment methods may be particularly useful. At the most basic level, interviews provide more than the narrative that the child, parent, or teacher provides in response to questions; observing the child's behavior during the interview is also informative. Systematic in-session observations typically have not been used during PTSD interviews, but some interviewers (e.g., ADIS-C) nonetheless incorporate interviewer observations into conclusions regarding symptoms and diagnosis (Stallings & March, 1995). For example, the interviewer may be able to see evidence of arousal or reexperiencing if the child becomes visibly upset when talking about the traumatic event. If the interviewer has prior knowledge of some aspects of the event from other sources, he or she may be able to note places where the child omits important details and, when questioned, appears not to remember them. The child may also simply refuse to talk about the experience, possibly reflecting avoidance. The use of play materials that could be used to reenact the trauma (e.g., toy villages that could be destroyed by a flood or fire or dolls that could be kidnapped or killed) can also prove informative. Play is a natural form of communication for children and may allow them the opportunity to express in behavior what they are less able or less comfortable expressing in words. One should be cautious when interpreting children's play behavior, however, to avoid overinterpreting simple fantasy play, and hypotheses formed during observation of children's play activity should be evaluated in the context of information from other sources.

Physiological and neurobiological assessments may also offer promise in evaluation of PTSD. For example, research has documented abnormal cortisol levels in traumatized children, although the specific nature of the abnormality (e.g., higher or lower) differs across studies and types of trauma and is not yet well understood (De Bellis et al., 1999; Goenjian et al., 1996; King, Mandansky, King, Fletcher, & Brewer, 2001). Similarly, functional MRI is emerging as a useful method of identifying brain function associated with different forms of psychopathology in youth (Vaidya et al., 2005; Viard et al., 2005) and may be applied to PTSD in the future.

SELECTION OF TREATMENT TARGETS AND REFERRAL

One major purpose of interviewing youth about their trauma experiences and responses is to guide treatment decisions. Initially, this involves deciding whether treatment is warranted. Conscientious adults may refer children for evaluation whom they know have been exposed to trauma, but exposure does not automatically indicate treatment. For example, although approximately one third of youth who are exposed to trauma develop PTSD (Fletcher, 2003), many trauma-exposed youth cope adaptively without treatment. In fact, recent evidence indicates that providing universal intervention to trauma-exposed individuals may be not only unnecessary but harmful (e.g., Critical Incident Stress Debriefing; Litz, 2004). If assessment indicates that the youth does not meet criteria for PTSD or for an acute stress response that is causing distress or impairment, treatment may not be needed. Even if a child is not in current need of treatment, however, psychoeducation can be useful to inform the youth and his or her parents about common trauma reactions (both adaptive and maladaptive) and potential changes over time and to encourage them to seek evaluation and treatment as issues arise in the future.

If the interview suggests that the youth is exhibiting significant distress or impairment, interview results can be used to identify treatment goals, targets, and approaches. Broadly speaking, the goal of PTSD treatment is to help the traumatized child survive and move on in an adaptive manner. Treatment cannot change the past and take away the child's trauma exposure, but it can reduce symptoms, strengthen adaptive coping, and help the child engage in life in a developmentally appropriate way. Treatment targets that can be clarified via interview include the specific reexperiencing, avoidance, and hyperarousal symptoms the youth is experiencing and the youth's personal and environmental resources that can help support his or her adjustment. For example, children and their parents and teachers can specify which symptoms are most disruptive to children's daily lives. Similarly, the interview process is useful for gaining information about children's support groups. Interviews with the child and important adults can provide clues about the nature of the child's relationships with these adults and about their potential for involvement in the child's treatment. When the interview reveals that parents have also been traumatized, successful treatment of children will most likely be linked closely with appropriate treatment for the parents. Thus, parent adjustment becomes a treatment target, addressed in conjunction with children's treatment or through a separate referral.

Specific treatment approaches can also be guided by interview results. In general, cognitive-behavioral therapy (CBT) approaches have been shown to be the most effective treatments for youth with PTSD (Cohen et al., 2004; March, Amaya-Jackson, Murray, & Schulte, 1998; Saigh, Yule, & Inamdar, 1996). These approaches incorporate psychoeducation, anxiety and anger management to address cognitive and physiological symptoms, gradual exposure to the trauma story or memory, and strategies for coping with grief and loss. Interviews can identify which treatment components may require greater attention for individual children and which might be less necessary. For example, for some youth, anger management may be a key component of treatment, but for others, grief and loss issues may be more important. Integral to the TF-CBT approach is a skill-building focus, helping youth cope positively with the trauma effects (symptoms and associated losses) and increasing personal control in their lives and environments. Interviews can also guide treatment by identifying areas in which the youth displays competence or by identifying individuals in the youth's family or peer group who can provide social support for positive coping.

Finally, interview and treatment are part of an iterative process. Used initially to diagnose and guide referral and treatment recommendations,

interviews are also useful in assessing treatment progress and outcomes and guiding longer-term courses of treatment. Although many youth show substantial improvement after a standard course of CBT (e.g., 12–20 sessions), other youth will benefit from longer courses of treatment that allow attention to particularly severe or chronic trauma (e.g., prolonged abuse) or that address issues that become more relevant at different points in the youth's development. For instance, a child whose functioning has stabilized after treatment for sexual abuse may experience renewed difficulty when she begins dating and forming intimate relationships. In PTSD treatment, the notion of "pulsed intervention" is particularly useful (McKnight, Compton, & March, 2004). Pulsed intervention provides episodic treatment, with each episode, or course of treatment, limited to developmentally appropriate and personally relevant issues. With pulsed interventions, ongoing assessment is critical to staying informed of the youth's current strengths and needs, in order to make decisions about when treatment can be suspended and when it should resume (Brewin, 2005). In this way, interviews become part of the youth's overall mental health maintenance regimen.

Several interviews reviewed in this chapter have versions that assess (or can be adapted to assess) current or past-year symptoms and can be used after initial diagnosis to assess functioning during and after treatment. Although comprehensive diagnostic interviews are typically too time-intensive to use frequently, the treating clinician can incorporate the briefer and more focused interviews into treatment on a regular basis as a way of assessing the youth's progress. At posttreatment and follow-up, using interviews to obtain a more complete diagnostic picture can help evaluate treatment effectiveness and identify additional treatment directions. Thus, PTSD interviews take multiple forms, including comprehensive and PTSD specific, structured and less structured, child and adult report, and, in combination, they play a central role in ongoing assessment of children coping with traumatic events.

REFERENCES

Achenbach, T. M. (1991). *Manual for the teacher's report form and 1991 profile*. Burlington: University of Vermont Department of Psychiatry.

Achenbach, T. M., McConaughy, S. H., & Howell, C. T. (1987). Child/adolescent behavioral and emotional problems: Implications of cross-informant correlations for situational specificity. *Psychological Bulletin, 101,* 213–232.

Ahmad, A., Sundelin-Wahlsten, V., Sofi, M. A., Qahar, J. A., & von Knorring, A. L. (2000). Reliability and validity of a child-specific cross-cultural instrument for assessing posttraumatic stress disorder. *European Child & Adolescent Psychiatry, 9,* 285–294.

Allwood, M. A. (2000). *The prevalence and implications of emotional numbing and PTSD in war-traumatized children from Bosnia.* Unpublished master's thesis, University of Missouri-Columbia.

Allwood, M. A. (2003, October). *Attention problems in war-traumatized Sarajevan Children.* Presentation at the 2003 Conference of Ford Foundation Fellows, San Juan, Puerto Rico.

Allwood, M. A. (2005). *The relation of violence exposure, trauma symptoms, and aggressive cognitions to youth violent behavior.* Unpublished doctoral dissertation, University of Missouri-Columbia.

Allwood, M. A., Bell-Dolan, D., & Husain, S. A. (2002). Children's trauma and adjustment reactions to violent and non-violent war experiences. *Journal of the American Academy of Child & Adolescent Psychiatry, 41,* 450–457.

Ambrosini, P. J. (2000). Historical development and present status of the Schedule for Affective Disorders and Schizophrenia for School-Age Children (K-SADS). *Journal of the American Academy of Child & Adolescent Psychiatry, 39,* 49–58.

American Academy of Child and Adolescent Psychiatry. (1998). Summary of the practice parameters for the assessment and treatment of children and adolescents with posttraumatic stress disorder. *Journal of the American Academy of Child & Adolescent Psychiatry, 37,* 997–1001.

American Psychiatric Association. (2000). *Diagnostic and statistical manual of mental disorders* (4th ed., Text rev.). Washington, DC: Author.

Angold A., & Costello, E. (1995). A test-retest reliability study of child-reported psychiatric symptoms and diagnoses using the Child and Adolescent Psychiatric Assessment. *Psychological Medicine, 25,* 755–762.

Angold, A., & Costello, E. J. (2000). The Child and Adolescent Psychiatric Assessment (CAPA). *Journal of the American Academy of Child & Adolescent Psychiatry, 39,* 39–48.

Atkinson, D. R., Morten, G., & Sue, D. W. (1998). *Counseling American minorities* (5th ed.). Boston: McGraw-Hill.

Barrios, B. A., & Hartmann, D. P. (1997). Fears and anxieties. In E. J. Mash & L. G. Terdal (Eds.), *Assessment of childhood disorders* (pp. 230–327). New York: Guilford Press.

Beidel, D. C., & Turner, S. C. (1998). *Shy children, phobic adults: Nature and treatment of social phobia.* New York: American Psychological Association.

Bell-Dolan, D., Luebbe, A., Allwood, M., & Swenson, L. (2002, November). *Informant effects on the relationships of children's general and social anxiety to cognitive, behavioral, and emotional adjustment.* Paper presented at the 36th Annual Meeting of the Association for the Advancement of Behavior Therapy, Reno, NV.

Bernstein, D. P., Fink, L., Handelsman, L., Foote, J., Lovejoy, M., Wenzel, K., et al. (1994). Initial reliability and validity of a new retrospective measure of child abuse and neglect. *American Journal of Psychiatry, 151,* 1132–1136.

Blake, D. D., Weathers, F. W., Nagy, L. M., Kaloupek, D. G., Klauminzer, G., Charney, D. S., et al. (1990). A clinician rating scale for assessing current and lifetime PTSD: The CAPS-1. *Behavior Therapy, 13,* 187–188.

Bravo, M., Ribera, J., Rubio-Stipec, M., Canino, G., Shrout, P., Ramirez, R., et al. (2001). Test-retest reliability of the Spanish version of the Diagnostic Interview Schedule for Children (DISC—IV). *Journal of Abnormal Child Psychology, 29,* 433–444.

Brent, D. A., Perper, J. A., Moritz, G., Liotus, L., Richardson, D., Canobbio, R., et al. (1995). Posttraumatic stress disorder in peers of adolescent suicide victims: Predisposing factors and phenomenology. *Journal of the American Academy of Child & Adolescent Psychiatry, 34,* 209–215.

Brewin, C. (2005, November 3). *Designing screen & treatment programme following 7/7 London bombings.* Paper presented at the International Society of Traumatic Stress Studies 21st Annual Meeting, Toronto, Canada.

Briere, J. (1996). *Trauma Symptom Checklist for Children professional manual.* Odessa, FL: Psychological Assessment Resources.

Cantwell, D. P., Lewinsohn, P. M., Rohde, P., & Seeley, J. R. (1997). Correspondence between adolescent report and parent report of psychiatric diagnostic data. *Journal of the American Academy of Child & Adolescent Psychiatry, 36,* 610–619.

Carrion, V. G., Weems, C. F., Ray, R., & Reiss, A. L. (2002). Toward an empirical definition of pediatric PTSD: The phenomenology of PTSD symptoms in youth. *Journal of the American Academy of Child & Adolescent Psychiatry, 41,* 166–173.

Chaffin, M., & Shultz, S. K. (2001). Psychometric evaluation of the Children's Impact of Traumatic Events Scale-Revised. *Child Abuse & Neglect, 25,* 401–411.

Chilcoat, H. D., & Breslau, N. (1998). Posttraumatic stress disorder and drug disorders: Testing causal pathways. *Archives of General Psychiatry, 55,* 913–917.

Cohen, J. A., Deblinger, E., Mannarino, A. P., & Steer, R. (2004). A Multi-site, randomized controlled trial for children with abuse-related PTSD symptoms. *Journal of the American Academy of Child & Adolescent Psychiatry, 43,* 393–402.

Cohen, J. A., & Mannarino, A. P. (2004). Posttraumatic stress disorder. In T. H. Ollendick & J. S. March (Eds.), *Phobic and anxiety disorders in childhood and adolescence* (pp. 405–432). New York: Oxford University Press.

Comer, J. S., & Kendall, P. C. (2004). A symptom-level examination of parent-child agreement in the diagnosis of anxious youths. *Journal of the American Academy of Child & Adolescent Psychiatry, 43,* 878–886.

Cooley, M. R., Turner, S. M., & Beidel, D. C. (1995). Assessing community violence: The children's report of exposure to violence. *Journal of the*

American Academy of Child & Adolescent Psychiatry, 34, 201–208.

Cortes, A. M., Saltzman, K. M., Weems, C. F., Regnault, H. P., Reiss, A. L., & Carrion, V. G. (2005). Development of anxiety disorders in a traumatized pediatric population: A preliminary longitudinal evaluation. *Child Abuse & Neglect, 29,* 905–914.

Costello, E. J., Angold, A., March, J., & Fairbank, J. (1998). Life events and posttraumatic stress: The development of a new measure for children and adolescents. *Psychological Medicine, 28,* 1275–1288.

De Bellis, M. D., Baum, A. S., Birmaher, B., Keshavan, M. S., Eccard, C. H., Boring, A. M., et al. (1999). Developmental traumatology: Part I. Biological stress systems. *Biological Psychiatry, 45,* 1259–1270.

Ellis, B. H., Lhewa, D., Charney, M., & Cabral, H. (in press). Screening for PTSD among Somali adolescent refugees: Psychometric properties of the UCLA PTSD Index. *Journal of Traumatic Stress.*

Endicott, J., & Spitzer, R. L. (1978). A diagnostic interview: The Schedule for Affective Disorders and Schizophrenia. *Archives of General Psychiatry, 35,* 837–844.

Esquilin, S. C. (1987). Family responses to the identification of extra-familial child sexual abuse. *Psychotherapy in Private Practice, 5,* 105–113.

Eth, S., & Pynoos, R. (1985). *Posttraumatic stress disorder in children.* Washington, DC: American Psychiatric Press.

Evans, A. S., Spirito, A., Celio, M., Dyl, J., & Hunt, J. (in press). Relation of substance use to trauma and conduct disorder in an adolescent psychiatric population. *Journal of Child and Adolescent Substance Use.*

Ezpetela, L., de la Osa, N., Domenech, J. M., Navarro, Jose, B., & Losilla, J. M. (1997). Diagnostic agreement between clinicians and the Diagnostic Interview for Children and Adolescents (DICA-R) in an outpatient sample. *Journal of Child Psychology and Psychiatry and Allied Disciplines, 38,* 431–440.

Fabrega, H., Mezzich, J., & Ulrich, R. F. (1988). Black and white differences in psychopathology in an urban psychiatric population. *Comprehensive Psychiatry, 29,* 285–297.

Fitzpatrick, K. M. (1993). Exposure to violence and presence of depression among low-income African American youth. *Journal of Consulting and Clinical Psychology, 61,* 528–531.

Fletcher, K. (1996). Psychometric review of the When Bad Things Happen Scale (WBTH). In B. H. Stamm (Ed.), *Measurement of stress, trauma, and adaptation* (pp. 435–437). Lutherville, MD: Sidran Press.

Fletcher, K. E. (2003). Childhood posttraumatic stress disorder. In E. J. Mash & R. A. Barkley (Eds.), *Child psychopathology* (2nd ed., pp. 330–371). New York: Guilford Press.

Foa, E. B., Johnson, K. M., Feeny, N. C., & Treadwell, K. R. (2001). The Child PTSD Symptom Scale: A preliminary examination of its psychometric properties. *Journal of Clinical Child Psychology, 30,* 376–384.

Ford, J. D., Racusin, R., Ellis, C. G., Daviss, W. B., Reiser, J., Fleisher, A., et al. (2000). Child maltreatment, other trauma exposure, and posttraumatic symptomatology among children with oppositional defiant and attention deficit hyperactivity disorders. *Child Maltreatment, 5,* 205–217.

Friedman, S. (2001). Cultural issues in the assessment of anxiety disorders. In M. M. Antomy, S. M. Orsillo, & L. Roemer (Eds.), *Practitioner's guide to empirically based measures of anxiety* (pp. 37–42). New York: Kluwer.

Fristad, M. A., Glickman, A. R., Verducci, J. S., Teare, M., Weller, E. B., & Weller, R. A. (1998). Study V: Children's Interview of Psychiatric Syndromes (ChIPS): Psychometrics in two communities. *Journal of Child and Adolescent Psychopharmacology, 8,* 237–245.

Fristad, M. A., Teare, M., Weller, E. B., Weller, R. A., & Salmon, P. (1998). Study III: Development and concurrent validity of the Children's Interview for Psychiatric Syndromes-Parent Version (P-ChIPS). *Journal of Child and Adolescent Psychopharmacology, 8,* 221–226.

Gee, S., & Pipe, M. E. (1995). Helping children to remember: The influence of object cues on children's accounts of a real event. *Developmental Psychology, 31,* 746–758.

Giaconia, R. M., Reinherz, H. Z., Silverman, A. B., Pakiz, B., Frost, A. K., & Cohen, E. (1995). Traumas and posttraumatic stress disorder in a community population of older adolescents. *Journal of the American Academy of Child & Adolescent Psychiatry, 34,* 1369–1380.

Goenjian, A. K., Yehuda, R., Pynoos, R. S., Steinberg, A. M., Tashjian, M., Yang, R. K., et al. (1996). Basal cortisol, dexamethasone suppression of cortisol, and MHPG in adolescents after the 1988 earthquake in Armenia. *American Journal of Psychiatry, 153,* 929–934.

Graham-Bermann, S. A., & Levendosky, A. A. (1998). Traumatic stress symptoms in children of battered women. *Journal of Interpersonal Violence, 13,* 111–128.

Gray, M. J., Litz, B. T., Hsu, J. L., & Lombardo, T. W. (2004). Psychometric properties of the Life Events Checklist. *Assessment, 11,* 330–341.

Grills, A. E., & Ollendick, T. H. (2002). Issues in parent-child agreement: The case of structured diagnostic interviews. *Clinical Child and Family Psychology Review, 5,* 57–83.

Grills, A. E., & Ollendick, T. H. (2003). Multiple informant agreement and the Anxiety Disorders Interview Schedule for parents and children. *Journal of the American Academy of Child & Adolescent Psychiatry, 42,* 30–40.

Hastings, T. L., & Kelley, M. L. (1997). Development and validation of the Screen for Adolescent Violence Exposure (SAVE). *Journal of Abnormal Child Psychology, 25,* 511–520.

Hill, H. M., & Jones, L. P. (1997). Children's and parents' perceptions of children's exposure to violence in urban neighborhoods. *Journal of the National Medical Association, 89,* 270–276.

Ho, M. K. (1992). *Minority children and adolescents in therapy.* Newbury Park, CA: Sage.

Ho, T., Leung, P. W., Lee, C., Tang, C., Hung, S., Kwong, S., et al. (2005). Test-retest reliability of the Chinese version of the Diagnostic Interview Schedule for Children-Version 4 (DISC-IV). *Journal of Child Psychology and Psychiatry, 46*, 1135–1138.

Hsu, C., Chong, M., Yang, P., & Yen, C. (2002). Posttraumatic stress disorder among adolescent earthquake victims in Taiwan. *Journal of the American Academy of Child & Adolescent Psychiatry, 41*, 875–881.

Jenkins, E. J., & Bell, C. C. (1994). Violence among inner city high school students and posttraumatic stress disorder. In S. Friedman (Ed.), *Anxiety disorders in African Americans* (pp. 76–88). New York: Springer.

Jones, R. T., Fletcher, K., & Ribbe, D. R. (2002). *Child's Reaction to Traumatic Events Scale-Revised (CRTES-R): A self-report traumatic stress measure.* Available from the first author, Department of Psychology, Stress and Coping Lab, Virginia Tech University, Blacksburg, VA 24060.

Kaufman, J., Birmaher, B., Brent, D., Rao, U., Flynn, C., Moreci, P., et al. (1997). Schedule for Affective Disorders and Schizophrenia for School-Age Children-Present and Lifetime Version (K-SADS-PL): Initial reliability and validity data. *Journal of the American Academy of Child & Adolescent Psychiatry, 36*, 980–988.

Kendall, P. C., Flannery-Schroeder, E. C., Panichelli-Mindell, S. M., Southam-Gerow, M., Henin, A., & Warman, M. (1997). Therapy for youths with anxiety disorders: A second randomized clinical trial. *Journal of Consulting and Clinical Psychology, 65*, 366–380.

Keppel-Benson, J. M., Ollendick, T. H., & Benson, M. J. (2002). Posttraumatic stress in children following motor vehicle accidents. *Journal of Child Psychology and Psychiatry, 43*, 203–212.

King, J., Mandansky, D., King, S., Fletcher, K. E., & Brewer, J. (2001). Early sexual abuse and low cortisol. *Psychiatry and Clinical Neurosciences, 55*, 71–74.

Kinzie, J. D. (1993). Posttraumatic effects and their treatment among Southeast Asian refugees. In J. P. Wilson & B. Raphael (Eds.), *International handbook of traumatic stress syndromes* (pp. 311–319). New York: Plenum Press.

Kroes, M., Kalff, A. C., Kessels, A. G. H., Steyaert, J., Feron, F. J. M., van Someren, A. J. W., et al. (2001). Child psychiatric diagnoses in a population of Dutch schoolchildren aged 6 to 8 years. *Journal of the American Academy of Child & Adolescent Psychiatry, 40*, 1401–1409.

La Greca, A. M., Silverman, W. K., & Wasserstein, S. B. (1998). Children's predisaster functioning as a predictor of posttraumatic stress following Hurricane Andrew. *Journal of Consulting and Clinical Psychology, 64*, 712–723.

Lahey, B. B., Flagg, E., W., Bird, H. R., & Schwab-Stone, M. E. (1996). The NIMH methods for the epidemiology of child and adolescent mental disorders (MECA) study: Background and methodology. *Journal of the American Academy of Child & Adolescent Psychiatry, 35*, 855–864.

Lambert, M. C., Puig, M., Lyubansky, M., Rowan, G. T., Hill, M., Milburn, B., et al. (2001). Child behavior and emotional problems in Jamaican classrooms: A multimethod study using direct observations and teacher reports for ages 6–11. *International Journal of Intercultural Relations, 25*, 545–562.

Levendosky, A. A., Huth-Bocks, A. C., Semel, M. A., & Shapiro, D. L. (2002). Trauma symptoms in preschool-age children exposed to domestic violence. *Journal of Interpersonal Violence, 17*, 150–164.

Litz, B. T. (Ed.). (2004). *Early intervention for trauma and traumatic loss.* New York: Guilford Press.

March, J. S., Amaya-Jackson, L., Murray, M. C., & Schulte, A. (1998). Cognitive behavioral psychotherapy for children and adolescents with posttraumatic stress disorder after a single incident stressor. *Journal of the American Academy of Child & Adolescent Psychiatry, 37*, 585–593.

March, J. S., Amaya-Jackson, L., Terry, R., & Costanzo, P. (1997). Posttraumatic stress in children and adolescents after an industrial fire. *Journal of the American Academy of Child & Adolescent Psychiatry, 36*, 554–565.

Mash, E. J., & Terdal, L. G. (Eds.). (1997). *Assessment of childhood disorders* (3rd ed.). New York: Guilford Press.

Matzner, F., Silva R., Silvan, M., Chowdhury, M., & Nastasi, L. (1997). *Preliminary test-retest reliability of the KID-SCID.* Scientific Proceedings, American Psychiatric Association Meeting, Washington, DC.

McCloskey, L. A., & Walker, W. (2000). Posttraumatic stress in children exposed to family violence and single event trauma. *Journal of the American Academy of Child & Adolescent Psychiatry, 39*, 108–115.

McFarlane, A. C., Policansky, S., & Irwin, C. P. (1987). A longitudinal study of the psychological morbidity in children due to a natural disaster. *Psychological Medicine, 17*, 727–738.

McKnight, C. D., Compton, S. N., & March, J. S. (2004). Posttraumatic stress disorder. In T. L. Morris & J. S. March (Eds.), *Anxiety disorders in childhood and adolescence* (pp. 241–262). New York: Oxford University Press.

Mesman, J., & Koot, H. M. (2000). Child-reported depression and anxiety in preadolescence: I. Associations with parent- and teacher-reported problems. *Journal of the American Academy of Child & Adolescent Psychiatry, 39*, 1371–1378.

Miller, K. E., Martell, Z. L., Pazdirek, L., Caruth, M., & Lopez, D. (2005). The role of interpreters in psychotherapy with refugees: An exploratory study. *American Journal of Orthopsychiatry, 75*, 27–39.

Moradi, A. R., Doost, H. T., Taghavi, M. R., Yule, W., & Dalgleish, T. (1999). Everyday memory deficits in children and adolescents with PTSD: Performance on the Rivermead Behavioral Memory Test. *Journal of Child Psychology and Psychiatry, 40*, 357–361.

Nader, K. O. (2004). Assessing traumatic experiences in children and adolescents: Self-reports of *DSM* PTSD criteria B-D symptoms. In J. Wilson & T. M. Keane (Eds.), *Assessing psychological trauma and PTSD* (2nd ed., pp. 513–537). New York: Guilford Press.

Nader, K. O., Kriegler, J. A., Blake, D. D., & Pynoos, R. S. (1994). *Clinician-Administered PTSD Scale-Child and Adolescent Version (CAPS-C).* White River Junction, VT: National Center for PTSD.

Nader, K. O., Newman, E., Weathers, F. W., Kaloupek, D. G., Kriegler, J. A., Blake, D. D., et al. (1998). *Clinician-Administered PTSD Scale for Children and Adolescents for (DSM-IV)*. White River Junction, VT: National Center for PTSD.

Nader, K. O., Pynoos, R. S., Fairbanks, L. A., A1-Ajeel, M., & Al-Asfour, A. (1993). A preliminary study of PTSD and grief among the children of Kuwait following the Gulf Crisis. *British Journal of Clinical Psychology, 32*, 407–416.

Ohan, J. L., Myers, K., & Collett, B. R. (2002). Ten-year review of rating scales. IV: Scales assessing trauma and its effects. *Journal of the American Academy of Child & Adolescent Psychiatry, 41*, 1401–1422.

Orvaschel, H. (1995). *Schedule for Affective Disorders and Schizophrenia for School-Age Children, Epidemiological Version*. Copyrighted Instrument, Nova Southeastern University, Ft. Lauderdale, FL.

Puig-Antich, J., & Chambers, W. (1978). *The Schedule of Affective Disorders and Schizophrenia for School Age Children (Kiddie-SADS)*. New York: New York State Psychiatric Institute.

Pynoos, R. S., Frederick, C., Nader, K., Arroyo, W., Steinberg, A., Eth, S., et al. (1987). Life threat and posttraumatic stress in school-age children. *Archives of General Psychiatry, 44*, 1057–1063.

Pynoos, R. S., Rodriquez, N., Steinberg, A. Stuber, M., & Fredrick, C. (1998). *UCLA PTSD Index for DSM-IV (Rev. 1)*. Los Angeles: UCLA Trauma Psychiatry Program.

Rapee, R. M., Barrett, P. M., Dadds, M. R., & Evans, L. (1994). Reliability of the *DSM-III-R* childhood anxiety disorders using structured interview: Interrater and parent-child agreement. *Journal of the American Academy of Child & Adolescent Psychiatry, 33*, 984–992.

Reebye, P., Moretti, M. M., Wiebe, V. J., & Lessard, J. C. (2000). Symptoms of posttraumatic stress disorder in adolescents with conduct disorder: Sex differences and onset patterns. *Canadian Journal of Psychiatry, 45*, 746–751.

Reich, W. (1998). *Diagnostic Interview for Children and Adolescents (DICA): DSM-IV version*. St Louis, MO: Washington University School of Medicine.

Reich, W. (2000). Diagnostic Interview for Children and Adolescents (DICA). *Journal of the American Academy of Child & Adolescent Psychiatry, 39*, 59–66.

Reich, W., Leacock, N., & Shanfield, C. (1994). *Diagnostic Interview for Children and Adolescents-Revised (DICA-R)*. St. Louis, MO: Washington University.

Ribbe, D. (1996). Psychometric review of Traumatic Event Screening Instrument [*sic*] for Children (TESI-C). In H. Stamm (Ed.), *Measurement of stress, trauma, and adaptation* (pp. 386–387). Lutherville, MD: Sidran Press.

Richters, J. E., & Martinez, P. (1993). The NIMH community violence project: I. Children as victims of and witness to violence. *Psychiatry, 56*, 7–21.

Sack, W. H., Seeley, J. R., & Clarke, G. N. (1997). Does PTSD transcend cultural barriers? A study from the Khmer adolescent refugee project. *Journal of the American Academy of Child & Adolescent Psychiatry, 36*, 49–54.

Saigh, P. A. (1989). The development and validation of the Children's Posttraumatic Stress Disorder Inventory. *International Journal of Special Education, 4*, 75–84.

Saigh, P. A. (1998). *Children's PTSD Inventory (DSM-IV Version)*. New York: Author.

Saigh, P. A. (2004). Assessment of PTSD in children and adolescents. In R. R. Silva (Ed.), *Posttraumatic stress disorders in children and adolescents: Handbook* (pp. 202–217). New York: Norton.

Saigh, P. A., & Bremner, J. D. (Eds.). (1999). *Posttraumatic stress disorder: A comprehensive text*. Needham Heights, MA: Allyn & Bacon.

Saigh, P. A., Yasik, A. E., Oberfield, R. A., Green, B. L., Halamandaris, P. V., Rubenstein, H., et al. (2000). The children's PTSD inventory: Development and reliability. *Journal of Traumatic Stress, 13*, 369–380.

Saigh, P. A., Yule, W., & Inamdar, S. C. (1996). Imaginal flooding of traumatized children and adolescents. *Journal of School Psychology, 34*, 163–183.

Saylor, C. F., Swenson, C. C., Reynolds, S. S., & Taylor, M. (1999). The Pediatric Emotional Distress Scale: A brief screening measure for young children exposed to traumatic events. *Journal of Clinical Child Psychology, 28*, 70–81.

Scheeringa, M. S., Zeanah, C. H., Drell, M. J., & Larrieu, J. A. (1995). Two approaches to the diagnosis of PTSD in infancy and early childhood. *Journal of the American Academy of Child & Adolescent Psychiatry, 34*, 191–200.

Shaffer, D., & Fisher, P. (1997). *NIMH Diagnostic Interview for Children: Child Informant*. New York: New York State Psychiatric Institute.

Shaffer, D., Fisher, P., Lucas, C. P., Dulcan, M. K., & Schwab-Stone, M. E. (2000). NIMH Diagnostic Interview Schedule for Children Version IV (NIMH DISC-IV): Description, differences from previous versions, and reliability of some common diagnoses. *Journal of the American Academy of Child & Adolescent Psychiatry, 39*, 28–38.

Shemesh, E., Yehuda, R., Rockmore, L., Shneider, B. L., Emre, S., Bartell, A. S., et al. (2005). Assessment of depression in medically ill children presenting to pediatric specialty clinics. *Journal of the American Academy of Child & Adolescent Psychiatry, 44*, 1249–1257.

Silverman, W. K., & Albano, A. M. 1996). *The Anxiety Disorders Interview Schedule for Children for DSM-IV: Child and Parent Versions*. San Antonio, TX: Psychological Corporation.

Silverman, W. K., Saavedra, L. M., & Pina, A. A. (2001). Test-retest reliability of anxiety symptoms and diagnoses with the Anxiety Disorders Interview Schedule for *DSM-IV*: Child and parent versions. *Journal of the American Academy of Child & Adolescent Psychiatry, 40*, 937–944.

Spitzer R. L., Williams, J., B., Gibbon, M., & First, M., B. (1990). *Structured Clinical Interview for DSM-III-R, patient edition/non-patient edition (SCID-P/SCID-NP)*. Washington, DC: American Psychiatric Press.

Stallings, P., March, J. S. (1995). Assessment. In J. S. March (Ed.), *Anxiety disorders in children and adolescents* (pp. 125–147). New York: Guilford Press.

Steinberg, A. M., Brymer, M. J., Decker, K. B., & Pynoos, R. S. (2004). University of California–Los Angeles Posttraumatic Stress Disorder Reaction Index. *Current Psychiatry Report, 6,* 96–100.

Steiner, H., Garcia, I. G., & Matthews, Z. (1997). Posttraumatic stress disorder in incarcerated juvenile delinquents. *Journal of the American Academy of Child & Adolescent Psychiatry, 36,* 357–365.

Sue, D. (1998). The interplay of sociocultural factors on the psychosocial development of Asians in America. In D. R. Atkinson, G. Morten, & D. W. Sue (Eds.), *Counseling American minorities* (5th ed., pp. 205–213). Boston: McGraw-Hill.

Switzer, G. E., Dew, M. A., Thompson, K., Goycoolea, J. M., Derricott, T., & Mullins, S. D. (1999). Posttraumatic stress disorder and service utilization among urban mental health center clients. *Journal of Traumatic Stress, 12,* 25–39.

Terr, L. C. (1990). *Too scared to cry: Psychic trauma in childhood.* New York: Harper & Row.

Terr, L. C. (1991). Childhood traumas: An outline and overview. *American Journal of Psychiatry, 148,* 10–20.

Timbremont, B., Braet, C., & Dreessen, L. (2004). Assessing depression in youth: Relation between the children's depression inventory and a structured interview. *Journal of Clinical Child and Adolescent Psychology, 33,* 149–157.

U.S. Census Bureau. (August 2004). *The foreign-born population in the United States: 2003.* Washington DC: U.S. Department of Commerce.

U.S. Department of Justice. (2001, March). *Bureau of Justice Statistics special report: Violent victimization by race, 1993–1998.* Retrieved March 23, 2002, from http://www.ojp.usdoj.gov/bjs/pub/pdf/vvr98.pdf

U.S. Department of Justice. (2003, August). *National Crime Victims Survey: Criminal victimization 2002.* Retrieved January 14, 2006 from http://www.ojp.gov/bjs/pub/pdf/cv03.pdf

U.S. Public Health Service. (2000). *Report of the Surgeon General's Conference on Children's Mental Health: A national action agenda.* Washington, DC: U.S. Department of Health and Human Services.

Vaidya, C. J., Bunge, S. A., Dudukovic, N. M., Zalecki, C. A., Elliott, G. R., & Gabrieli, J. D. E. (2005). Altered neural substrates of cognitive control in childhood ADHD: Evidence from functional magnetic resonance imaging. *American Journal of Psychiatry, 162,* 1605–1613.

Viard, A., Flament, M. F., Artiges, E., Dehaene, S., Naccache, L., Cohen, D., et al. (2005). Cognitive control in childhood-onset obsessive-compulsive disorder: A functional MRI study. *Psychological Medicine, 35,* 1007–1017.

Weathers, F. W., Keane, T. M., & Davidson, J. R. T. (2001). Clinician-Administered PTSD Scale: A review of the first ten years of research. *Depression and Anxiety, 13,* 132–156.

Wekerle, C., & Wolfe, D. A. (2003). Child maltreatment. In E. J. Mash & R. A. Barkley (Eds.), *Child psychopathology* (2nd ed., pp. 632–684). New York: Guilford Press.

Weller, E. B., Weller, R. A., Fristad, M. A., Rooney, M. T., & Schecter, J. (2000). Children's Interview for Psychiatric Syndrome (ChIPS). *Journal of the American Academy of Child & Adolescent Psychiatry, 39,* 76–84.

Weller, E. B., Weller, R. A., Rooney, M. T., & Fristad, M. A. (1999). *Children's Interview for Psychiatric Syndrome (ChIPS).* Washington, DC: American Psychiatric Association.

Wolfe, D. A., & McEachran, A. (1997). Child physical abuse and neglect. In E. J. Mash & L. G. Terdal (Eds.), *Assessment of childhood disorders* (3rd ed., pp. 523–568). New York: Guilford Press.

Wolfe, V. V., & Wolfe, D. A. (1997). Child sexual abuse. In E. J. Mash & L. G. Terdal (Eds.), *Assessment of childhood disorders* (pp. 569–623). New York: Guilford Press.

Wolfe, V. V., Gentile, C., Michienzi, T., Sas, L., & Wolfe, D. A. (1991). The Children's Impact of Traumatic Events Scale: A measure of post-sexual-abuse PTSD symptoms. *Behavioral Assessment, 13,* 359–383.

Wolfe, V. V., Gentile, C., & Wolfe, D. A. (1989). The impact of sexual abuse on children: A PTSD formulation. *Behavior Therapy, 20,* 215–228.

Wood, J. J., Piacentini, J. C., Bergman, R. L., McCracken, J., & Barrios, V. (2002). Concurrent validity of the anxiety disorders section of the Anxiety Disorders Interview Schedule for *DSM-IV*: Child and Parent Versions. *Journal of Clinical Child and Adolescent Psychology, 31,* 335–342.

World Health Organization. (1993). *The ICD-10 classification of mental and behavioural disorders: Diagnostic criteria for research.* Geneva: Author.

Wozniak, J., Crawford, M. H., Biederman, J., Faraone, S. V., Spencer, T. J., Taylor, et al. (1999). Antecedents and complications of trauma in boys with ADHD: Findings from a longitudinal study. *Journal of the American Academy of Child & Adolescent Psychiatry, 38,* 48–56.

Yule, W. (2001). Posttraumatic stress disorder in the general population and in children. *Journal of Clinical Psychiatry, 62,* 23–28.

Yule, W., & Canterbury, R. (1994). The treatment of posttraumatic stress disorder in children and adolescents. *International Review of Psychiatry, 6,* 141–151.

13

Pervasive Developmental Disorders

Lara Delmolino, Robert LaRue, Kate Fiske, Megan Martins, and Sandra L. Harris

Description of the Disorders

It has been more than 60 years since psychiatrist Leo Kanner first used the diagnosis of "early infantile autism" to describe a small group of children at the Phipps Clinic of Johns Hopkins University (Kanner, 1943, 1944). His astute clinical description of these youngsters captured many essential qualities of the pervasive developmental disorders (PDDs) that we use in current diagnostic practice. These disorders are labeled in various ways, including the terms *pervasive developmental disorders, autism spectrum disorders,* and *autism,* and with several official diagnostic categories found in the nomenclature of the American Psychiatric Association (APA, 2000). These five PDDs include autistic disorder, Asperger's disorder, pervasive developmental disorder-not otherwise specified, Rett's disorder, and childhood disintegrative disorder. The diagnostician's task is to discriminate among these categories as well as to differentiate PDDs from other conditions.

The PDDs, once thought to be relatively rare, are diagnosed more frequently today than was the case 60 years ago. Fombonne (2005) estimates the prevalence for all categories of PDDs, based on the most recent epidemiological studies, to be between 35/10,000 and 60/10,000 and notes there is variability around those figures in different studies. Given that prevalence, this is a diagnostic grouping that the clinical child psychologist or school psychologist can realistically expect to see in practice. It is important to be alert to the possibility that a child falls on this spectrum and to either make the appropriate diagnosis or refer the family to someone with expertise in the PDDs. Fortunately, there are good diagnostic tools available for identifying people on the autism spectrum and assessing their strengths and deficits. It is important to do a careful assessment of the child's clinical and educational needs so that appropriate intervention can begin as early as possible (National Research Council, 2001).

The present chapter first briefly describes the PDDs and then discusses the use of structured and unstructured interview strategies to diagnose and assess these conditions.

Key Features of PDDs

The symptoms of the PDDs fall into three broad categories: social interaction, communication, and stereotypic/repetitive behavior. The different diagnostic categories show these symptoms in different but overlapping ways.

A universal feature of the PDDs is significant impairment in social interaction. This may range from a very general lack of interest in or awareness of others to a somewhat more subtle lack of nuanced, empathic, or reciprocal response. The *DSM-IV-TR* (APA, 2000) points to several specific deficits in this domain, including (a) impairment in the use of multiple nonverbal gestures; (b) a lack of age-appropriate peer relationships; (c) a failure to share one's interests and pleasures with others by actions such as bringing an item, pointing to it, and establishing joint attention around an item or experience of interest; and (d) a deficit in social or emotional reciprocity as reflected, for example, in diminished empathy for another's distress or happiness.

People with PDDs are also challenged in the domain of communication (APA, 2000). This can include (a) a lack of language or a delay in its development, (b) an impaired ability to engage in an ongoing conversation exchange, and (c) the presence of idiosyncratic or stereotypic language. Also under the heading of communication, children on this spectrum do not typically demonstrate age-appropriate pretend/imaginary play.

In the third major cluster of symptoms, repetitive and stereotyped behavior (APA, 2000), individuals with PDDs may exhibit a variety of behaviors: (a) a fascination or preoccupation with an interest that is abnormal either in terms of the content (e.g., fire hydrants) or the intensity of the interest, (b) rigid following of rituals or routines, (c) stereotypic motor behavior (e.g., hand-flapping), and (d) a preoccupation with parts of objects (e.g., spinning the wheels of a toy truck).

The Categories of PDDs and Comorbid Disorders

Autistic disorder, with a prevalence rate of 13/10,000 (Fombonne, 2005), is characterized by an onset of symptoms before 36 months. The symptoms occur in all three categories: social, communication, and stereotypic/repetitive behavior. Mental retardation may also be present. The other frequent diagnosis, *pervasive developmental disorder-not otherwise specified* (PDD-NOS), has a prevalence of 20.8/10,000 and includes people on

the spectrum who have some but not all of the symptoms of another PDD or whose symptoms are less intense in nature. The term *atypical autism* is sometimes used to label these individuals as well. *Asperger's disorder* has an estimated prevalence of 4.3/10,000 (Fombonne, 2005), and although it includes deficits in social behavior and the presence of stereotypic/repetitive behavior, it does not include delays in language or the presence of mental retardation. Another less common condition under the PDD category is *Rett's disorder,* with an estimated prevalence of 1/22,800 girls (Van Acker, Loncola, & Van Acker, 2005). These girls have a typical early infancy followed by a decline in head growth; loss of purposeful hand movements and the onset of stereotypic handwringing; an early loss of social response that may improve later; and motor and language impairment (APA, 2000). *Childhood disintegrative disorder* is a relatively rare condition with a prevalence of approximately 1.9/100,000 (Fombonne, 2005). This is a later-onset disorder that appears between 2 and 10 years of age and is marked by a grave regression in functioning. Along with the appearance of abnormalities in social, communication, and/or restricted/stereotyped behaviors, there is a loss of skills such as bladder and motor control (APA, 2000).

Among the most common comorbid conditions one may identify in the PDDs are mental retardation, seizure disorders, fragile X syndrome, and tuberous sclerosis.

INTERVIEWING STRATEGIES

Unstructured Interviews

Until fairly recently, all diagnostic interviews for people on the autism spectrum and much of the interview-based assessment of skill deficits and problem behaviors were without widespread use of standardized tools. Senior clinicians might have had an implicit set of criteria based on the *Diagnostic and Statistical Manual of Mental Disorders (DSM)* in use at any given time, and those who were able to articulate those principles could train their students to use the same criteria. There was considerable room for error in this approach, however, and the development of highly effective tools to guide the interview process has made that degree of informality largely a thing of the past. To do justice to the needs of a person with a PDD, it is now essential that one use standardized diagnostic tools and established interview methods for assessment. These are the focus of the remainder of this section.

Structured Interviews

When describing structured interviews in the area of autism, one must keep in mind the special needs of the population. By definition, children with autism exhibit communication deficits that may make a structured interview impossible. As a result, assessment in children with autism is done primarily by observation. For that reason, while we have included descriptions of structured interviews that can be conducted with parents and caregivers, we have also included descriptions of structured observations that serve as "interviews" with the children in this population.

The structured interviews and observation schedules are many, including the Autism Behavior Checklist (Krug, Arick, & Almond, 1980), the Pervasive Developmental Disorder Screening Test (Siegel, Anders, Ciaranello, Bienenstock, & Kraemer, 1986), the Checklist for Autism in Toddlers (Baron-Cohen, Allen, & Gillberg, 1992), the Gilliam Autism Rating Scales (Gilliam, 1995), the Children's Social Behavior Questionnaire (Luteijn, Luteijn, Jackson, Volkmar, & Minderaa, 2000), the Autism Screening Questionnaire (Berument, Rutter, Lord, Pickles, & Bailey, 1999), and the Social Responsiveness Scale (Constantino et al., 2003). In this chapter, we describe three frequently used assessments, the Childhood Autism Rating Scale (CARS) (Schopler, Reichler, DeVellis & Daly, 1980), the Autism Diagnostic Observation Scale-Generic (ADOS-G) (Lord et al., 2000), and the Autism Diagnostic Interview-Revised (ADI-R) (Lord, Storoschuk, Rutter, & Pickles, 1993), as representations of the observations and interviews that are used in the field.

Early structured interviews for the classification of autism were developed using Kanner's (1943) definition of autism. These early interviews seemed incomplete, and in 1979, Reichler and Schopler developed what is currently known as the Childhood Autism Rating Scale (CARS). The CARS is used primarily as an observational tool, in which the child is observed and then rated in 15 different domains. The child is rated on the extent to which he or she relates to others; ability to engage in imitative behavior; range and appropriateness of emotional affect; body use and the presence of motor stereotypy; use of objects; adaptation to change; visual, auditory, and tactile responses; fear or anxiety; verbal and nonverbal communication; activity level; cognitive skills; and general impressions of the degree of autism observed. Raters assign a score on a scale from 1 to 4 for each domain, where 1 is coded for appropriate behavior and 4 is coded for extreme deviance within the domain. Children who score below 30 do not meet criteria for autism, while mild or moderate autism is classified between the scores of 30 and 36.5. Severe autism is classified for scores greater than 36.5 (Schopler et al., 1980). The CARS is available through Western Psychological Services.

The authors of the CARS initially reported good reliability and validity for their interview tool: Interrater reliability (the agreement between two independent raters) stood at .71, and the validity (the agreement between the CARS classification and a clinician's diagnosis) stood at .84 (Schopler et al., 1980). In the years following the development of the tool, however, the CARS was criticized because it was developed prior to the current *DSM* diagnostic criteria for autism and had thus lost some of its initial validity (Lord et al., 1993; Rellini, Tortolani, Trillo, Carbone, & Montecchi, 2004; Saemundsen, Magnusson, Smari, & Sigurdardottir, 2003).

While the CARS is still widely used, more recent interview tools have been constructed using the *DSM-IV* diagnostic criteria (APA, 1994) as well as the *ICD-10* diagnostic criteria (World Health Organization, 1993) for autism. Two such tools that are frequently used in tandem are the Autism Diagnostic Observation Schedule-Generic (ADOS-G) and the Autism Diagnostic Interview-Revised (ADI-R). The ADOS-G developed as an outgrowth of two prior diagnostic tools: the ADOS, an assessment tool for children aged 5 to 12 with expressive language, and the PL-ADOS, a downward extension of the ADOS for children younger than 5 or nonverbal children.

The ADOS-G is a semistructured assessment that examines a child's performance in a variety of domains, including language and communication, reciprocal social interaction, play, stereotyped behaviors and restricted interests, and other abnormal behavior, such as overactivity, aggressive and disruptive behavior, and anxiety.

During the observation, opportunities for social interaction and communication are created to elicit specific skills, such as initiations and joint attention. Structured play situations also elicit imaginative play and social play skills. The child is then rated on a scale from 0 to 3, where 0 is no evidence of abnormality related to autism and 3 is severe abnormality that interferes with observation. The assessment holds appeal in that it can be adapted to a child's level of language and development. Module 1 is used with children who do not exhibit consistent spontaneous speech, while Module 2 is used for children who exhibit flexible phrase speech but are not fluent in language. Module 3 is for verbally fluent children, and Module 4 is for verbally fluent adolescents and adults who may not be interested in the games and toys used during assessments with younger children (Lord et al., 2000). The ADOS-G and all testing materials are currently available as the ADOS, published by Western Psychological Services.

The ADOS-G reports excellent reliability and validity. The interrater reliability for Modules 1, 2, 3, and 4 falls above 88%; and the test-retest reliability shows excellent stability for the communication, social, and total scores and good stability for stereotyped behavior and restricted interests. The validity of the assessment is also excellent, with the percent agreement between the ADOS-G and clinical diagnosis standing at 95% for children with autism and 92% for children outside the spectrum (Lord et al., 2000). One benefit of the ADOS-G is that it classifies not only children with autism but also children with autism spectrum disorders other than autistic disorder. According to the authors, however, only 33% of individuals with PDD-NOS were classified as having nonautism ASD; 53% fell within the range of autism. While the ADOS-G is an excellent tool for discriminating autism and PDD-NOS from nonspectrum disorders, it is less useful in discriminating PDD-NOS from autism (Lord et al., 2000). This may be especially difficult in classifying PDD or other nonautism autism spectrum disorders in low-functioning children (de Bildt et al., 2004).

While the ADOS-G offers an ADOS classification, it alone cannot be used to determine a diagnosis of autism or a nonautism spectrum disorder, since it is based on only one observation of the child (Lord et al., 2000). For this reason, the ADI-R is usually administered to the primary caregiver of the child to gather information about behavior that cannot be observed during the observation. The semistructured interview consists of 111 items that fall within three domains: (1) qualities of reciprocal social interaction, (2) communication and language, and (3) restricted and repetitive stereotyped interests and behaviors. In addition, like the ADOS-G, it includes items regarding other abnormal behavior, such as self-injurious behavior. The primary caregiver is asked questions about each domain, and the interviewer then scores the responses on a scale from 0 to 3, where 0 indicates no relevant quality of autism and 3 indicates particularly severe abnormality (Lord et al., 1993). The ADI-R is available through Western Psychological Services.

While critics point out that the ADI-R can take upward of 2 hours to complete and the severity of a child's symptoms are acquired secondhand through ratings or parents' responses (Constantino et al., 2003), the ADI-R has excellent reliability and validity. Interrater agreement on all items averages 88% or above, and test-retest reliability averages 91% (Lord et al., 1993). With regard to validity, the authors (Lord et al., 1993) report that the assessment is able to differentiate preschool children with autism from mentally handicapped/language-impaired children, though with increased difficulty in low-functioning or nonverbal children. Lord, Rutter, and Couteur (1994) point out that while the ADI-R differentiates children with autism from children without autism on social and nonverbal communication domains, it shows poor differentiation in verbal communication domains, especially in low-functioning or nonverbal children. Differentiating between children with autism and children with nonautism autism spectrum disorders (e.g., PDD) also remains difficult, especially in low-functioning children (de Bildt et al., 2004).

INTERVIEWING OBSTACLES AND SOLUTIONS

The development of the above structured observation and assessment tools has improved the consistency and skill with which clinicians are now able to assess and diagnose the PDDs. The variable and pervasive nature of these disorders, however, continues to present challenges to even the most experienced clinicians.

One of the primary obstacles to conducting a traditional diagnostic interview with individuals with autism is the questionable utility of conducting a client interview with a child at such a young age who has significant communication deficits and often has cognitive impairment. These factors essentially make a client interview impossible in the conventional sense. In addition, given that the diagnosis of a PDD most often occurs before the age of three, it is extremely rare for direct client interview to be a primary part of the diagnostic process. Instead, observation of the child and interview with a parent or significant others are essential, primarily utilizing the tools described above. Issues specifically related to interviewing with parents and other caregivers are described below.

Client Interviews

Although most young children on the autism spectrum are not suitable for a direct interview, there are some people for whom an interview is helpful. This includes cases with an older child who has not been previously diagnosed with a PDD, possibly due to a lack of significant impairments of language and cognition. In such instances, social and communication deficits may not be evident at an early age without the use of structured interviews and observations, such as the ADI and ADOS, which are designed to specifically probe for the type of communication and social deficits involved in a PDD diagnosis.

In addition, it is also possible that older adolescents who have never received a PDD diagnosis in the past may be referred or seeking evaluation for assessment of a possible PDD or Asperger's disorder. Asperger's disorder is of particular relevance in this context because of its relatively recent presence in the *DSM*. Since Asperger's disorder was not included in the *DSM* until publication of the *DSM-IV*, in 1994, children meeting its diagnostic criteria may not have been identified prior to that time. For this subgroup of individuals, the primary deficits may be more subtle in the realm of social interaction and communication, without the accompanying language impairments and cognitive challenges seen in autism.

Interviewing an older child or adolescent for the assessment of a possible PDD (and most likely Asperger's disorder) presents a unique problem. Since core diagnostic characteristics of this disorder include conversational ability and social interaction, the interview process itself may be challenging, as it requires lengthy face-to-face interpersonal interaction and the ability to engage in conversation. In such cases, the context of the interview may also be considered a sample of behavior. In other words, the client's behavior and communication within the interview become an essential component of the diagnostic process, in addition to any information provided by the client. For example, a clinician would be able to (a) observe and assess the client's ability to engage in and sustain reciprocal conversation and offer information about a variety of topics or (b) note the presence of conversational rigidity. Other aspects of communication that could be observed within an interview context include the use of eye gaze, nonverbal behavior (body language and gestures), and qualitative aspects of speech, including tone and prosody. As described above, the higher modules of the ADOS, particularly Modules 3 and 4, could be well suited for this purpose.

Another related challenge is the possibility that an individual client may not have insight into the nature of his or her social and communicative difficulties or differences. This will vary depending on the age and experiences of an individual, but it is an important component to keep in mind. An individual may not report difficulties with peers or perceive a lack of peer relationships as problematic. A range of related behavioral, mood, or personality features may also be more evident in this type of diagnostic scenario and would require careful attention to issues of history and differential diagnosis.

Given these challenges, in addition to a client interview, it would be prudent to interview parents, teachers, and significant others to explore the history and scope of behavioral symptoms across settings.

INTERVIEW OF PARENTS AND TEACHERS

In addition to the challenges posed by directly interviewing an individual for assessment of a potential PDD, a clinician will also undoubtedly encounter obstacles related to interviewing caregivers. One initial and evident challenge is the length of the most comprehensive structured interview instruments, such as the ADI-R. One reason for this particular challenge is the broad scope of the disorder. Because the diagnosis affects development in such a pervasive way, it is not possible to focus an assessment interview on one specific problem or symptom. The clinician's challenge is to balance the need for thorough and structured methodology with clinical judgment. While the extensive scope of the ADI-R is essential to promote sound and accurate research and professional communication, it may be possible to isolate the aspects of the instrument most closely related to the diagnostic criteria (algorithm items) to streamline the interview process. It will be essential, however, for clinicians to guard against drift in interpretation and implementation of the instrument if they change the interview from its validated form.

Another related obstacle is the relative brevity of time and limitations of context that a clinician has to observe a child in a typical diagnostic assessment. A clinician may not be able to observe a child in a social environment with peers, which may be the most relevant setting for a particular child's manifestation of symptoms. In addition, a brief office visit may not be sufficient for an examiner to assess the presence of any unusual or stereotyped behaviors if the behaviors do not occur with extremely high frequency or are not evoked by the assessment environment. It is also possible that parents may not have experience with their children in particular settings or situations. For example, parents with a single child may not have the opportunity to observe the child with peers and may not be able to provide sufficient information about the presence or absence of social impairment with peers. In either of these cases, additional information from other sources is essential to obtain the most comprehensive and accurate information. Supplemental interview with day care providers or teachers may be needed to provide descriptions of the child's behavior in peer contexts.

When additional informants are utilized, it is possible that discrepancies may surface in the accounts of different reporters. In fact, this may not be unusual in cases of PDD, in which environmental variations may play a significant role in the child's behavior. If this occurs, such differences in behavior may be diagnostically significant and provide relevant information for the particular circumstances that are related to specific behavioral features. This is essential information that could be further evaluated through a behavioral assessment, as described later in the chapter.

It is also essential that an interviewer be attuned to the emotional state and anxiety that parents often experience throughout the process of assessment for PDD. Diagnosis on the autism spectrum suggests a profound lifelong disability and naturally initiates a grieving process for parents. In addition, the range of treatments available and reports of positive impact of early intensive intervention gives an added urgency to the need to obtain an accurate and timely diagnosis in order to begin treatment initiatives.

Also, given the behavioral nature of the PDD diagnoses and the lack of a medical "test" to confirm them, many parents struggle with the seemingly arbitrary or subjective diagnostic process. There are times when parents may openly disagree about the presence, absence, or severity of particular behavioral symptoms, which may often be subtle and qualitative. It is often helpful in these circumstances for clinicians to ask for clear examples and descriptions of specific instances of behavior, rather than asking parents to broadly endorse or agree with more general statements. These specific examples may then be explored through focused observation with the child.

Unfortunately, there may also be circumstances in which parents are responding to pressure from a variety of sources in order to obtain specific services for their children. In such cases, parents' perceptions and descriptions of the degree of their children's impairment may be affected. Again, specific examples paired with focused observation are vital in these cases.

Case Illustrations With Dialogue

Excerpts of ADI-R interview with Mr. and Mrs. Patterson (P), parents of Sean, age 2½:

Interviewer: I'd like to ask a little about Sean's early development. Can you tell me how old Sean was when you first worried that there may be something "not quite right" with his development?

P: Well, I guess we started to become concerned around his first birthday. He seemed to be behind what we were expecting and compared to his older sister with walking and other general milestones. We didn't really talk to his

I: And how old was he then?

P: In October? By then he was about 15 months. I think we spoke to the doctor about our concerns at his 15-month checkup.

I: And your primary concern at that time was the delay in walking and other milestones?

P: Well, that and he wasn't babbling at all or using any words. Our daughter had some language by that time, so we were just starting to wonder.

I: Tell me a little bit about his language now. For example, how does Sean usually let you know that he wants something?

P: Now? Or before he had any speech at all? He used to just scream and we could usually guess what he wanted, by the circumstances or because we knew the things he usually wanted. Sometimes now he'll pull us to what he wants, and if we ask him, he might use a word to tell us, like "juice" or something. Sometimes he still just screams and we have to remind him to show us or tell us. A lot of time he just goes and gets what he wants.

I: Sometimes, when children are just babbling or beginning to talk, they seem to make sounds just to be friendly or social, rather than to get something. Does Sean do this, or did he?

P: Oh, I know what you mean, our daughter used to do this all the time. Sean never did this type of babbling. He didn't babble at all. Even now that he's starting to babble, he seems to just babble to himself, he doesn't really come up to us and babble like he's talking to us. When he does talk to us, it is to ask for something that he wants, and we still have to remind him to do that.

I: Does Sean ever say the same thing over and over in almost exactly the same way?

P: No, not really, he still doesn't talk very much. But, he's very smart and knows all of the alphabet and numbers up to

20. Sometimes he repeats those while he's playing with letters or numbers.

I: Does Sean ever point at things around him, to get you to look at them or express interest?

P: Well, when he's looking at a book he always points to the letters and numbers on the pages. Sometimes he'll point to pictures in the book, especially if they are things we have pointed out to him before. So, he definitely points to things. He doesn't point to things like airplanes in the sky or anything. I don't think he is interested, really.

I: Does Sean ever bring you things to show you something that interests him? Like a new toy or something he is playing with?

P: Oh yes, all the time.

I: Can you describe an example?

P: Sure, like when he brings me a book and wants me to read it to him, or if he gets a new toy and doesn't know how to work it, he might bring it to me to fix it or get it to work.

I: Are there times that he might bring you things that you don't need to do anything except just look at what he's showing you and sort of acknowledge it?

P: Hmm . . . I'm not really sure. I don't think so, I think he usually wants us to do something.

I: What does Sean think of other children approximately the same age that he does not know? Is he interested in them? For example, what would Sean do at a playground with other children?

P: Oh, he'd be right in the middle of all the kids, he doesn't avoid children at all. He loves the playground.

I: Does he watch or try to approach the children in any way?

P: Well, he'd sort of just charge into the middle of the kids, I guess. Almost as if he was oblivious to them, really. He would be mostly interested in the slides and swings. I don't think he'd really watch or approach them, unless they were doing something that was really interesting to him or if they had something he wanted, he might approach them to try to get it.

I: Does Sean have any mannerisms or odd ways of moving his hands or fingers, such as twisting or flicking his fingers in front of his eyes?

P: Not really, although he is sort of clumsy with his hands.

I: What about complicated movements of his whole body, such as spinning, bouncing or waving his arms while rocking?

P: Well, sometimes when he's excited he'll sort of tense his arms out straight, like this [demonstrates] and rocks back and forth, sometimes going up on his toes. Sometimes he makes an excited sound when he does that, too.

I: Does that ever interfere with other things? What if you try to get him to stop?

P: It doesn't really interfere, it just sort of happens and then goes away. He doesn't really stop when we ask him, though, it's like he "finishes" and gets it out of his system. It does happen pretty frequently, though, and other kids sometimes ask why he does that. We just tell them that it is how Sean shows everybody he's excited.

Excerpts of ADOS Module 4 interview with Jordan Myles (J), 17, adolescent with a history of language delay, social impairment, restricted interests, and repetitive behavior:

I: Have you ever had problems getting along with people, at school, for example?

J: Umm . . . some, but I . . . haven't really had many problems. No.

I: Are there things that other people do that irritate or annoy you at times?

J: Some, but not always . . . but it's not always irritating.

I: Can you give me an example? What might be irritating sometimes?

J: Uhh, just tease me, you know, make fun of my name. [J imitates teasing] They keep on repeating it and saying it, you know, like the world's going to stop in a triple seconds.

I: Do you ever try to stop them when that's happening?

J: I do try to ask them to stop, yeah, but it's like the "Energizer bunny" that just keeps going and going and going and going and going.

I: Do you do anything that annoys other people?

J: Well, I do, I honestly do some things that might annoy other people, but, but I try not to.

I: What's one thing? Can you give me an example?

J: Well. [long pause] The sounds I do, I mean there are certain sounds so that I do though, that, I mean the kind of things that, that kind of makes me, that seems, that makes me one of a kind.

I: You make sounds that other people might find annoying?

J: Yeah, but I try not to.

I: What kind of things make you feel happy and cheerful?

J: Video games, video games, video games, of course! Are you mad?

I: Can you tell me what it feels like, when you're feeling happy and cheerful?

J: Pretty cheerful . . . like going to lend a helping hand, like I'm going to be able to do it. Cheerful.

I: Is there anything that makes you feel anxious or afraid?

J: Not really. . . . but there is one thing. I don't like people teasing me. I already told you!

I: How does it feel when you're anxious or afraid?

J: Like I don't want to have to, like I want to have to do something else.

I: People usually have things that make them sad or upset. Is there anything that makes you feel sad?

J: If there's a death.

I: That is very sad. What does it feel like to you when you're sad?

J: Just like a prison inside there. [touching chest]

I: Do you have any friends or a group of friends?

J: Umm, yeah.

I: Tell me about them.

J: It's hard to talk about really, but I mean, some of them are nice, some of them are friendly though I mean . . . I don't know. Some are boys, but mostly girls.

I: What are some things you do with your friends?

J: Well, mostly . . . just . . . I . . . just school, biology class, mostly.

I: What does it mean to be a friend?

J: To be trustworthy.

I: Do you ever think about getting married when you get older?

J: Kinda, I guess.

I: Why do some people get married, do you think?

J: So they, well. . . . if they, umm . . . [long pause] They can have sex.

I: What would be nice about it, about being married?

J: [long pause] Well, at least they wouldn't, they won't necessarily be committed of rape, at least in one sense.

I: What might be difficult about being married?

J: You'd probably have to pay for more things.

I: It would be expensive?

J: Yeah.

I: Do you ever get lonely sometimes?

J: Yeah.

I: Are there things that you can do that can make you feel better, when you feel lonely?

J: I guess just play games and stuff. Yeah, video games.

I: Does that help?

J: Yeah, video games.

I: Jordan, do you have any dreams for the future? Things you'd like to do or accomplish?

J: Oh, maybe a wrestler, or a singer like a performer . . . I don't know.

A programmer . . . like videos, a video game programmer.

I: What would that be like, to be a video game programmer or a singer?

J: It could be cool, I could, like . . . I would be able to put cheats in the game. You know, be able to put cheats in. If I was a singer, I could go to, umm, be at special events and things . . . have special remixes of songs.

I: Are there things you can do to prepare for those goals, to make things happen?

J: Umm, not really. Play video games, unless someone, you know, makes me do something else.

MULTICULTURAL AND DIVERSITY ISSUES

In clinical practice, psychologists and educators are faced with the demanding task of assessing children from diverse cultural backgrounds. This is another important factor to be considered while interviewing clients and caregivers about the possible presence of PDDs. It has been estimated that approximately one third of the young children in the United States today are from culturally or linguistically diverse backgrounds (Zhang & Bennet, 2003). Most research on interview and assessment methods with children with developmental disorders and their families, however, has been conducted from a Western cultural perspective (Dyches, Wilder, Sudweeks, Obiakor, & Algozzine, 2004). This means that, unfortunately, there is little research to guide professionals who routinely work with children from diverse backgrounds. Despite the lack of research in this area, it is important to consider multicultural issues because families from a nondominant culture may be experiencing overwhelming challenges and have complex needs.

It is also recommended that psychologists acknowledge the impact of a person's worldview on their psychological work (American Psychological Association, 2003). Since professionals are likely to encounter individuals from cultures widely different from their own, they are encouraged to recognize themselves as cultural beings who may hold attitudes, beliefs, and perceptions that may be detrimental to individuals with whom they work. Awareness of a professional's own assumptions about the differences between cultural groups will lead to more effective assessment practices (Butcher, Nezami, & Exner, 1998). People are motivated by different social processes, based upon their unique cultural experiences, and each client must be assessed in his or her own context.

Culture and Diagnosis

The diagnosis of children with PDDs is a complex task for a professional, but it is even more complicated when the client is from a linguistic or cultural background different from the clinician's. If the family's primary language is not English, it may be important to refer the family to a bilingual diagnostician, since it is certainly difficult to assess problems with language or social skills in a language with which the child is not familiar (Wilder, Dyches, Obiakor, & Algozinne, 2004). It is recommended that psychologists maintain an awareness of the limitations of assessment practices (American Psychological Association, 2003). Many commonly used assessment instruments have not been evaluated for use with groups outside the dominant culture and ought to be interpreted with caution.

In working with families from diverse cultures, practitioners may encounter various perceptions; for example, the association of certain behaviors with autism differs between cultures. Cultures hold various norms for behavior for social and communicative behaviors and may consider certain behavioral deficits or excesses usually associated with autism as more, or less, problematic. For example, children from Asian American families are less likely than children from European American families to use eye contact in their interactions with adults (Wilder et al., 2004). This complicates a diagnosis of autism, since it is difficult to determine whether problems in frequency of eye contact are due to cultural social norms or problems with social relatedness. Further, professionals and families from Asian Indian cultures hold the belief that young boys speak later and may not be concerned with early language delays (Daley & Sigman, 2002). Factors such as these may increase or decrease the likelihood that a child will be referred for treatment at an early age, and this complicates diagnosis. What an educator or psychologist notes as atypical behavior (e.g., lack of eye contact, delayed language) may be acceptable or even reinforced in the home.

Although most researchers maintain that autism is a universal disorder present in all cultures, there is some dispute regarding the prevalence rates of autism among different identity groups. It has been suggested that some discrepancies between groups are due to the fact that diagnosticians are more likely to diagnose autism in children from certain ethnic backgrounds. There is some support for this assertion in data obtained from the annual reporting of children served under the Individuals with Disabilities Education Act of 1997 (IDEA). In a summary of IDEA '97 data obtained from 1998 to 2000, Dyches et al. (2004) found that the identification of autism differs across racial categories. Black or Asian/Pacific Islander children were more likely than White children to be served with the label of autism. The lowest rates of identification were found among American Indian/Alaskan or Hispanic children. Although it is unknown if there are true differences between groups, it suggests that professionals need to maintain awareness of these issues when making diagnoses.

In addition to considering multicultural issues when determining an autism diagnosis, professionals should also acknowledge that families may have reactions to the diagnosis of a PDD that are unique to their cultures. Some families are more likely to appraise the stressor of a diagnosis more positively and some, more negatively. For example, some Latino families accept a child with a disability as a gift from God and a sign that they have been found worthy of taking on the responsibility of raising the child, while other Latino cultures consider a child with a disability as a punishment for the sins of the mother (Dyches et al., 2004). Some families from South Asia may not request a diagnosis or services for a daughter in order to avoid the accompanying stigma that will result in it being more difficult to arrange a marriage. These differing beliefs will significantly impact the way a family responds to the diagnosis of a PDD and what types of support a family may need.

Impact of Culture on Interviewing and Assessment

Building rapport is an essential interview and assessment practice that will lead to a more thorough assessment and more effective and relevant intervention plans. Unfortunately, many families from nondominant cultures do not feel respected or understood by professionals from the dominant culture, creating a barrier to creating effective interventions (Zionts, Zionts, Harrison, & Bellinger, 2003). A number of authors have recommended certain practices during initial client contact that enhance rapport building with families from linguistically and culturally diverse backgrounds (Santarelli, Koegel, Casas, & Koegel, 2001; Sheridan, 2000; Zhang & Bennet, 2003; Zionts et al., 2003). While these suggestions have been made with the client from a nondominant culture in mind, many of these practices are useful for building rapport in a variety of interview or assessment situations.

Some cultures value personal interaction over maintaining the boundaries of time and goals that are the focus of so much of Western professional interaction (Zhang & Bennet, 2003). During early contacts with a family, it may be important to spend some time engaged in casual conversation and personalize the interactions between the professional and family. This can help the families feel increasingly comfortable approaching psychologists and educators and accessing services for their children. Further, professionals should be careful during interviews not to ask questions that may shame the family for its approach to raising children. For example, families may spend more time or less time on academic tasks during the hours outside of school. Some families will react more positively to the question "Who spends the most time working on speech with Maria?" than to "Do you spend time working on speech with Maria?" Researchers have also found that individuals are more likely to consider a professional as multiculturally sensitive when he or she acknowledges diversity, rather trying to act "race-blind" (Sheridan, 2000, p. 351).

When interactions with clients are challenging due to language differences, it is especially important to not use jargon specific to the field of study (Sheridan, 2000). It may also be important to assess language goals for the family. For example, a family may desire that their child learn the language of the family as well as English, and assessments have to be conducted in both languages to determine levels of need. When an interpreter is needed, some professionals have recommended discussing the family's preferences about the interpreter. Some families may prefer that the interpreter be another family member, while others may prefer an unrelated individual, to protect confidentiality (Lopez, 2000)

In addition to increasing the focus on rapport building, professionals working with clients from diverse cultures may want to tailor other aspects of the interview process to ensure that they obtain information about the family's culture and goals. Professionals may choose to interview extended-family members or hold interviews when all family members are able to attend. Santarelli et al. (2001) highlight the differing role of the father in professional intervention. In the custom of some cultures, a father may leave more of the parenting activities to the mother, while in others, the father, as head of the household, may insist upon participating in all meetings that pertain to the family. Professionals may also need to ask additional questions to obtain more specific information about the family's culture as it relates to their routine. Rogers-Adkinson, Ochoa, and Delgado (2003) suggest regularly including questions in interviews such as "How long has your family lived in this country?" "Does your family maintain regular contact with your homeland?" "What holidays are most important to your family?" "How are meals prepared?" "Does your child participate in mealtime?" "How are the generations/extended family recognized?" (p. 6). Questions such as these make up an essential component of the assessment process and will lead to conclusions that accurately describe the needs of the family and interventions that will fit within the context of the client's environment (Santarelli et al., 2001).

DIFFERENTIAL DIAGNOSIS AND BEHAVIORAL ASSESSMENT

Practices and considerations to promote a thorough, accurate, and culturally sensitive client and/or caregiver interview have been the focus of this chapter thus far. In addition, further refinement of the interview and observation process to address questions of differential diagnosis is vital for maximizing appropriate assessment and treatment for individuals on the autism spectrum. The interview process should include in-depth questioning to differentiate a PDD from other disorders and to differentiate among the subtypes within the PDD diagnosis.

Many psychiatric disorders share common symptoms, such as hyperactivity, inattention, impulsivity, obsessive-compulsive behavior, cognitive delay, and behavioral problems. The distinction between a PDD and other disorders can be challenging and should be thoroughly explored in a clinical interview. Childhood behavior disorders that may share symptomatology similar to that of PDD include mental retardation (MR), attention-deficit/hyperactivity disorder (ADHD), selective mutism, communication disorders, and obsessive-compulsive disorder (OCD).

- *Mental Retardation:* MR and PDD often co-occur. Although PDDs frequently co-occur with significant cognitive delay and behavioral stereotypies similar to that of MR, social and communicative delays are not typically present in individuals with MR alone.

- *Attention-Deficit/Hyperactivity Disorder:* ADHD also shares some of the symptomatology associated with PDD. Both disorders may be characterized by hyperactivity, impulsivity, inattention, and impairments in social functioning. Unlike ADHD, however, PDD is associated with significant delays in communicative skill and a restricted repertoire of activities and interests.

- *Selective Mutism/Communication Disorders:* Selective mutism is another psychiatric disorder that often presents with symptoms that are topographically similar to those of the PDDs. The lack of speech in communication in selective mutism may be confused with impairments in the ability to communicate or social behavior. The lack of communication and social impairments in PDD, however, are the result of a skill deficit, whereas these impairments in selective mutism are not. Similarly, other communication disorders/problems (e.g., articulation problems, aphasia) may appear similar to a PDD but are not associated with impairments in social functioning and unusual restricted interests and behaviors.

- *Obsessive-Compulsive Disorder:* OCD is another disorder that often presents with symptoms similar to PDD. Individuals with OCD typically report unusual interests and behavior similar to that observed with individuals with PDD. Unlike PDD, however, social and language skills are typically unaffected.

The previous examples provide only a cursory glance of the psychiatric disorders that share similar symptoms with autism spectrum disorders. The purpose of the interview should be to at least begin to narrow down some of the diagnostic possibilities to make the intervention process more efficient. The ability to distinguish between PDDs and other disorders lies in the interviewer's ability to determine which symptoms are *primary* to the PDD diagnosis (social and communication impairments, restricted activities/interests) and which are features of a comorbid condition (e.g., hyperactivity, inattention).

Differential Diagnosis Within PDDs

As briefly described earlier in the chapter, there are five subtypes within the PDD diagnosis: autistic disorder, Asperger's syndrome (AS), Rett's syndrome, childhood disintegrative disorder (CDD), and pervasive developmental disorder-not otherwise specified (PDD-NOS). Each subtype shares similarities with the others:

1. *Autistic Disorder:* For a diagnosis of autistic disorder, impairments are observed in three main functioning areas: clinically significant impairments in social functioning, delays in communication/language, and restricted patterns of activities and interests or stereotypic/repetitive behavior (APA, 1994).

2. *Asperger's Syndrome:* Unlike the majority of individuals diagnosed with autistic disorder, individuals with AS typically have average to above-average cognitive ability. Although impairments in social interaction and a restricted pattern of interest and activities are present in AS, there is no clinically significant delay in language/communicative ability.

3. *Rett's Disorder:* Rett's Disorder is much less common than autistic disorder and has been documented almost exclusively in girls. There are, however, a few rare reports of boys with the diagnosis (e.g., Coleman, 1990). Rett's disorder can be differentiated from autistic disorder (and other PDDs) in that it is characterized by a period of normal functioning after birth, lasting approximately 5 months, which is followed by a specific pattern of regression from 5 to 48 months. This pattern of regression includes decelerated rate of head growth, loss of

purposeful hand movements, development of hand stereotypies (e.g., hand-wringing), poorly coordinated gait or trunk movements, and significant impairments in expressive and receptive language ability.

4. *Childhood Disintegrative Disorder:* CDD is characterized by a period of at least 2 years of typical development, followed by a regression in social interaction and communication and restricted, repetitive, and stereotypical patterns of behavior, interests, and activities. Autistic disorder differs from CDD in that CDD has a distinctive pattern of regression after the first 2 years of life, while autistic disorder is characterized by developmental abnormalities within the first year of life.

5. *Pervasive Developmental Disorder-Not Otherwise Specified:* PDD-NOS, the most frequent spectrum diagnosis (Fombonne, 2005), is characterized by a clinically significant impairment in the development of reciprocal social interaction or communication/language skills, or the presence of restricted patterns of behavior, interests, or activities. The diagnosis of PDD-NOS may be used when some, but not all, the necessary criteria for autistic disorder are met.

Behavioral Assessment of PDD and the Selection of Treatment Targets

Following diagnostic assessment, comprehensive behavioral assessment for learners with an autism spectrum disorder is essential for treatment. Clinical interviews provide practitioners with an opportunity to collect valuable assessment information that will help to assist in the intervention process. Accurate assessment information is vital for targeting the specific strengths and weaknesses of students and developing an effective, individualized plan or curriculum. Behavioral assessment can be broken down into two main components: the assessment of adaptive behavior (e.g., social skills, communication) and the assessment of maladaptive behavior (e.g., functional behavior assessment).

Behavioral Assessment of Adaptive Behavior

To select appropriate treatment targets, a thorough assessment of adaptive skills is extremely important. At the most basic level, it is important to assess learning-readiness skills, which include the student's ability to attend to stimuli in the environment (e.g., instructional materials), the ability to remain seated for any period of time, and the ability to acquire skills. Assessment should also address communicative ability, which may involve determining the current/preferred mode of communication (e.g., verbal speech, picture exchange, sign language), the breadth of communicative ability (number of words in one's communication repertoire), receptive (understanding of language) and expressive language (language production ability), and social communication (ability to coordinate receptive/expressive language and speak with others).

Several assessment instruments exist for the assessment of adaptive behavior. Commonly used instruments include the Adaptive Behavior Scale–Second Edition (ABS-2) (Lambert, Nihira, & Leland, 1993), the Vineland Adaptive Behavior Scales–Second Edition (VABS-II) (Sparrow, Balla, & Cicchetti, 2005), and the Scales of Independent Behavior–Revised (SIB-R) (Bruininks, Woodcock, Weatherman, & Hill, 1996). In addition, several assessment instruments that specifically target language and communication have been developed in recent years. These instruments include the Assessment of Basic Language and Learning Skills (ABLLS) (Sundberg & Partington, 1998a) and the Behavioral Language Assessment (BLA) (Sundberg & Partington, 1998b). The ABLLS is a comprehensive assessment and curriculum guide that provides practitioners with detailed information regarding a student's current functioning and guidelines for educational objectives. The BLA is a brief language assessment used to determine current language functioning levels.

The use of systematic assessment procedures during the interview process allows practitioners to match intervention to the specific strengths and weaknesses of the learner. The indirect methods described above, used in conjunction with other direct measures of adaptive behavior assessment, can be used for the subsequent selection of treatment targets, and provide useful information for the individualization of academic programming.

Behavioral Assessment of Maladaptive Behavior

Behavioral assessment should also involve a thorough assessment of maladaptive behavior.

The most appropriate way to assess maladaptive behavior is to conduct a functional behavioral assessment. Functional assessment is based on the premise that challenging behavior is acquired through the basic principles of learning and that the behavior is purposeful and may have a communicative function. Maladaptive behavior may be maintained by positive reinforcement (e.g., access to items, activities, access to social attention), negative reinforcement (e.g., escape from demands), or automatic reinforcement (e.g., not maintained by social factors). Functional assessment is a process of evaluating antecedent and consequent events to discover the factors that maintain maladaptive behavior. Revealing these relationships allows practitioners to maximize the efficiency and effectiveness of behavioral intervention. Functional assessment consists of three main components: indirect measures (interviews/rating scales), descriptive assessment, and functional analysis. Although all components are important, indirect models of functional assessment (e.g., structured interviews, rating scales) are discussed in this chapter.

Several useful indirect measures for assessing the function of maladaptive behavior have been developed in recent years.[1] Some commonly used structured interviews include the Functional Analysis Interview (FAI) (O'Neill et al., 1997), Functional Behavioral Assessment Screening Form (FBASF) (Watson & Steege, 2003), Antecedent Variables Assessment Form (AVAF) (Watson & Steege, 2003), Individual Variables Assessment Form (IVAF) (Watson & Steege, 2003), and Consequence Variables Assessment Form (CVAF) (Watson & Steege, 2003). In addition to structured interviews, a variety of functional assessment rating scales has been developed to determine the function of challenging behavior. Frequently used rating scales include the Functional Analysis Screening Tool (FAST) (Iwata & DeLeon, 1996), the Motivator Assessment Scale (MAS) (Durand & Crimmins, 1992), and the Problem Behavior Questionnaire (PBQ) (Lewis, Scott, & Sugai, 1994).

Functional assessment allows practitioners to select treatment targets that match the function or cause of problem behavior. Interventions that are based on the function of maladaptive behavior rather than its form are more likely to result in meaningful behavior change (Steege, Wacker, Berg, Cigrand, & Cooper, 1989). For example, if a functional assessment were to reveal that challenging behavior was maintained by escape from demands, the practitioner could determine ways to change the presentation of demands to make the behavior less likely to occur (e.g., provide frequent breaks), identify replacement behavior (e.g., a break request), and identify consequences to provide/not provide (e.g., no breaks/time-out contingent on challenging behavior).

REFERRAL

As most practitioners can easily understand, the diagnosis of an autism spectrum disorder has serious implications and should not be made without timely and thorough diagnostic assessment. Prompt diagnosis is important for enabling parents or guardians to be eligible for appropriate services and arranging early intervention at a potentially critical period in time. Diagnosing a PDD that is not present may have serious implications for the parents and lead to subsequent inaccurate labeling of the student throughout his or her academic career.

Prior to making a PDD diagnosis, it is important that practitioners consult other health care professionals, such as neurologists, developmental pediatricians, and child psychiatrists. Input from neurologists is valuable, given that they can rule out other neurological conditions that may be responsible for the symptomatology observed. Developmental pediatricians have an understanding of developmental variability that may account for the symptoms as well. In addition, child psychiatrists can help to rule out other conditions with overlapping symptoms (e.g., ADHD). Practitioners should take measures to ensure that the diagnostic process is a team effort, that children are diagnosed appropriately, and that parents are guided to the appropriate resources as early as possible.

In addition to the needs of the referred individual, practitioners should also consider the needs of the family. Family counseling may be an appropriate referral to help family members deal with anxiety and grief associated with the diagnosis of a PDD for a loved one. Practitioners should also refer parents to educational resources to help them to distinguish research-based approaches (e.g., applied behavior analysis, early intervention) from those that offer much promise but little empirical evidence of efficacy (e.g., holding therapy). In addition, practitioners/interviewers should attempt to direct parents to educational resources that provide information about the child's right to a "free and appropriate education" under the IDEA. Helping parents to effectively deal with stress and providing them with the resources to educate themselves will lead to more effective intervention for their children.

Note

1. Although indirect functional assessment strategies are commonly used and potentially extremely helpful, they should not be considered adequate for a functional assessment. Indirect measures are most effectively used in conjunction with more thorough procedures (direct observation, systematic environmental manipulations).

References

American Psychiatric Association. (1994). *Diagnostic and statistical manual of mental disorders* (4th ed.). Washington, DC: Author.

American Psychiatric Association. (2000). *Diagnostic and statistical manual of mental disorders* (4th ed., Text rev.). Washington, DC: Author.

American Psychological Association. (2003). Guidelines on multicultural education, training, research, practice and organizational change for psychologists. *American Psychologist, 58*, 377–402.

Baron-Cohen, S., Allen, J., & Gillberg, C. (1992). Can autism be detected at 18 months? The needle, the haystack, and the CHAT. *British Journal of Psychiatry, 161*, 839–843.

Berument, S. K., Rutter, M., Lord, C., Pickles, A., & Bailey, A. (1999). Autism screening questionnaire: Diagnostic validity. *British Journal of Psychiatry, 175*, 444–451.

Bruininks, R., Woodcock, R., Weatherman, R., & Hill, B. (1996). *Scales of Independent Behavior-Revised*. Park Allen, TX: DLM Teaching Resources.

Butcher, J. N., Nezami, E., & Exner, J. (1998). Psychological assessment of people in diverse cultures. In S. Kazarian & D. R. Evans (Eds.), *Cross-cultural clinical psychology* (pp. 61–105). New York: Oxford University Press.

Coleman, M. (1990). Is classical Rett syndrome ever present in males? *Brain Development, 12*, 31–32.

Constantino, J. N., Davis, S. A., Todd, R. D., Schindler, M. K., Gross, M. M., Brophy, et al. (2003). Validation of a brief quantitative measure of autistic traits: Comparison of the Social Responsiveness Scale with the Autism Diagnostic Interview-Revised. *Journal of Autism and Developmental Disorders, 33*, 427–433.

Daley, T. C., & Sigman, M. D. (2002). Diagnostic conceptualization of autism among Indian psychiatrists, psychologists, and pediatricians. *Journal of Autism and Developmental Disorders, 32*, 13–23.

de Bildt, A., Sytema, S., Ketelaars, C., Kraijer, D., Mulder, E., Volkmar, F., et al. (2004). Interrelationship between Autism Diagnostic Observation Schedule-Generic

(ADOS-G), Autism Diagnostic Interview-Revised (ADI-R), and the Diagnostic and Statistical Manual of Mental Disorders *(DSM-IV-TR)* classification in children and adolescents with mental retardation. *Journal of Autism and Developmental Disorders, 34*, 129–137.

Durand, V. M., & Crimmins, D. B. (1992). *The Motivation Assessment Scale* (MAS administration guide and score sheets). Topeka, KS: Monaco & Associates.

Dyches, T. T., Wilder, L. K., Sudweeks, R. R., Obiakor, F. E., & Algozzine, B. (2004). Multicultural issues in autism. *Journal of Autism and Developmental Disorders, 34*, 211–222.

Fombonne, E. (2005). Epidemiological studies of pervasive developmental disorders. In F. R. Volkmar, R. Paul, A. Klin, & D. Cohen (Eds.), *Handbook of autism and pervasive developmental disorders* (Vol. I., 3rd ed., pp. 42–69). Hoboken, NJ: Wiley.

Gilliam, J. E. (1995). *Gilliam Autism Rating Scale*. Austin, TX: ProEd.

Individuals with Disabilities Education Act, 20 U.S.C. § 1400 et seq. (1997).

Iwata, B. A., & DeLeon, I. (1996). *The functional analysis screening tool*. Gainesville: Florida Center on Self-Injury.

Kanner, L. (1943). Autistic disturbances of affective contact. *Nervous Child, 2*, 217–250.

Kanner, L. (1944). Early infantile autism. *Journal of Pediatrics, 25*, 211–217.

Krug, D. A., Arick, J. R., & Almond, P. J. (1980). Behavior checklist for identifying severely handicapped individuals with high levels of autistic behavior. *Journal of Child Psychology and Psychiatry, 21*, 221–229.

Lambert, N., Nihira, K., & Leland, H. (1993). *AAMR Adaptive Behavior Scale: 2nd Edition*. Austin, TX: Pro-Ed.

Lewis, T. J., Scott, T. M., & Sugai, G. M. (1994). The problem behavior questionnaire: A teacher-based instrument to develop functional hypotheses of problem behavior in general education classrooms. *Diagnostique, 19*, 103–115.

Lopez, E. C. (2000). Conducting instructional consultation through interpreters. *School Psychology Review, 29*, 378–388.

Lord, C., Risi, S., Lambrecht, L., Cook, E. H., Jr., Leventhal, B. L., DiLavore, et al. (2000). The Autism Diagnostic Observation Schedule-Generic: A standard measure of social and communication deficits associated with the spectrum of autism. *Journal of Autism and Developmental Disorders, 30*, 205–223.

Lord, C., Rutter, M., & Couteur, A. L. (1994). Autism Diagnostic Interview-Revised: A revised version of a diagnostic interview for caregivers of individuals with possible pervasive developmental disorders. *Journal of Autism and Developmental Disorders, 24*, 659–685.

Lord, C., Storoschuk, S., Rutter, M., & Pickles, A. (1993). Using the ADI-R to diagnose autism in preschool children. *Infant Mental Health Journal, 14*, 234–252.

Luteijn, E., Luteijn, F., Jackson, S., Volkmar, F. R., & Minderaa, R. B. (2000). The Children's Social Behavior Questionnaire for milder variants of PDD problems: Evaluation of the psychometric characteristics. *Journal of Autism and Developmental Disorders, 30,* 317–330.

National Research Council. (2001). *Educating children with autism* (Committee on Educational Interventions for Children With Autism, Division of Behavioral and Social Sciences and Education). Washington, DC: National Academy Press.

O'Neill, R., Horner, R., Albin, R., Sprague, J., Storey, K., & Newton, J. (1997). *Functional assessment and program development for problem behavior: A practical handbook.* Pacific Grove, CA: Brooks/Cole.

Rellini, E., Tortolani, D., Trillo, S. Carbone, S., & Montecchi, F. (2004). Childhood Autism Rating Scale (CARS) and Autism Behavior Checklist (ABC) correspondence and conflicts with *DSM-IV* criteria in diagnosis of autism. *Journal of Autism and Developmental Disorders, 34,* 703–708.

Rogers-Adkinson, D., Ochoa, T., & Delgado, B. M. (2003). Developing cross-cultural competence: Serving families of children with significant developmental needs. *Focus on Autism and Other Developmental Disabilities, 18,* 4–8.

Saemundsen, E., Magnusson, P., Smari, J., & Sigurdardottir, S. (2003). Autism Diagnostic Interview-Revised and the Childhood Autism Rating Scale: Convergence and discrepancy in diagnosing autism. *Journal of Autism and Developmental Disorders, 33,* 319–328.

Santarelli, G., Koegel, R. L., Casas, J. M., & Koegel, L. K. (2001). Culturally diverse families participating in behavior therapy parent education programs for children with developmental disabilities. *Journal of Positive Behavior Interventions, 3,* 120–123.

Schopler, E., Reichler, R. J., DeVellis, R. F., & Daly, K. (1980). Toward objective classification of childhood autism: Childhood Autism Rating Scale (CARS). *Journal of Autism and Developmental Disorders, 10,* 91–103.

Sheridan, S. M. (2000). Considerations of multiculturalism and diversity in behavioral consultation with parents and teachers. *School Psychology Review, 29,* 344–353.

Siegel, B., Anders, T. F., Ciaranello, R. D., Bienenstock, B., & Kraemer, H. D. (1986). Empirically derived classification of the autistic syndrome. *Journal of Autism and Developmental Disorders, 16,* 275–293.

Sparrow, S. S., Balla, D. A., & Cicchetti, D. V. (2005). *Vineland Adaptive Behavior Scales: Second Edition.* Circle Pines, MN: American Guidance.

Steege, M. W., Wacker, D. P., Berg, W. K., Cigrand, K. K., & Cooper, L. J. (1989). The use of behavioral assessment to prescribe and evaluate treatments for severely handicapped children. *Journal of Applied Behavior Analysis, 22,* 23–33.

Sundberg, M. L., & Partington, J. W. (1998a). *The Assessment of Basic Language and Learning Skills (the ABLLS).* Pleasant Hill, CA: Behavior Analysts.

Sundberg, M. L., & Partington, J. W. (1998b). *Teaching language to children with autism and other developmental disorders.* Pleasant Hill, CA: Behavior Analysts.

Van Acker, R., Loncola, J. A., & Van Acker, E. Y. (2005). Rett syndrome: A pervasive developmental disorder. In F. R. Volkmar, R. Paul, A. Klin, & D. Cohen (Eds.), *Handbook of autism and pervasive developmental disorders* (Vol. I., 3rd ed., pp. 126–156). Hoboken, NJ: Wiley.

Watson, T. S., & Steege, M. W. (2003). *Conducting school-based functional behavioral assessments: A practitioner's guide.* Guilford Press: New York.

Wilder, L. K., Dyches, T. T., Obiakor, F. E., & Algozinne, B. (2004). Multicultural perspectives on teaching students with autism. *Focus on Autism and Other Developmental Disabilities, 19,* 105–113.

World Health Organization. (1993). *The international classification of diseases-10th revision: Classification of mental and behavioral disorders.* Geneva, Switzerland: Author.

Zhang, C., & Bennett, T. (2003). Facilitating the meaningful participation of culturally and linguistically diverse families in the IFSP and IEP process. *Focus on Autism and Other Developmental Disabilities, 18,* 51–59.

Zionts, L. T., Zionts, P., Harrison, S., & Bellinger, O. (2003). Urban African American families' perceptions of cultural sensitivity within the special education system. *Focus on Autism and Other Developmental Disabilities, 18,* 41–51.

14

OPPOSITIONAL DEFIANT DISORDER AND CONDUCT DISORDER

MICHAEL L. HANDWERK

DESCRIPTION OF THE DISORDERS

Childhood defiance and conduct problems are some of the most costly mental health problems encountered in our society, both in terms of economic expenditures and human suffering (Connor, 2002). Childhood problems with defiance and conduct represent the majority of referrals to child-oriented practitioners, accounting for almost half of all clinical referrals and the majority of admissions for psychiatric inpatient hospitalizations (Kazdin, 1995; Lock & Strauss, 1994). Children who have serious oppositional and conduct problems are at high risk for an overabundance of negative short-term and long-term outcomes, including violent behaviors, mental health problems, school failure and dropout, chemical dependency, occupational difficulties, marital and family dysfunction, and criminal offending (Bloomquist & Schnell, 2002). Thus, the importance of appropriate recognition and assessment of childhood oppositional and conduct problems cannot be overstated.

As a primary goal of clinical interviewing and, more broadly, assessment is the classification of presenting problems, it is necessary to have an appropriate diagnostic framework. There are many formal and informal classification systems for childhood conduct problems. The most utilized diagnostic classification system in the United States is the *Diagnostic and Statistical Manual of Mental Disorders (DSM-IV)* (American Psychiatric Association [APA], 1994). As such, the majority of material presented in this chapter will utilize the *DSM* as the backdrop for discussions on childhood oppositional and conduct problems.

Definition

Formally, oppositional defiant disorder (ODD) and conduct disorder (CD) are the two disorders that best capture pediatric oppositional and conduct problems (see Tables 14.1 and 14.2 for *DSM-IV* criteria). According to the *DSM-IV*, the primary characteristic of ODD is a persistent and recurrent pattern of defiant, oppositional, and hostile behavior toward adult authority. Children with ODD frequently disobey established rules (e.g., not going to bed on time), refuse to comply with adult requests, resist adult directions, have difficulty compromising or negotiating, argue with adults, deliberately try to annoy others (adults and peers), and do not accept responsibility for their actions. They often seem "angry" and "resentful," frequently complaining about injustices perpetrated on them by adults. Diagnostic criteria state that at least four of the eight criteria must be present for at least 6 months.

The core characteristic of CD is chronic, serious violations of societal norms and rules that cause substantive problems in social relationships or academic/occupational functioning. Symptoms of CD have been clustered into four subcategories: aggression to people or animals, destruction of property, theft or deceitfulness, and major rules violations (e.g., staying out all night, skipping school, running away). Conceptually, CD is a more advanced variant of ODD (Quay, 1999). The *DSM-IV* states that when both ODD and CD are present, only CD is diagnosed, as it is assumed that a diagnosis of CD subsumes the features of ODD. Based on empirical evidence, around 75% to 95% of children with CD also demonstrate behaviors associated with ODD (Hinshaw & Anderson, 1996). Diagnostic criteria state that 3 of the 15 criteria must be present within the last year, with at least one symptom occurring within the last 6 months. Although not diagnostic, youth with CD often demonstrate associated features, such as early

onset or persistent drug and alcohol use, low self-esteem, school problems, low academic achievement, early sexual activity or persistent promiscuity, and legal problems (APA, 1994; Bloomquist & Schnell, 2002; Connor, 2002).

Critical in the *DSM* definitions for ODD and CD is that the behaviors must be present more frequently than would be expected given the child's age, developmental level, and sociocultural expectations. Many children at various ages occasionally demonstrate qualities associated with ODD and CD. Children frequently engage in oppositional behavior, including lying, noncompliance, destruction of property, and temper tantrums. Isolated acts of defiance and oppositional behavior can be developmentally normal, as evidenced by empirical studies of the prevalence of these behaviors in the general population. For example, at age 6, 53% of children were reported by their mothers to lie, and 20% of 5-year-olds were reported by parents to destroy others' things (Achenbach, 1991). Similarly, adolescents occasionally steal, stay out late, skip school, and engage in other antisocial behavior. In a large survey of adolescents conducted in 2003, approximately 33% of

---

Table 14.1   *DSM-IV* Criteria for Oppositional Defiant Disorder

A. Pattern of negativistic, hostile, and defiant behavior lasting at least 6 months, during which four (or more) of the following are present:

1. Often loses temper

2. Often argues with adults

3. Often actively defies or refuses to comply with adults' requests or rules

4. Often deliberately annoys people

5. Often blames others for his or her mistakes or misbehavior

6. Is often touchy or easily annoyed by others

7. Is often angry and resentful

8. Is often spiteful or vindictive

Note: Consider a criterion met only if the behavior occurs more frequently than is typically observed in individuals of comparable age and developmental levels.

B. The disturbance in behavior causes clinically significant impairment in social, academic, or occupational functioning.

C. The behaviors do not occur exclusively during the course of a psychotic or mood disorder.

D. Criteria are not met for conduct disorder, and if the individual is age 18 years or older, criteria are not met for antisocial personality disorder.

SOURCE: Reprinted with permission from the *Diagnostic and Statistical Manual of Mental Disorders, Fourth Edition, Text Revision* (Copyright 2000). American Psychiatric Association.

TABLE 14.2   *DSM Criteria for Conduct Disorder*

A repetitive and persistent pattern of behavior in which the basic rights of others or major age-appropriate societal norms or rules are violated, as manifested by the presence of three (or more) of the following criteria in the past 12 months, with at least one criterion present in the past 6 months:

Aggression to People and Animals

1. Often bullies, threatens, or intimidates others

2. Often initiates physical fights

3. Has used a weapon that can cause serious physical harm to others (e.g., a bat, brick, broken bottle, knife, gun)

4. Has been physically cruel to people

5. Has been physically cruel to animals

6. Has stolen while confronting a victim (e.g., mugging, purse snatching, extortion, armed robbery)

7. Has forced someone into sexual activity

Destruction of Property

8. Has deliberately engaged in fire setting with the intention of causing serious damage

9. Has deliberately destroyed others' property (other than by firesetting)

Deceitfulness or Theft

10. Has broken into someone else's house, building, or car

11. Often lies to obtain goods or favors or to avoid obligations (i.e., "cons" others)

12. Has stolen items of nontrivial value without confronting a victim (e.g., shoplifting, but without breaking and entering; forgery)

Serious Violations of Rules

13. Often stays out at night despite parental prohibitions, beginning before age 13

14. Has run away from home overnight at least twice while living in parental or parental surrogate home (or once without returning for a lengthy period)

15. Is often truant from school, beginning before age 13

The disturbance in behavior causes clinically significant impairment in social, academic, or occupational functioning.
If the individual is age 18 years or older, criteria are not met for antisocial personality disorder.

Specify Type (based on age at onset):

Childhood-Onset Type: onset of at least one criterion characteristic of conduct disorder prior to age 10
Adolescent-Onset Type: absence of any criteria characteristic of conduct disorder prior to age 10

Specify Severity:

Mild: few, if any, conduct problems in excess of those required to make the diagnosis; **and** conduct problems cause only minor harm to others

Moderate: number of conduct problems and effect on others intermediate between "mild" and "severe"

Severe: many conduct problems in excess of those required to make the diagnosis; **or** conduct problems cause considerable harm to others

SOURCE: Reprinted with permission from the *Diagnostic and Statistical Manual of Mental Disorders, Fourth Edition, Text Revision* (Copyright 2000). American Psychiatric Association.

high school students reported being in a physical fight at least once during the last year; 17% reported carrying a weapon within the last 30 days; 45% reported having at least one drink of alcohol within the last 30 days; and 22% indicated they had used marijuana at least once within the last 30 days (Grunbaum et al., 2004). CD is differentiated from developmentally "normal" antisocial activity by frequency and intensity, repetitiveness/chronicity, and impairment, which are operationalized in the *DSM-IV* by (a) the number of antisocial acts needed to meet criteria (i.e., 3 or more), (b) impairment in life activities, and (c) a severity rating (i.e., mild, moderate, and severe).

CD Subtypes

Because the core features of CD may manifest in a variety of conceptually unrelated behaviors (e.g., physical or verbal aggression, staying out late, bullying other children, torture of animals), several classification systems have been developed that attempt to capture more homogenous features of CD. These include age of onset (childhood versus adolescent onset), undersocialized versus socialized (i.e., individual versus group activity), relational versus direct aggression, covert versus overt antisocial behavior, proactive versus reactive aggression, and psychopathic aggression versus nonpsychopathic aggression (Frick, 1998). Many of these subtypes possess theoretical appeal, though only a few have received solid empirical support. The current *DSM-IV* includes only one subtype that is based on age of onset of the disorder. Childhood onset of the disorder is defined by the presence of at least one criterion being present before the age of 10. Early-onset CD is associated with more violent and aggressive behavior, lower academic achievement, solitary (as opposed to group) aggressive and antisocial activity, comorbid attention and neurological impairments, and a significantly poorer prognosis and outcome. In contrast, adolescent-onset CD is associated with less frequent violent and aggressive activity and better long-term prognosis of the disorder into adulthood (Connor, 2002; Hinshaw & Anderson, 1996).

Prevalence and Developmental Course

Rates of ODD and CD vary dramatically depending on the characteristics of the defining sample, including assessment methods, gender ratio of the sample, algorithms for combining informant data, geography, sampling time frame, as well as others. Rates of ODD range from 3% to 22%, with conservative estimates clustering around 6% to 10% (Costello, 1990; Lahey, Miller, Gordon, & Riley, 1999). There do not appear to be substantial age trends for the prevalence of ODD, as children at various ages tend to have similar rates of the disorder. Although the *DSM* indicates gender differences in the rates of disorder in prepubescent children, the preponderance of evidence indicates that rates of ODD are approximately equal between boys and girls across development (Lahey et al., 1999; Webster-Stratton, 1996), though boys clearly tend to be more aggressive than girls throughout the prepubescent and adolescent years (Bierman et al., 2004). Onset of ODD symptoms tends to peak around the age of 8, though it remains relatively high throughout childhood (Loeber, Lahey, & Thomas, 1991).

Between 2% and 16% of American youth are diagnosed with CD, with conservative estimates of the prevalence of CD of around 2% to 10% (Costello, 1990). Some evidence suggests prevalence rates may be higher in urban and lower socioeconomic status (SES) groups (Bloomquist & Schnell, 2002; Lahey et al., 1999). There is a substantial increase in the rates of CD in older children, with peak rates occurring around the ages of 10 and 13 (Lahey et al., 1999). The proportion of males to females diagnosed with CD is about 3:1 to 5:1, although this ratio tends to be more equal in adolescence (Zoccolillo, 1993). The primary reason for the narrowing of this gender gap appears to be an increase in girls' nonaggressive antisocial activity, not an increase in female aggression (Bierman et al., 2004; Hinshaw & Anderson, 1996). Earlier onset is associated with more severe symptomatology and poorer outcomes (Quay, 1999).

Stability of childhood oppositional and conduct problems has been measured in numerous longitudinal studies. Aggression, which is significantly correlated with both ODD and CD, is a highly stable phenomenon across childhood development, particularly for boys (Rutter, Giller, & Hagell, 1998). In terms of formal *DSM* categories, several longitudinal studies have documented that over a period of several years, only 25% of children diagnosed with ODD had the diagnosis remitted (Lahey, Loeber, Frick, Quay,

& Grimm, 1992). Of the other 75%, 50% continued to show behavior characteristic of ODD, while another 25% progressed into more serious antisocial behavior associated with CD.

CD seems to be a relatively stable condition (Lahey et al., 1995). Approximately 25% to 33% of children who are diagnosed with CD will continue to show persistent antisocial behavior into adulthood, as indicated by a diagnosis of antisocial personality disorder (APD), which is roughly the adult equivalent of CD (Robins, 1978; Zoccolillo, Pickels, Quinton, & Rutter, 1992). Even for youth with CD who do not meet all criteria for APD as adults, significant social, occupational, and personal impairment is likely. Adults who were diagnosed with CD as children are more likely to engage in criminal behavior, be alcoholics, have poorer work performance, and have other comorbid psychiatric diagnoses (Connor, 2002; Rutter et al., 1998). Early-onset CD is associated with more chronic and persistent negative outcomes, whereas late-onset CD tends to result in more time-limited problems (Caspi & Moffitt, 1995).

Comorbidity

ODD and CD have high rates of comorbidity with many other *DSM* disorders (Loeber & Keenan, 1994). Among the most frequent co-occurring diagnoses are attention-deficit/hyperactivity disorder (ADHD), substance abuse disorders, learning problems, anxiety disorders, and depressive disorders. ADHD is probably the most frequent co-occurring diagnosis in youth with ODD and CD, with comorbidity rates of around 40% to 75%. The combination of comorbid ODD/CD and ADHD seems to have the worst prognosis of all the potentially comorbid conditions (Lynam, 1996; Waschbusch, 2002). Children with ODD/CD and ADHD exhibit more physical aggression, a greater range and more severe forms of antisocial behavior, higher rates of peer rejection, higher rates of academic learning problems and learning disabilities, increased drug use, poorer prognosis in adolescence and adulthood, and increased rates of cognitive deficits. These deficits seem to be specific to comorbid ODD/CD and ADHD and do not appear when CD co-occurs with other comorbid conditions.

CD also has a high rate of comorbidity with substance use disorders (SUD), with rates of substance use in some samples being 2 to 9 times higher for youth with CD (Molina, Smith, & Pelham, 1999). Many studies report a higher proportion of males than females with CD having co-occurring SUD, though CD may be more of a risk factor for females for developing SUD (Loeber & Keenan, 1994). There is accumulating evidence of relatively high rates of comorbidity of CD with internalizing disorders, specifically depression and anxiety. Approximately a quarter to a third of youth diagnosed as CD have a co-occurring internalizing disorder (i.e., major depression, dysthymia, phobias, generalized anxiety, separation anxiety; Frick, 1998; Hinshaw & Anderson, 1996; Loeber & Keenan, 1994; Zoccolillo, 1992). Gender dramatically moderates this relationship, with females having approximately twice the rate of comorbid internalizing disorders. Comorbid CD and depression appear to be associated with increased risk of suicidal behavior. Children with comorbid CD and anxiety disorders seem to exhibit fewer symptoms of aggression and have fewer police arrests for violent offenses, suggesting a suppressing effect of anxiety on the expression of CD (Frick, 1998).

Historically, there has been a strong link between the disruptive behavior disorders (i.e., ADHD, ODD, and CD) and learning problems (LP) (Hinshaw & Anderson, 1996). A rather robust finding is that youth with CD demonstrate an IQ deficit of approximately 8 points, almost exclusively due to deficits in verbal (relative to performance) IQ (Moffitt, 1993). Recent examinations of the relationship between ADHD, CD/ODD, and LP have demonstrated that although higher-than-expected rates of LP occur in children with CD, this relationship is attributed primarily to comorbid attention deficits (Hogan, 1998).

Risk and Protective Factors

Risk factors are variables that have been associated with increased probability of a maladaptive developmental outcome (i.e., in this case, a child experiencing substantial problems with oppositional and conduct problems), whereas protective factors are variables that tend to minimize or reduce the probability of an individual experiencing a maladaptive outcome. Numerous risk factors have been identified for both ODD and CD, including child factors, parent/family factors, and environmental factors (Bloomquist & Schnell,

2002; Connor, 2002; Stouthamer-Loeber, Loeber, Wei, Farrington, & Wikstrom, 2002). Child factors include temperament/early development, peer relationships, and biological factors. Children who have been identified as having a "difficult temperament" (i.e., "fussy," irregular patterns of sleeping and eating, "underreactive" to external stimulus, high-motoric activity, low persistence) as infants and toddlers demonstrate higher rates of oppositional and conduct problems (as well as other forms of psychopathology) as children and adolescents. This relationship is relatively weak, however, and seems mediated by the presence of other risk factors (e.g., family dysfunction, parental psychopathology, etc.), as the overwhelming majority of children with a "difficult temperament" do not ultimately develop ODD or CD (Connor, 2002).

Children's peer relationships are also a risk (and protective factor) in the development of ODD and CD. Children who are socially rejected (i.e., actively disliked) by their peers are more at risk for psychopathology in general, though it is unclear whether peer rejection is specifically associated with increased risk for ODD and CD (Parker & Asher, 1987). It is apparent that children who show early trends toward aggression are more likely to be rejected, and this may subsequently increase social isolation and peer victimization. The combination of peer rejection and aggression does seem to have specific risk for later development of pathological antisocial behavior (i.e., ODD and CD), particularly for boys (Bloomquist & Schnell, 2002). As youth grow older, the influence of deviant peers on the development of aggression and CD can be substantial. Multiple studies have documented that association with delinquent peers increases the risk for subsequent antisocial behavior (Dishion, French, & Patterson, 1995). It is not clear, however, whether affiliation between antisocial youth is simply a product of mutual interest and/or social rejection by nonantisocial youth or whether deviant peer affiliation causally influences subsequent antisocial behavior. Further, many variables significantly moderate this effect, including parental monitoring and supervision (Ardelt & Day, 2002; Handwerk, Field, & Friman, 2000).

Familial factors that influence the development of oppositional and antisocial behavior include ineffective parenting practices, family functioning, family structure, and parental psychopathology. Parent-child interactions have moderate to strong relationships with children's antisocial behavior (McGee & Williams, 1999). A social-learning model accounting for the development of aggressive and antisocial behavior (coercion theory; Dishion et al., 1995; Patterson, 1982; Snyder, 1995) proposes that the interactional styles of families with an aggressive, oppositional child tend to be dominated by patterns of negative reinforcement captured by escalating child behaviors that terminate an aversive parental request (e.g., after asking for candy in a store and receiving a "no" response, the child throws a tantrum, causing the parents to give in and buy the candy to calm the child). Parents, too, escalate their reactions to their children's aggressive behavior with similarly aggressive, harsh, and punitive parenting. Over the course of the child's development, thousands of these interactions establish coercion as a prominent interactional style within the family. Research has demonstrated that families with aggressive children have far more coercive interactions than those without aggressive children (Dishion et al., 1995; Patterson, 1982; Snyder, 1995).

More generally, low levels of parental involvement and supervision and harsh and inconsistent discipline have been supported as risk factors for the development of oppositional and conduct problems (Burke, Loeber, & Birmaher, 2002; McMahon & Estes, 1997; Stouthamer-Loeber et al., 2002). In families with children diagnosed with ODD and CD, there tends to be less parental involvement (e.g., playing games, eating dinner together); less parental supervision (e.g., knowing where the children are, watching peer and sibling interactions); less warmth (e.g., fewer appropriate physical contacts, such as hugging, and positive verbalizations toward the child); and more harsh (e.g., excessive corporal punishment), inconsistent, and ineffective discipline (e.g., less use of time-out, response-cost, and grounding; more utilization of yelling, threatening, and belittling).

The presence of divorce and marital discord also increases the likelihood of a child receiving a diagnosis of ODD and CD (Bloomquist & Schnell, 2002; Lahey et al., 1999). In general, larger family size and being a middle child is associated with a diagnosis of CD. The effects of these variables on the development of CD seem to be mediated, however, by other contextual variables, such as parental availability, preexisting aggressive tendencies in children, and psychopathology of parents (Bloomquist & Schnell, 2002; Connor, 2002; Kazdin, 1995). Parental psychopathology also has a specific effect on development of childhood conduct problems. For example, parental antisocial personality is strongly related to childhood-onset CD. Children whose parents are alcoholic, engage in criminal behavior, or are diagnosed with APD are much more likely to be diagnosed with ODD/CD (Frick, 1998; Lahey et al., 1999; Rutter et al., 1998). Parental depression is also significantly correlated with the development of child psychopathology, though not necessarily exclusively antisocial behavior (Bloomquist & Schnell, 2002; Lahey et al., 1999).

Sociological variables that are related to the development of delinquency include peer associations, SES, and exposure to violence. SES shows a consistent relationship with delinquency (Lahey et al., 1999; Stouthamer-Loeber et al., 2002), though these effects interact with other environmental and parental variables (stage of developmental, parental monitoring). Exposure to domestic and neighborhood violence is also correlated with subsequent aggression and antisocial behavior, though the effects of these risk factors are not specific for disruptive behaviors (Bloomquist & Schnell, 2002).

Interviewing Strategies

General Considerations

Interviews constitute the primary method of obtaining information regarding childhood oppositional and conduct problems (Sattler, 1998). The essential purpose of clinical interviewing is to obtain accurate diagnosis, collect information regarding contextual variables that ameliorate or exacerbate the problem (e.g., family dynamics, peer interactions), assess the motivation and ability of the youth and family to engage in treatment, and inform intervention.

The informal clinical interview constitutes the preferred method of obtaining information by most clinicians (Watkins, Campbell, Nieberding, & Hallmark, 1995) because of the many advantages it possesses over other types of assessments (i.e., structured interviews, behavior ratings scales). Informal clinical interviews provide flexibility in content and time of the assessment, allow for detailed questioning in salient areas of concern, utilize clinical judgment and interpretation

in determining symptomatology, establish rapport and "connectedness" with the child and family that might lead to more valid information gathering, and set the stage for treatment planning and intervention. Despite the advantages and popularity of informal clinical interviews, they are not without problems.

Diagnostically, informal clinical interviews are notoriously unreliable (Rogers, 1995; Shaffer, Fisher, & Lucas, 1999). Part of the reason for this is that interviewers are influenced by their own personal and professional biases and theories. Further, clinicians who rely solely on informal clinical interviews often miss or do not assess for other potential comorbid problems or conditions (Jensen & Weisz, 2002). The reliability and validity of informal clinical interviews can be significantly enhanced when clinicians adhere closely to diagnostic criteria (Garb, 1998). Therefore, clinicians who are likely to conduct clinical interviews with youth who present with oppositional and conduct problems should thoroughly familiarize themselves with the diagnostic criteria for each disorder (as well as common differential diagnoses). As some aggression, oppositional behavior, and antisocial behavior are developmentally appropriate at certain age ranges and not indicative of psychopathology, clinicians should be aware of normal developmental expectations in the area of oppositional, antisocial, and aggressive behaviors. Although this was briefly covered earlier in this chapter, the interviewer may wish to seek further descriptions of developmental norms in these areas from other sources (e.g., Achenbach, 1991; Frick et al., 1994; Lahey & Loeber, 1994; Loeber et al., 1991).

To minimize potential problems associated with reliance on the informal clinical interview, when possible, it is highly recommended that other forms of standardized assessment accompany the clinical interview (Merrell, 2003). Given the comorbidity that occurs with ODD and CD, standardized measures of behavior and emotional functioning collected from multiple informants may help in determining other areas that may be of concern, such as the Child Behavior Checklist (CBCL) (Achenbach, 1991), Behavior Assessment System for Children (BASC) (Reynolds & Kamphaus, 2002), or the Strengths and Difficulties Questionnaire (SDQ) (Goodman, 1997), though any behavior checklist with broad coverage, adequate reliability and validity, and child, parent, and teacher versions would be sufficient. Specific standardized behavior checklists for externalizing problems should also be considered, to allow a normative basis for diagnostic decision making with respect to CD and ODD. Examples of such instruments include the Conners' Rating Scale (Conners, 2000) and Eyberg Child Behavior Inventory (Eyberg & Pincus, 1999), though many other instruments are available (Hinshaw & Nigg, 1999; McMahon & Estes, 1997).

Pragmatic Considerations

The recommendations presented in this chapter are specific to interviewing youth with ODD and CD. This presupposes that the clinician knows prior to conducting the initial clinical interview that he or she will be assessing for oppositional and conduct problems, which may not always be the case. Most clinics, however, have a prereferral process in which a brief assessment is conducted (usually over the phone) to collect information regarding why the family is seeking services. During the prereferral process, it is recommended that other methods of obtaining information be introduced that allow the interviewer to focus more exclusively on salient areas of concern during the initial interview (Barkley, Edwards, & Robin, 1999), such as areas relevant to the assessment of conduct problems, rather than spending time eliciting information that may not be particularly germane. For example, prior to the appointment, the family can complete a general questionnaire that covers essential background information, such as family structure, parental education and employment, psychiatric history, current medications, medical history, developmental history, and so on. At a convenient time prior to or during the interview, the clinician can review the information and query parents or the youth regarding anything that seems particularly remarkable. These sorts of peripheral informal assessments can be particularly effective at "ruling out" areas that do not need extensive follow-up.

Unstructured Versus Structured Interviews

Depending on the context of the assessment and the depth and breadth of information that is needed, the informal clinical interview can be supplemented with other more formal interviews. Primary among these would be the structured

clinical interview, such as the Diagnostic Interview Schedule for Children (DISC) (Shaffer, Fisher, Lucas, Dulcan, & Schwab-Stone, 2000). The advantage of utilizing a structured interview includes improving reliability of diagnoses, breadth of coverage, conformity of questions to formal diagnostic criteria, and formalization of diagnostic decision rules (Rogers, 1995). Relevant to ODD and CD, one study of youth placed in residential care examined the predictive validity of CD diagnoses generated by clinicians versus a structured interview (Jewell, Handwerk, Almquist, & Lucas, 2004). Youth who received a diagnosis of CD solely by a clinician demonstrated fewer incidents of conduct problems during their stay at the facility than those youth who obtained a CD diagnosis on a self-report structured interview. That is, the diagnosis of CD generated by the structured interview was more predictive of future incidents of CD.

The question of whether to utilize a traditional, informal clinical interview or a more structured interview seems a misguided question. Both have strengths and limitations. The obvious preference would be to utilize both an informal clinical interview and a structured interview. In the era of managed care, monetary and time factors often constrain this ideal. Thus, the more pertinent question is this: Under what circumstances should each be used? Unfortunately, there is no consensus answer to the question. A perspective that may be useful, however, is consideration of the purpose of the assessment (Haynes & O'Brien, 2000). If the interview primarily serves as the initial, information-gathering phase of what will be ongoing assessment and treatment, the unstructured interview may suffice. Problems associated with the unreliability and constricted diagnostic coverage inherent in informal interviews may be minimized as the dynamic process of assessment unfolds, especially if combined with other forms and types of assessment (e.g., broad-based and narrow-band rating scales, observations, teacher interviews). However, if the primary purpose of the assessment is to generate a formal report with *DSM* diagnoses for dissemination to another entity (e.g., psychiatrist, court, school), then it is highly recommended that a structured clinical interview be utilized.

There are numerous structured clinical interviews for children and adolescents, including the DISC, Schedule for Affective Disorders and Schizophrenia for School-Age Children (K-SADS)

(Kaufman et al., 1997), and the Diagnostic Interview for Children and Adolescents (DICA) (multiple versions; see Angold & Fisher, 1999). Although reviewing each of these interviews is beyond the scope of this chapter, a general comment regarding considerations of structured interviews is warranted.

Structured interviews can be classified on a continuum, from respondent-based interviews (RBI) to interviewer-based interviews (IBI). RBIs are highly structured, utilize precise scripts that are read to the informant with little or no variation, have limited response options (e.g., yes, no, sometimes), and offer little interviewer assistance (Shaffer et al., 1999). The "interviewer" utilizes little clinical judgment. (Some RBIs, such as the Voice DISC, utilize a computer as the "interviewer.") IBIs, on the other hand, are more flexible in their structure, allow variance in the question wording and order of administration, and provide no limitations on interviewee response options (the interviewee produces free-flowing speech for most questions).

What is "structured" in IBIs is usually symptom definition (Angold & Fisher, 1999). IBIs tend to be more time-intensive and effortful to administer and require specialized training; however, they minimize invalid responding by interviewees who misunderstand questions and can access nontraditional presentations of symptomatology that happened to fall outside the relatively limited scope of questions in an RBI. RBIs can be thought of as complex (often thousands of potential questions), nonlinear (hierarchically progressive questions; e.g., affirmation to the question "Have you felt sad or blue in the last 2 weeks?" leads to progressively more specific questions regarding negative affect), DSM-derived behavior checklists for children (Shaffer et al., 1999).

All the interviews described are appropriate for complementing the informal clinical interview, possess good reliability and validity, and provide broad coverage of childhood disorders. Most, however, are inappropriate for interviewing youth under 8 or 9 years of age.

One strategy that might allow for both structured and unstructured interviews to be conducted in a relatively efficient manner would be to have the youth complete a structured interview while the clinician is conducting the informal assessment with the parents, and then reverse the scenario (i.e., parents participate in the structured interview while the interviewer conducts the informal clinical interview with the youth). This assumes that the interviewer has help in administering the interviews or that the structured interview is computerized (which several are, e.g., Voice DISC, DICA). In our clinic, we have found that a combination of informal clinical interviews coupled with administration of an RBI (i.e., Voice DISC) has provided ample and diverse information to inform and improve diagnostic decision making without compromising the rich information and robust interactions obtained in informal clinical interviews, with relatively little additional staff effort.

Interview Content and Questions

The type of interview conducted with youth presenting with externalizing problems will vary depending on the theoretical orientation of the practitioner. A dynamic therapist will most likely spend significantly more time assessing early childhood experiences, whereas a behaviorally oriented psychologist will spend significantly more effort obtaining details surrounding the frequency and intensity of oppositional or delinquent behavior and the context surrounding the behavior (i.e., antecedents and consequences). Nevertheless, in the case of oppositional and conduct problems, the preference is for an interview that focuses on obtaining a clear definition of the problem behavior(s) and factors that may exacerbate or ameliorate the problem (Barkley et al., 2005; Haynes & O'Brien, 2000; McMahon & Estes, 1997; Merrell, 2003). The primary goals of the clinical interview with children presenting with oppositional and conduct problems and their families will be to elicit the type and frequency of behavioral problems, antecedent and consequence conditions surrounding the problem behaviors, contextual variables that contribute to the problems, how the behaviors interfere with and are influenced by relationships in the home and with other significant adults and peers, solutions that have been attempted in the past, the level of motivation of parents and children to participate in intervention, and obstacles to appropriate treatment.

Table 14.3 lists the primary content domains that should be assessed when interviewing youth who present with oppositional and conduct problems and their parents. Some of these categories are typical domains when interviewing any youth and their parents, regardless of the presenting problem (McConaughy, 2005; Sattler, 1998). It is important, however, to clearly assess each domain as it relates to the presenting problems of ODD and CD, as each of these domains has been implicated in the etiology, maintenance, or treatment of these problems. The domains and subcategories are simply presented as a general guide or structure when assessing for ODD and CD problems that are derived from multiple sources (Barkley et al., 1999; Bloomquist & Schnell, 2002; McMahon & Estes, 1997; McMahon & Forehand, 2003; Merrell, 2003; Robin & Foster, 1989). Of course, these domains are not exhaustive, and general information should be obtained on other areas as well, such as developmental milestones, family structure, medical history, trauma, living environment, environmental stressors, SES, education level of the parents, and family and community resources. The domains in Table 14.3, however, are considered critical for the assessment of ODD and CD and should receive the brunt of attention in the clinical interview.

The major domains in Table 14.3 contain subcategories, along with illustrative questions for each category. Although some of the illustrative questions have been worded to reflect how they might be asked of youth whereas others have a parent-interview perspective, each category could potentially be assessed from both parents and youth. Parental input is more essential for some categories, such as "ODD- and CD-Specific Behaviors" and "Parenting," as youth with ODD and CD often have difficulty reporting the antecedents and consequences surrounding their disruptive behaviors (see the "Parent Interview" section later in this chapter). Other domains, such as "Social Relationships," require (or least would substantially benefit from) youth input.

The questions for the subcategories are provided simply to illustrate how the information may be queried during an interview, but they should not be construed as concrete scripts. The exact form of the questions might vary dramatically depending on the personality and clinical skills of the interviewer, the presentation style of the child and parents (e.g., many "talkative" parents "answer" many of these questions in the general context of disclosure), the level of rapport established during the interview, the developmental level of the child, and the available information from other sources. Preferably, the questions would be asked in the context of an unfolding, naturally flowing conversation with the child or parents (Sattler, 1998).

As the primary purpose of the informal clinical interview is to obtain specific information for diagnosis and treatment, the interviewer should utilize strategies that maximize this goal. This requires a balance between the goals of obtaining critical information and "being natural" or personable in order to build rapport (Robin & Foster, 1989). Parents of children with ODD and CD often experience a sense of relief in sharing their frustrations of dealing with chronic problems in their parent-child relationship with a professional and will "unload" until they feel heard. While it is critical to validate the frustration of these families and establish a working relationship and rapport with the family, time limitations may require the interviewer to gently reengage the parents or youth from a conversation that has "gotten off task" to the goal of obtaining information in the various domains listed in Table 14.3.

The structure of Table 14.3 does not reflect the number of questions that should be devoted to each domain or subcategory. The interviewer should ask enough questions (or obtain enough information) to gain a clear understanding of how the child and family function relative to each domain and subcategory. Thus, the interviewer might ask many different questions in order to elicit a clear understanding of the quality of interactions that occur between the parents and the child. Conversely, the interviewer does not necessarily need to ask each (or any) member of the family a question assessing each subcategory. Depending on other available sources of data (e.g., prereferral questionnaire, standardized assessments), critical information regarding some domain items may be readily apparent. For example, if the interviewer has information from another information source that indicates the referred child is popular, has several best friends, is liked by most people in school, and is invited to other children's homes on a regular basis, it is unnecessary to spend any significant time asking the youth (or parents) questions about quantity of the peer friendships. Instead, resources of the interviewer and

TABLE 14.3   Interview Domains and Illustrative Questions for Youth With Oppositional and Conduct Problems

Domain	Illustrative Questions
ODD- & CD-Specific Behaviors	
Description of noncompliance/rule violations	You said he doesn't listen to you. . . . Can you tell me what that looks like? What do you do, Johnny, when you get angry with your parents?
Antecedents Situations most likely to occur Range of activities involving noncompliance/conduct	What's happening right before she throws a tantrum? When are you most likely to steal money from your parents? So from the ride home to dinner, it seems like he argues about everything. How about after dinner and in the morning? Does he argue then as well?
Types of requests/rules evoking noncompliance	When do you usually ignore your parents? Are there any other situations where he throws a temper tantrum?
Interaction during noncompliance	So what happens after you tell him to come to dinner and he doesn't come?
Parents' response	How do you respond when Arnold comes home after his curfew?
Youth's reaction	When your parents tell you to turn the computer off and you keep playing, what do they do then?
Escalation/intensity of noncompliance/conduct	After you tell him he's grounded, what does he do? How long do you argue with him about it?
Termination	After you and your parents have been arguing, do you finally sit down and do your homework? How do you get him to finally turn off his Game Boy?
Consequences	What do you typically do for discipline? When they tell you you're grounded, do they follow through?
Frequency of noncompliance/conduct	How often do you get detentions? How many times a day does he tell you "No"?
Types of requests/rules that evoke compliance	Are there times when he does listen? Is he noncompliant 24/7, or are there chores that he will do once in a while? Is anything different about those times he does his chores? For instance, do you ask him in a different tone? Or is he in a better mood?
Onset of problems	How long have these things been going on? When did this start?
Legal/criminal involvement	Have any of these problems caused him to get in trouble with the police?
Drug use	Have you ever consumed alcohol or used drugs?
Parenting/Family Relationships	
Quantity of interactions	What does the family do after dinner? Do you and your mom or dad ever spend any time together? Does your family do many activities that involve Brian?
Quality of interactions	When you're playing games with him, does he seem to like that? When do you have your best interactions with Mike? Do you feel like you can talk to your parents about important things?
Level of affection/positive interactions	Out of 10 interactions you have with Charles, how many would you say are positive? How often do your parents tell you they appreciate (are proud of) you?

Domain	Illustrative Questions
Attitude toward child/parent	What does Sammy do well? What do you like about Shyla? What do your parents do that you most admire?
Parental agreement	Do you and your husband agree on the . . . (problem, rules, expectations, consequences)? Does one of you tend to usually be the disciplinarian? When you have disagreements about how to deal with Jackie, how do you handle that?
Parental psychopathology	Were either of you "stubborn" as children like Johnny is with you? Is there anything that keeps you from being more effective in dealing with this problem?
Extra familial support	Are you ever able to get a break or get away for a while? Do you have relatives or friends that have been helpful in dealing with this?
Sibling interactions	How do you get along with your older brother? How has this problem with Jimmy affected Julie (sibling)?
Chores/responsibilities	Does Tabitha have to do any chores around the house? What time is your curfew on the weekends, Andrew?
Social Relationships: *Child & Friends*	
Number of friends	Does he have any friends? Does he have friends in the neighborhood, too?
Best/close friends	Of those, how many would you consider "best friends"?
Age of friends	Does he tend to play with kids who are his same age?
Type of friends	What type of groups do you hang out with (skaters, Goths, druggies)? Do any of his friends get in trouble too?
Contact with friends	How often do you and your buddies hang out? How often does she see her friends outside of school?
Skill in initiating/maintaining interactions	Does he make friends easily? How does she treat her friends?
Social rejection	Do people ever tease or make fun of you? Is he popular or well liked?
Educational/School	
Grades	How does he do academically? Do you care about how you do in school?
Homework	Do you have trouble getting him to do homework? How long does it take you to get your homework done?
Behavior problems in school	Do you ever get calls from school about Kim? Have the teachers ever complained about Jamir's behavior?
Similar behavior problems at school?	Are you talking back to your teachers the way you do with your parents?
Attendance	Do you skip school or some of your classes?

(Continued)

TABLE 14.3 (Continued)

Domain	Illustrative Questions
Extracurricular activities	Is she involved in any extracurricular activities at school, like Girl Scouts or a club?
Favorite school activities	What's your favorite class/subject? What does he enjoy most about school?
Previous Treatment	
Other interventions	Has anything you've tried been useful or helpful? I'm amazed the problem has gotten worse. . . . How have you managed to accomplish that? Have you seen anybody else about these problems? What have others (teachers/clinicians) suggested to try to help? Was it effective?
Previous diagnosis	Has she received any formal diagnoses?
Comorbidity	Are there any problems besides oppositional/conduct behavior (like anxiety, depression, etc.)?
Strengths & Prosocial Competencies	
Interests	What are your favorite things to do?
Hobbies	Does he have any hobbies?
Task engagement during free time	What do you like to do in your free time? After dinner, what does Danny do?
Extracurricular activities	Is he involved in any extracurricular activities (like sports or church groups)?
Presence of ODD/CD behaviors in those situations	How does he behave during those activities?
Vocation/work	Do you have a job? Do you get an allowance for doing chores? What does she spend her money on?
Level of empathy	Does he seem remorseful after you argue? Do you ever apologize to your mom?
Moral reasoning	Why do you think it's important to follow the rules?
Goals/Motivation	
Goals	What would it look like if these problems were gone? What are some goals for Rob and your family?
Expectations	How do expect LeRoy to treat you? What chores do you think are appropriate for Donna to do?
Treatment motivation	It seems like you're at your wits end. . . . Are you willing to try other things?

interviewee can be better spent obtaining more highly specified information within the domain (e.g., What activities do the child and peers typically engage in when together? How does the youth treat the parents of his or her best friends?) or simply assess other domains.

Structure of the Clinical Interview

There is no generally agreed-upon manner to structure the first (or subsequent) interview session (McMahon & Estes, 1997). Given that information should be obtained from multiple informants, however, one method that allows input from all salient parties would be to first have both the parents and the child together in the interview room, then interview each separately (Robin & Foster, 1989). This allows for assessment of how the problem is discussed in a family context, as well as obtaining more detailed information from each party in a confidential format. The following illustrates the recommended format:

1. Meet the family and introductions

2. Family interview (5–10 minutes)

3. Dismiss the child/adolescent and accompany him or her to alternative activities

4. Parent interview (40–50 minutes)

5. Child interview (10–20 minutes for children; 20–30 minutes for adolescents)

6. Observations (10–15 minutes)

7. Wrap-up and future plans

To initiate the interview, the interviewer should ask a general question, such as "Tell me what brings you here today?" or "What sort of problems are happening that had you make this appointment?" Usually, the parent(s) will initiate a response. Key in the assessment is how the parents generally talk about the problem with the child present (see the "Case Illustration and Dialogue" section later in this chapter). In families with chronic problems and coercive patterns of interacting, parents often utilize derogatory language, personalize the problem, exclusively fault the child for stressing the family, are excessively critical of the youth in front of a stranger, and divulge information that may be embarrassing to the child. None of these is particularly diagnostic of ODD

or CD, though each is critical in understanding the current functioning of the family. This phase of the interview is also an opportunity to evaluate the problem through informal observation of the presenting problem as it unfolds in the office (see the "Behavioral Observations" section later in this chapter).

If the youth has not responded or not had input during this phase, it is important to ask whether the youth generally agrees with his or her parents' response, with a question such as "So your parents think that you don't listen to them and that's causing problems for your family. What do you think about that?" Regardless of whether this produces agreement, disagreement, or indifference, it sets the stage for the youth interview by letting the child or adolescent know the interviewer is interested in his or her perspective. If the youth responds to this question affirmatively, it is important to validate him or her for acknowledging a problem exists (e.g., "Wow, I'm impressed you're mature enough to admit that!"). If the youth responds discordantly, this is an opportunity to get perspective on the family's problem while in the presence of the parents (e.g., "So, you don't agree with your parents that you're always breaking the rules of the house. So, what do you think is going on? Why do *you* think your parents made this appointment to come talk with me today?").

After the brief family interview, it is recommended that the parents be interviewed alone, first, without the child present (see the "Parent Interview" section later in this chapter; Barkley et al., 1999; McMahon & Estes, 1997; McMahon & Forehand, 2003). This is essential for a variety of reasons. First, conducting the interview with the parents in the presence of an oppositional child often leads to frequent disruption, potential embarrassment, and inhibition in disclosing information. These factors might affect not only the quality of the information obtained during the interview but also the rapport and alliance that can be developed with parents, which is critical in treatment success. Interviewing the parents first and alone helps to alleviate these problems.

Second, critical to the assessment of oppositional and conduct problems is the understanding that usually the child or adolescent's behavior is more troubling to adults than to the child. Unlike many internalizing disorders where children report significant internal "suffering," many children and adolescents exhibiting ODD and CD do not report impairment or even admit there is a problem. Often, it is necessary to obtain specific problem descriptions from the parents prior to interviewing the youth. If not, many times, children and adolescents will produce an "Everything's fine" response. If the interviewer knows of specific behavior problems that are provided by the parents, however, the interviewer can directly elicit the youth's response regarding these specific incidents or patterns (e.g., "What about last weekend? Your parents said you came home at 2:15 in the morning, and you and your dad almost came to blows"). In cases where a child or adolescent steadfastly denies the presence of behavior problems, it may be helpful to refer to the problem as one that the parents have with the youth, rather than directly implicating the youth. For example, the interviewer might say, "Well, I understand that you believe everything is going well for you, and you don't have any problems. But it seems as if your parents certainly have a problem with some things you are doing. I'm not saying they're right, John . . . but I'm guessing that them thinking you're the problem causes trouble for you. Like, I'm guessing you get in trouble a lot at home, maybe for things you don't think you should get in trouble for?" Usually, this will elicit some form of agreement, which will allow for questioning about the particulars, such as "What do you usually get in trouble for? How do you respond when your parents get angry at you?"

To introduce this transition from family interview to parent interview, it is a good idea for the interviewer to let everyone know that he or she wants to hear their individual perspectives on the problem. For example, the interviewer might say, "Well, I'd like to talk to your parents a little more, Jennifer, so I can get a better understanding of how they see the problem and how they describe your family. But, I really want to hear from you, too. So after I'm done talking to your parents, I'd like to talk to you . . . alone without your parents, so I can get a better idea of how you see what's happening at home and with your parents." For adolescents (and their parents), it is often beneficial to introduce the idea of the subjectivity of "truth" at this point. For example, the interviewer might have said something like the following:

It's okay that you don't agree with your folks. Everyone . . . you, your parents, me . . . we all see the world through our own eyes. We can't fully know what it looks like through someone else's eyes. So, we all have our "stories" about what the truth is. And because you don't have video monitors mounted all over your house, we'll never really know who did what when. Your parents have their story about what's going on, and they see life through their own little video camera [interviewer points to his eyes], and you have your story and see it through yours. I'm going to get their story first, but I really want to hear your story too . . . you cool with that?

This sets the occasion for the youth to know that although his or her parents will be sharing information privately with the interviewer, the interviewer is making no a priori judgments about the validity of any of the participants' reports and that the youth's perspective is equally valid. This is particularly important for older children and adolescents in order to establish rapport for the youth interview.

For younger children, conducting separate parent and child interviews during the first session creates some dilemmas. Obviously, if children are not going to be in the interview room with their parents, they need to be elsewhere, preferably supervised (as, by definition, they tend to be disruptive). Many larger clinics have a "playroom" that is adjacent to the interview offices/rooms that can be easily monitored by ancillary staff (or, if it is near the interview room, can simply have the door open so that activities and exiting can be partially monitored). If this is not feasible, the interviewer will need to decide whether to conduct parent interviews with the child present in the interview room. If so, the child should be allowed to engage in games and activities (McMahon & Forehand, 2003). Alternatively, the initial assessment can be conducted over two sessions, the first session being the parent interview and the second being the youth interview and observation session (McMahon & Estes, 1997). Many commercial insurance companies, however, will not reimburse sessions with the parents alone, without the child, so in private practice settings, the interviewer will have to develop a protocol that is both clinically informative and economically judicious.

If the youth interview is conducted after the parent interview, there may need to be a "transition device" from the parent to the child interview. For younger children 5 to 10 years old, often this can be as simple as "Well, your parents and I talked a lot about you. They had many good things to say about you, like you are really good at sports, and you're a good friend, and you like it when they play video games with you. As you heard when we were all together, they also said they thought you're not listening to them at home, and this is causing a lot of problems for them and for you. I want to ask you about that, but first I'd just like to get to know you a little better." Sometimes, for younger children in this age range (i.e., 5–8 years old), it may be more effective to simply begin the transition by using "warm-up questions" that engage them in familiar topics that are less problem focused, such as "What do you like to do after school?" "What's your favorite sport?" "What's your favorite cartoon?" "What sports do you like?" "What's your favorite thing to do at school?" and so on. These questions usually engage even the most reluctant younger oppositional child and serve to build momentum in regard to question answering.

There is no generally agreed-upon length for the initial clinical interview or even the number of sessions that should be considered. Generally, we have found that the initial clinical interview can be conducted in one session that lasts from 1½ to 2 hours.

Developmental Considerations

Interviewers will be faced with a wide chronological and developmental range when conducting clinical interviews with youth presenting with these problems, from preschoolers to high schoolers. As such, the interview needs to be tailored to developmental level of the youth. Younger children tend to lack advanced social skills, insight and perspective-taking capabilities, verbal ability, ability to sustain attention, and willingness to engage in a detailed conversation regarding their behavior. Adolescents may present with distrust, misconceptions, or motives that are contrary to the purpose of the interview. Excellent discussions of developmental considerations when conducting interviews with children and adolescents are provided by Jayne, Bethay, and Gross (see Chapter 4, this volume), Bierman (1988), McConaughy (2005), Merrell (2003), and Sattler (1998).

Interviews with younger children (less than 5 years old) tend not to produce substantial information relevant to the purpose of the clinical interview for ODD and CD. Children in this age range tend to have limited communication skills and limited memory capabilities and cannot engage in lengthy conversations. For these youth, it may be more useful and productive to spend the majority of the assessment period interviewing parents and conducting observations (see below). This is not to say that the interviewer should not spend time with the child who is younger than 5 years old, just that the domains in Table 14.3 may not be appropriate areas for an interview. Time with a child younger than 5 may be best spent engaged in an interesting activity (e.g., drawing, playing cards, throwing a ball) to facilitate a level of comfort with the interviewer and the setting. This is particularly important if the assessment is the initial phase of ongoing treatment.

Children in the elementary years (approximately 5–12 years old) have or are beginning to develop the abilities to be less egocentric, engage in perspective taking, regulate their emotions, and understand social conventions (i.e., right or wrong). They are better able to provide temporal structure to descriptions, describe themselves with normative considerations, and understand and describe emotions. With children in this age range, it is also important to remember their limitations. They have difficulty with contextual questions, particularly remembering and providing temporal information (e.g., "When did you start to have fights with your mother?" "How long has that been happening?"). Although they can be quite capable of providing input and descriptions for many of the questions listed in Table 14.3, they are generally not capable of engaging in prolonged questioning. Therefore, it is critical that the interviewer provide "breaks" in asking questions, insert validating reactions to the children's responses (e.g., "Oh, that's interesting"; "I never thought of that before"; "Wow, you've obviously thought a lot about this problem!"), allow them some "wondering" in their responses, engage their curiosity (e.g., the youth may ask questions about the interviewer or the room), and rephrase or simplify questions when the child doesn't understand or produces a response that is obviously indicative that he or she doesn't understand.

Open-ended questions tend to be the most appropriate for all ages and developmental levels, at least initially, as they tend to produce the most reliable answers (McConaughy, 2005; Sattler, 1998). For younger children, however, it may be necessary to utilize more "yes/no" or multiple-choice questions (e.g., "Would you say that you and your parents argue every day, a couple times a week, once a week, or once a month?") as follow-ups to open-ended questions. The interviewer should also avoid "why" questions regarding children's motives (e.g., "Why did you say that?" "How come you told your dad you hated him?"), as children at this age level lack advanced metacognitive skills (i.e., thinking about their own thinking) to reflect and answer these sorts of questions (McConaughy, 2005). "Why" questions tend to produce either "I don't know" responses (which are probably accurate responses for younger children), socially desirable responses based on preconventional moral reasoning that are not very helpful ("I know I shouldn't argue with mommy because it's wrong"), or defensiveness (Sattler, 1998). The interviewer should also avoid "rhetorical" types of questions with school-age children who are oppositional (e.g., "Would you like to tell me a little about yourself?"), as these tend to produce oppositional responses (e.g., "No").

Adolescents can think more abstractly than younger children and have sometimes devoted significant reflection to the problems that have brought the family to the interview. They are generally much more capable of describing themselves, relationships within the family, temporal sequences of events, how others view them, and reflections on their own thinking. Because of this, they are much more capable of participating in extended conversations and questioning about themselves and their families. They also can be very resistant or resentful for having to participate and thus can be very difficult to interview (see the "Problems and Obstacles" section later in this chapter). Further complicating this problem is that adolescents tend to be highly sensitive to criticism, due to increased self-awareness and insecure identities (McConaughy, 2005; Sattler, 1998). Thus, interviewing an adolescent is not equivalent to interviewing a "mini-adult."

If there is a golden rule to interviewing adolescents, it is to be respectful to adolescents during interviews. This can be accomplished by actively listening to their perspectives, being nonjudgmental, and validating their input as valuable. Adolescents tend to be more discerning consumers of psychological services than are younger children and perceive "typical" psychological questions to be annoying or, worse, demeaning (e.g., "How did that make you feel?" Edgette, 2002). It is also important for interviewers to avoid using "psychological jargon," even to establish themselves as credible or as experts (McConaughy, 2005). Even if adolescents understand such terms, such language tends to activate their already overactive self-evaluative nature and may cause resentment that the interviewer thinks "they're crazy" or that "they're the problem."

INTERVIEWING OBSTACLES AND SOLUTIONS

Engagement

Because of the nature of the problems associated with oppositional and antisocial behavior, interviewing youth with these problems can be a difficult and challenging task. They are, by definition, prone to stubbornness, defiance, hostility, and lying. In addition, because of the context of most referrals for ODD and CD, there are often disincentives for children and adolescents to fully participate in the assessments. Parents initiate the referral because they, not the child, want help for the "child's problem." It is not unusual for parents to have a difficult time just getting the adolescent to come to the initial appointment. Thus, the challenges to the interviewer can be enormous.

One philosophical and pragmatic implication of this challenge is for the interviewer to realize that the assessment of families with children presenting with ODD and CD behavior is not a static process, but rather dynamic and ongoing over multiple episodes. Children, especially adolescents, may be more willing to share their perspectives on their problems over time as they come to trust clinicians and form relationships with them. Similarly, parents may be more able to disclose sensitive information regarding their own behavior over time as a relationship is established with the clinician. For example, it is rare for parents to disclose that they slap, hit, or even frequently yell at their children when responding to the question "How do you discipline your child when they have misbehaved?" yet such discipline is fairly common (Whipple & Richey, 1997). If the clinician/interviewer is conducting the assessment only for dissemination of the information to others (e.g., courts, school, mental health agency) rather than as part of the initial phases of ongoing treatment with the clinician, conclusions regarding the functioning of the child and family must be more tentative. It is also desirable in such cases that the interview not be an isolated (i.e., one time) assessment, but that it span more than one session.

Problems with engagement can be potentially minimized by attending to the developmental considerations discussed previously and by interviewing the parents and the child separately. With adolescents, it is important to utilize more age-appropriate language and attend to issues that might be interesting to them (Robin & Foster, 1989). For example, instead of saying, "I see from information provided to me by your parents earlier that you have engaged in illicit substance use on numerous occasions during the past 6 months," the interviewer could say, "Your parents said they caught you smoking pot a couple times recently." Also, many adolescents "declare" their personalities through their clothes, music, and reading material. The interviewer should be attentive to these areas and other behaviors in order to be able to ask adolescents questions about topics that might be of interest to them, such as "I saw you were listening to music in the waiting area. . . . What music do you listen to?" or "I see you have a tongue piercing. . . . Did it hurt when you got it?"

A more severe problem of engagement that the interviewer may experience when interviewing the child or adolescent with ODD or CD is the "silent treatment." Any professional that has worked with children and adolescents for any length of time has experienced the child who refuses to answer questions or participate in the interview, which can be frustrating for even the most experienced clinician. For youth with ODD and CD, it is important to recognize that this is often their standard mode of interacting with the world, not a reflection on any personal or professional characteristic of the interviewer. The best advice to avoid the "silent treatment" is prevention. That is, communicating interest in the perspectives of youth, validating their responses, and communicating respect will go a long way in minimizing resistance.

Should these strategies still not produce participation, there are numerous strategies that have been suggested by interviewing experts, and picking an effective strategy will in large part depend on your assessment as to the function of the child's silence (Sattler, 1998). If the youth has been silent throughout all phases of the interview, the interviewer should reiterate how valuable his or her input will be. For older children and adolescents, the interviewer might even say something like, "Look, I know they were bashing you earlier. That's got to be embarrassing. But I know that it's never that simple. It takes two to tango. . . . There's always two sides to a story, and I'd really like to hear your side." Additional questions can acknowledge the youth's silence and empower him or her to change the situation: "I know you don't want to be here. I don't blame you. . . . I wouldn't want to be here either if I were you. Is there anything I can do to make this easier?" or "This doesn't seem to be going very well. Is there anything I can do differently?"

For younger children, silence may also be dealt with by introducing a fun activity, such as playing a game. Sometimes, children become silent after a period of participation. This might signal that the interviewer has somehow "offended" the child. In these situations, it is often useful to acknowledge the silence ("I notice that you've stopped talking"), ask whether the child feels offended ("Did I say something that made you mad?"), grant permission for silence to occur ("I understand. I didn't mean to upset you. Why don't we just stop talking for awhile?"), or try to gently change the subject ("Okay, I guess you don't want to talk about how you feel about your brother. . . . How about talking about the football game you have this weekend?").

For some older children and adolescents, the interviewer can elicit participation during the child interview by gently suggesting that if the youth doesn't participate, the interviewer will reintroduce the family to the assessment. For example, the interviewer might say, "Okay, I respect that you're angry and don't want to talk. So instead of wasting your time, I still have some questions that I want to ask your parents, and it may be important for you to hear what they say. So unless you're interested in talking to me alone, I'll go get your parents to rejoin us." For some youth, being in the room with their parents talking about them is more aversive than engaging in a dialogue with the interviewer.

Finally, it is important to realize that silence, though potentially uncomfortable, is very informative. Although it would be helpful to elicit information from the child, the youth's presentation is potentially indicative of how he or she treats other adults; silence is highly functional in coercive interactions with adults. In this case, the interviewer should simply respect the right of the child or adolescent not to speak: "Okay, Brody, I wish you would talk to me, but I understand that you're angry. Why don't we call it a day? We'll try it again next time." (This may be the one exception to the no-rhetorical-questions rule.)

Combining Information From Various Informants

Children are notoriously poor informants regarding their externalizing behavior problems (particularly for ADHD and ODD behaviors). Indices of agreement between parental and youth reports of their own behavior tend to be low in general, but particularly for externalizing problems (Handwerk, Larzelere, Soper, & Friman, 1999). Combining information from various sources in a meaningful way can be difficult. Many interviewers tend to rely most heavily on information from parents in formulating diagnostic impressions (Loeber, Green, & Lahey, 1990). While this is generally an acceptable strategy for externalizing problems, CD may represent an exception. For CD, youth input in the assessment process and diagnostic formulation is important if it can be obtained. Although youth may not be aware of or able to reliably report on their oppositional behavior or ADHD, research has indicated that adolescents tend to be valid informants regarding their antisocial behavior (Friman et al., 2000). Many parents are unaware of their children's covert disruptive behavior. It is not uncommon during the parent interview for parents to report primarily oppositional behaviors observed at home, and for adolescents to report more covert activity that is unknown to their parents.

There are no agreed-upon rules for dealing with discrepant information (see Reich & Earls, 1987). In general, however, information from parents regarding oppositional behavior tends to be more heavily weighted by most professionals than information obtained from children (Loeber et al., 1990). This is partially due to children's lack of reliability and validity when reporting on ODD symptoms. As children develop, the reliability of their reports tends to increase and become less discrepant with parental reports. A general recommendation would be to heavily weight parental reports of oppositional behavior relative to discrepant child reports, while giving more priority to adolescents' reports of covert antisocial activity.

There are some obvious exceptions to the general preference to weighting parental reports. For example, parental reports of a child's oppositional and defiant behavior may be obscured by their unrealistic and developmentally inappropriate expectations for the child (e.g., parents reporting their 6-year-old child is highly oppositional because he won't fold and put away his own laundry, won't complete 2 hours worth of homework without distractions every night, calls his sister names, and forgets to take his asthma medication each morning without being reminded). The developmental context of reports of oppositionality need to be considered in diagnostic formulation and treatment plan (e.g., educating the parents on developmentally appropriate expectations for behavior).

Confidentiality

The issue of confidentiality is always critical when working with children and their parents for any referral problem, but it is particularly important when working with children and adolescents with oppositional and conduct problems, because, as mentioned, adolescents with CD often engage in covert forms of antisocial behavior unbeknownst to their parents. Therefore, it is essential that confidentiality be discussed and agreed upon by parents and adolescents. *Confidentiality* refers to the ethical practice of maintaining the privacy of information (Sattler, 1998). *Privilege* is a legal right granted by states for certain communications that occur between individuals and select professions (e.g., lawyers, physicians, psychologists) to be held in confidence unless consent is granted by the authorized individual. Legal obligations supersede theoretical preferences in the arena of privileged communications and confidentiality, and the interviewer should be fully aware of state regulations and practice guidelines for his or her particular state.

In general, parents have a legal privilege to most records pertaining to their children, including information in assessments (e.g., school records, medical records). That means they also have a legal right to information recorded (i.e., contained in a written report) by the interviewer during an assessment. There are numerous exceptions to confidentiality and privilege that should be discussed with parents and youth, as outlined in Chapter 9 (Miller & Dodge) of this volume. There is less legal precedence and professional guidance, however, on how to handle communications that occur between the clinician and youth (and subsequent disclosure to parents) and between the clinician and parent (and subsequent disclosure to the youth). For example, what should the clinician do when after interviewing an adolescent, the parent asks, "Is he having sex with anyone?" or "Did she tell you if she still loves me?" or when the adolescent comes into the room and asks, "What did they say about me?" Assuming the interviewer knows, how should he or she respond? These situations can largely be avoided if confidentiality of communication between the parties and the interviewer is handled in a commonsense manner from the beginning. The interviewer can communicate to all parties (in a manner developmentally appropriate to children) how they would like to handle issues of confidentiality in the communications between each party and the interviewer. For example, the interviewer might say,

I need to discuss how I'd like to handle confidentiality. Of course, I will not release information to other parties without your consent [looking at the parents]. But I'm specifically referring to confidentiality between what Gene [adolescent] says to me and what I share with you, as well as what you tell me about Gene and I share with him. I know a lot of parents are curious about what their children say and do, and I'm guessing you are as well. I think it's important for parents to know what's going on with their children, too. After all, you're responsible for him, and I'm not. On the other hand, if Gene thinks that I'm going to blab every little detail of our conversations to both of you, he's not going to trust me or tell me anything. So, I'd like for us to agree that I will inform you [looking at parents] of important issues that Gene and I discuss, but *in general terms*. For example, if Gene tells me "I hate my parents," I'm *not* going to say to both of you, "Gene said he hates you." Rather, I'll say something to you like, "Gene indicated that his relationship with you is very strained right now." Of course, if Gene reports that he's doing something dangerous to himself or someone else, like he's thinking about hurting himself or he's carrying a weapon to school, I'm required by law to inform you. Can we all agree to that?

Usually, this will provide the parents with a sense that the clinician will inform them of critical issues that they need to know about, and it will also give the adolescent the sense that he or she can share potentially sensitive information with the interviewer.

Of course, this will not keep interviewers from being in difficult situations or ethical dilemmas, unless they specify everything that they consider to belong to the "dangerous" category (which, for many reasons, is not always practical). For example, during the interview process, it is not uncommon for adolescents to disclose sexual activity or drug use that their parents are unaware of. Are these "dangerous" activities that should be immediately reported to the parents? How the interviewer handles these situations will significantly determine whether the adolescent will continue to disclose sensitive information (either in the current interview or in subsequent therapy sessions). Unfortunately, there is little guidance in the professional literature regarding handling these sorts of communications (McConaughy, 2005; Robin & Foster, 1989).

When in doubt, it is advisable "to err" on the side of being liberal in disclosures of adolescents' "dangerous" activities to parents. Keeping an adolescent's behavior "confidential" from parents for the sake of maintaining rapport and trust (even for altruistic reasons, such as trying to obtain information about other, more serious suspected problems or trying to get the adolescent to attempt interventions to reduce the problem) can often backfire. If parents later discover that the adolescent disclosed the information to the clinician but the clinician did not disclose the information to them, there is the risk not only of destroying rapport and trust with the parents but also of the parents terminating their relationship with the clinician and the clinician subsequently not having any opportunity to work with the family.

Again, much of this can be averted by discussions at the beginning of the interview regarding how to handle child-therapist disclosure of sensitive information. In the illustration above, the interviewer can modify the dialogue to fit the parents' preferences on handling these disclosures. For example, the interviewer could provide more examples of what he or she considers "dangerous" behavior (e.g., drug use, unprotected sexual activity, carrying a weapon, etc.). This should also be discussed when the interview is being conducted for the primary purpose of producing a report or evaluation, as these sorts of disclosures during an interview in which the primary goal is a written evaluation for dissemination to parents or others tend to be utilized in the report (e.g., "John reports that he has stolen several items from teachers within the last year").

Should the interviewer decide that information divulged in the interview is important enough to warrant specific communication to the parents, the interviewer should immediately inform the adolescent of that decision. For example, suppose that halfway through the interview, an adolescent divulges that he is smoking marijuana daily and his parents are not aware of this. In this case, the interviewer should not wait until the end of the interview to state that he or she will be informing the adolescent's parents of this information—which would certainly damage trust and rapport and all but guarantee that future sessions with the adolescent would be unproductive. Instead, the interviewer might say this to the adolescent at the time of the disclosure:

Interviewer: Remember when I said that if you told me you were doing something dangerous, I'd have to tell your parents? Well, we're going to have to tell them you're smoking pot every day.

Adolescent: What? [in angry disbelief] Smoking weed's not dangerous! Come on, man! I can't believe this! Are you serious?!

Interviewer: I am serious, LeRoy. And I honestly believe you think that smoking pot every day is not dangerous. But, I think you're putting yourself in danger when you're buying it, when you're driving high, when you're at work stoned. You go to school high once in a while, too. I have to do what I think is best for you and your family to keep you safe. That's my number one priority, no matter what else happens, even if you resent me for telling. I'm not doing this to get you in trouble or because I side with your parents, but because I truly believe that you're putting yourself in danger. I realize that you don't like my decision and don't agree with me. But I couldn't bear it if something bad happened to you when you're high in those situations. And we have to tell your parents because they're responsible for you if anything bad happens.

Although adolescents will be upset regarding your decision to inform their parents, they can (occasionally) at least appreciate your reasons for doing so. At this point, the interviewer should allow some time for de-escalation, if needed, and then ask the adolescent whether or not he or she can continue with the interview. It is often necessary in such situations to terminate the youth interview because the adolescent either refuses to talk or is too upset to continue. Occasionally, however, interviewers can reengage adolescents in the interview process by indicating that there is important information they would still like to hear the adolescents' opinions about, particularly if it involves their opinions of their parents (and not their covert activities). Interviewers should also offer adolescents the chance to tell their parents, rather than the interviewers informing the parents, allowing them to take responsibility for the disclosure. If the adolescent chooses this option, it should be done with the interviewer present to ensure adequate detail in the disclosure. Although situations such as these are relatively rare, they will arise, and interviewers should be prepared regarding how they want to handle them. To reiterate, the interviewer should be very familiar with federal and state laws governing confidentiality.

Difficult Child Behavior During the Interview

Prior to beginning the youth interview, the interviewer may need to establish the guidelines for appropriate and inappropriate behavior during the interview, especially for younger children. Sometimes, the necessity of doing this can be gauged from the child's behavior at the beginning of the interview when all parties are together. If it is apparent that the child's behavior is not under instructional control (i.e., isn't staying seated, touching or picking up objects in the room, grabbing paperwork, etc.), the interviewer should communicate to the child (preferably with the parents present) guidelines for his or her conduct during the interview and consequences for rule violations. Usually, youth with ODD and CD are more cooperative when their parents are not present, but occasionally a child or adolescent may test the limits with the interviewer as well. There are no guidelines for room rules, as this will largely depend on the personal characteristics and tolerances of the interviewer. The interviewer should bear in mind, however, that tolerances established during the initial interview are a precedent and may linger if the family remains in treatment with the clinician. If the interviewer suspects that formal discipline may be needed (i.e., beyond simple redirection), he or she should discuss this with the parents. The following dialogue (between Mr. and Mrs. X and their 7-year-old daughter, Jenny) may serve as an example:

Interviewer: Jenny, before your parents leave the room, I have something very important to say. I really need you to listen to this. You've been standing up on the chair a couple times, trying to jump up and touch the clock. I'm guessing you won't do something like that when you and I are in here alone, but if you do, I'll have to stop you, just like your parents did, because that's dangerous. I don't want you to hurt yourself. Also, you can't pull any of the books off the bookshelf. [turning to the parents, but ensuring that Jenny can hear] Mr. and Mrs. R., when parents leave their child in someone else's care, even for a little while, like you're going to do today with Jenny and I, the issue of discipline can be a little touchy. During our interview, you said you sometimes use time-out when Jenny doesn't follow the rules. If Jenny doesn't follow the rules in here, I'm going to put her in time-out in here. Are you okay with that?

Mr. X: [a little startled at the request] Sure, I'm fine with that . . . is that okay with you, honey?

Mrs. X: Sure, if you think it will work . . .

Interviewer: Great . . . again, I don't think there'll be a problem, but just in case. Also, if Jenny does a good job following the rules, is it okay if we end a few minutes early and go outside and play Frisbee? [to Jenny] Jenny, do you like to play Frisbee? [to parents] It won't substantially lengthen the interview, and I'll get you out of here on time.

Mrs. X: Sure, fine with us.

Rarely will an interviewer need to resort to this, but anyone conducting interviews with children who are oppositional should have a plan to deal with misbehavior that occurs in the room. The specifics of the consequence should be agreeable with the parents, and in most cases the parents are simply grateful that the interviewer won't be afraid to deal with their children's misbehavior. Time-out is convenient because is it immediate and effective and most parents report they have utilized the procedure (though many report it doesn't work, usually because they have not implemented it effectively). Most children have also been "put in time-out" before and will generally avoid situations that will cause that to happen. For older children and adolescents, the threatened withdrawal of the interviewers' unadulterated attention and interest is often sufficiently powerful to serve as a motivator to cease inappropriate behavior (e.g., "Kiesha, I really like hearing your stories about what goes on in your house. But if you keep writing on the table with the pen, we'll have to stop talking"). Should parents not agree to a suggested reasonable consequence for misbehavior, the interviewer should ask the parents, "Well, do you have any ideas that we all can agree upon on how I can handle Jenny's disruptive behavior?"

Rarely will adolescents with even the most severe forms of CD pose a threat to an interviewer. In most cases, they will be appreciative that someone is interested in their side of the story. More than likely, if anything, they will simply refuse to comply or participate in the interview. Nevertheless, an interviewer who suspects that an adolescent poses a risk should take precautionary steps to ensure both his or her own safety as well as the adolescent's. When conducting interviews with high-risk adolescents, the interviewer should be close to the door so he or she can leave the situation if needed. Should an adolescent become agitated, hostile, or threatening during the interview, the interviewer should take steps to calm the adolescent down and restore emotional control to the situation, for example, by providing validating statements, empathetic comments, and even remorse for provoking agitation (Morrison, 1995). Usually, such responses do not "come out of nowhere." The interviewer can often ascertain when an adolescent is becoming emotionally aroused and hostile and intervene appropriately. If the adolescent is unable to calm down, however, or escalates to making threats or engages in physical posturing (e.g., standing up in a threatening manner), the interviewer should simply state to the adolescent that the interview is over, leave the room, and inform the parents (or police, if the adolescent is threatening violence).

To minimize potential "temptations" for youth with disruptive behaviors, the interviewer should attempt to "childproof" the room. Quite simply, this entails putting valuable or dangerous objects out of the reach of children. Pictures can be hung at a height that most children can't reach; family photos can be put in areas that do not allow for easy access; books can be placed on higher shelves; and files and paperwork can be placed in drawers. While most of this is common sense, even the most experienced interviewer can get "caught off guard" when an oppositional youth grabs the client file sitting on the table between them, and the interviewer should take simple steps to minimize the potential for these problems to occur. This should not be taken as a recommendation to "sterilize" the interview environment. In fact, the general recommendation is quite the opposite. It is preferable to have child-friendly stimuli in the room, such as drawings from other children, posters of child-friendly material, and so on. This helps establish the interview room as a warm, inviting environment and, more important, to establish the interviewer as "experienced" in the eyes of the parents and as affable in the eyes of the child. It is sometimes useful to have an assortment of small trinkets and toys that children can play with during the interview.

INTERVIEWING PARENTS AND TEACHERS

Interviewing parents is absolutely critical when assessing oppositional and conduct problems. In some sense, when parents seek treatment or an assessment because their child is noncompliant, defiant, or antisocial, the parents are the primary clients. The youth's behavior is most concerning to parents, not necessarily to the youth. Thus, it is critical to validate the parents' concerns in the interview, as well as assess the parental perceptions of the behavior problems (Barkley et al., 1999). It is also critical to engage parents in the initial interview, because most empirically supported interventions entail participation of the parents, often as the primary target of intervention (e.g., behavioral parent training).

When appropriate (i.e., dual-parent home), it is desirable that both parents be interviewed, preferably together. Even in situations of divorce or separation where the child spends significant time with both parents, it may be beneficial to have both parents together for at least part of the interview. The level of hostility that is present in a formal context of an initial interview, where there is a pull for socially desirable behaviors on the part of parents, can be highly indicative of parents' behavior in a less formal situation with no demand characteristics (i.e., in front of the child during typical interactions).

For parents of youth who are oppositional, a useful interview structure is the "typical-day" interview (see Mullis, 2002). The purpose of this interview is to obtain a comprehensive, detailed description of the child's life in a typical 24-hour period. Embedded in the typical-day interview, the interviewer obtains information regarding the areas of problematic functioning. The typical-day interview is the verbal equivalent of having a videotape of the child and family during a day. The interview is introduced by asking the parents to describe a typical day in the life of the identified child:

> I know there is no such thing as a "typical day," but to the best of your ability, could you describe an average day in Sam's life? I want to get a sense of what goes on in the family, as if I were somehow a fly on the wall that followed him around. Why don't we start in the evening, say bedtime. What time is bedtime for Sam?

The typical-day interview is a more sinuous version of standard formats described by McMahon and Forehand (2003) and Barkley et al. (1999), in which the interviewer probes for the presence of the problem in different situations.

In Table 14.3, all the items in the domain of "ODD- & CD-Specific Behaviors" lend themselves well to this type of interview. The interview proceeds in an "around-the-clock" format. Major domains to cover include typical problem areas for youth with ODD and CD, including prebedtime routine, bedtime, getting up in the morning, breakfast, getting dressed and ready for school, car ride to/from school, coming out of school, late-afternoon transition (i.e., time between arriving home from school/day care to dinner), playtime, dinner, homework, evening chores, and behavior in public places (see the case illustration following this section). Conducting the interview in this format will allow the interviewer to determine those times when the oppositional behavior is most likely to occur.

When parents are describing "a hot spot" (a time or activity, for example, bedtime, that tends to produce noncompliance or disruptive behavior), interviewers should ask questions from "ODD- & CD-Specific Behaviors" that allow them to obtain sufficient detail regarding interactions between the child and parents in that situation. An important component of the parent interview is to ascertain the level of agreement and cooperation and the roles of both the mother and father in discipline, supervision, and child interactions. These questions can simply be asked directly or can be embedded within the typical-day interview. For example, if one parent tends to be dominating the interview, the interviewer can ask the nonparticipating parent, "What are you doing when this is happening?" (See the case illustration following this section.)

Obtaining information from teachers can be particularly useful in identifying cross-situational specificity of ODD and CD behaviors. It would be unrealistic, however, for most interviewers to routinely conduct teacher interviews. A decisive parent question that might guide the decision regarding whether to interview a teacher would be "Do you get calls (or other forms of communication) regarding your child's behavior at school?" If affirmed, a teacher interview could be critical in eliciting similarities and differences in the child's behavior at school and at home.

Often, it can be sufficient to interview the teacher over the phone (or send rating scales through the mail), though a face-to-face meeting would be preferable. When interviewing teachers, the interviewer should obtain sufficient information to determine the type of oppositional behavior that occurs within the school environment, antecedents and consequences, whether any interventions have been helpful, and the child's preferred (and nonpreferred) activities. It may also be important to access information from school personnel regarding social relationships of the youth at school. This is often an area of significant discrepancy between parent and youth reports, as youth with externalizing disorders tend to have distorted views of their social relationships and parents simply lack the level of information to be reliable informants in this domain. Finally, it is important to gain the teacher's perspective on whether the parents are (or have been) willing to work with the teacher and school, as well as whether the teacher might be willing to participate in additional interventions (e.g., home-school notes).

CASE ILLUSTRATION WITH DIALOGUE

Sam is a 10-year-old male who was brought into a behavioral pediatric outpatient clinic by his mother and father (Mr. and Mrs. B) due to "temper tantrums, disobedience, and aggression." Sam has a previous diagnosis of ADHD given by a child psychiatrist and currently takes Adderall XR 20mg. He has an older brother (14) and a younger sister (8).

When the interviewer went into the waiting room to meet the family, Sam and his mother were arguing about Sam's homework. Sam's father was reading a magazine. Sam's mother was lecturing her son: "Sam, if you don't take your homework seriously, you're not going to do well in school. School is important." Sam angrily responded, "I hate school. I don't care about homework. Homework is stupid. I don't want to do homework." Mrs. B retorted, "Well, we think it's important. I really want you to do well in school. If you want to get into a good college, you need to start getting good grades *now!*"

The mother soon noticed the interviewer walking toward them, and she discontinued her dialogue with Sam. After an initial greeting, the family was asked to come back to the interviewer's office. Mrs. B asked Sam to put his homework back in his backpack and come with them. Sam responded, "This is stupid. If I didn't have to be here, I could be outside playing already." Mrs. B responded, "Sam, I already told you, this is something your mom and dad really want to do. Now would you please put your book away?" Sam fumbled with his book but did not put it in his bag. Mrs. B asked again, "Sam, would you please put your book away so we can go back and talk to Dr. H?" Sam said, "I don't want to!" Mr. B interjected somewhat harshly, "Sam, listen to your mother, or you'll be grounded when you get home." While huffing with frustration, Sam put his book in his backpack, and his mother responded, "Thanks, Sam. I'll get you something from McDonald's if you do a good job today."

Although brief, this interaction already provided some tentative insight and hypothesis regarding the family dynamics, parental discipline, and relationship variables. First, Sam's mother tended to use frequent rationales to persuade Sam to behave. There did not seem to be much limit setting, and no consequences were provided for Sam's inappropriate behavior (though his father threatened a consequence). While this may be a product of avoidance of "public parenting" (i.e., parents not wanting to give consequences to children in public), it may also represent typical dynamics in the home. It is also telling that Mrs. B asked Sam to put his book away rather than telling him. Finally, Mr. B tended to be distant through the entire interaction, until finally stepping in and telling Sam to listen to his mother or there would be consequences. A positive indication of potential treatment success was that Sam accommodated the request at this point.

Once in the interviewer's office, the interviewer explained that everyone would spend a few minutes together before splitting up. The interview began with the following:

Interviewer:	So, what brings you in today?
Mrs. B:	Well, we're having some problems at home with Sam. [Mom looks over at Sam, smiles, touches his arm . . . he pulls away.]
I:	What sort of problems are you having?
Mrs. B:	Well . . . he won't mind. It seems like everything is a fight. It's like if we say "black," he'll say "white." When we—[is interrupted]
Sam:	That's not true . . . I listen, but you guys aren't fair!
Mr. B:	[sternly] Sam, don't interrupt your mother.
S:	[Sam lets out an exasperated breath and leans back in his chair.]
Mrs. B:	Sam, it's not nice to talk over someone else when they're talking. We've discussed this a million times already. People aren't going to like you if you keep interrupting them. [Sam rolls his eyes and shakes his head.] It's like this all the time. It's just so frustrating. We thought that when he started taking Adderall, most of these problems would go away. And for a while, they did get better. But they seem worse now than ever before. We just don't know what to do. We fight all the time, and it's affecting the rest of the family . . . [Mrs. B begins to cry.]
S:	[to mom:] Can we go now?

The interview proceeds for about 5 minutes, with the interviewer sporadically interjecting very general questions. Primarily, as is typical, the parents occupy most of this time telling their story of Sam's misbehavior at home.

I:	Okay, so I think I have a pretty good overview of what's happening. Sam's having a hard time following instructions. Any other *big* things? [Mom and dad shake their heads.]
I:	Sam, what do you think about what your parents said? Do you think that you sometimes don't listen to what they're telling you to do?
S:	[Sam looks down at the floor, then at the clock.]
Mr. B:	Sam, answer the doctor.
S:	I guess . . . but Sally [Sam's younger sister] does it too . . . I don't know why I'm the one who has to be in this stupid office.
I:	Thanks for answering Sam. This can't be much fun for you, listening to us talk about you. I want to spend some time with your parents for a while, but after that, I'd like just to get your take on things too. It's really important that I get a chance to talk to everyone alone, especially you, Sam, because sometimes it's embarrassing to discuss these issues with your parents around. And sometimes kids want to say stuff but are afraid to say it in front of their parents.
S:	I'm not afraid of nothin.'
I:	I bet you're not Sam, and I hope you won't be afraid to talk to me in a little while.

Sam is escorted to a playroom by the interviewer; parent interview continues.

I:	Looks like you have your hands full. [parents chuckle] Okay, I have a good general sense of the problem. Now, I'd like to get some very detailed information. Are there any specific tasks that he won't do?
Mrs. B:	Pretty much anything we ask him to do that he doesn't want to do. He just thinks that he can do anything he wants and doesn't have to listen to us.
I:	Can you give me an example?
Mrs. B:	Well, we have trouble getting him into bed at night. He won't simply go to bed . . . he's got to come out of his room to ask for a

drink, complain that he's not tired, ask if he can have the TV on . . . it's maddening!

I: Anything else?

Mrs. B: Well, as you probably saw out there, homework. He hates doing homework. It's a fight to get him to sit down and do homework. And when we do finally get him to sit down, he won't stay there. And he's certainly not doing homework even if he's at his desk. Usually, he'll be playing with his Game Boy, or drawing, or just goofing off. So when we ask him to get back to homework, he throws a temper tantrum.

I: And what does that look like . . . his temper tantrums?

Mrs. B: He throws himself to the ground, kicks his feet, screams, flails his arms, curses, says he hates us.

I: Does he do that *every time* you ask him to get back to homework?

Mrs. B: No, not every time.

I: How often would you say he throws a tantrum during homework . . . once a day, once a week, once a month?

Mrs. B: Oh, probably a couple times a week?

I: Are there other situations when he'll throw a tantrum?

Mrs. B: Well . . . sometimes in the grocery store . . . if he wants something like Popsicles and we tell him no, he'll sometimes just plop down right there in the middle of the store and tantrum.

I: Are his tantrums the same in the store . . . flailing, and cursing, and screaming, "I hate you"?

Mrs. B: No, not exactly, he just drops to the floor and screams and cries, "I want some ice cream!"

I: So what do you do when he does that in the store?

Mrs. B: I try to tell him that it's inappropriate, that people will think he's a baby. I tell him that if he continues, he won't get any ice cream or whatever he's wanting.

I: And does that stop it?

Mrs. B: No, not usually.

I: Then what?

Mrs. B: Well, I get so exasperated that I tell him if he stops immediately, I'll get him the ice

cream. I know I shouldn't, but I don't know what else to do.

I: I understand. That's embarrassing when your kid's having a meltdown in the store . . . everyone looking at you like you're a terrible parent. Worse, they seem to feel sorry for your kid. [shakes head]

Mr. B: [laughs and nods]

Mrs. B: Really, I sometimes just want to say, "Then you take him . . . he's all yours!"

I: Mr. B., you really haven't said too much yet. And I've gotten the impression that you don't necessarily agree with everything that's been said. Am I wrong about that?

Mr. B: Well, I just think she babies him too much. I never would have even *thought* about talking to my parents the way he talks to us, but particularly his mother. But that's because I know what would have happened if I did. And I hate being the bad guy all time. I'm always the one who has to step in and get things done. If I don't, it just goes on and on and on. [Mom starts to cry.]

I: So you don't agree with the way Mrs. B disciplines Sam?

Mr. B: No, I don't. She tells me that we just need to explain things to him, that he'll eventually get it. Well, maybe that's true, but he sure ain't gettin' it now!

I: How do you think things should be different?

Mr. B: Well, if he's not listening, he shouldn't be allowed to play with all the crap he has in his room and around the house.

I: Do you two ever discuss your differences about dealing with Sam?

Mrs. B: Yes, but it usually leads to a fight, so we only talk about it when it gets real crazy.

I: Do you ever disagree about how to deal with Sam in front of him?

Mr. B: No, I'd never do that. We keep our differences from him for the most part.

I: For the most part?

Mrs. B: Well, about 3 months, ago, when Sam was being particularly cranky and disrespectful, he [Mr. B] yelled at me in front of Sam, told me that I was babying him, and that what Sam really needed was a "good ole' kick in the ass!"

Mr. B: I felt bad about it, and apologized later. But, she never lets me forget it and kinda holds it over me sometimes.

I: Is that true?

Mrs. B: Maybe, but that was entirely uncalled for . . . I mean, I pick them up, I cook dinner for the family, I get them ready for school, I wash their clothes, I do a lot for this family.

I: Dealing with a stubborn kid can often precipitate problems between parents. Are you two willing to try strategies where you can support each other?

The interview proceeds, eliciting information pertaining to "ODD- & CD-Specific Behaviors" in Table 14.3.

I: Okay, well I think I have a pretty good idea of the types of things Sam's doing that are causing you stress. I'd like to switch gears just a little and have you describe a typical day in Sam's life. I know there's no such thing as a "typical day," as every day tends to be unique, with different schedules and activities. But I want to get a sense of what Sam does most days, as if I had a video camera and were following him around. Okay? Let's start off with bedtime. I know you said that was a difficult time for Sam. What time is Sam's bedtime?

Mr. B: It's supposed to be 8:30.

Mrs. B: But we have a hard time with bedtime.

I: Okay, how do you initiate bedtime? I'm assuming he's doing something else and at 8:30 he doesn't run up to his room and yell to you two, "I'm ready for bed!" So how do you start the bedtime routine?

Mr. B: Well, usually she tells Sam it's time for bed around 8, 'cause we know it's going to be a struggle to get him there. Usually, I'm watching TV or working on a project, and hear the commotion and have to get involved.

Mrs. B: Sam's usually watching TV, and I give him warnings that "It's almost bedtime." Then, at 8:30, I tell him to turn the TV off and get ready for bed.

I: And what does he do then?

Mr. B: Doesn't listen.

Mrs. B: He says something like "Okay, Mom, right after SpongeBob is over" or "Just a minute."

I: And then what?

Mrs. B: I usually tell him, "No, *now*." And then the arguing starts.

Mr. B: And that's usually when I step in.

I: How does the arguing go?

Mrs. B: You know, typical stuff.

I: Well, would you mind getting real specific for me . . . like, do you raise your voice, does he raise his, is there name-calling, how long does it last?

This proceeds until a very concrete description is presented.

I: So, how do you finally get him into bed?

Mr. B: It's a constant back and forth . . . us telling him to get into bed, and him coming up with excuses or things to do instead.

I: I understand . . . but how do you finally get him to go to bed?

Mrs. B: I usually just get fed up and say, "Get in bed now . . . I mean it . . . I'm not playing around anymore" and threaten to take some of his favorite toys away.

I: Are there any occasions when you make that threat where he doesn't get in bed afterward?

Mrs. B: Yes, sometimes, though usually once I "lose it" he gets in bed . . . plus, it's 10 p.m., and he's pretty tired by then.

I: And on those occasions when it doesn't work, when you "lose it" and threaten to remove stuff but he still doesn't comply, do you take his toys?

Mrs. B: Usually not, because if I did, we'd have another 2 or 3 hours of dealing with "the monster."

I: Wow, you guys are fighting him every night for at least an hour! That's got to be frustrating and tiring for both of you. Okay, prior to all this, do you have a bedtime routine, like brushing teeth, pajamas, reading, prayers . . . anything like that?

Mrs. B: Well, we'd like to. But just getting him into his room and then into bed is hard enough. We don't even bother with that stuff at this point.

I: Okay, so you're finally able to get him to stay in his room and go sleep by around 9:30 or 10 on most nights. Then you two go to bed, is that pretty accurate? [parents nod in agreement] Okay, after that, what happens? Does he ever wake up in the middle of the night?

Mr. B: Occasionally, he'll get up and try to come into our bed. We don't want him to, but sometimes I don't hear him. And even when I do, if we put him back in his bed, we're in for another struggle, so we just let him curl up with us.

I: How often will he wake up and get into your bed?

Mrs. B: Once or twice a week.

I: Do you have any idea about what time in the night that occurs?

Mr. B: I'm out half the time

Mrs. B: Between midnight and 2 a.m., usually.

I: When you try to put him back in his bed, what happens?

The interview proceeds in this manner, covering critical periods in the day. At the completion of the parent interview, the interviewer walks Mr. and Mrs. B out of the office and down to the playroom.

Mrs. B: Okay, Sam, your turn. Pick up those toys and go with the doctor.

[Sam does not respond and continues to play with toys.]

Mrs. B: Sam, you need to go talk to the doctor.

[Sam still does not respond, never looking up from playing.]

Mrs. B: [very loudly] Sam, I'm not kidding around. Put your toys up and go with Dr. H! [more calmly] If you can be good, we'll get something from McDonald's on the way home.

[Sam looks around the room at the multitude of toys strewn over the floor. He picks up one toy, very slowly and deliberately, and puts it in a container, then very slowly reaches for another.]

Mr. B: [calmly, yet firmly] That's enough, Sam. Get up and go with the doctor or you'll be grounded when we get home . . . no TV or electronics.

S: But Mom told me to pick up the toys first.

Mrs. B: It's okay, sweetie, we'll pick up the toys . . . you go with the doctor now.

[Sam reluctantly walks with the interviewer back to the office.]

I: You know, if I were you, I wouldn't want to be here either. I'd rather be playing outside with my friends, watching TV, playing video games, or even watching grass grow than to be here . . . man, I might even want to do homework rather than be here.

S: Well, I don't know about that . . . [Sam smiles slightly. The interviewer takes the smile as an indication that Sam may be willing to participate.]

I: So, I really want to thank you before we begin for taking some time to talk to me. I don't want to keep you here long, Sam, so I'm hoping that we can get down to business. [The interviewer is trying to validate Sam's requests that he wants to go home yet also is communicating that they need to have a conversation first.] First, I heard a lot about how your parents feel about what's happening at home. You heard what they said when we were all in here together. They think that your family has some problems. [The interviewer is using language that avoids blaming Sam for the problems that are occurring.] That's why they made this appointment and came in today, and that's part of what I've been talking with them about while you were playing. I also want you to know that they had a lot of good things to say about you too. [Sam raises his eyebrows skeptically.] Now I know you don't know me, and it can be hard to talk about those sorts of things with someone you don't know, but I really want to get to know you a little better and how you see things. I think your mom and dad just want to figure out how to make things better at home. I really want to hear your side of the story, too, Sam. So do you think things could improve at home?

The interviewer is taking a calculated gamble that "small talk" with the child would be unproductive and potentially even counterproductive. The child has indicated, both verbally and nonverbally, that he would prefer to be elsewhere, so the interviewer decides to begin the child interview with a rather direct, potentially invasive question. In other situations, however, the interview with the child or adolescent might more appropriately begin with more benign questions, such as "I saw you reading out in the waiting area. What are you reading?" or, to the teenager with headphones on, "What sort of music do you like?"

S: Yeah, it's pretty bad. They yell at me all the time.

I: What do they yell at you for?

S: Not listening.

I: How often do you get in trouble for not listening?

S: All the time. I'm always in trouble.

I: What happens when you're in trouble?

S: What do mean, "What happens?"

I: Are you grounded, they yell at you, they take stuff away, won't let you do things?

S: Well, they try to take stuff away, but that doesn't work. Mostly, my mom just is griping and griping.

I: What did you mean when you said taking away stuff "doesn't work"?

S: 'Cause they forgot, or I just do it anyway.

I: Wow! I'm impressed that you're honest enough to admit that, Sam. You said your mom gripes. What does that look like?

S: [mimicking his mom's voice] "You ought to listen to your parents . . . doing your homework is important." You know, that kind of thing, only it's *all the time!*

At this point, Sam has become invested in "sharing his story" and appears to be able to provide information regarding specifics of interactions between himself and his parents. The interviewer continues to get Sam's perspective on the specifics on the interactions, as well as asking Sam questions about peer relationships, school, and interests.

MULTICULTURAL AND DIVERSITY ISSUES

Cultural issues permeate the identification of ODD and CD. For example, in some studies, average ratings of externalizing problems tend to be higher for African American and Hispanic youth relative to Caucasian youth, though this is not a consistent finding (Lahey et al., 1999). Further, in most studies, SES is confounded with ethnicity, which precludes any meaningful extrapolations regarding the effects of ethnicity on rates of externalizing problems. In general, cultural factors interact with many of the risk factors described previously, and thus need to be accounted for in the assessment of oppositional and conduct problems (McGee & Williams, 1999). In addition, cultural variables will likely impact the amount, type, and quality of information that is ascertained during the clinical interview. Cultural norms partially dictate the level of social communication and disclosure during the assessment. For example, some cultural norms dictate that sensitive disclosures about family functioning should generally be avoided (Ho, 1992). Culture also directly impacts parenting practices relevant to ODD and CD. For example, there is some evidence that more harsh and punitive parenting practices are more accepted, and potentially more effective, in some cultures (Ho, 1992; Polaha, Larzelere, Shapiro, & Pettit, 2004). Cultural biases can also potentially confound the judgments made by the interviewer. Cultural variables have been demonstrated to impact clinical decisions made regarding diagnostic status, course of treatment, and placement recommendations (Garb, 1998). Overt cultural characteristics of the child and family do not necessarily imply that cultural variables will be potent in case conceptualization. The influence of cultural variables will depend largely on the level of acculturation of child and family to the majority culture (Ho, 1992). It is always critical for the clinician working with children to be aware of how cultural factors impact the causes and expression of externalizing behaviors, the interactive processes during the interview, and personal biases that might affect judgments made about the information obtained.

DIFFERENTIAL DIAGNOSES AND BEHAVIORAL ASSESSMENT

Differential Diagnoses

Many characteristics associated with oppositional and antisocial behavior are also associated with other significant mental health problems. For example, oppositional behavior may be associated with adjustment problems, such as the loss of someone close. These other problems or disorders may have very different treatments. Thus, it is critical to effectively rule out differential diagnoses to ensure adequate treatment of the presenting problem(s).

A primary differential diagnosis that needs to be made with children who present with oppositional behaviors is ADHD (see Donohue, Simmons, & Devore, Chapter 16, this volume). The relationship between ADHD and ODD/CD is complex and controversial. It is not even universally accepted that they are distinct disorders (Quay, 1999). A large body of evidence, however, suggests that ADHD is often a precursor to later oppositional, delinquent, and aggressive behavior (Connor, 2002). Thus, if a child is presenting with behaviors associated with ODD or CD, the clinician should suspect and assess for ADHD.

ADHD involves chronic and pervasive problems with attention, concentration, and hyperactivity. Often, children with ADHD lack inhibition and engage in rule-breaking behaviors. Many also experience associated problems that are similar to problems experienced by youth with oppositional behavior, including peer/socialization problems, poor academic performance, and poor child-parent relationships. Thus, these disorders can have similar presentations.

To illustrate, the *DSM* criteria for ADHD include "often does not seem to listen when spoken to directly," "does not follow through on instructions," and "often interrupts or intrudes others." These are very similar to one of the criteria for ODD, "often actively defies or refuses to comply with adults' request or rules." So, if a child often "ignores" a request to engage in a parental request, is this ADHD or ODD? The answer lies in the broader sense of the definitions of the two disorders. Most telling will be the frequency, intensity, and "flavor" of rule violations. Youth with ODD/CD often violate rules, argue with adults, lose their tempers, and are irritable. These characteristics are not indicative of ADHD. Children with "pure" ADHD may fail to respond to requests (because they are inattentive), but when the request is repeated, they will not respond with anger or vengeance (e.g., "I heard you the first time, Mom! If you want it done so bad, you do it!").

It is probably more difficult to determine whether ADHD is present when the presence of ODD has already been established. That is, many times it will be clear that a particular child is oppositional; however, whether there is also co-occurring ADHD will be hard to disentangle: Is part of the reason they are behaving so defiantly because they also can't pay attention or are impulsive?

Perhaps a telling feature (though not purely diagnostic) will be to assess how the child behaves in different environments. ADHD, by definition, is a pervasive condition that is present in multiple domains (e.g., school, work, home). Thus, inattention and impulsivity may lead to infrequent rule violations being present in multiple environments. Conversely, youth with ODD and CD sometimes, though not always, demonstrate frequent rule violations in confined settings or contexts, such as with people they feel comfortable with, like parents. This is not to imply that youth with ODD or CD cannot or do not demonstrate oppositional, aggressive, or antisocial behavior in multiple environments, only that it tends to be much more pronounced in certain environments. Thus, if ODD symptoms are isolated to the home environment yet teachers report that the child frequently won't stay seated, can't seem to sit still, and so on, then it is likely that ADHD is also present.

Waldman and Lilienfeld (1991) analyzed symptoms of ADHD and ODD to determine which criteria were most predictive of each disorder. Symptoms that were most discriminating by teacher report included "difficulty waiting to take a turn," "blurts out answers," "shifts activities," "difficulty playing quietly," and "physically dangerous" for a diagnosis of ADHD and "angry/resentful," "spiteful," "actively defies," and "swears" for a diagnosis of ODD.

Youth with oppositional and conduct problems may also be demonstrating more transient symptoms associated with adjustment disorders (AD), particularly AD with disturbance of conduct. AD is defined as "the development of emotional or behavioral symptoms in response to an identifiable stressor(s) occurring within 3 months of the onset of the stressor(s) . . . and once the stressor has terminated, the symptoms do not persist for more than additional 6 months" (APA, 1994, p. 626). Disturbance of conduct is "when the predominant manifestation is [one] in which there is a violation of the rights of others or major age-appropriate societal norms and rules (e.g., truancy, vandalism, reckless driving, fighting)" (p. 624).

Children who are grieving, dealing with parental divorce, switching schools, experiencing relocations, or experiencing social problems may demonstrate symptoms similar to those characteristic of ODD or CD. The key distinguishing characteristic is whether there is a clear precipitating event. The length of the disruption can be acute (less than 6 months) or chronic (greater than 6 months, but only if the stressor is not terminated). Differential diagnosis of AD and ODD/CD is obtained primarily by a clearly identifiable stressor and chronicity. ODD symptoms must be present for at least 6 months, and while there is no specific chronicity specifier for CD, the disorder is defined as "a repetitive and persistent pattern" of antisocial behavior.

Recently, there has been a debate regarding the significance of overlap between the disruptive behavior disorders (ADHD, CD, ODD) and bipolar disorder (BD). Currently, pediatric BD is defined by the same *DSM* criteria for adult BD (Wozniak et al., 2005; Youngstrom, Findling, & Feeny, 2004). BD is defined in the *DSM* by an episode of mania (or hypomania) in which the individual displays an abnormally and persistently elevated, expansive, or irritable mood; grandiosity; decreased need for sleep; more talkativeness than usual; flights of ideas; distractibility; increase in goal-directed activity or psychomotor agitation; and excessive involvement in pleasurable activities. Symptoms must be present for 1 week, cause impairment in daily functioning, and represent a distinct change from an individual's normal mood. Depression may also be present but is not required for a diagnosis.

Oppositional and conduct problems can be similar to the presenting characteristics of pediatric BD, such as irritability, inflated self-esteem, disturbances in sleep, talkativeness, distractibility, psychomotor agitation, and pleasure seeking. Some research has suggested that elevated moods and emotional dysregulation associated with ADHD, CD, and ODD (e.g., temper tantrums, lack of inhibition) is the pediatric precursor of adult BD (Youngstrom et al., 2004). Thus, it is often difficult to differentiate between pediatric bipolar disorder and the common presentation associated with ODD. There is currently debate among experts regarding whether grandiosity or elevated mood or chronic irritability is the predominant presentation in pediatric BD (Wozniak et al., 2005; Youngstrom et al., 2004).

As the defining characteristics and clinical course of pediatric BD are still highly debated and largely unknown (Youngstrom et al., 2004), clinicians should carefully assess BD symptoms if they suspect mania might be present. There are currently no separate pediatric criteria for BD, so children and adolescents must demonstrate the core symptoms of adult BD for a diagnosis. Pediatric BD is a relatively rare phenomenon (prevalence rate less than 2%), so

there should be substantial evidence that the oppositional behaviors are clearly more indicative of BD (Youngstrom et al., 2004).

Several characteristic of BD may be useful to keep in mind for deferential diagnosis. First, BD has a high index of intergenerational transmission. If a parent has BD, the odds that the child will have BD increase fivefold. Thus, a positive family history of bipolar disorder, though not diagnostic, should be seriously considered if the child is demonstrating symptoms that are hard to differentiate. Nevertheless, even though this is a dramatic increase in the chances of a child demonstrating BD, only 5% of children who have parents with BD will demonstrate BD themselves (Youngstrom et al., 2004). Second, at least currently, the mood and behavioral disturbances must clearly differ from the individual's typical mood and behavior. This is usually not the case with ODD and CD. Usually, these behaviors are chronically present and do not show the episodic, cycling nature of mania.

Behavioral Assessment

A hallmark of behavioral assessment is direct observation (Haynes & O'Brien, 2000). Observation has been cited as being critical to valid assessment of oppositional behavior (McMahon & Forehand, 1988). Behavioral observation can take many forms, from very structured and formal systems of data collection to simple descriptions of behavior (Bloomquist & Schnell, 2002). Like structured interviews, formal observational coding systems tend to increase reliability of observations and allow for comparisons of observations across situations. Several formal, empirically validated systems of observational coding have been developed and extensively utilized with oppositional children, including the Dyadic Parent-Child Interaction Coding System (DPICS) (Eyberg & Robinson, 1983) and the Behavioral Coding System (BCS) (McMahon & Forehand, 2003). Most formal coding systems require a fair amount of training to master and have been limited to use in research settings. For example, the BCS typically requires about 20 to 30 hours of training to achieve mastery.

Most observational protocols involve several analog conditions (about 5 minutes each): a child-directed activity, a parent-directed activity, and a cleanup task. The child-directed activity involves having the parent allow the child to engage in any reasonable activity he or she chooses, while the parent watches or participates in the play activity. The parent-directed activity usually involves the parent issuing commands or instructions to the child, while the cleanup tasks involve what the name implies. Typically, partial-interval recording (i.e., whether a behavior occurs during a segment of time) or frequency counts are conducted, whereby parent behaviors and child behaviors are recorded on a coding sheet. Typical parent behaviors that are recorded include the use of commands, questions, rewards, praise statements, attending gestures, warnings, consequences, and physical interactions. Child behavior that is typically recorded includes compliance, noncompliance, inappropriate behavior, and aggressive behavior. Utilization of formal observational coding systems provides rich information on child and parent interactions, including the level of compliance. However, utilization of these coding systems is not very practical in most typical outpatient settings (McMahon & Estes, 1997).

Regardless of whether the interviewer uses a formal observational coding system, for children less than 10 years of age, it is recommended that the interview entail some form of observation. The tasks used in the formal observation systems described above can be informally utilized in any clinic setting (McMahon & Estes, 1997). The interviewer can ask the parents to engage in the three tasks described above while using a semistructured observation coding system (e.g., predetermined categories, such as "commands," "compliance," "attends/praise" can be recorded), or the interviewer can simply take notes on the observations, as illustrated below:

> Mrs. T issued multiple commands (approximately 35) during the 5-minute parent task, repeating the same command frequently, with escalating volume. This invariably resulted in noncompliance (daughter Emily complied with 6 or 7 commands). After Mrs. T reissued the command 2 to 3 times, she would start to count "1–2–3." About half the time, when she got to "3," Emily started to engage in the directive, but never completed it. The other half of the time, she simply ignored her mother. After Mrs. T got to "3," she threatened to remove a toy or put the child in time-out. However, on only one occasion did she actually follow through on this threat. On this occasion, she attempted to take a toy out of Emily's hand, which prompted Emily to scream and yell and pull away. During this interaction,

> Mrs. T said, "Okay, I'll let you keep it, but the next time I tell you to put a toy away, I want you to listen," and then gave the toy back to Emily.

Obviously, though the quantity and quality of data obtained utilizing a more informal observation protocol and recording method are far less sophisticated than that of data obtained with formal observational systems, they can still be very useful in capturing the nature of parent-child interactions.

Given the episodic and often covert nature of behavioral transgressions associated with CD, behavioral observations may be less fruitful in assessment of this particular disorder. Even with CD, however, informal observation may provide insight into the relationship dynamics between youth and their parents, interactional styles, levels of lax or punitive parenting, and levels of validation and positive reinforcement. A variant of the child observational tasks described above for adolescents involves having parents and adolescents talk about a neutral topic and a topic that is likely to produce conflict. For example, the interviewer may instruct the parents to engage the adolescent in a conversation relating to a recent accomplishment, a known interest, or a current event. The conflict discussion can relate to any disputed rules, expectations, or recent punishments. The interviewer should note who initiates the interactions, whether the parents and adolescent acknowledge each other's perspective, the acceleration of emotionality that occurs during the discussions, whether there is any resolution to task, the frequency of positive statements present in the communications, the relative rate of conversation by each parent, and how de-escalation occurs.

Behavioral observation has many advantages. First, it can be more objective than the information gathered from parents, children, and teachers during the interview process. Second, it potentially provides the interviewer with an in vivo demonstration of the presenting problem, giving much-needed depth and quality to the data collected in an interview. Third, it can provide data that can be useful in resolving discrepant information from different informants. Behavioral assessment also has disadvantages. Formal systems can be difficult to implement in a typical clinic setting, as they are rather time-intensive and require a moderate amount of training (and supervision if conducted by other staff). Further, formal coding systems may not accurately capture the behavior of concern. The child- and parent-directed tasks may not elicit the behavior of interest (e.g., the child may not "act up" during the observation). Behavioral observations are also affected by participant reactivity (e.g., parents and children "act differently" when being observed), even if the interviewer has the advantage of having a one-way mirror available. Because of these factors, it cannot be assumed that behavioral observations are more reliable or valid than other sources of data (see Sleator & Ullmann, 1981). Behavioral observations, like other data collected in the assessment, are another piece of information that can help with diagnostic formulations and treatment planning.

Observations are also part of more traditional orientations as well. For example, client observations are crucial in the mental status evaluation (see Palmer, Fiorito, & Tagliareni, Chapter 5, this volume; Rogers, 1995). When done for this purpose, observations should be recorded of the child's general physical appearance (appropriate attire, height and weight, motor coordination, salient physical features, such as acne, scars, disfigurement, etc.), overt behavior (activity level, attentiveness, interactiveness, cooperativeness, impulsiveness, gross and fine motor abilities), affective and social presentation (range of affect, appropriateness of affect, mood during the interview, reaction to praise, reaction to redirection, frustration tolerance, ability to carry a conversation, ease of separation from caretaker), and cognitive functioning (overall intellectual competencies, language and communication skills, insight into the problem, role in the problem, developmental appropriateness of logic and reasoning, fluency of thought).

SELECTION OF TREATMENT TARGETS AND REFERRAL

The selection of treatment targets will, of course, depend on the information that is obtained during the assessment and will invariably differ depending on the theoretical orientation of the treatment provider. Nevertheless, for youth with ODD and CD, there are some obvious treatment targets. Bloomquist and Schnell (2002) recommend selecting treatment targets that match the treatment to the pertinent risk and protective factors. Primary domains of risk and protective factors include parent variables, child variables, child-parent interactions, social/peer variables, and environmental/contextual variables. Through the interview, strengths and deficiencies in each of these areas should become apparent. For example, it should be evident as to what discipline strategies parents tend to utilize, whether they monitor and supervise appropriately, and whether they have developmentally appropriate expectations of their children. Child characteristics, such as level of insight, perspective-taking skills, socialization skills, attributions and locus of control, and moral reasoning, may also become obvious. Socialization factors, such as peer rejection and peer socialization, level of intimacy with same- and opposite-gender friends, and level of affiliation with other antisocial peers, are also potential targets. Thus, if the interviewer discovers that the level of parental monitoring is poor, that the parent utilizes less than effective discipline tactics, and the child is associating with delinquent peers, interventions would be targeted at these variables.

Another important consideration in selecting treatment targets would be consideration of effective interventions (Brosnan & Carr, 2000). Some of the more promising and empirically validated approaches include behavioral parent training, family therapy, and multisystemic therapy (MST). Although the content and methods of parent-training programs differ significantly, most programs tend to teach parents to (a) differentially attend to their children's positive behaviors, (b) selectively ignore minor to moderate misbehavior, and (c) apply consequences to more serious rules infractions (e.g., time-out, response cost, etc.).

The effectiveness of family therapy has been evaluated in numerous studies. Several variants of family therapy have been identified as potentially efficacious for treating adolescent CD (e.g., structural family therapy, functional family therapy), and most include elements of problem solving, communication training, reframing, and negotiation skills (Robin & Foster, 1989). Validated family therapy methods typically include teaching parents elements of behavioral management as well.

MST has received much support as an effective treatment approach for adolescent delinquency and CD. MST intensively targets multiple systems in the adolescent's life (e.g., family, school, peers, etc.), borrowing interventions from established, evidenced-based practice to engage participants embedded within these systems to effect change in the adolescent's life. MST requires extensive training and collaboration with its developers in order to implement, and thus would be a service that would likely require the family to be referred to an MST provider in the area. A hierarchical algorithm that may be helpful in determining treatment targets includes the following:

1. Dangerous behavior

2. Behavior that causes the highest level of risk for future problems

3. Behavior that is most stressful for the parents

4. Behavior that is most stressful for the child

5. Behaviors that most likely interfere with the parent-child relationship

6. The efficacy of treatments available for the target behavior

7. The level of motivation of parents to participate in intervention designed to ameliorate a treatment target

8. The level of motivation of the child to participate in intervention designed to ameliorate a treatment target

For example, suppose that data collected during the interview process reveal that a 7-year-old frequently runs out of the house, doesn't listen, won't stay in bed at bedtime, and has difficulty doing homework. Further, the parents report that the most "troubling" behavior on a daily basis is that the child throws himself on to the floor whenever they "insist that something get done." Using the algorithm described above, the primary treatment target would be running out of the house, as this is clearly a dangerous behavior. Next, bedtime might be targeted, as sleep deprivation can cause impairments in daily functioning that will interfere with the child's ability to attend and demonstrate emotional control. As the parents report that tantruming is the most stressful behavior, this might be targeted next. These treatment targets do not necessarily have to be sequentially targeted, though it is advisable to tailor intervention to the skills and motivation of the family. In reality, many of the interventions for ODD and CD will be applicable to all, if not most, of the treatment targets.

REFERENCES

Achenbach, T. M. (1991). *Manual for the Child Behavior Checklist/4–18 and 1991 Profile*. Burlington: University of Vermont, Department of Psychiatry.

American Psychiatric Association. (1994). *Diagnostic and statistical manual of mental disorders* (4th ed.). Washington, DC: Author.

Angold, A., & Fisher, P. W. (1999). Interviewer-based interviews. In D. Shaffer, C. P. Lucas, & J. E. Richters (Eds.), *Diagnostic assessment in child and adolescent psychopathology* (pp. 34–64). New York: Guilford Press.

Ardelt, M., & Day, L. (2002). Parents, siblings, and peers: Close social relationships and adolescent deviance. *Journal of Early Adolescence, 22*, 310–349.

Barkley, R. A., Edwards, G. H., & Robin, A. L. (1999). *Defiant teens: A clinician's manual for assessment and family intervention.* New York: Guilford Press.

Bierman, K. L. (1988). The clinical implications of children's conceptions of social relationships. In S. R Shirk (Ed.), *Cognitive development and child psychotherapy* (pp. 247–272). New York: Plenum Press.

Bierman, K. L., Bruschi, C., Domitrovich, C., Fang, G. Y., Miller-Johnson, S., & the Conduct Problems Prevention Research Group. (2004). Early disruptive behaviors associated with emerging antisocial behavior among girls. In M. Putallaz & K. L. Bierman (Eds.), *Aggression, antisocial behavior, and violence among girls* (pp. 137–161). New York: Guilford Press.

Bloomquist, M. L., & Schnell, S. V. (2002). *Helping children with aggression and conduct problems.* New York: Guilford Press.

Brosnan, R., & Carr, A. (2000). Adolescent conduct problems. In A. Carr (Ed.), *What works with children and adolescents? A critical review of psychological interventions with children, adolescents, and their families* (pp. 131–154). Philadelphia: Brunner-Routledge.

Burke, J. D., Loeber, R., & Birmaher, B. (2002). Oppositional defiant disorder and conduct disorder: A review of the past 10 years, Part II. *Journal of the American Academy of Child & Adolescent Psychiatry. 41*, 1275–1293.

Caspi, A., & Moffitt, T. E. (1995). The continuity of maladaptive behavior: From description to understanding in the study of antisocial behavior. In D. Cicchetti & D. J. Cohen (Eds.), *Developmental psychopathology: Vol. 2. Risk, disorder, and adaptation* (pp. 472–511). Oxford, UK: John Wiley & Sons.

Conners, C. K. (2000). *Conners' Rating Scales–Revised technical manual.* North Tonawanda, NY: Multi Health Systems.

Connor, D. F. (2002). *Aggression and antisocial behavior in children and adolescents: Research and treatment.* New York: Guilford Press.

Costello, E. J. (1990). Child psychiatric epidemiology: Implications for clinical research and practice. In B. B. Lahey & A. E. Kazdin (Eds.), *Advances in clinical child psychology* (Vol. 13, pp., 53–90). New York: Plenum Press.

Dishion, T. J., French, D. C., & Patterson, G. R. (1995). The development and ecology of antisocial behavior. In D. Cicchetti & D. J. Cohen (Eds.), *Developmental psychopathology: Vol. 2. Risk, disorder, and adaptation* (pp. 421–471). Oxford, UK: John Wiley & Sons.

Edgette, J. S. (2002). *Candor, connection, and enterprise in adolescent therapy.* New York: Norton.

Eyberg, S. M., & Pincus, D. (1999). *Eyberg Child Behavior Inventory and Sutter-Eyberg Student Behavior Inventory-Revised: Professional manual.* Odessa, FL: Psychological Assessment Resources.

Eyberg, S. M., & Robinson, E. A. (1983). Conduct problem behavior: Standardization of a behavioral rating scale with adolescents. *Journal of Clinical Child Psychology, 12,* 347–354.

Frick, P. J. (1998). *Conduct disorders and severe antisocial behavior.* New York: Plenum Press.

Frick, P. J., Lahey, B. B., Applegate, B., Kerdyck, L., Ollendick, T., Hynd, G., et al. (1994). *DSM-IV* field trials for the disruptive behavior disorders: Symptom utility estimates. *Journal of the American Academy of Child & Adolescent Psychiatry. 33,* 529–539.

Friman, P., Handwerk, M., Smith, G., Larzere, R., Lucas, C., & Shaffer, D. (2000). External validation of conduct and oppositional defiant disorders by the NIMH Diagnostic Interview Schedule for Children. *Journal of Abnormal Child Psychology, 28,* 277–286.

Garb, H. N. (1998). *Studying the clinician: Judgment research and psychological assessment.* Washington, DC: American Psychological Association.

Goodman, R. (1997). The Strengths and Difficulties Questionnaire: A research note. *Journal of Child Psychology and Psychiatry, 38,* 581–586.

Grunbaum, J., Kahn, L., Kinchen, S., Ross, J., Hawkin, J., Lowrey, R., et al. (2004). *Youth Risk Behavior Surveillance-United States, 2003.* Atlanta, GA: Centers for Disease Control.

Handwerk, M. L., Field, C., & Friman, P. C. (2000). The iatrogenic effects of group interventions: Premature extrapolations. *Journal of Behavioral Education, 10,* 223–238.

Handwerk, M., Larzelere, R., Soper, S., & Friman, P. (1999). Parent and child discrepancies in reporting behavior problems in three out-of-home placements. *Psychological Assessment, 11,* 14–23.

Haynes, S. N., & O'Brien, W. H. (2000). *Principles and practice of behavioral assessment.* New York: Kluwer Academic/Plenum.

Hinshaw, S. P., & Anderson, C. A. (1996). Conduct and oppositional defiant disorders. In E. J. Mash & R. A. Barkley (Eds.), *Child psychopathology* (pp. 113–149). New York: Guilford Press.

Hinshaw, S. P., & Nigg, J. T. (1999). Behavior rating scales in the assessment of disruptive behavior problems in childhood. In D. Shaffer, C. P. Lucas, & J. E. Richters (Eds.), *Diagnostic assessment in child and adolescent psychopathology* (pp. 91–126). New York: Guilford Press.

Ho, M. K. (1992). *Minority children and adolescents in therapy.* Newbury Park, CA: Sage.

Hogan, A. E. (1998). Cognitive functioning in children with oppositional defiant disorder and conduct disorder. In H. C. Quay & A. E. Hogan (Eds.), *Handbook of disruptive behavior disorders* (pp. 317–335). New York: Kluwer Academic/Plenum.

Jensen, A. L., & Weisz, J. R. (2002). Assessing match and mismatch between practitioner-generated and standardized interview-generated diagnoses for clinic-referred children and adolescents. *Journal of Consulting and Clinical Psychology, 70,* 158–168.

Jewell, J., Handwerk, M., Almquist, J., & Lucas, C. (2004). Comparing the validity of clinician-generated diagnosis of conduct disorder to the Diagnostic Interview Schedule for Children. *Journal of Clinical Child and Adolescent Psychology, 33,* 536–546.

Kaufman, J., Birmaher, B., Brent, D., Rao, U., Flynn, C., Moreci, P., et al. (1997), Schedule for Affective Disorders and Schizophrenia for School-Age Children-Present and Lifetime version (K-SADS-PL): Initial reliability and validity data. *Journal of the American Academy of Child & Adolescent Psychiatry, 36,* 980–988.

Kazdin, A. E. (1995). *Conduct disorders in childhood and adolescence* (2nd ed.). Thousand Oaks, CA: Sage.

Lahey, B. B., & Loeber, R. (1994). Framework for a developmental model of oppositional defiant disorder and conduct disorder. In D. K. Routh (Ed.), *Disruptive behavior disorders in childhood* (pp. 139–180). New York: Plenum Press.

Lahey, B. B., Loeber, R., Frick, P. J., Quay, H. C., & Grimm, J. (1992). Oppositional defiant and conduct disorders: Issues to be resolved for *DSM-IV. Journal of the American Academy of Child & Adolescent Psychiatry, 31,* 539–546.

Lahey, B. B., Loeber, R., Hart, E., Frick, P. J., Applegate, B., Zhang, Q., Green, S. M., & Russo, M. F. (1995). Four-year longitudinal study of conduct disorder in boys: Patterns and predictors of persistence. *Journal of Abnormal Psychology, 104,* 83–93.

Lahey, B. B., Miller, R., Gordon, R. A., & Riley, A.W. (1999). Developmental epidemiology of the disruptive behavior disorders. In H. C. Quay & A. E. Hogan (Eds.), *Handbook of disruptive behavior disorders* (pp. 23–48). New York: Kluwer Academic/Plenum.

Lock, J., & Strauss, G. D. (1994). Psychiatric hospitalization of adolescents for conduct disorder. *Hospital & Community Psychiatry, 45,* 925–928.

Loeber, R., Green, S. M., & Lahey, B. B. (1990). Mental health professionals' perception of the utility of children, mothers, and teachers as informants on childhood psychopathology. *Journal of Clinical Child Psychology, 19,* 136–143.

Loeber, R., & Keenan, K. (1994). Interaction between conduct disorder and its comorbid conditions: Effects of age and gender. *Clinical Psychology Review, 14,* 497–523.

Loeber, R., Lahey, B. B., & Thomas, C. (1991). Diagnostic conundrum of oppositional defiant disorder and conduct disorder. *Journal of Abnormal Psychology, 100,* 379–390.

Lynam, D. (1996). Early identification of chronic offenders: Who is the fledgling psychopath? *Psychological Bulletin, 120,* 209–234.

McConaughy, S. H. (2005). *Clinical interviews for children and adolescents: Assessment to intervention.* New York: Guilford Press.

McGee, R., & Williams, S. (1999). Environmental risk factors in oppositional-defiant disorder and conduct disorder. In H. C. Quay & A. E. Hogan (Eds.), *Handbook of disruptive behavior disorders* (pp. 419–440). New York: Kluwer Academic/Plenum.

McMahon, R. J., & Estes, A. M. (1997). Conduct problems. In E. J. Mash & L. G. Terdal (Eds.), *Assessment of childhood disorders* (3rd ed., pp. 130–193). New York: Guilford Press.

McMahon, R. J., & Forehand, R. (1988). Conduct disorders. In E. J. Mash & L. G. Terdal (Eds.), *Behavioral assessment of childhood disorders* (2nd ed., pp. 105–153). New York: Guilford Press.

McMahon, R. J., & Forehand, R. L. (2003). *Helping the noncompliant child: Family-based treatment for oppositional behavior* (2nd ed.). New York: Guilford Press.

Merrell, K. W. (2003). *Behavioral, social, and emotional assessment of children and adolescents.* Mahwah, NJ: Lawrence Erlbaum.

Moffitt, T. E. (1993). The neuropsychology of conduct disorder. *Development and Psychopathology, 5,* 135–151.

Molina, B. S. G., Smith, B. H., & Pelham, W. E. (1999). Interactive effects of attention deficit hyperactivity disorder and conduct disorder on early adolescent substance use. *Psychology of Addictive Behaviors, 13,* 348–358.

Morrison, J. (1995). *The first interview: Revised for DSM-IV.* New York: Guilford Press.

Mullis, F. (2002). How was your day? Using questions about the family's daily routine. In R. E. Watts & J. Carlson (Eds.), *Techniques in marriage and family counseling* (Vol. 2., pp. 133–138). Alexandria, VA: American Counseling Association.

Parker, J. G., & Asher, S. R. (1987). Peer relations and later personal adjustment: Are low-accepted children at risk? *Psychological Bulletin, 102,* 357–389.

Patterson, G. R. (1982). *Coercive family process: A social learning approach* (Vol. 3). Eugene, OR: Castalia.

Polaha, J., Larzelere, R. E., Shapiro, S. K., & Pettit, G. S. (2004). Physical discipline and child behavior problems: A study of ethnic group differences. *Parenting: Science and Practice, 4,* 339–360.

Quay, H. C. (1999). Classification of the disruptive behavior disorders. In H. C. Quay & A. E. Hogan (Eds.), *Handbook of disruptive behavior disorders* (pp. 3–21). New York: Kluwer Academic/Plenum.

Reich, W., & Earls, F. (1987). Rules for making psychiatric diagnoses in children on the basis of multiple sources of information: Preliminary strategies. *Journal of Abnormal Child Psychology, 15,* 601–616.

Reynolds, C. R., & Kamphaus, R. W. (2002). *A clinician's guide to the BASC.* New York: Guilford Press.

Robin, A. L., & Foster, S. L. (1989). *Negotiating parent-adolescent conflict.* New York: Guilford Press.

Robins, L. N. (1978). Sturdy childhood predictors of adult antisocial behaviour: Replications from longitudinal studies. *Psychological Medicine, 8,* 611–622.

Rogers, R. (1995). *Diagnostic and structured interviewing: A handbook for psychologists.* Odessa, FL: Psychological Assessment Resources.

Rutter, M., Giller, H., & Hagell, A. (1998). *Antisocial behavior by young people.* New York: Cambridge University Press.

Sattler, J. M. (1998). *Clinical and forensic interviewing of children and families.* San Diego, CA: Author.

Shaffer, D., Fisher, P. W., & Lucas, C. P. (1999). Respondent-based interviews. In D. Shaffer, C. P. Lucas, &

J. E. Richters (Eds.), *Diagnostic assessment in child and adolescent psychopathology* (pp. 3–33). New York: Guilford Press.

Shaffer, D., Fisher, P., Lucas, C., Dulcan, M., & Schwab-Stone, M. (2000). NIMH Diagnostic Interview Schedule for Children Version IV (NIMH DISC-IV): Description, differences from previous versions, and reliability of some common diagnoses. *Journal of the American Academy of Child & Adolescent Psychiatry, 39,* 28–38.

Sleator, E., & Ullmann, R. (1981). Can the physician diagnose hyperactivity in the office? *Pediatrics, 1,* 13–17.

Snyder, J. J. (1995). Coercion: A two-level theory of antisocial behavior. In W. O'Donohue & L. Krasner (Eds.), *Theories of behavior therapy: Exploring behavior change* (pp. 313–348). Washington, DC: American Psychological Association.

Stouthamer-Loeber, M., Loeber, R., Wei, E., Farrington, D. P., & Wikstrom, P. H. (2002). Risk and promotive effects in the explanation of persistent serious delinquency in boys. *Journal of Consulting and Clinical Psychology, 70,* 111–123.

Waldman, I. D., & Lilienfeld, S. O. (1991). Diagnostic efficiency of symptoms for oppositional defiant disorder and attention-deficit hyperactivity disorder. *Journal of Consulting and Clinical Psychology, 59,* 732–738.

Waschbusch, D. A. (2002). A meta-analytic examination of comorbid hyperactive-impulsive-attention problems and conduct problems. *Psychological Bulletin, 128,* 118–150.

Watkins, C. E., Campbell, V. L., Nieberding, R., & Hallmark, R. (1995). Contemporary practice of psychological assessment by clinical psychologists. *Professional Psychology: Research and Practice, 26,* 54–60.

Webster-Stratton, C. (1996). Early-onset conduct problems: Does gender make a difference? *Journal of Consulting and Clinical Psychology, 64,* 540–551.

Whipple, E. E., & Richey, C. A. (1997). Crossing the line from physical discipline to child abuse: How much is too much? *Child Abuse & Neglect, 21,* 431–444.

Wozniak, J., Biederman, J., Kwon, A., Mick, E., Faraone, S., Orlovsky, K., et al. (2005). How cardinal are cardinal symptoms in pediatric bipolar disorder? An examination of clinical correlates. *Biological Psychiatry, 58,* 583–588.

Youngstrom, E. A., Findling, R. L., & Feeny, N. (2004). Assessment of bipolar spectrum disorders in children and adolescents. In S. L. Johnson & R. L. Leahy (Eds.), *Psychological treatment of bipolar disorder* (pp. 58–82). New York: Guilford Press.

Zoccolillo, M. (1992). Co-occurrence of conduct disorder and its adult outcomes with depressive and anxiety disorders: A review. *Journal of the American Academy of Child & Adolescent Psychiatry, 31,* 547–556.

Zoccolillo, M. (1993). Gender and the development of conduct disorder. *Development and Psychopathology, 5,* 65–78.

Zoccolillo, M., Pickles, A., Quinton, D., & Rutter, M. (1992). The outcome of childhood conduct disorder: Implications for defining adult personality disorder and conduct disorder. *Psychological Medicine, 22,* 971–986.

15

LEARNING, MOTOR, AND COMMUNICATION DISORDERS

BENSON SCHAEFFER

Interviewing children and adolescents is both a craft and an art, a craft in the sense of techniques and an art in the sense of having an intuitive appreciation of the individual young person that allows the interviewer to ask questions in a way that elicits truly important information. In this chapter, I discuss the craft of interviewing young people and hope that I also capture and convey some of the art. Specifically, I discuss interviewing children and adolescents with learning, motor, and communication disorders in the context of a comprehensive evaluation, often termed *multiaxial* or *multimethod*, of their problems for the purpose of treatment planning and referral. The goal is to interview the young persons in a manner that yields information that helps inform treatment. I begin with a brief discussion of the disorders (from the viewpoint of diagnostic labels rather than the disorder's psychological structure) that I suspect most readers will already be very familiar with and perhaps not overly interested in, but with which I cannot dispense, then move on to the heart of chapter, actually interviewing children and adolescents with learning, motor, and communication disorders.

The focus of the chapter will be on elementary- and middle-school-age children and adolescents. As I write about interviewing children,

I will consistently try to maintain the larger purpose, treatment planning, as my interpretive framework, keeping in mind that the diagnosis is not the child and that one or more interviews with a child does not a comprehensive evaluation make. The material that follows, therefore, should be viewed as a set of suggestions and guidelines for interviewing children for the larger purpose of treatment planning and in the context of the child's unique individuality. Interviews are important components of the assessment process but must be interpreted in the light of all of the other data gathered. Hughes and Baker (1990), McConaughy (2005), Morrison and Anders (1999), and Zwiers and Morrissette (1999) discuss treatment-relevant, developmentally and situationally appropriate interviewing of children and adolescents and their parents; this chapter is informed by the ideas and material they present in their books.

DESCRIPTION OF THE DISORDERS

Learning, motor, and communication disorders in children and adolescents can be described in a variety of ways. The three most useful for psychologists are those given by the *Diagnostic and Statistical Manual of Mental Disorders*

(DSM-IV-TR) of the American Psychiatric Association (APA, 2000); the 2004 reauthorization of the Individuals with Disabilities Education Act (IDEA) (2005); and the 1990 Americans with Disabilities Act (ADA). The *DSM-IV-TR* presents diagnoses and the criteria for making them for psychologists, social workers, counselors, and psychiatrists in private practice; IDEA and ADA guide the determination of special education eligibility categories. These are the educational equivalents of *DSM-IV-TR* diagnoses and relate to the instruction and treatment provided by special educators, school psychologists, and counselors in the context of individual educational plans (IEPs) and educational support plans. The former are the central IDEA structure; the latter are the central ADA structure.

In the *DSM-IV-TR*, the disorders I will be considering in this chapter are labeled as follows:

1. Learning Disorders
   a. Reading Disorder (315.00)
   b. Mathematics Disorder (315.1)
   c. Disorder of Written Expression (315.2)
   d. Learning Disorder NOS (315.9)

2. Motor Disorder: Developmental Coordination Disorder (315.4)

3. Communication Disorders
   a. Expressive Language Disorder (315.31)
   b. Mixed Receptive-Expressive Language Disorder (315.31)
   c. Phonological Disorder (315.39)
   d. Stuttering (307.0)
   e. Communication Disorder NOS (307.9)

For IDEA and ADA, the disorders, known as *eligibility categories,* are Specific Learning Disability, which could be in reading, mathematics, or written language (the learning part), and Speech and Language Impairment (the communication part). Other problems are captured under the eligibility category Other Health Impaired, for attention deficits in particular, and the category Traumatic Brain Injury. There is not an eligibility category that corresponds specifically to a Developmental Coordination Disorder, though of course educators do deal with fine motor skill deficits, which impact writing, and gross motor skill deficits, which impact playground and sports activities. Occupational therapy services are provided for remediation of the fine motor skill deficits, and adaptive physical education and physical therapy are provided for remediation of the gross motor skill deficits. There is the IDEA eligibility category Orthopedic Impairment, but it is usually reserved for congenital and acquired physical conditions and problems more severe than those that are usually described as a Developmental Coordination Disorder, particularly cerebral palsy, although the less severe end of the Orthopedic Impairment and the more severe end of Developmental Coordination Disorder do overlap.

The *DSM-IV-TR* disorders that correspond to particular IDEA/ADA eligibility categories should be reasonably clear from the above listings. In the body of most of the chapter, I will therefore use *DSM-IV-TR* terminology, with the exception of the section on "Selection of Treatment Targets and Referral," where I will also employ IDEA language. This is because the treatment of children's and adolescents' learning, motor, and communication problems is provided not only by mental psychologists and other mental health professionals in private practice but also at school, by special educators, school psychologists, counselors, occupational therapists, and speech-language therapists, as specified in IEPs (IDEA) and educational support plans (ADA).

Further, I would also note that the above *DSM-IV-TR* disorders and IDEA/ADA eligibility categories are summary rather than fine-grained descriptions of the problems to which they relate. Each child's and each adolescent's problem has its own unique sources and structure, in terms of brain localization and function and the child's history. This generates unique patterns of information processing and social-emotional and temperamental responsivity. What the above means is that thorough treatment and educational planning must be based on a comprehensive, individualized assessment of the child's or adolescent's cognitive-developmental, social-emotional, and neurological strengths and weaknesses, not just the disorder or eligibility category, a summary descriptor of problems, or the results of one or more interviews with the child.

INTERVIEWING STRATEGIES

There is no single interviewing strategy appropriate for all children and all adolescents. The differences in age, cognitive levels, social-emotional maturity, and motor skills between first graders in elementary school and eighth graders in middle school make this obvious, and other considerations come into play as well. In this section, I discuss interviewing strategies; in the next, I take up more specific obstacles and solutions.

Perhaps the first things to note about interviewing are that (a) the way the interviewer structures the conversation with the child or adolescent will depend on the purpose for conducting the interview and that (b) the interview will likely have more than one goal or purpose. The central purpose will be treatment planning, but under this heading there may well be a number of subpurposes. These could include establishing, corroborating, and/or confirming a specific diagnosis; exploring and determining the impact of the problems on the young person's life; generating an overall picture of the young person's cognitive and social-emotional status and life situation; gaining an image of the young person's sense of self; and, more generally, entering vicariously into the young person's mind and heart with the goal of seeing the world from his of her point of view (Ginsburg, 1997).

Further, we cannot forget about the properties of the interviewer, so to speak. All clinicians who work with children and adolescents bring to each interview their histories of clinical experience and training and their own personal social-emotional and cognitive styles and characteristics. What this means is that each interviewer is a unique interviewing instrument and, as such, has a unique impact on the child or adolescent being interviewed. This confers either benefits, insofar as the clinician's history has well prepared him or her to interview the specific individual, or drawbacks, such that there is a lack of experience with the particular problem the clinician is asked to address or a lack of personal "clicking" with the young person being interviewed. I mention the almost necessarily multipurpose nature of interviews and the properties of the interviewer because their possible impact must be considered if the interviewer is to be able to rule out their possible negative effects, particularly narrowness of vision and the neglect of treatment possibilities, and, by ruling out such biases, to optimize treatment planning.

Structure: How Much?

First and foremost related to interviewing strategies, we must consider whether and to what degree the interview is structured. Most clinicians over time develop ways of interviewing children and adolescents that can be described as at least somewhat structured or semistructured. They tend to ask a relatively fixed set of questions or choose from a predetermined population questions that their clinical experience has led them to believe will generate valuable information, and to ask the questions in a relatively fixed order. Interviews can be more structured or less structured than this, however.

The clinical and research literature discusses a number of structured clinical interviews for children and adolescents designed to improve the reliability of *DSM-IV* diagnoses for epidemiological research, including the Diagnostic Interview for Children and Adolescents-Revised (DICA-R) (Reich, Shayka, & Taibleson, 1992); the NIMH Diagnostic Interview Schedule for Children (DISC-IV) (Shaffer, Fisher, Lucas, Dulcan, & Schwab-Stone, 2000); the Interview Schedule for children and adolescents (ISCA) (Sherrill & Kovacs, 2000); the Child Assessment Schedule (CAS) (Hodges, Kline, Stern, Cytryn, & McKnew, 1982); and the Schedule for Affective Disorders and Schizophrenia for School-Age Children (K-SADS) (McConaughy, 1996). Their length and primary focus on obtaining *DSM-IV* diagnoses (rather than treatment planning and special education eligibility) and their research (rather than clinical) emphasis, however, make them less than optimal for everyday clinical work.

By contrast, McConaughy and Achenbach (1996) discuss a semistructured interview for children and adolescents aged 6 to 18 and the Structured Clinical Interview for Children and Adolescents (SCICA), dealing primarily with data on the 6- to 12-year-old age group, which is more useful to the clinician; and McConaughy (1996) expands the consideration to include interviews of parents and teachers as well. The SCICA "contains open-ended questions and tasks covering eight broad areas: (a) activities, school, job; (b) friends; (c) family relations; (d) fantasies; (e) self-perception, feelings; (f) parent/teacher-reported problems; (g) achievement tests; and (h) screen for fine and gross motor abnormalities" (McConaughy, 1996, pp. 192, 193). As the list illustrates, the interview goes beyond interview data to problems reported by the adults in the child's or adolescent's life, measures of academic skills, and indices of motor function. This is important to note: The assessor must utilize more than interview data to assess and plan for the treatment of children's and adolescents' problems. Also important to note is the absence from the list of a set of questions specifically regarding information children and adolescents might be capable of providing regarding their learning, motor, and communication disorders.

I will take up the topic of what information young people are able to provide in an interview in the next section but wish to emphasize here that I have not found published structured sets of questions for clinicians to ask children and adolescents regarding their problems in the three domains addressed in this chapter (except for the "Reading Comprehension Interview," which is geared to obtaining students' perceptions of specific classroom reading tasks and therefore is not likely of more general clinical utility; Wilcoxin, Bosky, Yokum, & Alverman, 1984). This does not mean that clinicians do not ask young people such questions, only that the research literature does not as yet appear to provide interviewers with reliable tools of demonstrated validity for doing so.

McConaughy's and Achenbach's (1996) validation study of the SCICA, as indicated by the responses of children and adolescents to the interview questions, yielded significantly higher problem scores for learning-disabled children than for nonreferred children on the following factors: anxious/depressed, attention problems, overall internalizing and externalizing problems, total observations (of difficulties), and total self-reports (of difficulties). What this tells us is that children and adolescents with learning disabilities are aware of their problems, have strong negative feelings about them, and may have comorbid anxiety problems, depressive feelings, and attention difficulties. In some instances, these symptoms meet the criteria for a formal diagnosis of anxiety disorder-not otherwise specified (AD-NOS) or another anxiety diagnosis, dysthymic disorder or another depression diagnosis, or one or another variant of attention-deficit/hyperactivity disorder (ADHD).

Other investigators and authors also discuss the use of structured interviews. They conclude for the most part that semistructured interviews are more effective in eliciting information from children and adolescents than either highly structured or unstructured interviews. Calinoiu and McClellan (2004), for example, claim that semistructured interviews, which they call "interviewer-based tools," "allow clinical interpretation of responses as well as the incorporation of other sources of information, thereby making them more relevant for clinicians" than highly structured, what they call "respondent-based, young-person-led" measures (p. 88). And, according to Sternberg, Lamb, Orbach, and Esplin (2001), "protocol-guided interviews (in forensic settings) elicited more information using open-ended prompts and less information using option-posing and suggestive questions than did standard (more highly structured) interviews" (p. 997).

Overall, therefore, I would recommend, and the research and clinical literature supports, the use of semistructured rather than highly structured, symptom-specific interviews. It is a good idea to interview the parents of children and adolescents with learning, motor, and communication disorders before interviewing the young people. This is because parents usually have broader perspectives on their sons' and daughters' problems and life situations than do the children and adolescents themselves. Parents often bring up events, issues, and problems their sons and daughters are embarrassed about or would not think to mention. The information they provide, therefore, can help the clinician formulate questions to ask the young person or modify the questions he or she usually asks.

Whether or not to interview teachers and other adults in young people's lives, such as school counselors, therapists, and so on, before interviewing the young people themselves is less easy to decide. On one hand, they, like parents, may be able to provide information that could help the clinician formulate interview questions; on the other hand, the clinician may wish to have a sense of who the child or adolescent is, and enough information about the individual, to be able to know what questions to ask teachers and other adults involved in the young person's life.

Strategies

First of all, it is important that children or adolescents feel comfortable enough with and personally accepted, respected, and understood by interviewers to talk openly with them. Actively taking steps to build the young person's comfort in the interview situation and to establish rapport is therefore extremely important. Over time, experienced clinicians usually develop ways of building relationships with young people that fit with their (the clinicians') personal styles and promote emotional and informational openness. There is no guarantee, though, that the young person and the clinician will "click." The goal, however, is not a perfect match, but only that degree of social-emotional connectedness sufficient to allow young people to answer questions freely, elaborate on answers when asked to, and, it is hoped, spontaneously offer potentially treatment-relevant information about their world.

Perhaps the best way to increase the likelihood that young people will communicate freely and openly is for interviewers to take time to be with and talk with children or adolescents about personal interests and experiences before beginning to ask questions related to their problems, which most young people tend in general to be loathe to discuss. Taking time to be with and talk to young people means just that: taking time, waiting, not rushing; asking them about what is happening in their lives; allowing them to look around at the clinician's office if they wish, briefly examine the toys there (not so many that a child is distracted or an adolescent feels he or she is in a place for younger children), or sit quietly for a brief period, whatever the young person needs to do to become comfortable with the interviewer. This would optimally also include the clinician making contact with the young person at a nonverbal level, via smiles, shared eye contact, and conversation about things that interest the young person, prior to beginning to address the problems that will be the focus of the assessment. Also, the interviewer may wish to defer to the latter portion of the interview, or even to a second interview session, asking questions that may be difficult or uncomfortable for the young person to answer.

Only after taking the time to establish a positive relationship with the child or adolescent, so that both the young person and the clinician are comfortable in the situation, ought the interviewer to begin asking problem-related questions. And when the young person answers, the clinician would do well to encourage expatiation and elaboration, even if the information thus elicited is not always directly to the point. The interviewer will want not only to obtain the specific information needed to establish a precise diagnosis and plan treatment but also to get a sense of the child's life situation, both in relation to and independent of personal problems. Only when clinicians have such an understanding will they be able to plan treatment procedures that are likely to be accepted by children or adolescents and made part of their lives, and to be carried out by their parents and educators and other professionals.

Like most experienced psychologists, I use a semistructured set of sequenced questions in interviewing children and adolescents and interview young people after I have interviewed their parents. Below, I outline those questions (and later illustrate their use in the section describing a specific case). It is not my intent in presenting these questions to imply that others ought to use exactly the same ones, but only to suggest that establishing a sequenced set of questions is usually a good idea, for this will help clinicians avoid missing information about domains of function relevant to the problems being assessed. Further, if clinicians use such a semistructured interview format and the format fits with their personal styles, they will then be able to use themselves as reliable interview instruments, clearly distinguishing themselves from the young people's problems.

The questions I ask, the answers to which I often ask the child or adolescent to elaborate on, are as follows (in the order I generally use):

1. What do you like, really like, to do?

2. What don't you like to do, really not like to do, not enjoy doing at all?

3. When you grow up, after you finish school, what would you like to be, what job or career would you like to have?

4. If I were a magic genie, which of course I'm not, and I could give you three magic wishes, what would you wish for?

5. In school, what's the best part for you, the part of school you like best? Why?

6. What's the worst part of school for you, the part you like least? Why?

7. We all do some things well, what do you think you're best at doing?

8. We all have things that are problems for us, things we don't do well, or worry about, or

get angry about, or are just difficult for us. What problems do you have?

9. Subquestions following #8, to help the young person elaborate and be more specific, for all but the youngest children (Nancy Lamb, PhD, personal communication, May 5, 2005): What do you think would make things better? What do you need your teacher to do to help? What do you want your parents to do to make things better? What would you do to make things better?

I would note here, too, that I wait for the child or adolescent to respond, at his or her own pace, after asking a question, both to give the young person time to process the information in the question and find out about his or her style of responding. And, as noted earlier, I ask for elaboration, particularly of sparse responses (which is not always forthcoming) and watch for nonverbal cues that might give me information about the young person's deeper or hidden feelings about the topic. Further, when asking for elaboration of a reply, I try not to lead the child or adolescent. First, I prompt with open-ended questions and only gradually hone in on specifics that are important to me but which the young person may not mention. Last, I have also learned from clinician friends that it is often useful to help young people answer Question #8 by asking additional subquestions that help them elaborate and provide me with more specific and personalized information. In the following section, I more specifically consider the impact of young people's difficulties on the manner in and adequacy with which they are likely to answer questions.

Interviewing Obstacles and Solutions

A variety of specific obstacles related to children's and adolescent's learning, motor, and communication problems, and other problems as well, may interfere with interviewing or compromise information gathering during an interview. The obstacles I discuss here, for which I will suggest possible solutions, include the following, in four separable categories:

1. *Cognitive:* comprehension and response difficulties deriving from specific communication problems, low cognitive level,

young people's inability to reflect on and introspect about their information processing, actions and/or feelings, attention difficulties and hyperactivity

2. *Social-Emotional:* fear, anxiety, shyness, and concern about exposing oneself to criticism, censure, or ridicule; worries about betraying parents; poor self-concept; sullenness and anger, which often mask emotional insecurity; and cultural difference

3. *Trauma Related:* the aftereffects of trauma, abuse, in utero exposure to drugs and alcohol, and brain injury (which also produce cognitive obstacles)

4. *Suggestibility and Social Desirability Bias:* the tendency to answer in ways that the interviewer appears to suggest or want or that the interviewee feels is the socially approved fashion (related to social-emotional obstacles listed above)

Cognitive Obstacles and Solutions

The primary cognitive obstacles to interviewing children and adolescents relate to communication and speech/language difficulties and are often associated with low cognitive level. Children and adolescents with learning, motor, and communication disorders often have such problems. These difficulties could include one or more of several problems: Young people may poorly comprehend the questions asked; they may process spoken language very slowly; they may have difficulties processing amounts of spoken language that exceed immediate memory span and difficulties putting thoughts into words; they may produce utterances of limited intelligibility; and they may have weak English language skills because English is a second language. The negative effects of these difficulties can be minimized, though not eliminated, by the use of techniques that make it easier for the child or adolescent to understand, respond to, and elaborate on answers to questions. The list below derives from my own clinical experience and the literature on interviewing children and adolescents (particularly McConaughy, 1996 and 2005, who in this context also discusses the Youth Self-Report Form of the Child Behavior Checklist). For children with language and communication difficulties, it is important for the interviewer to follow guidelines that minimize the effects of the problems listed above. The clinician can do so by following the guidelines listed below:

- Speak slowly and distinctly and loudly enough to facilitate comprehension but not so loudly as to be unpleasant or off-putting.

- Ask only one question at a time and avoid embedding subquestions within larger questions, to avoid overwhelming the child's or adolescent's limited language-processing capacity.

- Allow sufficient time for the young person to process and respond to the question; do not assume noncomprehension because he or she does not respond immediately.

- Be ready for an answer produced after a delay; although the clinician has already moved on to another question or topic, a child or adolescent with a language-processing difficulty may keep thinking about and formulating an answer to the previous question for a period of time.

- Ask important questions several times and/or in a number of different formats if the young person does not respond, so that the child has the opportunity to consolidate the question in memory well enough to answer it and experience a variety of ways to think about and respond to it.

- In a related vein, ask young people to elaborate, paraphrase, or expand on their answers if it is not clear what they mean, to make sure to obtain enough information to understand the answer well, both specifically and in the larger context of the child's life at home and at school.

- Avoid yes/no questions, for such questions tend to foreclose discussion and elaboration and allow the shy, stubborn, or sullen young person to exercise influence or engage in a power struggle by refusing to answer.

- Follow the child's or adolescent's lead in the conversation, to allow a natural path of associations to unearth potentially important information that may prompt further questions.

- Use the young person's terms and language and people's names instead of pronouns, to maintain a personally relevant and comprehensible context for the conversation and clarity regarding reference.

- Avoid judgmental comments, rhetorical questions, "why" questions, and interpretations of what the young person says, for these ways of reacting tend to close off communication.

- Intersperse nonverbal activities among questions, a bit of lightness and play, and avoid responding to every answer with another question, to keep the interview sufficiently lighthearted and prevent communicative stress, boredom, or too high a level of seriousness from limiting or closing off communication.

- Allow the young person who seems to need to keep his hands busy or is fidgety to hold and "fiddle with" a small toy or other object during the conversation. This will help the young person remain calm and likely improve his or her ability to focus on the questions.

The above list of positive and negative recommendations may seem too long for any interviewer, however capable, to keep in mind, but don't worry: The clinician who follows a subset of the suggestions will almost automatically tend to follow the others as well, because they are mutually supportive, tend to entrain one another, and likely fit in with what he or she has learned over the years clinically.

In addition to communication-related difficulties, attention problems and hyperactivity can also be obstacles to interviewing. The recommendations outlined above for dealing with communication difficulties are, in general, good ways of reducing these problems as well, especially when they are related to low cognitive level. And for reducing the effects of inability to introspect, that is, metacognitive self-monitoring difficulties, the interviewer may also wish to introduce miniature versions of the young person's problems before asking about them. This can be accomplished, for example, by the interviewer asking the child or adolescent with reading problems to read parts of a simple book aloud prior to discussing his or her problems in learning to read or doing schoolwork that entails reading; asking the young person with arithmetic problems to play a brief board game that involves counting; or asking the youngster with fine motor skills difficulties to play with Legos (a construction block toy). Such activities may make it easier for the young person to introspect about personal problems and, in addition, introduce interesting variety into the interview and give the clinician a sense of the impact of the young person's problems in nonschool play settings.

Last, when interviewing a child or adolescent with attention difficulties who may also be hyperactive, the clinician would do well to remove toys and objects on desks, tables, and shelves from the office or interview room that might distract the young person from the questions being asked. The interviewer would also do well to try to make certain he or she has the young person's attention before asking a question. This can be accomplished by catching the child's or adolescent's eye before speaking, and addressing the youngster by name when querying. Also, the clinician can sit close enough to the young person to be directly in his or her line of sight (though of course not so close as to invade the youngster's personal space).

Social-Emotional Obstacles and Solutions

More than cognitive obstacles, social-emotional obstacles to communicative openness interfere with and compromise the results of interviews of children and adolescents. A young person who is emotionally closed in the interview setting because he or she feels uncomfortable will not answer questions and provide the clinician with the necessary information. Even when the young people do not suffer from the sorts of cognitive difficulties that interfere with understanding questions and conversation (as outlined above), if they feel discomfort or unease, they will function as if there were comprehension and communication difficulties, and solely cognitive solutions (as outlined above) are unlikely to solve the problems. Ways of minimizing social-emotional obstacles have been carefully discussed in the literature on interviewing abused and traumatized children and adolescents, especially forensically (Hynan, 1999; Mordock, 2001; Sternberg et al., 2001; Zwiers & Morrissette, 1999), and my recommendations draw on this work.

There are a variety of ways the interviewer can work to minimize the possible negative effects of troubling emotions that reduce or close off communicative openness, such as fear; anxiety; shyness; concern about exposure of oneself to criticism, censure, or ridicule; worries about betraying parents; poor self-concept; and anger and sullenness. To minimize the negative effects of troubling emotions, the clinician would do well to follow the recommendations listed below:

- Arrange for more than one interview session, to give the child or adolescent the opportunity to become familiar with and warm up to the clinician.

- Briefly talk with the young person about what will take place in the interview.

- Describe what sorts of questions will be asked and explain to the young person that it is permissible to ask the clinician to clarify a query or terms he or she does not understand, that it is permissible to say "I don't know" or "I can't remember" if such is the case (something I routinely do, though very few young people take me up on it), and that it is also permissible to ask questions of the interviewer.

- Briefly talk over confidentiality issues, namely, that details the young person reveals about his or her life will be kept confidential where appropriate, with the exception of comments about self-harm, harming others, or engaging in illegal behavior. Even young children are put at ease by a brief discussion, at a level they can understand, of confidentiality issues, because such discussions create a stronger sense of personal freedom to respond or not.

- Carefully follow those guidelines related to cognitive obstacles that also relate to social-emotional obstacles, particularly following the young person's lead in conversation and avoiding judgmental comments and interpretations.

Trauma-Related Obstacles and Solutions

A proportion of children and adolescents with learning, motor, and/or communication disorders the clinician interviews are likely to have experienced abuse or other traumas (such as the death of a parent, chronic illness, out-of-home placement), and these traumas may, in fact are likely to, inhibit open communication with the interviewer. To minimize the resulting decline in communicative openness, the clinician would do well to carefully follow the recommendations outlined above for minimizing cognitive and social-emotional obstacles and to constantly keep in mind the child's or adolescent's emotional fragility. Also, as there may be events young people are afraid to tell their parents or an authority figure such as the interviewer about, the clinician querying previously traumatized children or adolescents will want to stress the value of their uniqueness and to strengthen their sense of self and may also wish to revisit confidentiality issues more than once, to help youngsters feel safer talking about emotionally sensitive issues.

Suggestibility- and Social-Desirability-Related Obstacles and Solutions

Children and adolescents often want so much to please clinicians that they say what they think clinicians want to hear rather than what they know to be true, or they say what they think is socially proper and appropriate. The ways to minimize such distorting effects on the interview process and on the information the young person provides are to carefully follow the guidelines outlined above for dealing with social-emotional obstacles, for it is often small-scale social or emotional discomfort in the interview setting that potentiates young people's suggestibility and social desirability tendencies.

Last, two considerations cut across obstacle domains: (1) temperament and (2) pace and rhythm. As each young person has a unique temperament and pace and rhythm of responding to questions, it is important for the clinician to attend to these sources of individuality and carefully adjust to them. This means taking into account the child or adolescent's momentary microemotional state—happy, sad, inhibited, energized, and so on—while asking questions; being sensitive to the youngster's pace of responding; and allowing periods for emotional recuperation between questions when dealing with emotionally sensitive material.

INTERVIEWING PARENTS AND TEACHERS

Parents have much information to offer the clinician about their sons' and daughters' learning,

motor, and communication disorders, and teachers have much information about how the disorders express themselves in the school setting.

Interviewing Parents

As caretakers who live with young people day in and day out, parents have more detailed information than other adults in children's or adolescents' lives about their problems and the problems' impact on all areas of life, a very special database the clinician would do well to mine carefully and an expertise deserving of respect and acceptance. Parents do not typically, however, have the broad comparative perspective on their offsprings' problems and breadth, as do clinicians who have assessed and worked with a wide variety of children and adolescents with similar problems over a span of many years. Therefore, the clinician ought to both diligently gather the valuable information parents have to offer and weigh the meaning of that information carefully. The information parents provide can be of critical importance. Sometimes, though, parents may wish to deny aspects of their sons' and daughters' problems; worry about possible stigmatization they and their children may be subject to upon exposure of these problems; have incomplete or distorted views of the problems; or be unable to describe the problems accurately because they are unable to separate their interpretations and conceptualizations of the problems from their actual expression. For all of these reasons and despite parents' strong desires to help their children work through and overcome their problems, the task of gathering information about problems from parents and teachers must be approached with an awareness of the possible complications involved. What this means, in practice, is that it is best for the clinician when interviewing parents to follow the same general guidelines for dealing with cognitive, social-emotional, trauma-related, and suggestibility- and social-desirability-related obstacles that he or she follows with their children.

McConaughy (1996) offers an excellent discussion of parent interviewing, within the general framework of the data generated by responses to the Parent Report Form and the Teacher Report Form, of the Child Behavior Checklist. Taylor (1988) outlines an interview for parents of children and adolescents with learning disabilities; and Kadesjo et al. (2004)

and Trillingsgaard et al. (2004) discuss and present data on the Five to Fifteen (FTF) questionnaire for parents of young people with learning and attention difficulties. My discussion of parent interviewing below is closely informed by the work and thought of these investigators.

As McConaughy (1996) notes, the clinician interviewing the parents of a child or adolescent with learning, motor, and/or communication problems ought to begin by explaining the goals of the interview and asking parents what their goals are for the evaluation and what their hopes and worries are for their child's future. After thus setting the stage, taking into account parents' hopes and fears, the clinician can then proceed to gather information about the details of the young person's problems, including specifically how the learning, motor, and/or communication problems are expressed; what they look like (literally) in terms of daily functioning; how they impact social-emotional and adaptive function; the history of the problems, including family history and current health and medical and developmental history; information gathered from previous assessments; and interventions attempted, with outcomes, and the feasibility of as yet untried interventions.

McConaughy (1996) makes the very good point that it is a good idea for the clinician to ask parents questions about "antecedent, sequential and consequential conditions that precipitate and sustain the [problem] behaviors" (p. 207) in a way that would, if possible, permit a functional behavioral analysis of the young person's problems. This is particularly important since the clinician wishes to develop an understanding of the social-emotional and adaptive impact of learning, motor, and/or communication problems on the young person's life. Furthermore, as IDEA very strongly promotes the performing of functional behavior assessments (FBAs), very nearly requiring them prior to the development of a behavior intervention plan to deal with problem behaviors and emotional reactions and outbursts at school, the generation of FBAs by professionals in private practice is likely to be of assistance to school staff who work with the child and to fit with their typical ways of thinking about the social-emotional impact of learning, motor, and/or communication problems.

I usually interview parents before interviewing their children, because parents are likely to have broader perspectives on young people's lives and problems than children themselves do, which may well help individualize the questions I typically ask and/or suggest important questions I would otherwise not have thought of. Also, this allows me to gather information about an issue often of importance to parents, family mental health history and the child's or adolescent's psychological resemblance to one or the other parent or member(s) of the extended family. Further, after I interview a child, I may go back and ask the parents to help me clarify the meaning of the young person's answers to interview questions or discuss issues the young person's answers raised that I had not thought to ask the parents.

Regarding questionnaires, my usual strategy is to ask parents to fill out the one I choose, perhaps the Child Behavior Checklist/4–18, after I interview them. If their responses raise new questions or are inconsistent with the information they offered in the interview, I then reinterview them, sometimes in person, sometimes by phone.

Last, I consider how the FTF questionnaire for parents of a young person with cognitive and/or motor skill problems (Kadesjo et al., 2004; Trillingsgaard et al., 2004) might be employed as a child and adolescent interview enhancer. This written questionnaire has 17 motor skills, 25 executive function, 18 perception, 11 memory, 21 language, and 27 social skills items. An interesting possibility to explore would be whether the clinician would gain more or better information about a child's learning, motor, and/or communication problems if (a) the clinician does the interview after reading the parents' responses to FTF items and in part basing his or her interview questions on them or (b) the clinician actually rephrases and asks as questions FTF items that discriminate statistically between groups of children with different types of problems.

Interviewing Teachers

As with parents, the clinician interviewing the child or adolescent's teachers and other school staff would do well to keep in mind and respect these important individuals' special expertise. Teachers know a great deal about how young people's learning, motor, and communication problems are expressed at school and about the social-emotional impact on the youngsters' lives with their peers, whether or not they have peer friends, and how well integrated they are into the larger social world of the school as a whole. Further, and very important, teachers can offer information about a young person's performance in the problem domain compared with that of same-age classmates, which often helps the clinician gain a clearer sense of the real impact of the problems and ideas for interventions, based on a long history and expertise in dealing with children and adolescents with similar problems.

McConaughy (1996) discusses teacher interviews within the framework provided by Gutkin and Curtis (1990). This framework posits "seven problem-solving steps for teacher interviews" (McConaughy, 1996, p. 212). I discuss only the first three of the seven steps here; the last four relate to the process of consultation to the school and are beyond the purview of the present chapter.

The first step is to ask the teacher for a detailed description of the young person's learning, motor, and/or communication problems. During this step, it is important for the interviewer to attempt to identify possible hidden agendas the teacher may have that could bias interview results, such as the desire to have parents told that the young person needs medication or to move the child out of the teacher's class.

The second step is to ask questions about the problem behaviors and emotional reactions the young person evidences at school, the social-emotional impact of learning, motor, and/or communication problems and their antecedent, sequential, and consequent conditions, with a view toward enabling the clinician and school staff to do FBAs. During this step, it is important for the clinician to ask questions about the teacher's feelings about and expectations of the young person, to determine how best to interpret the teacher's comments about the problems.

The third step is to brainstorm alternative educational and treatment strategies with the teacher. This would include discussion of interventions already tried, the teacher's ideas about what could be tried, and joint teacher-clinician consideration of new and as yet untried interventions and their possible feasibility. Brainstorming with the teacher can lead to the generation of new treatment ideas and shows respect for the teacher's special knowledge of the young person and expertise in dealing with young people's problems of the sort the student in question displays. The clinician should be careful, however, to explain to the teacher that brainstorming is just the beginning of the process of figuring out how to help the young person, so that the teacher is not left with the impression of commitment to a specific course of action.

As with parents, I usually ask the teacher to fill out the questionnaire I use, perhaps the Teacher Report Form (Achenbach, 1991), after the interview, then briefly reinterview the teacher in person or by phone if the responses to the questionnaire raise new questions or are inconsistent with the information the teacher offered in the interview.

Case Illustration With Dialogue

In the following section, I present and discuss a case illustration. I start with referral questions and information, then move on to the interview with the young person, background information, the interview with his foster parent and the school vice principal, academic and cognitive test data, test data on social understanding, diagnostic formulation, and educational and treatment recommendations.

Referral Questions and Information

Ty, a 12-year, 8-month-old adolescent, had a learning disability in reading and was on an IEP. His caseworker referred him for evaluation because she wanted answers to two questions: (1) What was the nature of Ty's learning disability in reading/reading disorder, and what could be done to reduce it? and (2) what were the sources and structure of the child's anger management problems with aggressive outbursts, and what could be done to reduce them? The problems were especially hard to understand given Ty's history of trauma, and the caseworker also wanted to know how the aftereffects of the trauma might be exacerbating Ty's other problems. The confluence of more than one referral concern or problem with a history of trauma is not unusual in a case where the clinician is asked to evaluate whether or not a young person has a learning, motor, and/or communication disorder; the confluence makes interpretation of the data both more complex and difficult than it would otherwise be, but at the same time also a more interesting puzzle.

Due to a precipitating event involving aggression toward two girls in the middle school, Ty had recently been sent from his middle school to an alternative education program, let's call it "New Day," for adolescents with behavioral and emotional problems. Staff expected Ty to return to the middle school after a short stay of several months in the alternative education program.

In doing the evaluation, I reviewed background information and a previous psychological assessment, interviewed Ty's foster mother and the vice principal in charge of discipline at the alternative education program, interviewed Ty, did cognitive neuropsychological testing, assessed his level of social-emotional understanding, offered a formulation of his problems, and made psychoeducational and treatment recommendations. Below, I present excerpts from the interview with Ty, taken from my verbatim notes, followed by excerpts from other parts of my report and discussion of the various data sources and how they related to one another. In the last two sections of the chapter, I then discuss at a theoretical level "Differential Diagnosis and Behavioral Assessment" and "Selection of Treatment Targets and Referral," exemplified in the evaluation of Ty at a practical clinical level.

Interview With Ty (Excerpts)

Ty brought his plastic-encased Michael Jordan basketball cards into my office and showed them to me. He was warm and open with me, answered questions freely, spontaneously offered information about himself and his world, and evidenced an interest in the photos in my office and aspects of my personal life. In what follows, my questions are in italics, and Ty's answers immediately follow.

What do you like to do? Get in my room [in his foster home] and play with my Sega [a computerized game toy] . . . And in the future, be in the NBA [a professional basketball player] . . . I like goin' to the mall and card shops [for basketball and other cards] and CD places . . . And I like to collect jewelry and basketball cards . . . Just plain chains, when you're wearing chains more people see it.

What don't you like to do? Sometimes, clean my room . . . But sometimes I like cleanin' my room . . . [and Ty does not like] Someone tells me to do stuff and I'm busy.

What is New Day? [the alternative education program Ty was attending] An alternative school, sorta like a jail. You stay in one class, 10 people in each class, and they don't want two classes passing each other [in the halls]. You watch movies telling you not to do drugs . . . I think I learn not to be bad from that school.

What's the best part of New Day? When we do OA [outdoor activities] . . . it's like gym sorta, you play soccer and basketball in the gym.

The worst part? Morning routine, you have to do like a lot of stuff in a short period of time.

How is reading for you? Not so good, I guess, I don't really like it.

What is it that you don't like about it? I don't know, I just don't like it . . . It's sorta hard, and I don't do good . . . They help me [assistance from an educational assistant], but it don't work.

Do you understand what you read? Not so good, it's hard, not so much the words . . . I just don't remember what I read.

Do you mean "don't remember" or "don't understand"? I don't remember [ambiguous but seemed to mean that he did not understand].

Given three magic wishes, Ty asked for "a wife and a boy and a girl, kids," "a big house," and to "be in the NBA so I have money to support my family."

What do you do best? I think math and basketball.

What are your problems, you know, like things that you don't do well or worry about or get angry and in trouble about? Arguing. I argue with my brothers and sister [biological, who live in the same foster home] all the time, I wanna work on stoppin' arguin' a lot.

Do you get in fights? People in my school be too bully, they pick on me and I talk back, I say stuff I don't supposed to.

How come you followed those two girls into the bathroom? [the incident of aggression at school for which Ty was suspended] We were talking about a teacher, she [one of the two girls] hit me and I chased her to the bathroom. She had her back to the door to keep me from getting in 'cause I's gonna hit her.

Why did you hit her? I would tell her about the teacher. From the fourth to the seventh grade I have problems with her . . . [but] we was friends at one time.

Do you have a short fuse, a bad temper? When people call me names, I get mad in my body and I want to hit 'em, but outside I don't, but sometimes I get angry in school and I fight when they hit me and call me names, like "You're really stupid!" My body tells me to, like if she say sothin' inappropriate I just get mad.

Does not reading too well also make you angry? I don't think so, why should it?

As can be seen, Ty was reasonably articulate in talking about most aspects of his life, but not when talking about his reading problems and their possible impact on his emotions. This is not uncommon. It is difficult for children and adolescents to introspect closely about the thinking processes they go through as they use academic skills and about the emotional impact of their learning, motor, and/or communication problems on other aspects of their lives. As the interview also demonstrates, Ty spoke nonstandard English. The precise sources of this were not initially clear from the interview—whether his nonstandard English resulted primarily from growing up with individuals who spoke nonstandard English or was a consequence of intrinsic language-processing problems. Testing suggested, though (see farther on in this section), the presence of a possible mild mixed receptive-expressive language disorder and pointed to specific neuropsychological deficits that would be expected to result in reading difficulties. As noted, too, the interview does not clarify the issue of the degree to which frustrations and disappointments related to Ty's reading disorder impacted his ability to manage anger.

Background Information

The available data on Ty's early history suggest probable in utero exposure to drugs and alcohol and clearly point to neglect and physical abuse in the home of his biological parents, who were allegedly drug dependent and engaged in criminal activities. Ty was removed from his parents' home at age 2½ and moved to his present foster home at age 8½ because of physical abuse at his previous foster home. He was argumentative and aggressive when he first entered his present foster home, but these problems had decreased very noticeably since that time. As noted, his three biological siblings and his foster mother's 17-year-old biological son lived with Ty in the foster home.

Ty's traumatic early history would be predictive of behavioral and emotional problems and tend to increase the likelihood of his having a learning and/or communication disorder.

Interview With Foster Mother

Ty's foster mother stated that Ty had "a caring side for people," was a good worker and volunteered to help when he visited her at her job, and was good at drawing. Further, he had friends in the neighborhood and evidenced empathy when his foster mother was ill or hurt. Ty had a fierce, quick temper: He had frequent verbal and physical fights with his three biological siblings: Ursula, 14 years old; Virginia, 11; and Wayne, 10; and he often did not understand what he was told and got frustrated and angry when this happened. His foster mother viewed Ty as having become more aggressive as he had gotten older, and she noted that he was suspended from school six to seven times during the last school year because of his aggressiveness. Regarding the incident with the two female students this school year (mentioned in the interview with Ty, above) that resulted in his being placed at New Day, she stated that Ty claimed, counter to fact, that he had not actually followed the two girls into the bathroom (yet in the interview, he admitted doing so).

Regarding reading, Ty's foster mother said she knew reading was difficult for him but did not know exactly why, and she considered his difficulties in managing his anger a much bigger problem; she did not appear to think the two problems were linked. Her responses to the items of the Child Behavior Checklist yielded high scores on Aggressive, Delinquent, and Hostile Withdrawal, consistent with the problems she described, and an elevated score on Obsessive-Compulsive, because of Ty's inability to "let go" of issues, and Hyperactive, because of his school problems. Her responses also yielded low Social Competence scores but did not highlight his reading difficulties.

The interview with Ty's foster mother corroborated the presence of a pervasive anger management problem but shed little light on his reading disorder. Her statement about often not understanding what was told to him, though, raised the possibility of receptive language problems.

Interview With Vice Principal

The vice principal at the alternative education program stated that he was told Ty had improved his behavior in middle school over the course of the year, compared to the previous year, and was not having problems during class, only during unstructured periods, such as recess, lunch, and transitions between periods. He also said that the teachers in the middle school liked Ty and were looking forward to having him back in their classrooms. The vice principal said that Ty was a "nice kid" who had difficulties with social-emotional cause-and-effect reasoning, that he didn't "get it," and that he had significant behavior and anger management issues. When asked about Ty's reading problems, he stated that he did not know about them, because the teachers (at the alternative education program) focused on Ty's anger management problems and "didn't make a big deal out of them" (his reading problems). He also noted that he thought Ty was receiving small-group instruction in reading (at the alternative education program). The vice principal did not return the Teacher Report Form I sent him.

This interview indicated that school staff were at times unaware of or underestimated the extent and impact of a student's learning, motor, and/or communication difficulties, especially when those difficulties were associated with concomitant social-emotional problems.

Previous Evaluation

Ty obtained a Full Scale IQ of 96 on the Wechsler Intelligence Scale for Children-Third Edition (WISC-III) (Wechsler, 1991), in the normal range. Given his possible mild mixed receptive-expressive language disorder, though, this result might underestimate his true overall level of intellectual function. Academic testing indicated grade-level mathematics skills (Woodcock-Johnson, Revised Broad Math Score 100), but a learning disability in reading/reading disorder (Woodcock-Johnson, Revised Broad Reading

Score 74) and weakness in written spelling (Woodcock-Johnson, Revised Spelling Score 80). The previous evaluator did not view Ty as basically antisocial, but as acting aggressively to defend himself and his pride against injury. She suggested that the sources of his aggression lay in the effects of the early abuse, neglect, and deprivation he had suffered; strong competitive feelings; hypersensitivity to issues of fairness and justice; feelings of vulnerability because he was of small stature; and perhaps most important, a lack of well-formed internal structures for behavioral and emotional self-regulation.

It should also be noted that the data indicating a learning disability in reading had not been acted on and were consistent with Ty's foster mother's and school staff's focus on his anger management problems.

Present Evaluation: Academic and Cognitive Test Results

To corroborate the presence of a reading disorder, I readministered the Woodcock-Johnson-IV reading tests. Ty obtained a Broad Reading Score of 73, essentially the same score he had obtained a year earlier (see above), with individual tests scores of 74 on letter-word identification, single-word recognition; 81 on reading fluency, the speeded answering of single-sentence true-false questions; 70 on passage comprehension, stating the word missing in a sentence; and 82 on word attack, reading phonically readable and pronounceable nonsense words. These scores suggested that Ty was beginning to develop phonic reading skills (word attack) but was having difficulties understanding what he read (passage comprehension). I would note, too, that as Ty took the reading subtests, he appeared at times somewhat uneasy, as if he were worried about the quality of his performance.

To determine the possible sources of Ty's reading disorder, I administered a number of neuropsychological tests. Ty scored in the bright normal range on the Tower of London, a test of efficient mind's-eye visual-spatial problem solving that demands planning ahead, a score consistent with his at-grade-level mathematics skills and in the normal range on the California Verbal Learning Test-Children's Version, suggesting that he has intact rote auditory-verbal learning and memorization skills. His pattern of scores on the Neuropsychological Test Battery for Children

(NEPSY) (Korkman, Kirk, & Kemp, 1998) sub-tests I administered, however, indicated deficits consistent with difficulties in learning to read. His scaled scores on the NEPSY subtests, with percentiles, were as follows.

Subtest	Scaled Score	Percentile
Visual Attention	11	63
Visuomotor Precision	8	25
Auditory Attention & Response Set	11	63
Comprehension of Instructions	11	63
Verbal Fluency	11	63
Sentence Repetition	7	16
Narrative Memory	5	5
Phonological Processing	3	1

The above scores suggested that the sources of Ty's reading disorder were likely a deficit in phonemic awareness, reading-related speech sound analysis and synthesis (phonological processing); a deficit in the ability to process amounts of meaningful auditory-verbal information that exceed immediate memory span (narrative memory); and a weakness in rote short-term auditory-verbal working memory (sentence memory). These deficits and weakness were consistent with Ty's great difficulties learning to read and learning disability in reading/reading disorder. Further, the effects of the deficits were likely significantly compounded by the large-scale negative effects of the abuse and trauma he had suffered; probable disruptions in schooling as a function of changes in living situation; and his use of nonstandard English and its use by the people with whom he was living. Further, the deficits and weaknesses, particularly Ty's difficulty processing amounts of information that exceed immediate memory span, were also consistent with his at times significant difficulties understanding conversations and instructions, especially under conditions of emotional stress.

Social-Emotional Understanding

Ty obtained a standard score of 90, at the 25th percentile for 11-year, 6-month-olds on the Test of Problem Solving, Elementary Level. Given that he was 12 years, 8 months old at the time of testing (I did not administer the adolescent version because it requires the young person to listen to a story read by the evaluator and

simultaneously read along, a multitasking demand I thought might prove too complex for Ty), this score indicates a deficit in verbally expressed social-emotional understanding consistent with a lack of well-formed internal structures for behavioral and emotional self-regulation.

Diagnostic Formulation

The five-axis *DSM-IV-TR* diagnostic profile I gave Ty was as follows.

Axis I	309.81	Posttraumatic Stress Disorder, Chronic and Severe
	313.81	Oppositional Defiant Disorder (by History)
	315.0	Reading Disorder (Learning Disability in Reading)
	315.39	Mixed Receptive-Expressive Language Disorder, Mild (Speech and Language Impairment, by History)
Axis II	V71.09	No Diagnosis
Axis III		No Reported Medical Problems
Axis IV		History of Neglect and Physical Abuse, Stresses of Reading Problems
Axis V		GAF = 53 (Current)

I also noted in my report, as did the previous evaluator in hers, that I found Ty warm-hearted and wanting to do well, fit in with his peers, and succeed at the tasks he attempted. Like the previous evaluator, I did not view him as basically antisocial, despite his anger management problems.

Regarding differential diagnoses related to Ty's documented reading disorder (I consider differential diagnosis at a theoretical level in the next section of the chapter), two questions arose: Did Ty's receptive and expressive language problems rise to the level of a formal diagnosis of mixed receptive-expressive language disorder, mild? Were his specific neuropsychological deficits part of that disorder, or did they constitute a relatively independent problem that would be more appropriately labeled a learning disorder–not otherwise specified (*DSM-IV-TR* 315.9)? I would note, too, regarding Ty's anger management problems and aggressive outbursts, that because I did not view him as antisocial, I decided to use oppositional defiant disorder as a descriptor rather than conduct disorder. I freely admit, though, that I chose to diagnose as I did on the basis of clinical judgment and that the above diagnoses were based on my integrated conceptualization of all of the information I gathered, including the interview and test data, and on my overall impression of Ty.

Regarding behavioral assessment (which I also consider at a theoretical level in the next section), I would note primarily that the exigencies of time were such that I did not visit Ty in school to observe him there, either in class when he was doing academic work or in unstructured situations where his behavioral and emotional difficulties were more likely to show themselves. Had I been able to, I might have gained a better understanding of how he functioned in complex social situations with many distracting stimuli and a relatively high noise level (compared with my office) and of the interface between his reading and behavioral/emotional problems. The lack of enough time to do extensive behavioral assessment, particularly observational, is a generic problem in private practice, a problem often faced by the clinician doing an evaluation.

Educational and Treatment Recommendations

On the basis of the information and data I gathered and my formulation of Ty's difficulties, I made the following educational and treatment recommendations. I wrote them with the audience of the report in mind, specifically, Ty's teachers, educational assistants, and caseworker; his foster mother; his potential therapist; and his potential prescribing physician (I discuss audience and related issues at a general level in the last section of the chapter).

1. Ty would likely benefit, as part of his IEP, from Orton-Gillingham (a combined phonics- and visual-memory-based) reading instruction and/or sight vocabulary instruction, to allow him to at least partially bypass his deficit in phonemic awareness. A published Orton-Gillingham curriculum and either of two sight-reading curricula could be used to structure this teaching. The phonic instruction Ty has received seems to be beginning to take, but overfocusing on phonics, I think, will keep Ty subvocalizing more than is optimal and interfere with the development of fluent, automated reading skills.

2. Ty would benefit, also as part of his IEP, from individual one-to-one, as opposed to group, tutoring in reading on a daily or every-other-day basis, if possible, by a warmhearted, experienced, talented tutor who is able to link instruction to Ty's personal interests, particularly basketball. His reading problems are severe enough, in my view, that Ty will likely be able to begin overcoming them only in a close relationship with a caring tutor who can gently correct him at the right susceptible moment, to the fraction of a second, and make reading a personally rewarding and meaningful experience for him.

3. Ty would benefit at school, again, as part of his IEP and in addition to individual tutoring in reading, from instruction in anger management; negotiating differences of opinion and conflict; how to talk about his feelings; how to understand complex language-based emotions related to social emotions, such as shame, pride, self-satisfaction, and so on; as well as role-playing exercises to help him learn to deal prosocially with emotional stress. Social stories and comic strip conversations could at times be used as tools.

4. Ty would benefit at school from having a safe place to repair to when he feels stressed.

5. Ty would benefit from individual therapy, if possible, with a male therapist with whom he could identify, to help him understand the sources and structure of his anger management problems and aggression, learn new ways of responding to social-emotional stresses, develop a more positive self-concept and greater self-esteem, and explore his negative feelings about reading and their relation to his other problems.

6. Ty would benefit from a psychiatric medication evaluation. He might very well be greatly helped in his efforts to modulate his anger by an appropriately chosen psychotropic that mutes the intensity of his emotional reactions to social-emotional stresses. A carefully monitored, medically supervised clinical trial on the medication his physician chooses appears warranted.

DIFFERENTIAL DIAGNOSIS AND BEHAVIORAL ASSESSMENT

Because very few cases are perfectly clear-cut, the clinician evaluating a child or adolescent with a learning, motor, and/or communication disorder will almost always of necessity be faced with issues related to differential diagnosis and behavioral assessment, and the issues will not be independent of one another. Good differential diagnosis requires, first, a picture of the complete range of diagnostic possibilities and, second, sufficient behavioral assessment to enable the psychologist to discriminate accurately between the various possible diagnoses. Further, differential diagnosis is present as an issue at both the macro *DSM-IV-TR* or IDEA/ADA level and at the micro-information-processing and social-emotional reactivity-and-response level.

Behavioral assessment, in the sense I am using the term here, encompasses the data gathered from a broad range of information sources the clinician can potentially access, including the interview with the young person; the young person's responses to questionnaires, such as the Youth Self-Report Questionnaire (Achenbach, 1991); interviews with parents, teachers, and other adults involved in the young person's life; these adults' responses to behavior questionnaires; intellectual/cognitive, neuropsychological, speech-language, occupational therapy, physical therapy, academic, and social-emotional/personality testing; and home, classroom, and other observations. Since every life is an entire encyclopedia of detail, however, and time exigencies are an inevitable part of clinical work, there are limits to how much behavioral assessment the psychologist will realistically be able to do. I would note, too, regarding both differential diagnosis and behavioral assessment, that slightly different considerations come into play when the focus is *DSM-IV-TR*-based treatment by professionals in private practice and when it is IDEA/ADA-, IEP-, and educational-support-plan-based psychoeducational treatment at school. Last, it must be noted, too, that differential diagnosis and behavioral assessment are always informed by the clinician's overall formulation of the young person's problems. They do not flow directly from the interview, testing, and observational data; interpretation and conceptualization intervene.

Regarding differential diagnosis, there are two very important points to make. First, the clinician needs to make an explicit plan for differential diagnosis, laying out all the possibilities—not create one on the fly as new diagnostic possibilities arise in the course of the evaluation. Second,

the clinician would do well to keep in mind that learning, motor, and communication disorders almost always have social-emotional problems associated with them and that this necessitates careful differential social-emotional, as well as learning-motor communication, diagnosis. Without an explicit plan to do differential diagnosis and a comprehensive list of diagnostic possibilities, the clinician will be likely to miss subtle or hidden diagnoses, especially in complex evaluations. Further, without a steady focus on the social-emotional aspects of disorders, as well as their academic, cognitive, and fine and gross motor aspects, the clinician will likely not generate a broad enough picture of the young person's problems to be able to select the most appropriate and effective treatment targets and make the most appropriate and effective referrals.

Even after the clinician settles on a formal diagnosis, or diagnoses, however, the issue of differential diagnosis remains. This is because the issue exists at both a macrolevel and a microlevel. To take one example, consider the child with a reading disorder. The child's reading problems may have arisen as a result of a deficit in phonemic awareness and speeded speech sound processing, receptive language, expressive language, short-term auditory-verbal memory, long-term auditory-verbal memory, visual memory, and/or visual scanning, as well as attention problems that interfered with the automation of reading skills and the development of reading fluency, or as a result of a combination of these deficits and attention difficulties. Further, the problems may impact single-word recognition, phonic reading, oral (as opposed to silent) reading, reading rate, reading comprehension, or a combination of reading subdomains. And this is not all.

The impact of a child's reading problems will vary, especially in the social-emotional realm, depending on his or her temperament, family or other living situation, developmental and trauma history, and the range of opportunities for learning to read that were made available to the child. The clinician must therefore consider the nature and impact of all of these factors when doing differential diagnosis, for they can all have implications for the selection of treatment targets and referrals. Further, as the report the evaluator writes will likely be read by teachers and other school staff, even if it is written primarily for the child's or adolescent's parents and therapist, it is usually good practice to suggest IDEA-based as well as *DSM-IV-TR*-based psychological diagnoses. I usually present educational diagnoses as possible special education eligibility categories, because these are the terms school staff use and the terms that will appear on the young person's IEP.

Regarding specifically behavioral, that is, observational, assessment, the basic decision the clinician will need to make is "How much?" Since evaluations, particularly when the clinician is asked to be comprehensive, routinely include an interview with the young person; interviews with adult caregivers, teachers, and professionals involved in the young person's life; and formal cognitive, academic, and social-emotional testing, the question as to how much behavioral assessment to do often comes down to how many situations to observe the child or adolescent in and how many questionnaires to ask the adults involved to respond to. There are no hard-and-fast answers to these questions. The guideline the clinician would do well to follow in making the decision, and this will of necessity be a matter of clinical and practical judgment, is the number of observations and questionnaires necessary to accurately distinguish between the range of diagnostic possibilities.

I should mention, for the sake of completeness, that it is possible to do too much behavioral assessment. Beyond a certain number of observations and a certain number of tests, the possibility of obtaining fluky results that distort or cannot be integrated with the other data the clinician gathered, the probability of a type I error, rises above an acceptable level.

I would like to mention, too, that behavioral assessment can have different meanings within a IDEA/IEP as opposed to a *DSM-IV-TR* framework. Within IDEA, the presumption is that observational assessments to establish special education eligibility will be done in more than one setting; this is a desideratum but does not necessarily occur in the private practice world outside of school. Furthermore, behavioral assessments for the establishment of eligibility are increasingly likely, these days, to involve assessment of what is termed "response to intervention," that is, how well or poorly the young person responds to an intervention designed to decrease language, motor, and/or communication problems and reduce associated behavior

and emotional problems. Unfortunately, to my way of thinking, responses to intervention assessments are not commonly done as part of evaluations conducted by professionals in private practice, often because there is not enough time or because they cannot be funded; they are not "usual and customary."

Last is the formulation of the children's or adolescents' problems. The way clinicians do differential diagnosis and what kind and how much behavioral assessment they do depends, of necessity, on their way of formulating, or conceptualizing, the problems of young people and the effects of these problems on young people's lives. Even when the clinician does not explicitly spell out a formulation, an implicit formulation guides what he or she does. For this reason, it is in my view a good idea, even obligatory, for the clinician to attempt to make his or her formulation explicit and to continue refining it throughout the process of evaluation. This is true for reasons similar to those that make careful differential diagnosis necessary: Without a well-thought-through formulation of the young person's problems, the psychologist will be less able to select optimal treatment targets and make optimal referrals.

SELECTION OF TREATMENT TARGETS AND REFERRAL

The reason for doing an evaluation of a young person's learning, motor, and/or communication problems is to be able to help the child or adolescent overcome them by selecting appropriate treatment targets, suggesting appropriate treatments, and referring the young person and his or her family to appropriate professionals and service agencies. If they follow the clinician's recommendations, the young person and his or her family will normally move from evaluation to sustained work with a psychologist, speech/language pathologist, occupational therapist, physical therapist, or special educator in a private practice setting or at school as part of the implementation of an IEP or educational support plan.

The basis for selecting treatment targets and making referrals, as noted earlier, is the clinician's formulation, or conceptualization, of the young person's problems. What I will therefore do here is present an ordered outline of issues to consider that I believe will help the clinician develop a comprehensive formulation relevant for treatment and referral:

1. Cognitive
   a. Overall level of cognitive function, cognitive adaptation level
   b. Cognitive-neuropsychological strengths
   c. Effects of strengths on daily adaptive and intellectual/academic function
   d. Cognitive-neuropsychological weaknesses
   e. Effects of weaknesses on daily adaptive and intellectual/academic function
   f. Interactions between strengths and weaknesses
   g. Effects of interaction between strengths and weaknesses on daily adaptive and intellectual/academic function

2. Social-Emotional
   a. Temperament and personality characteristics
   b. Social and emotional strengths
   c. Effects of strengths on daily social-emotional, adaptive, and academic function
   d. Social and emotional weaknesses
   e. Effects of weaknesses on daily social-emotional, adaptive, and academic function
   f. Interactions between strengths and weaknesses
   g. Effects of interactions between strengths and weaknesses on daily social-emotional, adaptive, and academic function

3. Impact of Problems: impact of learning, motor, and/or communication problems on daily social-emotional/adaptive and intellectual/academic function in the context of the young person's social and emotional strengths and weaknesses; FBAs that have been done; and academic, intellectual, motor, and/or social-emotional interventions that have been attempted.

The above outline for a formulation will, I believe, help the clinician reason in a comprehensive, inclusive, and logical fashion without leaving out important issues. With a carefully developed, comprehensive formulation of the nature, sources, and effects of the young person's problems in hand and a good knowledge of the resources available for implementation of the proposed treatment, or treatments, the clinician will be in a good position to select specific treatment targets, suggest treatment strategies, either begin treatment or make appropriate referrals, and work with the other professionals who will end up being part of the young person's treatment team.

SUMMARY

After writing the previous sections, I asked myself the following question: How do interview information and impressions influence the subsequent development of a formulation, selection of treatment targets and techniques, and the making of appropriate referrals?

The answer that came to mind surprised me a bit, for it implied that the value of the interview, though a central element of the evaluation, was likely in the end to be as much indirect as direct. The answer was that I hoped that as a result of interviewing the young person, the clinician develops a deep sense of the person as a unique individual and that this impression informs the clinician in developing a formulation of the child's or adolescent's learning, motor, and/or communication problems; selection of treatment targets; and techniques of making appropriate referrals. It is my firm belief that the treatment that works best for a young person is the one that fits with who the individual most deeply is, so that it promotes not only problem resolution but also the young person's growth as a human being.

REFERENCES

Achenbach, T. M. (1991). *Integrative guide for the 1991 CBCL/4–18, YSR, and TRF profiles.* Burlington: University of Vermont Department of Psychiatry.

American Psychiatric Association. (2000). *Diagnostic and statistical manual of mental disorders* (4th ed., Text rev.). Washington, DC: Author.

Americans with Disabilities Act, 42 U.S.C. § 12101 (July 26, 1990).

Calinoiu, I., & McClellan, J. (2004). Diagnostic interviews. *Current Psychiatry Reports, 6,* 88–95.

Ginsburg, H. P. (1997). *Entering the child's mind: The clinical interview in psychological research and practice.* New York: Cambridge University Press.

Gutkin, T. B., & Curtis, M. J. (1990). School-based consultation: Theory, techniques, and research. In T. B. Gutkin & C. R. Reynolds (Eds.), *The handbook of school psychology* (pp. 577–611). New York: Wiley.

Hodges, K., Kline, J., Stern, L., Cytryn, L., & McKnew, D. (1982). The Child Assessment Schedule (CAS) diagnostic interview: A report on reliability and validity. *Journal of the American Academy of Child & Adolescent Psychiatry, 21,* 468–473.

Hughes, J. N., & Baker, D. B. (1990). *The clinical child interview.* New York: Guilford Press.

Hynan, D. J. (1999, March/April). Interviewing: Forensic psychological interviews with children. *Forensic Examiner, 3*(2), 25–28.

Individuals with Disabilities Education Act, 2004 Reauthorization, 20 U.S.C. § 1400 et seq. (June 21, 2005).

Kadesjo, B., Janois, L.-O., Korkman, M., Mickelsson, K., Strand, G., Trillingsgaard, A., et al. (2004). The FTF (Five to Fifteen): The development of a parent questionnaire for the assessment of ADHD and comorbid conditions. *European Child and Adolescent Psychiatry, 13,* 3–13.

Korkman, M., Kirk, U., & Kemp, S. J. (1998). *NEPSY- A developmental neuropsychological assessment.* San Antonio, TX: Psychological Corporation.

McConaughy, S. H. (1996). The interview process. In M. J. Breen & C. R. Fiedler (Eds.), *Behavioral approach to assessment of youth with emotional/behavioral disorders: A Handbook for school-based practitioners* (pp. 181–223). Austin, TX: Pro-Ed.

McConaughy, S. H. (2005). *Clinical interviews for children and adolescents: Assessment to intervention.* New York: Guilford Press.

McConaughy, S. H., & Achenbach, T. M. (1996). Contributions of a child interview to multimethod assessment of children with EBD and LD. *School Psychology Review, 25,* 24–39.

Mordock, J. B. (2001). Interviewing abused and traumatized children. *Clinical Child Psychology and Psychiatry, 6,* 271–291.

Morrison, J., & Anders, T. F. (1999). *Interviewing children and adolescents: Skills and strategies of effective DSM-IV diagnosis.* New York: Guilford Press.

Reich, W., Shayka, J. J., & Taibleson, C. C. (1992). *Diagnostic interview for children and adolescents-revised.*

St. Louis, MO: Washington University, Division of Child Psychiatry.

Shaffer, D, Fisher, P., Lucas, C. P., Dulcan, M. K., & Schwab-Stone, M. E. (2000). NIMH Diagnostic Interview Schedule for Children-Version IV (NIMH DISC-IV): Description, differences from previous versions, and reliability of some common diagnoses. *Journal of the American Academy of Child & Adolescent Psychiatry, 39,* 28–38.

Sherrill, J. T., & Kovacs, M. (2000). Interview Schedule for Children and Adolescents (ISCA). *Journal of the American Academy of Child & Adolescent Psychiatry, 39,* 67–75.

Sternberg, K. J., Lamb, M. E., Orbach, Y., & Esplin, P. W. (2001). Use of a structured investigative protocol enhances young children's responses to free-recall prompts in the course of forensic interviews. *Journal of Applied Psychology, 86,* 997–1005.

Taylor, H. G. (1988). Learning disabilities. In E. J. Mash & L. G. Terdal (Eds.), *Behavioral assessment of childhood disorders* (2nd ed., pp. 402–450). New York: Guilford Press.

Trillingsgaard, A., Damm, D., Sommer, S., Jepsen, J. R. M., Ostergaard, O., Frydenberg, M., et al. (2004). Developmental profiles on the basis of the FTF (Five to Fifteen) questionnaire: Clinical validity and utility of the FTF in a child psychiatric sample. *European Child and Adolescent Psychiatry, 13,* 39–51.

Wechsler, D. (1991). *Wechsler Intelligence Scale for Children-Third Edition: Manual.* San Antonio, TX: Psychological Corporation.

Wilcoxin, K. K., Bosky, A. B., Yokum, M. N., & Alverman, D. E. (1984). An interview assessing students' perceptions of classroom reading tasks. *The Reading Teacher, 18,* 346–352.

Zwiers, M. L., & Morrissette, P. J. (1999). *Effective interviewing of children: A Comprehensive guide for counselors and human service workers.* Ann Arbor, MI: Taylor & Francis.

16

ATTENTION-DEFICIT/ HYPERACTIVITY DISORDER

BRAD C. DONOHUE, RACHEL E. SIMMONS, AND STEPHANIE A. DEVORE

DESCRIPTION OF THE DISORDER

Attention-deficit/hyperactivity disorder (ADHD) is a frequently diagnosed childhood behavioral condition that has a particularly negative influence on learning disabilities and conduct disorders (Quinn, 1997). In this disorder, abnormalities in the executive functions of the prefrontal cortex and limbic systems of the frontal lobes as well as the reticular activating system are found in affected youth (Barkley, Grodzinsky, & DuPaul, 1992; National Institutes of Health [NIH], 2000; Quinn, 1997), resulting in deficits in attention, activity level, and impulsivity (Barnett & Labellarte, 2002). Monozygotic and dizygotic twin studies suggest ADHD is genetically transmitted (Cantwell, 1972; Morrison & Stewart, 1971, 1973). As in many psychological disorders, it is not currently known whether the presence of ADHD symptoms represents the presence of a discrete disease or a continuum of characteristics. Nevertheless, the utility of diagnosis and treatment are evident in ameliorating the disorder's effects (NIH, 2000).

Diagnostic Criteria

The American Psychiatric Association's *Diagnostic and Statistical Manual of Mental Disorders, Fourth Edition, Text Revision (DSM-IV-TR)* (APA, 2000) outlines the diagnostic criteria for three subtypes of ADHD: primarily inattentive (ADHD-I), primarily hyperactive (ADHD-H), and combined (ADHD-C). Symptoms for diagnosis of any of the subtypes (see below) must be present prior to age 7 and persist for a minimum of 6 months at a level that is maladaptive and inconsistent with the child's developmental level. In addition, symptoms must be present in two or more settings and cause significant impairment in social, academic, or occupational functioning. The symptoms cannot occur exclusively during the course of a pervasive developmental disorder, schizophrenia, or psychotic disorders and are not better accounted for by another disorder.

Primarily Inattentive (ADHD-I). ADHD-I requires the presence of at least six symptoms consistent with inattention (e.g., does not listen when spoken to directly, forgetful in daily activities, loses things) but less than six hyperactive-impulsive symptoms (e.g., has difficulty awaiting turn, talks excessively, interrupts others). Descriptions of children with ADHD often include symptoms from this subtype, which all exhibit diminished facility for attention. Children usually do not evidence symptoms of inattention during play activities. Rather, they manifest them during tasks that require sustained activity and that are less appealing (Anastopoulos & Shelton, 2001). Inability to sustain attention during task-oriented activities inevitably results in academic difficulties and subsequent ADHD-I evaluation (Barkley, 1998; Root & Resnick, 2003). Although some have purported the ADHD-I constellation may be a distinct disorder (Barkley, Fischer, Edelbrock, & Smallish, 1991; Goodyear & Hynd, 1992; Quinn, 1997), the results of factor analyses have demonstrated two distinct independent dimensions inherent in ADHD, supporting the conceptualization that is offered in the *DSM-IV-TR* (DuPaul, 2003; Lahey & Carlson, 1992).

Primarily Hyperactive (ADHD-H). ADHD-H requires the presence of at least six hyperactive-impulsive symptoms but less than six inattentive symptoms. Although children often express these symptoms physically (in extreme cases, the child may appear to be in "constant motion"), they can also manifest verbally through incessant talking. Hallmark symptoms include extremes in task-irrelevant and developmentally inappropriate behavior (Anastopoulos & Shelton, 2001). Characterized by gross disinhibition, children with ADHD-H evidence poor delay in gratification, often resulting in weak interpersonal relationships. Compared with children with ADHD-H, children with ADHD-I tend to have less severe conduct problems, less impulsivity, and suffer less peer rejection. They are more withdrawn, sluggish, and drowsy. They also appear to experience fewer pre- and perinatal complications; neurological abnormalities; and impairments in reading, visual perception, and visual and auditory memory than do children with ADHD-H (Quinn, 1997).

Combined (ADHD-C). Diagnosis of ADHD-C requires the presence of at least six hyperactive-impulsive and six inattentive symptoms.

Prevalence

Investigators involved in the Pediatric Research in Office Settings (PROS) study reported that only 38% of 3,900 clinicians use *DSM* criteria when diagnosing AHDH (Wasserman et al., 1999), suggesting there may be significant variability in the diagnosis of ADHD in clinical settings. Although up to 15% of youth are diagnosed with ADHD, well-controlled studies indicate that the true prevalence of ADHD in the United States ranges from 3% to 7% of school-age children and that the disorder is more prevalent among boys than girls (Cantwell, 1996).

Comorbidity

When ADHD is present, 44% of the time there is another *DSM* disorder present, 33% of the time there are two *DSM* disorders, and 10% of the time there are three *DSM* disorders present, with conduct (CD) disorder and oppositional defiant disorder (ODD) being the most common comorbid disorders (APA, 2000; Barkley, 1998; Root & Resnick, 2003). Prevalence rates for comorbidity with ADHD-I are lower than for the other two ADHD subtypes (Barkley & Mash, 2003).

Conduct Disorder (CD) and Oppositional Defiant Disorder (ODD). Estimates of comorbidity with CD or ODD are estimated to range from 30% to 50% of children diagnosed with ADHD (Barnett & Labellarte, 2002; Jensen, Martin, & Cantwell, 1997). These children exhibit more severe symptoms, experience greater cognitive impairment, display poorer school achievement, and have more social difficulties than those evidencing only ADHD symptoms (Harada, Yamazaki, & Saitoh, 2002; Werry, Elkind, & Reeves, 1987).

Substance Abuse. Some studies indicate adverse outcomes, such as substance abuse, for individuals diagnosed with ADHD (Lambert & Hartsough, 1998). Indeed, untreated ADHD has consistently been linked to substance use disorders in early adulthood (Chilcoat & Breslau, 1999; Hart, Lahey, Loeber, Applegate, & Frick, 1995). Conversely, another study indicated that the occurrence of substance abuse disorders is more highly associated with the presence of comorbid CD than ADHD (Disney, Elkins, McGue, & Iacono, 1999).

Mood Disorders. Approximately 15% of children and adolescents diagnosed with ADHD evidence mood disorders (Barnett & Labellarte, 2002). Comorbidity of ADHD and depressive disorders is higher for ADHD-I than the other ADHD subtypes (Lahey & Carlson, 1992). Similarities between symptoms of ADHD-I and symptoms of depression (i.e., irritability, fatigue or loss of energy, and diminished ability to think) make differential diagnosis difficult (Salend & Rohena, 2003). Bipolar disorder is also highly comorbid with ADHD, and when coexisting with ADHD, it is very difficult to treat (Biederman, Faraone, & Lapey, 1992).

Anxiety Disorders. Anxiety disorders occur in approximately 25% of ADHD cases. These disorders are more prevalent for children with ADHD-I diagnoses than with ADHD-H or ADHD-C (Barnett & Labellarte, 2002; Lahey & Carlson, 1992). Youth with comorbid ADHD and obsessive-compulsive disorder (OCD) compared with youth who are diagnosed with ADHD alone have evidenced greater social problems, attention deficit, delinquency, and aggression (Geller et al., 2004).

Learning Disorders (LD). Although the majority of children with ADHD do not have a learning disorder, there is a high rate of comorbidity between learning disorders and ADHD (Biederman et al., 1992). The learning profiles for children with ADHD, LD, behavioral disorders, and reading difficulties are similar; thus, differentiating between them can be complex (Salend & Rohena, 2003). A significant number of children with ADHD also show evidence of deficits in auditory-linguistic areas and with basic reading skills mastery (Riccio & Jamison, 1998; Schwanz & Kamphaus, 1997).

Associated Features

Features associated with the presence of ADHD (e.g., low frustration tolerance, temper outbursts, stubbornness, and bossiness) are developmentally influenced. These children are also more prone to accidental injury (which may be a result of their impulsivity and poor planning skills) and more likely to experience mood liability, demoralization, dysphoria, peer rejection, and poor self-esteem (Barkley, 1998). For instance, the rates of injury for these children are estimated to be 10 times that of children without ADHD (DiScala, Lescohier, Barthel, & Li, 1998).

Between 30% and 70% of youth will continue to manifest ADHD symptoms in adulthood (Barnett & Labellarte, 2002). Of those who continue to maintain this diagnosis, slightly less than half develop comorbid disorders, most often including substance abuse and antisocial personality disorder (Cantwell, 1985; Manuzza, Klein, & Bessler, 1993). Others, however, develop coping strategies that effectively manage their symptoms (Barnett & Labellarte, 2002). Others often misinterpret symptoms of ADHD as character flaws (e.g., laziness, irresponsibility, oppositional behaviors), leading ADHD children to experience social and occupational problems. Conflict with authority figures in the family or at school, in addition to attention deficits, can negatively impact children academically. Impairments in academic achievement are common for children diagnosed with ADHD, particularly those diagnosed with ADHD-I (Cantwell, 1996). Individuals whose ADHD symptoms persist into adulthood often have poorer vocational achievement in comparison to their peers and have a tendency to choose careers for which the effects of ADHD are not as contributory (Barnett & Labellarte, 2002).

INTERVIEWING STRATEGIES

The interview is the keystone of ADHD assessment and should include a detailed and comprehensive psychosocial, developmental, and medical history obtained from both parents, if available (Barnett & Labellarte, 2002). A review of medical records should occur, whenever possible, including a medical referral to rule out medical causes for symptoms (Douglas & Parry, 1994). A single interview and observational session is insufficient to determine ADHD, as behaviors may be exacerbated, restricted, or otherwise modified due to the interview environment (Barnett & Labellarte, 2002). Therefore, multiple interviewing methods, including unstructured, semistructured, and structured components, are quintessential elements of a comprehensive assessment (Magyary & Brandt, 2002).

Observation

The interview begins in the waiting room with a careful observation of the child's behavior (Root & Resnick, 2003). Through observation, the interviewer can assess problems with disinhibition, as evidenced by fidgeting, not staying seated, moving around, running and climbing, noisy playing, excessive talking, and interrupting others' activities. In addition, familial interactions can be a rich source of information about the parents' reactions to the child's behavior, which may not be evident during the parent interview. The child's appearance, attitude, affect, speech, and language should be examined to assist in differential diagnosis (Barnett & Labellarte, 2002).

Rapport

Assessment is dependent on a positive relationship between the client and interviewer (i.e., rapport), particularly when working in ADHD populations. Fortunately, interviewers may utilize several methods to facilitate the acquisition of rapport, including effective structuring of interviews. Indeed, the initial interview ideally includes the parent(s), target child, and relevant others (i.e., teacher, grandparent) whenever possible (Barnett & Labellarte, 2002). Assessment is guided by initial observations and responses to the interviewer's queries that occur with the parent(s) and youth together. The youth should then be briefly seen individually, followed by a more extensive interview with the parent(s) alone, as parents are the primary informants when assessing ADHD, due to the developmental limitations of the child. Younger children, particularly under 5 years of age, may be interviewed in the presence of a parent while playing interactive games, in lieu of a formal interview. Initial interviews with ADHD children are usually briefer than adult interviews (i.e., 10 to 25 minutes).

Children should be praised throughout the interview, particularly regarding desirable behaviors and attributes that are likely to be seldom reinforced by others (e.g., paying attention, showing interest). Indeed, the initial child interview should be chiefly focused on establishing rapport. Parents are usually responsive to being praised for behaviors that may be seldom reinforced, as well (e.g., parenting techniques, using succinct instructions or praise that is specific). It is often helpful to establish rapport by giving the child an inexpensive gift for attending the session or promising the child token prizes consequent to socially appropriate behavior. Eliciting information about activities the child enjoys, including negative and positive consequences for those activities, provides insightful information regarding potential reinforcers and acts to enhance rapport.

The initial interview with the child should probably exclude an assessment of problem behavior, as such inquiry has a tendency to decrease input from the child early on and may negatively influence child enthusiasm and responsiveness to subsequent intervention. Indeed, youth are often classically conditioned to react negatively to questions that are pertinent to their undesired behaviors, and this information can be easily obtained from others.

Affect

The interviewer should pay careful attention to the child's affect throughout the interview process. Indeed, children with ADHD often experience difficulties regulating emotion, and they evidence labile affect, irritability, and hostility (Barkley et al., 1991). They may become excitable in response to rewards and easily annoyed or discouraged when rates of reinforcement decline (Douglas & Parry, 1994). In addition, they often experience problems interpreting the affect of others, thus contributing to poor social-perspective-taking skills (Barkley & Mash, 2003).

Friendships

Children with ADHD evidence problems in peer rejection and social interactions because of their symptoms, necessitating assessment of both quantity and quality of their friendships and interpersonal skills. For instance, problems with impulse control may result in premature decision making, use of profanity, or other expressions of anger, thus taxing friendships. Results from the child's interview should be integrated with parent and teacher reports to gain a full and accurate perspective of the child's friendships.

Academia

Inquiries into the child's educational level and the effects of ADHD on educational attainment should be correlated with school records, achievement tests, and teacher and parental reports. Questions should be designed to minimize embarrassment related to possible educational deficits and should assess educational strengths. Schoolteachers are often stretched and may regard ADHD children with negative biases. Therefore, interviewers should query teachers about their expectations of the target child, including both their personal and professional relationships with the child. Indeed, negative expectations have been shown to limit educational achievement (Madon, Jussim, & Eccles, 1997). It is also important to assess the teacher's willingness to employ specialized interventions, such as the home-based token economy. In this intervention, parents are provided progress notes that are completed by the teacher regarding the conduct or school performance of the child on a regular basis. The parents then reinforce desired performance or punish undesired performance (failure of the child to provide the progress note to the parent results in a negative consequence).

Mental State

Observations of the child's response patterns can be clues to the child's mental state, as children with ADHD-I are characterized as having a sluggish cognitive style and problems with memory retrieval (Barkley & Mash, 2003). Inquiries about the child's thoughts during classroom situations or the interview itself may reveal anxiety or mood-based explanations for apparent cognitive deficits or memory difficulties (Stein, 2004). Difficulties with receptive language or hearing may become apparent during such lines of inquiry (Stein, 2004). Youth who are found to evidence cognitive dysfunctions that negatively influence attention may be particularly responsive to self-instructional training strategies during treatment (i.e., teaching the child to utilize self-instructions that are relevant to on-task behavior; Meichenbaum & Goodman, 1971).

Unstructured Interview

In conducting unstructured interviews, the interviewer is not limited in content or method of inquiry. The unstructured interview guides further assessment by indicating which specific measures will be included in the assessment process (Barkley, 1997). Along these lines, every interview should incorporate an unstructured interview to some extent, particularly since this format assists in developing rapport (Barnett & Labellarte, 2002). This interview format is useful in identifying and broadly understanding clinical problems evidenced by the child, as well as gaining a better global perspective of the child's environment (Barkley, 1997). The unstructured format emphasizes broad-based questions and can take a seemingly unlimited number of directions as interviewee responses guide the interview.

Despite enhanced flexibility, the interviewer should begin the interview with an a priori agenda designed to touch upon the interviewee's perception of the reason for referral, as well as ADHD symptoms and pertinent domains in the child's life, including academic performance, sport participation and exercise, diet, medications/medical status, family, social skills, and friendships. Interviewees should be queried if behavioral problems vary by situation or have changed over time. It is also important to query for times of the day when symptoms are exacerbated, individuals with whom symptoms are less evident in their presence, and how significant others perceive and react to behavioral symptoms. Of course, the preceding lines of inquiry assist in determining antecedent and consequent stimuli that maintain ADHD symptoms (Magyary & Brandt, 2002).

Structured Interview

Contrary to the unstructured interview, the structured interview consists of a set of predetermined questions occurring in a prescribed order (Barkley, 1997). This process yields categorical responses that indicate the presence or absence of a disorder (Anastopoulos & Shelton, 2001). Structured interviews also result in increased specificity and facilitate differential diagnosis. Structured interviews are useful both in clinical practice and in research, particularly when diagnostic reliability is important (Anastopoulos & Shelton, 2001).

The Diagnostic Interview Schedule for Children-Version 4 (DISC-IV) (Shaffer, Fisher, Lucas, Dulcan, & Schwab-Stone, 2000) is a structured interview that is organized in six major sections: anxiety disorders, mood disorders, disruptive disorders, substance use disorders, schizophrenia, and miscellaneous disorders. Two versions exist, one for parents and one for adolescents aged 9 to 17 years. The format consists of question stems that may be utilized to direct the interviewer to disorder-salient questions contingent upon previous answers. Although potentially time-consuming to administer (about an hour), computer scoring is available, and it is not necessary to administer all modules (when assessing ADHD, the disruptive disorders section must be included).

Information gathered in the unstructured interview can be used in selecting modules for administration, and standard questions facilitate reliable assessment. Indeed, most federal funding agencies (e.g., NIH) now require investigators to propose the employment of structured interviews when funding is solicited to conduct studies that necessitate mental health diagnoses. Familiarity with structured interviews through practice inevitably enhances administration and decreases robotic responses that deter from effective rapport building.

Semistructured Interview

The semistructured interview often includes a list of questions pertinent to ADHD symptoms. The interviewer chooses which questions to ask and which areas to further probe with follow-up questions (Barkley, 1997). This format is particularly useful when interviewing very young children who may not respond well to the more rigorous structured format. It also is useful in eliciting information about symptom severity and offers guidelines for scoring or interpreting responses (Anastopoulos & Shelton, 2001). The Diagnostic Interview for Children and Adolescents (DICA-IV) (Reich, Welner, Herjanic, & MultiHealth System Staff, 1996) is similar in question format to the DISC-IV, although it is less structured (Reich, 2000). It incorporates a critical-items checklist for high-risk behaviors, and the parent version contains sections on pregnancy, birth, and early development. The child version may be administered to children 6 to 17 years old. Sections of specific interest for ADHD assessment include behavior at home and school, interpersonal relationships with peers, and mental status.

Rating Scales

Rating scales provide a structured format for collecting data on the child's behavior. Rating scales may be either broad (i.e., Achenbach system) or narrow (i.e., ADHD Symptom Checklist-4) in scope (see Table 16.1). Broad-band scales assess different disorders, and narrow-band scales facilitate the collection of information relevant to one particular disorder. Many of the scales have multiple versions for children, parents, and teachers to complete, and most can be self-administered. It is parsimonious to instruct clients to complete these scales in the waiting room prior to the interview or while others are being interviewed. Item

analyses, in which respondents are queried to provide additional information, may occur upon completion and scoring of relevant subscales, particularly those subscales that are elevated. For instance, if a parent endorsed that her child often "dawdles" in getting ready for school, the parent might be asked to report strategies that may have helped her motivate the child to attend school on time (consequences) or instructions she may have used to inform the child to get ready (antecedent stimuli). Table 16.1 describes some of the more commonly used rating scales.

INTERVIEWING OBSTACLES AND SOLUTIONS

Inattention and Hyperactivity

Children with ADHD engage in a wide array of problem behaviors that interfere with the interviewing process. Some of the symptoms (i.e., inattention, hyperactivity) can be overcome with frequent scheduling of breaks during the interview, using age-appropriate language, keeping questions brief, and incorporating interactive games.

Interviewer

Response reactivity occurs when the interviewee adjusts his or her method of responding to the interviewer in a manner that is ingenuous, usually to impress the interviewer. ADHD children may try to please the interviewer by endorsing symptoms they believe the interviewer finds desirable. The interviewer can usually reduce such responding by avoiding leading questions (e.g., "You have trouble sitting still, don't you?") and maintaining neutrality when responding to answers (e.g., "I see what you mean").

Symptom Inconsistency

ADHD symptoms are not always consistent across settings. In the novel and highly structured environment of the therapist's office, symptoms may be less apparent than they would be in the child's natural environment, where task demands are more intense or such behavior has a history of receiving reinforcement or punishment. Whenever possible, observations should

TABLE 16.1   Brief Description of Commonly Employed Measures Available to Assist in the Assessment of ADHD

Rating Scale	Age Range	Informant/Number of Items	Completion Time	Interrater Reliability	Subscales
Broad-Band Measures					
Child Behavior Checklists (CBCL; Achenbach, 1991, in Sattler, 2002)	4–18	Teacher (TRF)–120 Parent (CBCL)–120 Youth (YSR)–119	10–15 minutes	Teacher: –.05 to .81 Mother/Father: .26 to .86 Youth: Not reported	Withdrawn; Somatic; Social Problems; Anxious/Depressed; Thought Problems; Attention Problems; Delinquent Behavior; Aggression; Sex Problems (CBCL only); Self-Destructive/Identity Problems (YSR-boys only)
Conners' Rating Scales-Revised (CRS-R; Conners, 1997)	Parents/ Teachers 3–17 Students 12–17	Short Forms: Teacher–28; Parent–27 Student–27 Long Forms: Teacher–59; Parent–80 Student–87	10–20 minutes	Not reported	Hyperactivity; Social Problems; Oppositional; Cognitive/ Inattention; Anxious-Shy; Perfectionism; ADHD Index; Psychosomatic; Global Index; *DSM-IV* Symptom Subscales
Narrow-Band ADHD Measures					
ADHD Rating Scale-IV (ADHD-IV; Angello et al., 2003; DuPaul et al., 1998)	5–18	Teacher–18 Parent –18	10 minutes	Teacher & Parent: .41–.45	Hyperactivity/Impulsivity; Inattention; Total
ADHD Symptom Checklist-4 (SC-4; Gadow & Sprafkin, 1997)	3–18	Teacher–50 Parent–50	10–15 minutes	Teacher: .23–.46 Parent: .23–.46	Hyperactive/Impulsive; Inattentive; ODD; Peer Conflict; Stimulant Side Effects
Attention Deficit Disorders Evaluation Scale (ACTeRS; Angello et al., 2003; Ullman et al., 1997)	5–14	Teacher–24 Parent–25	10 minutes	Teacher: .51–.73 Parent: not reported	Hyperactive/Impulsive; Inattentive
Attention Deficit Disorders Evaluation Scale (ADDES; 2nd ed.; Angello et al., 2003; McCarney, 1995)	4–18 Teachers 3–18 Parents	Teacher–60 Parent–46	15–20 minutes	Teacher: .81–.90 Parent:.80–.84	Hyperactive/Impulsive; Inattentive
BASC Monitor for ADHD (BASC-M; Angello et al., 2003; Kamphaus & Reynolds, 1998)	4–18	Teacher–47 Parent–46	10–15 minutes	Not reported	Hyperactivity; Attention Problems; Internalizing Problems; Adaptive Skills
School Situations Questionnaire (Barkley et al., 1992)	4–11 Teachers	Teacher–12	5 minutes	Not reported	Inattentive
Home Situations Questionnaire (Barkley, 1990)	4–11 Parents	Parent–16	5 minutes	Not reported	Inattentive
Swanson, Nolan, & Pelham Rating Scale (SNAP-IV; Swanson, 1992)	6–18	Teacher–90 Parent–90	10 minutes	Not reported	Hyperactive/Impulsive; Inattention; CD; ODD; Tourette's; Stereotypic Movement Disorder; OCD; GAD; Narcolepsy; Manic Episode; MDD; Dysthymic Disorder

be conducted in the child's natural environment (i.e., school, home, sport leagues, playgrounds). Situations that provide opportunities to compare the child's behaviors with that of same-age peers (e.g., recess at school) are extremely valuable (Brown, 2000), particularly when the assessor is inexperienced in child development. With careful discretion, these children may be informally queried about general relationships, activities, and issues relevant to the overall culture in the classroom (e.g., how less popular youth are treated; gender, income, and racial prejudices). In doing so, it is imperative to maintain the target child's confidentiality.

Self-Report Inaccuracy

Child self-reports of ADHD symptoms are sometimes inaccurate (Barkley, 1998). Therefore, interviews with multiple informants, such as the child's parents and teachers who are familiar with the child's daily behavior, are extremely valuable sources of information (Zametkin & Ernst, 1999). When inconsistencies are noted, it is important to conduct further inquiry with all involved parties. Indeed, interviewees are often misunderstood, and ADHD symptoms are often controlled in some situations but not others, due to varying levels of tolerance and enforcement of consequences by adult monitors. For instance, a mother may report less severe symptoms of impulsive behavior than the child's teacher does because task demands at home are less than at school and the child receives severe and consistent beatings at home when impulsive behaviors occur. Conversely, this same mother may report more severe symptoms of inattention by the child than the teacher does because the child often worries about "getting a spanking" at home.

Misinformation

Parents may be overly concerned about the risks of medications used to treat ADHD. They may fear negative pressure from family or friends due to social stigma associated with ADHD, resulting in subsequent inhibition to pursue therapy (Neophytou & Webber, 2005; NIH, 2000). Most of these fears can be eliminated or reduced through psychoeducation. Indeed, the assessor should always provide ample opportunities for family members and teachers to ask questions

throughout the assessment process, including prompts to ensure that interviewees fully understand the topic at hand (e.g., "Tell me what you believe causes ADHD"; "What is your understanding of the consequences of the stimulant medications?").

Misunderstanding Interview Items

Because ADHD symptoms are transgenerational (Barkley et al., 1991; Biederman et al., 1992; Taylor, Sandberg, Thurley, & Giles, 1991), children afflicted with ADHD often have parents who experience difficulties reading instructions, understanding vocabulary words, and maintaining attention. Therefore, it is very important to clarify instructions and question items (Burns, Gomez, Walsh, & de Moura, 2003). Indeed, some interviewers read instructions and question stems and instruct the client to explain the response set, prior to attempting the first item. The latter strategy is particularly important when standardized assessment measures are administered in research settings.

It is important to query as to whether interviewees had personally witnessed ADHD symptoms and in what settings, particularly since ADHD symptoms must occur in at least two settings. For instance, a teacher informs a father that his son has exhibited symptoms of ADHD in school. The father has not witnessed such symptoms at home. When queried during an interview, however, the father reports that his child exhibits ADHD symptoms. The parent does not volunteer that the symptoms were observed by someone else, because he does not think it is important to qualify his response. Unless the parent is queried to disclose where the behaviors occurred, the assessor may erroneously form an impression that these symptoms were evidenced at home rather than at school.

INTERVIEWING PARENTS AND TEACHERS

Magyary and Brandt (2002) suggested that interviews occur with the target child, the target child's parents, and other significant others (e.g., teacher) and that the resulting content be reviewed for consistencies and discrepancies. Indeed, when ADHD is diagnosed on the basis of only one informant, the diagnoses tend to reveal either ADHD-I or ADHD-H. When reports from multiple informants are considered together, however, relatively more ADHD-C diagnoses are made (Mitsis, McKay, Schulz, Newcorn, & Halperin, 2000). The latter finding suggests enhanced sensitivity to the detection of ADHD symptoms when multiple informants are utilized.

Parents

Family History. It has long been established that ADHD is genetically transmitted (Cantwell, 1972; Morrison & Stewart, 1971, 1973; NIH, 2000). Therefore, a detailed family history should be obtained during the parent's interview. Several studies suggest the families of children with ADHD-I have fewer psychiatric diagnoses than families of children with ADHD-C but are more likely to have higher rates of anxiety disorders and learning problems than families of children with ADHD-H. Moreover, families of children with ADHD-H have higher rates of aggression and substance abuse than families of children with ADHD-I (Barkley et al., 1991; Biederman et al., 1992; Taylor et al., 1991). Therefore, the assessment of psychopathology, particularly among parents and siblings, is critically important. Other important factors include the presence of recent or major familial stressors (e.g., child maltreatment, divorce, integration of new family members: Magyary & Brandt, 2002). Another familial factor to consider is the level of parental education, as parents with fewer years of education typically underreport ADHD-I symptoms (Weckerly et al., 2005).

Medical History. The interviewer should obtain a comprehensive medical history detailing any problems that may have neurological ramifications, such as a history of seizures, head injury, loss of consciousness, or infections that may have a negative influence on the central nervous system (e.g., encephalitis or meningitis). Of significant importance is the date of last physical examination. If recent medical records are not available, the child should be referred for a thorough examination to rule out biological causes for symptoms (e.g., apparent inattentive or oppositional behavior due to a hearing impairment). In addition, parents should be queried about their children's recurrent illnesses (e.g., ear infections), hospitalizations, medications used, and operations.

Developmental History. The developmental history should include information on the child's attainment of developmental milestones and assessment of potential sensory, language, and perceptual problems. Interestingly, some studies have shown a correlation between sleep disorders and future manifestations of ADHD. For instance, approximately 25% of infants who have severe sleep problems are diagnosed with ADHD at 5 years of age (Thunstrom, 2002).

Education. The interviewer should include questions about the child's educational attainment, subjects in school that are particularly problematic (e.g., math, science), study habits (location, time of day, and availability of assistance), organizational skills, and ability to complete assignments. A release of information should be obtained by the legal guardian to obtain school records, including school performance (i.e., grades) and results of standardized testing.

Mood. As mentioned previously, children with ADHD have difficulty regulating emotions. Therefore, parents should be queried about the child's mood, including potential fluctuations in mood, general daily mood, and how the child handles adversity. As children often exhibit depression as irritability, the existence and duration of irritable or depressed moods should be carefully evaluated, including their consequences. For some children with ADHD, symptoms of ADHD may lead to negative experiences with others and ultimately result in depressed and irritable mood. Youth should be queried about these potential consequences. Indeed, later in treatment, the relationship between ADHD symptoms, the environment, and depressed mood may be reported to youth to encourage active participation in treatment (i.e., enhance motivation for change).

Social Effects. As mentioned previously, hyperactive and impulsive symptoms of ADHD often negatively affect how others perceive and react to children with ADHD. Parents should be queried to report the number of friends the child has and how the child's behavior affects friendships. In soliciting such information, parents should be queried to summarize observations of social interactions involving their children at sleepovers, birthday parties, and local sport clubs and leagues. Relevant to the treatment plan, it is important to assess the motivation of the child to participate in such activities, as later participation in these activities may be utilized to reinforce efforts in treatment and provide opportunities to practice therapy assignments.

Target Behavior. The parent should be queried to report when ADHD symptoms were first noticed, whether symptoms vary by situation, how symptoms may have changed over time, times in the day when symptoms are most and least prevalent, and events that are associated with symptom intensity (including absence of symptoms). It is also important to assess how people in the child's life perceive and react to the behavioral symptoms, as well as other consequences and antecedents that help maintain the behaviors (Magyary & Brandt, 2002).

Teachers

In diagnosing ADHD, teachers are often the best individuals to interview (Barnett & Labellarte, 2002), probably because they have ample opportunities to observe children in high- and low-structure activities, they are involved with children on a daily basis, and they are usually quite familiar with developmentally appropriate behavior (Barkley, 1998). Teachers should be queried about the target child's strengths and specific problem behaviors in various school settings (e.g., recess, formal classroom settings, lunch). In doing so, it is possible to compare conduct during academically oriented tasks (e.g., performing math problems) with conduct during nonacademically oriented tasks (e.g., free play). Behaviors that are consistent with *DSM-IV-TR* symptoms of ADHD should be emphasized, including potential reinforcers and behaviors that are often included in the treatment plan (e.g., academic, social, and play skills). School-based assessment should also shed light on teacher interactions with children (Magyary & Brandt, 2002). The class structure, including teacher-to-student ratio, types of activities, and teaching style, may all influence teacher perspectives on ADHD. For instance, a didactic teaching style with few options for physical activity combined with a large class may inappropriately cast a child with a kinetic learning style as exhibiting hyperactive symptoms.

CASE ILLUSTRATION WITH DIALOGUE

Enrique was a 10-year-old Caucasian male referred by his teacher for a second time to the school counselor for "poor academic performance." When asked to elaborate on the most recent referral, Enrique's teacher reported, "This child can't sit still for 5 seconds, he doesn't complete his homework, and he's failing most of his courses." Knowing that Enrique's mother was a 28-year-old single parent with a history of methlydioxymethamphetamine (MDMA) dependence, the counselor scheduled a meeting with the mother to occur during the following week and immediately conducted a 25-minute unstructured interview with Enrique (consent and assent for treatment forms were completed during the initial referral). To facilitate the assessment process, the counselor mailed Enrique's mother a demographic and background information form as well as a widely used standardized questionnaire to assess Enrique's conduct at home (i.e., Child Behavior Checklist, see Table 16.1). The mother was instructed to complete these forms and return them to the school prior to her scheduled session. The counselor also asked the teacher to complete a similar form relevant to Enrique's conduct in the classroom and arranged a meeting with the teacher to discuss Enrique's classroom behavior. Along these lines, the counselor arranged to observe Enrique in class during formal (math) and informal (gym) instruction.

Enrique presented to the interview wearing an untucked shirt and unkempt hair. Throughout the interview, he nervously jerked his left leg up and down and frequently tapped his index finger on his right knee. When asked to elaborate on the presenting problem, Enrique quickly retorted, "My teacher hates me." The counselor informed Enrique that she was interested in learning more about his hobbies and interests, his relationships with family and school, and things he would like to receive more often when doing well in school.

The counselor initiated the interview by asking Enrique to describe things he liked to do for fun. Enrique immediately reported, "I like to play Little League Football. I also like to play baseball in the park at home with my friends." He went on to describe other activities he enjoyed and often bragged about his athletic abilities. To facilitate rapport, the counselor frequently praised Enrique for his athletic prowess and queried what he liked and disliked about his friends. He appeared to have intimate friendships, and his play activities were unremarkable. In general, he seemed to have good relationships at school. He was particularly fond of his teacher, although he reported that his teacher thought he was a "dummy." When asked to disclose the people in his family he spent the most time with, he reported, "I don't have any family but my mother. Everyone in my family is dead or won't talk with me or my mother." The counselor queried Enrique to elaborate on these circumstances and to indicate the things he liked and disliked about his mother and family members he missed the most. Based on his reports, his maternal grandparents had died in a car accident when he was 5 years of age, and his paternal relatives (including his biological father) had "disowned" his mother because she used drugs when he was a baby.

In an attempt to gain a broad understanding of Enrique's social skills, the counselor presented Enrique with two social skills scenarios. One of the scenarios was relevant to negative assertion (i.e., response to being teased), and the other was relevant to positive assertion (i.e., request to play baseball). In both scenarios, the counselor depicted a hypothetical scenario to Enrique and instructed him to respond to the counselor's prompts as if the counselor were his friend and Enrique were in that situation: for instance, "In a moment, I'm going to pretend to be a boy who is teasing you. I want you to act just like you would in that situation. Here I go. You're a terrible baseball player." The child remained motionless for a few seconds and then exclaimed, "Leave me alone or I'll smack you in the head!" The counselor then instructed the child to pretend that the counselor was a friend and requested that Enrique attempt to get this friend to play baseball. Enrique responded, "I haven't seen you around for a while. Would you like to play baseball? We'll have a lot of fun." After the counselor indicated that he did not want to play because he was not feeling well, Enrique looked disappointed and replied, "I'd really like to play, but if you're not feeling well, let's do something else."

Hypothesizing that Enrique experienced problems with negative assertion but not positive assertion, the counselor initiated a conversation about Enrique's personal experiences with teasing and being told to do things he did not want to do. This discussion supported the counselor's hypothesis that Enrique appeared to be overly aggressive in responding to friends when he did not "get his way." The counselor presented Enrique with a list of rewards that are common for preadolescent children. He was instructed to rate his desire for each of the listed reinforcers, utilizing a scale of 1 (extremely undesired) to 5 (extremely desired). He was also encouraged to list additional rewards. Permission to have a friend spend the night at his home and ability to play outside after school were both extremely desired. He also indicated that he liked to be captain of the after-school kickball teams. The counselor noted these rewards as potential reinforcers for the parent and teacher to consider in the soon-to-be developed treatment plan.

MULTICULTURAL AND DIVERSITY ISSUES

Age

The expression of ADHD symptoms varies over the lifespan. As a result, several age-related issues involved in properly diagnosing ADHD are inherent in the diagnostic criteria. A diagnosis of ADHD is difficult to determine when children are younger than 4 or 5 years of age, as ADHD characteristic behaviors tend to be developmentally appropriate for children this age. Preschoolers are normally energetic and have few requirements in the accomplishment of tasks. They may also lack opportunities to meet criteria for the prerequisite number of symptoms necessary to evidence ADHD. In addition, when children get older (i.e., elementary school years), most are able to control behaviors that are consistent with ADHD; hence, the prevalence of ADHD generally decreases into adulthood. The onset of adolescence marks the first time most children who evidence ADHD symptoms are able to reliably report inner feelings of restlessness or jitteriness (Barnett & Labellarte, 2002), thus assisting in differential diagnosis.

Ethnicity and Culture

When assessing ADHD, it is important to consider the child's cultural perspective and how that perspective affects the child's behavior (Salend & Taylor, 2002). Although ADHD is found in all ethnic groups and countries studied to date, the rate of ADHD diagnosis in the United States is higher for African American children than for Hispanic or European American children (Barkley & Mash, 2003). Gilbert and Gay (1989, as cited in Salend & Rohena, 2003) theorized that these higher prevalence rates might be due to teachers' misattribution of culturally based stage-setting behaviors. It should be mentioned, however, that these stage-setting behaviors may be evidenced among non–African American students as well and may include the following:

> Such activities as looking over the assignment in its entirety; rearranging posture, elaborately checking pencils, paper, and writing space; asking teachers to repeat directions that have just been given; and checking perceptions of neighboring students. To the black student these are necessary maneuvers in preparing for performance; to the teacher they may appear as avoidance tactics, inattentiveness, disruptions, or evidence of not being prepared to do the assigned task. (Gilbert & Gay, 1989, p. 277, as cited in Salend & Rohena, 2003)

As another example of potential cultural influence in the diagnosis of ADHD, difficulties inherent in learning a second language may cause students who are in the process of learning English to present as inattentive and withdrawn. Thus, it is important to determine how the child's cultural or linguistic abilities may be influencing the expression of behavior (Damico, 1991; Pennsylvania Department of Education, 1997).

Gender

There are gender differences in both prevalence rates for ADHD diagnosis and subtypes diagnosed. Prevalence rates range from 2:1 to 9:1 (males: females), with diagnosis of ADHD-I being less prevalent than the other ADHD subtypes (APA, 2000). Interestingly, females tend to evidence higher rates of anxiety and depression, which are often overlooked in the diagnosis of ADHD (Brown, Abramowitz, Madan-Swain, Eckstrand, & Duncan, 1989).

DIFFERENTIAL DIAGNOSIS

Symptoms of ADHD may be situation specific, environmentally caused, or indicative of another disorder (Barnett & Labellarte, 2002), most often conduct, mood, anxiety, and learning disorders. *Differential diagnosis* concerns deriving the correct mental health diagnosis when symptoms are

consistent with more than one disorder. Along these lines, if a child were reported to experience difficulties remaining in his seat (a symptom of ADHD), the interviewer would need to eliminate the possibility that this symptom was not due to another disorder (e.g., noncompliance consistent with oppositional defiant disorder).

Conduct Disorder (CD) and Oppositional Defiant Disorder (ODD)

Many symptoms of ADHD are similar to symptoms making up the conduct disorders (e.g., ignoring parental instructions). Frequent comorbidity of the conduct disorders with ADHD (Azrin et al., 2001) also complicates differential diagnosis. To assist in differential diagnosis, the child's intentions offer insight. For instance, conduct disorders are often diagnosed when children purposefully fail to initiate tasks, whereas children with ADHD more often fail to initiate tasks because they are concerned their performance will be judged poorly. Children with ADHD, compared with children with conduct disorders, also agree to start tasks and then lose interest or get distracted from their commitments, whereas children with CDs are more likely to refuse tasks at the onset.

Mood Disorders

ADHD symptoms are often erroneously attributed to depressive disorders (Brown et al., 1989). For instance, irritability in children often occurs in both depressive and ADHD disorders. Although the duration of irritability in depressive disorders is less chronic compared with ADHD, the severity is greater (Mick, Spencer, Wozniak, & Biederman, 2005). Similarly, symptoms of distractibility, psychomotor agitation, talking more than usual or pressured speech, and decreased need for sleep are all manifested in bipolar disorder and ADHD (Barnett & Labellarte, 2002). Bipolar disorder rarely occurs before age 7. Therefore, the interviewer can easily rule out bipolar disorder if the onset of these symptoms occurs prior to 7 years of age.

Anxiety Disorders

Similarly, ADHD and anxiety disorders share some symptoms, particularly those associated with distractibility and restlessness. Children with anxiety disorders are less likely than children with

ADHD to be socially disruptive, impulsive, or aggressive and more likely to be socially inhibited. They are more likely to have problems focusing their attention than sustaining it, and their restlessness results from internal worried states rather than excessive energy (Barkley, 1998). Parental and teacher reports are good sources of information about the child's visible symptoms. However, the child's internal states must be assessed during the child interview.

Learning Disorders

Children with learning disorders score significantly lower (+1 standard deviation) on achievement tests relative to IQ tests, do not have an early history of hyperactivity and attention problems, are not impulsive or disinhibited, and are not socially disruptive. Their attentional problems are task specific or subject specific and usually become apparent in middle childhood, whereas children with ADHD are more likely to evidence problems in all areas of academics and have an onset prior to 7 years (Barkley, 1998). Interestingly, however, it should be mentioned that many ADHD children later develop learning disorders. Thus, learning disabilities should be emphasized in all behavioral interviews involving ADHD children.

Other Disorders

One of the first indications of psychotic disorders concerns problems with attention (Barnett & Labellarte, 2002). However, the presence of psychosis (e.g., odd thoughts, social aloofness, or unusual sensory reactions) helps to distinguish between ADHD and psychotic disorders (Barkley, 1998). Excessive motor movements associated with ADHD are differentiated from excessive movements due to stereotypic movement disorder, as stereotypies are generally focused and fixed, not generalized as in ADHD. Other medical disorders (cortical lesions, fetal alcohol syndrome, thyroid disorders, or genetic disorders; Barnett & Labellarte, 2002) can mimic ADHD symptoms and are more difficult for mental health professionals to identify. Thus, it is always important to consider medical referrals and medical history reports when attempting to diagnosis ADHD.

BEHAVIORAL ASSESSMENT

Information gathered during the interview process is incorporated in the Functional Behavioral Assessment (FBA) (Salend & Taylor, 2002) with other assessment tools. FBA is used to identify the child's maladaptive behaviors and to identify factors that maintain ADHD symptoms (Sugai, Horner, & Sprague, 1999).

In this process, it helps to make a list of all target problem behaviors, particularly behavioral deficits that will likely impede treatment. Whenever possible, similar target behaviors may be grouped together. For instance, failure to perform homework assignments and dysfunctional study habits might be grouped together due to their functional similarity, whereas cutting in line at school and blurting out answers, both classic examples of impulsive behavior, are functionally distinct and thus would probably need to be listed separately. Antecedent stimuli (e.g., learning disabilities, parenting deficits, poor social skills, irritability) and behavioral consequences (e.g., yelling, school detention, teasing, laughing) determined in the assessment process to maintain target problem behaviors can then be recorded (antecedent stimuli to the left of their respective target behaviors, consequences to the right). This process permits the interviewer to objectively conceptualize factors that contribute most to target problem behaviors, as well as to understand how the environment acts to shape problem behavior.

Interestingly, stimuli that are chiefly implicated in the development and maintenance of ADHD symptoms often contribute to more than one target problem behavior or may be implicated as both antecedent stimuli and behavioral consequences. For instance, yelling may cause a child to be anxious (i.e., antecedent condition), thus contributing to inattentiveness (i.e., target behavior). Yelling may also occur after the target behavior, however, thus contributing to other problem behaviors (e.g., aggression). The latter example suggests it may be important to prioritize "yelling" as a primary goal for treatment, since this stimulus appears to influence multiple problem behaviors.

The FBA also makes it easy to quickly identify areas or gaps in the case that will need further clarification or additional inquiry. For instance, if antecedent stimuli were not identified for the target behavior "argues with classmates," the interviewer might spend additional time interviewing the child to determine stimuli that occur prior to the child's arguments with classmates (e.g., social skills deficits, teasing by others, tension). Therefore, the interviewer can utilize information gained from the FBA to objectively determine appropriate diagnosis, select treatment targets, and make appropriate referrals.

SELECTION OF TREATMENT TARGETS AND REFERRAL

The determination of treatment targets and referrals is complicated and necessitates diplomacy. Indeed, the child, parent, and referring agency (usually an administrator or teacher from the child's school) may have separate agendas influencing the treatment plan. In determining treatment plans, the preliminary goals of the target child and all significant others with roles in the child's life should be integrated and subsequently listed in degree of relative priority. This may initially occur based on the interviewer's impressions resulting from the behavioral assessment and later be substantiated by all involved parties during individual interviews.

Along these lines, the interviewer should first demonstrate how antecedent stimuli and consequences relate to target behaviors utilizing the FBA model. Age-appropriate sensitivity should be considered in disseminating this information to the target child and, separately, to significant others involved in the child's treatment plan. To the extent possible, all involved parties should be involved in the prioritization of treatment goals. Family members should be encouraged to consider the likelihood of change when prioritizing target problem behaviors, because it is important for the child to experience success early in treatment. Developmental considerations will obviously compromise the extent to which children are involved in this process.

Once behavioral problems are prioritized in treatment planning, the interviewer should assist the family in scheduling appointments with referral agents. As earlier indicated, most children with ADHD should be referred to a physician for a medical checkup to rule out potential medical conditions that may be contributing to the constellation of symptoms. Medical practitioners should also be considered for potential medication management (e.g., stimulant drugs), as these drugs have consistently been shown to be at least as effective as the behavioral therapies (Carlson, Pelham, Milich, & Dixon, 1992; Horn et al., 1991). Recommendations for school tutors or intensive school guidance programs are often useful, particularly for older children evidencing ADHD symptoms and academic difficulties.

REFERENCES

American Psychiatric Association. (2000). *Diagnostic and statistical manual of mental disorders* (4th ed., Text rev.). Washington, DC: Author.

Anastopoulos, A. D., & Shelton, T. L. (2001). *Assessing attention-deficit/hyperactivity disorder.* New York: Kluwer/Plenum.

Angello, L. M., Volpe, R. J., DiPerna, J. C., Gureasko-Moore, S. P., Gureasko-Moore, D. P., Nebrig, M. R., et al. (2003). Assessment of attention-deficit/hyperactivity disorder: An evaluation of six published rating scales. *School Psychology Review, 32,* 241–262.

Azrin, N. H., Donohue, B., Teichner, G., Crum, T., Howell, J., & DeCato, L. (2001). A controlled evaluation and description of individual-cognitive problem solving and family-behavioral therapies in conduct-disordered and substance dependent youth. *Journal of Child and Adolescent Substance Abuse, 11,* 1–43.

Barkley, R. A. (1990). *Attention-deficit hyperactivity disorder: A handbook for diagnosis and treatment.* New York: Guilford Press.

Barkley, R. A. (1997). *ADHD and the nature of self-control.* New York: Guilford Press.

Barkley, R. A. (1998). *Attention-deficit hyperactivity disorder: A handbook for diagnosis and treatment* (2nd ed.). New York: Guilford Press.

Barkley, R. A., Fischer, M., Edelbrock, C. S., & Smallish, L. (1991). The adolescent outcome of hyperactive children diagnosed by research criteria: Mother-child interactions, family conflicts, and material psychopathology. *Journal of Child Psychology and Psychiatry, 32,* 233–256.

Barkley, R. A., Grodzinsky, G., & DuPaul, G. (1992). Frontal lobe functions in attention deficit disorder with and without hyperactivity: A review and research report. *Journal of Abnormal Child Psychology, 20,* 163–188.

Barkley, R. A., & Mash, E. J. (2003). *Child psychopathology* (2nd ed.). New York: Guilford Press.

Barnett, S. R., & Labellarte, M. J. (2002). Practical assessment and treatment of attention-deficit/hyperactivity disorder. *Adolescent Psychiatry, 26,* 181–225.

Biederman, J., Faraone, S. V., & Lapey, K. (1992). Comorbidity of diagnosis in attention-deficit hyperactivity disorder. In G. Weiss (Ed.), *Child and adolescent psychiatry clinics of North America: Attention deficit hyperactivity disorder* (pp. 335–360). Philadelphia: Saunders.

Brown, M. (2000). Diagnosis and treatment of children and adolescents with attention-deficit/hyperactivity disorder. *Journal of Counseling & Development, 78*, 195–203.

Brown, R. T., Abramowitz, A. J., Madan-Swain, A., Eckstrand, D., & Duncan, M. (1989). *ADHD gender differences in a clinical referral sample.* Paper presented at the Annual Meeting of the American Academy of Child and Adolescent Psychiatry, New York.

Burns, G. L., Gomez, R., Walsh, J. A., & de Moura, M. A. (2003). Understanding source effects in ADHD rating scales: Reply to DuPaul (2003). *Psychological Assessment, 15*, 118–119.

Cantwell, D. P. (1972). Psychiatric illness in families of hyperactive children. *Archives of General Psychiatry, 27*, 414–417.

Cantwell, D. P. (1985). Hyperactive children have grown up: What have we learned about what happens to them? *Archives of General Psychiatry, 42*, 1026–1028.

Cantwell, D. P. (1996). Attention deficit disorder: A review of the past 10 years. *Journal of the American Academy of Child & Adolescent Psychiatry, 35*, 978–987.

Carlson, C. L., Pelham, W. E., Jr., Milich, R., & Dixon, J. (1992). Single and combined effects of methylphenidate and behavior therapy on the classroom performance of children with attention-deficit hyperactivity disorder. *Journal of Abnormal Child Psychology, 20*, 213–232.

Chilcoat, H. D., & Breslau, N. (1999). Pathways from ADHD to early drug use. *Journal of the American Academy of Child & Adolescent Psychiatry, 38*, 1347–1354.

Conners, C. K. (1997). *Conners' Parent and Teacher Rating Scales Revised.* North Tonawanda, NY: Multi-Health Systems.

Damico, J. S. (1991). Descriptive assessment of communicative ability in limited English proficient students. In E. V. Hamayan & J. S. Damico (Eds.), *Limiting bias in the assessment of bilingual students* (pp. 157–218). Austin: Pro-ed.

DiScala, C., Lescohier, I., Barthel, M., & Li, G. (1998). Injuries to children with attention deficit hyperactivity disorder. *Pediatrics, 102*, 1415–1421.

Disney, E. R., Elkins, I. J., McGue, M., & Iacono, W. G. (1999). Effects of ADHD, Conduct disorder, and gender on substance use and abuse in adolescence. *American Journal of Psychiatry, 156*, 1515–1521.

Douglas, V. I., & Parry, P. A. (1994). Effects of rewards and non-reward on attention and frustration in attention deficit disorder. *Journal of Abnormal Child Psychology, 22*, 281–302.

DuPaul, G. J. (2003). Assessment of ADHD symptoms: Comment on Gomez et al. (2003). *Psychological Assessment, 15*, 115–117.

DuPaul, G. J., Power, T. J., & McGoey, K. E. (1998). Reliability and validity of parent and teacher rating of attention-deficit/hyperactivity disorder symptoms. *Journal of Psychoeducational Assessment, 16*, 55–68.

Gadow, K. D., & Sprafkin, J. (1997). *ADHD Symptom Checklists-4: Manual.* Stony Brook, NY: Checkmate Plus.

Geller, D. A., Biederman, J., Faraone, S., Spencer, T., Doyle, R., Mullin, B., et al. (2004). Re-examining comorbidity of obsessive compulsive and attention-deficit hyperactivity disorder using an empirically derived taxonomy. *European Child and Adolescent Psychiatry, 13*, 83–91.

Goodyear, P., & Hynd, G. (1992). Attention deficit disorder with (ADD/H) and without (ADD/WO) hyperactivity: Behavioral and neuropsychology differentiation. *Journal of Clinical Child Psychology, 21*, 273–304.

Harada, Y., Yamazaki, T., & Saitoh, K. (2002). Psychosocial problems in attention-deficit hyperactivity disorder with oppositional defiant disorder. *Psychiatry and Clinical Neurosciences, 56*, 365–369.

Hart, E. L., Lahey, B. B., Loeber, R., Applegate, B., & Frick, P. J. (1995). Developmental change in attention-deficit hyperactivity disorder in boys: A four-year longitudinal study. *Journal of Abnormal Child Psychology, 23*, 729–749.

Horn, W. F., Ialongo, N., Pascoe, J. M., Greenberg, G., Packard, T., Lopez, M., et al. (1991). Additive effects of psychostimulants, parent training, and self-control therapy with ADHD children. *Journal of the American Academy of Child & Adolescent Psychiatry, 30*, 233–240.

Jensen, P. S., Martin, D., & Cantwell, D. P. (1997). Comorbidity in ADHD: Implications for research, practice and *DSM-V. Journal of American Academy of Child & Adolescent Psychiatry, 36*, 1065–1079.

Kamphaus, R. W., & Reynolds, C. R. (1998). *Behavior Assessment System for Children: Monitor for ADHD manual.* Circle Pines, MN: American Guidance Service.

Lahey, B. B., & Carlson, C. L. (1992). Validity of the diagnostic category of attention deficit disorder without hyperactivity: A review of the literature. In S. E. Shaywitz & B. A. Shaywitz (Eds.), *Attention deficit disorder comes of age: Toward the twenty-first century* (pp. 119–144). Austin, TX: Pro-Ed.

Lambert, N., & Hartsough, C. (1998). Prospective study of tobacco and substance dependencies among samples of ADHD and non-ADHD participants. *Journal of Learning Disabilities, 31*, 533–544.

Madon, S., Jussim, L., & Eccles, J. (1997). In search of the powerful self-fulfilling prophecy. *Journal of Personality & Social Psychology, 72*, 791–809.

Magyary, D., & Brandt, P. (2002). A decision tree and clinical paths for the assessment and management of children with ADHD. *Issues in Mental Health Nursing, 23*, 553–566.

Manuzza, S., Klein, R. G., & Bessler, A. (1993). Adult outcome of hyperactive boys. *Archives of General Psychiatry, 50*, 565–576.

McCarney, S. B. (1995). *Attention Deficit Disorders Evaluation Scale School Version* (2nd ed.). Columbia, MO: Hawthorne.

Meichenbaum, D., & Goodman, J. (1971). Training impulsive children to talk to themselves: A means of developing self-control. *Journal of Abnormal Psychology, 77*, 115–126.

Mick, E., Spencer, T., Wozniak, J., & Biederman, J. (2005). Heterogeneity of irritability in attention-deficit/hyperactivity disorder subjects with and without mood disorders. *Biological Psychiatry,* *58,* 576–582.

Mitsis, E. M., McKay, K. E., Schulz, K. P., Newcorn, J. H., & Halperin, J. M. (2000). Parent-teacher concordance for *DSM-IV* attention-deficit/hyperactivity disorder in a clinic-referred sample. *Journal of American Academy of Child & Adolescent Psychiatry,* *38,* 308–313.

Morrison, J. R., & Stewart, M. A. (1971). A family study of the hyperactive child syndrome. *Biological Psychiatry,* *3,* 189–195.

Morrison, J. R., & Stewart, M. A. (1973). Evidence for a polygenetic inheritance in the hyperactive child syndrome. *American Journal of Psychiatry,* *130,* 791–792.

National Institutes of Health. (2000). National Institutes of Health consensus development conference statement: Diagnosis and treatment of attention-deficit/hyperactivity disorder (ADHD). *Journal of American Academy of Child & Adolescent Psychiatry,* *39,* 182–193.

Neophytou, K., & Webber, R. (2005). Attention deficit hyperactivity disorder: The family and social context. *Australian Social Work,* *58,* 313–325.

Pennsylvania Department of Education. (1997). *Instructional support for students who are culturally and linguistically diverse: A collection of background information and training materials.* Harrisburg, PA: Author.

Quinn, P. O. (1997). *Attention deficit disorder: Diagnosis and treatment from infancy to adulthood.* New York: Brunner/Mazel.

Reich, W. (2000). Diagnostic Interview for Children and Adolescents (DICA). *Journal of the American Academy of Child & Adolescent Psychiatry,* *39,* 59–67.

Reich, W., Welner, Z., Herjanic, B., & MultiHealth System Staff. (1996). *Diagnostic Interview for Children and Adolescents-IV Computer Program (DICA-IV).* New York: MultiHealth Systems.

Riccio, C. A., & Jemison, S. J. (1998). ADHD and emergent literacy: Influence of language factors. *Reading and Writing Quarterly: Overcoming Learning Difficulties,* *14,* 43–58.

Root, R. W., & Resnick, R.J. (2003). An update on the diagnosis and treatment of attention-deficit/hyperactivity disorder in children. *Professional Psychology: Research and Practice,* *34,* 34–41.

Salend, S. J., & Rohena, E. (2003). Students with attention deficit disorders: An overview. *Intervention in School and Clinic,* *38,* 259–266.

Salend, S. J., & Taylor, L. S. (2002). Cultural perspectives: Missing pieces in the functional assessment process. *Intervention in School and Clinic,* *38,* 104–112.

Sattler, J. M. (2002). *Assessment of children: Behavioral and clinical applications* (4th ed.). San Diego, CA: Sattler.

Schwanz, K. A., & Kamphaus, R. W. (1997). Assessment and diagnosis of ADHD. In W. M. Bender (Ed.), *Understanding ADHD: A practical guide for teachers and parents* (pp. 81–122). Columbus, OH: Merrill/Prentice Hall.

Shaffer, D., Fisher, P., Lucas, C. P., Dulcan, M. K., & Schwab-Stone, M. E. (2000). NIMH Diagnostic Interview Schedule for Children Version IV (NIMH DISC-IV): Description, differences from previous versions, and reliability of some common diagnoses. *Journal of American Academy of Child & Adolescent Psychiatry,* *39,* 28–38.

Stein, M. P. (2004). Attention-deficit/hyperactivity disorder: The diagnostic process from different perspectives. *Journal of Developmental Behavior Pediatrics,* *25,* 53–57.

Sugai, G. A., Horner, R. H., & Sprague, J. R. (1999). Functional-assessment-based behavior support planning: Research to practice to research. *Behavioral Disorders,* *24,* 253–257.

Swanson, J. M. (1992). *School-based assessments for ADD students.* Irvine, CA: K.C. Publishing.

Taylor, E., Sandberg, S., Thurley, G., & Giles, S. (1991). *The epidemiology of childhood hyperactivity.* London: Oxford University Press.

Thunstrom, M. T. (2002). Severe sleep problems in infancy associated with subsequent development of attention-deficit/hyperactivity disorder at 5.5 years of age. *Acta Paediatrica,* *91,* 584–593.

Ullman, R. K., Sleator, E. K., & Sprague, R. L. (1997). *ACTeRS teacher and parent forms manual.* Champaign, IL: MetriTech.

Wasserman, R. C., Kelleher, K. J., Bocian, A., Baker, A., Childs, G. E., Indacochea, F., et al. (1999). Identification of attentional and hyperactivity problems in primary care: A report from pediatric research in office settings and the ambulatory sentinel practice network. *Pediatrics,* *103,* e38.

Weckerly, J., Aarons, G. A., Leslie, L. K., Garland, A. F., Landsverk, J., & Hough, R. L. (2005). Attention on inattention: The differential effect of caregiver education on endorsement of ADHD symptoms. *Developmental and Behavioral Pediatrics,* *26,* 201–208.

Werry, J. S., Elkind, G. S., & Reeves, J. S. (1987). Attention deficit, conduct, oppositional, and anxiety disorders in children: Laboratory differences. *Journal of Abnormal Child Psychology,* *15,* 409–428.

Zametkin, A. J., & Ernst, M. (1999). Problems in the management of attention-deficit-hyperactivity disorder. *New England Journal of Medicine 340,* 40–46.

17

EATING DISORDERS

MICHELLE HEFFNER MACERA AND J. SCOTT MIZES

DESCRIPTION OF THE DISORDERS

The start of an Olympic dream began when Christy Henrich enrolled in her first gymnastics class at age 4. Twelve years later, 16-year-old Christy wanted to compete at the 1988 Olympics, but her 10th-place finish at the U.S. Olympic Gymnastics Trials was .395 of a point too low to earn a spot on the six-member team. Amid the disappointment, Christy was determined to continue training for the 1992 Olympic games. To boost her scores, Christy considered some advice that a judge gave her to lose weight. Christy stopped eating and burned calories in grueling training sessions. If she did eat, she limited her daily caloric intake to one apple—sometimes an apple slice—and then forced herself to vomit or take laxatives. Initially, the gymnastics community praised Christy as her body transformed from a muscular build into a thinner, more "pixie" shape. In 1989, she placed second at the U.S. National Championships and was selected to compete at the World Championships. Soon, however, the toll of caloric deprivation, excessive exercise, self-induced vomiting, and laxative abuse took its toll on Christy's body, and she became too weak to perform gymnastics. In 1992, instead of performing in the Barcelona Olympics, Christy was repeatedly hospitalized for anorexia.

In a newspaper article, a U.S. gymnastics official described a 1994 phone conversation with Christy ("Illness Attacks Mind and Body," 1994). The official asked Christy, "How are you doing?" Christy replied, "Sometimes I have good days. Sometimes I have bad days, but I'm doing better." The official was encouraged by Christy's comment and believed that Christy was recovering. Less than 1 month after this phone conversation, Christy lapsed into a coma and died of multiple organ failure at a weight of 61 lbs. Christy's words to the gymnastics official provide a glimpse into one of the intricacies of interviewing children and adolescents with eating disorders, who may minimize or deny symptoms with responses such as "I'm doing better" or "I'm fine." The purpose of this chapter is to inform clinicians of how to cope with potential obstacles and adequately interview children and adolescents who present with eating disorders. The *Diagnostic and Statistical Manual for Mental Disorders, Fourth Edition, Text Revision (DSM-IV-TR)* (American Psychiatric Association [APA], 2000a) lists three types of eating disorders: anorexia nervosa (AN), bulimia nervosa (BN), and eating disorder-not otherwise specified (ED-NOS).

Of the three diagnoses, AN is most commonly associated with adolescence, with an average age of onset between 15 to 19 years (Bulik, Reba,

Siega-Riz, & Reichborn-Kjennerud, 2005). Symptoms of AN include abnormally low body weight, fear of weight gain, and body image disturbance (APA, 2000a). Body image disturbance can include body avoidance behaviors, perceptual distortions of body size, dissatisfaction with weight/shape, and reliance on weight/shape as a basis for self-esteem (Crowther & Sherwood, 1997). The *DSM* diagnostic criteria also require the absence of three consecutive menstrual periods, but this criterion applies only to postmenarchal females. Unfortunately, menstrual irregularity is difficult to determine for adolescents who may not have established regular menstrual cycles (Robin, Gilroy, & Dennis, 1998). Another problem with the amennorhea criterion is that hormonal birth control pills regulate the menstrual cycle and may induce menstruation in clients who would otherwise have amennorhea. Clinicians typically disregard the amenorrhea criterion if the client is using birth control pills. (Walsh & Garner, 1997). Clients who meet the diagnostic criteria for AN can be classified with either restricting or binge-purge subtype. The restricting subtype is assigned if dietary restraint is the method of weight loss. The binge-purge subtype is assigned if eating episodes are followed by compensatory behaviors, such as excessive exercise, self-induced vomiting, laxative abuse, and use of diet pills and/or diuretics.

AN binge-purge subtype can be distinguished from bulimia nervosa (BN) based upon body weight. Although body weight must be abnormally low for the diagnosis of AN, there is no body weight requirement for BN, and many clients with BN are normal or overweight. It is important to note that AN and BN cannot be simultaneously diagnosed, and the diagnosis of AN takes precedence over the diagnosis of BN (Walsh & Garner, 1997). Therefore, a client with low body weight, body image disturbance, amennorhea, and binge-purge behaviors should be diagnosed with AN binge-purge subtype, even if the binging and compensatory behavior satisfy all of the BN criteria.

The diagnosis of BN in preadolescent children is extremely rare, and the average age of onset for the majority of BN cases is between 15 and 27 years (Kendler et al., 1991). The *DSM* (2000a) diagnostic criteria for BN include symptoms of body image disturbance, binge eating, and compensatory behaviors that occur at least twice per week for 3 months. *Binge eating* is defined as eating an abnormally large amount of food in a discrete time period, with a lack of control over eating. To compensate for the excessive food intake, the client engages in compensatory behaviors, such as self-induced vomiting, laxative abuse, enema use, diet pills, excessive exercise, and fasting. Based on the type of compensatory behavior, the client can be diagnosed with either purging or nonpurging subtype. The purging subtype is diagnosed if compensatory behaviors include vomiting, laxatives, enema use, and/or diuretics. The nonpurging subtype is diagnosed in cases of fasting or excessive exercise.

Cases of binge eating without engagement in compensatory behavior are diagnosed as ED-NOS. The category of binge-eating disorder (BED) is being considered but requires further study before it is officially included in the *DSM*. Currently, BED symptoms include binge eating twice per week for 6 months, with associated symptoms, such as rapid eating, eating when not hungry, eating alone to avoid embarrassment, eating until uncomfortably full, and guilt following a binge.

The category of ED-NOS also applies to cases of partial-symptom AN or BN. Especially with BN, adolescents are more likely to present with partial symptoms that do not satisfy all *DSM* criteria for BN. Up to 15% of all adolescents engage in some form of subthreshold binge eating and purging behaviors (Schneider, 2003). Although they do not engage in the binge-purge episodes frequently enough to meet the diagnostic criteria, adolescents with partial-symptom BN report similar levels of self-esteem problems, depression, dietary restraint, and body dissatisfaction as those who meet full BN criteria (Le Grange, Loeb, Van Orman, & Jellar, 2004). Thus, treatment is necessary even if the binge-purge behavior does not fit precisely into the mold of the *DSM* criteria.

Interviewing Strategies

Structured Interviews

Several structured interviews have been developed to assess a wide range of *DSM-IV* psychiatric disorders, including eating disorders, in children and adolescents: Diagnostic Interview Schedule for Children (DISC) (Shaffer, Fisher, & Lucas, 2000), Kiddie Schedule for Affective Disorders and Schizophrenia Present and Lifetime Version (K-SADS-PL) (Kaufman et al., 1997), Diagnostic Interview for Children and Adolescents (DICA) (Reich, 2000), and Child and Adolescent Psychiatric Assessment (CAPA) (Angold & Costello, 2000). All four structured interviews include parent versions to gather diagnostic information from the parent or to compare parent-child agreement. An advantage of these interviews is the assessment of eating disorders plus possible comorbid Axis I conditions that may be treatment targets. Some of the most common comorbid conditions include anxiety disorders and mood disorders (Herpertz-Dahlmann, Wewetzer, Schulz, & Remschmidt, 1996).

In addition to these more global interviews, interviews that focus specifically on eating disorder symptoms are also available. The most commonly used interview for the diagnosis of eating disorders in children is the Eating Disorder Examination Adapted for Children (ChEDE) (Bryant-Waugh, Cooper, Taylor, & Lask, 1996; Watkins, Frampton, Lask, & Bryant-Waugh, 2005), a child version of the Eating Disorder Examination Interview for Adults (Cooper & Fairburn, 1987). In addition to wording modifications, the ChEDE also includes a sorting task in which the child rank orders values, including the value of weight and shape. Other structured eating disorder interviews have been developed and normed for use with adults but not modified for children. These include the Interview for Diagnosis of Eating Disorders-IV (Kutlesic, Williamson, Gleaves, Barbin, & Murphy-Eberenz, 1998), Clinical Eating Disorder Rating Instrument (Palmer, Robertson, Cain, & Black, 1996), and Structured Interview for Anorexia and Bulimia Nervosa (Fichter et al., 1991).

Administration of structured diagnostic interviews requires extensive training and may be time-consuming. The ChEDE, for example, requires 1 hour of administration, which may encompass the entire intake session. In addition, structured interviews can be inflexible and disruptive to rapport building. The interview is the client's first impression of the therapeutic relationship and may be an adolescent's first clinical experience. Therefore, building rapport to engage the client in the session should be the main goal of an initial interview, and this goal can be more effectively achieved through unstructured interviews.

Unstructured Interviews

To allot clinical time to build rapport, we recommend that the clinician administer intake questionnaires prior to the interview to gather background information and diagnostic data (see Table 17.1). The clinician can review the questionnaire data prior to the interview to gather an initial clinical impression and follow up with clarification questions during the interview. The intake questionnaire can be supplemented with standardized self-report measures, as described in Macera and Mizes (2006). During the course of the interview, the following topics should be assessed: binge eating, dietary restraint, body image, and weight history.

Binge Eating. Assessment of binge eating is less straightforward than it may appear. Consider this case example: After dinner, Pat ate one slice of pecan pie. Pat did not intend to eat any dessert but could not resist the urge to have just one bite. One bite led to another, and Pat just could not stop until the whole slice was gone. For AN, the *DSM* (2000a) criteria do not define binge-eating frequency, duration, or quantity for the diagnosis of the binge-purge subtype. Thus, relatively small quantities of food (e.g., one slice of pie) may qualify as a subjective binge-eating episode for a client with AN. For BN and BED, however, the *DSM* (2000a) criteria define a binge as consumption of a larger amount of food than what most people would eat under similar circumstances. Thus, eating a slice of pie is a normal dessert for most people and would not meet the definition of binge eating for BED or BN.

Assessment of binge eating is subjective for clients and clinicians alike. Between people, there are wide variations in the amount of calories each person consumes during a binge. Even within the same client, caloric intake can vary from binge to binge. Asking a client what and how much was eaten during the most recent binge can aid in determining whether binge eating is occurring. It is also helpful to ask whether eating is followed by compensatory behavior (exercise, skipping meals, etc.). Compensatory behavior is not likely to be

TABLE 17.1   Sample Questions to Include on a Preintake Questionnaire Form

Name _____   Age _____   Birthdate _____

Who referred you to our eating disorder clinic?

Tell us about the reason for your visit today.

Living Situation

Who is living in the home with you?

Are your parents married?

If your parents are married, how long have they been married?

If your parents divorced, how old were you when they divorced?

If your parents never married or divorced, what is the custody/visitation arrangement?

How would you describe the relationships among people living in your home?

Does anyone in your biological family have a problem with substance abuse or mental illness?

Education History

What is your grade in school?

Have you ever failed, repeated, or skipped a grade?

How are your grades in school?

Have there been any changes in your grades or academic performance?

Do you like school?

What activities are you involved in at school?

How would you describe your relationship with your classmates?

Medical History

Provide the name and phone number of your primary care physician (family doctor).

When was your most recent medical checkup or evaluation?

Have you ever been hospitalized for a medical problem? If so, when and where?

Are you taking medications for medical problems? (State medication, dosage, and prescriber)

Date of last menstrual period: _____

Place a check next to each medical problem you have:

Irregular periods

Excess body hair or a "peach fuzz" hair growth on parts of your body

Brittle hair or hair falling out

Orthostatic hypotension

Constipation

Dizziness

Dental cavities

Swollen cheeks

Burning/sore throat

Rapid/irregular heartbeats

Dry skin

Edema (swelling) in hands or feet

Coldness in hands or feet

Other medical problems:

Mental Health

Have you ever seen a counselor for emotional problems?

Are you currently taking medication for psychological/emotional problems?

Have you ever taken medication for psychological/emotional problems? If so, what medication and when?

Have you ever been a patient in a psychiatric hospital?

Have you ever been hospitalized for an eating disorder?

Do you think of suicide? If so, describe your plan.

Have you ever made a suicide attempt?

Have you ever experienced a traumatic event? Have you ever been abused or neglected?

(Continued)

TABLE 17.1 (Continued)

How much alcohol do you drink?
Do you use illegal drugs?
Do you smoke?

Eating Behavior

When did your eating problems begin?
Give an estimate of how many calories you eat each day. Do you limit your calories?
How much caffeine do you use?
Do you ever feel that your eating is out of control and you binge?
If yes, describe how much you ate during a recent binge.
If yes, how often do you binge?
Do you use any of the following methods to control your weight?

_____ Vomiting (How often? _____ Age Begun_____)

_____ Laxatives

_____ Diuretics

_____ Diet Pills

_____ Fasting

_____ Exercise

Weight History

What is your current height?
What is your current weight?
How often do you weigh yourself?
What is the most you have ever weighed? _____ How old were you when weighed this much?
What is your goal weight?

present in persons with BED since they do not, by definition, engage in compensatory behaviors. Thus, they are more likely to have one binge flow into the next binge, with no "punctuating" behavior to distinguish one binge from the next. Indeed, this is why the *DSM-IV* criteria for BED specify the number of days that binging occurs in order to meet the diagnostic criteria, rather than number of binge episodes, as is done for BN. For AN or BN, compensatory behavior indicates that the client perceives the eating to be a binge episode, even though compensatory behavior per se does not definitely indicate that a binge has occurred. Beglin and Fairburn (1992) introduced the useful terminology of subjective versus objective binge episodes. *Objective binge episodes* are those where a large amount of food is consumed. A *subjective binge episode* is one where very small amounts of "forbidden food" are eaten. The subjective versus objective binge distinction may be useful because different treatment approaches are needed for the two types of binges. For objective binges, the goal is to eliminate the binge. For subjective binges, the goal is to have the person tolerate, without guilt or self-criticism, the eating of forbidden foods.

Loss of control during a binge is described in the *DSM* (2000a) as patients feeling that they cannot stop eating or control the amount they eat. Many patients will report feeling a loss of control while binge eating. Some patients, however, are hesitant to report a loss of control. Some may say that they skipped breakfast and lunch and planned to binge when they got home from school. Or they may say that they could have stopped eating during the binge but chose not to. Others have described their binge eating as a habit more than a loss of control (which is more likely with persons with long histories of binge eating). In this situation, we rely on behavioral indicators of loss of control, rather than verbal reports. Many of these behavioral indications are drawn from behavioral descriptors of binge eating in the current *DSM-IV* criteria (and, interestingly, were part of the diagnostic criteria for BN in earlier versions of the *DSM*). We ask questions to determine how the binge ends. Binge eating is considered when the episode ends based on "external" factors other than normal satiation. Sample questions include the following:

- Do you eat more rapidly than usual during a binge?

- Do you eat until you are uncomfortably full and cannot eat any more?

- Do you eat all of the food that is available (e.g., an entire package of cookies)?

- Would you stop eating if someone discovered you eating?

- Even if you planned to binge, would you find it difficult to stop eating before consuming all that you had planned to eat?

Dietary Restraint and Forbidden-Food Rules. *Dietary restraint* refers to a conscious intent to restrict food intake, whether or not the person is successful in doing so. Persons high in dietary restraint have a variety of rules that define "safe" versus "unsafe" or "forbidden" eating, relative to the fear of gaining weight. When interviewing about forbidden-food rules, we ask about rules related to three general types of food rules, drawn from our clinical experience: type of food, amount of food, or some aspect of the timing of eating. Questions may include the following:

- What types of food do you feel you should almost never eat?

This may include high-calorie foods, such as ice cream, cakes, and even red meat. Vegetarianism is often a "smokescreen" for an eating disorder, and female high school students who adhere to a vegetarian diet report more eating disorder attitudes than their nonvegetarian peers (Lindeman, Stark, & Latvala, 2000).

- Do you have any limit for how much food you can eat?

Some clients may define a specific quantity or calorie limit. Others will define a subjective limit based on feeling of fullness in the stomach, feeling that their stomach is sticking out, or their pants are getting tight.

- Do you avoid eating any meals (breakfast, lunch, dinner)? Do you avoid eating at any times of day (morning, late at night)? How do you react if you eat during a forbidden meal or time period?

Body Image. Symptoms of both AN and BN include body image disturbance, but the diagnostic criteria for BED is silent on the issue of body image. Nonetheless, many adolescents with BED "feel fat," and many are, in fact, obese. Many of those with BED, though not all, report a high degree of shape and weight dissatisfaction, which may or may not have significant effects on self-esteem. In general, those with BN are more likely than those with AN to easily state that they feel fat and that this has a negative effect on their self-esteem. More difficulties are encountered when assessing body image in AN patients. For adolescents, this is sometimes due to a refusal to admit to symptoms of AN as part of the denial of the seriousness of low body weight. Others may not feel "fat" at that moment because their weight is at or below their self-defined ideal weight (Mizes, 1992). The problem, of course, is that their ideal weight is unrealistically low, often 30 pounds lower than a medically accepted normal or expected weight (Mizes, 1992). To assess body image in clients who deny body image problems, the following questions are helpful:

- How would you feel if you weighed 1, 5, or 10 pounds more than you currently weigh?

- How would you feel after eating a "forbidden food"?

- What would it be like if you had to wear size 4 jeans?

The body image assessment should also explore body image avoidance behaviors. These are behaviors that reduce the feeling of being fat or other distress associated with appearance, shape, and weight. For example, clients may experience marked discomfort or refuse to look at themselves, clothed or unclothed, in a full-length mirror. Others will look in a mirror but avert their eyes and not look at the body areas that bother them. Other behaviors involve wearing excessively baggy clothes or refusing to wear shorts, bathing suits, short-sleeved shirts, or other clothing that reveals shape or weight. Among patients who are sexually active (or potentially sexually active), some may abstain from sexual contact to avoid their partners seeing them unclothed, or have sex with the lights off. Many patients report feeling uncomfortable being touched by their partners, especially if the partner touches body areas that the person feels are fat and unattractive. A thorough assessment of body image behaviors is important to gain a complete picture of the specific patient's body image concerns. In addition, it is an important part of treatment planning for treating body image directly. Due to the high prevalence of body image concerns and their effects on self-esteem among adolescents, it can be difficult to determine whether negative body image and low self-esteem are more extreme than what is normative. Other patients may have difficulty describing the effects of their negative body image on their self-esteem. The extent to which they engage in body image avoidance behaviors is good behavioral evidence of the degree of body dissatisfaction and negative effects on self-esteem.

Interviewing about previous or current teasing or criticism about shape and weight assists in identifying personal experiences that have contributed to negative body image. Teasing or criticism may come from school peers, siblings, parents, or other family members. Persons who are overweight or obese may hear negative comments from complete strangers when in public. Comments from parents or even health care professionals may not be meant as critical, but may reflect realistic or unrealistic health concerns for the child or adolescent. Nonetheless, frequently bringing up the topic of needing to lose weight and diet is hurtful to many children. Parents, sometimes mothers, may also impose or model their own overemphasis on weight and thinness, dieting, and negative body image on their daughters. Early pubertal development in girls has been shown to be a risk factor for developing an eating disorder (Smolak, Levine, & Gralen, 1993). Early pubertal physical changes can result in unwanted attention to their bodies by peers and family, or teasing and criticism. It is possible that girls who mature early and have more significant breast development are more likely to have these experiences.

It is equally important for the interviewer to ask about positive experiences during weight loss. Persons with AN, in particular, may receive substantial positive attention in the early phases of their weight loss. For example, one adolescent was overweight and socially ridiculed throughout middle school. She became depressed and lost her appetite, which led to weight loss. When peers complimented, rather than criticized, her appearance, she intentionally began to restrict her dietary intake and developed an eating disorder to maintain a thinner body and social acceptance. As weight gets dangerously low, the positive attention gives way to expressions of concern or criticism for being too thin. Although persons with BN are usually in the normal weight range, they may have had periods of modest weight loss that resulted in positive attention. Persons who binge eat and are obese may have had periods of substantial weight loss, perhaps by participating in a formal weight loss program. Substantial positive attention for the weight loss often occurs. These reactions can underscore the importance of shape and weight in being approved of by others. Patients may also report feeling differently about themselves, such as feeling more confident, more attractive, more assertive, or that they have more self-control or discipline. All of these internal reactions highlight the extent to which shape and weight have become important components of self-esteem.

Weight History. Finally, it is helpful to gather a weight history and learn the client's current weight, highest lifetime weight (and age at which that weight was achieved), and self-stated goal weight. Being weighed can be a stressful experience for the client, and the clinician needs to approach this topic in a compassionate manner. For some clients, getting weighed and knowing the weight is so anxiety provoking that they refuse to be weighed. In these cases, we ask clients to be weighed but agree to not reveal their weight to them. For medical reasons, it is important to get an accurate weight, especially for anorexic clients. For very hesitant clients, we will explain that obtaining an accurate weight is part of good medical care. Thus, it is no different than when heart rate, pulse, and temperature are taken during a routine visit to their physicians. The goal is to obtain the needed weight information but not have clients so upset that they have difficulty with other parts of the interview. We also do not want the clients to find this part of the interview so aversive that they will not return to therapy. If being weighed is a difficult experience for the client, it is helpful to offer an opportunity to discuss the client's thoughts, feelings, and other reactions to being weighed. Partly, this is for clinicians to be empathetic and convey to clients that they understand how much body image and fear of weight gain is an issue for them. The task of weighing the client, however, also serves as a brief behavioral assessment of the severity of the client's body image disturbance and fear of weight gain.

In some cases, measuring an accurate weight can be a challenge. Clients with AN who are extremely underweight may intentionally distort weigh-ins to appear heavier to maintain a stance of "I'm fine" or to avoid treatment. To distort weight, they may drink a large amount of water to fluid load prior to the interview or put heavy objects in their pockets or underwear. When conducting a weigh-in, ask the client, "When was the last time you ate or drank anything?" If there is any concern that the client drank fluids 1 hour prior to the interview, ask the client to use the bathroom prior to being weighed. Also ask them to empty their pockets and remove any unnecessary clothing (e.g., belts, jewelry, jackets). In some cases, it may be necessary to have clients weighed in a physician's office, after voiding, wearing only a hospital gown.

Clinicians should ask clients whether they weigh themselves and how often. Some clients avoid weighing themselves, while others weigh themselves repeatedly. Repeated weighing can be an antecedent to eating disorder behavior. If the weight is higher than expected, the client may react with "I'm not dieting enough" and increase the eating disorder behavior, such as food restriction or increased exercise. If the weight is lower or consistent with what is desired, the client receives reinforcement for continued eating disorder behavior. Also, repeated self-weighing can reinforce purging or compensatory behavior. For example, a client may binge eat, weigh herself, vomit, then weigh herself again. Any drop in weight after vomiting will result in relief for the client and reinforce the vomiting behavior. If the client self-weighs, the interviewer should secure the agreement of the client and/or parents to remove the scale from the home and eliminate this behavior early in treatment.

The *DSM-IV* diagnostic weight criterion for AN is weight loss or failure to gain weight such that the person's weight is 85% or less of "expected weight." The *DSM-IV*, however, does not clearly define "expected weight," which is particularly problematic for children and adolescents. Issues include a normal lower relative body weight in adolescents compared with adults, differences in the growth rate, and difficulties estimating the projected weight when there is a failure to gain weight. The timing of puberty is important, as a girl who has reached puberty would be expected to weigh more and have more body fat than another girl of the same age and height who has not reached puberty. Also, there are differences in what is a normal weight for that individual. Some people's natural body weight may be under or over what is considered an average weight on a given weight chart.

In addition to 85% of expected weight, a body mass index (BMI) of 17.5 is considered to meet the weight criterion for AN (World Health Organization, 1992). BMI is a ratio of height and weight, and normal BMI ranges from 20 to 25 for adults. The normal BMI ranges for adolescents and children are lower than for adults, making the 17.5 BMI criterion inappropriate. Thus, some have suggested using the BMI that corresponds to the 5th percentile on standard growth charts (Robin et al., 1998), such as the Centers for Disease Control (CDC) growth charts. The CDC developed growth charts that include body weight percentiles for children aged 2 to 20 (Kuczmarski et al., 2000). Abnormal weight loss can also be detected by plotting any dramatic changes in the child's body weight percentile on the CDC growth chart over time. For example, the child's weight may have been in the 50th percentile for her age last year but dropped to the 10th percentile this year.

Body weight, although important to consider, is only one factor related to medical complications, and body weight alone is not useful, as clients with "normal" body weight can still experience serious medical problems. Regardless of body weight, clinicians should ask about medical complications and ask parents to consent to release their children's medical records. Refer to the "Medical History" section of Table 17.1 for a sample of medical issues to consider during the interview.

INTERVIEWING OBSTACLES AND SOLUTIONS

Patients under the age of 18 and living with their parents are often brought to the initial interview against their will. One obstacle to interviewing adolescents with eating disorders is their firm resistance to treatment and their belief that they do not have a problem. This is particularly true of those with AN, less so for BN. Among a sample of eating disorder patients, including adolescents, 23% of those with AN were precontemplative about change, and 3% of those with BN were precontemplative (Blake, Turnbull, & Treasure, 1997). *Precontemplation* is a stage of change in which the person has no intention of change, being unaware or in denial of a problem (Prochaska & DiClemente, 1982).

Gowers and Smyth (2004) administered a motivational interview to 42 adolescents with AN. The interview addressed ambivalence by asking the adolescent to discuss the advantages and disadvantages of having an eating disorder. Following the motivational interview, scores on motivation questionnaires increased compared with preinterview scores, and higher motivation scores were related to less likelihood of treatment dropout. Thus, an interviewing style that addresses ambivalence and enhances client motivation to change can be beneficial to the treatment process. The first topic addressed is the patient's view of the circumstances of how they were brought to treatment and how they feel about it. Often, they are moderately to very angry. Many are angry about arguments with their parents about eating-disordered behaviors, such as purging or eating small amounts at meals. Many feel that they are constantly being watched for evidence of eating disorder behavior. In maintaining that they do not have a problem, many adolescents will assert that their dieting and food restriction, as well as their body image concerns, are no more intense than those of their same-age female peers.

When interviewing about these issues, the goal is to encourage patients to express their anger (or other emotional reactions) as well as the reasons that they feel that they do not have a problem. If appropriate, we acknowledge that their parents may have done some things in reacting to the eating disorder that were not helpful, or were even harmful. We try to reframe this as the parents being very frightened by the possibility that their child has an eating disorder and that frightened people often do desperate things. Also, we indicate that their parents do not know what to do to be helpful, nor should they be expected to understand something they know little about. We indicate that it is our job to help their parents be more adaptively helpful. Thus, we are letting patients know that participating in treatment may help reduce the frequent conflict they have with their parents. Most adolescents are interested in "getting their parents off their backs."

In terms of addressing the belief of patients that they are no different from their female peers, we take an empirical approach. That is, we ask the adolescent whether they are open to getting concrete information (i.e., test results) that would show whether or not they are similar to eating disorder clients. An important part of making this agreement is letting the patient know that if the test results indicate that there is not an eating disorder problem, we will be happy to say so and communicate that to their parents. Part of the agreement, however, is that they will be open to the possibility that they have an eating disorder if that is what the testing suggests.

We use the Eating Disorders Inventory-III, a measure of primary and secondary eating disorder symptoms, which has norms for females as young as age 11 (EDI-III) (Garner, 2004). Although only females were included in the normative sample, the EDI-III can also be administered to males. The EDI-III authors report that males and females with anorexia respond similarly to this measure and the adolescent norms are applicable to both males and females (Garner, 2004). In addition to the EDI-III, we also recommend administration of the Revised Restraint Scale (RRS) (Herman, Polivy, Pliner, Threkheld, & Munic, 1978) and the Mizes Anorectic Cognitions Questionnaire (MAC) (Mizes & Klesges, 1989). The MAC requires a sixth-grade reading level (Pike, Wolk, Gluck, & Walsh, 2000), and a modified version of the MAC has shown good concurrent validity in a sample of middle school students as young as 14 (Guillard, 2002).

We use these self-report measures because they assess constructs central to a cognitive-behavioral conceptualization of eating disorders. Thus, the feedback process educates the patient about ideas that will be central parts of treatment and areas targeted for change. Also, teaching patients these concepts and ideas within the context of their own personal experience (as reflected by their test scores) often facilitates greater understanding. Alternatively, a variety of other questionnaires and measures for children and adolescents can be used (Macera & Mizes, 2006).

If the adolescent does have an eating disorder, the feedback on the testing is that the patient is much more extreme on the test scores than same-age peers. Thus, for example, they can be shown that their body image dissatisfaction score is much higher than scores of peers without eating disorders. It is also important to have adolescents provide input into the feedback process regarding how the test results are reflected in their own experience. For example, when providing feedback on the RRS, patients can be told that high scorers on the RRS typically have a variety of black-and-white "forbidden-food" rules. Patients are asked to give examples of their own forbidden-food rules. This helps reduce resistance by showing them that therapists really do understand their eating disorders and how they feel. This often stands in stark contrast to the reaction of family and friends, who think the solution to the problem is to "just eat" or to "get over feeling fat."

By giving nonjudgmental feedback of how the patient's experience is the same as eating disorder patients, patients can begin to acknowledge that they do have eating disorders. That does not mean that they are ready to change their eating disorder behavior, but at least the hurdle of whether or not they have an eating disorder has been cleared. Of course, feedback on psychological testing is only one way to elicit the patient's experience and how that mirrors that of eating disorder patients. This process is woven into the initial interview and also much of the early treatment sessions.

We avoid attempts to provide feedback about medical consequences, especially risk of death, that scare the patients into changing their behavior. This is rarely helpful. In fact, some patients intensify their resistance in the face of such pressure. Death is extremely rare among persons with BN. Although death is a possibility with AN, it typically is not an imminent issue for patients in this age group. We also do not confront them with statements that their weight is too low and they are not fat, or in the case of BN, that they are not fat even though they are normal weight. We also do not confront them about their daily intake being too low. These are simply arguments that cannot be won. This is not to say that these issues are not addressed later in therapy. They are definitely part of the psychoeducation that occurs in treatment. Rather, the idea is to avoid trying to forcefully overcome the patient's resistance by bringing up these issues.

Early in the interview process, in fact, we acknowledge that there are significant benefits of the eating disorder from the patients' point of view. We also let them know that under these circumstances, their resistance is not only likely but also understandable. Why should they change something that is often one of the few ways that they know how to feel good about themselves? This acknowledgment of the benefits of the eating disorder is often markedly different from what they have heard from family and friends and even some health care professionals. This not only gives the patient one less thing to fight against but also communicates that the therapist really understands the patient and the eating disorder. In the initial interviews, we ask the patients preliminary questions about how the eating disorder benefits them. Guided questioning is often needed to elicit from them that the most important benefits are the positive effects on self-worth. This is often a preliminary discussion of the benefits of the eating disorder, with more detailed discussion coming in later therapy sessions. The goal at this point is to communicate to the patient that the therapist understands these perceived benefits, not to examine or challenge the perceived benefits.

As part of efforts to engage the patients in therapy (or sometimes just to get them to more willingly agree to come back to a second session after the initial interview!), it is important to assess patients' fears about therapy and about changing their eating disorder behaviors. Many patients fear that the prime goal of therapy, to use their words, "is to fatten me up." We openly acknowledge that it is not reasonable to help them get to, or accept, a healthy weight and then to leave them feeling fat and horrible about themselves. Not only would they be miserable, but it would be a matter of time before they relapsed. We clearly let them know that one of our goals is to help them achieve and maintain a healthy body weight and to help them to feel good about their bodies and themselves at that weight, even though they may not feel this is possible. In early interviews, we purposely avoid discussing what we would see as a healthy body weight. At this point, we do not want to get into disagreement with the patients on what a healthy body weight is for them.

Another way to approach engaging patients in therapy is to ask whether they would be interested in treatment if it could achieve certain benefits that they would find positive. The benefits that are asked about are often based on what they have indicated are benefits of the eating disorder, as well as aspects of the eating disorder they do not like. For example, we might ask questions such as the following: Would you be interested in treatment . . .

- if it could help you feel good about your body?

- if it could help you feel good about yourself, even if your weight changes?

- if it could get the constant thinking about food and weight to go away? or

- if you could eat foods you like without feeling fat and horrible about yourself and feeling like you have to vomit?

Some patients will say that they are interested. Many, however, will assert that these things are simply not possible. We tell them that we understand that since they have an eating disorder, these things will seem impossible to them. We ask them to set these beliefs aside for a moment. Rather, just for an idea to consider, we ask them to assume that treatment could accomplish the benefits described. Would they be interested in treatment then?

INTERVIEWING PARENTS AND TEACHERS

For the initial interview, our approach is to briefly interview the parents (or parent) and the adolescent together before interviewing the adolescent individually. We ask the parents what led them to be concerned about a potential eating disorder. Also, we ask them whether there are any specific questions or concerns that they would like to discuss in the first visit. Many times, the questions are about how to handle certain situations, such as meal times. At a later point in treatment, we will address how to handle these issues with their child or adolescent.

When families enter the therapy setting for the first visit, they desire information, resources, and support (McMaster, Beale, Hillege, & Nagy, 2004; Winn, Perkins, Murray, Murphy, & Schmidt, 2004). The therapist needs to be cautious not to convey a blaming tone. Parents of eating disorder clients view a provider as "not helpful" if the provider conveys that the parents are to blame for the child's eating disorder (McMaster et al., 2004; Sharkey-Orgnero, 1999). To assist parents in this regard, we often discuss the rapidly emerging evidence of a strong genetic component for risk of developing an eating disorder (Kendler et al., 1991). As well, we acknowledge that although research has identified risk factors for eating disorders, there is no way to determine exactly why

their children developed eating disorders. It is also important to discuss the possibility that current family interaction problems can be a reaction to, rather than a cause of, having a child with an eating disorder. Parents are not equipped with specialized knowledge on how to react to an eating disorder, and they are frequently very frightened by the potential medical consequences. Under these circumstances, it is understandable that they would react in ways that are not helpful, or are unintentionally harmful.

Finally, assuming that family problems did contribute to the development of the eating disorder, we clarify that we are not interested in blame and that we have a forward-looking focus. Specifically, the issue is how we can assist them now to be most helpful to their child. This approach helps reduce parents' resistance and facilitates their more productive involvement in family treatment.

We typically involve the parents in family therapy, as family therapy is more effective than individual therapy for younger eating disorder clients (Russell, Szmukler, Dare, & Eisler, 1987). Our approach is to see the parents in sessions separate from the adolescent. In these sessions, interviewing often focuses on each parent's relationship with the child historically and currently, their interactions regarding eating disorder behavior (vomiting, refusing to eat at meals), and significant family events, such as divorce or other traumatic events (see Table 17.2). Of particular interest is the assessment of how well the parents work together as a team in parenting their child. It is particularly important to assess for any major disagreements in their general approach to parenting and how they resolve disagreements—if, in fact, disagreements are resolved. It is important to identify where there are significant concerns as to one parent regarding the parenting practices of the other parent. For example, does one parent become more protective of the child to compensate for feeling that the other parent is overly hostile? Does one parent undermine and not support the other in decisions about the child? In general, we are assessing for any number of factors that interfere with the parents working together as a team that presents a united front to the child. To have parents working together as an effective team is essential to their implementation of the parental aspects of the treatment plan.

Another way to assess for family problems is to administer the Parent-Child Boundaries Scale

TABLE 17.2   Sample Questions to Include in a Parent Interview

Are you the biological parent?
If yes, how old were you when the child was born?
If not, how long have you been involved in the child's life?
If the child was adopted, at what age and under what circumstances?

Family Relationships

How many siblings does (Name of Client) have? What are their names, and how old are they?
Include deceased siblings and miscarriages by mother.
What hopes or expectations do you have for the child?
How would you describe your relationship with your child?

Family History

Describe loss or trauma experienced by your child or in your family during the child's lifetime.
Are there any family members with an eating disorder?
Do any family members have substance abuse problems?
Any other psychiatric problems in family members?

Eating Behavior

When did the eating problems begin?
What are your main concerns for your child at this time?
How have you already tried to address this problem, and what were the results?

Verify any information that the child has provided (see questions listed in Table 17.1).

(PBS-II) (Kerig, 2001). This self-report measure contains 51 items that cover a range of parent-child boundary violations that may disrupt the family dynamics. The subscales and items include the following:

- Intrusiveness ("My mother wants me to tell her everything I think and feel.")

- Psychological Control ("If I hurt my mother's feelings, she stops talking to me until I please her again.")

- Role Reversal: Parentification ("I feel like my mother is the kid and I am the parent.")

- Role Reversal: Adultification ("My mother talks to me about her worries.")

- Enmeshment ("My mother likes to feel that she and I are exactly alike.")

- Hostile Spousification ("When my mother gets mad at me, she says I am just like my father.")

- Affectionate Spousification ("My mother acts toward me in a way that is like flirting.")

- Protectiveness ("My mother tries to keep me from worrying about grown-up things.")

The PBS-II is completed by the child, and two versions of this measure are available for the child to rate the mother's behavior and another for the child to rate the father's behavior on the same items. Items can also be reworded for parents to evaluate themselves by changing "my parent" to "I" and "me" to "my child." The responses to this questionnaire can be used to introduce family issues in a sensitive, objective manner: "I noticed on the PBS-II questionnaire you reported that . . . Tell me more about that." During the course of the discussion about the item, the parent or child may identify how the behavior or expectation is interfering with their relationship. Ideally, the interviewer should allow the family to arrive at this conclusion on their own rather than confronting the family with boundary violations they are committing.

During parental sessions, it is important to give information and answer questions. We have found it useful to explain eating disorder symptoms, especially the psychological causes of eating disorder behavior and resistance to change by the patient. One of the most important ideas to convey is the central importance that body shape and weight have in the child's overall self-concept. It is important that parents come to understand how this results in a tremendous fear of weight gain and reluctance by patients to stop all forms of weight regulation in which they are engaged. We discuss at length that it is natural and normal for anyone to resist changing or losing something that is a fundamental part of his or her self-esteem and self-concept. Thus, in the case of a daughter, for example, we would explain that rather than being manipulative, deceitful, or a liar, she is trying to hang on to something that has become a central part of her self-esteem, because to lose it would mean she felt like nothing. This is even more frightening for the patient because she does not know any alternative, healthy ways to feel good about herself. For an overview of the general aspects of treatment, parents can benefit from reading patient-oriented treatment workbooks (Heffner & Eifert, 2004; Treasure, 1997).

While interviewing parents is an important part of an eating disorder assessment, interviews with teachers for assessment purposes are not routinely conducted. It may be useful, however, to talk with school nurses or teachers to assist in implementing the treatment plan. It is not uncommon to have school personnel monitor the patient's access to the bathroom after meals to prevent purging or to verify the amount and types of food eaten at school.

Case Illustration With Dialogue

During a clinical interview, adolescents with eating disorders, especially AN, may be resistant and deny disordered-eating symptoms. In the following section, we describe an interview example that demonstrates the use of reflection and empathy to enhance client motivation to participate in the interviewing process. This is a fictional adolescent eating disorder case based on actual clients we have assessed. The client, Courtney, is a 16-year-old high school sophomore who weighs 89 pounds (4 foot, 11 inches; BMI = 17.9). Courtney and her parents completed a preintake questionnaire packet that indicates that she was referred by her primary care physician for an eating disorder assessment due to weight loss and osteoporosis.

Therapist: Hello, Courtney. It's nice to meet you. Please tell me more about why you are here today.

Client: Well, my mom made me come because my doctor said I have to. The doctor thinks I have some kind of bone problem, but I haven't figured out how talking to you is going to make my bones stronger. Anyway, I'm young and I'm sure they have some kind of medicine to help my bones get stronger so it's no big deal. I just think it would be better if the doctor gave me a prescription instead of making me come here.

T: It sounds like you don't want to be here and don't understand how our time together will be helpful for you.

C: Well, I guess you're nice and all. I'm sorry if this hurts your feelings, but I don't really think there's much to talk about.

T: I can understand that you may not want to be here today. You know, I don't like to be forced to do anything that I don't want to do either.

C: Yeah. It sucks.

T: Thank you for saying that. If you believe that it sucks to be here, I am glad you shared that. You are being honest and authentic, and I appreciate that very much. During this meeting, you are free to say exactly how you feel, and all of your feelings are welcome here.

C: Okay. Thanks. To be even more honest, I don't like any of this. It's wasting time that I don't have and money that my parents don't have. This is so stupid! There is nothing wrong with me. [becomes teary and agitated] Everyone keeps telling me that I don't eat enough, but I do. God, I eat more than all the other girls at school, and their parents don't force them to come see a psychologist. It's so not fair.

T: I can understand why you are angry and confused about coming here. It just doesn't make sense when you look around and see other people eating less than you do. It's really hard to figure out why you are being singled out.

C: Yeah. Seriously, I am not one of those anorexic girls you see on TV. I eat food every single day. Every day. Every meal. I don't see what the problem is. [Intake paperwork indicates that Courtney typically eats an apple for breakfast, a handful of sprouts for lunch, and soup for dinner.]

At this point, Courtney remains resistant. It will be more helpful to offer reflection, rather than confront Courtney about her irrational belief that she is eating enough at each meal.

T: Even though you eat every day, other people worry about how much you are eating. I imagine that you are annoyed or bothered by everyone else's concern.

C: You can say that. Sometimes, I have to eat more when my parents are hawking me at the dinner table just to get them off my back. It makes me feel sick when I stuff myself like that. It's disgusting to feel all that food sitting in my stomach. I feel like a bloated pig. Uhh! It's so gross. I hate to pig out like that.

T: I noticed on your questionnaires that sometime when you feel sick like this you throw up? That's been happening about twice per week for the last 6 months?

C: That's right.

T: It sounds like you are describing a chain of events. First, your parents worry about your eating. Next, your parents react to that anxiety by pressuring you to eat. Then, you react to your parents' pressure by eating more than you normally eat. That leads you to feeling disgusted. Then, you vomit to feel less disgusted. This whole scenario is one stressful event after another. I imagine that it's very hard to be caught up in this cycle.

C: Yeah. I guess that's how one thing leads to another. I wish it would stop.

T: You wish it would stop. If I asked you to rate, from 0 to 10, how much you want to end this scenario, this scenario that starts with your parents worrying and ends with you vomiting, what rating would you give? 0 is no desire to change, and 10 is a really, really strong desire to change.

C: I'd say a 10. But just because I want to change it doesn't mean it will happen.

T: So, you feel discouraged about the possibility that you and your family could have a normal meal together. You'd like for the situation to change, but you're not confident that this whole chain of events will end? Let's take out that 0 to 10 scale again, where 0 is absolutely no confidence and 10 is extreme confidence, how confident are you that you can change?

C: I think something like a 2.

T: And why are you at a 2 and not a 0? [This question allows the client to recognize that verbalizing even the most minimal amount of hope means she is not entirely hopeless about change. Be cautious not to reverse the question by asking, "Why are you not at 10?" which will lead the client to verbalize how far away from changing she is (Miller & Rollnick, 2002).]

C: Well, every once in a while, my parents don't start off with staring at my plate and making dumb comments like, "Is that all you're eating?" or "I can't take this anorexia anymore." It's not like an everyday thing. Thankfully.

T: Well, you and your parents have the option of doing family therapy, which can be really helpful for situations like this. It sounds like your parents are really worried. When people worry too much, they panic and do things or say things out of desperation that may not be helpful. Right now, your parents may be confused about what to say or do. Family therapy can help them to understand you better and respond to you in a more effective way.

C: Yeah. They need help with all their worry. I don't know why they worry. I am fine. Will you tell them that?

T: Yes. I would really like to tell them that you are fine, but I need more information to show me that you are fine. Right now, it would not be responsible for me to make a rash decision after just 10 minutes of talking to you. Talking like this is one way to figure out if you are fine. Another way is to look at your questionnaire results. Earlier today, you said that you feel your eating is no different than your classmates.' In fact, you feel you eat better than they do. The questionnaire results will let us explore that belief further and give us an idea as to whether your eating is "normal" or not. If the test results show that you do not have a problem with eating, we will tell that to your parents. However, if there appears to be problems with your eating, I'd really like to talk more with you about that. Is that okay with you?

C: Yeah. I want to see what they show.

At this point, the therapist reviews questionnaire results and elicits a discussion with the client about the eating disorder and body image symptoms that are measured on each questionnaire.

DIFFERENTIAL DIAGNOSIS AND BEHAVIORAL ASSESSMENT

The current *DSM* diagnostic criteria do not adequately capture the symptoms of eating disorders among children and adolescents. In fact, only half of 7- to 15-year-old children referred for eating disorder treatment meet full criteria for AN or BN (Bryant-Waugh & Lask, 1995). The other half experience disordered-eating patterns not represented in the *DSM*. To enhance the classification of childhood eating disorders, Lask and Bryant-Waugh (2000) proposed the Great Ormond Street (GOS) criteria, named after the pediatric hospital where they conducted their research. The GOS criteria include four types of disordered-eating problems, in addition to AN and BN, that children may present with: selective eating, food avoidance emotional disorder, functional dysphagia, and pervasive refusal syndrome (Lask & Bryant-Waugh, 2000; Nicholls, Carter, & Lask, 2000). For all of these disordered-eating patterns, there is dietary restraint without the body image disturbance required for the diagnosis of AN and BN.

Selective eating occurs when a child refuses to eat a varied diet (e.g., "picky eaters"). *Functional dysphagia* is an anxiety reaction that occurs when a child refuses to eat due to fears of choking or vomiting. *Food avoidance emotional disorder* occurs when a child loses weight and refuses to eat in reaction to a mood disturbance other than major depression or other Axis I mood disorders. *Pervasive refusal syndrome* is a generalized pattern of refusal to engage in any self-care activity, including eating or drinking. Unless the eating disorder behavior functions as a means of avoiding weight gain or relieving body image distress, an eating disorder cannot be diagnosed. If there is no evidence of body image disturbance, the clinician should consider other functions of disordered-eating behavior. During the interview, the clinician will identify not only "what" the eating disorder symptoms are, but must also ask "why" the symptoms occur.

In some cases, medical conditions can lead to weight loss, vomiting, and other symptoms that appear to be eating disordered. For example,

Richterich, Brunner, and Resch (2003) described the case of a 9-year-old girl who lost 20 pounds in 1 year. Although she was participating in weekly outpatient psychotherapy for AN purging type, her dietary restraint and purging behaviors were not consistent with an eating disorder. Instead, she described purging as uncontrollable, including unintentional vomiting while asleep. Likewise, her fluid restriction was the result of physical difficulty swallowing liquids rather than an intentional means of avoiding weight gain. After her medical doctor ordered a chest X-ray and barium swallow, the girl was diagnosed with esophageal achalasia. After being treated for this medical condition, she gained weight and was discharged in stable condition.

In other cases, the clinician should rule out other psychiatric disorders that may underlie an eating or weight problem. Jaffe and Singer (1989) described eight children, average age of 8.5 years, who were hospitalized for disordered-eating patterns and weight loss. None of the children reported fear of weight gain consistent with a diagnosis of AN or BN. Instead, the researchers concluded that the eating problems were not isolated problems, but occurred in the context of other psychiatric conditions, including thought disorder, obsessive-compulsive disorder, dysthymic disorder, overanxious disorder, possible major depression, adjustment disorder with mixed emotional features, and oppositional defiant disorder.

During the course of the interview, the clinician should assess whether the eating problems are suggestive of another psychiatric problem, especially anxiety and depression. Depression symptoms include psychomotor retardation (e.g., eating slowly, "picking" at food) and loss of appetite. In AN, there is usually intense hunger, whereas during the course of depression, there is a loss of interest in food and lack of appetite. Likewise, an anxiety disorder may be present if there is evidence of a specific phobia of choking, obsessive-compulsive fear that food is contaminated, or anxiety-related gastrointestinal distress.

The following case of an adolescent with significant weight loss due to significant anxiety illustrates a common referral for differential diagnosis. "Amy" was a 17-year-old girl who had lost 28 pounds over 11 months. At 5 foot, 4 inches, her weight had dropped from 117 pounds (BMI = 20) to 89 pounds (BMI = 15.2) when she was admitted to the pediatric medical unit. Amy complained of abdominal pain upon eating, but numerous medical tests did not find any specific medical cause for her abdominal pain. The eating disorder service was consulted to rule out AN. Although guarded during the interview, Amy denied avoidance of food due to fear of weight gain, but indicated that she avoided food due to abdominal distress. She also consistently stated that she wanted to gain weight. Routine eating disorder questionnaires showed no evidence of an eating disorder. Although her MMPI-A was within normal limits, she did show a strong tendency toward repression and a tendency to develop physical symptoms due to anxiety. Behaviorally, she was cooperative with her meal plan, especially when a prescription antacid was started for her abdominal pain. During the course of a 10-day hospitalization, she was able to gain 3.7 pounds with little difficulty. Our opinion was that Amy did not have AN, but rather had food avoidance and weight loss secondary to psychosomatic gastrointestinal distress. Although not present in this case, we have seen several cases where the psychosomatic gastrointestinal distress was sufficient to cause vomiting upon eating, which can further add to the picture of an eating disorder when one is not actually present.

Behavioral assessment can be useful in the differential diagnosis of eating disorders. This can be particularly useful when trying to determine whether the patient is denying eating disorder symptoms such as body image disturbance or avoidance of food due to fear of weight gain. For body image disturbance, patients can be asked to engage in several common body image avoidance behaviors. Examples include being weighed and being told their weight, or looking at themselves in the mirror while focusing on common body areas that are associated with body shape and weight concerns (e.g., stomach, thighs, buttocks). A patient who is denying an eating disorder will typically show clear evidence of anxiety and distress, as well as some evidence of avoidance behaviors. A patient who does not have AN or BN will be able to perform these behavioral "tests" with little to no distress or avoidance.

Patients can also be asked to eat food typically avoided by eating disorder patients, such as high-calorie foods that are typically viewed as fattening. It is important to make clear that there will be no opportunity to "get rid" of the food by purging or other compensatory behavior. Eating

disorder patients will be quite distressed and anxious and will eat very small amounts of the food or refuse completely. It is important to assess the patients' thoughts while they are attempting to eat the food. Eating disorder patients will report fears about gaining weight or feeling fat in certain parts of their body, as well as a strong urge to get rid of the food in their typical manner. Patients with other eating concerns may often avoid eating the food but will report entirely different thoughts. For example, they may report that they are afraid they will get sick to their stomach or that they may vomit. Patients who can easily eat the food do not have an eating disorder.

Finally, a functional analysis of behavior can also assist in differential diagnosis. Often, it is the consequences of not eating or vomiting that reinforce the behavior. For example, one of the authors (JSM) treated a young teenage girl who would eat only small amounts of food and only with her mother's reassurance. She complained that she felt sick to her stomach and feared that she would vomit. On occasion, she actually did vomit. Eventually, it was discovered that when the girl would refuse to eat, her mother would spend a great deal of time with her, including brushing the patient's hair. This pattern had started during a time when the girl did have an illness that resulted in her vomiting. She began eating normally again once the excessive attention after not eating was stopped, and her mother was taught how to implement firm limits on the patient eating appropriately.

SELECTION OF TREATMENT TARGETS AND REFERRAL

Treatment must be implemented by a multidisciplinary team consisting of nutritionists, psychotherapists, and medical doctors who specialize in eating disorders. In some cases, medical specialists, such as cardiologists or gynecologists, will need to be consulted. It is important to refer the client to providers who are experienced at treating the unique and complex physical and psychological problems associated with eating disorders. Not all physicians, nutritionists, and psychologists are trained to treat eating disorder clients. In fact, most training programs do not require coursework or practical training in eating disorders. Some of our clients have reported negative experiences with nonspecialist providers who make misinformed comments such as "Just go eat more yogurt" or "You could afford to lose 5 or 10 more pounds."

For AN, the primary treatment target is weight restoration. We typically expect the client to achieve a body mass index (BMI) of at least 18, which is approximately 90% of expected body weight. As discussed previously, however, BMI is not always appropriate for child or adolescent clients. Therefore, weight restoration goals may include restoration of menses, increased body fat percentage, or increased expected body weight percentile. In severe cases, medical hospitalization may be necessary to achieve weight restoration. The APA practice guidelines (APA, 2000b) recommend inpatient hospitalization if an adolescent client has had an acute decline in body weight, refuses to participate in weight restoration, and has poor vital signs (e.g., heart rate in the 40s, blood pressure below 80/50).

For all eating disorder clients, treatment targets include normalization of eating and body image acceptance. For child and adolescent clients, the treatment plan should also include family communication, problem solving, and relationship enhancement. Treatment goals related to normalization of eating target the extremes of disordered eating: restriction and binge eating. To address this goal, the client learns to eat three meals and snacks per day to prevent caloric restriction. When working with severely malnourished clients, caloric intake needs to be increased gradually, under the supervision of nutritionists and doctors who specialize in eating disorders. When severely malnourished clients begin to increase dietary consumption, they are at risk for developing *refeeding syndrome,* which can lead to cardiac and electrolyte problems (Katzman, 2005; Mehler & Crews, 2001).

For clients with BN and binge-eating problems, regularly scheduled meals can prevent binge eating triggered by extreme hunger that results from prolonged restriction. Other clients, who often describe themselves as "emotional eaters," binge eat in response to anxiety, anger, and other unwanted emotions and benefit from learning coping skills to better manage emotional states. To help clients normalize eating, gradual exposure to forbidden foods can be implemented to treat the anxiety and cognitive distortions

associated with specific food items. Underlying the disordered-eating behavior is body image disturbance. Treatment goals to improve body image acceptance include exposure techniques, cognitive restructuring, and positive body experiences, such as massage (Rosen, 1997).

REFERENCES

American Psychiatric Association. (2000a). *Diagnostic and statistical manual of mental disorders* (4th ed., Text rev.). Washington, DC: Author.

American Psychiatric Association. (2000b). *Practice guidelines for the treatment of patients with eating disorders* (2nd ed.). Washington, DC: Author.

Angold, A., & Costello, E. J. (2000). The child and adolescent psychiatric assessment (CAPA). *Journal of the American Academy of Child & Adolescent Psychiatry, 39,* 39–48.

Beglin, S. J., & Fairburn, C. G. (1992). What is meant by the term "binge"? *American Journal of Psychiatry, 149,* 123–124.

Blake, W., Turnbull, S., & Treasure, J. L. (1997). Stages and processes of change in eating disorders. Implications for therapy. *Clinical Psychology and Psychotherapy, 4,* 186–191.

Bryant-Waugh, R. J., Cooper, P. J., Taylor, C. L., & Lask, B. D. (1996). The use of the eating disorder examination with children: A pilot study. *International Journal of Eating Disorders, 19,* 391–397.

Bryant-Waugh, R. J., & Lask, B. (1995). Eating disorders in children. *Journal of Child Psychology and Psychiatry, 36,* 191–202.

Bulik, C. M., Reba, L., Siega-Riz, A. M., & Reichborn-Kjennerud, T. (2005). Anorexia nervosa: Definition, epidemiology, and cycle of risk. *International Journal of Eating Disorders, 37,* S2–S9.

Cooper, Z., & Fairburn, C. (1987). The Eating Disorders Examination: A semi-structured interview for the assessment of specific psychopathology of eating disorders. *International Journal of Eating Disorders, 6,* 1–8.

Crowther, J. H., & Sherwood, N.E. (1997). Assessment. In D. M. Garner & P. E. Garfinkel (Eds.), *Handbook for treatment for eating disorders* (pp. 34–49). New York: Guilford Press.

Fichter, M. M., Elron, M., Engel, K., Meyer, A., Mall, H., & Poustka, F. (1991). Structured interview for anorexia and bulimia nervosa (SIAB): Development of a new instrument for the assessment of eating disorders. *International Journal of Eating Disorders, 10,* 571–592.

Garner, D. M. (2004). *Eating Disorder Inventory-3: Professional manual.* Lutz, FL: Psychological Assessment Resources.

Gowers, S. G., & Smyth, B. (2004). The impact of a motivational assessment interview on initial response to treatment in adolescent anorexia nervosa. *European Eating Disorders Review, 12,* 87–93.

Guillard, R. P. (2002). *The validity of the Mizes Anorectic Cognitions Questionnaire-Revised with a racially* mixed, nonclinical population of 14–19-year-old adolescents. Doctoral dissertation, Philadelphia College of Osteopathic Medicine, Philadelphia, PA.

Heffner, M., & Eifert, G. H. (2004). The anorexia workbook. Oakland, CA: New Harbinger.

Herman, C. P., Polivy, J., Pliner, P., Threkheld, J., & Munic, J. (1978). Distractibility in dieters and non-dieters: An alternative view of externality. Journal of Personality and Social Psychology, 36, 536–548.

Herpertz-Dahlmann, B. M., Wewetzer, C., Schulz, E., & Remschmidt, H. (1996). Course and outcome in adolescent anorexia nervosa. International Journal of Eating Disorders, 19, 335–345.

Illness attacks mind and body: Eating disorder killed world-class gymnast. (1994, July 29). St. Louis Post-Dispatch, p. 5B.

Jaffe, A. C., & Singer, L. T. (1989). Atypical eating disorders in young children. International Journal of Eating Disorders, 8, 575–582.

Katzman, D. K. (2005). Medical complications in adolescents with anorexia nervosa: A review of the literature. International Journal of Eating Disorders, 37, 52–59.

Kaufman, J., Birmaher, B., Brent, D., Rao, U., Flynn, C., Moreci, P., Williamson, D., et al. (1997). Schedule for Affective Disorders and Schizophrenia for School-Age Children-Present and Lifetime Version (K-SADS-PL): Initial reliability and validity data. Journal of the American Academy of Child & Adolescent Psychiatry, 36, 980–988.

Kendler, K. S., MacLean, C., Neale, B. A., Kessler, R., Heath, A., & Eaves, L. (1991). The genetic epidemiology of bulimia nervosa. American Journal of Psychiatry, 148, 1627–1637.

Kerig, P. K. (2001). Validation of a measure of parent-child boundary dissolution. University Research Council Grant, University of North Carolina at Chapel Hill.

Kuczmarski, R. J., Ogden, C. L., Grummer-Strawn, L. M., Flegal, K. M., Guo, S. S., Mei, Z., et al. (2000). CDC growth charts: United States. Hyattsville, MD: National Center for Health Statistics. Retrieved February 8, 2007, from http://www.cdc.gov/nchs/data/ad/ad314.pdf

Kutlesic, V., Williamson, D. A., Gleaves, D. H., Barbin, J. M., & Murphy-Eberenz, K. P. (1998). The interview for the diagnosis of eating disorders IV: Application to the DSM-IV diagnostic criteria. Psychological Assessment, 10, 41–48.

Lask, B., & Bryant-Waugh, R. (Eds.). (2000). Anorexia nervosa and related eating disorders in children and adolescence (2nd ed.). Hove, UK: Psychology Press.

Le Grange, D., Loeb, K. L., Van Orman, S., & Jellar, C. C. (2004). Bulimia nervosa in adolescents. Archives of Pediatrics and Adolescent Medicine, 158, 478–482.

Lindeman, M., Stark, K., & Latvala, K. (2000). Vegetarianism and eating-disordered thinking. Eating Disorders, 8, 157–165.

Macera, M. H., & Mizes, J. S. (2006). Eating disorders. In M. Hersen (Ed.), Clinician's handbook of child behavioral assessment (pp. 437–457). San Diego, CA: Elsevier.

McMaster, R., Beale, B., Hillege, S., & Nagy, S. (2004). The parent experience of eating disorders: Interactions with health professionals. International Journal of Mental Health Nursing, 13, 67–73.

Mehler, P. S., & Crews, C. K. (2001). Refeeding the patient with anorexia nervosa. Eating Disorders, 9, 167–171.

Miller, W. R., & Rollnick, S. (2002). Motivational interviewing: Preparing people for change (2nd ed.). New York: Guilford Press.

Mizes, J. S. (1992). The Body Image Detection Device versus subjective measures of weight dissatisfaction: A validity comparison. Addictive Behaviors, 17, 125–136.

Mizes, J. S., & Klesges, R. C. (1989). Validity, reliability, and factor structure of the Mizes Anorectic Cognitions Questionnaire. Addictive Behaviors, 14, 589–594.

Nicholls, D., Carter, R., & Lask, B. (2000). Children into DSM don't go: A comparison of classification systems for eating disorders in childhood and early adolescence. International Journal of Eating Disorders, 28, 317–324.

Palmer, R., Robertson, D., Cain, M., & Black, S. (1996). The clinical eating disorders rating instrument (CEDRI): A validation study. European Eating Disorders Review, 4, 149–156.

Pike, K. M., Wolk, S. L., Gluck, M., & Walsh, B. T. (2000). Eating disorder measures. In American Psychiatric Association (Eds.), Handbook of psychiatric measures (pp. 647–671). Washington, DC: American Psychiatric Association.

Prochaska, J. O., & DiClemente, C. C. (1982). Transtheoretical therapy: Toward a more integrative model of change. Psychotherapy: Theory, Research, and Practice, 19, 276–288.

Reich, W. (2000). Diagnostic interview for children and adolescents (DICA). Journal of the American Academy of Child & Adolescent Psychiatry, 39, 59–66.

Richterich, A., Brunner, R., & Resch, F. (2003). Achalasia mimicking prepubertal anorexia nervosa. International Journal of Eating Disorders, 33, 356–359.

Robin, A. L., Gilroy, M., & Dennis, A. B. (1998). Treatment of eating disorders in children and adolescents. Clinical Psychology Review, 18, 421–446.

Rosen, J. C. (1997). Cognitive-behavioral body image therapy. In D. M. Garner & P. E. Garfinkel (Eds.), Handbook for treatment for eating disorders (pp. 188–201). New York: Guilford Press.

Russell, G. F. M., Szmukler, G. I., Dare, C., & Eisler, I. (1987). An evaluation of family therapy in anorexia nervosa and bulimia nervosa. Archives of General Psychiatry, 44, 1047–1056.

Schneider, M. (2003). Bulimia nervosa and binge eating disorder in adolescents. Adolescent Medicine, 14, 119–131.

Shaffer, D., Fisher, P., & Lucas, C. P. (2000). NIMH Diagnostic Interview Schedule for Children Version IV (NIMH DISC-IV): Description, differences for previous versions, and reliability of some common diagnoses. Journal of the American Academy of Child & Adolescent Psychiatry, 39, 28–38.

Sharkey-Orgnero, M. I. (1999). Anorexia nervosa: A qualitative analysis of parents' perspectives on recovery. Eating Disorders, 7, 123–141.

Smolak, L., Levine, M. P., & Gralen, S. (1993). The impact of puberty and dating on eating problems among middle school girls. *Journal of Youth and Adolescence, 22,* 355–368.

Treasure, J. (1997). *Anorexia nervosa: A survival guide for family, friends, and sufferers.* Hove, UK: Psychology Press.

Walsh, B. T., & Garner, D. M. (1997). Diagnostic issues. In D. M. Garner & P. E. Garfinkel (Eds.), *Handbook for treatment for eating disorders* (pp. 25–33). New York: Guilford Press.

Watkins, B., Frampton, I., Lask, B., & Bryant-Waugh, R. (2005). Reliability and validity of the child version of the eating disorder examination: A preliminary investigation. *International Journal of Eating Disorders, 38,* 183–187.

Winn, S., Perkins, S., Murray, J., Murphy, R., & Schmidt, U. (2004). A qualitative study of the experience of caring for a person with bulimia nervosa. *International Journal of Eating Disorders, 36,* 256–279.

World Health Organization. (1992). *ICD-10 classification of mental and behavioral disorders: Clinical descriptions and diagnostic guidelines.* Geneva, Switzerland: Author.

18

SUBSTANCE USE DISORDERS

BRAD C. DONOHUE, HEATHER H. HILL, AND DANIELLE KNATZ

DESCRIPTION OF THE DISORDERS

There are two primary substance use disorders, substance abuse and substance dependence, and symptom criteria for these disorders are the same for both adults and adolescents. According to the *Diagnostic and Statistical Manual of Mental Disorders, Fourth Edition, Text Revised (DSM-IV-TR)* (APA, 2000), substance abuse is diagnosed when at least one of the following leads to clinically significant distress or impairment and occurs within a 12-month period: (a) Substance use interferes with responsibilities and obligations at school, home, or work; (b) substance use occurs in hazardous situations; (c) legal problems occur as a result of substance use; and (d) substance use continues despite recurring problems. Substance dependence, a more severe diagnosis, is diagnosed when three or more of the following occur within a 12-month period: (a) unintentional increases in the amount and frequency of substance use; (b) unsuccessful attempts to reduce or eliminate substance use; (c) a significant amount of time is spent obtaining, using, and recovering from the negative effects of substances; (d) continued use of substances causes significant distress in social, occupational, and recreational activities; and (e) use of substances continues despite recurring problems caused by the substances. The diagnosis of

substance dependence also includes both tolerance and withdrawal as symptoms. Tolerance occurs when the individual experiences a reduced effect of the substances despite continued use of the same amount. Tolerance can occur when an adolescent requires greater amounts of the substance to achieve intoxication or previously perceived effects. Withdrawal occurs when physiological symptoms arise when the particular substance is abruptly discontinued. Withdrawal effects are often substance specific. That is, particular substances may produce effects different from other substances.

The prevalence of substance use in adolescent populations remains relatively high, although rates have decreased slightly within the last decade. For instance, according to the U.S. Centers for Disease Control (CDC, 2003), 75% of the adolescent population reported using alcohol at least once in their lifetime, while 45% reported having used alcohol during the past 30 days. Marijuana use was reported by 40% of the youth population to have occurred at least once in their lifetime, while 22% of these youth reported marijuana use during the past 30 days. In addition, 5% to 9% of the youth reported hard drug use at least once in their lifetime, and 2% to 5% of the sample reported using hard drugs within the past 30 days.

In general, the greater the number of risk factors an adolescent is exposed to, the greater the risk of substance abuse or dependence. Therefore, when attempting to determine the extent of substance use involvement, it is important for clinicians to be knowledgeable about the various factors that place adolescents at risk. In their review of various substance abuse risk factors, Hawkins, Catalano, and Miller (1992) found 17 categories that place adolescents at an increased risk. These risk factors include temperament and genetic predisposition, early and persistent problem behaviors, poor parenting skills, family conflict, low family bonding, peer rejection in early childhood, deviant peer group membership in adolescence, alienation and rebelliousness, favorable attitudes to drug use, early poverty, neighborhood disorganization, academic failure, low commitment to school, family drug-taking behavior, early onset of drug use, laws and norms favorable to substance use, and substance availability. Some of these risk factors should be addressed during the course of the clinical interview, while others are more specific to substance use.

Substance use disorders in children and adolescents often comorbidly exist with severe behavioral problems (e.g., academic troubles, relationship problems with family members and authority figures). Psychiatric disorders, including disruptive disorders (oppositional defiant disorder, conduct disorder, attention-deficit/hyperactivity disorder), personality disorders (antisocial personality disorder), mood disorders (major depressive disorder, anxiety disorders, bipolar disorder), and adjustment disorders are also found to commonly occur in adolescents with substance use disorders (Garland et al., 2001; Wise, Cuffe, & Fischer, 2001). Therefore, identification of these disorders should act to signal the necessity of assessing substance abuse and dependence.

Habitual drug use in adolescence appears to negatively affect a wide range of life domains, including impairments in mental and physical health, romantic and familial relationships, employment stability, and educational endeavors (Newcomb & Bentler, 1988). Adolescents with substance use disorders often engage in risky sexual practices and continue to engage in these practices while abusing substances. For example, Tapert, Aarons, Sedlar, and Brown (2001) collected assessments on sexual behaviors and substance use in a sample of adolescent

substance abusers and matched controls at 2-, 4-, and 6-year intervals after their initial assessment. Results indicated that compared with controls, the substance-abusing sample engaged in sexual activity at an earlier age, had more sexual partners, used condoms less consistently, and had higher rates of sexually transmitted diseases (STDs). In addition, higher rates of STDs and pregnancies were reported by substance-abusing females than by females in the control group. Therefore, the results of this study suggest that whenever possible, substance-abusing adolescents should be assessed for various STDs (American Academy of Child and Adolescent Psychiatry, 2005).

Adolescents who abuse substances often engage in risk-taking behaviors despite being knowledgeable of negative consequences. For instance, Deas-Nesmith, Brady, White, and Campbell (1999) found substance-abusing adolescents were significantly more likely than age- and gender-matched controls to engage in risky behaviors related to HIV/AIDS infection. These behaviors include engaging in intercourse without using a condom and with higher-risk individuals (e.g., acquaintances, prostitutes). Interestingly, however, the authors found no differences between the two groups with regard to knowledge about the transmission of HIV/AIDS. These findings suggest that substance use may interfere with decision making and judgment even when the youth possesses the proper knowledge base to make safe decisions.

Adolescent substance abuse is also related to additional risky behaviors, including drinking and driving. For example, approximately half (45%) of all traffic fatalities involve the use of alcohol, and an estimated 18% of adolescent drivers between the ages of 16 and 20 drive under the influence of alcohol (Center for Substance Abuse Treatment, 1999). Alcohol use has also been shown to be associated with both delinquent and violent behaviors (Komro et al., 1999). Finally, using alcohol at earlier ages increases the risk of developing alcohol use disorders in adulthood. Grant and Dawson (1997) found that age of initial use of alcohol was a significant predictor of the development of lifetime alcohol abuse and alcohol dependence. Indeed, a person who first drinks alcohol at age 13 is 4 times more likely than someone who first drinks at age 21 to develop alcohol dependence at some point in his or her life.

INTERVIEWING STRATEGIES

An interview is used to diagnose and conceptualize problems and, to a lesser extent, achievements. Information obtained from the interview is used to guide the intervention plan and determine targets for intervention. For substance-abusing youth, the primary target for intervention is almost always substance use, although other problem areas may also be of great concern, including aggression, noncompliance to adult instructions, truancy, and social skills deficits. Interviews are often used to ascertain program placements and to assist in judicial decisions. The interview may occur in many different settings, such as inpatient or outpatient medical facilities, detention centers, correctional facilities, and homes. It is also preferable to interview family members, teachers, and other significant others whenever possible. The interview length varies depending on the purpose of the interview but generally ranges from 10 or 15 minutes (e.g., psychiatric or medical examinations) to 2 hours (e.g., comprehensive psychological assessments, neurological examinations).

Prior to the first session, the clinician should review pertinent available records, including psychological and psychiatric reports, medical and psychiatric charts, treatment plans, completed questionnaires, case progress reports, and school records. This review of records will assist in identifying and conceptualizing problems and can aid in creating an agenda for the first session. First-session agendas may include a description of the purpose of the interview, a listing of topic areas to be reviewed during the assessment, and an estimate of the duration of time to be spent reviewing each topic area. Another step that should be performed prior to the interview is telephoning the family to remind them of the session, problem solve any barriers that may interfere with session attendance, and instill hope (see Donohue, Karmely, & Strada, 2006). Research has shown that telephoning the youth and parent(s) prior to the first session significantly increases attendance rates in adolescent substance abusers (Donohue et al., 1998).

When beginning the interview, the legal guardian should be given an opportunity to provide informed consent for treatment, and the youth should be involved in providing youth assent. An attempt should be made for parents and youth to mutually determine what information will be shared, what information will be kept confidential between the clinician and the youth, and what information will not be privileged (e.g., danger to self or others, child and elder abuse, court mandate, duty to warn). This agreement may help in establishing open communication between the youth and the clinician. The interviewer should initiate the session with all interviewees seen together (youth, parents, other significant others), thereby permitting an assessment of family interactions. Most intervention content, however, should be obtained during separate interviews with the parent(s) and substance-abusing youth, thus eliminating audience control. Interview methods in the assessment of adolescent substance abuse are typically classified into three main approaches, unstructured, semistructured, and structured, which often occur in combination to some extent.

Unstructured Interviews

An unstructured interview provides the clinician flexibility to identify and broadly understand problems and to review domains indirectly related to substance use. This type of interview usually involves the utilization of broad questions that facilitate discussion and the identification of key problem areas that may otherwise have been ignored. The unstructured interview is notoriously unreliable, as interviewers will vary in the questions they ask and the responses they record. In most cases, poor reliability between interviewers is not a concern, as the interview format may need to support the interviewer's unique style or theoretical orientation. Due to poor reliability, however, unstructured interviews are often excluded from research settings, although this format facilitates rapport, as it permits the interviewer to loosely explore areas that are pleasant to discuss (e.g., hobbies, interests, rewards, ambitions, things liked and disliked about relationships). Moreover, unstructured interviews often enable experienced clinicians to quickly intuit domains that are worthy of exploration and similarly abandon topic areas that elicit upset.

During the unstructured interview, it has become conventional to assess reasons for the referral, history of the presenting problem, the client's mental status, medical history, social and academic history, social supports, social skills, hobbies, family background, relative client strengths, and goals for therapy. The child's substance use should be discussed throughout the interview. In doing so, the interview should initially be focused on broadly identifying problems and developing rapport. Gradually, more detailed information about substance use and related problem behaviors should be explored. As the interview is unstructured, the interviewer may tailor domains to fit the needs of each family.

In examining life domains, there are some hallmark domains to assess that are specific to substance use. For instance, when assessing medical history, it is important to review medical conditions that may be related to substance use or exacerbated by substance use (see Donohue et al., 2006). Indeed, referrals to medical examinations are strongly recommended, particularly when prescribed medications are indicated. When youth are prescribed medications, the interviewer should assess the interactive history between prescription and illicit substances. Substance-abusing youth are at a higher risk of committing suicide. Therefore, clinicians need to emphasize the assessment of suicide risk factors, such as certain demographic indicators (e.g., being a male, 15–24 years old, Caucasian, low socioeconomic status, few social supports); history of suicide attempts; plan, intent, and means to commit suicide; and lack of future orientation. Along these lines, suicidal risk is exacerbated during intoxication. The interviewer should also assess homicidal ideation.

It is important to assess the affect of substance-abusing youth, as well as disorganized, irrational, and psychotic thought patterns and regulatory skills associated with emotional control. The lifestyle of substance abusers is often distinct from that of non–substance abusers. Compared with non-substance-abusing adolescents, substance-abusing youth are more likely to spend time engaged in solitary activities, engage in vandalism, and demonstrate poor social skills when interacting with authority figures. Therefore, the interviewer should query peer relationships before and after the onset of substance use problems. It is important to obtain a list of friends who do not use substances and those friends who do use substances, particularly those who influence the youth to use substances.

Along a different vein, academic performance should be fully explored, including an examination of activities and events that are liked and disliked about school or work, if applicable. Assessment of the family system is of paramount importance when conducting interviews with substance-abusing youth. Indeed, a dysfunctional family system exerts tremendous negative influence on youth to use substances. Some target topics within this domain include household membership, severe illnesses or disabilities of family members, psychopathology, criminality, unemployment among caregivers, separation of loved ones, frequent residential changes, strengths and skills, supportive and stressful relationships, method of caregivers' discipline, and the youth's response to discipline. Spousal abuse, child abuse, and child neglect occur in the vast majority of adolescent substance abusers (Dennis & Stevens, 2003), necessitating a thorough examination.

Youth ambitions should be emphasized in the unstructured interview, including youth goals for treatment. Indeed, many ambitions of adolescent substance abusers (e.g., playing the guitar, doing artwork, racing cars, building model airplanes, cooking) are often ignored or dismissed as nonproductive. Youth goals for therapy are often inconsistent with those of adult authority figures. Therefore, the interviewer will need to assess the reactions of others to youth ambitions, in addition to motivation of the youth to decrease or eliminate substance use, improve school or vocational performance, comply with curfews, and spend less time with delinquent and substance-abusing youth. Interviewers need to support youth when discussing their ambitions, as they may be mandated to attend therapy by others and have little or no desire to change their behavioral patterns. Interviewers may need to acknowledge that treatment is imposed on adolescents by parents and court officials, and empathize with their plight. The interviewer should attempt to elicit negative outcomes of substance use (e.g. physical effects, nagging parents, poor school performance, poor relationship with family), as these consequences will likely be used later in therapy to bring about youth motivation to decrease or abstain from substances.

One of the chief goals to accomplish during the unstructured interview is the establishment of rapport. Along these lines, it is important to be genuine, warm, empathic, and nonjudgmental (Donohue et al., 2006). Interviewers should advise youth to indicate when they do not feel comfortable talking about particular topics, thus preventing opportunities for youth to lie (Morrison & Anders, 1999). Discussing interests and hobbies with youth may enhance their comfort level when discussing difficult topics, such as substance use and dating. Sincere compliments usually assist in accomplishing rapport. As the substance-abusing youth has likely had negative experiences with authority figures, it is sometimes helpful to permit youth to refer to the interviewer by first name, allow profanity during the interview, and indicate an awareness that most teens have experimented with alcohol, tobacco, and marijuana (Morrison & Anders, 1999). Motivational-interviewing techniques can also be used in the unstructured interview to establish rapport, increase youth incentive to provide relevant information, and lead to immediate therapeutic effects (Miller & Rollnick, 2002).

The clinician will need to determine frequency and duration of substance use. Along these lines, the Timeline Followback (TLFB) procedure is best used during the unstructured portion of the interview (Sobell & Sobell, 1996). The TLFB is the most extensively evaluated procedure for determining retrospective self-report estimates of substance use and was originally created to measure alcohol use for research protocols (Sobell, Agrawal, & Annis, 2001). Briefly, youth are provided with a blank calendar and instructed to fill in information about the days they used substances, which substances were used, and the settings where the substance use occurred. To aid in recall, holidays and dates of personal interest to the participant (e.g., birthdays, parties, employment, illnesses, and arrests) are recorded on the calendar to serve as memory triggers (Ehrman & Robbins, 1994). Administration times vary due to the extent of substance use and duration of time interval assessed (i.e., the TLFB can be used to assess intervals up to 12 months in the past, which can take approximately 30 minutes to complete; Sobell, Brown, Leo, & Sobell, 1996). Other substance use behavior patterns and comorbid events and activities can be monitored utilizing the TLFB, such as days incarcerated, days employed, days attending school, and days institutionalized. Thus, antecedent stimuli and consequences to substance use can be better identified. The TLFB can also be administered to parents to increase the likelihood of substance use detection (Donohue et al., 2004).

Semistructured Interviews

Typically, unstructured interviews are the most frequently used interviews in the assessment of substance abuse disorders; information on published semistructured interviews is given in Table 18.1. However, in circumstances where validity and reliability are imperative (i.e., forensic court involvement, research studies), semistructured and structured interviews are of greater utility. In a semistructured interview, a flexible format is utilized in which the interviewer chooses, and is able to modify, the interview questions from a prearranged set of questions, with each question being pertinent to relevant topics (e.g., criteria for substance use disorders). Guidelines are utilized to assist in scoring and interpretation of youth responses. The Teen Addiction Severity Index (T-ASI) (Kaminer, Bukstein, & Tarter, 1991; Kaminer, Wagner, Plummer, & Seifer, 1993) is a semistructured interview specifically designed for adolescents. Adapted from the Addiction Severity Index (McLellan, Luborsky, O'Brien, & Woody, 1980), the T-ASI evaluates severity of adolescent alcohol and drug use and problem domains, including school status, employment, family relationships, peer and social relationships, legal status, and psychiatric disturbances. The T-ASI interview has demonstrated adequate psychometric properties (Kaminer et al., 1991; Kaminer et al., 1993) and has recently demonstrated validity in self-report formats utilizing both Internet and interactive voice response automated-telephone technologies (Brodey et al., 2005).

The Schedule for Affective Disorders and Schizophrenia for School-Age Children-Present and Lifetime Version (K-SADS-PL) (Kaufman et al., 1997) is a semistructured diagnostic interview designed to assess both current and past episodes of psychopathology in children and adolescents (Kaufman et al., 1997). This instrument may be utilized to assess disorders according to both the *DSM-III-R* and the *DSM-IV* criteria and includes three sections pertaining to current and past substance abuse, alcohol abuse, and cigarette use (Kaufman et al., 1997).

Structured Interviews

Structured interviews are particularly effective in establishing substance use diagnoses in research settings. Table 18.1 provides summary information on published structured interview protocols. These interviews are made up of a prescribed set of questions that are administered in a prearranged and specified order. Youth responses to the questions are recorded according to standard

TABLE 18.1   Structured and Semistructured Interviews for Adolescent Substance Abuse

Semistructured Interviews

Interview Name	Assessment Domain/Purpose	Description	Administration
Teen Addiction Severity Index (T-ASI; Kaminer, Bukstein, Tarter, 1991; Kaminer, Wagner, Plummer, & Seifer, 1993)	Used for periodic evaluation of adolescent substance abuse problems	Contains seven domains: alcohol and drug use severity, school status, employment, family relationships, peer and social relationships, legal status, and psychiatric disturbances	Clinician administered; 30 minutes or less to administer; youth self-report Internet and telephone voice response formats available
Schedule for Affective Disorders and Schizophrenia for School-Age Children-Present and Lifetime (K-SADS-PL; Kaufman et al., 1997)	*DSM-III-R* and *DSM-IV* criteria of 32 Axis I child psychiatric diagnoses	Contains an introductory interview; a screening interview; five diagnostic supplements: affective disorders, psychotic disorders, anxiety disorders, behavioral disorders, and substance abuse, eating, and tic disorders; and parent and youth interviews	Clinician administered; 1.25 hours each to administer parent and child interviews in psychiatric patients
Timeline Followback (TLFB) Sobell & Sobell, 1996	Provides estimates of daily alcohol drinking and/or drug use	Semistructured interview 12-month calendar with memory aids to help adolescent recall past alcohol and/or drug use Appropriate for ages 14 years and older Spanish, French, Swedish, and Polish versions available Free use of this copyright-protected scale is allowed by test developers	Self-report, paper/pencil or computer version; 10 to 30 minutes to administer

Structured Interviews

The Structured Clinical Interview for the *DSM-IV* Axis I disorders (SCID-IV; First, Spitzer, Gibbon, & Williams, 1996)	*DSM-IV* criteria for most Axis I disorders, including substance use disorders	Includes six modules: substance use disorders, mood episodes, psychotic symptoms, psychotic disorders, mood disorders, anxiety and adjustment disorder	Clinician administered; 30 to 120 minutes to administer
National Institute of Mental Health Diagnostic Interview Schedule for Children-Version IV (NIMH DISC-IV; Shaffer, Fisher, Lucas, Dulcan, & Schwab-Stone, 2000)	*DSM-IV* and *ICD-10* criteria of over 30 psychiatric disorders in children and adolescents	Contains an introductory module that includes demographic information and an instructional component, then has six modules containing diagnoses related to anxiety, mood, disruptive, substance use, schizophrenia, and miscellaneous disorders; English and Spanish language versions available; parent and youth interviews	Clinician administered; 70 minutes per informant and approximately 90 to 120 minutes for known patients; however, interviewer can drop diagnostic modules that are not relevant to a particular setting to shorten administration time; can be administered by lay interviewers after minimal training; computer-assisted scoring available

Interview Name	Assessment Domain/Purpose	Description	Administration
Structured Clinical Interview for Adolescents (SCI; Brown, Creamer, & Stetson, 1987; Brown, Vik, & Creamer, 1989)	Assessment of adolescent functioning in major life domains	Includes assessment of academic, interpersonal, and psychosocial functioning; information relevant to adolescent substance use includes previous treatment, current motivation for entering treatment and reducing substance use, peer substance use, and assessment of familial history of substance abuse	Clinician administered
Adolescent Diagnostic Interview (ADI; Winters & Henly, 1993)	DSM-III-R and DSM-IV criteria for substance use disorders	Includes clinical sections, such as sociodemographics, psychosocial stressors, substance use frequency and duration, alcohol symptoms, cannabis symptoms, other substance symptoms, and level of functioning; contains appendix with orientation and memory screen	Clinician administered; 45 minutes to administer; should be performed by well-trained paraprofessionals or professionals

response format, thereby yielding indices concerning the presence or absence of substance use disorders. These interviews have excellent psychometric support. Administration of these instruments can interfere with the establishment of rapport when the interviewer is not practiced in the instrument. Extensive training, experience, and inclusion of an additional unstructured component during the interview process usually work to eliminate this latter problem.

The Structured Clinical Interview for the DSM-IV Axis I Disorders (SCID-IV) (First, Spitzer, Gibbon, & Williams, 1996) is a commonly utilized structured interview that assesses most of the major Axis I DSM-IV disorders, including the substance use disorders. The SCID-IV has been found to be a reliable instrument in controlled-treatment outcome studies involving substance-abusing and dependent youth (e.g., Azrin et al., 2001).

The National Institute of Mental Health Diagnostic Interview Schedule for Children Version IV (NIMH DISC-IV) (Shaffer, Fisher, Lucas, Dulcan, & Schwab-Stone, 2000) is a highly structured clinical interview that is capable of being utilized to assess more than 30 psychiatric diagnoses in children and adolescents, including the substance use disorders. English and Spanish versions are available (Shaffer et al., 2000).

The Structured Clinical Interview for Adolescents (SCI) (Brown, Creamer, & Stetson, 1987; Brown, Vik, & Creamer, 1989) is a structured interview that may be utilized to obtain information relevant to the adolescent's academic, interpersonal, and psychosocial functioning. Information relevant to adolescent substance use includes previous treatment for substance use disorders, motivation for entering treatment, peer substance use, motivation for reducing current substance use, and a comprehensive assessment of familial history of substance use and abuse. Assessment of its psychometric properties is warranted; it appears to have great promise (Myers, Brown, & Vik, 1998).

The Adolescent Diagnostic Interview (ADI) (Winters & Henly, 1993) is a structured interview that assesses the criteria of substance use disorders in adolescents according to both the DSM-III-R and the DSM-IV. The interview may be utilized to assess problems commonly associated with substance abuse, substance use consumption, psychosocial stressors, school and interpersonal functioning, and cognitive impairment. Only well-trained paraprofessionals or mental health professionals should administer this interview. Its psychometric properties are well supported, including adequate test-retest reliability, interrater agreement, and discrimination on alternative measures of problem severity (Winters, Stinchfield, Fulkerson, & Henly, 1993; Winters, Stinchfield, & Henly, 1993).

INTERVIEWING OBSTACLES AND SOLUTIONS

Adolescent substance abuse is one of the most difficult mental health disorders to interview. Indeed, the interviewer must be prepared to manage a lack of motivation, developmental and medical complications, arguments between family members, strong negative emotions, reporting inconsistencies, and deceit. Moreover, it is likely the youth has experienced negative responses from parents and teachers when discussing substance use and related issues, and therefore these youth often have a tendency to minimize or deny substance use. The first step in overcoming the latter obstacle is to spend time at the outset of the interview establishing rapport (later establishing trust, which is difficult to accomplish in the initial interviewing process). A detailed explanation of the purpose of the interview session is likely to be helpful, as the youth may erroneously believe that admitting to or discussing substance use may lead to negative sanctions. Along these lines, youth should be prompted to clarify roles and expectations relevant to sharing information.

Youth often disclose substance-specific information when prompted to discuss the benefits of using substances, and the interviewer should respond to their statements in a nonjudgmental manner. Questions and statements should be phrased so negative connotations for substance use are avoided. For instance, instead of asking, "Why do you use drugs?" the interviewer might ask, "What are some positive things drug use is able to provide you?" When youth deny substance use that has been evidenced to occur, the interviewer may ask the youth to assist the interviewer in understanding how the inconsistency may have occurred, gently confronting the youth about conflicting evidence (Morrison & Anders, 1999). The TLFB (Sobell & Sobell, 1996), mentioned previously, is a proven self-report method of obtaining accurate reports of substance use frequency for up to 12 months. This method has demonstrated excellent psychometric support (Donohue et al., 2004; Sobell & Sobell, 1996) and may be particularly useful when urinalysis testing is employed (Williams & Nowatzki, 2005).

Interviewers must also be careful to avoid leading questions (e.g., "Do you think using drugs is wrong?") that may influence youth response reactivity. Instead, interviewers should utilize open-ended questions (e.g., "How do you feel about using drugs?"). If it is discovered that the youth has been deceitful in substance use reporting, it is often prudent to make a note of the contradictory information and continue the interview without confrontation. Indeed, confrontation early in the interviewing process will usually damage rapport and result in future defensiveness. When accurate information is critical, however, it may be helpful for the interviewer to neutrally present the contradictory information to the youth and ask for assistance in understanding the situation (e.g., "You said you typically use marijuana once a week, and your mother says you use marijuana almost every day. Help me to understand why the reports are so different."). When deceit occurs, it is sometimes helpful to ask the youth to explain contradictory information after an opportunity is provided by the interviewer to assist in removing responsibility from the youth (e.g., "I've asked you so many questions, I think I may have confused you . . .").

Interestingly, substance-abusing youth are more likely to admit use of alcohol and marijuana during an interview format than on a self-administered questionnaire (Stone & Latimer, 2005). Also, there is the influence of third parties on the self-reporting of substance use. For instance, one study found that when a parent was present during the interview, youth were less likely to report the use of alcohol or marijuana and that this parental influence was stronger for youth aged 12 to 18 years than for young adults aged 19 to 34 years (Aquilino, Wright, & Supple, 2000). This supports the idea that youth should be interviewed alone when attempting to obtain youth self-reports of their frequency of substance use.

Drug urinalysis testing is an objective biological indicator of drug use (Kaminer, Burleson, Blitz, Sussman, & Rounsaville, 1998) that is relatively accurate in determining the presence or absence of substances in a particular specimen (Cook, Bernstein, Arrington, Andrews, & Marshall, 1995). The implementation of drug testing is often problematic because positive drug-testing results are tied to negative legal consequences (e.g., extended treatment, prison sentencing, loss of privileges) and youth are aware of these consequences. Biological measures are outside the focus of this chapter; however, discussion of this topic will be difficult and may impact rapport, especially if the interviewer will be the person responsible for conducting the tests. In these situations, an explanation of the urinalysis technique as well as its purpose and potential consequences will be helpful in establishing honesty with the youth. The interviewer may solicit the youth's feelings or concerns about being subjected to this form of drug screening (e.g., feeling like they are not going to be believed or trusted) and empathize with solicited feelings.

Minimizing or denying substance use often leads to arguments and negative emotions among family members and lack of motivation. When confronted with low motivation, the interviewer should immediately provide empathy and remain nonjudgmental in determining the etiology of this concern. Sometimes it helps to initiate discussion about youth goals, including how accomplishment of these goals is beneficial. During the interview, serious arguments between family members may arise, or a family member may express strong negative emotions. The interviewer may avoid arguments by obtaining commitments from participants, at the start of the interview, to attempt to comply with communication guidelines and to redirect faulty communication before it is permitted to escalate, and by instructing family members who violate communication guidelines to practice appropriate communication skills, after being reminded of their commitments. If arguments spontaneously occur, interviewers may need to separate family members, to prevent escalation of undesired behavior, and discuss solutions separately. The interviewer should provide empathy and acknowledge the importance of hearing all perspectives while remaining neutral.

Another interviewing obstacle is youth nonattendance to the scheduled interview. As mentioned above, attendance rates increase if the clinician proactively telephones the youth and parents 2 or 3 days prior to the scheduled interview (Donohue et al., 1998). In the event of session nonattendance, the youth and parents should be telephoned, and problem-solving interventions should be employed to assist in deterring future nonattendance (see Lefforge, Donohue, & Strada, 2007). When practical difficulties prevent the family from attending an interview (e.g., no transportation available, disability), the clinician may need to consider a home interview (Carr, 1999).

If developmental and medical complications arise, a referral to a physician may be appropriate.

INTERVIEWING PARENTS AND TEACHERS

To obtain a complete picture of the youth's substance use problems, it is essential to obtain information from multiple informants, including parents, teachers, and additional family members, whenever possible, as each of these informants provides unique information concerning the youth's behavior in varying contexts (Achenbach, McConaughy, & Howell, 1987). There is some support to suggest relatively mild agreement among the ratings of different types of informants (Achenbach et al., 1987). When these relationships have been low, however, informants have been found to provide unique information concerning the presenting problem behavior (Van der Ende & Verhulst, 2005).

The initial contact with parents of substance-abusing youth typically occurs in a phone call scheduling the first session. In this population, attendance at this first session has been found to be less than 50% (Gariti et al., 1995). Therefore, it is essential to explicitly employ strategies that have been shown to increase attendance in controlled trials. For instance, a brief 10- to 15-minute telephone call involving both the parent and the youth prior to the initial scheduled session has been found to increase initial session attendance by 29% (Donohue et al., 1998). Topics include discussing each person's perspective of the presenting problem, empathizing with presenting concerns, reviewing and problem solving potential difficulties in attending the session, and reviewing specific directions to the facility. Similar, albeit less involved, procedures have been shown to improve subsequent sessions, suggesting telephone interviews should be employed between sessions whenever possible (Donohue et al., 1998).

The initial session should be spent with all family members assessing the reasons for referral and observing various interactions among family members. The youth and parent(s) should then be interviewed independently. The family should be asked to decide which member will be seen independently first, and session time should be distributed equally across family members. When family members indicate ambivalence regarding the order of interviews, the youth should be seen first.

The primary purpose of the parent interview is to enlist family support and to determine the parents' perspectives of the presenting problem. To enhance the therapeutic relationship and alliance, the interviewer should first empathize with parental complaints or concerns. Programmatic issues should be addressed, including consent to conduct the interview, credentials of the treatment provider, hours of clinician availability, duration of sessions, procedures for canceling sessions, and limits of confidentiality. Whenever possible, an attempt should be made to mutually determine what information will be disclosed to the parents and what information will be held confidential (i.e., parent holds privilege). Unless the referral is mandated, it is generally important to keep all information reported by the youth confidential, with the exception of legal mandates.

A description of the interviewing process should be fully delineated to the parent, including the purpose of the assessment and interview, how the information will be used to conceptualize the presenting problems, and methods of developing the treatment plan. The clinician should structure the parent interview to collect information relevant to identifying the reasons for seeking treatment, past psychiatric and medical history and treatment (including medications), disciplining strategies utilized, behavior problems and skills of the youth, quality of parents' relationships with the youth, family history of drug use/abuse, and current mental status.

The session should conclude by reconvening the family to discuss their satisfaction with the interview process, so potential concerns may be addressed. An appointment card with contact information and the time of the next appointment should be provided to both the youth and legal guardian. Finally, a routine 5-minute follow-up telephone call should be provided to both the parent and youth within 24 hours of the session to reinforce their participation, express positive qualities about their family, and to answer additional questions. As previously mentioned, these procedures have been effectively utilized to increase subsequent session attendance (Donohue et al., 1998) and can demonstrate a continued interest in the family.

Subsequent interviews may be conducted with additional informants, including the adolescent's teachers, preferably teachers who know the adolescent well. Whenever possible, clinicians should distribute various teacher rating forms (e.g., Achenbach's Child Teachers' Report Form [TRF], Achenbach, 1991; BASC Teacher Rating Scale, Reynolds & Kamphaus, 1992) to the adolescent's teachers prior to the initial interview. If possible, it is helpful to gather information from teachers of the adolescent's best and worst classes. Common information elicited from teachers includes the adolescent's current and past academic achievements; performance in nonacademic activities; relationships with teachers, staff, and peers; the teachers' beliefs about the substance problems and their ideas for resolution; the degree of parent-teacher cooperation; and the teachers' style (e.g., use of positive reinforcement; Carr, 1999).

CASE ILLUSTRATION WITH DIALOGUE

Robert was a 16-year-old Caucasian male referred to his counselor by his mother after being arrested for possession of marijuana. After reviewing court records, it was determined that this was Robert's first arrest. Robert's school records indicated he was an honor student less than a year prior to the arrest.

Robert and his mother arrived for their appointment on time. Once brief introductions were made, an agenda of the interview was reviewed with the family. Robert provided study assent, and his mother provided study consent. The clinician met with both individuals to mutually determine what information disclosed by Robert would be kept confidential and what information would not be privileged (i.e., danger to self or others, child and elder abuse, court mandate, duty to warn). During this discussion, the clinician carefully observed the interactions between Robert and his mother. Next, the clinician excused the mother and met with Robert alone for a 20-minute unstructured interview.

When asked to elaborate on the presenting problem, Robert reported, "There is no problem, I just got caught with a little bit of weed. It's not a big deal. My mom's freaking out about nothing." The counselor then informed Robert that she was interested in learning more about his hobbies and interests. Among other things, Robert stated, "Well, I'm really good at football and even made the JV team this year, but my mom told my coach about the weed, and now I can't play again until next year." To facilitate rapport, the counselor praised Robert for his athletic abilities and instructed him to disclose what he liked and disliked about his friends. Robert reported having many different groups of friends, including friends from his football team and more recent friendships with the individuals who had sold him the marijuana that led to the referral. Robert reported that his friends on the football team did not use drugs, but "like to have fun drinking lots of beer at parties."

When asked about his school performance, Robert acknowledged decreased performance since he began using marijuana. However, he stated, "I can get my grades back up with no problem. I just want my mom to stop nagging me about them. Then maybe I'll try harder." When asked about his goals for treatment, Robert stated, "I want to get my mom off my back, and I want to be able to play football again." The counselor praised Robert for his desire to participate in sports and acknowledged that substance use can often result in the negative outcomes that Robert mentioned (e.g., nagging parents, poor academic performance, loss of privileges). The counselor informed Robert that his goals for treatment were achievable.

When asked to report on his relationships with his family members, Robert stated, "I used to be close to my dad, but since my parents divorced, I don't see him that much. He's always with his new girlfriend." When asked to elaborate on the divorce, Robert disclosed that his parents had divorced 3 months prior to the interview and that he visited his father only every other weekend. He was also asked to disclose information on what he liked and disliked most about his relationships with both his mother and father.

Robert denied any suicidal ideation and did not appear to exhibit irrational thought patterns. To determine the frequency and duration of Robert's substance use, the Timeline Followback interview was administered to assess substance use frequency during the past 6 months. The clinician paid special attention to Robert's substance use patterns before and after his parents were divorced. Next, the clinician administered the Teen Addiction Severity Index to assist in a possible substance use diagnosis.

After excusing Robert, the clinician conducted a brief unstructured interview with Robert's mother. This interview primarily focused on her perspectives on the presenting problem; her relationship with Robert; onset of the substance use; recent stressors, including the divorce; and family history of substance use. The clinician also asked Robert's mother to discuss potential reinforcers that might be utilized in Robert's treatment plan (e.g., playing football if substance use decreased and grades improved).

MULTICULTURAL AND DIVERSITY ISSUES

Ethnic identity is emerging as an important developmental consideration in adolescents and relates to psychological wellness and sense of self (James, Kim, & Armijo, 2000). Indeed, some investigators have considered ethnicity when evaluating evidence-based interventions for adolescent substance abuse (see Strada, Donohue, & Lefforge, 2006, for extensive review), and there is some support that the use of substances is related to ethnic identity and level of acculturation. For instance, alcohol use has been linked to conflicts in cultural identity among Native Americans (Sue & Sue, 2003), and stress associated with acculturation has helped to explain the extent of substance use in Hispanic adolescents. Hispanic bilingual adolescents have been found to use more alcohol than more acculturated (English-language-only) adolescents (Epstein, Botvin, & Diaz, 2000). In language spoken with parents, Hispanic bilingual adolescents were shown to use more alcohol than less acculturated (Spanish-language-only) adolescents (Epstein et al., 2000). In an examination of Asian and Pacific Islander youth, it was found that cultural identification is a protective factor leading to lower alcohol use (James, Kim, & Moore, 1997). In terms of substance use treatment, one study found substance-abusing African American youth to be less motivated than Caucasian youth to remain in treatment, due to external influences, mainly because of less fear among African American youth of being incarcerated (Breda & Heflinger, 2004). In consideration of these research findings, it may be important for the interviewer to determine motivation for treatment in ethnic-minority youth and to use motivational interviewing to assist youth in appreciating the benefits of abstinence rather than using external threats to cease substance use.

Ethnic-minority substance-abusing youth may have culturally related concerns about the interview and treatment. One study found that ethnic-minority individuals referred to substance abuse treatment programs were concerned that they would be the only ethnic minority in the program (Alvarez, Jason, Davis, Ferrari, & Olson, 2004). If a youth will be entering a substance abuse treatment program, it may be beneficial in the interview to address any concerns related to ethnicity that the youth may have about the program.

The youth's substance use may have disgraced the family, and the interviewer should invite discussion of these possible concerns. It may be appropriate to disseminate psychoeducational information about substance use among youth, with the intent to instill hope, instead of minimizing the problem. Another cultural consideration is that substances, such as alcohol, may be used in tribal and family customs or traditions (Sue & Sue, 2003). The clinician should ask about such use and should incorporate these cultural considerations into the interviewing process.

When involving family members in the interview, the impact of cultural norms and perspectives should be regarded. Indeed, it is important that ethnic parents who value strict family hierarchies perceive interviewers as respectful of their cultures, particularly among Asian and Hispanic parents (Sue & Sue, 2003). Along different lines, ethnic mistrust appears to compromise treatment outcomes in substance-abusing Hispanic adolescents, whereas high levels of ethnic pride and ethnic orientation are related to greater response to treatment (Gil, Wagner, & Tubman, 2004). Thus, it is imperative that adolescent substance abusers perceive the interviewer as respectful and complimentary of their ethnic cultures. Therefore, when interviewing ethnic-minority substance-abusing youth, it is probably particularly important to assess the extent to which they identify with the dominant culture. There are scales that can be used to determine acculturation; however, these scales offer little clinical utility.

An evidence-based, 7-item scale with an accompanying semistructured interview, the Semi-Structured Interview for Consideration of Ethnic Culture in Therapy Scale (SSICECTS) (Donohue et al., 2006), is now available and may be utilized to assess the extent to which culture is perceived to be important, as well as the extent to which problems are experienced due to ethnic culture. The scale component requires less than a minute to complete, and the semistructured interview lasts approximately 10 to 20 minutes. Two

factors have been substantiated in a nonclinical sample, problems due to ethnic culture and importance of ethnic culture, with each factor demonstrating excellent internal consistency and concurrent validity. In a controlled trial, interviewers who utilized the SSICECTS were perceived by participants as having greater knowledge and respect of participants' cultures compared with interviewers who used a parallel semistructured interview that was relevant to exercise/sports participation (Donohue et al., 2006). Content of the SSICECTS appears to be relevant to adolescent substance abusers, although studies have yet to be specifically conducted in substance-abusing samples.

Although limited, there is some information to suggest gay and lesbian teenagers may be more at risk than matched controls to use substances (Olson, 2000), perhaps because these youth are more likely to evidence negative experiences, such as ridicule, feeling physically unsafe in their environments, and having difficulties developing a sense of self (Olson, 2000). As these stress experiences are likely an antecedent to substance use, clinicians should query sexual activity and identity in the interview process and make no assumptions about the sexual orientation of adolescent substance abusers. Moreover, given potential consequences of admitting to be of homosexual orientation, confidentiality may need to be revisited when discussing these topics.

DIFFERENTIAL DIAGNOSIS

A frequent problem interviewers encounter is being able to correctly differentiate between the diagnoses of substance abuse and substance dependence. Therefore, it should be reiterated that substance dependence is a more severe diagnosis that includes tolerance and withdrawal symptoms. Interviewers must also carefully distinguish between symptoms due to substance use and symptoms that resemble other psychological disorders. For example, frequent use of substances may cause shifts in mood resembling major depression, dysthymia, and bipolar disorder.

In general, the interviewer can distinguish between substance use disorders and mood disorders by determining whether the physiological consequences of the substance are causing the change in mood (APA, 2000). For instance, if the frequent use of alcohol is causing depressive symptoms, then a substance-induced mood disorder would be diagnosed, rather than a major depressive disorder. If onset of depression consistently occurs consequent to substance use, substance abuse and dependence should be considered, rather than mood disorders. It is important to consider, however, that about a quarter of adolescents entering substance abuse treatment programs evidence comorbid mood disorders (Azrin et al., 2001). It is also difficult to differentiate between substance use disorders and externalizing disorders (i.e., oppositional defiant disorder, conduct disorder, attention-deficit/ hyperactivity disorder), particularly when substance-abusing adolescents deny use of substances. Indeed, these disorders to some extent often involve noncompliance to adult instructions, school performance deficits, and poor relationships with authority figures. Nevertheless, the diagnosis of substance abuse or dependence is made when substance use results in poor social or occupational deficits in functioning.

Substance abusers evidence impulsive behavior; however, these impulsive behavioral patterns are typically limited to the acquisition and use of substances, whereas youth with ADHD engage in widespread impulsive behavior. Similarly, substance-abusing youth experience significant impairments in attention when intoxicated or "high," whereas youth with ADHD usually evidence extreme difficulties maintaining attention in multiple tasks that are perceived to be "boring."

BEHAVIORAL ASSESSMENT

The primary purpose of the behavioral assessment of adolescent substance abuse is to identify and understand behaviors and thoughts that maintain substance use. This assessment strongly relies upon behavioral observation, role plays, and standardized inventories and should ideally be performed by the clinician who will conduct treatment.

Functional analysis is a critical component of the behavioral interview and has received greater empirical validation compared with its less directive counterparts (Haynes, 1998; Newcomer & Lewis, 2004). Functional analysis includes a detailed query of specific factors that act to maintain substance use. Substance use is conceptualized

to occur as a result of its interactions with environmental antecedents and consequences. Antecedent stimuli that trigger substance use include exposure to other substance users, sensing substances through sight or smell, locations where substances are known to occur, having a lot of money immediately available to pay for substances, boredom, emotional arousal, stressors, parties, and celebrations. Consequences of substance use include reduction of anxiety or stress, pleasurable physiological sensations, esteemed social acknowledgment, and assertiveness. Once antecedent stimuli and consequences that appear to maintain substance use are determined, the interviewer should identify competing repertoires and stimuli that are incompatible with substance use (Azrin, Donohue, Besalel, Kogan, & Acierno, 1994). The interviewer may utilize information gathered from the behavioral assessment to objectively determine appropriate diagnosis, select treatment targets, and make appropriate referrals.

SELECTION OF TREATMENT TARGETS AND REFERRAL

After all interviews have been conducted, the clinician should focus on selecting appropriate treatment targets for the youth and family. Selection of treatment targets is largely based on information gathered from the behavioral assessment that is performed with the youth and from relevant parties (e.g., parents, teachers). When determining treatment targets, the interviewer should demonstrate how antecedent stimuli and consequences relate to substance use. For instance, identification of antecedent stimuli will include monitoring the specific stimuli (i.e., person, places, activities) that place the adolescent at an increased risk to use substances, as well as the specific stimuli that place the youth at a decreased risk. Treatment targets can also include the identification of competing stimuli and teaching skills that can be utilized to decrease risk associated with substance use, particularly when moderation of substance use is a treatment goal.

It is essential that the youth and family be involved in mutually determining treatment goals. The first step includes the clinician presenting an explanation and rationale for a variety of empirically supported interventions to the parent(s) and youth independently. The interviewer should present only those interventions the counselor is competent to administer and that appear most relevant to the case. As an example, the interviewer could briefly describe Family Behavior Therapy (FBT) (Azrin et al., 1996; Azrin, Donohue et al., 1994; Azrin et al., 2001; Azrin, McMahon et al., 1994), Multidimensional Family Therapy (MDFT) (Liddle, 1992; Liddle, Dakof, & Diamond, 1991), and Multi-Systemic Therapy (MST) (Henggeler, Schoenwald, Borduin, Rowland, & Cunningham, 1998), all of which have been shown to be effective.

Various components from these empirically supported interventions can be applied to the specific needs and desires of the case. For instance, multisystemic therapists conduct intervention where the problem behavior is found to be most problematic (i.e., the family's home). Therefore, this intervention would be particularly beneficial when resources permit therapist travel. Similarly, the self-control procedure of FBT can be employed chiefly with adolescents who evidence cravings for substances. Indeed, youth who consume alcohol only during parties to be "part of the crowd" may benefit most from social components of the self-control procedure, whereas youth who abuse methamphetamines due to strong physiological cravings may benefit most from the initial cognitive steps of the self-control procedure, which serve to refocus the adolescent to substance-incompatible activities.

After a rationale for each intervention is presented independently to both the parents and the youth, the clinician should elicit discussion in which the parents and the youth describe positive and negative aspects associated with each intervention. This discussion allows parents and youth to conceptualize potential intervention components and to feel a sense of control in the treatment planning. In addition, parents and youth will be able to more clearly understand the treatment targets, including potential obstacles to accomplishing these goals. Clinicians should have parents and youth prioritize the interventions independently, and reconvene to discuss their choices. During this time, the clinician should emphasize commonalities between the parents' and the youth's intervention options. Once intervention options have been agreed upon, the interviewer should assist the family in scheduling appointments with referral agents.

REFERENCES

Achenbach, T. M. (1991). *Manual for the Teacher's Report Form and 1991 Profile.* Burlington: University of Vermont, Department of Psychiatry.

Achenbach, T. M., McConaughy, S. H., & Howell, C. T. (1987). Child/adolescent behavioral and emotional problems: Implications of cross-informant correlations for situational specificity. *Psychological Bulletin, 101,* 213–232.

Alvarez, J., Jason, L. A., Davis, M. I., Ferrari, J. R., & Olson, B. D. (2004). Latinos and Latinas in Oxford House: Perceptions of barriers and opportunities. *Journal of Ethnicity in Substance Abuse, 3,* 17–32.

American Academy of Child and Adolescent Psychiatry. (2005). Practice parameter for the assessment and treatment of children and adolescents with substance use disorders. *Journal of the American Academy of Child & Adolescent Psychiatry, 44,* 609–621.

American Psychiatric Association. (2000). *Diagnostic and statistical manual of mental disorders* (4th ed., Text rev.). Washington, DC: Author.

Aquilino, W. S., Wright, D. L., & Supple, A. J. (2000). Response effects due to bystander presence in CASI and paper-and-pencil surveys of drug use and alcohol use. *Substance Use and Misuse, 35,* 845–867.

Azrin, N., Acierno, R., Kogan, E. S., Donohue, B., Besalel, V., & McMahon, P. T. (1996). Follow-up results of supportive versus behavioral therapy for illicit drug use. *Behaviour Research and Therapy, 34,* 41–46.

Azrin, N. H., Donohue, B., Besalel, V., Kogan, E., & Acierno, R. (1994). Youth drug abuse treatment: A controlled outcome study. *Journal of Child and Adolescent Substance Abuse, 3*(3), 1–16.

Azrin, N. H., Donohue, B., Teichner, G. A., Crum, T., Howell, J., & DeCato, L. A. (2001). A controlled evaluation and description of individual-cognitive problem solving and family-behavior therapies in dually-diagnosed conduct-disordered and substance-dependent youth. *Journal of Child and Adolescent Substance Abuse, 11,* 1–43.

Azrin, N. H., McMahon, P., Donohue, B., Besalel, V., Lapinski, K., Kogan, E., et al. (1994). Behavior therapy of drug abuse: A controlled outcome study. *Behavior Research and Therapy, 11,* 857–866.

Breda, C., & Heflinger, C. A. (2004). Predicting incentives to change among adolescents with substance abuse disorder. *American Journal of Drug and Alcohol Abuse, 30,* 251–267.

Brodey, B. B., Rosen, C. S., Winters, K. C., Brodey, I. S., Sheetz, B. M., Steinfeld, R. R., et al. (2005). Conversion and validation of the Teen-Addiction Severity Index (T-ASI) for Internet and automated-telephone self-report administration. *Psychology of Addictive Behaviors, 19,* 54–61.

Brown, S. A., Creamer, V. A., & Stetson, B. A. (1987). Adolescent alcohol expectancies in relation to personal and parental drinking patterns. *Journal of Abnormal Psychology, 96,* 117–121.

Brown, S. A., Vik, P. W., & Creamer, V. A. (1989). Characteristics of relapse following adolescent substance abuse treatment. *Addictive Behaviors, 14,* 291–300.

Carr, A. (1999). *The handbook of child and adolescent clinical psychology: A contextual approach.* New York: Routledge.

Center for Substance Abuse Treatment. (1999).*Treatment of adolescents with substance abuse problems.* Treatment Improvement Protocol (TIP) Series, No. 32. DHHS Publication No. (SMA) 99-3283. Rockville, MD: Substance Abuse and Mental Health Services Administration.

Cook, R. F., Bernstein, A. D., Arrington, T. L., Andrews, C. M., & Marshall, G. A. (1995). Methods for assessing drug use prevalence in the workplace: A comparison of self-report, urinalysis, and hair analysis. *International Journal of Addictions, 30,* 403–426.

Deas-Nesmith, D., Brady, K. T., & White, R., & Campbell, S. (1999). HIV-risk behaviors in adolescent substance abusers. *Journal of Substance Abuse Treatment, 16,* 169–172.

Dennis, M. L., & Stevens, S. J. (2003). Maltreatment issues and outcome of adolescents enrolled in substance abuse treatment. *Child Maltreatment: Journal of the American Professional Society on the Abuse of Children, 8,* 3–6.

Donohue, B., Azrin, N. H., Lawson, H., Friedlander, J., Teichner, G., & Rindsberg, J. (1998). Improving initial session attendance of substance abusing and conduct disordered: A controlled study. *Journal of Child and Adolescent Substance Abuse, 8*(1), 1–13.

Donohue, B., Azrin, N. H., Strada, M. J., Silver, N. C., Teichner, G., & Murphy, H. (2004). Psychometric evaluation of self- and collateral timeline follow-back reports of drug and alcohol use in a sample of drug-abusing and conduct-disordered adolescents and their parents. *Psychology of Addictive Behaviors, 18,* 184–189.

Donohue, B., Karmely, J., & Strada, M. J. (2006). Substance abuse. In M. Hersen (Ed.), *Clinical handbook of behavioral assessment: Vol. 2. Child assessment* (pp. 337–372). Hoboken, NJ: Wiley.

Donohue, B., Strada, M.J., Rosales, R., Taylor-Caldwell, A., Ingham, D., Ahmad, S., et al. (2006). The semi-structured interview for consideration of ethnic culture in therapy scale: Initial psychometric and outcome support. *Behavior Modification, 30,* 867–891.

Ehrman, R. N., & Robbins, S. J. (1994). Reliability and validity of 6-month timeline reports of cocaine and heroin use in a methadone population. *Journal of Consulting and Clinical Psychology, 62,* 843–850.

Epstein, J. A., Botvin, G. J., & Diaz, T. (2000). Alcohol use among Hispanic adolescents: Role of linguistic acculturation and gender. *Journal of Alcohol and Drug Education, 45,* 18–32.

First, M. B., Spitzer, R. L, Gibbon, M., & Williams, J. B. W. (1996). Structured Clinical Interview for *DSM-IV* Axis I Disorders, Clinician Version (SCID-IV). Washington, DC: American Psychiatric Press.

Gariti, P., Alterman, A. I., Holub-Beyer, E., Volpicelli, J. R., Prentice, N., & O'Brien, C. (1995). Effects of an appointment reminder call on patient show rates. *Journal of Substance Abuse Treatment, 12,* 207–212.

Garland, A. F., Hough, R. L., McCabe, K. M., Yeh, M., Wood, P. A., & Aarons, G. A. (2001). Prevalence of psychiatric disorders in youths across five sectors of care. *Journal of the American Academy of Child & Adolescent Psychiatry, 40,* 409–418.

Gil, A. G., Wagner, E. F., & Tubman, J. G. (2004). Culturally sensitive substance abuse intervention for Hispanic and African American adolescents: Empirical examples from the Alcohol Treatment Targeting Adolescents in Need (ATTAIN) Project. *Addiction, 99,* 140–150.

Grant, B. F., & Dawson, D. A. (1997). Age at onset of alcohol use and its association with *DSM-IV* alcohol abuse and dependence. *Journal of Substance Abuse, 9,* 103–110.

Hawkins, J., Catalano, R. F., & Miller, J. Y. (1992). Risk and protective factors for alcohol and other drug problems in adolescence and early adulthood: Implications for substance abuse prevention. *Psychological Bulletin, 112,* 64–105.

Haynes, S. N. (1998). The assessment-treatment relationship and functional analysis in behavior therapy. *European Journal of Psychological Assessment, 14,* 26–35.

Henggeler, S. W., Schoenwald, S. K., Borduin, C. M., Rowland, M. D., & Cunningham, P. B. (1998). *Multisystemic treatment of antisocial behavior in children and adolescents.* New York: Guilford Press.

James, W. H., Kim, G. K., & Armijo, E. (2000). The influence of ethnic identity on drug use among ethnic minority adolescents. *Journal of Drug Education, 30,* 265–280.

James, W. H., Kim, G. K., & Moore, D. D. (1997). Examining racial and ethnic differences in Asian adolescent drug use: The contributions of culture, background, and lifestyle. *Drugs, Educations, Prevention, and Policy, 4,* 39–51.

Kaminer, Y., Bukstein, O., & Tarter, R. E. (1991). The teen-addiction severity index: Rationale and reliability. *International Journal of the Addictions, 26,* 219–226.

Kaminer, Y., Buleson, J. A., Blitz, C., Sussman, J., & Rounsaville, B. J. (1998). Psychotherapies for adolescent substance abusers: A pilot study. *Journal of Nervous and Mental Disease, 186,* 684–690.

Kaminer, Y., Wagner, E., Plummer, B., & Seifer, R. (1993). Validation of the Teen Addiction Severity Index (T-ASI): Preliminary findings. *American Journal on Addictions, 2,* 250–254.

Kaufman, J., Birmaher, B., Brent, D., Rao, U., Flynn, C., Moreci, P., et al. (1997). Schedule for Affective Disorders and Schizophrenia for School-Age Children-Present and Lifetime Version (K-SADS-PL): Initial reliability and validity data. *Journal of the American Academy of Child & Adolescent Psychiatry, 36,* 980–989.

Komro, K. A., Williams, C. L., Forster, J. L., Perry, C. L., Farbakhsh, K., & Stigler, M. H. (1999). The relationship between adolescent alcohol use and delinquency and violent behaviors. *Journal of Child and Adolescent Substance Abuse, 9*(2), 3–28.

Lefforge, N., Donohue, B., & Strada, M. (2007). Improving session attendance in mental health and substance abuse settings: A review of controlled studies. *Behavior Therapy, 38,* 1–22.

Liddle, H. A. (1992). A multidimensional model for treating the adolescent drug abuser. In W. Snyder & T. Ooms (Eds.), *Empowering families, helping adolescents: Family-centered treatment of adolescents with mental health and substance abuse problems* (pp. 91–100). Washington, DC: U.S. Government Printing Office.

Liddle, H. A., Dakof, G. A., & Diamond, G. (1991). Adolescent substance abuse: Multidimensional family therapy in action. In E. Kaufman & P. Kaufman (Eds.), *Family therapy of drug and alcohol abuse* (pp. 120–171). Boston: Allyn & Bacon.

McLellan, A. T., Luborsky, L., O'Brien, C. P., & Woody, G. E. (1980). An improved diagnostic instrument for substance abuse patients: The Addiction Severity Index. *Journal of Nervous and Mental Diseases, 168,* 26–33.

Miller, W. R., & Rollnick, S. (2002). *Motivational interviewing: Preparing people for change* (2nd ed.). New York: Guilford Press.

Morrison, J., & Anders, T. F. (1999). *Interviewing children and adolescents: Skills and strategies for effective DSM-IV diagnosis.* New York: Guilford Press.

Myers, M. G., Brown, S. A., & Vik, P. W. (1998). Adolescent substance use problems. In E. J. Mash & R. A. Barkley (Eds.), *Treatment of childhood disorders* (2nd ed., pp. 692–729). New York: Guilford Press.

Newcomb, M. D., & Bentler, P. M. (1988). Impact of adolescent drug use and social support on problems of young adults: A longitudinal study. *Journal of Abnormal Psychology, 97,* 64–75.

Newcomer, L. L., & Lewis, T. J. (2004). Functional behavioral Assessment: An investigation of assessment reliability and effectiveness of function-based interventions. *Journal of Emotional & Behavioral Disorders, 12,* 168–181.

Olson, E. D. (2000). Gay teens and substance use disorders: Assessment and treatment. *Journal of Gay and Lesbian Psychotherapy, 3,* 69–80.

Reynolds, C. R., & Kamphaus, R. W. (1992). *Behavioral assessment system for children.* Circle Pines, MN: American Guidance Service.

Shaffer, D., Fisher, P., Lucas, C., Dulcan, M. K., & Schwab-Stone, M. E. (2000). NIMH DISC-IV: Description, differences from previous versions, and reliability of some common diagnoses. *Journal of the American Academy of Child & Adolescent Psychiatry, 40,* 1228–1231.

Sobell, L. C., Agrawal, S., & Annis, H. (2001). Cross-cultural evaluation of two drinking assessment instruments: Alcohol timeline followback and inventory of drinking situations. *Substance Use and Misuse, 36,* 313–331.

Sobell, L. C., Brown, J., Leo, G. I., & Sobell, M. B. (1996). The reliability of the alcohol timeline followback when administered by telephone and by computer. *Alcohol Dependence, 42*(1), 49–54.

Sobell, L. C., & Sobell, M. B. (1996). Timeline followback: A technique for assessing self-reported consumption. In R. Litten & J. Allen (Eds.), *Measuring alcohol consumption* (pp. 41–72). Totowa, NJ: Humana Press.

Stone, A. L., & Latimer, W. W. (2005). Adolescent substance use assessment: Concordance between tools using self-administered and interview format. *Substance Use and Misuse, 40,* 1865–1874.

Strada, M., Donohue, B., & Lefforge, N. (2006). Examination of ethnicity in controlled treatment outcome studies involving adolescent substance abusers: A comprehensive literature review. *Psychology of Addictive Behaviors, 20,* 11–27.

Sue, D. W., & Sue, D. (2003). *Counseling the culturally diverse: Theory and practice* (4th ed.). New York: Wiley.

Tapert, S. F., Aarons, G. A., Sedlar, G. R., & Brown, S. A. (2001). Adolescent substance use and sexual risk-taking behavior. *Journal of Adolescent Health, 28,* 181–189.

U.S. Centers for Disease Control. (2003). *Youth Risk Behavior Surveillance System.* Retrieved November 15, 2005, from http://www.cdc.gov/HealthyYouth/yrbs/index.htm

Van der Ende, J., & Verhulst, F. C. (2005). Informant, gender and age differences in ratings of adolescent problem behaviour. *European Child & Adolescent Psychiatry, 14,* 117–126.

Williams, R. J., & Nowatzki, N. (2005). Validity of adolescent self-report of substance use. *Substance Use and Misuse, 40,* 299–311.

Winters, K., & Henly, G. (1993). *Adolescent Diagnostic Interview (ADI) manual.* Los Angeles: Western Psychological Services.

Winters, K. C., Stinchfield, R. D., Fulkerson, J., & Henly, G. A. (1993). Measuring alcohol and cannabis use disorders in an adolescent clinical sample. *Psychology of Addictive Behaviors, 7,* 185–196.

Winters, K. C., Stinchfield, R. D., & Henly, G. A. (1993). Further validation of new scales measuring adolescent alcohol and other drug abuse. *Journal of Studies on Alcohol, 54,* 534–541.

Wise, B. K., Cuffe, S. P., & Fischer, T. (2001). Dual diagnosis and successful participation of adolescents in substance abuse treatment. *Journal of Substance Abuse Treatment, 21,* 161–165.

19

SCHIZOPHRENIA

RACHEL L. LOEWY AND CINDY M. YEE-BRADBURY

DESCRIPTION OF THE DISORDER

Schizophrenia is a severe and debilitating disorder that affects approximately 1% of the population and typically begins in late adolescence or early adulthood (Di Maggio, Martinez, Menard, Petit, & Thibaut, 2001; Regier et al., 1988). *Childhood-onset schizophrenia* (COS) refers to onset of the disorder by age 13 and is a much more rare condition than the adolescent- (prior to age 17) or adult-onset forms of the illness (Remschmidt, Schulz, Martin, Warnke, & Trott, 1994; Thomsen, 1996). Comprehensive epidemiological studies have yet to determine the prevalence of COS, but it is estimated to be less than 1 in 10,000 (Thomsen, 1996). Although a very early onset of schizophrenia occurs infrequently, children and adolescents do present with psychotic symptoms in mental health settings with some regularity. Among patients with schizophrenia, 23% of females and 39% of males develop the illness before the age of 19 (Loranger, 1984). In addition, 4% to 8% of children in clinical settings exhibit psychotic symptoms that are associated with other psychiatric disorders (Biederman, Petty, Faraone, & Seidman, 2004; Ulloa et al., 2000). This chapter, therefore, focuses on schizophrenia as the prototype of psychotic disorders but also considers other forms of psychosis seen in youth.

Diagnosis and Symptomatology

According to the *Diagnostic and Statistical Manual of Mental Disorders, Fourth Edition (DSM-IV)* (American Psychiatric Association [APA], 1994), the diagnostic criteria for schizophrenia are the same for youth and adults. The characteristic symptoms of schizophrenia include hallucinations, delusions, and/or disorganized thinking and behavior. The clinician looks for evidence of these as well as indications of duration (at least 6 months total, with a minimum of 1 month of active psychotic symptoms), social or occupational (for children, school) disruption, and reasons to rule out this diagnosis in favor of another. The suggestion that childhood- and adult-onset schizophrenia are continuous versions of the same disorder is supported by clinical and neurobiological similarities across the two conditions (Kumra, Shaw, Merka, Nakayama, & Augustin, 2001; Nicolson et al., 2000), although COS may have a more insidious onset (Eggers, Bunk, & Krause, 2000), with greater impairment in premorbid functioning (Alaghband-Rad et al., 1995; Nicolson et al., 2000), poorer outcome (Hollis, 2000), and more pronounced structural brain abnormalities (Jacobsen et al., 1997) than the adult-onset disorder. Etiological models also are similar for the child- and adult-onset forms of the illness, pointing to largely genetic and early environmental (e.g., prenatal) risk factors, with onset triggered by maturational processes and psychosocial stressors (see Walker, Kestler, Bollini, & Hochman, 2004, for a review). Limited evidence suggests that COS carries a larger genetic component than the adult form, with a greater proportion of schizophrenia spectrum disorders present among first-degree relatives (Nicolson et al., 2003; Nicolson et al., 2000).

Symptoms of schizophrenia are typically distributed along three dimensions: positive symptoms, negative symptoms, and disorganization. *Positive symptoms* refer to experiences that are in excess of normal functioning, such as hallucinations and delusions, and also are referred to as *psychotic symptoms*. Hallucinations are sensory perceptions experienced without any external stimulus. They can occur in auditory, visual, olfactory, gustatory, or tactile domains, although auditory hallucination (e.g., hearing voices) is the most frequent psychotic symptom in children (Eggers et al., 2000; Russell, 1994). Delusions are unrealistic ideas in which the child has complete conviction despite evidence to the contrary. Delusions often focus on themes of persecution, religion, or supernatural experiences. In youth, delusions and hallucinations may reflect relationships in the child's life and are often developmentally relevant, with a focus on monsters, pets, toys, religious figures, or aspects of identity, and tend to increase in complexity with age (Russell, Bott, & Sammons, 1989; Volkmar, 1996). When delusions reflect processes that are not physically possible, such as the belief that aliens have replaced a real sibling with a false imposter, those delusions would be labeled as *bizarre*.

Negative symptoms refer to a loss of normal functions, including social withdrawal, diminished emotional expression, lack of motivation, reduction in motor movements, and decreased number or quality of thoughts. Although negative symptoms are not required for a diagnosis of schizophrenia, they are experienced by most children and adults with the disorder, may be less responsive to treatment with antipsychotic medication (Arango, Buchanan, Kirkpatrick, & Carpenter, 2004), and are associated with poorer outcome and quality of life (Mueser, Douglas, Bellack, & Morrison, 1991). Disorganized speech and behavior represent a third symptom dimension of schizophrenia, and examples range from dressing strangely (e.g., wearing a helmet and

seven layers of clothing to school) to speaking unintelligibly (e.g., interspersing speech with animal sounds).

A *DSM-IV* diagnosis of schizophrenia requires a constellation of symptoms that persists for at least 1 month and is associated with impaired social or occupational/academic functioning, with related symptoms lasting at least 6 months; the latter may occur preonset (prodromal) or postepisode (residual). A diagnosis of schizophrenia also can be made on the basis of only one symptom if it is a bizarre delusion (e.g., an adolescent believes he is the father of a football), auditory hallucinations that consist of two voices conversing with each other (e.g., "He should walk on the line." "He can't or it will break his mother's spine." "Walking on the line will not break her spine. . . ."), or a voice providing a running commentary on the patient's behavior (e.g., "Now she's looking through her sock drawer, oh, she's so stupid because she can't find her socks. . . ."). Full positive symptoms that present for less than 1 month warrant a schizophreniform diagnosis, while a brief psychotic episode is diagnosed if the child returns to normal functioning within a month of psychosis onset. A delusional disorder requires the presence of a single delusion without any other positive, negative, or disorganized symptoms, although some brief hallucinations may present that are related to the delusion. *Schizoaffective disorder* refers to psychotic symptoms along with a diagnosed mood disorder, but the psychotic symptoms must occur at some point in the absence of prominent mood symptoms. *Psychosis NOS* refers to other psychotic disorders that do not fit into any of the categories described.

Associated Features

In addition to positive symptoms, negative symptoms, and disorganization, youth with psychotic disorders frequently experience other types of psychiatric symptoms, cognitive problems, and impairment in role functioning. Comorbid disorders are the rule rather than the exception in childhood-onset psychosis. In a recent study, the most common comorbid disorders in children with psychosis who presented for psychiatric treatment were, in order of prevalence, oppositional defiant disorder, attention-deficit/hyperactivity disorder, anxiety disorders, bipolar disorder, and major depression (Biederman et al., 2004). Youth with all types of psychotic disorders also are likely to present with behavior problems and impaired functioning, although youth with schizophrenia or schizoaffective disorder tend to experience worse social and academic functioning than children with bipolar disorder or psychosis NOS (Biederman et al., 2004; McClellan, McCurry, Snell, & DuBose, 1999).

Various cognitive difficulties occur in schizophrenia and are considered part of the pathophysiology of the disorder. Similar to adult-onset schizophrenia, global intelligence is often impaired in COS, as IQ scores appear to deteriorate over the 2-year period prior to psychosis onset and for up to several years after (Gochman et al., 2005). Specific neuropsychological deficits that are present in adult schizophrenia also are apparent in children and adolescents, including problems with attention, memory, and abstraction (Brickman et al., 2004; Hoff et al., 1996; Kumra et al., 2000; Rhinewine et al., 2005; Strandburg, Marsh, Brown, Asarnow, & Guthrie, 1994; Thaden et al., 2006).

Course and Outcome

Given the rarity of childhood-onset schizophrenia, few longitudinal studies are available that examine the full course and outcome of the disorder. Retrospective accounts, however, have documented poor overall functioning and frequent developmental abnormalities in children even prior to the onset of schizophrenia, including motor abnormalities, delays in language development, speech and language disorders, learning disorders, and disruptive-behavior disorders (Alaghband-Rad et al., 1995; Asarnow & Ben-Meir, 1988; Nicolson et al., 2000). The course of child- and adult-onset schizophrenia is typically episodic, with increased periods of positive symptom exacerbation, while negative symptoms and cognitive problems may be more chronic. COS often has a more insidious onset of symptoms than adult-onset cases (Eggers et al., 2000; Green, Padron-Gayol, Hardesty, & Bassiri, 1992), while those with adolescent onset fall in between (Ballageer, Malla, Manchanda, Takhar, & Haricharan, 2005; Ropcke & Eggers, 2005). Although onset before the age of 6 is extremely rare, cases of preschool-age children with fully psychotic delusions, hallucinations,

and disorganization have been documented (Beresford, Hepburn, & Ross, 2005).

At onset, the first symptoms seen in children are generally nonspecific behavioral changes, such as school problems, inattention, social withdrawal, depression, anxiety, and aggressive behavior (Eggers et al., 2000; Schaeffer & Ross, 2002). Of the psychotic symptoms, auditory hallucinations are the most common at onset (Eggers et al., 2000; Kemph, 1987; Russell, 1994; Ulloa et al., 2000). Because children with psychosis are generally more impaired in their overall functioning, they are more likely than children with other psychiatric conditions to be in need of inpatient hospitalization (Biederman et al., 2004).

Several studies have documented poor outcomes for child- and adolescent-onset schizophrenia, with some evidence that outcomes may be worse than for those with an onset in adulthood (Hollis, 2000). Premorbid functioning and insidious onset are the strongest predictors of symptom severity and overall functioning in adolescence and adulthood (Fleischhaker et al., 2005; Ropcke & Eggers, 2005; Stayer et al., 2005; Werry, McClellan, Andrews, & Ham, 1994), with the majority of cases continuing to experience impairing symptoms and at least 50% of patients showing serious social disability in adulthood (Gillberg, Hellgren, & Gillberg, 1993; Lay, Blanz, Hartmann, & Schmidt, 2000; Werry, McClellan, & Chard, 1991). On the basis of one long-term study, 25% of COS cases were determined to be in complete remission at follow-up 27 years later (Eggers & Bunk, 1997).

Differential Diagnosis and Prediction

Similar to findings with adults, recent research has revealed that a much larger proportion of children experience psychosis than originally believed, with approximately 4% to 8% of children who present in clinical settings exhibiting at least one psychotic symptom (Biederman et al., 2004; Ulloa et al., 2000). In addition to occurring in schizophrenia and schizoaffective disorder, psychotic symptoms may be present in a variety of psychiatric disorders in childhood and adolescence, including mood disorders, anxiety disorders, pervasive developmental disorder, conduct disorder, and substance abuse (Biederman et al., 2004). Children with histories of trauma and abuse are also more likely to experience hallucinations (see Schreier, 1999, for a review) but in some cases without increased risk of an eventual psychotic disorder diagnosis (Garralda, 1984). In one clinical sample, over 70% of children who reported psychotic symptoms at age 11 experienced hallucinations and delusions at age 26, but only 25% met the functional impairment criterion necessary for a diagnosis of schizophreniform disorder (Poulton et al., 2000).

Compared with those with atypical psychosis, youth initially diagnosed with schizophrenia are more likely to (a) display odd behavior during the premorbid phase, (b) exhibit a stable level of impairment, (c) maintain a diagnosis of schizophrenia into adulthood, and (d) experience a worse outcome (McClellan, Werry, & Ham, 1993; Ropcke & Eggers, 2005). Children with psychosis who develop schizoaffective disorder tend to fall between the schizophrenia and atypical psychosis groups, with better premorbid adjustment and a higher rate of affective psychoses in relatives than that found among children with schizophrenia (Eggers, 1989). Few samples of children with psychosis have been followed for more than 10 years, however, and the level of risk for psychotic disorders over the lifespan of these children is still unclear.

Interviewing Strategies

Assessment

A comprehensive assessment of psychosis should include a detailed evaluation of symptom presentation, course of illness, comorbid symptoms (e.g., mood and anxiety, developmental problems, substance use), and family psychiatric history, along with a mental status exam (McClellan & Werry, 1994). The criteria differentiating psychotic disorders from other conditions are complicated, and clinicians therefore should thoroughly assess the longitudinal course of several domains, including relevant symptoms, substance use, stressors, and role functioning, in order to determine a definitive diagnosis.

Semistructured Interviews

A variety of semistructured interviews are available to formally assess for psychotic disorders in children. At present, the interview most

commonly used in psychosis research with children is the Schedule for Affective Disorders and Schizophrenia in School-Age Children (Kiddie-SADS-PL) (Kaufman, Birmaher, Brent, et al., 1997). Different versions of the K-SADS are available for use in various settings, such as epidemiological research, clinical research, and clinic settings. Other semistructured interviews include the Structured Clinical Interview for *DSM-IV* for Children (KID-SCID) (Hien et al., 1999), the Diagnostic Interview for Children and Adolescents (DICA) (Reich, 2000), and the Diagnostic Interview Schedule for Children (DISC-IV) (Shaffer et al., 2000).

Two instruments are available for assessing the psychosis prodrome among adolescents, but they have yet to be validated specifically with children. These semistructured interviews focus upon attenuated psychotic symptoms or very brief fully psychotic symptoms that may be indicative of high risk for developing a full psychotic disorder. They are the Structured Interview for Prodromal Syndromes (SIPS) (Miller et al., 1999) and the Comprehensive Assessment of At-Risk Mental States (CAARMS) (Yung et al., 2005). While a detailed description of each interview listed above is beyond the scope of this chapter, we recommend perusing one of these interviews to anyone who will be regularly assessing children for psychosis. Structured interviews typically require formal training and are the gold standard for psychodiagnostic assessments in research, but they can be useful in clinical practice as well (Doss, 2005). Even if structured interviews are not utilized in their entirety, we have found that it is useful in clinical practice to be familiar with the variety of questions that can probe for psychotic symptoms.

Other Tests

Although projective tests have been used in clinical settings to assess for schizophrenia and other psychoses, there is currently no evidence supporting their use as diagnostic tests. They may be used to assess a child's reality testing by allowing more open-ended expression of internal processes. Commonly used tests are the Rorschach Inkblot Test, the Thematic Apperception Test (TAT), the Children's Apperception Test (CAT), and the Draw-a-Person test (Bellack, 1986; Exner & Erdberg, 2005; Goodenough, 1926). These tests may provide a different route toward accessing a child's perspective, but their results can be used only in conjunction with a careful and thorough clinical interview to form a comprehensive picture of the child's symptoms and functioning and to rule out other possible causes.

Symptom Assessment

Regardless of whether an interview is structured or not, there are various practical strategies for gathering information about psychotic symptoms that can inform diagnostic decisions. Obtaining specific details regarding symptom onset, frequency, duration, and severity is crucial for determining psychiatric diagnoses. For every symptom a child endorses, follow-up questions should address when the symptom began, how often it occurs, and how long it lasts.

When assessing symptom severity, questions should be posed to address the child's level of conviction in psychotic experiences, which, in turn, determines whether the symptom is considered to be fully psychotic. For example, does the child believe that the hallucination is real? How does he or she explain it? Such questions often elicit delusional explanations for hallucinatory experiences, such as "The cat knows what I'm thinking. That's why she follows me around the house and talks to me." If it appears that the child firmly believes the experience is real, the interviewer should offer alternative explanations or hypotheses, such as "Is it possible it's just your imagination?" or "Are you sure she's talking to you, or do you think it could be your mind playing tricks on you?" Preoccupation with a symptom suggests greater severity, which can be assessed by asking, "How often do you think about the cat?" Symptoms are also considered to be more severe or fully psychotic if they affect the child's behavior, which can be assessed by asking, "Do you do anything differently because of it?" A child who reports that "I don't want to leave my room because I'm afraid the cat will find me" may exhibit functional impairment or distress due to the symptoms, further supporting a possible psychiatric diagnosis.

Once the current level of severity has been established, the course of the symptom should be characterized, including when the symptom started becoming more severe or occurring more frequently, whether it ever disappeared entirely or lessened, and what may have helped

to relieve it. Identifying triggers for worsening or improvement of symptoms is useful for ruling out other potential causes of the symptoms, such as substance use, and for eventual treatment planning.

Often, children are reticent to discuss the presence of psychotic symptoms due to a variety of factors, including paranoia, disorganized thinking and communication, and the distrust typical of some adolescents when speaking to an authority figure. Assessments of psychosis are typically lengthy, which can be challenging for children (Irwin & Johnson, 2005), particularly for those with thought disorder. It is often necessary and helpful, therefore, to perform multiple assessments before determining a final diagnosis.

Interview Process

Gathering information may be the main goal of the interview, but it cannot be achieved without awareness of the interview process. While rapport is essential to any clinical interaction (Irwin & Johnson, 2005), it is especially important to help children feel comfortable discussing experiences that they may recognize as strange or unusual. The interview should be prefaced with a general statement, such as "We ask a lot of different questions to get to know you. Some might be things you've thought or felt before, others might not." Typically, questions should be asked in order of increasing severity or related anxiety, possibly beginning the interview with questions about the child's general level of functioning at school, with family and friends, and then progressing to questions about mood and anxiety symptoms or learning problems.

Once rapport has been established, introduce questions about psychotic symptoms. To normalize what might be perceived as abnormal experiences, these items should be asked with the same tone of voice and style of presentation as any other questions. Children will typically follow the interviewer's approach and be sensitive to the interviewer's reactions. In fact, we often find that the interviewer is more apprehensive about asking children questions about psychosis than children are about answering. Novice interviewers or clinicians who have limited experience with psychotic disorders may find it helpful to practice with peers or colleagues before interviewing patients so as to become more comfortable with the questions. In exploring delusional beliefs and the strength of conviction with which they are held, it is important not to challenge these beliefs, as this usually will increase a child's anxiety.

Children may express their unease with either nonverbal expression, such as changes in body posture, or direct comments such as "That's crazy! Do you think I'm crazy?" If children do react with discomfort to questions, it provides an opportunity for reassurance. Examples of such statements include "Lots of kids hear a voice at some point. It doesn't mean that they're crazy" or "Well, sometimes people see things that no one else sees. Has that ever happened to you?" It is important not to support a perspective that some questions are about "crazy" symptoms or to assume that a child who does not "seem crazy" would not have psychotic or quasi-psychotic experiences. Many children experience psychotic symptoms without the knowledge of their treating clinicians, who simply fail to ask about them (Schreier, 1999).

Asking psychotic children questions about their symptoms can raise substantial anxiety for children who may already have a limited ability to tolerate anxiety. Older children and adolescents may be better able to directly report their anxiety and discomfort, but many psychotic children may be unaware of their feelings or have great difficulty expressing them directly. Therefore, it is important to monitor any indirect expressions of anxiety, which may manifest as fidgeting; avoiding eye contact; changing the subject; requesting to leave, see a parent, or use the bathroom; or refusing to answer questions.

Anxiety may be reduced by taking frequent breaks or talking to the child while playing with toys and games or while taking a walk. Encouraging a child to draw a picture in response to questions and then asking about the picture also may ease anxiety when a child is unable to tolerate direct questioning. Although play may reduce anxiety for some children, it should not be assumed that children will be unable to respond to direct questioning (Harden, Scott, Backett-Milburn, & Jackson, 2000). In addition, using more structured, closed-ended questions can contain anxiety (e.g., asking, "Did you see the ghost when you were in Mrs. Lampert's class?" rather than "Tell me about the ghost") and may be less challenging for children's cognitive abilities (Irwin & Johnson, 2005). Caution is required,

however, when using closed-ended questions, to avoid leading questions that may encourage children to falsely endorse experiences in order to please the interviewer or a parent, to gain attention or other secondary benefit, or to provide a response when the meaning of a question is not fully understood. A leading question might ask, "Didn't you skip school because you were afraid of the other kids?" rather than asking "Did you skip school because you were afraid of the other kids?" Balancing questions about symptomatology with questions about a child's interests, hobbies, and achievements also can alleviate discomfort or a sense of being pathologized. In addition to increasing rapport, asking about a child's strengths will be invaluable when recommending interventions.

Risk Assessment

While assessment of child abuse and potential harm to self or others is part of any comprehensive clinical evaluation, these risks are higher for children with psychosis. Among an inpatient sample, children experiencing psychotic symptoms were 3 times more likely than children without psychotic symptoms to have attempted or threatened suicide (Livingston & Bracha, 1992). Psychotic patients, in general, are at greatly increased risk for suicide: Up to 30% of schizophrenia patients attempt suicide at some point in their lives (Radomsky, Haas, Mann, & Sweeney, 1999).

While aggression in psychotic children has not been systematically studied, there is a small but significantly increased risk for committing violent acts among adult schizophrenia patients (Angermeyer, 2000) that may be associated with delusional thoughts (Buchanan et al., 1993; Wessely et al., 1993). Limited research suggests that adult violence may be predated by childhood aggression and psychotic symptoms (Arseneault et al., 2003), although the risk of violence toward others is often exaggerated by the media and contributes to social stigma (Angermeyer, 2000). In addition, patients with schizophrenia are more likely to be victims of violence (Hiroeh, Appleby, Mortensen, & Dunn, 2001) and to have experienced childhood sexual and physical abuse (Janssen et al., 2004). Children who have experienced trauma, in turn, are more likely to develop psychotic symptoms (Read, van Os,

Morrison, & Ross, 2005). Given these data, risk assessment becomes especially important with psychotic children. When children experience auditory hallucinations, interviewers should inquire about the presence of command hallucinations that instruct the child to hurt himself or someone else, as well as potential risk related to perceived threats from others that may be part of persecutory delusions.

Rates of substance abuse are higher among psychotic patients (Batel, 2000) and also significantly related to violence or aggression in schizophrenia (Schwartz, Reynolds, Austin, & Petersen, 2003), so a comprehensive assessment of substance use should be included in any risk evaluation, particularly with older children and adolescents. Unfortunately, some children (and many adults) hesitate to discuss their symptoms because they are concerned that the admission of any psychotic symptom would trigger a psychiatric hospitalization. In that case, the interviewer must communicate directly and honestly with the patient about what constitutes a safety risk. As with all children, every attempt should be made to involve trusted family members and relevant health care providers as soon as possible if any safety concerns arise.

Providing Feedback

Ultimately, the course of psychotic symptoms may change over time as children mature. Consequently, any feedback to children and their families should include caveats about the importance of monitoring symptoms over time. Partnering with families to monitor a child's symptoms and reassess them at regular intervals can help to keep diagnoses accurate and to facilitate early intervention if symptoms should worsen.

INTERVIEWING OBSTACLES AND SOLUTIONS

A variety of challenges are commonly encountered when interviewing psychotic youth that may reflect the presenting symptoms of the disorder or associated cognitive, social, and emotional difficulties. The very nature of thought disorder impacts the interview process, as expressed in hallucinations, delusions, negative symptoms, and disorganized thinking and communication.

Interviewers may also find themselves experiencing a variety of personal reactions when working with psychotic youth, as a result of their backgrounds or prior experiences and in the context of societal perspectives on schizophrenia. We will address obstacles to interviewing from each of these areas, as well as suggestions for overcoming them.

Interference of Positive Symptoms

A frequent set of challenges arises from the presence of active psychotic symptoms and may be similar for psychotic adults, adolescents, and children. Clients who are experiencing hallucinations during the interview often appear preoccupied and distracted. They may glance at empty areas of the room repeatedly, laugh or smile at odd moments, or appear not to hear the interviewer; these all may be signs that the youth is responding to internally generated stimuli, typically a voice or an image. Often, it is useful to simply ask the child if he or she is listening to something or seeing something, as this may elicit a description of the hallucination. If the child has already described hallucinatory symptoms, the clinician might inquire further (e.g., "You described a bad man who speaks to you, but no one else hears him. Is he talking to you right now?"). If the symptoms have been adequately described but are now disrupting the interview, it may help to ask the child to try to focus on the interviewer's questions or to take a break from interviewing, as you would with any child who is struggling to pay attention.

A specific delusion that is most likely to affect interviewing is the presence of paranoia. Patients may be extremely guarded, refusing to answer questions or providing only minimal answers. At times, the child's fear can be lessened through reassurance that the interviewer does not intend to harm the patient but, instead, hopes to help. If the client has described a specific suspicion about health care providers (e.g., "Doctors are spying on me and want to kidnap me"), checking with the child periodically and offering reassurance may help to dissuade his or her fear. Clients can also be encouraged to tell the interviewer if they start feeling scared or suspicious or to ask questions of the interviewer. If it helps to ease a child's fear and discomfort, another possibility is to interview children with parents present. As is true for all child interviews, a parent's presence may either inhibit or enhance the child's freedom to respond, and this must be determined individually in each case (Irwin & Johnson, 2005).

In general, suspiciousness is likely to recede somewhat once rapport is established, although it may resurface or persist in varying degrees. Some patients may hide the presence of psychotic symptoms from others for a long period of time, until trust has been developed; this is especially true of children speaking to unfamiliar adults (Ross et al., 2003). A series of interviews or inpatient observations can be helpful in situations where severe paranoia must be overcome. Adolescents are often guarded with adults, regardless of the presence of psychosis, and it may be difficult at first to distinguish between a typical adolescent presentation and paranoia-driven reticence. Parental and teacher reports can be helpful in such situations.

Interference of Negative Symptoms

Youth struggling with negative symptoms may present as unmotivated, apathetic, affectively flat or blunted, socially and emotionally disconnected, and unresponsive. Adapting an interview to a patient's negative symptoms requires patience, given long delays in responding, and supportive probing when children have difficulty formulating answers. Interviews may need to be scheduled during the afternoon if a patient has difficulty waking up in the morning. Interviewers should keep in mind that negative symptoms are part of the disorder and not necessarily willful oppositional behaviors.

Interference of Disorganized Symptoms

Disorganized communication can include subtle signs (e.g., odd word choices), moderate impairment (e.g., tangential responses), or severe disorganization (e.g., speech is incomprehensible). Thought disorder, expressed through the disorganized communication that characterizes psychotic children, includes illogical thinking, loosening of associations, incoherence, and poverty of content of speech (Caplan, 1994).

In practice, understanding children despite these communication deficits requires interviewer patience, as well as applying a specific

structure to the interview. In these situations, short, specific, closed-ended questions are generally useful (e.g., "How long does it take you to fall asleep at night?"). Unclear answers may require probing and summarizing (e.g., "Let's make sure that I understand. You said it might take longer to fall asleep if you're at camp but that you've never been to camp. What's the longest that it's taken you to fall asleep at home? What's the shortest time? What is typical or usual?"). With tangential or circumstantial answers, repeating questions or redirecting the line of inquiry may be necessary (e.g., "We've gotten a little off the track. The first question I asked you was, 'When were you feeling the most down and sad?'"). Respectful, firm redirection is often appreciated by patients of any age, who may be aware they have difficulty communicating clearly. Another aspect of thought disorder is thought blocking, which can cause long latencies before a child responds to questions, and verbal expression may be reduced, with repeated answers of "I don't know." Although this can be frustrating for the interviewer, some patients may simply need more time to formulate answers.

Interference of Cognitive Deficits

The cognitive deficits associated with schizophrenia frequently contribute to the challenges encountered during an interview. As described previously, psychotic children often have difficulty with attention, abstraction, and memory, in addition to a generally lower IQ, all of which clearly impact a child's ability to comprehend and respond to interview questions. Therefore, clear and simple language is especially important with this population. When memory problems are apparent, temporal landmarks are helpful (e.g., "Did the monster show up before school started last fall, when you were still on summer vacation?"). In addition, children with schizophrenia may appear to be younger than their chronological age, both cognitively and emotionally. They may engage in behavior inappropriate for an older child (e.g., picking their noses, jumping around the room) and may require the interviewing strategies typically used with younger children, such as redirection, setting firm boundaries, and frequent breaks. Taking walks or playing games while talking may be especially helpful in these cases.

Interviewer Reactions

Working with psychotic children can elicit a variety of feelings in interviewers, including anxiety, fear, pity, discomfort, and even disgust. Due to potentially delayed social development or cognitive difficulties, patients may engage in behaviors typical of younger children, such as asking personal questions, being attentive to bodily functions, or engaging in other unusual behavior that is exhibited without an awareness of social propriety, which can be disconcerting to interviewers. Odd behavior such as talking to themselves or displaying unusual motor movements is not uncommon and may be more striking in older children and adolescents.

Psychotic children may also experience intense anxiety or paranoia that is difficult to contain, and, in some cases, they may decompensate over the course of an interview if the symptoms are severe, raising the interviewer's anxiety as well. Risk issues presented by a youth with schizophrenia should not be minimized and can present challenges for the novice or experienced interviewer. In all cases, discussing personal reactions with an attentive supervisor or colleague can ease the interviewer's discomfort. In addition to discomfort and anxiety, interviewers may experience a desire to rescue "helpless" children or may have difficulty tolerating patients' apparent psychological pain. Parents and other family members may be critical and blaming of what they believe is the child's "willful" behavior, and interviewers may find it difficult to engage empathically with such parents.

Finally, fear of the prognosis or stigma attached to a diagnosis of schizophrenia can prompt clinicians to ignore, deny, or misread signs of psychosis in an attempt to normalize the child's behavior. Instead, they may blame external situations or parents for psychotic behavior, dismissing its significance, or proceed under the misassumption that a psychotic disorder diagnosis prohibits any chance of a "normal" life for the child. Such reactions may occur outside of awareness but can be detected and processed in helpful ways under supervision or in peer consultation.

INTERVIEWING PARENTS AND TEACHERS

The child is the most important source of information but, in general, should not be the sole supplier of information. Parents and other family members as well as other important figures in the child's life, such as teachers, can provide different perspectives on the child's behavior and mental or emotional state.

Interviewing Parents and Family Members

Interviewing parents or other informants is crucial to diagnosing psychotic disorders in children and adolescents. Some evidence points to greater utility for parental report than for self-report of youth with serious mental illnesses (Youngstrom et al., 2004). Parents are especially helpful in developing a picture of the long-term course of their children's behavior, such as highlighting points of change or deterioration. They can assist with determining the extent to which a youth has ever developed the ability to reality test and question perceptions and whether psychotic experiences represent a change from previous functioning. In addition, parents can describe the familial and subcultural social environment, providing a context for the child's behavior to help inform the distinction between psychotic beliefs and normal cultural or religious practices. Parents also are often in a position to describe the child's behavior in ways that the child may be unable to express due to age or level of insight.

There are several additional considerations when interviewing parents of children with psychotic symptoms. First, parents may have high levels of anxiety around the possibility that their child has a psychotic disorder. They may wish to deny or minimize the child's problems, seeing psychotic symptoms as an expression of "normal" adolescence or adjustment difficulties. Understandably, parents often fear the stigma that may be attached to the presence of a psychotic disorder in their children or family, and they frequently struggle with feelings of guilt about the potential cause of a child's illness. Unfortunately, prior misconceptions of mothers as a potential cause of schizophrenia have led some parents to fear criticism and blame from clinicians (Hartwell, 1996). They may also fear that any chance for a "normal" future is doomed if their child is labeled with "psychosis" or "schizophrenia." These anxieties and reactions must be taken into careful consideration from the moment the parent walks into the interview room.

Given the high heritability of schizophrenia, it is not uncommon for a parent to suffer from a schizophrenia spectrum disorder or to know another family member who does. If the parent has a related disorder, this should be considered sensitively when interviewing the parent. In such cases, it may be necessary to interview the other parent or a close family member.

Prior experience with psychoses in another family member may alter parental expectations for the child's behavior, such that parents underreport due to difficulty identifying some behaviors as abnormal or overreport due to sensitivity to seemingly unusual behavior (Hambrecht, 1995). Most important, they are likely to have strong reactions to a psychotic diagnosis in their child and, possibly, to mental health professionals. For example, a father whose sister was diagnosed with schizophrenia several decades ago and institutionalized as a child may expect the same prognosis for his daughter and be unaware of the recent treatment advances that offer better outcomes for patients. Or a mother may believe that her father's symptoms of bipolar disorder were willful and might assume that her son does not need medication, but can simply choose to behave more appropriately, feel motivated, or stop his "crazy talk." Assessing parental expectations is especially important when providing diagnostic feedback and should be handled in each case with sensitivity and care.

Informant Discrepancies

Although parental report is critical when assessing childhood psychosis, it is well established that different informants (parents, teachers, and children) rarely agree about the child's symptoms or diagnoses across all forms of psychopathology (see De Los Reyes & Kazdin, 2005, for a review).

Results of meta-analytic studies of child psychopathology suggest that parent-child agreement is higher for externalizing behaviors that are readily apparent to observers, such as aggression or hyperactivity, compared with internalizing symptoms, such as depression and anxiety (Achenbach, McConaughy, & Howell, 1987; Duhig, Renk, Epstein, & Phares, 2000). Available evidence suggests that this rule holds for psychosis as well. In an assessment of the early signs of psychosis, greatest agreement was found for observable symptoms, such as substance abuse, suicidal behavior, parental and marital role deficits, and paranoid delusions (Hambrecht,

Hafner, & Loffler, 1994). In addition, in a sample of adolescents and young adults with attenuated psychotic syndromes, greater informant-patient agreement has been found for odd behavior than for bizarre thinking, with only moderate agreement across most symptom categories (Bearden et al., 2004). A mother, for example, might describe her child's odd facial expressions or social behavior, about which the child lacks awareness and insight. Alternatively, an adolescent may endorse hearing voices for months without any awareness on his parents' part that he has been experiencing auditory hallucinations.

Although diagnoses based only on an informant's report might be inaccurate, symptoms reported by informants should not be dismissed if they are denied by the patient, because they may represent clinically significant phenomena that the youth is unable or unwilling to endorse (Jensen et al., 1999). This is especially true when diagnosing psychotic disorders, which do not require that the child display a symptom across multiple settings, as is the case for attention-deficit/hyperactivity disorder. Rather, the experience of any psychotic symptoms that are impairing or distressing is enough for the symptom to be judged as present. In general, a reasonable criterion that can be applied to assessments of psychotic and prepsychotic children is the "either/or" rule, where a symptom reported by either the patient or a reliable informant is judged to be present (Ross et al., 2003).

It is important to keep in mind that youth (as well as adults) often experience hallucinations and delusions without the awareness of others. In one study, 57% of mothers were previously unaware of psychotic symptoms in their adolescent children who had recently been admitted to the hospital for a first episode of psychosis (de Haan, Welborn, Krikke, & Linszen, 2004). When a child reports thoughts, beliefs, or experiences that are judged by the clinician to be psychotic, it usually provides a sufficient basis for making a diagnosis, using parental reports to corroborate the impact of the internal symptoms on the child's level of functioning. Alternatively, many youth will fail to report a psychotic symptom that a parent readily describes, possibly because of discomfort talking with strangers, level of cognitive development, limited insight, preference for social desirability, or oppositional attitudes (Ross et al., 2003).

One approach toward resolving such a discrepancy is to discuss the parental report with the child and invite his or her perspective. An interviewer might gently confront a youngster by saying, "So, your mom says sometimes she sees you yelling, 'Go away!' Do you remember doing that? Who were you talking to?" This approach, however, can increase the likelihood that children will feel compelled to agree with their parents (De Los Reyes & Kazdin, 2005). It also is the case with psychotic children that their perceptions of reality may differ significantly from their parents' perspectives. Any initial confrontation about discrepant reports, therefore, should emphasize the child's observable behavior (e.g., "Your mom has seen you yelling, 'Go away!'"), without reference to the parents' beliefs or attributions (e.g., that no real person is in the room). This approach emphasizes allowing for disagreement between reporters without leading the child into agreement with the parent (Edwards, 2005). Support for the views of both parties can be maintained by explaining, "In families, sometimes people remember things differently or have different experiences of the same event. So, it's okay if you and your mom don't agree about what happened last week. It doesn't mean someone is wrong, it just means you have different perspectives."

Once the child's experience has been established, gentle confrontation that incorporates the parents' beliefs can help to gauge the child's sense of reality, such as "Your mom doesn't see anyone in the room when you yell. Do you know why that might be?" In some cases, however, confrontation can increase anxiety to the point that a psychotic child becomes unresponsive. Therefore, sensitivity, a gentle approach, and close monitoring of the patient's reactions is advisable whenever confronting a patient about positive symptoms.

Interviewing Teachers

Youth with schizophrenia often present for clinical services when they are acutely ill, and clinicians must assess for symptoms and functioning without access to informants other than the child's primary caretaker(s). When at all possible, it is extremely helpful to obtain information from teachers. As noted earlier, initial signs of psychosis often include problems with school functioning. Teachers are in a unique position to judge a child's academic performance and social functioning compared with his or her peers, and

they may be able to identify cognitive problems, communication difficulties, social deficits, or odd behaviors that are less salient in other situations. As is the case with parent-child disagreement, discrepant reports must be clarified, but teacher information is essential in determining a child's global functioning. Interviews should cover all symptom and behavior domains and may be useful in identifying a child's interests and strengths. Confidentiality limits the feedback that assessors can provide to teachers, particularly during the initial assessment, and parents may be especially concerned that their child not be labeled as "psychotic" or "schizophrenic" by schoolteachers and officials. Once treatment planning begins, however, teachers become critical partners in developing plans that are integrated with school services. Most youth contending with schizophrenia or even subsyndromal psychotic symptoms require special education services for both cognitive and emotional difficulties, which is discussed as part of treatment planning later in this chapter.

Other Informants

In addition to parents and teachers, reports should be obtained from as many other sources as possible, including school counselors and previous treating clinicians. A clinician may report that he or she failed to observe any psychotic symptoms, even though a child now meets diagnostic criteria for a psychotic disorder, because the child was experiencing low-level prodromal symptoms at the time, the treatment format did not provide opportunities for expression of psychotic symptoms, or the informants had different conceptualizations of the child's behavior. When clinicians have been aware of psychotic symptoms, their report can help identify the course of illness, which, in turn, may be instrumental in making a differential diagnosis. In cases where a child has an ongoing treatment provider, the clinician's input is critical for evaluation purposes and collaborative treatment planning.

CASE ILLUSTRATION WITH DIALOGUE

Chris, a 12-year-old boy, was referred because of increasingly withdrawn behavior, inconsistent peer relationships, distractibility, and a dramatic decline in school performance. In recent months, he had begun making excuses to avoid after-school or weekend activities, preferring to remain alone in his bedroom. When his parents questioned the amount of time Chris spent on his computer, he responded with intense angry outbursts. His parents noted that Chris also appeared to be tired much of the time, yawning often and falling asleep even during short car rides. Prior to sixth grade, Chris was an outgoing child who formed friendships easily. He consistently performed well in school and was involved in a variety of extracurricular activities. A complete physical examination by his pediatrician failed to reveal a medical condition that might account for Chris's lethargy and changes in behavior.

Interviewer: Hi, Chris. I'm Dr. Capps, and I'll be spending some time talking with you today. I'll be asking a lot of different questions as I get to know you and find out how things are going at home and at school, and to see what we can do to help make things better. Some of the areas that we'll cover might be things you've thought of or felt before, and others might not.

Chris: [nods]

I: So, if it's okay with you, I'd like to take some notes to help me keep all of your information straight.

C: Yeah, okay.

I: Great. Let's start with how old you are.

C: Twelve.

I: And, when was your birthday?

C: December 26th.

I: Where do you live, and who do you live with?

C: I live in Oak Glen with my mom, dad, brother, and dog.

I: Where do you go to school? And what grade are you in?

C: I'm in the sixth grade at Chalmers School.

I: Have you always gone to Chalmers School?

C: No, I started in second grade because we used to live in Boston.

I: What are your favorite classes?

C: Science, reading, and art. I guess that's it. Oh, and I like P.E.

I: Are there particular sports that you like?

C: Yeah, soccer and handball.

I: How about kids that you like to spend time with at school?

C: I have two friends at school, but my best friend lives next door and he goes to a different school.

I: What do you and your friends like to do?

C: We play handball and talk. Sometimes they come over to my house or I go to their house and we play on the computer.

I: We'll talk more about what you like to do at home, but first, let me ask how school is going for you.

C: Fine. [pauses] Well, not so good. I guess my mom told you that I'm getting C's and D's. Except in art and P.E., I still get A's.

I: What do you think is going on?

C: I sometimes forget to do the homework.

I: How does that happen?

C: [shrugs.] I guess I get busy with other stuff.

I: Your mom mentioned that your teacher thought you also seemed tired a lot.

C: I guess.

I: Are you having trouble sleeping at night?

C: Not really. Sometimes, I have to stay up to do stuff on my computer.

I: What kind of stuff?

C: Not games. And, my parents won't let me IM or go to MySpace. They're kind of strict.

I: So, what do you do on your computer at night?

C: You wouldn't understand.

I: How about if you try me?

C: [long pause] Well, one time I accidentally got onto this guy's Web page when I was using Google for a science project and [looks away] now I don't have my own brain anymore. I'm not sure how he did it but the guy replaced my brain with someone else's. The thing is, I can keep my own thoughts if the brain that's in my head stays charged up. I just have to make sure to watch the download bar as it fills up; the longer it takes, the more brainpower I get. Before I go to sleep, I download really big files or games to make sure that I'll have enough brainpower until morning. Sometimes, it doesn't work and I have to get up to recharge.

I: That all sounds pretty frightening. Have you ever tried not recharging?

C: No, I have to do it! You don't know what it's like. Sometimes at school, I can't get to a computer and then all these weird thoughts start slipping in and I can't stop them except by recharging. My friends think I'm a freak because I can't do stuff with them but I have to get to my computer.

I: How long has this been going on?

C: When I started my science project at the end of winter break.

I: So, it started at the end of December or beginning of January?

C: Yeah. It's been a really long time.

I: More than 2 months.

C: [nods]

I: Sometimes people have more than one unusual experience that might not make sense or that they can't control or that's frightening. I'm wondering if that might be happening with you.

C: Like what kind of stuff?

I: Oh, sometimes kids might hear a voice or see things that no one else sees.

C: Yeah, sometimes I hear my name but when I ask people, they look at me like I'm weird. Or, when it's really quiet I can hear waves, like when you listen to a seashell but it doesn't bother me because I like those sounds when we go to the beach.

I: How long has all of that been going on?

C: The wave sounds have been forever; I can't remember when they started. I'm not sure about the name thing, it's usually just whispery. Do we have to talk about this?

I: Okay, how about if we take a short break? Your mom said it would be fine if you have a snack, so let me show you what we have.

I: [after returning from break] Okay, Chris, I just have a few more specific questions to ask you. Do you ever feel like people can read your mind or that you can read other people's minds?

C: Uh . . . not people, but sometimes our dog Ace looks at me funny, like he knows what I'm thinking.

I: Oh, yeah? Do you think he really does know what you're thinking?

C: Nah, I don't think he really does, it just sort of feels like it for a second.

I: Have you ever talked to anyone about this or done anything differently because of it?

C: Nah, it's not a big deal, it just feels kind of weird. But I like Ace, so it's okay.

I: When did you first feel like Ace could tell what you're thinking?

C: I don't know, maybe last summer.

I: And how often does that happen now?

C: Not much. Just once in a while when we're the only ones there.

I: Has it happened this week?

C: No, maybe last month around Valentine's.

Commentary

Chris meets diagnostic criteria for schizophrenia on the basis of firmly holding a bizarre delusion for more than 1 month, experiencing mild auditory hallucinations for more than 6 months, and exhibiting a decline in academic functioning, along with increased social isolation. The symptom involving mind reading is considered to be subsyndromal because the patient is not fully convinced that it is true. In the remainder of the interview, inquiries should be made regarding other delusions that may be present; tactile, olfactory, and gustatory hallucinations; mood symptoms; substance use; risk; and any other relevant areas.

MULTICULTURAL AND DIVERSITY ISSUES

Although schizophrenia is experienced by children worldwide, cultures vary in categorizing and labeling psychotic experiences, adhering to different explanatory models for psychosis and adopting different approaches to treatment. It is with this awareness in mind that clinicians must assess children from cultures other than their own. While familiarity with specific cultural perspectives can be helpful, each case must be considered individually and without resorting to stereotypes or overgeneralizations. The best sources of information regarding cultural experiences, beliefs, and attitudes related to psychosis are children and their families. Asking children's parents about their views provides an opportunity to not only gather information but also begin the collaborative process necessary for effective treatment of youth.

The most basic way that inaccuracies occur in clinical assessments is that the clinician does not speak the primary language of the child and his or her parents. When a clinician or interpreter who is fluent in the patient's language is not available, misunderstanding is probable. Even with bilingual children, misunderstandings can occur, due to confusion between word choice in one language versus the other and when describing symptoms that are understood from one cultural perspective and are not easy to express in the language of another culture. Such misunderstandings can occur even when the child and clinician are from the same culture (Irwin & Johnson, 2005). Extreme care, therefore, is necessary to ascertain the true intent of a child's words, rather than to assume his or her meaning.

Beyond language, culture has many influences on the experience of mental illness. In non-Western cultures, psychotic symptoms may present in conditions not formally recognized in the

DSM-IV or *ICD-10*. For example, *Qi-gong psychotic reaction* refers to a brief psychotic reaction characterized by dissociative, paranoid, or other psychotic symptoms that may occur in patients who practice the Chinese health-enhancing folk remedy of *Qi-gong* ("exercise of vital energy") (APA, 1994). A variety of other culture-specific disorders have been documented that include dissociative and psychotic symptoms (Findling, Schulz, Kashani, & Harlan, 2001). Although these symptoms may appear in culturally accepted forms, they still can represent a psychotic break with reality that requires some form of intervention. In other instances, psychotic experiences may be culturally normative. Hallucinations can occur outside the context of psychosis, for instance, particularly in non-White cultures (Johns, Nazroo, Bebbington, & Kuipers, 2002). Sociocultural factors also need to be considered. African Americans have been found to score higher on measures of paranoia, possibly in response to actual experiences of racism and discrimination (Combs, Penn, & Fenigstein, 2002). These examples underscore the importance of considering cultural experiences when differentiating psychosis from normal experience.

Culture becomes particularly salient when distinguishing between normal religious beliefs or experiences and religious delusions or related hallucinations. A particular danger is the tendency of clinicians to judge religious beliefs or experiences outside of their own religious perspective as irrational and psychotic (O'Connor & Vandenberg, 2005). It has been recommended that religious experiences and practices be viewed as existing on a continuum from normal to psychotic and that their relative positions on the continuum be judged by assessing the elements of conviction in the experience, preoccupation, and impact on an individual's functioning and relationships (Pierre, 2001). Parents can be especially helpful by informing the clinician about their family's religious beliefs and practices, to help determine beliefs that begin to depart from the child's traditional cultural experience.

Because not all cultures view psychosis as an internally generated psychiatric condition or illness, treatment recommendations need to be informed by cultural beliefs. When providing diagnostic feedback and agreeing on treatment goals with families who possess alternative belief systems, for example, it is often helpful to discuss therapeutic goals at least partially from within the families' cultural perspectives so as to increase the likelihood that they will adhere to the treatment plan. Some families may also pursue alternative treatments that can exacerbate the child's condition, such as giving natural remedies with psychoactive properties that may exacerbate the youth's condition. Thus, a culturally sensitive approach to treatment planning that attempts to maintain points of contact between the clinician's belief system and the patient's is the most likely to succeed (Martinez-Taboas, 2005).

DIFFERENTIAL DIAGNOSIS AND BEHAVIORAL ASSESSMENT

Diagnosis of specific psychotic disorders is difficult even with adults, in part because the term *schizophrenia* refers to a variety of similar disabling mental conditions that represent a severe break with reality but may be caused by somewhat different etiological factors (Tsuang & Faraone, 1995). The clinical presentation of schizophrenia is extremely heterogeneous, and the symptom presentations of any two patients may differ remarkably. Diagnosis of psychotic disorders in children is especially complex, and misdiagnosis is common (Stayer et al., 2005). An accurate diagnosis can be established, however, through a careful distinction between schizophrenia and other psychiatric or developmental disorders, medical and neurological conditions, substance abuse, and normal patterns of development.

Normal Development

With youth, especially very young children, it can be difficult to distinguish between imaginative fantasy and psychotic symptoms. Young children do not have an adult sense of reality and logic, which can make it difficult to assess for psychosis (Volkmar, 1996). Illogical thinking and loosening of associations tend to decrease in normal children by the age of 7 and are extremely rare by 10 years of age (Caplan, 1994). Although illogical thinking and loose associations do occur in healthy 4- to 6-year-olds, the rate of these thought disorder indices is much higher in youth with COS (Caplan, Guthrie, Fish, Tanguay, & David-Lando, 1989). Incoherence and poverty of speech are rare even in children with schizophrenia and should be taken as serious signs of disturbance when they appear (Caplan et al., 1989).

The presence of imaginary companions is normative for young children, with these experiences typically diminishing by adolescence. In an unselected sample of 12-year-olds, 9% reported the experience of an imaginary friend (Pearson et al., 2001). Had formal interviews been conducted, it is possible that many of the youth would have described their imaginary companions as "not real," ruling out fully psychotic hallucinatory experiences. In addition to inquiring about the level of conviction with which a belief is held, clinicians should look for signs of cognitive or behavioral disorganization, assess the impact of psychotic-like experiences on the child's level of functioning, and inquire about associated distress in order to distinguish normal developmental events from psychiatric symptomatology.

During adolescence, normal developmental patterns such as separation from parents and individuation of the self often result in experimentation and enthusiasm for ideas and behavior that may seem unusual. Similar to assessing young children, the key features differentiating normal adolescent development from psychosis rests on the level of conviction about experiences, the extent of preoccupation, the presence of associated distress, and impact on the young person's functioning. For example, a teenager who becomes interested in unusual religious or political ideologies (e.g., anarchism or magic) may do so within a group of peers who share the beliefs, without interference in family and school functioning. These beliefs, however, should be judged as psychotic when their practice is accompanied by delusional conviction or hallucinations (e.g., a teen is convinced that a spell was placed on her by a peer and is causing her to be confused and fail classes, denying any possibility of another explanation) and interferes with relationships, school performance, or attendance.

As noted earlier, it is vital to investigate the beliefs held by the child's immediate family and friends to determine whether the child's beliefs are consistent with subcultural or family norms or whether they represent unusual ideas not held by others close to them. Finally, there is evidence that a substantial minority of adults in nonclinical samples experiences psychotic symptoms, such as verbal hallucinations, with no apparent relationship to current psychopathology or level of social conformity (Barrett & Etheridge, 1992; Verdoux & van Os, 2002). The presence of self-reported attenuated psychotic experiences has also been well documented in nonclinical samples of adolescents (McGorry et al., 1995) but has yet to be examined in children. In sum, psychotic experiences can occur outside the context of psychopathology across the lifespan, and a careful distinction must be made between psychotic experiences and psychotic symptoms that are associated with psychiatric syndromes, distress, and impairment.

Schizotypal Personality Disorder and Prodromal Psychosis

Although attenuated forms of psychotic symptoms may not fulfill criteria for schizophrenia, they can mark the prodromal phase of the illness if they are of recent onset, especially during adolescence (Miller et al., 1999; Yung et al., 2005). When attenuated symptoms are mild and long-standing, they may be better accounted for with a diagnosis of schizotypal personality disorder (SPD). These symptoms include social withdrawal, odd behavior, and magical thinking that are not considered fully psychotic. Because 25% of children diagnosed with SPD later develop a full psychotic disorder (Asarnow, 2005), identification of subthreshold psychotic symptoms may be of critical importance for early diagnosis and intervention. Given the lack of prognostic clarity for these children, however, assessing for subthreshold psychosis must be conducted without attaching stigma or a premature prognosis to children who experience such symptoms.

Intellectual Disability and Developmental Disorders

Determining the difference between psychosis and developmental delays can be difficult in children, especially young children, and may be impossible in children with very low IQs due to their restricted verbal abilities. Twenty percent of children and adolescents with psychotic disorders have an IQ below 80 (Werry et al., 1994), and thought disorder is often observed in both pervasive developmental disorder (PDD) and COS patients (van der Gaag, Caplan, van Engeland, Loman, & Buitelaar, 2005). Because children with intellectual disability or PDDs are at an elevated risk for developing psychotic symptoms, it has been suggested that PDD diagnoses prior to the onset of COS mark a manifestation of severe abnormal early development (Sporn et al., 2004). The course of illness for these children is not clear, and, in some cases, the psychosis may resolve (Friedlander & Donnelly, 2004). When there is sufficient evidence of hallucinations and delusions, however, an additional diagnosis of schizophrenia can be made in children with a low IQ or PDD.

The process of making a diagnosis is facilitated when the psychotic symptoms first present in late childhood or adolescence and there is a change from the previous level of functioning. Psychotic diagnoses are extremely difficult to determine in autistic or otherwise developmentally delayed children who exhibit minor variations in level of functioning or appear never to develop full reality testing. If possible, these children should be referred for evaluation by a clinician who is experienced in working with developmentally delayed children.

Primary Mood Disorders

Differentiating between primary mood disorders with psychotic features and schizophrenia spectrum disorders is challenging in youth, especially when children are acutely psychotic or when psychosis onset is recent (Carlson, Fennig, & Bromet, 1994). Hallucinations are present in 9% to 27% of children with major depressive disorder, but delusions are found in only 6% of these children (Ryan et al., 1987; Ulloa et al., 2000). Psychotic features in major depressive disorder may signal risk for later development of bipolar disorder (Strober & Carlson, 1982). In pediatric bipolar disorder, documented rates of psychotic symptoms are high but vary widely, ranging from 16% to 75% of study samples, and are more common in adolescents than in young children (Biederman et al., 2004; Ketter, Wang, Becker, Nowakowska, & Yang, 2004; Pavuluri, Herbener, & Sweeney, 2004). When both mood and psychotic symptoms are prominent, it is often necessary to follow the course of the illness over time to determine the diagnosis.

Although determining a differential diagnosis may be challenging, diagnoses involving mood disorders and psychotic symptoms are typically reliable. The most common psychotic symptoms in depression and mania are mood congruent, including auditory hallucinations (e.g., a child hears commands to punish or kill himself), grandiose delusions (e.g., having supernatural powers), or loosening of associations (Calderoni et al., 2001; Pavuluri et al., 2004). The overlap in symptoms may be explained by evidence for some shared genetic contributions to bipolar disorder and schizophrenia, with the closest relationship between schizoaffective and bipolar disorders (Maier, Hofgen, Zobel, & Rietschel, 2005). Ascertaining an accurate diagnosis, therefore, requires determining the exact temporal relationship between mood and psychotic symptoms, as psychotic symptoms must occur at some point in the absence of prominent mood symptoms for schizophrenia or schizoaffective disorder to be diagnosed (APA, 1994).

Obsessive-Compulsive Disorder

Clinical research on childhood obsessive-compulsive disorder (OCD) and psychosis is limited, so we draw somewhat from the available literature on adults. Adults with schizophrenia frequently display symptoms of OCD (for a review, see Bottas, Cooke, & Richter, 2005), and in a study of adolescents with schizophrenia, a corresponding rate of 26% with OCD has been documented (Nechmad et al., 2003). Adults with OCD may have an increased risk for a comorbid diagnosis of SPD (see Poyurovsky & Koran, 2005, for a review), but the rate of schizophrenia in their families is consistent with that of the general population, suggesting the absence of a genetic association (Nestadt et al., 2001).

A critical difference between OCD and psychosis is that OCD patients have insight into the excessive nature of their symptoms at some point during the course of the disorder (APA, 1994), although clinical research studies indicate that many patients with OCD may lack such insight (Eisen et al., 2001; Foa et al., 1995; Kozak & Foa, 1994). Patients with OCD can also develop delusions that meet diagnostic criteria for a brief psychotic disorder or delusional disorder but may be best understood as an "obsessive-compulsive psychosis" (Insel & Akiskal, 1986). In cases where the only psychotic symptom appears in the form of a delusional obsession (e.g., delusional fear of contamination), the indication of insight at any point in time would distinguish OCD from psychosis. Following such children over time is necessary to determine whether the delusional intensity of the obsession is transient or indicative of a long-term psychotic disorder.

Trauma: Posttraumatic Stress Disorder and Dissociative Disorders

Youth who have been physically or sexually maltreated are at heightened risk for developing psychotic symptoms in childhood and as adults (see Read et al., 2005, for a review). Hallucinations and delusions can be present in dissociative disorders and posttraumatic stress disorder (PTSD), making them difficult to differentiate from a schizophrenic psychosis. Children with dissociative disorders, however, have periods of trancelike states and do not typically exhibit formal thought disorder with disorganized communication (Caplan, 1995). Children with PTSD or borderline personality disorder (BPD) may have brief states of confusion and transient hallucinations or paranoid delusions centered around traumatic themes of harm or persecution, but they do not typically have bizarre delusions or formal thought disorder, hear voices with running commentary, or exhibit persistent negative symptoms or disorganized behavior (Findling et al., 2001; Kaufman, Birmaher, Clayton, Retano, & Wongchaowart, 1997). For many children with PTSD, BPD, or brief psychotic symptoms in relation to intense stress or trauma, the symptoms may resolve once treatment has been initiated and the child feels safe and supported (Mertin & Hartwig, 2004).

Shared Psychotic Disorder

Shared psychotic disorder is the rare presentation of delusions and/or hallucinations reported by a "secondary" person due to the shared reality with a psychotic family member or "primary" patient. In children, the primary patient is likely to be a parent, most often the mother or a sibling. In one sample, persecutory delusions were the focal symptoms in 75% of cases across all age groups, with 29% of the secondary patients reporting hallucinations (Silveira & Seeman, 1995).

In instances of a shared psychotic disorder, the pair tends to be extremely socially isolated, which may be a key contributing factor to the development of the delusions (Silveira & Seeman, 1995). When there is suspicion of a shared psychotic disorder between a parent and child, it is helpful to conduct an interview with the psychotic parent as well as with another informant, such as another family member or spouse, who can describe the impact of the parent's psychosis on the child's symptoms and functioning. When both the youth and a family member present similar delusional beliefs, it may be difficult to distinguish a shared psychotic disorder from two primary psychotic disorders (Reif & Pfuhlmann, 2004). In true cases of shared psychotic disorder, the symptoms typically resolve once the child has spent sufficient time apart from the psychotic family member and has begun engaging in a broader social environment (APA, 1994).

Substance Abuse

Adolescence, in particular, is a period of vulnerability for developing psychotic disorders and substance abuse problems. The relationship between psychotic symptoms and substance use is especially tricky to untangle in youth who may not have a long history of either problem or who present during acutely intoxicated states. Dual diagnosis is quite common, with approximately 50% of schizophrenia patients using substances at some point in their life (Regier et al., 1990). Alternatively, a number of substances can be associated with psychosis during use and/or withdrawal, especially stimulants (e.g., cocaine, methamphetamines) or hallucinogens (e.g., PCP and LSD). Substance use strongly predicts a worse course for psychotic patients (Swofford, Kasckow, Scheller-Gilkey, & Inderbitzin, 1996), and increasing evidence suggests that substance use, particularly marijuana, contributes to risk for developing schizophrenia (Hambrecht & Hafner, 2000; Kumra, Thaden, DeThomas, & Kranzler, 2005).

In diagnostic assessments, primary psychotic disorders must be differentiated from substance-induced psychosis. Psychotic symptoms that are present only during acute intoxication or withdrawal are assigned a diagnosis of substance-induced psychosis, while substances are considered precipitants to a primary psychotic disorder when symptoms linger long after the substance use. Although shared biological vulnerability, reactions to psychosocial stress, and self-medication have been hypothesized to account for the association between substance abuse and psychosis (van Nimwegen, de Haan, van Beveren, van den Brink, & Linszen, 2005; Verdoux, Tournier, & Cougnard, 2005), the temporal relationship between substance use and psychotic symptoms ultimately determines the formal psychiatric diagnosis.

Assessing for substance use is critical in any psychotic disorder evaluation, regardless of a child's age. The average age of first substance use in the United States is now between 11 and 12 years (Solhkhah, 2003). Patients of any age often minimize their drug use, and youth may specifically fear parental punishment for admitting use. Many young patients will admit the full extent of their use only after developing trust with a clinician over time, so extending assessments over a period of time along with conferring with the child's therapist may be helpful. When patients present in acute psychotic states, laboratory tests should be ordered to assess for substance use.

Medical and Neurological Conditions

A variety of medical conditions can also lead to psychotic symptoms, including tumors, infections, central nervous system lesions, metabolic disorders, seizure disorders, and the adverse effects of prescribed medications (APA, 1994; McClellan & Werry, 1994; Pellock, 2004). Therefore, it is critical to include a thorough physical examination to rule out organic causes of psychosis. Often, specific laboratory tests and procedures are needed, such as neuroimaging, toxicology screens, or assessment of renal functioning (McClellan & Werry, 1994). An integrated team approach is often indicated when assessing for psychoses, drawing upon the expertise of mental health specialists, neurologists, and the patient's primary care provider.

SELECTION OF TREATMENT TARGETS AND REFERRAL

Treatment Targets

Although positive symptoms define the presence of psychosis, we have previously described the wider array of symptoms and problems associated with schizophrenia in youth, including negative symptoms, disorganization, mood and anxiety disturbances, risk issues, cognitive problems, and impaired social and academic functioning. Any and all of these areas may be targets for treatment. Treatment goals, for instance, might include reduction of auditory hallucinations, improved mood, better school attendance, decreased fighting with family members, and increased tolerance of challenging social situations. Due to cognitive impairments and possible developmental delays, children with psychosis often have poor insight, impaired judgment, and a reduced ability to plan and predict consequences. These factors place them at increased risk for abuse, substance use, pregnancy, or engaging in physical violence. They may also have more difficulty navigating social relationships compared with their peers, yet be in school and social settings that require complex judgments, especially in adolescence. Treatment goals should extend to the entire family system, as parents and siblings likely require psychoeducation, support for themselves, and expert assistance in addressing specific challenges that a child with psychosis will encounter.

The three-phase model of schizophrenia treatment (Goldstein & Miklowitz, 1995) has been recommended for use with children (Asarnow, Tompson, & McGrath, 2004). It involves relying upon (1) medication and inpatient care to reduce psychotic symptoms during the *acute phase,* (2) outpatient medication management and psychosocial interventions during the *stabilization phase,* and (3) multimodal outpatient treatment (e.g., psychopharmacology, family psychotherapy, skills building) during the *maintenance phase.* Similar to treatment of other severe mental disorders and psychosis in adults, the most effective strategy for treating psychotic youth is a combination of medication and psychotherapy (e.g., Linszen, Lenior, De Haan, Dingemans, & Gersons, 1998; Mojtabai, Nicholson, & Carpenter, 1998; Rund et al., 1994).

Pharmacological Interventions

While psychopharmacology is the primary form of treatment for schizophrenia, little data are available assessing the efficacy and safety of these medications in youth. When taken by adult patients, atypical antipsychotic medications largely reduce positive symptoms and have fewer side effects than the older generation of typical neuroleptic medications, although they retain the risk of sedation, motor problems, and metabolic changes (e.g., weight gain or diabetes) that often lead patients to stop taking their medications (Lieberman et al., 2005).

Overall, antipsychotic medications appear to provide similar benefits in reducing psychotic symptoms in youth but carry an even greater risk for side effects (Armenteros, Whitaker, Welikson, Stedge, & Gorman, 1997; Kumra et al., 1996; Remschmidt, Martin, Hennighausen, & Schulz, 2001; Sikich, 2005). Close monitoring of side effects and open communication with youth and their parents are crucial, therefore, to maintaining treatment adherence with effective and tolerable doses. Adolescents can be especially sensitive to weight gain and may require behavioral interventions to assist with weight reduction if medications lacking this side effect are not effective for them. If clinically indicated, youth may also benefit from antidepressants, mood stabilizers, or antianxiety medications. The use of psychostimulants is controversial because some evidence suggests that these stimulants may precipitate or exacerbate psychotic symptoms (Cherland & Fitzpatrick, 1999; Tossell et al., 2004).

Psychotherapy

Although antipsychotic medications are often the "front line" treatment for treating acute schizophrenia, behavioral interventions are necessary for helping psychotic patients to cope with and reduce symptoms and to improve their social, academic, and occupational functioning over the course of their lives (Asarnow et al., 2004; Mojtabai et al., 1998; Tolbert, 1996). In cases of severe symptoms or risk of harm, hospitalization may be necessary to provide a highly structured environment, with close monitoring during medication trials and risk periods. Upon stabilization or with moderate levels of symptoms and risk, day treatment programs can be a useful option. For youth who cannot be maintained safely at home due to risk or symptom severity, residential treatment may be necessary for short or long periods of time. Once stabilized, children can attend outpatient family, group, or individual therapy.

Individual and group psychotherapy that involves a skills-building approach is often a primary intervention for adults with schizophrenia. Although empirical evidence supporting the efficacy of psychosocial rehabilitation with psychotic children is still forthcoming, helping youth to improve their coping, social, problem-solving, and emotion regulation skills is often necessary. Social skills training has been shown to be especially effective for younger adults with schizophrenia and children with nonpsychotic disorders, suggesting its potential utility with psychotic children (Gresham, Cook,

Crews, & Kern, 2004; Marder, Wirshing, Mintz, & McKenzie, 1996). Cognitive therapy can be used to target specific symptoms, ranging from auditory hallucinations to lack of motivation (Kingdon & Turkington, 2005) and may be helpful for youth with sufficient intellectual development and verbal skills (Sikich, 2005). Psychodynamic approaches with psychotic children often require a supportive rather than "uncovering" approach (Mueser & Berenbaum, 1990; Scott & Dixon, 1995). This approach provides external structure to assist children with containing a frightening and disorganized internal world, while supporting them in establishing reality-based relationships and navigating developmental challenges. Across all psychotherapies adapted from adult interventions for schizophrenia, the developmental stage of the child must, of course, be taken into account.

Family therapy and psychoeducation are also extremely important, especially with newly diagnosed children. Parents and siblings are often in a state of crisis, upset and uncertain of a child's condition and future. They may require support for themselves as well as instruction in ways to assist the ill youth and to prepare for the future. Siblings in particular are often overlooked, although they may be frightened and unsure of how to act with the psychotic child. Once an acute phase has been resolved, parents are then confronted with the challenge of helping their child to continue to achieve developmental and academic goals and often require the assistance of expert clinicians as they navigate various options and obstacles. A positive family environment, reflected in parental warmth and positive statements, is associated with improved symptoms and social functioning in adolescents with attenuated psychotic symptoms (O'Brien et al., 2006). Therefore, families should be supported to recognize their children's positive qualities without focusing exclusively on problematic symptoms. Multifamily groups offered by clinicians (McFarlane, 2002) or support groups, such as those associated with the National Alliance on Mental Illness (NAMI), can be extremely effective in bringing together families who are struggling with similar issues and in providing support and education.

Other Services

Children and adolescents with psychotic disorders often require special educational services or school settings designed for children with emotional difficulties that offer smaller classes or flexible class scheduling. Sensory stimulation, stress, and social relationships can be quite challenging, and some youth may be able to tolerate only a few classes a day without becoming overwhelmed and experiencing increased symptoms. Continued and open communication with teachers and school staff to help them understand and manage a psychotic child's particular problems is essential (Sikich, 2005). Children with psychosis may also qualify for state or federal disability or health insurance, assisted housing, or other social services, and they often require a case manager or social worker to assist with coordinating their care effectively.

Summary

Because psychotic disorders affect a broad range of functioning in children and adolescents, proper assessment and treatment of affected youth require comprehensive psychological and medical evaluations. The interview is a key means of gathering information about these disorders, and in this chapter, we outlined common challenges and difficulties that clinicians face when working with individuals experiencing symptoms of psychosis. The aim of this chapter is to introduce novice practitioners to common challenges that arise when conducting interviews with this population and to provide practical guidelines for overcoming these difficulties. At the same time, this chapter is intended to provide seasoned clinicians with new tools and perspectives. Although childhood psychosis is an unusually difficult and debilitating human experience, well-conducted interviews enable early, accurate diagnoses that can vastly improve outcomes for youth and the families who care for them.

References

Achenbach, T. M., McConaughy, S. H., & Howell, C. T. (1987). Child/adolescent behavioral and emotional problems: Implications of cross-informant correlations for situational specificity. *Psychology Bulletin, 101,* 213–232.

Alaghband-Rad, J., McKenna, K., Gordon, C. T., Albus, K. E., Hamburger, S. D., Rumsey, J. M., et al. (1995). Childhood-onset schizophrenia: The severity of premorbid course. *Journal of the American Academy of Child & Adolescent Psychiatry, 34,* 1273–1283.

American Psychiatric Association. (1994). *Diagnostic and statistical manual of mental disorders* (4th ed.). Washington, DC: Author.

Angermeyer, M. C. (2000). Schizophrenia and violence. *Acta Psychiatrica Scandinavica, 102*(Suppl. 407), 63–67.

Arango, C., Buchanan, R. W., Kirkpatrick, B., & Carpenter, W. T. (2004). The deficit syndrome in schizophrenia: Implications for the treatment of negative symptoms. *European Psychiatry, 19*, 21–26.

Armenteros, J. L., Whitaker, A. H., Welikson, M., Stedge, D. J., & Gorman, J. (1997). Risperidone in adolescents with schizophrenia: An open pilot study. *Journal of the American Academy of Child & Adolescent Psychiatry, 36*, 694–700.

Arseneault, L., Cannon, M., Murray, R., Poulton, R., Caspi, A., & Moffitt, T. E. (2003). Childhood origins of violent behaviour in adults with schizophreniform disorder. *British Journal of Psychiatry, 183*, 520–525.

Asarnow, J. R. (2005). Childhood-onset schizotypal disorder: A follow-up study and comparison with childhood-onset schizophrenia. *Journal of Child and Adolescent Psychopharmacology, 15*, 395–402.

Asarnow, J. R., & Ben-Meir, S. (1988). Children with schizophrenia spectrum and depressive disorders: A comparative study of premorbid adjustment, onset pattern, and severity of impairment. *Journal of Child Psychology and Psychiatry, 29*, 477–488.

Asarnow, J. R., Tompson, M. C., & McGrath, E. P. (2004). Annotation: Childhood-onset schizophrenia: Clinical and treatment issues. *Journal of Child Psychology and Psychiatry, 45*, 180–194.

Ballageer, T., Malla, A., Manchanda, R., Takhar, J., & Haricharan, R. (2005). Is adolescent-onset first-episode psychosis different from adult onset? *Journal of the American Academy of Child & Adolescent Psychiatry, 44*, 782–789.

Barrett, T. R., & Etheridge, J. B. (1992). Verbal hallucinations in normals: I. People who hear "voices." *Applied Cognitive Psychology, 6*, 379–387.

Batel, P. (2000). Addiction and schizophrenia. *European Psychiatry, 15*, 115–122.

Bearden, C. E., Meyer, S. E., Gordon, J. L., O'Brien, M., Johnson, J. K., Loewy, R. L., et al. (2004, September). *Is parental report critical for diagnosing a prodromal state in adolescents?* Paper presented at the 4th International Conference on Early Psychosis, Vancouver, Canada.

Bellack, L. (1986). *The TAT, CAT, and SAT in clinical use.* New York: Grune & Stratton.

Beresford, C., Hepburn, S., & Ross, R. G. (2005). Schizophrenia in pre-school children: Two case reports with longitudinal follow-up for 6 and 8 years. *Clinical Child Psychology and Psychiatry, 10*, 429–439.

Biederman, J., Petty, C., Faraone, S. V., & Seidman, L. (2004). Phenomenology of childhood psychosis: Findings from a large sample of psychiatrically referred youth. *Journal of Nervous and Mental Disease, 192*, 607–614.

Bottas, A., Cooke, R. G., & Richter, M. A. (2005). Comorbidity and pathophysiology of obsessive-compulsive disorder in schizophrenia: Is there evidence for a schizo-obsessive subtype of schizophrenia? *Journal of Psychiatry & Neuroscience, 30*, 187–193.

Brickman, A. M., Buchsbaum, M. S., Bloom, R., Bokhoven, P., Paul-Odouard, R., Haznedar, M. M. et al. (2004). Neuropsychological functioning in first-break, never-medicated adolescents with psychosis. *Journal of Nervous and Mental Disease, 192*, 615–622.

Buchanan, A., Reed, A., Wessely, S., Garety, P., Taylor, P., Grubin, D., et al. (1993). Acting on delusions. II: The phenomenological correlates of acting on delusions. *British Journal of Psychiatry, 163*, 77–81.

Calderoni, D., Wudarsky, M., Bhangoo, R., Dell, M. L., Nicolson, R., Hamburger, S. D., et al. (2001). Differentiating childhood-onset schizophrenia from psychotic mood disorders. *Journal of the American Academy of Child & Adolescent Psychiatry, 40*, 1190–1196.

Caplan, R. (1994). Communication deficits in childhood schizophrenia spectrum disorders. *Schizophrenia Bulletin, 20*, 671–683.

Caplan, R. (1995). "Environmental trauma and psychosis": Response. *Journal of the American Academy of Child & Adolescent Psychiatry, 34*, 1258–1259.

Caplan, R., Guthrie, D., Fish, B., Tanguay, P. E., & David-Lando, G. (1989). The Kiddie Formal Thought Disorder Rating Scale: Clinical assessment, reliability, and validity. *Journal of the American Academy of Child & Adolescent Psychiatry, 28*, 408–416.

Carlson, G. A., Fennig, S., & Bromet, E. J. (1994). The confusion between bipolar disorder and schizophrenia in youth: Where does it stand in the 1990s? *Journal of the American Academy of Child & Adolescent Psychiatry, 33*, 453–460.

Cherland, E., & Fitzpatrick, R. (1999). Psychotic side effects of psychostimulants: A 5-year review. *Canadian Journal of Psychiatry, 44*, 811–813.

Combs, D. R., Penn, D. L., & Fenigstein, A. (2002). Ethnic differences in subclinical paranoia: An expansion of norms of the paranoia scale. *Cultural Diversity and Ethnic Minority Psychology, 8*, 248–256.

de Haan, L., Welborn, K., Krikke, M., & Linszen, D. H. (2004). Opinions of mothers on the first psychotic episode and the start of treatment of their child. *European Psychiatry, 19*, 226–229.

De Los Reyes, A., & Kazdin, A. E. (2005). Informant discrepancies in the assessment of childhood psychopathology: A critical review, theoretical framework, and recommendations for further study. *Psychological Bulletin, 131*, 483–509.

Di Maggio, C., Martinez, M., Menard, J. F., Petit, M., & Thibaut, F. (2001). Evidence of a cohort effect for age at onset of schizophrenia. *American Journal of Psychiatry, 158*, 489–492.

Doss, A. J. (2005). Evidence-based diagnosis: Incorporating diagnostic instruments into clinical practice. *Journal of the American Academy of Child & Adolescent Psychiatry, 44*, 947–952.

Duhig, A. M., Renk, K., Epstein, M. K., & Phares, V. (2000). Interparental agreement on internalizing, externalizing, and total behavior problems: A meta-analysis. *Clinical Psychology: Science and Practice, 7*, 435–453.

Edwards, M. C. (2005). Test of time: Agreeing about disagreements: A personal reflection on Achenbach, McConaughy, and Howell (1987). *Clinical Child Psychology and Psychiatry, 10*, 440–445.

Eggers, C. (1989). Schizo-affective psychoses in childhood: A follow-up study. *Journal of Autism and Developmental Disorders, 19,* 327–342.

Eggers, C., & Bunk, D. (1997). The long-term course of childhood-onset schizophrenia: A 42-year follow-up. *Schizophrenia Bulletin, 23,* 105–117.

Eggers, C., Bunk, D., & Krause, D. (2000). Schizophrenia with onset before the age of eleven: Clinical characteristics of onset and course. *Journal of Autism and Developmental Disorders, 30,* 29–38.

Eisen, J. L., Rasmussen, S. A., Phillips, K. A., Price, L. H., Davidson, J., Lydiard, R. B., et al. (2001). Insight and treatment outcome in obsessive-compulsive disorder. *Comprehensive Psychiatry, 42,* 494–497.

Exner, J. E., Jr., & Erdberg, P. (2005). *The Rorschach: A comprehensive system* (3rd ed., Vol. 2). Hoboken, NJ: Wiley.

Findling, R. L., Schulz, S. C., Kashani, J. H., & Harlan, E. (2001). *Psychotic disorders in children and adolescents.* Thousand Oaks, CA: Sage.

Fleischhaker, C., Schulz, E., Tepper, K., Martin, M., Hennighausen, K., & Remschmidt, H. (2005). Long-term course of adolescent schizophrenia. *Schizophrenia Bulletin, 31,* 769–780.

Foa, E. B., Kozak, M. J., Goodman, W. K., Hollander, E., Jenike, M. A., & Rasmussen, S. A. (1995). *DSM-IV* field trial: Obsessive-compulsive disorder. *American Journal of Psychiatry, 152,* 90–96.

Friedlander, R. I., & Donnelly, T. (2004). Early-onset psychosis in youth with intellectual disability. *Journal of Intellectual Disability Research, 48,* 540–547.

Garralda, M. E. (1984). Hallucinations in children with conduct and emotional disorders: II. The follow-up study. *Psychological Medicine, 14,* 597–604.

Gillberg, I. C., Hellgren, L., & Gillberg, C. (1993). Psychotic disorders diagnosed in adolescence. Outcome at age 30 years. *Journal of Child Psychology and Psychiatry, 34,* 1173–1185.

Gochman, P. A., Greenstein, D., Sporn, A., Gogtay, N., Keller, B., Shaw, P., et al. (2005). IQ stabilization in childhood-onset schizophrenia. *Schizophrenia Research, 77,* 271–277.

Goldstein, M. J., & Miklowitz, D. J. (1995). The effectiveness of psychoeducational family therapy in the treatment of schizophrenic disorders. *Journal of Marital and Family Therapy, 21,* 361–376.

Goodenough, F. L. (1926). *Measurement of intelligence by drawings.* New York: Yonkers World Book.

Green, W. H., Padron-Gayol, M., Hardesty, A. S., & Bassiri, M. (1992). Schizophrenia with childhood onset: A phenomenological study of 38 cases. *Journal of the American Academy of Child & Adolescent Psychiatry, 31,* 968–976.

Gresham, F. M., Cook, C. R., Crews, S. D., & Kern, L. (2004). Social skills training for children and youth with emotional and behavioral disorders: Validity considerations and future directions. *Behavioral Disorders (Special Issue): Elucidating Precision and Rigor in EBD Research, 30,* 32–46.

Hambrecht, M. (1995). A second case of schizophrenia in the family: Is it observed differently? *European Archives of Psychiatry and Clinical Neuroscience, 245,* 267–269.

Hambrecht, M., & Hafner, H. (2000). Cannabis, vulnerability, and the onset of schizophrenia: An epidemiological perspective. *Australian and New Zealand Journal of Psychiatry, 34,* 468–475.

Hambrecht, M., Hafner, H., & Loffler, W. (1994). Beginning schizophrenia observed by significant others. *Social Psychiatry and Psychiatric Epidemiology, 29,* 53–60.

Harden, J., Scott, S., Backett-Milburn, K., & Jackson, S. (2000). Can't talk, won't talk? Methodological issues in researching children. *Sociological Research Online, 5*(2). Retrieved from http://www.socresonline.org .uk/5/2/harden.html

Hartwell, C. E. (1996). The schizophrenogenic mother concept in American psychiatry. *Psychiatry, 59,* 274–297.

Hien, D., Matzner, J. J., First, M. B., Spitzer, R. L., Gibbon, M., & Williams, J. B. W. (1999). Structured clinical interview for *DSM-IV*—Child edition (KID-SCID version 1.0). New York: Columbia University.

Hiroeh, U., Appleby, L., Mortensen, P. B., & Dunn, G. (2001). Death by homicide, suicide, and other unnatural causes in people with mental illness: A population-based study. *Lancet, 358,* 2110–2112.

Hoff, A. L., Harris, D., Faustman, W. O., Beal, M., DeVilliers, D., Mone, R. D., et al. (1996). A neuropsychological study of early onset schizophrenia. *Schizophrenia Research, 20,* 21–28.

Hollis, C. (2000). Adult outcomes of child- and adolescent-onset schizophrenia: Diagnostic stability and predictive validity. *American Journal of Psychiatry, 157,* 1652–1659.

Insel, T. R., & Akiskal, H. S. (1986). Obsessive-compulsive disorder with psychotic features: A phenomenologic analysis. *American Journal of Psychiatry, 143,* 1527–1533.

Irwin, L. G., & Johnson, J. (2005). Interviewing young children: Explicating our practices and dilemmas. *Qualitative Health Research, 15,* 821–831.

Jacobsen, L. K., Giedd, J. N., Berquin, P. C., Krain, A. L., Hamburger, S. D., Kumra, S., et al. (1997). Quantitative morphology of the cerebellum and fourth ventricle in childhood-onset schizophrenia. *American Journal of Psychiatry, 154,* 1663–1669.

Janssen, I., Krabbendam, L., Bak, M., Hanssen, M., Vollebergh, W., de Graaf, R., et al. (2004). Childhood abuse as a risk factor for psychotic experiences. *Acta Psychiatrica Scandinavica, 109,* 38–45.

Jensen, P. S., Rubio-Stipec, M., Canino, G., Bird, H. R., Dulcan, M. K., Schwab-Stone, M. E., et al. (1999). Parent and child contributions to diagnosis of mental disorder: Are both informants always necessary? *Journal of the American Academy of Child & Adolescent Psychiatry, 38,* 1569–1579.

Johns, L. C., Nazroo, J. Y., Bebbington, P., & Kuipers, E. (2002). Occurrence of hallucinatory experiences in a community sample and ethnic variations. *British Journal of Psychiatry, 180,* 174–178.

Kaufman, J., Birmaher, B., Brent, D., Rao, U., Flynn, C., Moreci, P., et al. (1997). Schedule for Affective Disorders and Schizophrenia for School-Age Children-Present and Lifetime Version (K-SADS-PL): Initial reliability and validity data. *Journal of the American Academy of Child & Adolescent Psychiatry, 36,* 980–988.

Kaufman, J., Birmaher, B., Clayton, S., Retano, A., & Wongchaowart, B. (1997). Case study: Trauma-related hallucinations. *Journal of the American Academy of Child & Adolescent Psychiatry, 36,* 1602–1605.

Kemph, J. P. (1987). Hallucinations in psychotic children. *Journal of the American Academy of Child & Adolescent Psychiatry, 26,* 556–559.

Ketter, T. A., Wang, P. W., Becker, O. V., Nowakowska, C., & Yang, Y.-S. (2004). Psychotic bipolar disorders: Dimensionally similar to or categorically different from schizophrenia? *Journal of Psychiatric Research, 38,* 47–61.

Kingdon, D. G., & Turkington, D. (2005). *Cognitive therapy of schizophrenia.* New York: Guilford Press.

Kozak, M. J., & Foa, E. B. (1994). Obsessions, overvalued ideas, and delusions in obsessive-compulsive disorder. *Behaviour Research and Therapy, 32,* 343–353.

Kumra, S., Frazier, J. A., Jacobsen, L. K., McKenna, K., Gordon, C. T., Lenane, M. C., et al. (1996). Childhood-onset schizophrenia. A double-blind clozapine-haloperidol comparison. *Archives of General Psychiatry, 53,* 1090–1097.

Kumra, S., Shaw, M., Merka, P., Nakayama, E., & Augustin, R. (2001). Childhood-onset schizophrenia: Research update. *Canadian Journal of Psychiatry, 46,* 923–930.

Kumra, S., Thaden, E., DeThomas, C., & Kranzler, H. (2005). Correlates of substance abuse in adolescents with treatment-refractory schizophrenia and schizoaffective disorder. *Schizophrenia Research, 73,* 369–371.

Kumra, S., Wiggs, E., Bedwell, J., Smith, A. K., Arling, E., Albus, K., et al. (2000). Neuropsychological deficits in pediatric patients with childhood-onset schizophrenia and psychotic disorder not otherwise specified. *Schizophrenia Research, 42,* 135–144.

Lay, B., Blanz, B., Hartmann, M., & Schmidt, M. H. (2000). The psychosocial outcome of adolescent-onset schizophrenia: A 12-year follow-up. *Schizophrenia Bulletin, 26,* 801–816.

Lieberman, J. A., Stroup, T. S., McEvoy, J. P., Swartz, M. S., Rosenheck, R. A., Perkins, D. O., et al. (2005). Effectiveness of antipsychotic drugs in patients with chronic schizophrenia. *New England Journal of Medicine, 353,* 1209–1223.

Linszen, D., Lenior, M., De Haan, L., Dingemans, P., & Gersons, B. (1998). Early intervention, untreated psychosis and the course of early schizophrenia. *British Journal of Psychiatry, 33*(Suppl. 172), 84–89.

Livingston, R., & Bracha, H. S. (1992). Psychotic symptoms and suicidal behavior in hospitalized children. *American Journal of Psychiatry, 149,* 1585–1586.

Loranger, A. W. (1984). Sex difference in age at onset of schizophrenia. *Archives of General Psychiatry, 41,* 157–161.

Maier, W., Hofgen, B., Zobel, A., & Rietschel, M. (2005). Genetic models of schizophrenia and bipolar disorder: Overlapping inheritance or discrete genotypes? *European Archives of Psychiatry and Clinical Neuroscience, 255,* 159–166.

Marder, S. R., Wirshing, W. C., Mintz, J., & McKenzie, J. (1996). Two-year outcome of social skills training and group psychotherapy for outpatients with schizophrenia. *American Journal of Psychiatry, 153,* 1585–1592.

Martinez-Taboas, A. (2005). The plural world of culturally sensitive psychotherapy: A response to Castro-Blanco's (2005) comments. *Psychotherapy: Theory, Research, Practice, Training, 42,* 17–19.

McClellan, J., McCurry, C., Snell, J., & DuBose, A. (1999). Early-onset psychotic disorders: Course and outcome over a 2-year period. *Journal of the American Academy of Child & Adolescent Psychiatry, 38,* 1380–1388.

McClellan, J., & Werry, J. (1994). Practice parameters for the assessment and treatment of children and adolescents with schizophrenia. *Journal of the American Academy of Child & Adolescent Psychiatry, 33,* 616–635.

McClellan, J. M., Werry, J. S., & Ham, M. (1993). A follow-up study of early onset psychosis: Comparison between outcome diagnoses of schizophrenia, mood disorders, and personality disorders. *Journal of Autism and Developmental Disorders, 23,* 243–262.

McFarlane, W. R. (2002). *Multifamily groups in the treatment of severe psychiatric disorders.* New York: Guilford Press.

McGorry, P. D., McFarlane, C., Patton, G. C., Bell, R., Hibbert, M. E., Jackson, H. J., et al. (1995). The prevalence of prodromal features of schizophrenia in adolescence: A preliminary survey. *Acta Psychiatrica Scandinavica, 92,* 241–249.

Mertin, P., & Hartwig, S. (2004). Auditory hallucinations in nonpsychotic children: Diagnostic considerations. *Child and Adolescent Mental Health, 9,* 9–14.

Miller, T. J., McGlashan, T. H., Woods, S. W., Stein, K., Driesen, N., Corcoran, C. M., et al. (1999). Symptom assessment in schizophrenic prodromal states. *Psychiatric Quarterly, 70,* 273–287.

Mojtabai, R., Nicholson, R. A., & Carpenter, B. N. (1998). Role of psychosocial treatments in management of schizophrenia: A meta-analytic review of controlled outcome studies. *Schizophrenia Bulletin, 24,* 569–587.

Mueser, K. T., & Berenbaum, H. (1990). Psychodynamic treatment of schizophrenia: Is there a future? *Psychological Medicine, 20,* 253–262.

Mueser, K. T., Douglas, M. S., Bellack, A. S., & Morrison, R. L. (1991). Assessment of enduring deficit and negative symptom subtypes in schizophrenia. *Schizophrenia Bulletin, 17,* 565–582.

Nechmad, A., Ratzoni, G., Poyurovsky, M., Meged, S., Avidan, G., Fuchs, C., et al. (2003). Obsessive-compulsive disorder in adolescent schizophrenia patients. *American Journal of Psychiatry, 160,* 1002–1004.

Nestadt, G., Samuels, J., Riddle, M. A., Liang, K. Y., Bienvenu, O. J., Hoehn-Saric, R., et al. (2001). The relationship between obsessive-compulsive disorder and anxiety and affective disorders: Results from the Johns Hopkins OCD Family Study. *Psychological Medicine, 31,* 481–487.

Nicolson, R., Brookner, F. B., Lenane, M., Gochman, P., Ingraham, L. J., Egan, M. F., et al. (2003). Parental schizophrenia spectrum disorders in childhood-onset and adult-onset schizophrenia. *American Journal of Psychiatry, 160,* 490–495.

Nicolson, R., Lenane, M., Hamburger, S. D., Fernandez, T., Bedwell, J., & Rapoport, J. L. (2000). Lessons from childhood-onset schizophrenia. *Brain Research Reviews, 31,* 147–156.

O'Brien, M. P., Gordon, J. L., Bearden, C. E., Lopez, S. R., Kopelowicz, A., & Cannon, T. D. (2006). Positive family environment predicts improvement in symptoms and social functioning among adolescents at imminent risk for onset of psychosis. *Schizophrenia Research, 81,* 269–275.

O'Connor, S., & Vandenberg, B. (2005). Psychosis or faith? Clinicians' assessment of religious beliefs. *Journal of Consulting and Clinical Psychology, 73,* 610–616.

Pavuluri, M. N., Herbener, E. S., & Sweeney, J. A. (2004). Psychotic symptoms in pediatric bipolar disorder. *Journal of Affective Disorders, 80,* 19–28.

Pearson, D., Rouse, H., Doswell, S., Ainsworth, C., Dawson, O., Simms, K., et al. (2001). Prevalence of imaginary companions in a normal child population. *Child Care Health Development, 27,* 13–22.

Pellock, J. M. (2004). Defining the problem: Psychiatric and behavioral comorbidity in children and adolescents with epilepsy. *Epilepsy & Behavior (Special Issue): Psychiatric Comorbidity in Children and Adolescents With Epilepsy, 5*(Suppl. 3), S3–S9.

Pierre, J. M. (2001). Faith or delusion? At the crossroads of religion and psychosis. *Journal of Psychiatry Practice, 7,* 163–172.

Poulton, R., Caspi, A., Moffitt, T. E., Cannon, M., Murray, R., & Harrington, H. (2000). Children's self-reported psychotic symptoms and adult schizophreniform disorder: A 15-year longitudinal study. *Archives of General Psychiatry, 57,* 1053–1058.

Poyurovsky, M., & Koran, L. M. (2005). Obsessive-compulsive disorder (OCD) with schizotypy vs. schizophrenia with OCD: Diagnostic dilemmas and therapeutic implications. *Journal Psychiatric Research, 39,* 399–408.

Radomsky, E. D., Haas, G. L., Mann, J. J., & Sweeney, J. A. (1999). Suicidal behavior in patients with schizophrenia and other psychotic disorders. *American Journal of Psychiatry, 156,* 1590–1595.

Read, J., van Os, J., Morrison, A. P., & Ross, C. A. (2005). Childhood trauma, psychosis and schizophrenia: A literature review with theoretical and clinical implications. *Acta Psychiatrica Scandinavica, 112,* 330–350.

Regier, D. A., Boyd, J. H., Burke, J. D., Jr., Rae, D. S., Myers, J. K., et al. (1988). One-month prevalence of mental disorders in the United States. Based on five epidemiologic catchment area sites. *Archives of General Psychiatry, 45,* 977–986.

Regier, D. A., Farmer, M. E., Rae, D. S., Locke, B. Z., Keith, S. J., Judd, L. L., et al. (1990). Comorbidity of mental disorders with alcohol and other drug abuse. Results from the Epidemiologic Catchment Area (ECA) Study. *Journal of the American Medical Association, 264,* 2511–2518.

Reich, W. (2000). Diagnostic interview for children and adolescents (DICA). *Journal of the American Academy of Child & Adolescent Psychiatry, 39,* 59–66.

Reif, A., & Pfuhlmann, B. (2004). Folie a deux versus genetically driven delusional disorder: Case reports and nosological considerations. *Comprehensive Psychiatry, 45,* 155–160.

Remschmidt, H., Martin, M., Hennighausen, K., & Schulz, E. (2001). Treatment and rehabilitation. In H. Remschmidt (Ed.), *Schizophrenia in children and adolescents* (pp. 192–267). Cambridge, NY: Cambridge University Press.

Remschmidt, H. E., Schulz, E., Martin, M., Warnke, A., & Trott, G. E. (1994). Childhood-onset schizophrenia: History of the concept and recent studies. *Schizophrenia Bulletin, 20,* 727–745.

Rhinewine, J. P., Lencz, T., Thaden, E. P., Cervellione, K. L., Burdick, K. E., Henderson, I., et al. (2005). Neurocognitive profile in adolescents with early-onset schizophrenia: Clinical correlates. *Biological Psychiatry, 58,* 705–712.

Ropcke, B., & Eggers, C. (2005). Early-onset schizophrenia: A 15-year follow-up. *European Child & Adolescent Psychiatry, 14,* 341–350.

Ross, R. G., Schaeffer, J., Compagnon, N., Heinlein, S., Beresford, C., & Farley, G. (2003). Creating school age versions of semistructured interviews for the prodrome to schizophrenia: Lessons from case reviews. *Schizophrenia Bulletin, 29,* 729–735.

Rund, B. R., Moe, L., Sollien, T., Fjell, A., Borchgrevink, T., Hallert, M., et al. (1994). The Psychosis Project: Outcome and cost-effectiveness of a psychoeducational treatment programme for schizophrenic adolescents. *Acta Psychiatrica Scandinavica, 89,* 211–218.

Russell, A. T. (1994). The clinical presentation of childhood-onset schizophrenia. *Schizophrenia Bulletin, 20,* 631–646.

Russell, A. T., Bott, L., & Sammons, C. (1989). The phenomenology of schizophrenia occurring in childhood. *Journal of the American Academy of Child & Adolescent Psychiatry, 28,* 399–407.

Ryan, N. D., Puig-Antich, J., Ambrosini, P., Rabinovich, H., Robinson, D., Nelson, B., et al. (1987). The clinical picture of major depression in children and adolescents. *Archives of General Psychiatry, 44,* 854–861.

Schaeffer, J. L., & Ross, R. G. (2002). Childhood-onset schizophrenia: Premorbid and prodromal diagnostic and treatment histories. *Journal of the American Academy of Child & Adolescent Psychiatry, 41,* 538–545.

Schreier, H. A. (1999). Hallucinations in nonpsychotic children: More common than we think? *Journal of the American Academy of Child & Adolescent Psychiatry, 38,* 623–625.

Schwartz, R. C., Reynolds, C. A., Austin, J. F., & Petersen, S. (2003). Homicidality in schizophrenia: A replication study. *American Journal of Orthopsychiatry, 73,* 74–77.

Scott, J. E., & Dixon, L. B. (1995). Psychological interventions for schizophrenia. *Schizophrenia Bulletin, 21,* 621–630.

Shaffer, D., Fisher, P., Lucas, C. P., Dulcan, M. K., & Schwab-Stone, M. E. (2000). NIMH Diagnostic Interview Schedule for Children-Version IV (NIMH DISC-IV): Description, differences from previous versions, and reliability of some common diagnoses. *Journal of the American Academy of Child & Adolescent Psychiatry, 39,* 28–38.

Sikich, L. (2005). Individual psychotherapy and school interventions for psychotic youth. In R. L. Findling & S. C. Schulz (Eds.), *Juvenile-onset schizophrenia: Assessment, neurobiology, and treatment* (pp. 257–287). Baltimore: Johns Hopkins University Press.

Silveira, J. M., & Seeman, M. V. (1995). Shared psychotic disorder: A critical review of the literature. *Canadian Journal of Psychiatry, 4,* 389–395.

Solhkhah, R. (2003). The psychotic child. *Child and Adolescent Psychiatric Clinics of North America, 12,* 693–722.

Sporn, A. L., Addington, A. M., Gogtay, N., Ordonez, A. E., Gornick, M., Clasen, L., et al. (2004). Pervasive developmental disorder and childhood-onset schizophrenia: Comorbid disorder or a phenotypic variant of a very early onset illness? *Biological Psychiatry, 55,* 989–994.

Stayer, C., Sporn, A., Gogtay, N., Tossell, J. W., Lenane, M., Gochman, P., et al. (2005). Multidimensionally impaired: The good news. *Journal of Child and Adolescent Psychopharmacology, 15,* 510–519.

Strandburg, R. J., Marsh, J. T., Brown, W. S., Asarnow, R. F., & Guthrie, D. (1994). Information-processing deficits across childhood- and adult-onset schizophrenia. *Schizophrenia Bulletin, 20,* 685–695.

Strober, M., & Carlson, G. (1982). Bipolar illness in adolescents with major depression: Clinical, genetic, and psychopharmacologic predictors in a three- to four-year prospective follow-up investigation. *Archives of General Psychiatry, 39,* 549–555.

Swofford, C. D., Kasckow, J. W., Scheller-Gilkey, G., & Inderbitzin, L. B. (1996). Substance use: A powerful predictor of relapse in schizophrenia. *Schizophrenia Research, 20,* 145–151.

Thaden, E., Rhinewine, J. P., Lencz, T., Kester, H., Cervellione, K. L., Henderson, I., et al. (2006). Early-onset schizophrenia is associated with impaired adolescent development of attentional capacity using the identical pairs continuous performance test. *Schizophrenia Research, 81,* 157–166.

Thomsen, P. H. (1996). Schizophrenia with childhood and adolescent onset: A nationwide register-based study. *Acta Psychiatrica Scandinavica, 94,* 187–193.

Tolbert, H. A. (1996). Psychoses in children and adolescents: A review. *Journal of Clinical Psychiatry, 57*(Suppl. 3), 4–8; discussion 46–47.

Tossell, J. W., Greenstein, D. K., Davidson, A. L., Job, S. B., Gochman, P., Lenane, M., et al. (2004). Stimulant drug treatment in childhood-onset schizophrenia with comorbid ADHD: An open-label case series. *Journal of Child and Adolescent Psychopharmacology, 14,* 448–454.

Tsuang, M. T., & Faraone, S. V. (1995). The case for heterogeneity in the etiology of schizophrenia. *Schizophrenia Research, 17,* 161–175.

Ulloa, R. E., Birmaher, B., Axelson, D., Williamson, D. E., Brent, D. A., Ryan, N. D., et al. (2000). Psychosis in a pediatric mood and anxiety disorders clinic: Phenomenology and correlates. *Journal of the American Academy of Child & Adolescent Psychiatry, 39,* 337–345.

van der Gaag, R. J., Caplan, R., van Engeland, H., Loman, F., & Buitelaar, J. K. (2005). A controlled study of formal thought disorder in children with autism and multiple complex developmental disorders. *Journal of Child and Adolescent Psychopharmacology, 15,* 465–476.

van Nimwegen, L., de Haan, L., van Beveren, N., van den Brink, W., & Linszen, D. (2005). Adolescence, schizophrenia and drug abuse: A window of vulnerability. *Acta Psychiatrica Scandinavica, 111,* 35–42.

Verdoux, H., Tournier, M., & Cougnard, A. (2005). Impact of substance use on the onset and course of early psychosis. *Schizophrenia Research, 79,* 69–75.

Verdoux, H., & van Os, J. (2002). Psychotic symptoms in non-clinical populations and the continuum of psychosis. *Schizophrenia Research, 54,* 59–65.

Volkmar, F. R. (1996). Childhood and adolescent psychosis: A review of the past 10 years. *Journal of the American Academy of Child & Adolescent Psychiatry, 35,* 843–851.

Walker, E., Kestler, L., Bollini, A., & Hochman, K. M. (2004). Schizophrenia: Etiology and course. *Annual Review of Psychology, 55,* 401–430.

Werry, J. S., McClellan, J. M., Andrews, L. K., & Ham, M. (1994). Clinical features and outcome of child and adolescent schizophrenia. *Schizophrenia Bulletin, 20,* 619–630.

Werry, J. S., McClellan, J. M., & Chard, L. (1991). Childhood and adolescent schizophrenic, bipolar, and schizoaffective disorders: A clinical and outcome study. *Journal of the American Academy of Child & Adolescent Psychiatry, 30,* 457–465.

Wessely, S., Buchanan, A., Reed, A., Cutting, J., Everitt, B., Garety, P., et al. (1993). Acting on delusions I: Prevalence. *British Journal of Psychiatry, 163,* 69–76.

Youngstrom, E. A., Findling, R. L., Calabrese, J. R., Gracious, B. L., Demeter, C., Bedoya, D. D., et al. (2004). Comparing the diagnostic accuracy of six potential screening instruments for bipolar disorder in youths aged 5 to 17 years. *Journal of the American Academy of Child & Adolescent Psychiatry, 43,* 847–858.

Yung, A. R., Yuen, H. P., McGorry, P. D., Phillips, L. J., Kelly, D., Dell'Olio, M., et al. (2005). Mapping the onset of psychosis: The comprehensive assessment of at-risk mental states. *Australian and New Zealand Journal of Psychiatry, 39,* 964–971.

PART III

SPECIAL POPULATIONS AND ISSUES

20

Neglected, Physically Abused, and Sexually Abused Children

Deborah Wise, Christina Wilder, and Alison Brodhagen

Description of the Problem

Interviewing children who have been neglected, physically abused, and/or sexually abused can be complex. Interviews may be undertaken for different and potentially conflicting purposes; definitions of abuse vary by state; and the structure and content of interviews should be modified to address the wide variety of psychological symptoms experienced by children who have been abused. Therefore, prior to initiating interviews about child abuse, clinicians should clarify interview goals, be familiar with legal definitions of child abuse, and be knowledgeable about potential outcomes of child abuse.

Interviewing children about abuse experiences can be undertaken either (a) to evaluate allegations of neglect, physical abuse, and sexual abuse, or a combination of all of these types of abuse, so as to contribute to legal decision making, or (b) to determine psychological adjustment following abuse experiences. Given these potentially divergent purposes, it is essential to clarify the purpose of each interview and the consequent role of the interviewer at the outset of the evaluation process (American Professional Society on the Abuse of Children [APSAC], 1997). Goals of forensic interviews of child abuse include offering an opinion as to whether or not abuse has occurred, determining a child's competency to stand trial, and addressing a child's credibility (Myers, 1998). On the other hand, goals of therapeutic interviews include evaluating a child's level of psychological adjustment, informing treatment planning, and determining the effectiveness of treatments (Friedrich, 2002). Due to the potential ethical conflicts inherent in dual forensic and therapeutic roles, these roles should be kept separate (American Psychological Association [APA], 2002; Myers, 2002).

Child abuse may comprise several distinct incidents and may reflect different types of abuse, including neglect and physical and/or sexual abuse. Moreover, definitions of various types of child abuse vary widely. Child abuse is legally defined in each state, and therefore definitions of child abuse frequently vary between states and across studies of child abuse. Clinicians should become familiar with the legal statutes of the states in which they practice so that they can understand the parameters of child abuse and their roles as mandated reporters. For the purpose of this chapter, child abuse will be defined in a manner consistent with the APSAC (Berliner & Elliot, 2002; Erickson & Egeland, 2002; Hart, Brassard, Binggeli, & Davidson, 2002; Kolko,

2002). Child abuse includes neglect, physical abuse, and sexual abuse.

Child neglect is failure by caregivers to provide needed, age-appropriate care given adequate financial resources (U.S. Department of Health and Human Services, Administration on Children, Youth, and Families, 2003). There are several subtypes of neglect, including physical, emotional, medical, mental health, and educational neglect (Erickson & Egeland, 2002). *Physical neglect* is the failure to protect a child from physical harm or to provide adequate food, shelter, or clothing. *Emotional neglect* is the failure of a caretaker to provide for the basic emotional needs of the child. Although emotional neglect is clearly difficult to substantiate, this type of abuse can be devastating. Emotional neglect is implicated as one of the primary causes of nonorganic failure to thrive, which connotes lack of appropriate growth in infants (Iwaniec, 1997). *Medical neglect* is the failure to meet a child's medical needs, such as withholding immunizations, medications, surgeries, or other medical interventions (Erickson & Egeland, 2002). *Mental health neglect* refers to lack of compliance with mental health interventions. Finally, *educational neglect* includes failure to ensure school attendance.

Child physical abuse includes injury or risk of injury as a result of being hit by a hand or object or being kicked, shaken, thrown, burned, or stabbed by a parent or caretaker (Sedlak & Broadhurst, 1996). Child physical abuse is often the easiest type of maltreatment to identify because it may be evidenced by physical injury.

Child sexual abuse includes sexual activity with a child without the child's consent or when a significant difference in age, size, or developmental stage precludes consent (Berliner & Elliot, 2002). Child sexual abuse includes sexual contact events, such as penetration and fondling the child's or the perpetrator's genitalia, and noncontact events, including exposure or voyeurism.

The prevalence of child abuse is surprisingly high. Based on reports to child protective services (CPS) agencies in the United States during 2001, approximately 903,000 children experienced or were at risk for child abuse and/or neglect (U.S. Department of Health and Human Services, Administration on Children, Youth and Families, 2003). Among these reports of child abuse, 59% of victims suffered neglect (including medical neglect); 19% were physically abused; and 10% were sexually abused. Given the high prevalence

of child abuse, it is likely that at some point in their careers, clinicians will interview a child who has been abused.

Unfortunately, actual rates of abuse may be much higher than statistics reported by the U.S. Department of Health and Human Services because not all suspected cases of abuse are reported to CPS (Finkelhor, Hotaling, Lewis, & Smith, 1990). In the Third National Incidence Study of Child Abuse and Neglect (NIS-3), data on child abuse prevalence was gathered from CPS agencies and from community professionals (Sedlak & Broadhurst, 1996). Based on this survey, an estimated 1,553,800 children in the United States were neglected or abused in 1993. Among these numbers, approximately 338,900 were physically neglected; 212,800 were emotionally neglected; 381,700 were physically abused; and 217,700 were sexually abused. Given the likelihood that the prevalence of child abuse is higher than reports of abuse to CPS workers, teachers, therapists, doctors, and caregivers, skillful interviewing of children with abuse histories is particularly important.

The sequelae of child abuse also highlight the importance of skillful interviews with children who may have been abused. The impact of child abuse can be devastating; according to reports to CPS, in 2001, 1,300 children died from maltreatment, and among these deaths, 26% were due to physical abuse, and 35% were due to neglect (U.S. Department of Health and Human Services, Administration on Children, Youth and Families, 2003). Moreover, child abuse is associated with a wide range of psychological sympotomatology. Neglect has been associated with attachment difficulties, attention problems, aggression, internalizing problems, social skills deficits, language delays, poor grades, and failure to thrive (Erickson & Egeland, 1996, 2002; Iwaniec, 1997; Katz, 1992; Kendall-Tackett & Eckenrode, 1996). Physical abuse is associated with various difficulties, including physical injuries, heightened aggression, oppositional behavior, delinquency, substance abuse, depression, posttraumatic stress disorder (PTSD), academic achievement deficits, and interpersonal difficulties (Boney-McCoy, & Finkelhor, 1995; Eckenrode, Laird, & Doris, 1993; Hotaling, Straus, & Lincoln, 1990; Kaplan, Pelcovitz, Salzinger, Mandel, & Weiner, 1998; Kilpatrick, Saunders, & Smith, 2003; Kolko, Moser, & Weldy, 1990; Pelcovitz, Kaplan, Goldenberg, & Mandel, 1994; Rogosch, Cicchetti,

& Abre, 1995; Sedlack & Broadhurst, 1996; Wolfe, Wekerle, Reitzel-Jaffe, & Lefebvre, 1998).

Child sexual abuse is associated with a wide range of emotional and behavioral problems; however, PTSD and sexual-acting-out behaviors are among the most consistently reported (Kendall-Tackett, Williams, & Finkelhor, 1993; Paolucci, Genuis, & Violato, 2001). Other sequelae of child sexual abuse include depression, anxiety, low self-esteem, running away, eating disorders, substance use, and academic and social problems (Boney-McCoy & Finkelhor, 1995; Hibbard, Ingersoll, & Orr, 1990; Kendall-Tackett et al., 1993; Kilpatrick et al., 2003; Mannarino & Cohen, 1996a, 1996b; McLeer, Deblinger, Atkins, Foa, & Ralphe, 1988; McLeer et al., 1998). Interviewers need to be familiar with the sequelae of child abuse so that they can adapt the structure and content of interviews to meet children's needs.

Although a wide range of emotional, behavioral, and physical symptoms has been observed among groups of children with histories of child abuse, it is important to retain an idiographic approach to interviewing. Many symptoms that are commonly associated with abuse histories can also be observed among nonabused populations (Friedrich et al., 2001; Gordon, Schroeder & Hawk, 1993). For example, although sexual acting out is commonly associated with experiences of sexual abuse (Kendall-Tackett et al., 1993), many sexual-acting-out behaviors are observed among nonabused populations (Friedrich et al., 2001). Moreover, children who have experienced child abuse may also manifest symptoms that are commonly observed among nonabused populations. For example, although a child who has experienced child sexual abuse may have sleep difficulties, this symptom is commonly observed among children who have not been sexually abused (Horn & Dollinger, 1995). To further complicate the issue, many children who have experienced abuse appear to be asymptomatic (Caffaro-Rouget, Lang, & van Santen, 1989; Conte & Scheurman, 1987; Finkelhor & Berliner, 1995; Kendall-Tackett et al., 1993; Mannarino & Cohen, 1986). Clearly, an idiographic approach is essential for gathering reliable and valid information.

In summary, interviews of children about abuse can be complex. To competently proceed with such interviews, clinicians should clearly define the goals of the interview and their roles with respect to the interview and be knowledgeable about definitions of child abuse as defined by state statutes, laws on child abuse reporting, common sequelae of child abuse, and idiographic aspects of each child's presentation.

INTERVIEWING STRATEGIES

Children are one of the most important sources of information about abuse history and impact (Lamb, 1994). They are highly reliable reporters of abuse. In fact, only between 4.7% and 7.6% of allegations of child abuse are estimated to be false (Everson & Boat, 1989). Given the importance of interviewing children, clinicians should carefully determine the format of interviews and endeavor to master strategies to conduct abuse-related interviews.

Interview Formats

Prior to conducting abuse-related interviews, clinicians must determine whether to use structured or unstructured interview formats. Structured interview formats consist of lists of questions from which clinicians do not deviate unless necessary to clarify a response. With unstructured interview formats, clinicians themselves determine the content and order of questions.

Structured Interview Formats

The primary advantage of structured over unstructured interview formats is that clinicians are less likely to introduce biases or make suggestive comments to children because the same questions are asked of every child (Orbach et al., 2000). In addition, clinicians are unlikely to neglect important domains of functioning because relevant content is likely to be included in interview schedules. Therefore, structured interviews can be especially helpful for use by clinicians who do not have a lot of experience in conducting interviews with abused children. Another advantage of structured interviews is that they may provide more reliable diagnostic information than do unstructured interviews (Miller, Dasher, Collins, Griffiths, & Brown, 2001). For example, clinicians are more likely to diagnose PTSD when using structured versus unstructured interview formats

(Davidson & Smith, 1990; Zimmerman & Mattia, 1999). Given these advantages, clinicians should consider employing structured interview formats when assessing abuse and abuse-related symptomatology.

There are several structured interview protocols available to clinicians. The National Institute of Child Health and Human Development (NICHD) Investigative Protocol (Orbach et al., 2000) is a structured interview created to elicit information about abuse from children. Despite the fact that the beginning of the NICHD protocol includes open-ended questions to encourage spontaneous recall of abuse experiences, this portion of the interview is followed by structured interview questions to elicit information missing from children's reports. Several other structured interviews, such as the Brief Assessment of Traumatic Events (BATE) (Lipovsky & Hanson, 1992) and the Abuse Dimensions Inventory (ADI) (Chaffin, Wherry, Newlin, Crutchfield, & Dykman, 1997), also provide interview probes for clinicians who are assessing physical and sexual abuse among children.

Unstructured Interview Formats

Although a number of structured interviews are available, many clinicians take an unstructured approach to interviewing abused children. The principle advantages of unstructured interviews are that clinicians can tailor questions to a child's specific circumstances and adjust questions according to how a child responds to questions. This allows abused children to control the pace of their discussions of trauma-specific information (Pearlman & McCann, 1994). Nonetheless, because clinicians must decide which questions to ask and in what order to ask them, unstructured interview formats may require more skill and training than structured interview formats to employ effectively.

When conducting unstructured interviews, clinicians should ask open-ended questions about the following topics: number of abusive episodes; where abuse occurred; who perpetrated abuse; where the child's primary caregiver or parent (if different from the perpetrator) was when the abuse occurred; antecedents and consequences of abuse, including threats made by the perpetrator; when and with whom the child has discussed abuse; and how the child feels about abuse experiences (Mannarino & Cohen, 2003). Specific questions that should be asked during unstructured interviews, however, will vary depending on the nature of each case. Likewise, the order of questions should depend on children's responses to questions.

Interviewing Strategies

Regardless of choice of interview format, there are several strategies that can facilitate successful interviewing of children who may have been abused. These strategies include preparation, clarification of the parameters of interviews, use of strategies to facilitate disclosures, and careful documentation of information.

Preparing for Interviews

Preparation may increase the likelihood of successful interviews. There are a number of steps that clinicians can take to prepare for interviews, including reviewing case material, considering who will be present during interviews, determining the location of interviews, and estimating the number of sessions for interviews.

The first step in preparing for interviews is to review information about the child and the alleged abuse. Although some argue that reviewing case information should be avoided because it could bias clinicians (Cantlon, Payne, & Erbaugh, 1996), most agree that reviewing case information can be valuable because this enables clinicians prior to interviews to prepare questions specific to each child and alleged abuse incident (Bourg et al., 1999). It is important to review information about the child (e.g., age, gender) and the child's home environment (e.g., names and relationships of people who live in the home), as well as previous abuse or neglect interviews, police and social service reports, psychological evaluations, medical exams, mental health treatment records, school records, and evaluations and records of family members that are relevant to the present evaluation (Bourg et al., 1999; Melton, Petrila, Poythress, & Slobogin, 1997; Morgan, 1995, Righthand, Kerr, & Drach, 2003). In particular, clinicians should attend to how abuse was initially discovered, whether or not the perpetrator of abuse has been identified and prosecuted, whether or not the child has discussed abuse with others, how others have reacted to learning about abuse allegations, and what words the child has used to describe abuse (Bourg et al., 1999; Morgan, 1995). Although information from the child's records can be helpful, it should be noted that the presence or absence of information on abuse in records does not constitute definitive evidence that abuse has or has not occurred (Lamb, 1994).

The second step in preparing for interviews is to determine the interview location. Interviews should not occur in settings where abuse may have taken place, such as a child's home, as this could reduce the likelihood of disclosure (Bourg et al., 1999). Instead, interviews should take place in settings that are comfortable for children and conducive to interviews. Interview rooms should have child-sized furniture; outside noise should be minimal; video- and audio-recording equipment should be placed in unobtrusive locations; and if interview aids or play materials are to be used, they should be kept out of sight until the time comes to use them, so as to avoid distracting children from the interview (Morgan, 1995).

The third step in preparing for an interview is to estimate the number of interviews that will be needed, and schedule appointments. There are several factors that influence the number of interviews that will have to be conducted with children, including the goal of the interview (i.e., to substantiate an allegation versus to develop a treatment plan), the age of the child, the willingness of the child to discuss abuse and abuse-related symptoms, and the child's safety (Bourg et al., 1999). When determining the number of interviews to schedule, clinicians should be aware that too many interviews might unduly influence children's responses (American Academy of Child and Adolescent Psychiatry [AACAP], 1990). On the other hand, two or more sessions are often necessary for full disclosures of abuse (APSAC, 1990; Sorenson & Snow, 1991). When setting up initial interviews, clinicians may want to instruct adults accompanying children to interviews to refrain from describing the nature of interviews in detail and instead to encourage children to talk openly and freely with clinicians (Bourg et al., 1999; Walker, 1988).

The final step in preparing for interviews with allegedly abused children is to consider who may be present. The alleged perpetrator of abuse should not be present during such interviews (Mannarino & Cohen, 2003). It may be that other people, such as police officers or social workers, want to be present. Given that children commonly request that nonabusive parents or caretakers be present during interviews, clinicians should recognize the drawbacks associated with such arrangements. Children may be reluctant to disclose or to discuss abuse in front of parents or caretakers or may feel compelled to say what they believe parents or caretakers want to hear (Mannarino & Cohen, 2003; Walker 1988). Another disadvantage to allowing parents to be present during interviews is that they may try to answer questions on behalf of their children (Aldridge & Wood, 1998; Bourg et al., 1999). Moreover, the presence of others in the room during interviews may increase the number of suggestive statements or questions made by clinicians (Santilla, Korkman, & Sandnabba, 2004). Given these drawbacks, it is recommended that clinicians make every effort to interview children alone. If nonabusive parents or caretakers must be present during interviews, however, they should be instructed to sit to the side, refrain from answering questions posed by the clinician to the child, and avoid giving nonverbal cues to the child (Bourg et al., 1999; Jones & McQuiston, 1988).

Clarifying Interview Parameters

After thorough preparation for the interview, clinicians are ready to initiate the interview process. A number of points should be emphasized at the beginning of the interview. First, clinicians should define their role to children as people who talk with and listen to children (Bourg et al., 1999). Clinicians may also want to ask about children's understanding of the clinician's role so as to correct misconceptions at the onset of the interview. Second, clinicians should inform children of the general purpose of the interview, the duration of the interview, and how information gathered during the interview will be used. When clarifying the purpose of the interview, clinicians may want to emphasize that children are not "in trouble." Third, clinicians should provide information about confidentiality and limits of confidentiality in a developmentally appropriate manner (APA Committee on Professional Practice and Standards, 1998). Although clinicians want to encourage children to feel comfortable discussing abuse, they should avoid promising to keep information secret (Bourg et al., 1999; Jones & McQuiston, 1988).

Furthermore, if clinicians plan to audiotape, videotape, or have someone observe the interview, children must be informed of the intended practice. Fourth, clinicians should outline expectations of children during the interview. For instance, clinicians should emphasize the importance of telling the truth and saying "I don't know," rather than guessing. In addition, clinicians should explain to children that asking questions more than once does not mean they have answered questions incorrectly. Moreover, clinicians should encourage children to correct them if they incorrectly paraphrase responses or make other mistakes (Poole & Lamb, 1998). By outlining these expectations to children, clinicians can reduce suggestibility (Bourg et al., 1999). Finally, and perhaps most important, clinicians should emphasize children's control over the interview process. Clinicians should explain to children that they may take breaks, leave the room, or terminate interviews when desired.

Facilitating Accurate Reports

In addition to preparing for and clarifying the parameters of interviews, several strategies may be employed to facilitate accurate reports from children. Clinicians should carefully attend to rapport building, pacing, and questioning style and consider the use of interview aids, as these strategies might impact the accuracy and level of detail of abuse disclosures.

Rapport Building. It is crucial that clinicians take time to build rapport and trust with children prior to interviews (Daly, 1991). Rapport can increase the likelihood of obtaining accurate information from children (Bourg et al., 1999). In many cases, discussing the clinician's role, purpose of the interview, and limits of confidentiality will aid in building rapport with children (Jones & McQuiston, 1988). In addition, clinicians should offer ample opportunities for children to ask questions about the interview process (Morgan, 1995). If appropriate, clinicians may want to acknowledge that such interviews may be frightening for children. Using such strategies, clinicians can demonstrate honesty, openness, and empathy. Another simple way to establish rapport is to inquire about neutral topics, such as favorite hobbies, and to convey interest in children's answers (Aldridge & Wood, 1998; Bourg et al., 1999; Jones & McQuiston, 1988).

When interviewing young children, a "free-play period" can be effective for building rapport and observing children's developmental levels (Aldridge & Wood, 1998; Morgan, 1995). Of course, clinical judgment should be used to ensure that rapport-building activities, such as discussing neutral topics or engaging children in play, are not so lengthy that children become bored or suspicious of clinicians (Jones & McQuiston, 1988; Morgan, 1995). Ideally, rapport-building activities provide a natural segue into interviews.

Pacing. Clinicians should allow ample time for interviews so that children do not feel rushed to discuss abuse. Children should dictate the pace of questions and should be given ample time to respond to questions (Bourg et al., 1999). Clinicians can best facilitate disclosures by being mindful of the difficulties in discussing abuse experiences and remaining sensitive to children's needs. If children become overly distressed, clinicians may consider delaying or terminating interviews (Briere, 1997).

Questioning Style. The manner in which clinicians ask questions and respond to answers can impact the quality of interviews of abuse. Clinicians should remain flexible and use different types of questions and words to elicit information (Bourg et al., 1999). Once children begin to discuss abuse, clinicians should avoid interrupting, correcting, or challenging their reports. Instead, clinicians can clarify information at later points in interviews. When children discuss abuse experiences, it is crucial that clinicians refrain from making judgmental comments (e.g., "Sometimes people do bad things to children"), because this is likely to increase children's discomfort and damage rapport (Jones & McQuiston, 1988, Mannarino & Cohen, 2003). Moreover, clinicians should avoid touching children or engaging in prolonged direct eye-to-eye contact with them, as these behaviors may be viewed as intrusive (Jones & McQuiston, 1988).

Clinicians must also be careful to avoid making biased or suggestive comments to children during interviews. Leading and coercive questions, such as "Your father touched your private parts, didn't he?" should be avoided, because this can increase suggestibility and decrease the accuracy of children's reports (APSAC, 1990; Morgan, 1995). For this reason, clinicians should endeavor to pose as many open-ended questions as possible. Open-ended questions and prompts give little direction as to the content of responses and therefore minimize bias and suggestibility (Bourg et al., 1999). If children do not offer important information about abuse spontaneously, clinicians may eventually have to use direct, closed, or multiple-choice questions that limit the content of their answers. Clinicians should, however, use direct, closed, and multiple-choice questions sparingly and only when necessary, as these types of questions may increase suggestibility and inaccuracy of reports. Similarly, clinicians should avoid repeating open-ended, direct, closed, or multiple-choice questions, because repeating questions can increase suggestibility.

Clinicians can increase the likelihood that children can accurately respond to questions by wording questions in such a way that children can understand. Clinicians should use words that match children's vocabularies and language abilities so that they can accurately respond to questions (Jones & McQuiston, 1988; Morgan, 1995; Saywitz, 1995). Other strategies to increase children's comprehension of questions include using simple, short questions composed of one- or two-syllable words; using proper names instead of pronouns; mentioning the names of items or places, instead of referents such as "this," "that," or "here"; limiting "why" questions; using active rather than passive voice; avoiding questions that contain double positives or negatives; refraining from asking questions that require children to assume the perspectives of others; and making clear transitions when changing to a new line of questioning (Aldridge & Wood, 1998; Bourg et al., 1999; Hewitt, 1999; Jones & McQuiston, 1988; Saywitz, 1995).

Reinforcement. One strategy to facilitate accurate reports from children is to regularly praise children for their efforts in discussing difficult information (Sattler, 2002). For example, clinicians may state, "It can be hard to talk about these things, but you are doing fine." Clinicians should, however, be careful not to praise the content of children's statements, as this practice could increase suggestibility.

Interview Aids. Clinicians frequently use interview aids, such as anatomically correct dolls or drawing materials, to elicit information from children about abuse. Interview aids are most commonly used with children who are young or nonverbal or have limited language abilities, developmental disorders, or emotional problems, such as anxiety (Jones & McQuiston, 1988). Children can use interview aids to circumvent language barriers, so as to demonstrate their knowledge of body parts, show abuse experiences, cue recall of abuse experiences, spontaneously demonstrate sexual knowledge, or become comfortable discussing sexual knowledge and experiences (APSAC, 1995; Faller, 1996a; Morgan, 1995).

Although there are advantages to using interview aids, there is a great deal of controversy on their use. One of the primary concerns about the use of anatomically correct dolls is that the presence of genitalia is suggestive and can lead to false reports of abuse among children. Results of a study (Goodman & Aman, 1990), however, indicate that anatomically correct dolls per se do not foster false reports of abuse among children. It may be that clinicians are more likely to make leading or suggestive statements to children when using anatomically correct dolls than when not using such interview aids (Santilla et al., 2004). To reduce the likelihood of asking leading or suggestive questions, clinicians should receive special training in the use of interview aids (Morgan, 1995). In addition, interview aids should not be used as the initial or sole means of inquiry (APSAC, 1995; Jones & McQuiston, 1988). Instead, clinicians should give children opportunities to describe abuse experiences and address questions prior to introducing interview aids. Furthermore, clinicians should interpret sexualized play with interview aids cautiously and in combination with other information gathered within the context of the interview (Mordock, 2001).

Documentation

Based upon guidelines on interviewing children who have been abused (AACAP, 1990; APSAC, 1990), clinicians must employ some method of documenting information during interviews. Commonly used methods of documenting information include taking notes, videotaping, audiotaping, having a professional record information from behind a one-way mirror, and having a professional take notes in the interview room (Conte, Sorenson, Fogarty, &

Dalla Rosa, 1991). According to the APSAC (1990) guidelines, clinicians should at least take written notes and may want to audiotape or videotape interviews. In the AACAP (1990), guidelines, an emphasis is placed on videotaping interviews.

There are both advantages and disadvantages to videotaping. Videotaping may reduce the need for multiple interviews or interviewers, provide complete documentation of interviews if children's statements or interviewers' techniques are challenged in court, and substitute for children's testimony in court (AACAP, 1990; Gordon, Schroeder, Ornstein, & Baker-Ward, 1995). Disadvantages or risks associated with the use of video documentation are that video cameras may negatively impact children's spontaneity or disclosures during interviews, and videotapes may be shown out of context or without concern for children's best interests (AACAP, 1990; Jones & McQuiston, 1988; Myers, 1992). Clinicians should consider both advantages and disadvantages when deciding whether or not to videotape interviews.

Several rules should be followed regardless of which documentation method is selected. First, clinicians should be aware of state laws with regard to documentation (Bourg et al., 1999). Second, clinicians should always inform children and their legal guardians that interviews will be documented (AACAP, 1990; APSAC, 1990). Third, clinicians should endeavor to document both their questions and children's responses, so it is clear that disclosures do not stem from leading questions. Fourth, clinicians should document direct observations of children's behaviors, because these are important facets of such interviews (Jones & McQuiston, 1988). Specifically, clinicians should document overt behavior changes and mood shifts in response to interview questions, such as instances when children cry when asked directly about abuse. Clinicians should attend to how children interact with them and also to children's levels of attention, quality of speech, affect, and skills used to cope with distress. Clearly, careful documentation of interviews of abuse is essential.

In summary, to increase the likelihood of conducting valid interviews of children who may have been abused, clinicians should endeavor to master a broad array of strategies. Given the complexity of developing such interview skills, well-trained and experienced interviewers are best able to conduct interviews of children's abuse experiences or abuse-related symptoms.

INTERVIEWING OBSTACLES AND SOLUTIONS

A number of obstacles may arise during the course of interviewing children about abuse and abuse-related symptomatology. Emotional, linguistic, and cognitive factors may present obstacles to interviewing strategies. Clinicians who are aware of challenges that could hinder the interview process are better able to address and to resolve these issues when they arise.

Emotional Barriers to Abuse Disclosures

One of the most common obstacles to clinicians is that children who have experienced child abuse may not admit to the experiences. Among 116 cases of confirmed child sexual abuse, 79% of children initially denied or were tentative about disclosing abuse (Sorenson & Snow, 1991). This tendency is particularly problematic given that often little or no physical evidence of sexual abuse is available and therefore confirmation of sexual abuse is often based upon children's disclosures during interviews (Bussey & Grimbeek, 1995; Sauzier, 1989). Nonetheless, children often deny abuse experiences due to feelings of fear, embarrassment, and guilt.

Anxiety about the impact of disclosures may hinder the interview process. Children who have been threatened with physical harm to themselves, family members, or pets are likely to deny abuse experiences (Steward, Bussey, Goodman, & Saywitz, 1993). Similarly, children who fear that disclosures will yield negative consequences, such as getting into trouble, being removed from home, losing love from family members, or having a caregiver sent to jail, are often hesitant to disclose abuse experiences. Finally, children may be afraid of not being listened to or believed by clinicians, particularly if previous disclosures were subject to doubt by family members (Bourg et al., 1999).

There is a great deal of societal stigma associated with sexual acts and poor living conditions. Therefore, children may be embarrassed to talk about these issues with clinicians (Bourg et al., 1999). In addition, children may be concerned about how others, particularly peers, might react to such information; children may be embarrassed and worried about being labeled, called names, or ridiculed (Bourg et al., 1999; Morgan, 1995).

Guilt may impede children's willingness to disclose abuse. Many children attribute the cause of their victimization to internal rather than external events (Mannarino & Cohen, 1996a). Young children are particularly prone to thinking that they caused their abuse experiences (Goodman-Brown, Edelstein, Goodman, Jones, & Gordon, 2003). Older children may also feel guilty about abuse experiences. For example, sexually abused adolescents often attribute sexual abuse experiences to their own sexual development or curiosity (Bourg et al., 1999; Celano, 1992).

Clinicians who are aware of potential emotional barriers to disclosures are better able to take steps to prevent these barriers and thereby facilitate open discussions of abuse experiences. Clinicians can facilitate open communications by children through using various strategies to facilitate disclosures, such as spending adequate time building rapport, clarifying their roles in the interview processes, discussing confidentiality policies, establishing rules for interviews, and describing potential outcomes of interviews.

In the event that children remain reluctant to discuss abuse experiences despite having implemented these strategies, clinicians should develop hypotheses about the roots of children's reluctance so as to generate appropriate solutions. In many cases, directly acknowledging children's difficulty with discussing abuse-related memories may help. For example, if clinicians suspect that children feel guilty about their abuse, they may share this hypothesis by explaining, "Sometimes children don't want to talk about things that have happened to them because they think they made these things happen. Have you ever felt that way?" When sharing hypotheses about reluctance to discuss abuse experiences, clinicians should remain flexible and empathetic toward children (U.S. Department of Justice, Office of Juvenile Justice and Delinquency Prevention, 2002). Children should never feel rushed or forced to disclose information about abuse. If this is the case, interviews should be rescheduled to accommodate children's needs. Finally, negative reactions from interviewers may heighten children's emotional discomfort and thereby fuel their reluctance to discuss the abuse experiences (Mannarino & Cohen, 2003). Therefore, clinicians should display a neutral affect and avoid negative reactions (e.g., disgust) to children's descriptions of abuse.

Linguistic Barriers to Abuse Disclosures

Limited language development may be an obstacle to obtaining valid information about abuse. Language ability and vocabulary can affect the quantity and the quality of information obtained during interviews in several ways. First, children may lack the words necessary to adequately describe abuse (Faller, 1996b). Second, children may be unable to put words together in a cohesive manner to describe abuse experiences. Finally, children may misunderstand questions posed by clinicians. Even adolescents may struggle to comprehend some of the questions asked during interviews. Therefore, clinicians should always assess for language and vocabulary ability during interviews, regardless of children's ages.

A number of techniques can be used to assess language abilities among children. One of the simplest and most informative techniques of assessing language ability is to listen carefully to children's speech during the initial, rapport-building phase of interviews. For example, clinicians can learn a lot about children's vocabularies by asking them to describe favorite activities and listening to responses to general, open-ended questions. Clinicians should pay particular attention to the type and variety of words spoken by children, as well as length of sentences (Hewitt, 1999). Another method of assessing children's understanding of terms prior to interviews is to ask directly about the meaning of terms. For example, clinicians could ask, "What does 'touch' mean?" In the case of sexual abuse evaluations, it can be especially important to have children define terms, because they may use idiosyncratic names for private parts or sexual behaviors (Bourg et al., 1999; Steward et al., 1993). In addition to attending to verbal responses, clinicians should also watch for nonverbal cues indicative of confusion, such as gaze aversion (Morgan, 1995). If children are unable to respond to straightforward, neutral questions, clinicians should consider terminating interviews and instead rely on other methods of data gathering, such as interviewing collateral sources (Hewitt, 1999).

Clinicians should adjust questioning strategies based upon children's language abilities. As mentioned, clinicians should ask short, simple questions composed of one- and two-syllable words (Bourg et al., 1999). In addition, whenever possible, clinicians should frame questions using children's own words or phrases (Jones & McQuiston, 1988; Morgan, 1995).

Clinicians should also carefully attend to children's responses to questions and to follow up as necessary. When children cannot comprehend questions, they often use compensatory strategies, such as responding as if a different question had been asked, ignoring part of a question, or giving stereotypical responses (Aldridge & Wood, 1998). For example, if asked, "When and with whom do you go to bed?" a child who does not understand the question may answer part of this question with a response such as "With my teddy bear" or "In my room." Similarly, children may respond, "I don't know" when presented with a question that they do not understand. Whenever children give inconsistent, vague, out-of-context, or difficult-to-understand responses, clinicians should ask questions again in a different way or with different wording (Bourg et al., 1999; U.S. Department of Justice, Office of Juvenile Justice and Delinquency Prevention, 2002). Clinicians also may use nonverbal techniques, such as having children draw pictures or point to body parts, to clarify responses.

Cognitive Barriers to Abuse Disclosures

Clinicians should be aware of cognitive impediments to gathering aggregate and authentic accounts from children during interviews. Children's inability to remember aspects of abuse experiences, difficulty with attention, susceptibility to suggestion, and propensity to fantasize, lie, or be coached may serve as barriers to obtaining valid accounts of abuse.

Memory Deficits

There are a number of reasons that children may have difficulty remembering aspects of abuse experiences. Children may not encode experiences, such as abuse, that they cannot understand (Faller, 1996b). Similarly, children may not encode details about abuse because they do not recognize these details as important. Moreover, children may struggle to recall information that has been encoded nonverbally when it is prompted verbally in interviews (Bourg et al., 1999). Moreover, due to their stages of development, children may not have acquired effective memory-retrieval strategies (Bourg et al., 1999). Children may also have trouble recalling experiences that happened

months or years ago due to memory deterioration over time (Faller, 1996b). Despite these potential obstacles to recall, even young children can remember past events, and children 10 years old and older can typically remember events as well as adults can (Hewitt, 1999).

Several interviewing strategies can be used by clinicians to facilitate children's recall of abuse experiences. Children recall more information about abuse experiences when asked open-ended questions (Sternberg et al., 1997). After providing opportunities for children to describe abuse experiences, clinicians can follow up with more focused, nonleading questions that include words already used by children (Aldridge & Wood, 1998; Morgan, 1995). Nonetheless, clinicians may have to employ more focused questions with preschool children (Hewitt, 1999). Another strategy to improve children's recall is to pose questions that reference the context of abuse experiences (Bourg et al., 1999; Steward et al., 1993). Children frequently remember abuse experiences as deviations from routine activities (Mordock, 2001). Therefore, questions such as "What happened after you heard the bedtime story?" may prompt recall. Asking children to describe details of rooms or objects present during abuse experiences may also aid with recall (Daly, 1991). Alternatively, providing cards to cue children to report information on who, where, when, what, and how may also aid with recall (Hewitt, 1999). The use of nonverbal props, such as dolls or drawing materials, may also assist with recall of abuse experiences (Aldridge & Wood, 1998; Bourg et al., 1999). Finally, multiple interviews may aid clinicians in gathering complete accounts of abuse from children (Hewitt, 1999).

Attention Deficits

Children vary in terms of attention and concentration skills. If children struggle to pay attention during interviews, they may have difficulty accurately responding to questions. Therefore, clinicians should ensure that children pay attention to questions by repeating them or gently prompting children to make eye contact and listen carefully (Hewitt, 1999). Clinicians may also want to allow additional time for breaks from the interview. Clinicians might also consider alternating between asking questions and engaging children in activities, such as drawing (Morgan,

1995). In certain cases, clinicians should schedule interviews over the course of several days. If children are obviously disinterested, unwilling, or unable to stay focused during interviews, clinicians should not try to force them to answer questions, because this increases the risk of obtaining invalid information (Hewitt, 1999).

Suggestibility

Although children are credible sources of information, there is some evidence that children's recounting of events may be vulnerable to suggested information (Ceci & Bruck, 1995; Everson & Boat, 1989; Reed, 1996). Preschool children are more vulnerable to suggestion than school-age children or adults (Ceci & Bruck, 1995).

Under certain conditions, children may be particularly vulnerable to suggestibility. Leading questions such as "Did your dad touch you in a bad way?" can elicit false positives from children who feel compelled to answer affirmatively to please clinicians (Mannarino & Cohen, 2003). Similarly, when clinicians interject information into questions, they may color children's memories of abuse experiences (Faller, 1996a). For example, if a child who indicated that he was hit with a broom is asked, "Tell me about when you were hit with the baseball bat," this child might change his account of the abuse to match the clinician's suggestion. Furthermore, clinicians can affect accounts of abuse by selectively praising or reinforcing children. Finally, children may be more susceptible to suggestibility when intimidated by interviewers (Reed, 1996). Overall, clinicians are more prone to using leading techniques at the end of interviews, when employing anatomically correct dolls, and during follow-up or repeat interviews (Bourg et al., 1999; Hewitt, 1999; Santilla et al., 2004).

To reduce the chance of reports colored by processes of suggestibility, child abuse assessments should be conducted in settings that are comfortable for children (Bourg et al., 1999). In addition, assessments should be conducted by interviewers who are friendly and encourage children to tell the truth and to let them know when they are confused, do not know the answers to questions, disagree with the interviewers, or do not want to answer questions (Ceci & Bruck, 1995; Hewitt, 1999; Reed, 1996). It may be helpful to have children practice such responses while discussing non-abuse-related information.

Moreover, interviewers should avoid leading and suggestive questions (Faller, 1996a). Instead, the interviewer should ask open questions that are sensitive to the cognitive and linguistic developmental level of the child. In addition, clinicians should praise children's efforts rather than specific statements (Mannarino & Cohen, 2003; Melton et al., 1997). Documenting interviews with audio- or videotape will diminish the number of interviews to which a child is exposed and may allow the interviewer to review the interview to assess for the presence of conditions that may heighten suggestibility (Gordon et al., 1995).

False Allegations and Fantasies

Despite the fact that false allegations of abuse are rare, it is possible that children could be coached or influenced by others about abuse-related information (Bourg et al., 1999; Faller, 1996a; Mannarino & Cohen, 2003). Likewise, children may have personal motives to make false reports, such as a dislike of perpetrators (Bourg et al., 1999; Faller, 1996a). Moreover, young children may have difficulty differentiating between fact and fantasy (Faller, 1996a).

To promote truthful reports by children, during the initial phase of interviews, clinicians should emphasize the importance of telling the truth (Aldridge & Wood, 1998). Clinicians should also assess whether children can differentiate between truth and lies. Typically, children do not fully understand the concept of lies until the age of 4 (Steward et al., 1993). In addition, clinicians should listen to the quality and consistency of accounts of abuse. Children who have not actually experienced abuse, including those who are lying, have been coached, or are fantasizing, are likely to have difficulty providing vivid details and maintaining accounts of abuse (Faller, 1988; Jones & McGraw, 1987; Risin & McNamara, 1989). Inconsistencies in stories are common among younger children, however, and therefore should not necessarily call into question their credibility (Bourg et al., 1999; Mannarino & Cohen, 2003; Risin & McNamara, 1989). Nonetheless, clinicians should follow up on inconsistencies, particularly if they are numerous or pertaining to significant elements of the abuse. Likewise, clinicians should address instances in which children use vocabulary to describe abuse that is inconsistent with their developmental levels (Jones & McGraw, 1987;

Mannarino & Cohen, 2003). To assess whether children have been coached, clinicians could also ask what children have been told of the interview beforehand, including possible outcomes. Clinicians could also ask about sources of information: "Did you see your brother get hit, or did someone tell you about it?" (Bourg et al., 1999). Depending on the response, clinicians may want to further question those (children or adults) who did the coaching concerning their motives for alleging abuse (Mannarino & Cohen, 2003). However, clinicians should refrain from confronting children or adults about the validity of abuse allegations until interviews have been completed, and, even then, clinicians should proceed with caution, because this could be harmful to children (Bourg et al., 1999).

Despite potential emotional, linguistic, and cognitive factors that may hinder the interviewer's ability to obtain accurate accounts of abuse and symptomatology, several strategies may be used to resolve these barriers when they arise. The complexity of mastering such strategies highlights the importance of careful training of interviewers.

INTERVIEWING PARENTS AND TEACHERS

Clinicians should gather information on abuse experiences from multiple informants (AACAP, 1990; APASC, 1997; APA Committee on Professional Practice and Standards, 1998). Parents and teachers are among the most valuable sources of information on abuse and associated symptomatology. Information from various sources should be considered simultaneously.

Primary Caregivers

Parents or primary caregivers are important sources of information and potential partners during subsequent treatment (Sattler, 2002). Therefore, clinicians should strive to establish collaborative working relationships with parents. Clinicians should refrain from asking questions in such a way that implies blame or criticism of parents. Instead, clinicians should empathize with parental concerns and be sensitive to their needs.

Parents may differ from one another in their views on the abuse, particularly if one was involved in the abuse perpetration. For this reason, parents should be questioned separately for at least a portion of the interview.

There might also be disparities between parent and child reports of abuse and abuse-related symptomatology. As previously mentioned, children may not provide accurate reports of abuse because they are afraid, embarrassed, or unable to describe experiences due to vocabulary deficits. Similarly, parents may also be reluctant or unable to describe details of abuse. For instance, parents who played a role in abuse perpetration may be reluctant to discuss abuse due to their fear of the consequences. Parents may also lack information about their children's experiences or internal states. As a result of these factors, it is not uncommon for disparities to be found between parent and child reports of abuse (e.g., Cohen & Mannarino, 1988; Kiser, Heston, Millsap, & Pruitt, 1991; Mannarino, Cohen, Smith, & Moore-Motily, 1991; Tong, Oates, & McDowell, 1987; Wolfe, Gentile, & Wolfe, 1989). Although clinicians should explore such disparities during interviews, they should refrain from viewing disparities as conclusive evidence that the abuse did not occur.

Unstructured Interview Methods

Topics routinely addressed with parents in clinical interviews should also be addressed in cases of alleged abuse. Topics that should be addressed include the child's developmental history (e.g., pre- and postnatal care, birth information, achievement of milestones), medical history (e.g., illnesses, surgeries, hospitalizations, dates of recent examinations, names of physicians), educational history (e.g., names of schools and teachers, grades, suspensions and expulsions, learning disabilities), social history (e.g., number of friends, frequency of contact with friends), recent family stressors or changes, and perceptions of the child's strengths (Bourg et al., 1999; Sattler, 2002). In addition, parents should be asked about behavioral or emotional problems exhibited by their children, including onsets, frequencies, severities, antecedents, and consequences. Clinicians should also obtain a complete family history (e.g., names and ages of siblings, dates of divorces or separations, names of current and past caregivers, names of parents' current and past partners, and names of others who have lived in the home). Furthermore, clinicians should inquire about parents' own medical or mental health problems, alcohol or substance use problems, abuse or neglect histories, legal or financial problems, communication and decision-making processes, approaches to discipline, coping strategies, and social support network (Bourg et al., 1999; Melton et al., 1997; Sattler, 2002). Nonetheless, clinicians should recognize that some questions, such as those about substance use, might be difficult for parents to answer (Dryer, 1999).

In addition to questions that are typical of clinical interviews, clinicians should ask about topics that are specific to allegations of abuse. Parents should be asked to describe children's daily routines, with particular attention to sleep and bath routines (Bourg et al., 1999). In addition, because children often know abuse perpetrators, it is vital to inquire about names, nicknames, and relationships of people with whom the child has had contact. Some topics addressed in interviews will depend on the nature of the abuse allegations. For example, in cases of allegations of sexual abuse, clinicians should ask about children's exposure to pornography, adult television programming, parental sexual activity, and nudity. Clinicians should also ask about previous disclosures and parental reactions to those disclosures.

In cases of allegations of physical abuse, clinicians should explore parental views and use of corporal punishment and details of children's medical histories. Clinicians should also inquire about when parents first noticed children's illnesses or injuries, what they observed, and what they believed caused these illnesses or injuries (Parrish, n.d.).

In cases of allegations of neglect, clinicians should ask about children's eating habits (including daily number and content of meals and who purchases food) and living conditions (including where children sleep and what the bedroom looks like) (Iwaniec, 1995). In cases of allegations of medical neglect, clinicians could ask parents how they might respond to hypothetical situations in which children need medical intervention.

Observation Methods

Observations of parent-child interactions are useful because they can provide an index of parental behaviors in situations in which parents are presumably demonstrating optimum caregiving skills, as well as an example of children's

behaviors with parents, so as to inform treatment (Budd, 2001). Observations in the family home are particularly helpful because these provide opportunities to note living conditions and familial relationships. If home observations are not feasible, however, valuable information can still be obtained by observing parent-child interactions in the assessment setting.

Clinicians can observe parent-child interactions during structured tasks or free play. Clinicians can ask parents and children to perform tasks together, such as demonstrating mealtime routines or cleaning up playrooms. Several structured observation methods can be used to track behaviors during parent-child interactions, such as the Dyadic Parent-Child Interaction Coding System II (DPICS II) (Eyberg, Bessmer, Newcombe, Edward, & Robinson, 1994) and the HOME Inventory (Caldwell & Bradley, 1984). In addition, clinicians can informally observe and record behaviors of interest throughout the assessment process. For example, when greeting families in waiting rooms, clinicians can observe the physical distance between family members. During interviews, the clinicians can record parental responsiveness to children's physical and safety needs. Clinicians can also record the frequency with which children display affection toward parents (Hewitt, 1999).

Teachers

Teachers are ideal informants about children's functioning in academic and social settings because they have extensive opportunities to observe children throughout the course of the school day (Busse & Beaver, 2000). Teachers may be more likely than parents to report internalizing behaviors (Stockhammer, Salzinger, Feldman, Mojica, & Primavera, 2001). Teachers also have opportunities to observe numerous children, and due to this basis for comparison, they may be particularly able to identify behaviors that are notably different from those of other children of the same developmental level.

Information obtained from interviews with teachers can be extremely valuable when clarifying the nature and impact of abuse on children. Clinicians should ask teachers about the nature and length of their relationships with the child, the child's academic performance, social skills with peers and adults, behaviors throughout the course of the school day, and strengths and weaknesses (Sattler, 2002). Teachers' observations of the onset, antecedents, and consequences of problematic behaviors can be particularly helpful. In addition, teachers are particularly proficient at comparing the frequency, duration, and intensity of problematic behaviors with those of the child's same-age peers. Based upon their observations of family interactions during parent-teacher conferences and other contacts with parents, teachers should be asked about perceptions of the child's family and home environment. Finally, teachers should be asked whether they have noticed anything unusual or disconcerting about the child's physical appearance, such as cuts or bruises.

Information from parents and teachers can highlight the nature of and impact of abuse on children. Information from these collateral sources should be considered along with information gathered from children during interviews.

CASE ILLUSTRATION WITH DIALOGUE

The case of Valerie Jones, a 6-year-old Caucasian girl, illustrates several facets of careful interviewing practices. Valerie was referred to a children's advocacy center to assess allegations of sexual abuse perpetrated by her biological father. Prior to initiating the interview, her clinician, Beth Smith, met with a team assigned to conduct the forensic evaluation, including a CPS worker, a district attorney, a police officer, and a therapist assigned to interview the nonoffending parent. The CPS worker, Lisa Blue, explained that this was the first time that a report on Valerie had been made to CPS. Ms. Blue clarified that the previous day, Valerie had tearfully told her teacher that she hurt because her father had touched her "pee pee" with his "thing," and her teacher, as a mandated reporter, had contacted CPS. She added that Valerie's mother had agreed to leave the home and stay with family friends until the completion of this interview.

Following this brief meeting, the CPS worker, district attorney, and police officer sat behind a two-way mirror to observe the interview. Beth Smith inserted a small earpiece in her left ear so that the observers could suggest questions during the interview without Beth having to leave the room to get their input. Near the ceiling at the corner of the interview room, a small video recorder was set up to document the contents of the interview.

Beth went to the waiting room to greet Valerie and her mother: "Hi, I'm Beth. I talk with children about problems that they might have, so I can help them. Let me show you where we will talk today." Beth showed Valerie and her mother the interview room and another room in which Valerie's mother would be interviewed. Beth explained that, first, she would speak with Valerie and her mother together, and then if Valerie felt comfortable, she would speak with Valerie alone. Beth asked Valerie of her understanding of what she was doing at the children's advocacy center. Valerie shyly shrugged her shoulders and hid behind her mother's skirt. Beth carefully repeated her role in the interview process and added that she would be talking with Valerie today for about 1 hour. Beth explained, "Valerie, I will share the things that you tell me with your Mom and Ms. Blue. But, I won't talk to your friends or anyone else that you know about the things that you tell me. You know, you are not in trouble. We are just going to talk today."

Beth showed Valerie around the interview room and pointed out the video camera. Valerie smiled as Beth invited both her and her mother to sit at the child-sized table and chairs. Beth explained, "In this room, we talk only about things that have really happened. If I ask you about things that you don't know about, please just say 'I don't know,' and don't make guesses." Beth posed questions to Valerie to make sure that she understood the concept of truth and would give responses only to questions to which she knew the answers. Beth added, "If you feel uncomfortable at any time, please tell me or make a stop sign with your hand. You can take a break, leave the room, or stop our talk at any time." Beth had Valerie practice making stop signs. She explored Valerie's understanding of her role, the interview process, and the limits of confidentiality. Beth also asked Valerie whether she had any questions. After clarifying the parameters of the interview, Beth asked whether Valerie was comfortable speaking with her alone, and Valerie assented.

For the remainder of the interview, Beth met with Valerie alone, and her mother met with another therapist. Beth talked with Valerie about her favorite hobby, which was drawing, and then pulled crayons and paper out of a box and asked Valerie to draw a picture for her. Beth then showed Valerie drawings of a girl's and a boy's body and asked her to name various body parts.

Valerie explained that girls' genitals were called "pee pees," whereas boys' genitals were called "things." Beth proceeded to gently ask open-ended questions about the alleged abuse, careful to use terms that Valerie had supplied and to phrase questions in a developmentally appropriate manner. Beth queried about the number, location, antecedents, and consequences of abuse incidents. Valerie explained that her father had touched her more than three times on her genitals and that he penetrated her vagina with his penis two nights ago for the first and only time. She added that all of the incidents occurred in her bedroom on top of her pink bedspread. Valerie explained that she had been afraid to disclose the abuse because her father had threatened to kill her dog and added that she had told her teacher only because "my pee pee hurt." Valerie began crying and said that she did not want to talk about this any more. Beth told her that she understood that this might be scary to talk about and normalized Valerie's reaction to her disclosure by explaining that many children feel afraid when this happens. Then, the interview was terminated.

Following the interview, Valerie's father was arrested. Valerie was referred for a medical examination and for psychological treatment. Beth and other members of the team continued to gather information by interviewing collateral sources.

MULTICULTURAL AND DIVERSITY ISSUES

Child abuse interviews should be conducted within a culturally sensitive developmental framework. Developing cognitive and linguistic skills may impact the ability of children to respond to the demands of an assessment situation, and therefore clinicians should be knowledgeable about normative development (Hewitt, 1999). Considerations of developmental level and culture should inform both the content and structure of interviews.

Cognitive developmental level impacts the ability of children to accurately understand and, in turn, report abuse experiences. Children may struggle with coordinating multiple aspects of relationships among people, events, and objects, and this may impair their ability to understand and describe complex social situations, such as abuse experiences (Fischer & Pipp, 1984). For example, due to their inability to comprehend abstractions, in cases of sexual abuse children lack the cognitive ability to differentiate between concrete acts of agreement and the abstract concept of informed consent (Celano, 1992). In addition, children younger than age 8 may struggle with taking others' perspectives (Morgan, 1995). To avoid confusing young children, clinicians should limit questions to children's subjective experiences and vantage points. Moreover, because they maintain respect for rules and fair play (Piaget, 1954), children may blame themselves for participating in child sexual abuse, because of their "initial consent." As children get older and internalize standards of conduct for members of the community, they may feel ashamed for having participated in an act that society deems wrong (Celano, 1992). Difficulties with the complexity of abuse experiences and emerging self-blame and feelings of shame may impact the reporting of such experiences.

As previously described, language development may also impact the reporting of abuse experiences. Children may employ language concepts before they comprehend their meaning (Walker, 1994). For example, a child may report that she was abused last year without fully understanding the meaning of the word *year*. In general, children younger than age 10 often struggle with estimates of time, kinship, dimensions, and quantity, and preschool-age children often struggle with prepositions (Bourg et al., 1999; Walker, 1994). To address these issues, interviewers should carefully examine children's understanding and use of terminology to ensure that both the child and interviewer share the same meaning. For example, although an interviewer may use the term *private parts*, a child may not know the parts of the body to which this refers (Goodman & Aman, 1990). Therefore, interviewers should use short, open-ended questions that employ clear, concrete, and developmentally appropriate vocabulary.

Although adolescents' cognitive and language development promotes their ability to understand complex concepts and address questions imbued with abstractions and complex vocabulary, accurate self-assessment is particularly challenging during this period of cognitive development (Elkind, 1978). Adolescents have an increasing sense of self-awareness and self-evaluation. Therefore, they may critically evaluate their responsibility for the abuse. For example, a sexually abused adolescent may think that if she were less developed or less sexually curious, abuse would not have occurred (Celano, 1992). Young adolescents cannot relate abstractions to fully comprehend concepts, such as intentionality and responsibility. Instead, they tend to engage in self-blame for sexual abuse experiences. In addition, because they often engage in all-or-none thinking, they have difficulty coping with conflicting perspectives about perpetrators. These cognitive developmental factors likely color an adolescent's perspective and reporting of abuse experiences.

The quality of child abuse assessments can also be impacted by cultural competence (for a detailed discussion of culturally competent interviewing of abuse children, see Fontes, 2005). Culture may impact child-rearing practices, reactions to child abuse and child abuse assessments, communication styles, the expression of symptoms, and approaches to mental health treatment (Azar & Benjet, 1994; Fontes, 1995). Culture may also inform beliefs related to child abuse, including beliefs about parent-child relationships, discipline practices, boundaries, sexuality, nudity, and virginity (Fontes, 1995). Cultural awareness and sensitivity should inform the choice of informants and psychological measures. For example, the importance of interviewing extended-family members such as grandparents will vary by cultural and familial norms. Therefore, evaluators should endeavor to enhance their cultural competence by becoming familiar with the culture of the family being assessed, being knowledgeable with regard to issues of cultural oppression and consulting, and referring as needed (APA, 2002).

Overall, an awareness of developmental and cultural norms should inform interviews of child abuse and related symptomatology. The extent to which interviews of child abuse yield information that is useful for forensic or treatment planning purposes may hinge upon these competencies.

DIFFERENTIAL DIAGNOSIS AND BEHAVIORAL ASSESSMENT

Children who have been neglected, physically abused, and/or sexually abused may meet criteria for several *DSM-IV-TR* diagnoses (American Psychiatric Association, 2000). Common diagnoses among maltreated children include sexual abuse of child, neglect of child, physical abuse of child, PTSD, acute stress disorder, major depressive disorder, adjustment disorder, oppositional defiant disorder, and attention-deficit/hyperactivity disorder (Morrison & Anders, 1999). It is also possible that maltreated children will not meet criteria for any diagnoses (Azar & Wolfe, 1998).

Behavioral assessment can be undertaken either to evaluate abuse allegations or to determine psychological adjustment following abuse experiences. Behavioral assessment should address multiple domains of functioning, use multiple informants, and employ multiple assessment measures (see Wise, 2006, for further details about behavioral assessment of child abuse). Through the behavioral assessment process, clinicians should endeavor to identify risk and protective factors among children, their families, and other systems that might impact their functioning (Davies, 2004; Sameroff & Fiese, 2000; Werner, 2000). Certain factors may heighten the risk or impact of child maltreatment, whereas protective factors may reduce the risk or impact of such maltreatment. Risk factors include child vulnerabilities, such as mental retardation, medical problems, or a lack of coping skills; parental vulnerabilities, such as impaired parenting due to familial conflict, psychopathology, substance abuse, inadequate parenting skills, or parental history of maltreatment; and family system vulnerabilities due to socioeconomic and institutional factors, such as poverty and exposure to community violence. Protective factors include child strengths, such as health, intelligence, and coping skills; parental strengths, such as household rules, structure and close monitoring of the child, stable familial relationships, appropriate expectations of the child, and good problem-solving skills; and family system strengths due to socioeconomic and institutional factors, such as economic resources, access to health care services, consistent employment, adequate housing, and the presence of an adequate social support network. For example, because facing skeptical and adversarial attorneys or reliving abuse experiences in a court context may exacerbate a child's experience of stress, this may serve as a risk factor for deterioration in the child's functioning (Higgins, 1988). Conversely, because social support is associated with improved functioning, this may serve as a protective factor in the child's functioning (Everson, Hunter, Runyon, Edelsohn, & Coulter, 1989). A comprehensive behavioral assessment of child abuse should include an assessment of risk and protective factors across the child's domains of functioning.

Self-Report Measures

Although interviewing and behavioral observations play a central role in behavioral assessment, self-report measures should also be used to gather information about abuse and current functioning. Standardized self-report measures can be used to inform the content of interviews, provide a quick and efficient method of gathering information across various domains of functioning, and yield a basis for comparison with abused and nonabused children. In addition, respondents who are reluctant to disclose sensitive information in face-to-face conversations may be more comfortable sharing information in the context of self-report measures. Self-report measures can also be repeatedly administered throughout treatment to assess progress. Given these advantages, it is recommended that clinicians routinely administer standardized self-report measures as part of abuse interviews.

Standardized Self-Report Measures for Children

A number of standardized measures can be used to gather detailed information from children on abuse experiences. For example, the Record of Maltreatment Experiences (ROME) (McGee, Wolfe, & Wilson, 1997) can be used to obtain frequency ratings for various behaviors that may indicate maltreatment. Similarly, the Dimensions of Stressful Events (DOSE) (Fletcher, 1991) can be employed to gather information about a range of traumatic events (e.g., sexual abuse, exposure to violence, serious physical injury) and characteristics of these events (e.g., frequency, duration, perceptions of control).

Because internalizing and externalizing behaviors are common among children who have been abused, broad-band measures of functioning may be particularly useful. The Youth Self-Report (YSR) (Achenbach, 1991c) is one such broadband self-report measure of internalizing and externalizing behaviors among children aged 11 to 18.

Given the prevalence of posttraumatic stress symptoms among children who have experienced abuse, it is particularly important to assess such symptoms (Kendall-Tackett et al., 1993; Paolucci et al., 2001; Pelcovitz et al., 1994). The Clinician-Administered PTSD Scale for Children (CAPS-C) (Nader, Kriegler, Blake, & Pynoos, 1994) is a measure of *DSM-IV* diagnostic criteria for PTSD and related symptoms. The CAPS-C is a method of evaluating the frequency and intensity of symptoms, as well as the impact of symptoms on functioning. The Trauma Symptom Checklist for Children (TSCC) (Briere, 1996) is another measure frequently used as part of child abuse interviews. The TSCC is a 54-item self-report designed to measure posttraumatic distress and related symptomatology in children aged 8 to 16. The TSCC includes questions about sexual abuse experiences, and the TSCC-A is an alternate form of this measure that excludes questions about sexual abuse experiences. Additional self-report measures designed to assess posttraumatic stress and related symptomatology are the Child's Reaction to Traumatic Events Scale (CRTES) (Jones, 1994) and the When Bad Things Happen Scale (WBTH) (Fletcher, 1991). Although these measures can provide valuable information about posttraumatic stress symptoms, it is important to note that none of them should be used to give definitive diagnoses of PTSD in the absence of information from other sources (e.g., interviews with children and parents).

Symptomatology among children who have experienced abuse or neglect may be moderated by cognitive attributions. For example, self-blame among sexually abused children and adolescents has been associated with heightened depression anxiety, posttraumatic stress symptoms, and self-esteem deficits (Mannarino & Cohen, 1996a; Taska & Feiring, 2000; Wolfe, Sas, & Wekerle, 1994). Therefore, measures of cognitive attributions can be beneficial supplements to child abuse interviews. Two measures of cognitive attributions have been developed for use with children who have been sexually abused. The Children's Impact of Traumatic Events Scale-Revised (CITES-R) (Wolfe, Gentile, Michienzi, Sas, & Wolfe, 1991) is a 78-item measure in which the impact of sexual abuse among children aged 8 to 16 can be assessed. The Children's Attribution and Perceptions Scale (CAPS) (Mannarino, Cohen, & Berman, 1994) is another self-report measure designed to assess abuse-related attributions and perceptions among sexually abused children aged 7 to 14. The CAPS is an 18-item scale that yields information on perceptions of being different from peers and attributions for negative events, credibility, and interpersonal trust.

Standardized Self-Report Measures for Caregivers

Several measures are designed to be administered to caregivers of children who may have been abused. For example, the Child Well-Being Scales (Magura & Moses, 1986) and the Ontario Child Neglect Index (Trocome, 1996) are measures of the type and severity of neglect. The Maltreatment Classification System (MSC) (Barnett, Manly, & Cicchetti, 1993) was developed to identify specific aspects of physical or sexual abuse history (e.g., frequency, severity, duration). The Child Abuse Potential Inventory (CAP) (Milner, 1986) is a 160-item measure for the detection of physical abuse.

There are several measures for evaluating risk of parental abuse. For example, the Parenting Stress Index (PSI) (Abidin, 1995) is designed to measure dysfunctional parent-child relationships. The Weekly Report of Abuse Indicators (WRAI) (Kolko, 1996) can be administered to evaluate high-risk parental behaviors in a short time frame. The Child Abuse Potential Interview (CAPI) (Milner, 1986, 1994) is a standardized measure created to evaluate parental risk of physically abusing a child. Similarly, the Conflict Tactics Scales (CTSPC) (Staus, Hambly, Finkelhor, Moore, & Runyan, 1998) is a measure of parental involvement in various violent behaviors directed at children.

Measures of family functioning, parental expectations of child behaviors, and parenting practices can also provide useful information. Some of the most commonly used instruments to assess family functioning are the Family Adaptability and Cohesion Evaluation Scales-Third Edition (FACES-III) (Olson, Portner, & Lavee, 1985) and the Family Environment Scale (FES) (Moos, Insel, & Humphrey, 1974). The Parent Opinion Questionnaire (PTQ) (Azar, Robinson, Hekimian, & Twentyman, 1984) and the Parent Attribution Test (PAT) (Bugental, Mantyla, & Lewis, 1989) can be used to evaluate parental expectations of child behaviors. Although there are no specific measures to evaluate parenting practices, some instruments, such

as the Alabama Parenting Questionnaire (APQ) (Shelton, Frick, & Wooten, 1996) and the Parenting Scale (PS) (Arnold, O'Leary, Wolfe, & Acker, 1993) contain subscales designed to provide a measure of parental practices (e.g., monitoring, discipline).

Caregivers are also valuable sources of information on children's current functioning. The Child Behavior Checklist, a broadband measure of symptoms, is a checklist of internalizing and externalizing behaviors among children aged 2 through 18 (CBCL) (Achenbach, 1991a). Results from the CBCL provide a broad array of information on problems in the parent-child relationship, school behaviors, and developmental delays. Although efforts have been made to develop a PTSD scale from the CBCL, this scale has poor concurrent and discriminant validity (Ruggiero & McLeer, 2000). Nonetheless, given the range of behavior problems that have been observed among children who have been abused, this measure may provide information important for treatment planning. To access information about the child's functioning in school, a version to be completed by the child's teachers, Teacher's Report Form, is also available (Achenbach, 1991b).

There are several measures of abuse-related symptomatology. The Child Sexual Behavior Inventory (CSBI) (Friedrich, 1997) is a 38-item measure of sexual behaviors of children aged 2 to 18. Using this measure, clinicians can evaluate whether sexual behaviors of children are within a normal range of behaviors among abused and nonabused populations. Although sexually abused children commonly display unusual sexual-acting-out behaviors, these behaviors may also be due to exposure to sexual material rather than to sexual abuse (Elliot, O'Donohue, & Nickerson, 1993).

Despite the value of self-report information from collateral sources, no single test can be used to substantiate child abuse or adequately assess the impact of child abuse. Therefore, it is important to gather information from a variety of sources (AACAP, 1990; APSAC, 1997).

Functional Analysis

In addition to gathering data from interviews, observations, and questionnaires, functional analysis can provide information on how problematic behaviors develop and are maintained.

A *functional analysis* is a process in which antecedents and consequences of problematic behaviors are identified so as to reduce problematic behaviors (Freeman & Miller, 2002). Information yielded by functional analysis can facilitate the identification of targets and inform treatment planning and referral processes.

SELECTION OF TREATMENT TARGETS AND REFERRAL

Treatment targets flow logically from findings from interviews, behavioral assessments, and diagnoses. Selection of treatment targets can be conceptualized as a multistage process (Azar & Wolfe, 1998). First, to ensure the welfare of the child, risk factors that reflect ongoing threats to a child's physical and emotional safety should be assessed and addressed. For example, if children are at imminent risk for being reabused due to living with perpetrators, making housing recommendations and/or developing family safety plans will be a top priority. Second, treatment goals should be developed so as to bolster protective factors and diminish risk factors (Kolko, 1996). It is particularly important to assess risk and protective factors among children, their families, and communities, because transactions between children and their environments impact the course of development, and therefore the effects of these risk and protective factors may be far-reaching (Cicchetti & Olson, 1990; Davies, 2004; Sroufe, 1997). Treatment goals will vary, based on presenting problems and risk and protective factors unique to children and caregivers.

Factors that are commonly addressed during treatment for children who have been maltreated can be divided between *child needs* and *caregiver needs* (Azar & Wolfe, 1998). Parents may be provided with information about how they can positively influence their children's behaviors and emotions by altering their own behaviors, thoughts, and coping skills. Psychoeducation, cognitive restructuring, role plays, and modeling may be used to teach child management strategies to parents. Children who have been maltreated are commonly removed from abusive situations. They often benefit from learning skills to identify and communicate emotions, cope with distress, understand abuse, challenge abuse-related cognitive distortions,

and cope with memories of traumatic events (Cohen, Deblinger, & Mannarino, 2005).

Children who have experienced abuse also may benefit from referrals for further assessment or treatment services. For example, if children have not already had physical exams, it can be helpful to refer them to physicians or agencies experienced in working with children who have been abused, to assess for physical damage caused by abuse or neglect (James, 1996). Physical examinations can also rule out organic causes of symptoms, offer reassurance to children that they are not damaged, and provide physical evidence of abuse for use in court settings (Azar & Wolfe, 1998; James, 1996). In addition, if a therapist is not competent to treat a child due to lack of expertise, it is important to refer the child to mental health providers that have adequate qualifications and experience to meet the needs of that child. Finally, if conducting an evaluation of a child or parent for forensic purposes, clinicians should avoid taking on an additional treatment role with the child or family (APA, 2002; APA Committee on Professional Practice and Standards, 1998; Myers, 2002). In this case, clinicians should refer the child or family out for treatment.

SUMMARY

Regardless of whether interviews of abuse are for forensic, research, or treatment-planning purposes, the overarching goal of every interview should be to promote the health and welfare of each child (APA Committee on Professional Practice and Standards, 1998). To achieve this goal, clinicians should develop a broad array of skills to competently interview children about abuse; clinicians should be knowledgeable of state laws on child abuse, psychological problems associated with child abuse, strategies to facilitate accurate reports from children, developmental norms, culturally competent assessment strategies, and treatment of abused children. Moreover, clinicians should employ multiple methods and gather information from multiple sources of information. Using these strategies, repeated assessments of psychological functioning should inform case conceptualization, treatment planning, and referral processes. Overall, the extent to which interviews of child abuse yield information that is useful for forensic or treatment planning purposes may hinge upon these competencies. Given the complexity of these assessment strategies, well-trained and experienced interviewers are best able to conduct interviews of child abuse experiences and abuse-related symptoms.

REFERENCES

Abidin, R. R. (1995). *Parenting stress inventory* (3rd ed.). Odessa, FL: Psychological Assessment Resources.

Achenbach, T. M. (1991a). *Manual for the child behavior checklist/4–18 and 1991 profile.* Burlington: University of Vermont, Department of Psychiatry.

Achenbach, T. M. (1991b). *Manual for the teacher's report form and 1991 profile.* Burlington: University of Vermont, Department of Psychiatry.

Achenbach, T. M. (1991c). *Manual for the youth self-report and 1991 profile.* Burlington: University of Vermont, Department of Psychiatry.

Aldridge, M., & Wood, J. (1998). *Interviewing children: A guide for childcare and forensic practitioners.* Chichester, UK: John Wiley & Sons.

American Academy of Child and Adolescent Psychiatry. (1990). *Guidelines for the evaluation of child and adolescent sexual abuse.* Washington, DC: Author.

American Professional Society on the Abuse of Children. (1990). *Guidelines for the psychosocial evaluation of suspected sexual abuse in young children.* Chicago: Author.

American Professional Society on the Abuse of Children. (1995). Guidelines for the clinical evaluation of child and adolescent sexual abuse. *Journal of the American Academy of Child & Adolescent Psychiatry, 27,* 655–657.

American Professional Society on the Abuse of Children. (1997). *Practice guidelines: Psychosocial evaluation of suspected sexual abuse in children* (2nd ed.). Oklahoma City, OK: Author.

American Psychiatric Association. (2000). *Diagnostic and statistical manual of mental disorders* (4th ed., Text rev.). Washington, DC: Author.

American Psychological Association. (2002). Ethical principles of psychologists and code of conduct. *American Psychologist, 57,* 1060–1073.

American Psychological Association Committee on Professional Practice and Standards. (1998). *Guidelines for psychological evaluations in child protection matters.* Washington, DC: Author.

Arnold, D. S., O'Leary, S. G., Wolff, L. S., & Acker, M. M. (1993). The parenting scale: A measure of dysfunctional parenting in discipline situations. *Psychological Assessment, 5,* 137–144.

Azar, S. T., & Benjet, C. L. (1994). A cognitive perspective on ethnicity, race, and termination of parental rights. *Law & Human Behavior, 18,* 249–268.

Azar, S. T., Robinson, D. R., Hekimian, E., & Twentyman, C. T. (1984). Unrealistic expectations and problem-solving ability in maltreating and comparison mothers. *Journal of Consulting and Clinical Psychology, 52,* 687–691.

Azar, S. T., & Wolfe, D. A. (1998). Child physical abuse and neglect. In E. J. Mash & R. A. Barkley (Eds.), *Treatment of childhood disorders* (pp. 501–544). New York: Guilford Press.

Barnett, D., Manly, J. T., & Cicchetti, D. (1993). Defining child maltreatment: The interface between policy and research. In D. Cicchetti & S. L. Toth (Eds.), *Child abuse, child development, and social policy* (pp. 7–73). Norwood, NJ: Ablex.

Berliner, L., & Elliot, D. M. (2002). Sexual abuse of children. In J. Myers, L. Berliner, J. Briere, C. T. Hendrix, C. Jenny, & T. A. Reid (Eds.), *The APSAC handbook on child maltreatment* (2nd ed., pp. 55–78). Thousand Oaks, CA: Sage.

Boney-McCoy, S., & Finklehor, D. (1995). Psychosocial sequelae of violent victimization in a national youth sample. *Journal of Consulting and Clinical Psychology, 63,* 726–736.

Bourg, W., Broderick, R., Flagor, R., Kelly, D. M., Ervin, D. L., & Butler, J. (1999). *A child interviewer's guidebook.* Thousand Oaks, CA: Sage.

Briere, J. (1996). *Trauma symptom checklist for children: Professional manual.* Odessa, FL: Psychological Assessment Resources.

Briere, J. (1997). *Psychological assessment of adult posttraumatic states.* Washington, DC: APA.

Budd, K. S. (2001). Assessing parenting competence in child protection □cases: A clinical practice model. *Clinical Child and Family Psychology Review, 4,* 1–18.

Bugental, D. B., Mantyla, S. M., & Lewis, J. (1989). Parental attributions as moderators of affective communication to children at risk for physical abuse. In D. Cicchetti & V. Carlson (Eds.), *Child maltreatment: Theory and research on the causes and the consequences of abuse and neglect* (pp. 254–279). New York: Cambridge University Press.

Busse, R. T., & Beaver, B. R. (2000). Informant report: Parent and teacher interview. In E. Shapiro & T. R. Kratochwill (Eds.), *Conducting school-based assessment of child and adolescent behavior* (pp. 235–273). New York: Guilford Press.

Bussey, K., & Grimbeek, E. J. (1995). Disclosure processes: Issues for child sexual abuse victims. In K. Rotenberg (Ed.), *Disclosure processes in children and adolescents* (pp. 166–203). New York: Cambridge University Press.

Caffaro-Rouget, A., Lang, R. A., & van Santen, V. (1989). The impact of child sexual abuse. *Annals of Sex Research, 2,* 29–47.

Caldwell, B. M., & Bradley, R. H. (1984). *Home observation for the measurement of the environment: Administration manual* (Rev. ed.). Little Rock: University of Arkansas.

Cantlon, J., Payne, G., & Erbaugh, C. (1996). Outcome-based practice: Disclosure rates of child sexual abuse comparing allegation blind and allegation informed structured interviews. *Child Abuse & Neglect, 20,* 1113–1120.

Ceci, S. J., & Bruck, M. (1995). *Jeopardy in the courtroom: A scientific analysis of children's testimony.* Washington, DC: American Psychological Association.

Celano, M. (1992). A developmental model of victims' internal attributions of responsibility for sexual abuse. *Journal of Interpersonal Violence, 7,* 57–69.

Chaffin, M., Wherry, J. N., Newlin, C., Crutchfield, A., & Dykman, R. (1997). The abuse dimensions inventory: Initial data on a research measure of abuse severity. *Journal of Interpersonal Violence, 12,* 569–589.

Cicchetti, D., & Olson, K. (1990). The developmental psychopathology of child maltreatment. In M. Lewis & S. M. Miller (Eds.), *Handbook of developmental psychopathology* (pp. 261–279). New York: Plenum Press.

Cohen, J. A., Deblinger, E., & Mannarino, A. P. (2005). Trauma-focused cognitive-behavioral therapy for sexually abused children. In E. D. Hibbs & P. S. Jensen (Eds.), *Psychosocial treatments for child and adolescent disorders: Empirically based strategies for clinical practice* (pp. 743–765). Washington, DC: American Psychological Association.

Cohen, J. A., & Mannarino, A. P. (1988). Psychological symptoms in sexually abused girls. *Child Abuse & Neglect, 12,* 571–577.

Conte, J. R., & Scheurman, J. R. (1987). The effects of sexual abuse on children: A multi-dimensional view. *Journal of Interpersonal Violence, 2,* 380–390.

Conte, J., Sorenson, E., Fogarty, L., & Dalla Rosa, J. (1991). Evaluating reports of sexual abuse: Results from a survey of professionals. *American Journal of Orthopsychiatry, 61,* 428–437.

Daly, L. W. (1991). The essentials of child abuse investigation and child interviews. *Issues in Child Abuse Accusations, 3*(2). Retrieved September 1, 2005, from http://www.ipt-forensics.com/journal/volume3/j3_2_2.htm

Davidson, J. R. T., & Smith, R. D. (1990). Traumatic experiences in psychiatric inpatients. *Journal of Traumatic Stress, 3,* 459–475.

Davies, D. (2004). *Child development: A practitioner's guide* (2nd ed.). New York: Guilford Press.

Dryer, F. J. (1999). *Psychological consultation in parental rights cases.* New York: Guilford Press.

Eckenrode, J., Laird, M., & Doris, J. (1993). School performance and disciplinary problems among abused and neglected children. *Developmental Psychology, 29,* 63–77.

Elkind, D. (1978). Understanding the young adolescent. *Adolescence, 13,* 127–134.

Elliot, A. N., O'Donohue, W. T., & Nickerson, M. A. (1993). The use of sexually anatomically detailed dolls in the assessment of sexual abuse. *Clinical Psychology Review, 13,* 207–221.

Erickson, M. R., & Egeland, B. (1996). Child neglect. In J. Briere, L. Berliner, J. Bulkley, C. Jenney, & T. Reid (Eds.), *The APSAC handbook on child maltreatment* (pp. 4–20). Thousand Oaks, CA: Sage.

Erickson, M. R., & Egeland, B. (2002). Child neglect. In J. Myers, L. Berliner, J. Briere, C. T. Hendrix, C. Jenny, & T. A. Reid (Eds.), *The APSAC handbook on child maltreatment* (2nd ed., pp. 3–20). Thousand Oaks, CA: Sage.

Everson, M. D., & Boat, B. W. (1989). False allegations of sexual abuse by children and adolescents. *Journal of the American Academy of Child & Adolescent Psychiatry, 28,* 230–235.

Everson, M. D., Hunter, W. M., Runyon, D. K., Edelsohn, G. A., & Coulter, M. L. (1989). Maternal support following

disclosure of incest. *American Journal of Orthopsychiatry, 59,* 197–207.

Eyberg, S., Bessmer, J., Newcombe, K., Edward, D., & Robinson, E. (1994). *Dydactic parent-child interaction coding system II: A manual.* Unpublished manuscript, University of Florida, Department of Clinical Health Psychology.

Faller, K. C. (1996a). *Evaluating children suspected of having been sexually abused.* Chicago: American Professional Society on the Abuse of Children.

Faller, K. C. (1996b). Interviewing children who may have been abused: A historical perspective and overview of controversies. *Child Maltreatment, 1,* 83–95.

Finkelhor, D., & Berliner, L. (1995). Research on the treatment of sexually abused children: A review and recommendations. *Journal of the American Academy of Child & Adolescent Psychiatry, 34,* 1408–1423.

Finkelhor, D., Hotaling, G., Lewis, I. A., & Smith, C. (1990). Sexual abuse in a national survey of adult men and women: Prevalence, characteristics, and risk factors. *Child Abuse & Neglect, 14,* 19–28.

Fischer, K., & Pipp, S. (1984). Development of structures of unconscious thought. In K. Bowers & D. Meichenbaum (Eds.), *The unconscious reconsidered* (pp. 88–148). New York: Wiley.

Fletcher, K. (1991). *When bad things happen scale.* Worcester, MA: Author.

Fontes, L. A. (Ed.). (1995). *Sexual abuse in nine North American cultures: Treatment and prevention.* Thousand Oaks, CA: Sage.

Fontes, L. A. (2005). *Child abuse and culture.* New York: Guilford Press.

Freeman, K. A., & Miller, C. A. (2002). Behavioral case conceptualization for children and adolescents. In M. Hersen (Ed.), *Clinical behavior therapy: Adults and children* (pp. 239–255). New York: Wiley.

Friedrich, W. N. (1997). *Child sexual behavior inventory.* Odessa, FL: Psychological Assessment Resources.

Friedrich, W. N. (2002). *Psychological assessment of sexually abused children and their families.* Thousand Oaks, CA: Sage.

Friedrich, W. N., Fisher, J. L., Dittner, C. A., Acton, R., Berliner, L., Butler, J., et al. (2001). Child sexual behavior inventory: Normative, psychiatric, and sexual abuse comparisons. *Child Maltreatment: Journal of the American Professional Society on the Abuse of Children, 6,* 37–49.

Goodman, G. S., & Aman, C. (1990). Children's use of anatomically detailed dolls to recount an event. *Child Development, 61,* 1859–1871.

Goodman-Brown, T. B., Edelstein, R. S., Goodman, G. S., Jones, D., & Gordon, D. S. (2003). Why children tell: A model of children's disclosure of sexual abuse. *Child Abuse & Neglect, 27,* 525–540.

Gordon, B. N., Schroeder, C. S., & Hawk, B. (1993). Clinical problems of the preschool child. In C. E. Walker & M. C. Roberts (Eds.), *Handbook of clinical child psychology* (pp. 296–334). New York: Wiley.

Gordon, B. N., Schroeder, C. S., Ornstein, P. A., & Baker-Ward, L. E. (1995). Clinical implications for research on memory development. In T. Ney (Ed.), *True and false allegations of child sexual abuse: Assessment and case management* (pp. 99–124). New York: Brunner/Mazel.

Hart, S. N., Brassard, M. R., Binggeli, N. J., & Davidson, H. A. (2002). Psychological maltreatment. In J. Myers, L. Berliner, J. Briere, C. T. Hendrix, C. Jenny, & T. A. Reid (Eds.), *The APSAC handbook on child maltreatment* (2nd ed., pp. 79–103). Thousand Oaks, CA: Sage.

Hewitt, S. K. (1999). *Assessing allegations of sexual abuse in preschool children.* Thousand Oaks, CA: Sage.

Hibbard, R. A., Ingersoll, G. M., & Orr, D. P. (1990). Behavior risk, emotional risk, and child abuse among adolescents in a nonclinical setting. *Pediatrics, 86,* 896–901.

Higgins, R. B. (1988). Child victims as witnesses. *Law & Psychology Review, 12,* 159–166.

Horn, J. L., & Dollinger, S. J. (1995). Sleep disturbances in children. In M. C. Roberts (Ed.), *Handbook of pediatric psychology* (2nd ed., pp. 575–588). New York: Guilford Press.

Hotaling, G. T. Straus, M. A., & Lincoln, A. J. (1990). Intrafamily violence and crime and violence outside the family. In M. A. Straus & R. J. Gelles (Eds.), *Physical violence in American families: Risk factors and adaptations to violence in 8,145 families* (pp. 431–470). New Brunswick, NJ: Transaction Publishers.

Iwaniec, D. (1995). *The emotionally abused and neglected child.* New York: Wiley.

Iwaniec, D. (1997). An overview of emotional maltreatment and failure-to-thrive. *Child Abuse Review, 6,* 370–388.

James, B. (1996). *Treating traumatized children: New insights and creative interventions.* New York: Free Press.

Jones, D., & McGraw, J. M. (1987). Reliable and fictitious accounts of sexual abuse to children. *Journal of Interpersonal Violence, 2,* 27–45.

Jones, D., & McQuiston, M. G. (1988). *Interviewing the sexually abused child* (3rd ed.). London: Royal College of Psychiatrists.

Jones, R. T. (1994). *Children's reaction to traumatic events scale: A self-report traumatic stress measure.* Blacksburg, VA: Author.

Kaplan, S., Pelcovitz, D., Salzinger, S., Mandel, F. S., & Weiner, M. (1998). Adolescent physical abuse: Risk for adolescent psychiatric disorders. *American Journal of Psychiatry, 36,* 799–808.

Katz, K. (1992). Communication problems in maltreated children: A tutorial. *Journal of Childhood Communication Disorders, 14,* 147–163.

Kendall-Tackett, K. A., & Eckenrode, J. (1996). The effects of neglect on academic achievement and disciplinary problems: A developmental perspective. *Child Abuse & Neglect, 20,* 161–169.

Kendall-Tackett, K. A., Williams, L. M., & Finkelhor, D. (1993). Impact of sexual abuse on children: A review and synthesis of recent empirical studies. *Psychological Bulletin, 113,* 164–180.

Kilpatrick, D. G., Saunders, B., E., & Smith, D. (2003). *Youth victimization: Prevalence and implications.* Washington, DC: U.S. Department of Justice.

Kiser, L. J., Heston, J., Millsap, P. A., & Pruitt, D. B. (1991). Physical and sexual abuse in childhood: Relationship with posttraumatic stress disorder. *Journal of the American Academy of Child & Adolescent Psychiatry, 30,* 776–783.

Kolko, D. J. (1996). Clinical monitoring of treatment course in child physical abuse: Child and parent reports. *Child Abuse & Neglect, 20,* 23–43.

Kolko, D. J. (2002). Child physical abuse. In J. Myers, L. Berliner, J. Briere, C. T. Hendrix, C. Jenny, & T. A. Reid (Eds.), *APSAC handbook on child maltreatment* (2nd ed., pp. 21–54). Thousand Oaks, CA: Sage.

Kolko, D. J., Moser, J. T., & Weldy, S. R. (1990). Medical/health histories and physical evaluation of physically and sexually abused child psychiatric patients: A controlled study. *Journal of Family Violence, 5,* 249–267.

Lamb, M. E. (1994). The investigation of child sexual abuse: An interdisciplinary consensus statement. *Journal of Child Sexual Abuse, 3,* 93–106.

Lipovsky, J. A., & Hanson, R. F. (1992, October). *Multiple traumas in histories of child/adolescent psychiatric inpatients.* Paper presented at the annual meeting of the International Society for Traumatic Stress Studies, Los Angeles.

Magura, S., & Moses, B. (1986). *Outcome measures for child welfare services.* Washington, DC: National Association of Social Workers.

Mannarino, A. P., & Cohen, J. A. (1986). A clinical-demographic study of sexually abused children. *Child Abuse & Neglect, 10,* 17–23.

Mannarino, A. P., & Cohen, J. A. (1996a). Abuse-related attributions and perceptions, general attributions, and locus of control in sexually abused girls. *Journal of Interpersonal Violence, 11,* 162–180.

Mannarino, A. P., & Cohen, J. A. (1996b). A follow-up study of factors that mediate the development of psychological symptomatology in sexually abused girls. *Child Maltreatment, 1,* 246–260.

Mannarino, A. P., & Cohen, J. A. (2003). Sexually and physically abused children. In M. Hersen & S. Turner (Eds.), *Diagnostic interviewing* (pp. 415–432). New York: Kluwer Academic/Plenum.

Mannarino, A., Cohen, J., & Berman, S. (1994). The children's attributions and perceptions scale: A new measure of sexual abuse-related factors. *Journal of Child Clinical Psychology, 23,* 204–211.

Mannarino, A. P., Cohen, J. A., Smith, J. A., & Moore-Motily, S. (1991). Six-and twelve-month follow-up of sexually abused girls. *Journal of Interpersonal Violence, 6,* 494–511.

McGee, R. A., Wolfe, D. A., & Wilson, S. K. (1997). Multiple maltreatment experiences and adolescent behavior problems: Adolescents' perspectives. *Developmental and Psychopathology, 9,* 131–149.

McLeer, S. V., Deblinger, E., Atkins, M. S., Foa, E. B., & Ralphe, D. L. (1988). Post-traumatic stress disorder in sexually abused children. *Journal of the American Academy of Child and Adolescent Psychiatry, 27,* 650–654.

McLeer, S. V., Dixon, J. F., Henry, D., Ruggerio, K., Escovitz, K., Niedda, T., & Scholle, R. (1998). Psychopathology in non-clinically referred sexually abused children. *Journal of the American Academy of Child & Adolescent Psychiatry, 37,* 1326–1333.

Melton, G. B., Petrila, J., Poythress, N. G., & Slobogin, C. (1997). *Psychological evaluations for the courts:*

A handbook for mental health professionals and lawyers (2nd ed.). New York: Guilford Press.

Miller, P. R., Dasher, R., Collins, R., Griffiths, P., & Brown, F. (2001). Inpatient diagnostic assessments: Accuracy of structured versus unstructured interviews. *Psychiatry Research, 105,* 255–264.

Milner, J. S. (1986). *The child abuse potential inventory: Manual* (2nd ed.). Webster, NC: Psyctec.

Milner, J. S. (1994). Assessing physical child abuse risk: The Child Abuse Potential Inventory. *Clinical Psychology Review, 14,* 547–583.

Moos, R. H., Insel, P. M., & Humphrey, B. (1974). *Family work and group environment scales.* Palo Alto, CA: Consulting Psychologists Press.

Mordock, J. B. (2001). Interviewing abused and traumatized children. *Clinical Child Psychology and Psychiatry, 6,* 271–292.

Morgan, M. (1995). *How to interview sexual abuse victims: Including the use of anatomical dolls.* Thousand Oaks, CA: Sage.

Morrison, J., & Anders, T. F. (1999). *Interviewing children and adolescents.* New York: Guilford Press.

Myers, J. E. B. (1992). *Legal issues in child abuse and neglect.* Newbury Park, CA: Sage.

Myers, J. E. B. (1998). *Legal issues in child abuse and neglect* (2nd ed.). Thousand Oaks, CA: Sage.

Myers, J. E. B. (2002). Risk management for professionals working with maltreated children and adult survivors. In J. Myers, L. Berliner, J. Briere, C. T. Hendrix, C. Jenny, & T. A. Reid (Eds.), *The APSAC handbook on child maltreatment* (2nd ed., pp. 379–401). Thousand Oaks, CA: Sage.

Nader, K. O., Kriegler, J. A., Blake, D. D., & Pynoos, R. S. (1994). *Clinician administered PTSD scale: Child and adolescent version (CAPS-C).* White River Junction, VT: National Center for PTSD.

Olson, D., Portner, J., & Lavee, Y. (1985). *FACES-III.* St. Paul: University of Minnesota, Department of Family Social Services.

Orbach, Y., Hershkowitz, I., Lamb, M. E., Sternberg, K. J., Esplin, P. W., & Horowitz, D. (2000). Assessing the value of structured protocols for forensic interviews of alleged child abuse victims. *Child Abuse & Neglect, 24,* 733–752.

Paolucci, E. O., Genuis, M. L., & Violato, C. (2001). A meta-analysis of the published research on the effects of child sexual abuse. *Journal of Psychology, 135,* 17–36.

Parrish, R. (n.d.). *Battered child syndrome: Investigating physical abuse and homicide.* Salt Lake City, UT: U.S. Department of Justice, Office of Justice Programs, Office of Juvenile Justice and Delinquency Prevention.

Pearlman, L. A., & McCann I. L. (1994). Integrating structured and unstructured approaches to taking a trauma history. In M. B. Williams & J. F. Sommer Jr. (Eds.), *Handbook of posttraumatic therapy* (pp. 38–48). Westport, CT: Greenwood Press.

Pelcovitz, D., Kaplan, S., Goldenberg, B., & Mandel, F. (1994). Posttraumatic stress disorder in physically abused adolescents. *Journal of the American Academy of Child & Adolescent Psychiatry, 33,* 305–312.

Piaget, J. (1954). *The construction of reality in the child.* New York: Basic Books.

Poole, D. A., & Lamb, M. E. (1998). *Investigative interviews of children: A guide for helping professionals.* Washington, DC: American Psychological Association.

Reed, L. D. (1996). Findings from research on children's suggestibility and implications for conducting child interviews. *Child Maltreatment, 1,* 105–120.

Righthand, S., Kerr, B., & Drach, K. (2003). *Child maltreatment risk assessments: An evaluation guide.* New York: Haworth Maltreatment and Trauma Press.

Risin, L. I., & McNamara, R. (1989). Validation of child sexual abuse: The psychologist's role. *Journal of Clinical Psychology, 45,* 175–183.

Rogosch, F., Cicchetti, D., & Abre, J. L. (1995). The role of child maltreatment in early deviations in cognitive and affective processing abilities and later peer relationship problems. *Development and Psychopathology, 7,* 591–609.

Ruggiero, K. J., & McLeer, S. V. (2000). PTSD Scale of the Child Behavior Checklist: Concurrent and discriminant validity with non-clinic-referred sexually abused children. *Journal of Traumatic Stress, 13,* 287–299.

Sameroff, A. J., & Fiese, B. H. (2000). Transactional regulation: The developmental ecology of early intervention. In J. P. Shonkoff & S. J. Meisels (Eds.), *Handbook of early childhood intervention* (2nd ed., pp. 135–159). Cambridge, UK: Cambridge University Press.

Santilla, P., Korkman, J., & Sandnabba, N. K. (2004). Effects of interview phase, repeated interviewing, presence of a support person, and anatomically detailed dolls on child sexual abuse interviews. *Psychology, Crime, & Law, 10,* 21–35.

Sattler, J. M. (2002). *Assessment of children: Behavioral and clinical applications* (4th ed.). San Diego, CA: Author.

Sauzier, M. (1989). Disclosure of child sexual abuse: For better or for worse. *Psychiatric Clinics of North America, 12,* 455–469.

Saywitz, K. J. (1995). Improving children's testimony. In M. S. Zaragoza, J. R. Graham, G. C. N. Hall, R. Hirschman, & Y. S. Ben-Porath (Eds.), *Memory and testimony in the child witness* (pp. 113–140). Thousand Oaks: CA: Sage.

Sedlack, A. J., & Broadhurst, D. D. (1996). *Executive summary of the third national incidence study of child abuse and neglect.* Washington, DC: U.S. Department of Health and Human Services.

Shelton, K. K., Frick, P. J., & Wooten, J. (1996). Assessment of parenting practices in families of elementary school-age children. *Journal of Clinical Child Psychology, 25,* 317–329.

Sorenson, T., & Snow, B. (1991). How children tell: The process of disclosure in child sexual abuse. *Child Welfare, 70,* 3–15.

Sroufe, L. A. (1997). Psychopathology as an outcome of development. *Development and Psychopathology, 9,* 251–268.

Staus, M. A., Hamby, S. L., Finkelhor, D., Moore, D. W., & Runyan, D. (1998). Identification of child maltreatment with the parent-child conflict tactics scales: Development and psychometric data for a national sample of American parents. *Child Abuse & Neglect, 22,* 249–270.

Sternberg, K., Lamb, M., Hershkowitz, I., Yudilevitch, L., Orbach, Y., Esplin, P., et al. (1997). Effects of introductory style of children's abilities to describe experiences of sexual abuse. *Child Abuse & Neglect, 21,* 1133–1146.

Steward, M. A., Bussey, K., Goodman, G. S., & Saywitz, K. J. (1993). Implications of developmental research for interviewing children. *Child Abuse & Neglect, 17,* 25–37.

Stockhammer, T. F., Salzinger, S., Feldman, R. S., Mojica, E., & Primavera, L. H. (2001). Assessment of the effect of physical child abuse within an ecological framework: Measurement issues. *Journal of Community Psychology, 29,* 319–344.

Taska, L., & Feiring, C. (2000). *Why do bad things happen? Attributions and symptom development following sexual abuse.* Paper presented at the San Diego Conference on Responding to Child Maltreatment, San Diego, CA.

Tong, L., Oates, K., & McDowell, M. (1987). Personality development following sexual abuse. *Child Abuse & Neglect, 11,* 371–383.

Trocome, N. (1996). Development and preliminary evaluation of the Ontario child neglect index. *Child Maltreatment: Journal of the American Professional Society on the Abuse of Children, 1,* 145–155.

U.S. Department of Health and Human Services, Administration on Children, Youth and Families. (2003). *Child maltreatment 2001.* Washington, DC: U.S. Government Printing Office.

U.S. Department of Justice, Office of Juvenile Justice and Delinquency Prevention. (2002). *Interviewing child witness and victims of sexual abuse: Portable guides to investigating child abuse.* Washington, DC: Author.

Walker, A. G. (1994). *Handbook on questioning children: A linguistic perspective.* Washington, DC: American Bar Association Center on Children and the Law.

Walker, L. E. (1988). New techniques for assessment and evaluation of child sexual abuse victims: Using anatomically "correct" dolls and videotape procedures. In L. E. Walker (Ed.), *Handbook on sexual abuse of children: Assessment and treatment* (pp. 175–197). New York: Springer.

Werner, E. E. (2000). Protective factors and individual resilience. In J. P. Shonkoff & S. J. Meisels (Eds.), *Handbook of early childhood intervention* (2nd ed., pp. 115–132). Cambridge, UK: Cambridge University Press.

Wise, D. (2006). Child abuse assessment. In M. Hersen (Ed.), *Clinician's handbook of child behavioral assessment.* New York: Elsevier.

Wolfe, D., Wekerle, C., Reitzel-Jaffe, D., & Lefebvre, L. (1998). Factors associated with abusive relationships among maltreated and nonmaltreated youth. *Development and Psychopathology, 10,* 61–85.

Wolfe, V. V., Gentile, C., Michienzi, T., Sas, L., & Wolfe, D. A. (1991). The Children's Impact of Traumatic Events Scale: A measure of post-sexual abuse PTSD symptoms. *Behavioral Assessment, 13,* 159–383.

Wolfe, V. V., Gentile, C., & Wolfe, D. A. (1989). The impact of sexual abuse on children: A PTSD formulation. *Behavior Therapy, 20,* 215–228.

Wolfe, V. V., Sas, L., & Wekerle, C. (1994). Factors associated with the development of posttraumatic stress disorder among child victims of sexual abuse. *Child Abuse & Neglect, 18,* 37–50.

Zimmerman, M., & Mattia, J. I. (1999). Is posttraumatic stress underdiagnosed in routine clinical settings? *Journal of Nervous and Mental Disease, 187,* 420–428.

21

HABIT DISORDERS

Tics, Trichotillomania

DOUGLAS W. WOODS, CHRISTOPHER A. FLESSNER,
AND AMANDA C. ADCOCK

I n this chapter, we discuss the assessment and
diagnosis of trichotillomania (TTM) and tic
disorders. In particular, we focus on various
interview strategies and considerations. After a
brief introduction to these disorders, we discuss
structured and unstructured methods of interviewing children and adolescents (hereafter
referred to as "children") with these concerns,
obstacles during the interview process, solutions
to these obstacles, and guidelines for interviewing parents and teachers. In addition, we present
a comprehensive case illustration of a child with
Tourette's disorder (TD) and address relevant
multicultural issues. The chapter concludes with
a discussion of differential diagnoses, behavioral
assessment, the selection of appropriate target
behaviors, and referral to local physicians and/or
clinicians.

DESCRIPTION OF THE DISORDERS

Habit disorders involve a variety of repetitive
behaviors (Teng, Woods, Twohig, & Marcks,
2002). Examples include tic disorders, TTM, nail
biting, skin picking, and chewing on the mouth or
lips that result in negative physical and/or social
consequences for the individual. In recent years,
there has been a steady increase in literature examining the assessment, phenomenology, functional
impact, and treatment of these problems (Flessner
& Woods, 2006; Flessner et al., 2005; Flessner,
Woods, Franklin, Cashin, & Keuthen, in press;
Woods, Flessner, Franklin, Keuthen, et al., 2006;
Woods, Wetterneck, & Flessner, 2006), with most
attention given to TTM and tic disorders.

Trichotillomania (TTM)

TTM is characterized by the recurrent pulling
out of one's hair, an increasing sense of tension
prior to or while attempting to resist pulling, and
a feeling of gratification, relief, or pleasure following pulling. In addition, pulling must be
accompanied by clinically significant impairment
or distress in social, occupational, or academic
functioning and must not be better accounted for
by another mental health condition (American
Psychiatric Association [APA], 2000). Debate
about the utility of the tension and tension reduction criteria have led some to diagnose TTM in
the absence of reported antecedent tension and

subsequent relief (Diefenbach, Tolin, Crocetto, Maltby, & Hannan, 2005; Rapp, Miltenberger, Long, Elliot, & Lumley, 1998; Watson & Allen, 1993; Watson, Dittmer, & Ray, 2000).

Hair may be pulled from anywhere on the body, including the scalp, eyebrows, eyelashes, and pubic area. Very young children (e.g., toddlers) typically pull from only the scalp (Cohen et al., 1995; Wright & Holmes, 2003). Research has suggested that TTM occurs in 1% to 5% of the population and is more prevalent among females (Graber & Arndt, 1993). The prevalence of childhood TTM is unclear, although some believe the disorder is more prevalent in children than in adults (Mehregan, 1970) and that the female-to-male ratio may be lower in children (Cohen et al., 1995). Repetitive hair manipulation may also occur in conjunction with hair pulling (Miltenberger, Long, Rapp, Lumley, & Elliot, 1998; Rapp, Miltenberger, Galensky, Ellingson, & Long, 1999), with prevalence estimates ranging from 14.9% (Woods, Miltenberger, & Flach, 1996) to 70.6% (Hansen, Tishelman, Hawkins, & Doepke, 1990).

Cohen et al. (1995) surveyed 123 individuals with TTM and found that pulling typically began at approximately 11 years of age. Other studies have found that age of onset ranges from 9 to 14 years (Christenson, Mackenzie, & Mitchell, 1991; King et al., 1995; Reeve, Bernstein, & Christenson, 1992; Woods, Flessner, Franklin, Keuthen, et al., 2006). Research using less stringent research methodology has demonstrated that hair pulling can begin at as young as 18 months (Watson et al., 2000; Wright & Holmes, 2003).

Aside from hair loss, TTM is not thought to have many serious physical consequences. Nevertheless, a significant number of individuals with TTM also bite, chew on, and occasionally swallow their hair (Woods, Friman, & Teng, 2001), which can cause physical problems. Swallowing one's hair can result in trichobezoars (i.e., hairballs), and although not very common, those with TTM can develop repetitive strain injuries such as carpal tunnel syndrome (O'Sullivan, Keuthen, Jenike, & Gumley, 1996) and dental erosion from biting hair (Christenson & Mansueto, 1999).

Research has also suggested a number of social consequences to TTM. Boudjouk, Woods, Miltenberger, and Long (2000) found that child actors exhibiting hair pulling were perceived as less socially acceptable by their peers, a finding replicated in other studies (Long, Woods, Miltenberger, Fuqua, & Boudjouk, 1999; Woods, Fuqua, & Outman, 1999). To minimize the social impact, children with TTM attempt to conceal the physical consequences of hair pulling by wearing hats or bandannas, makeup, hair extensions, certain hair styles, glasses, or wigs (Christenson et al., 1991; Schlosser, Black, Blum, & Goldstein, 1994).

Although data are limited, research has suggested that comorbid psychiatric diagnoses may be common in older children diagnosed with TTM. Reeve et al. (1992) examined clinical characteristics and psychiatric comorbidity in 10 children with TTM and found that 70% had at least one additional psychiatric diagnosis. Overanxious disorder and dysthymia were the most common comorbid diagnoses, and subsequent research showed similar rates of anxiety and mood disorders in children (King et al., 1995). The aforementioned patterns of comorbidity are similar to patterns found in adults with TTM (Lochner, Simeon, Niehaus, & Stein, 2002; Schlosser et al., 1994; Woods, Flessner, Franklin, Keuthen, et al., 2006).

Research examining the phenomenology of TTM has suggested that different subtypes or dimensions of hair pulling may exist (Christenson & Mackenzie, 1994; Christenson et al., 1991; Diefenbach, Mouton-Odum, & Stanley, 2002; du Toit, van Kradenburg, Niehaus, & Stein, 2001). Christenson and Mackenzie (1994) referred to these dimensions as "automatic" and "focused" pulling. "Automatic" pulling is characterized by pulling that occurs primarily out of an individual's awareness (e.g., client pulls while watching television, reading a book, or listening to the radio). Often, the person engaging in automatic pulling does not know he or she has done the behavior until it has been completed (e.g., the client sees hair on his or her lap). "Focused" pulling is characterized by pulling with an almost compulsive quality and seems to involve pulling in response to a negative emotion (e.g., anxiety, stress, anger) or an intense urge. Recent research suggests that focused pulling may represent an attempt to decrease levels of negative affect (e.g., unpleasant sensations, anxiety, specific hair-related cognitions; Begotka, Woods, & Wetterneck, 2004; Woods et al., 2006).

It is unclear to what extent the focused and automatic distinctions apply to children. Reeve et al. (1992) found that none of the 10 children assessed in their study reported pulling of a compulsive quality, suggesting that children do not experience or may be unable to identify focused pulling.

Tic Disorders

Tics are "sudden, rapid, recurrent, nonrhythmic, stereotyped motor movements or vocalizations" (APA, 2000, p. 108). There are four tic disorder diagnoses: tic disorder-not otherwise specified, transient tic disorder, chronic motor or vocal tic disorders (CTD), and Tourette's disorder (TD). Single or multiple motor or vocal tics, but not both, that persist for at least 1 year characterize CTD, while single or multiple motor tics and one or more vocal tic that persist for at least 1 year characterize TD. Both disorder characterizations require onset before age 18 (APA, 2000).

At any one time, as many as 6.6% of children and adolescents may be diagnosed with tic disorders (Khalifa & Knorring, 2003). Although data on the prevalence of CTD are sparse, research suggests that approximately 0.8% of the population suffers from motor tics and 0.5% suffers from vocal tics (Khalifa & Knorring, 2003). Prevalence estimates for TD vary from about 0.04% to 3.0% (APA, 2000; Hornsey, Banerjee, Zeitlan, & Robertson, 2001; Khalifa & Knorring, 2003; Mason, Banerjee, Eapen, Zeitlin, & Robertson, 1998).

Individuals diagnosed with tic disorders can suffer negative physical consequences. Tics involving repetitive lip or cheek biting can result in oral inflammation or infection, and tics that are directed toward oneself can result in abrasions and fractures. When the tic involves the eyes, ocular injury can result (e.g., blindness from detached retina; Leckman, King, & Cohen, 1999). Tics representing different topographies can result in additional injuries. Although there is no documented evidence suggesting physical consequences from vocal tics, clients in the first author's clinic have reported physical consequences such as sore throats and difficulty speaking due to repeated vocalization (e.g., throat-clearing tics).

Individuals with tic disorders can also experience a variety of social consequences. Research examining the social acceptability of individuals with tic disorders has found those with tics to be viewed as less socially acceptable than tic-free peers (Boudjouk et al., 2000; Friedrich, Morgan, & Divine, 1996; Long et al., 1999; Woods et al., 1999; Woods, Koch, & Miltenberger, 2003). Recent research suggests that educational information about TD (e.g., a 13-minute video provided by the Tourette's Syndrome Association) may increase the social acceptability and tolerance of persons with TD (Woods et al., 2003).

Perhaps a greater concern than tics in predicting social impairment is the presence of comorbid conditions (Cohen, Friedhoff, Leckman, & Chase, 1992; Gadow, Nolan, Sprafkin, & Schwarz, 2002). Up to 95% of those with tic disorders meet diagnostic criteria for another psychiatric condition (Coffey, Biederman, Smoller, et al., 2000), the most common being attention-deficit/hyperactivity disorder (ADHD) and obsessive-compulsive disorder (OCD) (Cohen et al., 1992; Comings & Comings, 1985). Research has suggested that ADHD may be diagnosed in 64% to 76% of children with tic disorders and OCD in 25% to 38% (Coffey, Biederman, Smoller, et al., 2000; Comings & Comings, 1985; Kadesjo & Gillberg, 2000).

Children diagnosed with tic disorders may also suffer from a variety of additional mental health concerns, including depression (20%–49%), simple phobia (13%–35%), and overanxious disorder (7%–36%). Children with tic disorders may also experience a variety of disruptive behavior problems, such as conduct disorder (15%–40%) and oppositional defiant disorder (59%–81%). Although not as common, children diagnosed with tic disorders may also experience increased rates of learning disorders (e.g., dyslexia; 7%–36%) (Carter, Pauls, Leckman, & Cohen, 1994; Coffey, Biederman, Geller, et al., 2000; Coffey, Biederman, Smoller, et al., 2000; Kadesjo & Gillberg, 2000; Mason et al., 1998; Spencer, Biederman, Harding, Wilens, & Faraone, 1995).

One phenomenological characteristic of tic disorders that has received increasing attention recently is the premonitory urge (Woods, Piacentini, Himle, & Chang, 2005). A *premonitory urge* can best be described as an itching, pressure, or tingling sensation in the region of the body where a tic is about to occur or as a mental awareness of an impending tic (Leckman et al., 1999; Leckman, Peterson, Pauls, & Cohen, 1997; Leckman, Walker, & Cohen, 1993). Premonitory urges are typically experienced by older children and adults (e.g., 10 years of age or older), although children as young as 7 years old may report such urges (Leckman et al., 1999). Leckman et al. (1993) found that as many as 93% ($N = 123$) of persons diagnosed with a tic disorder report experiencing some form of urge, feeling, or "need" to engage in a tic. This may explain the perceived "voluntary" nature of tics that some clients report (Leckman et al., 1997). Typically, the urge temporarily dissipates after engaging in a tic, only to reemerge a short time later.

INTERVIEWING STRATEGIES

Clinicians seeking to assess and diagnosis children presenting with behaviors characteristic of TTM or tic disorders may choose from several structured, semistructured, and unstructured interviewing strategies.

Structured Interviews

A number of structured/semistructured interviews exist to aide in the assessment and diagnosis of both TTM and tic disorders. In addition to structured diagnostic interviews, clinician-administered semistructured instruments can be used to assess tic and TTM severity. Such measures include the Yale Global Tic Severity Scale (YGTSS) (Leckman et al., 1989) and the National Institute of Mental Health (NIMH) Trichotillomania Impairment Scale (NIMH-TIS) (Swedo et al., 1989). These interviews are described below, and, where possible, psychometric properties are reported.

Establishing Diagnoses. Any number of structured interviews can be used to establish a diagnosis of tic disorder and/or TTM and comorbid diagnoses. Examples include the Anxiety Disorders Interview Schedule for *DSM-IV* (ADIS) (Silverman & Albano, 1996), the Kiddie Schedule for Affective Disorders and Schizophrenia for School-Age Children (6–18 years)–Lifetime Version (K-SADS) (Kaufman et al., 1997), and the NIMH Diagnostic Interview Schedule for Children– Version IV (NIMH DISC-IV) (Shaffer, Fisher, Lucas, Dulcan, & Schwab-Stone, 2000). We provide more detail on the DISC as one option for diagnosing tics and discuss the Trichotillomania Diagnostic Interview (TDI) (Rothbaum & Ninan, 1994) as a method for diagnosing TTM.

The DISC is a structured diagnostic interview assessing for more than 30 psychiatric diagnoses in children. The DISC uses diagnostic criteria set forth by the *Diagnostic and Statistical Manual of Mental Health Disorders, Fourth Edition (DSM-IV)* (APA, 1994) and the *International Classification of Diseases, 10th Edition (ICD-10)* (World Health Organization, 1993). The parent version of the DISC (DISC-P) is designed for administration to the parent, legal guardian, or primary caretaker of children between the ages of 6 and 17, while the youth version (DISC-Y) is designed for direct administration to children between the ages of 9 and 17. Data from these interviews can be interpreted either together or separately.

Questions from the DISC are short (e.g., primarily "yes" or "no" responses), include very few open-ended questions, and are worded in a manner allowing clinicians to confer diagnoses both at the present and in the past. To aid in interview administration and to enhance the accuracy of diagnosis, a computerized version of the DISC (C-DISC) is available. The C-DISC allows clinicians to select specific modules they feel are most important to their clients. For example, modules assessing disruptive behavior disorders (e.g., ADHD, conduct disorder, oppositional defiant disorder), anxiety disorders (e.g., OCD), and tic disorders may be administered for children presenting with tics. An additional benefit of the DISC is that the structured interview takes only 90 to 120 minutes to administer.

Although the DISC has several advantages supporting its use in the assessment and diagnosis of both TTM and tic disorders in children, the structured interview also has several limitations. Specifically, the DISC does not allow presentation of atypical behaviors (e.g., behaviors outside the scope of the *DSM-IV* and *ICD-10*), and the interview is unable to address invalid responses provided by a client who misunderstands a question (Shaffer et al., 2000). The DISC-P has shown moderate to good test-retest reliability (k = 0.45 – 0.68), while the DISC-Y has shown substantially poorer temporal stability (k = 0.10 – 0.64) in community samples. However, both the DISC-P and DISC-Y have demonstrated higher temporal stability in clinical samples (k = 0.43 – 0.96 and 0.25 – 0.92, respectively), and past versions of the DISC have demonstrated moderate to very good concurrent validity and good to excellent sensitivity in the diagnosis of uncommon psychiatric disorders. Unfortunately, research has yet to examine the psychometric properties of either the TTM or tic disorder sections of the DISC.

In diagnosing TTM, we have found the TDI to be quite helpful. The TDI provides a standardized assessment instrument for the diagnosis of TTM modeled after the Structured Clinical Interview for *DSM-III-R* (SCID) (Spitzer, Williams, Gibbon, & First, 1990). The TDI includes a 3-point clinician-rated scale (e.g., threshold, subthreshold, and below threshold) for each of several questions designed to assess diagnostic criteria for TTM set forth by the *DSM*. Although the TDI provides an excellent and efficient means by which to formally assess TTM in clients, the psychometric properties of the interview have yet to be examined. Therefore, the reliability and validity of the TDI for use with either children or adults should be approached with caution.

Ratings of Severity. After establishing a diagnosis, it is useful to quantify the severity of the disorder. To aid in this quantification, a number of interview-based instruments may be helpful. To assess the severity of tic disorders, the Yale Global Tic Severity Scale (YGTSS) (Leckman et al., 1989) may be useful. The YGTSS is a clinician-administered interview in which motor and vocal tics are rated separately across several domains of severity, including tic number, frequency, complexity, intensity, and amount of interference produced. The scores are summed to yield a total tic severity score, and clinicians can also provide a separate global impairment rating. The YGTSS has demonstrated adequate to excellent internal consistency (Leckman et al., 1989; Storch et al., 2005) and fair to excellent temporal stability across motor, vocal, and total tic scores (Storch et al., 2005). In addition, the YGTSS has demonstrated strong convergent validity and adequate to strong discriminant validity (Leckman et al., 1989; Storch et al., 2005). One factor not assessed by the YGTSS is the premonitory urge phenomenon. The recently developed Premonitory Urge for Tics Scale (PUTS) may be useful in this regard (Woods et al., 2005).

To measure the severity of TTM, the NIMH Trichotillomania Impairment Scale (NIMH-TIS) (Swedo et al., 1989) may be used. The NIMH-TIS provides a single impairment rating completed by a clinician. This rating is based on the damage resulting from pulling (as measured by direct observation), time spent pulling or concealing damage to the area, and the individual's ability to control his or her hair pulling.

The NIMH-TIS is rated on a 0- to 10-point scale, with a rating of 0 representing no impairment, ratings from 1 to 3 representing minimal impairment, 4 to 6 representing mild impairment, and 7 to 10 representing moderate to severe impairment. The NIMH-TIS has shown minimally acceptable ($r = 0.71$) (Stanley, Breckenridge, Snyder, & Novy, 1999) to excellent ($r = 0.94$) (Crocetto, Diefenbach, Tolin, & Maltby, 2003) interrater reliability and good to very good concurrent validity with measures of hair damage ($r = 0.77$) and ratings of pulling severity obtained via assessment interview ($r = 0.87$) (Stanley et al., 1999). The psychometric properties of the NIMH-TIS have yet to be examined for children.

Unstructured Interviews

Unstructured interviews are used for multiple purposes, but in the assessment of habit disorders, the most pressing information involves understanding the impact of the problem on the lives of those with the diagnosis and their families, establishing family and disorder history, differentially diagnosing the conditions, and conducting a functional assessment.

Functional Impact. In the assessment of both tic disorders and TTM, clinicians should explore possible impairment in social, academic, or family functioning. Children with these disorders may experience significant teasing and, consequently, may have begun to avoid social situations or become isolated from peers. Likewise, the unstructured interview should explore possible academic impairments that may be created by the habit disorder. For example, pulling may be happening with such frequency that studying becomes disrupted. Finally, the clinician should examine the possible negative physical effects of the disorder, as described earlier.

Establishing Family History and History of the Disorder. For both tic disorders and TTM, questions assessing the age of onset; longest period of time the child has gone without the habit; and family history of TTM, tic disorders, and closely related conditions can be helpful. In addition, it is very important to assess the treatment history surrounding the disorder. Many individuals with these disorders will have been treated ineffectively by practitioners not familiar with such symptom presentations. Consequently, a good deal of reeducation about what may and may not be effective may be required. Finally, assessing for beliefs about the cause and intentionality of the disorders on the part of the parent and child can be helpful in treatment planning. For example, if parents think the child is doing the behavior intentionally and should be punished for doing so, such beliefs may need to be addressed prior to starting treatment.

Differential Diagnosis. Differential diagnoses are discussed in more detail later in this chapter, but it is worthwhile to note that tic disorders and TTM can easily be confused with a host of other physical and psychiatric conditions. The astute clinician should take care to make accurate differential diagnoses.

Functional Assessment

In the assessment of both tic disorders and TTM, functional assessment (FA) is an important aspect of the interview process. As mentioned previously, children diagnosed with these disorders often experience a variety of social and/or physical consequences associated with the disorder (e.g., teasing from peers, sensory stimulation from manipulating the pulled hair, physical pain, etc.). Information of this nature, along with other antecedents and consequences to the child's habit behavior and the setting in which these events occur, can be assessed thoroughly in a proper FA. The information obtained can then be used in conjunction with an empirically supported treatment that the clinician deems appropriate. The information described above, along with demographic information (e.g., age, race, etc.), family history, and level of education will prove beneficial in not only the assessment and diagnosis but also the development of treatment recommendations for children diagnosed with tic disorders or TTM.

INTERVIEWING OBSTACLES AND SOLUTIONS

A number of obstacles can be encountered when assessing a child with tic disorders or TTM. What follows is a brief description of some obstacles we have encountered and possible solutions.

Parent and Child Disagreement

Many children (especially younger ones) do not present at clinic because they see their TTM or tic disorders as a problem. Often the parents, who have grown increasingly worried or concerned about their children's behavior, initiate the assessment process. Consequently, the parents and child may express disparate interpretations or descriptions of (a) the child's behavior, (b) situations exacerbating the child's behavior, (c) impairment resulting from the behavior, and (d) reasons as to why the child engages in the behavior.

It is critically important for clinicians, parents, and children to understand the importance of both the parents' and children's perspectives in the assessment process. Parents must understand that their children are not engaging in this behavior (e.g., tics or hair pulling) to "annoy" them, and children must understand that their parents are not just "nagging" them. Instead, clinicians must set a tone of mutual cooperation between parents and children as they work together to overcome the problem. In parallel, children must understand that the information they provide will be listened to and held in as much regard as the information provided by their parents.

Children's Embarrassment About Being Assessed

Initially, children may be apprehensive or embarrassed discussing hair pulling or tics with clinicians. Children who pull their hair will likely be hesitant to show the areas from which they pull and may engage in a variety of behaviors to conceal their pulling during the interview (e.g., makeup, hair styles, etc.) (Christenson et al., 1991). Children who exhibit tics may be embarrassed about the number, severity, and/or topography of tics they experience (e.g., they are teased at school because of certain tics). Although these obstacles may be difficult to overcome, clinicians can employ a number of strategies to reduce clients' embarrassment or apprehension.

During the interview, the clinician must create a safe environment where the child can disclose potentially embarrassing aspects of the condition and its physical and social effects. This can be done by normalizing the child's embarrassment and parents' frustration and by reassuring the child and parents as to the clinician's level of experience in dealing with tics, hair pulling, and similar problems. Sometimes watching brief films or television programs about TD or TTM can help facilitate more open disclosure.

Diagnostic Conundrums for TTM and Tic Disorders

TTM. Although researchers have become increasingly skeptical as to the importance of Criteria B (e.g., tension prior to or while resisting the urge to pulling) and C (e.g., gratification, pleasure, or relief following pulling; Christenson & Crow, 1996; Christenson, Ristvedt, & Mackenzie, 1993; Reeve et al., 1992), both are still required for a diagnosis of TTM. This creates a potential problem in that some children may not be able to report or fully understand what is meant by terms such as *tension* or *urge*. As a result, it is increasingly important for the clinician to have a list of available synonyms for words such as *urge, tension, pleasure,* or *gratification* suitable for the child's age and level of intelligence. If the use of alternate language does not yield an adequate understanding of the disorder, many in clinical practice have simply discarded the use of the tension and tension reduction criteria and diagnosed TTM when repetitive pulling resulting in notable hair loss is present.

Tic Disorders. Perhaps the most difficult aspect in the assessment of tic disorders is the similarity between complex tics and symptoms of OCD. Ambiguity as to which category a child's behavior should be classified in can have important implications for both diagnosis and treatment. A child who repeatedly taps, touches, or rubs objects could be said to be engaging in a complex tic or behavior characteristic of OCD. To differentiate between the two, a clinician should consider the antecedents to the repetitive behavior. Studies done to differentiate between complex tics and OCD have found that complex tics are more likely to be preceded by sensory phenomena (e.g., bodily and mental sensations; Mansueto & Keuler, 2005; Miguel et al., 1997; Miguel et al., 2000). In contrast, repetitive behaviors associated with OCD are more likely to be preceded by particular cognitions or physiological anxiety. A thorough interview and examination of the child's behavior is necessary to fully understand the variables maintaining the behavior.

INTERVIEWING PARENTS AND TEACHERS

Obtaining information from both parents and teachers can prove beneficial in conceptualizing the child's case. Parents can provide information about symptom presentation that the child may be unable to provide. For example, parents may be more aware of when tics occur, situations that exacerbate tics, and consequences of tics (e.g., attention, social withdrawal, scolding). Due to the private nature of TTM, parents often provide limited information about situations that exacerbate pulling, the frequency of pulling, and settings in which pulling is most likely to occur. Parents of children with TTM, however, are typically good reporters on the extent of pulling (e.g., amount of hair loss on visible parts of the body).

To ensure that each party contributes fully to the assessment, parent(s) and children should be interviewed together and separately. Separate interviews allow the parents and child to discuss sensitive topics without the other being present. For example, the parent may express concern over whether or not the child's hair will ever grow back or whether the child's tics will continue to get worse if nothing is done to stop them. Likewise, in the presence of her parents, the teenage daughter may be highly embarrassed about reporting the pulling of pubic hair. Combined interviews can be particularly helpful in examining the family interaction patterns surrounding the tics or pulling.

Because TTM is often a private behavior, teachers will likely not add to information provided by the child's parents. However, teachers may be able to provide information regarding the frequency, severity, and situations exacerbating the child's tics at school. For example, Watson, Dufrene, Weaver, Butler, and Meeks (2005) interviewed the teachers of two students diagnosed with TD, to obtain operational definitions of each child's tics and determine the times or situations when the tics were most likely to occur. Interviewing each student's primary teacher, obtaining information as to the child's tics during school, and subsequently implementing treatment based upon the results of interviews conducted with both the child and teacher resulted in significant decreases in the child's tics. For both TTM and tic disorder cases, teachers can be quite helpful in providing information about the child's socializing behavior, his or her ability to make and sustain friends, and problems with homework or classes.

CASE ILLUSTRATION WITH DIALOGUE

In the following case illustration, we demonstrate an excerpt of an initial interview with a young child presenting with both motor and vocal tics (e.g., TD).

Max was a 10-year-old male presenting with several tic-like behaviors he had demonstrated over a 5-year span. Max was the oldest in a sibling strip of three and lived with his biological parents. Both parents denied a family history of tic disorders, but Max's father was observed to exhibit subtle facial tics during the interview. To aide in Max's assessment, both clinical and structured interviews (the ADIS) along with the YGTSS were given to establish tic and comorbid diagnoses and tic severity. Due to Max's age, his parents were present throughout the duration of the interview. What follows is an abridged excerpt from the ADIS-P conducted during Max's clinical assessment:

Clinician: I would first like to ask you for a brief description of any problems Max has been having recently.

Mother: Max has been snorting a lot since Christmas. He's been doing it since he was like 4 or 5 years old, but it has gotten really bad more recently.

C: Has Max ever demonstrated any jerky or involuntary movements, twitches, or spasms? [motor tics] Some common examples include eye blinks, neck jerks, facial twitches, arm or leg movements, stomach tightening, or shoulder shrugs. Or he may complain that other parts of the body tic involuntarily.

M: Yes.

C: Could you tell me about that?

M: He has had a bunch of different things, like blinking his eyes really quickly, shaking his hands, and, like I said earlier, snorting. I guess he has been doing one or more of these things since he was about 4 or 5.

C: Okay, now I'd like to find out about each of the problems you just told me about, and also to see if there are other tics that Max may have. Now, I am going to read you a list of a few common motor tics. First, I want you to tell me "yes" or "no" as to whether your child has the tic.

The clinician then proceeded through a list of motor tics from the ADIS. Max's mother reported five motor tics, including eye blinking, facial grimacing, tongue movements, stomach tensing, and hand shaking. She went on to report that each of these tics happened several times per day. The clinician then administered the "Feelings Thermometer" to Max's mother to determine how much the tics bothered Max and discovered that the tics were quite intense and difficult for Max to control.

C: Did these tics occur many times a day, nearly every day, for at least 4 weeks?

M: The tics started when Max was about 4 or 5 and always get worse when he goes back to school. It started with eye blinking, but other ones soon showed up. He normally has the tics until he gets adjusted to going to school and classes, but this year he just keeps having them every day, both in school and after school. I think he does pretty good at stopping them during the day, but he always has them when we are at home.

C: Did these tics occur for as long as a year?

M: Yes, I guess.

C: Was there a time during the year when Max was tic free for at least 3 months?

M: No way. He has at least one tic or another pretty much every day.

Further inquiry into Max's vocal tics revealed that Max engaged in several vocalizations, including sniffing, snorting, and throat clearing. Administration of the "Feelings Thermometer" revealed that Max's mother thought Max's vocal tics were very intense and difficult for him to control. The interview then proceeded as follows:

C: Have you ever consulted a doctor because you were worried about the motor or vocal tics?

M: Yes. We first went to an eye doctor when we noticed the blinking, but his eyes were okay. We went to our pediatrician when he first started snorting a few years ago.

We thought he had sinus or allergy problems, but allergy tests didn't show anything. Eventually, we took him to a neurologist because we saw something about Tourette's on TV. The neurologist ran a bunch of tests, but they all came back normal.

Completion of the ADIS revealed no additional psychiatric diagnoses. Based upon the results of the ADIS, Max met diagnostic criteria for TD. To aide in the conceptualization of Max's case and to quantify the severity of his tics, the therapist administered the YGTSS, which revealed mild to moderate levels of tic severity. Max's PUTS score was a 26, indicating the presence of a significant premonitory urge.

The above case illustration provides an outline for how to conduct both a clinical and structured interview with the parent of a child who exhibits tics. Much of what has been discussed thus far in this chapter has focused on the problem behaviors themselves, rather than important demographic characteristics that may influence not only the interpretation of the interview but also the manner in which questions are asked and presented. The next section examines the role multicultural and diversity issues may play in the interview process.

MULTICULTURAL AND DIVERSITY ISSUES

Unfortunately, the literature on multicultural issues in tic disorders and TTM is scarce, and nonexistent with respect to informing clinical interviewing. With tics, existing research suggests no significant differences in the prevalence of tics between Caucasians and other minorities. For example, African Americans and European Americans are equally likely to exhibit symptoms of tic disorders (Lapouse & Monk, 1964). Still, a recent study conducted by Gadow et al. (2002) suggested that young African American children may experience more severe symptoms of TD.

To date, only two empirical studies have addressed multicultural issues in TTM. In the first, King et al. (1995) examined the relative prevalence of TTM among 794 Israeli Jewish adolescents and found prevalence rates comparable to those found among college students in the United States, 0.5% versus 0.6%, respectively (Christenson et al., 1991). In the second,

Neal-Barnett, Ward-Brown, Mitchell, and Krownapple (2000) found that African Americans were more likely to report and receive treatment from hairdressers for help for hair pulling than to go to a psychiatrist or psychologist. Until research further examines ethnic and cultural differences in TTM and tic disorders, clinicians are urged to use cultural sensitivity in their interviewing strategies, being careful to remain respectful of clients' ethnic and cultural heritage.

DIFFERENTIAL DIAGNOSIS

As discussed earlier, a number of possible differential diagnoses must be considered in the assessment of TTM and tic disorders. A number of medical and neurological concerns may explain the development of tic-like behaviors in some children, including postencephalitis, head injury, carbon monoxide poisoning, and neuroacanthocytosis. At least two cases have been reported in which behaviors characteristic of TD (e.g., coughing, weezing, and grunting) have been misinterpreted as symptoms of asthma (Hogan & Wilson, 1999), and allergic conditions may also mimic vocal tic symptoms. The clinician must also be careful to rule out abnormal movement characteristic of disorders such as Sydenham's chorea or Huntington's disease (APA, 2000). Tics must also be differentiated from stereotyped movements associated with pervasive developmental disabilities. Other psychiatric disorders to consider for differential diagnosis include ADHD and OCD.

With respect to TTM, loss of hair may result in a number of medical concerns, such as alopecia areata, traction alopecia, loose anagen hair, tinea capitis, telogen effluvium, and pseudopelade (O'Sullivan & Redmond, 2001). In addition to ruling out these medical concerns, the clinician must also make every effort to rule out a variety of mental health concerns, including OCD and body dysmorphic disorder (BDD).

BEHAVIORAL ASSESSMENT

In addition to conducting a thorough interview, behavioral assessment is a useful method for measuring TTM and tic disorders. Three primary behavioral assessment strategies have been employed to assess the frequency/severity of hair pulling and tics, including self-monitoring, direct observation, and product recording. With self-monitoring, the child is asked to record either the number of hairs pulled or the number of tics he or she exhibits during a specified amount of time (for very frequent behavior) or throughout the entire day (for less frequent behavior). At the end of the week the child can report the collected data to the therapist. Self-monitoring can be easily used in clinical practice and requires little or no expense (e.g., the child can use a piece of paper, golf counter, etc.). Although self-monitoring may be limited by the participant's lack of awareness or reporting biases, it has been used to measure hair pulling severity and the occurrence of tics in several treatment studies (e.g., Azrin & Nunn, 1973; Kohen, 1996; Rosenbaum, 1982). Self-monitoring may have the added benefit of decreasing the target behavior (e.g., Woods, Miltenberger, & Lumley, 1996).

Direct observation can also be used in the assessment of habit disorders (e.g., Deaver, Miltenberger, & Stricker, 2001; Miltenberger, Long, Rapp, et al., 1998; Woods, Twohig, Flessner, & Roloff, 2003). Typically, direct observation involves taping the child either at home or the clinic for a specified period of time (e.g., 15–30 minutes), and these videotaped segments are recorded for the number of occurrences of the child's problem behavior. It should be noted that direct observation may be of limited utility for some children with TTM, due to the private nature of hair pulling. In addition, videotaped assessment is moderately time-consuming and more costly than data obtained via an interview.

The final method of behavioral assessment for TTM involves product-based recording. Two examples of product-based recording include collecting and counting or weighing pulled hairs (e.g., Byrd, Richards, Hove, & Friman, 2002) and photographing pulled areas to assess severity of damage resulting from hair pulling (Winchel et al., 1992). Unfortunately, product-based measurements are not without their faults. Collecting pulled hairs may be limited by both reactivity and the child's failure to accurately collect hairs, and photographing pulled areas may be limited due to practical or ethical reasons (e.g., areas from the body that cannot be photographed, such as the pubic region, chest, legs).

Although a variety of methods exist to assess both TTM and tic disorders, limitations exist for many of the methods described above. It is the job of the clinician to examine the pros and cons of each method and choose the methods that will work best for the client. In the first author's clinic, videotaped assessment is almost exclusively used to assess the severity of children with tic disorders and is often used in conjunction with self-monitoring. Conversely, the method of assessment for children diagnosed with TTM will depend greatly on the child's age and the area(s) from which he or she pulls most frequently. The clinician must weigh these options and choose the method of assessment that will provide the most valid information about and description of the child's hair pulling.

SELECTION OF TREATMENT TARGETS AND REFERRAL

Selecting treatment targets depends largely on the clinician's own conceptualization of the case. When treating a child with TTM or tic disorders, however, we follow a general sequence of treatment considerations and make referrals where appropriate.

Assuming other physical and psychiatric explanations for the behavior have been ruled out and a tic disorder or TTM diagnosis has been confirmed, we first examine the pattern of comorbidity exhibited by the child. As mentioned previously, children with TTM or tic disorders are likely to exhibit behaviors associated with comorbid conditions. Especially with tic disorders, these comorbid conditions (e.g., ADHD) may put the child at greater risk of future psychosocial difficulties than the tics themselves. Likewise, a child who is highly depressed will be unlikely to implement many of the treatment strategies we use when treating TTM. As a result, we suggest that the comorbid condition(s) as the primary diagnosis be managed first.

After comorbid conditions have been stabilized, we suggest a three-pronged approach to treatment. First, we suggest that the child and his or her parents receive extensive psychoeducation about the disorders from the therapist and that the family be encouraged to seek information on its own. It is helpful to guide parents to specific patient organizations and associated Web sites, which prove useful in obtaining reliable and accurate information about the disorders. For TTM, we recommend the Trichotillomania Learning Center Web site (http://www.trich.org), and for tic disorders, we recommend families visit the Tourette Syndrome Association Web site (http://www.tsa-usa.org) or the TS+ Web site (http://www.tourettesyndrome.net).

After the child and his or her family have received psychoeducation, we suggest that the environment be modified in ways that may lead to decreases in pulling or tics. Depending on the results of the functional assessment, any number of environmental modifications could occur, but the general strategy involves limiting access to high-risk settings, alleviating sensory reinforcers for the behavior (e.g., wearing Band-Aids on fingers to decrease tactile stimuli derived from rubbing the pulled hair), and changing the consequences for engaging in the behavior (e.g., asking parents to stop comforting the child when he or she tics or asking teachers to stop sending the child out of the classroom because of tics).

The final target for treatment is to teach the child strategies to anticipate and control the tics or pulling. The most common strategy, and the one we use in our clinic, is *habit reversal* (HR) (Azrin & Nunn, 1973). As HR has been described and reviewed extensively in recent publications (e.g., Carr & Chong, 2005; Miltenberger, Fuqua, & Woods, 1998; Woods, Flessner, Franklin, Wetterneck, et al., 2006; Woods & Miltenberger, 1995), it will not be described in detail here. Nevertheless, the procedure involves three primary components. *Awareness training* is done to make the child more aware of when the tic or pulling is occurring and to increase awareness of the antecedent sensory stimuli or settings that may predict increased pulling. After awareness training, *competing-response training* is implemented, which involves teaching the child to engage in a behavior that is physically incompatible with the habit behavior for 1 minute, contingent on becoming aware of the behavior or one of its precursors. Finally, *social support* is implemented by training the parents to praise the child for correctly implementing the competing response and prompting the child to use the competing response when the child is found engaging in the habit but not using the competing behavior. Typically, HR is implemented in 3 to 10 weekly sessions. If the child has multiple tics or pulls from multiple areas, it is often useful to focus on one tic or one area at a time and add tics or areas in a cumulative fashion as the child meets with success.

One issue that has not been addressed in our discussion of treatment is pharmacotherapy. For more severe cases of tic disorders or for cases where functional impairment due to tics is evidenced, a referral to a psychiatrist or neurologist would be warranted. Unfortunately, evidence supporting the use of pharmacotherapy to treat TTM in children is poor (Woods, Flessner, Franklin, Keuthen, et al., 2006). Although medications may be useful in addressing some of the precipitants to pulling (e.g., anxiety, depression), they have not been found to be effective in the treatment of pulling.

SUMMARY

In summary, the current chapter has sought to describe a comprehensive interview/assessment strategy for children with tic disorders and TTM. Given the diverse symptom presentation often found in these disorders, along with high comorbidity rates, assessment and subsequent treatment planning can be quite challenging. Our hope is that this chapter will facilitate useful assessment of these children, which will ultimately result in the delivery of better services.

REFERENCES

American Psychiatric Association. (1994). *Diagnostic and statistical manual of mental disorders* (4th ed.). Washington, DC: Author.

American Psychiatric Association. (2000). *Diagnostic and statistical manual of mental disorders* (4th ed., Text rev.). Washington, DC: Author.

Azrin, N. H., & Nunn, R. G. (1973). Habit reversal: A method of eliminating nervous habits and tics. *Behaviour Research and Therapy, 11,* 619–628.

Begotka, A. M., Woods, D. W., & Wetterneck, C. T. (2004). The relationship between experiential avoidance and the severity of trichotillomania in a non-referred population. *Journal of Behavior Therapy and Experimental Psychiatry, 35,* 17–24.

Boudjouk, P. J., Woods, D. W., Miltenberger, R. G., & Long, E. S. (2000). Negative peer evaluations in adolescents: Effects of tic disorders and trichotillomania. *Child & Family Behavior Therapy, 22*(1), 17–28.

Byrd, M. R., Richards, D. F., Hove, G., & Friman, P. C. (2002). Treatment of early onset hair pulling as a simple habit. *Behavior Modification, 26,* 400–411.

Carr, J. E., & Chong, I. M. (2005). Habit reversal treatment of tic disorders: A methodological critique of the literature. *Behavior Modification, 29,* 858–875.

Carter, A. S., Pauls, D. L., Leckman, J. F., & Cohen, D. J. (1994). A prospective longitudinal study of Gilles de la Tourette's Syndrome. *Journal of the American Academy of Child & Adolescent Psychiatry, 33,* 377–385.

Christenson, G. A., & Crow, S. J. (1996). The characterization and treatment of trichotillomania. *Journal of Clinical Psychiatry, 57*(Suppl. 8), 42–49.

Christenson, G. A., & Mackenzie, T. B. (1994). Trichotillomania. In M. Hersen & R. T. Ammerman (Eds.), *Handbook of prescriptive treatment for adults* (pp. 217–235). New York: Plenum Press.

Christenson, G. A., Mackenzie, T. B., & Mitchell, J. E. (1991). Characteristics of 60 adult chronic hair pullers. *American Journal of Psychiatry, 148,* 365–370.

Christenson, G. A., & Mansueto, C. S. (1999). Trichotillomania: Descriptive characteristics and phenomenology. In D. J. Stein, G. A. Christenson, & E. Hollander (Eds.), *Trichotillomania* (pp. 1–42). Washington, DC: American Psychiatric Press.

Christenson, G. A., Ristvedt, S. L., & Mackenzie, T. B. (1993). Identification of trichotillomania cue profiles. *Behaviour Research and Therapy, 31,* 315–320.

Coffey, B. A., Biederman, J., Geller, D. A., Spe, T. J., Kim, G. S., Bellordre, C. A., et al. (2000). Distinguishing illness severity from tic severity in children and adolescents with Tourette's disorder. *Journal of the American Academy of Child & Adolescent Psychiatry, 39,* 556–561.

Coffey, B. A., Biederman, J., Smoller, J. W., Geller, D. A., Sarin, P., Schwartz, S., et al. (2000). Anxiety disorders and tic severity in juveniles with Tourette's disorder. *Journal of the American Academy of Child & Adolescent Psychiatry, 39,* 562–568.

Cohen, D. J., Friedhoff, A. J., Leckman, J. F., & Chase, T. N. (1992). Tourette syndrome: Extending basic research to clinical care. In T. N. Chase, A. J. Friedhoff, & D. J. Cohen (Eds.), *Advances in neurology* (pp. 341–362). New York: Raven Press.

Cohen, L. J., Stein, D. J., Simeon, D., Spadaccini, E., Rosen, J., Aronowitz, B., et al. (1995). Clinical profile, comorbidity, and treatment history in 123 hair pullers: A survey study. *Journal of Clinical Psychiatry, 56,* 319–326.

Comings, D. E., & Comings, B. G. (1985). Tourette syndrome: Clinical and psychological aspects of 250 cases. *American Journal of Human Genetics, 37,* 435–450.

Crocetto, J. S., Diefenbach, G. J., Tolin, D. F., & Maltby, N. (2003, November). *Self-report and clinician-rated hair pulling scales: A psychometric evaluation.* Poster presented at the 37th Annual Meeting of the Association of the Advancement of Behavior Therapy, Boston.

Deaver, C. M., Miltenberger, R. G., & Stricker, J. M. (2001). Functional analysis and treatment of hair twirling in a young child. *Journal of Applied Behavior Analysis, 34,* 535–538.

Diefenbach, G. J., Mouton-Odom, S., & Stanley, M. A. (2002). Affective correlates of trichotillomania. *Behaviour Research and Therapy, 40,* 1305–1315.

Diefenbach, G. J., Tolin, D. F., Crocetto, J., Maltby, N., & Hannan, S. (2005). Assessment of trichotillomania: A psychometric evaluation of hair-pulling scales. *Journal of Psychopathology and Behavioral Assessment, 27,* 169–178.

du Toit, P. L., van Kradenburg, J., Niehaus, D. J. H., & Stein, D. J. (2001). Characteristics and phenomenology of hair-pulling: An exploration of subtypes. *Comprehensive Psychiatry, 42,* 247–256.

Flessner, C. A., Miltenberger, R. G., Egemo, K., Kelso, P., Jostad, C., Johnson, B., Gatheridge, B. J., et al. (2005). An evaluation of the social support component of simplified habit reversal for the treatment of nail biting. *Behavior Therapy, 36,* 35–42.

Flessner, C. A., & Woods, D. W. (2006). Phenomenological characteristics, social problems, and the economic impact associated with chronic skin picking. *Behavior Modification, 30,* 944–963.

Flessner, C. A., Woods, D. W., Franklin, M. E., Cashin, S. E., & Keuthen, N. J. (in press). The Milwaukee-Dimensions of Trichotillomania Scale (M-DOTS): Development, exploratory factor analysis, and psychometric properties. *Journal of Psychopathology and Behavioral Assessment.*

Friedrich, S., Morgan, S. B., & Devine, C. (1996). Children's attitudes and behavioral interventions towards a peer with Tourette's Syndrome. *Journal of Pediatric Psychology, 21,* 307–319.

Gadow, K. D., Nolan, E. E., Sprafkin, J., & Schwarz, J. (2002). Tics and comorbidity in children and adolescents. *Developmental Medicine & Child Neurology, 44,* 330–338.

Graber, J., & Arndt, W. B. (1993). Trichotillomania. *Comprehensive Psychiatry, 34,* 340–346.

Hansen, D. J., Tishelman, A. C., Hawkins, R. P., & Doepke, K. J. (1990). Habits with potential as disorders: Prevalence, severity, and other characteristics among college students. *Behavior Modification, 14,* 66–80.

Hogan, M. B., & Wilson, N. W. (1999). Tourette's syndrome mimicking asthma. *Journal of Asthma, 36,* 253–256.

Hornsey, H., Banerjee, S., Zeitlin, H., & Robertson, M. (2001). The prevalence of Tourette syndrome in 13–to 14-year-olds in mainstream schools, *Journal of Child Psychotherapy and Psychiatry, 42,* 1035–1039.

Kadesjo, B., & Gillberg, C. (2000). Tourette disorder: Epidemiology and comorbidity in primary school children. *Journal of the American Academy of Child & Adolescent Psychiatry, 39,* 545–555.

Kaufman, J., Birmaher, B., Brent, D., Rao, U., Flynn, C., Moreci, P., et al. (1997). Schedule for Affective Disorders and Schizophrenia for School-Age Children-Present and Lifetime Version (K-SADS-PL): Initial reliability and validity data. *Journal of the American Academy of Child & Adolescent Psychiatry, 36,* 980–988.

Khalifa, N., & Knorring, A. (2003). Prevalence of tic disorders and Tourette syndrome in a Swedish population. *Developmental Medicine & Child Neurology, 45,* 315–319.

King, R. A., Scahill, L., Vitulano, L. A., Schwab-Stone, M., Tercyak, K. P., & Riddle, M. A. (1995). Childhood trichotillomania: Clinical phenomenology, comorbidity, and family genetic. *Journal of the American Academy of Child & Adolescent Psychiatry, 34,* 1451–1459.

Kohen, D. P. (1996). Hypnotherapeutic management of pediatric and adolescent trichotillomania. *Journal of Developmental and Behavioral Pediatrics, 17,* 328–334.

Lapouse, R., & Monk, M. A. (1964). Behavioral deviations in a representative sample of children. Variation by sex, age, race, social class and family size. *American Journal of Orthopsychiatry, 3,* 436–446.

Leckman, J. F., King, R. A., & Cohen, D. J. (1999). Tics and tic disorders. In J. F. Leckman (Ed.), *Tourette's syndrome–Tics, obsessions, compulsions: Developmental psychopathology and clinical care* (pp. 23–42). Hoboken, NJ: Wiley.

Leckman, J. F., Peterson, B. S., Pauls, D. L., & Cohen, D. J. (1997). Tic disorders. *Psychiatric Clinics of North America, 20,* 839–861.

Leckman, J. F., Riddle, M. A., Hardin, M. T., Ort, S. I., Swartz, K. L., Stevenson, J., et al. (1989). The Yale Global Tic Severity Scale: Initial testing of a clinician-rated scale of tic severity. *Journal of the American Academy of Child & Adolescent Psychiatry, 28,* 566–573.

Leckman, J. F., Walker, D. E., & Cohen, D. J. (1993). Premonitory urges in Tourette's syndrome. *American Journal of Psychiatry, 151,* 98–102.

Lochner, C., Simeon, D., Niehaus, D. J. H., & Stein, D. J. (2002). Trichotillomania and skin-picking: A phenomenological comparison. *Depression and Anxiety, 15,* 83–86.

Long, E. S., Woods, D. W., Miltenberger, R. G., Fuqua, R. W., & Boudjouk, P. J. (1999). Examining the social effects of habit behaviors exhibited by individuals with mental retardation. *Journal of developmental and Physical Disabilities, 11,* 295–312.

Mansueto, C. S., & Keuler, D. J. (2005). Tic or compulsion? *Behavior Modification, 29,* 784–799.

Mason, A., Banerjee, S., Eapen, V., Zeitlin, H., & Robertson, M. M. (1998). The prevalence of Tourette syndrome in a mainstream school population. *Developmental Medicine & Child Neurology, 40,* 292–296.

Mehregan, A. M. (1970). Trichotillomania. *Archives of Dermatology, 102,* 129–133.

Miguel, E. C., Baer, L., Coffey, B. J., Rauch, S. L., Savage, C. R., O'Sullivan, R. L., et al. (1997). Phenomenological differences appearing with repetitive behaviors in obsessive-compulsive disorder and Gilles de la Tourette's syndrome. *British Journal of Psychiatry, 170,* 140–145.

Miguel, E. C., Rosario-Campos, M. C., da Silva Prado, H., Valle, R., Rauch, S. L., Coffey, B. J., et al. (2000). Sensory phenomena in obsessive-compulsive disorder and Tourette's Disorder. *Journal of Clinical Psychiatry, 61,* 150–156.

Miltenberger, R. G., Fuqua, R. W., & Woods, D. W. (1998). Applying behavior analysis with clinical problems: Review and analysis of habit reversal. *Journal of Applied Behavior Analysis, 31,* 447–469.

Miltenberger, R. G., Long, E. S., Rapp, J. T., Lumley, V., & Elliot, A. J. (1998). Evaluating the function of hair pulling: A preliminary investigation. *Behavior Therapy, 29,* 211–219.

Neal-Barnett, A. M., Ward-Brown, B. J., Mitchell, M., & Krownapple, M. (2000). Hair pulling in African-Americans: Only your hairdresser knows for sure: An exploratory study. *Cultural Diversity and Ethnic Minority Psychology, 6,* 352–362.

O'Sullivan, M. J., & Redmond, H. P. (2001). Trichotillomania. *Irish Journal of Psychological Medicine, 18,* 137–139.

O'Sullivan, R. L., Keuthen, N. J., Jenike, M. A., & Gumley, G. (1996). Trichotillomania and carpal tunnel syndrome. *Journal of Clinical Psychiatry, 57,* 174.

Rapp, J. T., Miltenberger, R. G., Galensky, T. L., Ellingson, S. A., & Long, E. S. (1999). A functional analysis of hair pulling. *Journal of Applied Behavior Analysis, 32,* 329–337.

Rapp, J. T., Miltenberger, R. G., Long, E. S., Elliot, A. J., & Lumley, A. (1998). Simplified habit reversal treatment for chronic hair pulling in three adolescents: A clinical replication with direct observation. *Journal of Applied Behavior Analysis, 31,* 299–302.

Reeve, E. A., Bernstein, G. A., & Christenson, G. A. (1992). Clinical characteristics and psychiatric comorbidity in children with trichotillomania. *Journal of the American Academy of Child & Adolescent Psychiatry, 31,* 132–138.

Rosenbaum, M. S. (1982). Treating hair pulling in a 7-year-old male: Modified habit reversal for use in pediatric settings. *Journal of Developmental and Behavioral Pediatrics, 3,* 241–243.

Rothbaum, B. O., & Ninan, P. T. (1994). The assessment of trichotillomania. *Behavior Therapy and Research, 32,* 651–662.

Schlosser, S., Black, D. W., Blum, N., & Goldstein, R. B. (1994). The demography, phenomenology, and family history of 22 persons with compulsive hair pulling. *Annals of Clinical Psychiatry, 6,* 147–152.

Shaffer, D., Fisher, P., Lucas, C. P., Dulcan, M. K., & Schwab-Stone, M. E. (2000). NIMH Diagnostic Interview Schedule for Children Version IV (NIMH DISC IV): Description, differences from previous versions, and reliability of some common diagnoses. *Journal of the American Academy of Child & Adolescent Psychiatry, 39,* 28–38.

Silverman, W. K., & Albano, A. M. (1996). *The Anxiety Disorders Interview Schedule for Children for DSM-IV: Child and Parent Versions.* San Antonio, TX: Psychological Corporation.

Spitzer, R. L., Williams, J. B. W., Gibbon, M., & First, M. B. (1990). *User's guide for the structure clinical interview for DSM-III-R: SCID.* Washington, DC: America Psychiatric Association.

Spencer, T., Biederman, J., Harding, M., Wilens, T., & Faraone, S. (1995). The relationship between tic disorders and Tourette's syndrome revisited. *Journal of the American Academy of Child & Adolescent Psychiatry, 34,* 1133–1139.

Stanley, M. A., Breckenridge, J. K., Snyder, A. G., & Novy, D. M. (1999). Clinician-rated measures of hairpulling: A preliminary psychometric evaluation. *Journal of Psychopathology and Behavioral Assessment, 21,* 157–182.

Storch, E. A., Murphy, T. K., Geffken, G. R., Sajid, M., Allen, P., Robertsi, J. W., et al. (2005). Reliability and validity of the Yale Global Tic Severity Scale. *Psychological Assessment, 17,* 486–491.

Swedo, S. E., Leonard, H. L., Rapoport, J. L., Lenane, M. C., Goldberger, E. L., & Cheslow, D. L. (1989).

A double-blind comparison of clomipramine and desipramine in the treatment of trichotillomania (hair pulling). *New England Journal of Medicine, 321,* 497–501.

Teng, E. J., Woods, D. W., Twohig, M. P., & Marcks, B. A. (2002). Body-focused repetitive behavior problems: Prevalence in a nonrefferred population and differences in perceived somatic activity. *Behavior Modification, 26,* 340–360.

Watson, T. S., & Allen, K. D. (1993). Elimination of thumb-sucking as a treatment for severe trichotillomania. *Journal of the American Academy of Child & Adolescent Psychiatry, 32,* 830–835.

Watson, T. S., Dittmer, K. I., & Ray, K. P. (2000). Treating trichotillomania in a toddler: Variations on effective treatments. *Child & Family Behavior Therapy, 22*(4), 29–40.

Watson, T. S., Dufrene, B., Weaver, B., Butler, T., & Meeks, C. (2005). Brief antecedent and treatment of tics in the general education classroom. *Behavior Modification, 29,* 839–857.

Winchel, R. M., Jones, J. S., Molcho, A., Parson, B., Stanley, B., & Stanley, M. (1992). Rating the severity of trichotillomania: Methods and problems. *Psychopharmacology Bulletin, 28,* 457–462.

Woods, D. W., Flessner, C. A., Franklin, M. E., Keuthen, N. J., Goodwin, R., Stein, D. J., Walther, M., & Trichotillomania Learning Center-SAB. (2006). The trichotillomania impact project (TIP): Exploring phenomenology, functional impairment, and treatment utilization. *Journal of Clinical Psychiatry, 67,* 1877–1888.

Woods, D. W., Flessner, C. A., Franklin, M. E., Wetterneck, C. T., Walther, M., Anderson, E. R., & Cardona, D. (2006). Understanding and treating Trichotillomania: What we know and what we don't know. *Psychiatric Clinics of North America, 29,* 487–501.

Woods, D. W., Friman, P. C., & Teng, E. J. (2001). Physical and social impairments in persons with repetitive behavior disorders. In D. W. Woods & R. G. Miltenberger (Eds.), *Tic disorders, trichotillomania, and other repetitive behavior disorders: Behavioral approaches to analysis and treatment* (pp. 33–51). Boston: Kluwer Academic.

Woods, D. W., Fuqua, R. W., & Outman, R. C. (1999). Evaluating the social acceptability of person with habit disorders: The effects of topography, frequency, and gender. *Journal of Psychopathology and Behavioral Assessment, 21,* 1–18

Woods, D. W., Koch, M., & Miltenberger, R. G. (2003). The impact of tic severity on the effects of peer education about Tourette's Syndrome. *Journal of Developmental and Physical Disabilities, 15,* 67–78.

Woods, D. W., & Miltenberger, R. G. (1995). Habit reversal: A review of applications and variations. *Journal of Behavior Therapy and Experimental Psychiatry, 26,* 123–131.

Woods, D. W., Miltenberger, R. G., & Flach, A. D. (1996). Habits, tics, and stuttering: Prevalence and relation to anxiety and somatic awareness. *Behavior Modification, 20,* 216–225.

Woods, D. W., Miltenberger, R. G., & Lumley, V. A. (1996). Sequential application of major habit reversal components to treat motor tics in children. *Journal of Applied Behavior Analysis, 29,* 483–493.

Woods, D. W., Piacentini, J. C., Himle, M. B., & Chang, S. (2005). Premonitory Urge for Tics Scale (PUTS): Initial psychometric results and examination of the premonitory urge phenomenon in children with tic disorders. *Journal of Developmental and Behavioral Pediatrics, 26,* 397–403.

Woods, D. W., Twohig, M. P., Flessner, C., & Roloff, T. J. (2003). Treatment of vocal tics in children with Tourette's syndrome: Investigating the efficacy of habit reversal. *Journal of Applied Behavior Analysis, 36,* 109–112.

Woods, D. W., Wetterneck, C. T., & Flessner, C. A. (2006). A controlled evaluation of acceptance and commitment therapy plus habit reversal as a treatment for trichotillomania, *Behaviour Research and Therapy, 44,* 639–656.

World Health Organization. (1993). *ICD-10 classification of mental and behavioural disorders: Diagnostic criteria for research.* Geneva, Switzerland: Author.

Wright, H. H., & Holmes, G. R. (2003). Trichotillomania (hair pulling) in toddlers. *Psychological Reports, 92,* 231–233.

22

JUVENILE FIRESETTING

MICHAEL SLAVKIN

Jordan and Jalyn, a 4-year-old and 9-month-old from Boulder, Colorado, were put to bed by their parents on a Sunday evening. The parents went about the business of closing up the house for the night and went to bed themselves around 11:00 p.m. At 2:00 in the morning, Jordan woke his parents, screaming and crying hysterically. The parents immediately smelled smoke, and, upon entering the hallway that separates their bedroom from that of their children, they were immobilized by smoke and flames. The parents and Jordan jumped from their second-story window, leaving Jalyn in her crib. Her lifeless body was found hours later, charred and covered by ashen blankets. The source of the fire was later found to have been a lighter that the parents left on their nightstand, which had been used to set fire to Jordan's stuffed animal.

Are these children arsonists, or are they just passing through a developmental phase? Will they grow up to be arsonists? Were their fathers arsonists as children? Should they be in juvenile hall or hospitalized? Perhaps their parents should be jailed. These are the types of questions that clinicians, fire service personnel, law enforcement, and juvenile justice must answer on an ongoing basis.

Each year, fires set by juveniles account for a large portion of fire-related public property damage and deaths. Fires set by children and adolescents are more likely than any other household disaster to result in death (National Fire Protection Association [NFPA], 1999). Though the majority of arson cases in the United States are caused by juveniles, approximately 60% according to John Hall (2003) of the NFPA, the public is most likely to think of adult offenders when arson is mentioned. Moreover, most people fail to view the severity of this problem; while they would be unlikely to leave a loaded gun on a coffee table, they see no problem leaving a pack of matches on a table or a lighter in an open purse. Despite this lack of recognition of the problem, juvenile firesetting and adult arson are serious concerns. In 2003, children playing with fire started approximately 67,490 fires, resulting in 232 civilian deaths, 1,805 civilian injuries, and $234.7 million in direct property damage (NFPA, 2003). Most of those killed in child-set fires were under 6 years of age.

Despite the costs and impact of juvenile firesetting and adult arson, the behavior remains a little-studied and marginally reviewed area of research, though a great amount of investigation has occurred on other aspects in the past two decades. Acts of arson have often been reviewed as differing based on the motive or intent of the firesetter, and category systems have been organized around these motives (Fineman, 1995). While these categories may hold some predictive validity in determining repeat firesetting (recidivism), few longitudinal studies have been performed that link recidivist tendencies with these categories. Appropriate categorization, however, can be helpful both clinically and in the research domain, as some qualitative research and phenomenological data stemming from case studies and other treatment programs have shown differences between nonpathological and pathological groups with respect to repeat firesetting, with pathological types often making up the majority of repeat firesetters (see Slavkin, 2000).

It is important to note that to clinicians and interventionists of all types, firesetting and arson are challenging areas of investigation. While other crimes typically have clear definitions (for example, the presence of drugs, the presence of interpersonal aggressive behaviors, the presence of deviant sexual behaviors), arson and intentional firesetting are not so easily defined. Is a fire an accident or arson? In some instances, juveniles with access to incendiary devices such as matches will burn them without lighting any other object on fire. Others will demonstrate a stronger intent, lighting toys or household objects on fire. Some adolescents are likely to destroy the personal property of others as crimes of revenge, while others in that same age group use fire to demonstrate pain and anxiety by burning their own items.

The bulk of the research literature on outcomes of treatment for firesetters relates to children and adolescents (Barnett & Spitzer, 1994). A number of studies have described systemic and behavioral approaches to treatment for child and adolescent firesetters. These have included family therapy (Eisler, 1972); implosion and aversion therapies (Cowell, 1985; Carstens, 1982); stimulus satiation (Wolff, 1984); differential reinforcement of more positive behaviors (Adler, Nunn, Laverick, & Ross, 1988); covert sensitization; and combined approaches (McGrath, Marshall, & Prior, 1979). As Adler et al. (1988) concluded, however, a high proportion of children can be expected to stop setting fires even if they receive no intervention, due to the effects of maturation.

DESCRIPTION OF THE PROBLEM

This chapter is based on the premise that aberrant behavior, such as firesetting, occurs when children and adolescents suffer from weak or nonexistent bonds to family or society. The limited ability to interact with family, schools, or peers reduces their chances to learn or engage in traditional methods of emotional expression. That, in turn, leads them to behave in socially unacceptable ways.

Juvenile firesetters are typically defined as children or adolescents who engage in firesetting. Beyond its tautological character, such a definition implies a singularity about firesetting in children and adolescents. It should be made clear at the beginning of this review, however, that this is an extremely complex behavior, with different risk factors and predictors based on the motives and age of the firesetter. To recognize the complexity of this behavior, it is more appropriate for professionals who work with juveniles to distinguish among the types of juvenile firesetters. Previous classifications of juvenile firesetters have been based on individual characteristics (e.g., personal motives, physical problems, interpersonal ineffectiveness/skills deficits, and covert antisocial behavior excesses) as well as environmental characteristics (e.g., limited supervision and monitoring, parental distance and lack of involvement, parental pathology and limitations, and the presence of crisis or trauma; Fineman, 1995; Kolko & Kazdin, 1992).

An adequate understanding of juvenile firesetting is contingent upon the simultaneous examination of individual and environmental factors (Barnett, Richter, Sigmund, & Spitzer, 1997). Without an examination of both interindividual and intraindividual factors, a professional will tend to have a limited view of a juvenile's firesetting behavior and will be less likely to effectively intervene on the firesetter's behalf.

INDIVIDUAL FACTORS

Individual Characteristics

Factors within firesetters are used to predict and explain the maladaptive patterns of firesetting (Showers & Pickrell, 1987). Individual characteristics examined in this chapter include a discussion of both behavior patterns and personality factors that appear to predict whether firesetting is likely to be evidenced in a youth. Individual personality factors such as the tendency toward aggression, high levels of impulsivity, high levels of delinquency, a general affinity for fire, and social skills deficits are commonly reviewed when discussing youthful firesetting, Moreover, the presence of individual behavioral characteristics, such as an externalization of emotions (e.g., fighting), attention-seeking behaviors, and engaging in risky behaviors are behavior patterns that may be predictors for juvenile firesetting.

Individual Personality Factors

To recognize the potential risk for use of fire in youth or adults, it is imperative that the personality of the individual be examined. More often than not, the public believes that juveniles who set fires are pathological, thinking of films like *Backdraft* or *The Burning Bed,* when, in fact, most youth who set fires do so for reasons other than pathological impulses. It is fairly clear, however, that there is an age-related tendency for pathology to increase as the age of the firesetter increases, with adolescents and adults demonstrating more pathology than younger firesetters (Slavkin, 2000).

Rather than concluding that psychopathology is the controlling issue, professionals should consider that juvenile firesetting and adult arson begin with a personality characteristic that is often shared by members of our communities: an affinity for or a curiosity about fire. Curiosity about fire is a common characteristic of all human beings, a primeval element, the possession of which historically represents safety, security, support, and perhaps control over the elements. Beyond these characteristics, fire may symbolize a variety of cognitive states, including power and control. Yet for most children, fire represents a fascinating and ever-changing phenomenon—the child sees and is reinforced by the flicker of an enticing flame, one that ebbs and flows and changes according to the elements used to feed the flame. In addition to a curiosity or fascination for fire, there are other characteristics that are likely to support a juvenile being drawn to use fire. These include a tendency toward aggression, high levels of delinquency and impulsivity, and social skills deficits.

General Affinity for Fire. Most children and adults have a general curiosity about fire. It is a function of our past that fire holds metaphors of both power as well as rebirth. Children are drawn to fire and often are inquisitive about the ways

that fire works and its various uses. Beyond simple curiosity, however, some firesetters actually seek an explanation for these characteristics, tempting the risk of personal injury/death, family and peer injury/death, as well as monetary loss from damage. Such experimentation may originate out of curiosity, but the innocence of this personality characteristic may result in great damage and injury/death. The individual with the strongest affinity for fire is often a young firesetter who experiments to gain insight into the science of fire. In fact, fires set by young children are more likely than those set by any other age group to result in extensive damage and death, as the young children who set them often do so in private places where they play (e.g., in their bedrooms or playrooms, away from prying adult eyes) (Federal Emergency Management Agency, 1995). Such clandestine actions increase the likelihood that these fires will not be discovered until the damage is significant and the ability to escape the fire safely is greatly reduced.

Tendency Toward Aggression. Aggression in youth typically is not seen as a developmental difficulty until it is either evidenced in tandem with behaviors of noncompliance and disruption or it occurs at a frequent or intense level. Early childhood noncompliance and aggression have been identified as indicators of lifelong difficulty with aggression if interventions are not initiated (Carey, 1997; DeSalvatore & Hornstein, 1991). Firesetting has been closely related to antisocial behaviors in youth (Fineman, 1980, 1995; Raines & Foy, 1994). As an individual increases in age, the likelihood is that aggressive tendencies will take on a more deviant and disruptive tone; adult arsonists often represent the "worst of the worst" (if an adult continues to utilize such maladaptive behaviors, irrespective of the rationale for behaving this way, this is evidence of great deviance).

Rice and Harris (1996) found that among adolescent male firesetters at a maximum-security psychiatric hospital, one third of firesetters had also been reported to engage in other aggressive and violent offences. In addition, Kolko and Kazdin (1991) reported a relationship between early childhood firesetting, heightened aggression, and social skills deficits (also see Forehand, Wierson, Frame, Kemptom, & Armistead, 1991). Slavkin (2000) also found a greater likelihood that preadolescent and adolescent juvenile firesetters, in contrast with early childhood and elementary-age firesetters, set fires as a result of anger or aggressive tendencies. Similar findings have been shown by Loeber and Stouthamer-Loeber (1998), who reviewed the literature on juvenile aggression and violent behavior and identified a number of age-related patterns in their development. The authors found that there is a discontinuous relationship between early childhood aggression and aggression in early adulthood.

Professionals who work with firesetters should keep in mind that as the age of the firesetter increases, there is an increased likelihood that their firesetting is an externalization of their anger. A critical part of intervention and prevention of recidivist behaviors would require an anger management component, regardless of age.

High Levels of Delinquency. Firesetting research has neglected the connections between juvenile-firesetting recidivism and patterns of delinquency. Burgess and Akers (1966) and Junger and Wiegersma (1995) stated that aberrant criminal behavior is a shaped response to cultural and environmental stimuli. Social learning theory asserts that individuals learn how to behave and respond to environmental stimulation by watching others' behavior and by imagining themselves performing similar behaviors (Bandura, 1977; Nielsen, Harrington, Sack, & Latham, 1985).

Deviance and Vandalism. Firesetting has long been considered a form of social deviance in youth (Fineman, 1997). Loeber, DeLamatre, Keenan, and Zhang (1998) asserted that *deviance* can be classified as behaviors that are bothersome to adult caregivers (e.g., highly stubborn behavior, lying, truancy, running away from home) or that inflict harm or property loss on others (e.g., physical aggression, vandalism, theft, violent acts). Kazdin (1990) posited that deviance in early childhood is most closely connected with a diagnosis of conduct disorder (also see Barnett et al., 1997). Early childhood deviance is often revealed in disobedience and unmanageability during early childhood and preschool (age 2–5 years).

While 10% of juveniles who are arrested are juvenile firesetters, juvenile firesetters are more likely to be arrested overall compared with juveniles who engage in other maladaptive behaviors. Firesetters also engage in property destruction and crimes of physical aggression, such as forcible rape (11%), nonviolent sexual offenses (18%), vandalism (19%), and arson for hire (35%) (Williams, 1998).

High Levels of Impulsivity. A frequent declaration from the mental health and fire professionals who work with juvenile firesetters relates to the preponderance of children with high levels of impulsivity. Kolko's (1985) publication called attention to the connection between aggression, psychopathology, and social skills deficits in juvenile firesetters. It is noteworthy that many firesetters have difficulty controlling their thoughts and behaviors. Analyses reported by Kolko indicated that when firesetters from inpatient populations are compared with other juvenile inpatients, they tend to show higher levels of behavioral dysfunction and impulsivity. When this is paired with their lower levels of assertiveness and social skills deficits, one may hypothesize that some firesetters lack the cognitive capacity to recognize the dangerousness of their behaviors and also lack a set of skills that would enable them to stop fire-related deviant behavior before it starts.

Social Skills Deficits. Kolko and Kazdin (1991) reported a relationship between early childhood firesetting, heightened aggression, and social skills deficits (also see Forehand et al., 1991). Further, Fineman (1995) called attention to the relationship between poor social skills in childhood and the development of firesetting in children and adults.

Many in the field believe that some children are drawn to fire as a way of sharing emotions. Most juveniles in primary and intermediate grades do not have the language abilities to share complex emotions and relate them to their thoughts. Thus, sharing emotions through fire, though a very maladaptive approach to sharing significant events in one's life, is a powerful form of communication. Children might express pain or anxiety, for example, by burning the house down or trying to let the authorities know about sexual abuse by burning their parents' bed.

Externalization of Emotions. Firesetters tend to have conduct problems, such as disobedience and aggressiveness. It is thought that these maladaptive behaviors are juvenile firesetters' primary method for externalizing, or expressing, feelings (Forehand et al., 1991; Thomas & Grimes, 1994). Sakheim, Vidgor, Gordon, and Helprin (1985) also found that firesetters had feelings of anger and resentment over parental rejection and that such feelings were frequently expressed covertly through the use of fire (Fineman, 1995; Sakheim & Osborn, 1999; Thomas & Grimes, 1994). Children and adolescents who set fires are identified as having poor social awareness and limited ability or opportunity to express themselves.

Kolko and Kazdin (1986a, 1986b) found that early childhood firesetters can be characterized as having multiple behavior problems, with few internalizing behaviors, such as depression, but many externalizing behaviors, such as rule breaking, aggression, and destruction. Prior examinations of youthful firesetting have emphasized the intraindividual dynamics of children, focusing on the firesetting problem by relating it to some internal dysfunction that is either genetic or due to a developmental anomaly (Raines & Foy, 1994). The firesetting of most juveniles, however, is most likely the result of environmental influences and limited coping skills (Fineman, 1980; Kolko & Kazdin, 1991).

Attention-Seeking Behavior. Though largely ignored by research, attention-seeking behavior is a factor often involved in juvenile firesetting, as is the desire to get a reaction from parents, authorities, and emergency services (Schwartzman, Stambaugh, & Kimball, 1994). Most attention-seeking behavior is classified according to the functions of the behavior (Lee & Miltenberger, 1996). Although no studies of attention-seeking behavior in juvenile firesetters have been performed, Luby, Reich, and Earls (1995) and Taylor and Carr (1994) found that children involved in neglectful environments were more likely than children in traditional supervised settings to engage in attention-seeking behavior. Fineman (1980, 1995, 1997) noted that the attention-getting elements of firesetting were extremely powerful reinforcers, especially with adolescents.

Engagement in Risky Behaviors. Firesetting may be a risky behavior that draws youthful interest as a way of creating relationships. Many hyperactive and attention-seeking youth elicit attention through externalization of behaviors; as such, firesetting can easily meet a variety of needs. To such juveniles, firesetting provides an opportunity to obtain extensive attention: negative attention from adults and positive attention from peers. This maladaptive process can require little effort on the part of the juvenile firesetter.

Personality traits such as the need for attention from external sources, impulse control disorders, and defiance are found in firesetters; such traits tend to be found in risk takers as well. Adult firesetters, compared with nonfiresetters, tend to be risk takers who are extraverted, compulsive, and defiant. As firesetters get older, it is probable that their firesetting is related to compulsive emotions and defiant behaviors. Without intervention, it is unlikely that such impulses to engage in risky behaviors will stop.

ENVIRONMENTAL FACTORS

Environmental characteristics are defined as supports, controls, models, and expectations of others that are thought to be meaningful phenomena to the juvenile (Jessor, 1987). Achenbach's (1966) theory is similar to the tentative risk model originally identified by Kolko and Kazdin (1986a), in that both subscribe to an interactive relationship between individual characteristics and environmental factors. When intraindividual factors are viewed in concert with a combination of environmental factors, such as interpersonal difficulties, the presence of abusive adults, and problems with home and school, environmental influences appear to be more predictive than intraindividual factors of youthful firesetting, adult violence, and criminality (Justice, Justice, & Kraft, 1974).

Jessor and Jessor (1973) and Jessor (1981) have argued that differences in problem behaviors stem largely from the delinquent's perceptions of environmental characteristics: that which the individual believes about his or her environment tends to mitigate or reduce problem behaviors. *Proximal controls* refer to the prevalence or models and supports for problem behavior. Environmental proximal controls that were examined in this chapter include family problems and economic stressors. Environmental distal controls that were examined in this chapter include school problems and peer problems.

Environmental Proximal Controls for Firesetting

Family Problems. Kolko and Kazdin (1994) asserted that parent and family characteristics promote firesetting and a continuation of patterns of firesetting. Moderate firesetting by youth has been associated with limited family sociability, whereas recidivism has been associated with lax discipline, family conflict, limited parental acceptance, and family affiliation (Kolko & Kazdin, 1994). Parental influences such as limited supervision and monitoring, early learning experiences and cues with fire, parental distance and uninvolvement, and parental pathology have been identified as predictors of juvenile firesetting (Fineman, 1980, 1995, Kolko & Kazdin, 1986a, 1991).

There are correlates between parental maladaptive behaviors and child maladaptive behaviors, especially as related to firesetting (Fineman, 1980; Kolko & Kazdin, 1988, 1991). Few professionals, however, examine such environmental conditions when working with firesetters (Federal Emergency Management Agency, 1995; Gaynor, 2002). In reviewing the relations between family dynamics and juvenile firesetting, Squires and Busuttil (1995) determined that a significant number of house fires were directly related to the activities of adults in the home. Poor supervision and a lax child care environment were found to be better predictors of recidivism in children than were intraindividual factors (also see Kolko & Kazdin, 1988; Showers & Pickrell, 1987). Moreover, adults were found to spend a limited amount of time keeping track of incendiaries in the home, which increased juvenile access and ability to set fires (Squires & Busuttil, 1995).

Firesetting in young children has been identified as being largely the result of a neglectful family environment (Gaynor & Hatcher, 1987). Macht and Mack (1968) asserted that the family environment of the early childhood firesetter is likely to be chaotic and limited in nurturing behaviors. Patterson (1982) maintained that early childhood firesetters show the beginnings of antisocial behaviors and that the externalization of emotions through firesetting resembles behavior in adolescents who are victims of abuse and neglect. According to these theories, unwanted and unacceptable early childhood behaviors are thought to be largely the result of a neglectful and abusive home environment.

Some firesetting juveniles engage in destructive behaviors as a result of family context. Psychosocial maladjustment has been related to family dysfunction (Bumpass, Fagelman, & Brix, 1983; Fineman, 1980, 1995; Kazdin, 1990; Kolko & Kazdin, 1992). Saunders and Awad (1991) asserted that adolescent firesetters are likely to experience parental separation, violence within the home, parental alcohol and drug abuse, or some form of physical or sexual abuse. Firesetters experience significantly more emotional neglect and physical abuse than other children of similar socioeconomic and geographic backgrounds (Thomas & Grimes, 1994). These juveniles are also more likely to have parents with limited parenting skills, limiting their chances to learn adequate coping skills (Swaffer & Hollin, 1995). Firesetters and their parents are similar on measures of aggression, hostility, involvement in maladaptive behaviors, and difficult temperament (Kolko & Kazdin, 1991).

Economic Stressors

Stressful environmental circumstances, individual crises, and limited support at home are often the precursors to property damage through use of fire. Low socioeconomic stability has been identified as a prime stressor that can affect the behaviors of juveniles (Schaenman, Hall, Schainblatt, Swartz, & Karter, 1977). Lower levels of income are directly correlated with an increased risk of residential fire. Schaenman et al. (1977) found that intercity comparisons of fire rates were not as useful as census tracks that identified variables connected with socioeconomic status, such as (a) parental presence, or the percentage of children under the age of 18 years living with both parents; (b) poverty, defined as the percentage of persons whose incomes fell below the poverty line; and (c) undereducation, or the percentage of persons over the age of 25 years who had fewer than 8 years of schooling. In this study (Schaenman et al., 1977), 39% of the variance in fire rates could be connected with these three variables.

Environmental Distal Controls for Firesetting

School Problems. At the present time, limited information exists about firesetters' experiences with school and its importance as a socializing agent—for example, the influence of peers and teachers on the behavior of firesetters. Many school-age juveniles who are drawn to using fire for whatever reason tend to do so in public places where it is likely to be noticed (as opposed to younger, preschool-age juveniles who tend to use fire in private). School is a powerful place to communicate using fire, as it is likely to elicit much attention and receive negative retribution. Further, for those students who are being victimized at home or in their neighborhoods, school is perhaps one of the safest environments. That feeling of safety could provide them the stability to share such trauma and indicates a powerful need for counseling as a preventative system.

Peer Problems. Juvenile firesetters are often found to have difficulty interacting with others, including family, peers, and teachers (Showers & Pickrell, 1987). These limitations in their ability to communicate thoughts and emotions are likely to reduce the opportunity for these youth to develop normal socialization skills (Kazdin, 1990). Such limited opportunities for communication and camaraderie may limit the psychosocial stability of these individuals, furthering their firesetting tendencies and other maladaptive behaviors (Heaven, 1994; Kazdin, 1990; Levin, 1976; Vandersall & Wiener, 1970).

Vandersall and Wiener (1970) asserted that young firesetters rarely have significant friendships. Juvenile firesetters have been identified as viewing themselves as loners, living outside their families or communities. Some firesetters indicate that they engage in firesetting to impress peers. Others have stated that they set fires because they did not have peers to play with and engaged in firesetting as a way to pass the time (Blumenberg, 1981; Fineman, 1995; Kolko & Kazdin, 1986b). Vandersall and Wiener (1970) asserted that many teenagers receive incendiaries from peers, which are later used to start fires. The presence of peers who smoke, peers who play with fire, peer pressure to participate in firesetting, or materials left around by parents or peers can all be factors that presage the setting of a fire (Kolko & Kazdin, 1986a).

FIRESETTING ACROSS EARLY CHILDHOOD AND ADOLESCENCE

Examination of the differences between age groups will improve professionals' understanding of this maladaptive behavior. Though a largely unexplored area of study, it is believed that maladaptive firesetting and the reasons for firesetting differ across early childhood and adolescence as a result of developmental changes (Jackson, Hope, & Glass, 1987; Kolko, 1983).

Patterson (1982) asserted that firesetters of different types and ages require different explanations for their behavior. Previous studies have suggested that as children get older, their firesetting is directed away from their homes, toward neighborhood buildings, dumpsters, automobiles, and schools (Schwartzman et al., 1994). It is hypothesized that juvenile firesetting follows an age-related developmental trend, with children aged 7 to 10 showing greater levels of firesetting than other age groups. Further, it is hypothesized that firesetting in young children is more likely to result in greater destructiveness to property and loss of life than firesetting in any other age group (for further elaboration, see Federal Emergency Management Agency, 1995; Hall, 2003).

Firesetting in Young Children (Ages 3 to 6 Years)

Studies of firesetting behavior in children are limited, even though firesetting in young children constitutes a fairly frequent and dangerous set of early childhood behaviors (Moore, Thompson-Pope, & Whited, 1996). In connection with an orientation to psychodynamic ideas, firesetting in early childhood is often assumed to involve some inherent or biological (primary/instinctual) drive (Levin, 1976). As mentioned, firesetting in young children is also more likely to result in greater destructiveness to property and loss of life than the firesetting in any other age group (Slavkin, 2000; Showers & Pickrell, 1987).

Hanson, MacKay, Atkinson, and Staley (1994) strongly advised against limiting the opportunity for mental health involvement following the firesetting act. Limited access to counseling may increase the likelihood that the firesetter will continue to engage in destructive behaviors (Hanson et al., 1994).

Firesetting in Children (Ages 7 to 10 Years)

The primary source of information on firesetting behavior initiated by children is found within the Uniform Crime Report. The most recent Uniform Crime Report indicates that 11,000 juveniles were arrested for arson and firesetting in 1998. Firesetting behaviors are not typical behaviors for children or adolescents (Levin, 1976). Because many firesetters under the age of 12 years are diverted from the juvenile justice system, the real incidence of child firesetters is unknown (Federal Emergency Management Agency, 1995). Children between the ages of 7 and 12 years are the most understudied group of all firesetters (Kolko, 1985). Fineman (1988) described various characteristics of the preadolescent firesetter and the manner in which those characteristics can be assessed.

Firesetting in Early Adolescents (Ages 11 to 14 Years)

Firesetting behavior in this age group has been found to differ from that in earlier age groups, for motivational reasons. Showers and Pickrell (1987) found that those over the age of 12 years are motivated to use fire for revenge. Achenbach (1966) theorized that internalization or externalization of behaviors largely impacts aggression in children and early adolescents. Early adolescents who internalize emotions tend to report depressive or somatic symptoms, while juveniles who externalize emotions through their behaviors show a higher level of acting out against others. Achenbach placed maladaptive firesetting behaviors within this category. Kolko and Kazdin (1991) have supported these findings, reporting higher levels of antisocial behaviors, higher levels of behavioral problems, and higher levels of hostility and aggression in early adolescent firesetters. Examination of this age group shows that most adolescent firesetters are at the lower end of the age group, around 11 years of age (Schwartzman et al., 1994).

Firesetting in Late Adolescents (Ages 15 to 18 Years)

Firesetting among late adolescents typically involves delinquent activities and usually occurs as a result of peer pressure or group-oriented activities. Attention-seeking behaviors are often a factor involved in their firesetting, as is the desire to evoke a reaction from parents, authorities, and emergency services (Schwartzman et al., 1994). Research indicates that a subgroup of antisocial recidivist firesetters exists among young offenders (Hanson et al., 1994). Late adolescents who set fires often start with small and insignificant fires and then move onto larger and more destructive fires as they gain confidence and experience. Teenagers are also more likely than younger children to involve peers in their firesetting and to brag about their destructive behaviors.

INTERVIEWING STRATEGIES

While investigative and interviewing methods of arson detection and juvenile firesetting continue to improve, sufficient evidence is generated to proceed to court in only a small number of cases. The number of offenders found guilty or cautioned has remained relatively static in recent years. Further, firesetting and arson remain understudied areas. The last significant reviews by Kolko (1983) and Fineman (1980, 1995) concluded that the firesetter's personality characteristics and environment are related to firesetting and recidivism. Most attention to firesetting has been subsumed within broader categories of delinquency and aggression in children (Kazdin, 1990). No separate review of firesetting from a developmental framework has been performed, however.

Interviewing strategies should be based on two primary modes of investigation: (1) a general review of the firesetter's individual factors and (2) a general review of the firesetter's environmental factors. Without a critical examination of both areas, it is unlikely that a clear understanding of the behavior can be found.

Interview Strategies Via the Typology of Juvenile and Adult Firesetters/Arsonists

Patterson (1982) asserted that firesetters of different types and ages require different explanations for their firesetting behaviors. Fineman (1980) stated that the use of only one construct or motive when trying to understand the complexities of firesetting is problematic in that one cannot assume that all who set fires must have similar backgrounds, motives, drive, or reinforcement histories. Thus, professionals will find it helpful to identify the type of firesetters they are working with. Though some in the field have differentiated between firesetters based on severe versus nonsevere groupings (Sakheim & Osborn, 1999), other classification systems have been suggested as being more helpful to fire professionals and mental health workers. Jones, Ribbe, and Cunningham (1994) suggested that systems of classification parallel the motivations that spur juvenile firesetters. Fineman (1995) offered eight commonly identified types. These are presented as follows.

The Curiosity Firesetter. Curious firesetters are typically 3 to 9 years old, and are often young children from 3 to 6 years old. They engage in firesetting as experimentation. When asked why they started fires, curiosity firesetters tend to respond that they did so in a desire to watch the flames. In some instances, hyperactivity or attention-deficit disorder (ADD) may be present. Curiosity firesetters hold no intent to cause harm. Curiosity firesetting is the traditional early childhood diagnosis for most firesetting children aged 7 years and younger. Fineman et al. (1979, 1981) described prominent characteristics of curiosity firesetters and the manner in which they can be assessed.

Curiosity firesetters usually show remorse for their behaviors following the incident and tend not to understand the consequences of their behaviors. It is thought that most children are inherently curious about fire. Curiosity firesetters, however, are likely to have early involvement with fireplay or firesetting. Some may be more interested in fire than are other types of juvenile firesetters (Kolko & Kazdin, 1991). Fineman (1980, 1995) described the characteristics of curiosity firesetters. He asserted that perhaps 60% of the juveniles who set fires are curiosity firesetters, as opposed to manifesting significant psychopathology.

Because curiosity firesetters are more often than not following impulses and not reacting to environmental situations, interviews should focus on the consequences of firesetting, not the firesetters themselves. In most circumstances, curiosity firesetters can work with helping professionals in fire service or mental health fields to discuss and learn more about the implications of fireplay and the impact of such actions on personal property and individual/family safety. Use of informational videos, handouts, general statistics, and general review about the implications of the fire act are appropriate interview strategies.

Accidental Firesetter. Accidental firesetters are usually children under 11 years old. This category of firesetters, however, may also include teenagers engaging in experimental firesetting or those "playing scientist." Adult accidents or adult carelessness may fall into this group. Accidental firesetters do not intend to cause harm. For the most part, accidental firesetting is not the result of neglectful or abusive home environments (Canter & Frizon, 1998; Federal Emergency Management Agency, 1995).

As with curiosity firesetters, strategies that follow the firesetting event should focus on the implications of the act and the serious nature of playing with fire. Fire should be understood by young people to be an adult tool, but many accidental firesetters are early adolescents or adolescents, and they are likely to have greater access to fire sources. As such, the interviewer should spend time identifying the firesetter's access to fire sources. Time should be included in a meeting to work with the youth and the parents on appropriate storage of incendiary devices, including matches, lighters, grill lighters, and fireworks. Parents should be aware that in most states, they will be considered financially responsible for any damage that stems from a youth-set fire—oftentimes, this knowledge can assist parents in recognizing the need for greater diligence in reducing access to incendiary devices. In some cases with curiosity and accidental firesetters, a greater preponderance of ADD has been shown to exist in children 3 to 12 years old who set fires; as such, interviewers would be wise to examine whether characteristics of ADD are present and whether a referral for ADD testing is warranted. Storytelling techniques and rehearsal of social situations have been found to be effective with adolescent accidental firesetters, as well as assertiveness training and social skills training.

The Cry-for-Help Firesetter. The "cry-for-help" firesetter is often diagnosed with attention-deficit/hyperactivity disorder (ADHD), depression not otherwise specified, major depression, oppositional defiant disorder, or posttraumatic stress disorder (PTSD). These children and adolescents may engage in maladaptive firesetting behaviors in a conscious or unconscious attempt to bring attention to their parental or familial dysfunction (Fineman, 1995; Fineman et al., 1979, 1981). Although some of these firesetters may not attempt to cause harm or significant damage (Federal Emergency Management Agency, 1995), their inability to appropriately express themselves can cause serious personal or property injury. Cry-for-help firesetters generally have a positive prognosis for treatment (Fineman, 1995).

Most cry-for-help firesetters have prior histories of fireplay, and as such, interviews should include reviews of previous acts of fireplay or prior histories related to fire. Bumpass and colleagues (1983) developed a charting process that is very helpful with most cry-for-help firesetters, in which the juvenile can concretely visualize the events causing particular feelings leading up to firesetting. The juveniles are taught to recognize these triggering emotions early in the sequence so that they can interrupt them and choose more productive responses to difficult emotions. This is essentially a graph, with the events and feelings, in chronological order, written along the x-axis and the magnitude of the emotion indicated along the y-axis.

In an interview, the juvenile is asked to describe all the events that occurred on the day of a particular fire. These are listed sequentially, with the fire incident in the center. The events are reviewed, and the juvenile is asked to describe his or her thoughts and feelings for each of the events. A corresponding line is drawn on the graph indicating the duration and intensity of the feelings involved in the events. The therapist can assist by prompting for fuller descriptions and helping to label emotions. Once the juvenile and parents understand and can identify this sequence, positive responses and behaviors to cope with these feelings are generated and listed. The juvenile is instructed to employ the alternative behavior instead of firesetting the next time these initial feelings are experienced. In a study of 29 patients (ranging from 5 to 14 years of age) treated with this method, Bumpass and associates (1983) reported that only 2 set subsequent fires. Follow-up periods were from 6 months to 8 years, with an average of 2.5 years. The method was demonstrated to be an intervention that can alter dangerous firesetting behavior quickly and early in the intervention process.

Interview strategies with these clients should follow traditionally tested mental health strategies. In families where juveniles turn to firesetting, there is usually a serious deficit in communication and problem-solving skills. Emphasis on teaching communication can help these juveniles develop more effective ways to express their feelings and frustrations. Aggression replacement training or anger management skills train juveniles to express anger in less violent and more socially acceptable ways. Social skills building will be used to replace socially unacceptable behaviors with those that do not violate social or legal standards.

Juveniles who resort to firesetting to bring attention to difficult situations often do so because they feel helpless and powerless. Very often, they simply cannot think of anything else

to do. These juveniles and their families demonstrate poor problem-solving and decision-making skills. In such cases, family problem-solving techniques, which have been used and evaluated in a variety of settings and with a variety of clinical populations, may be effective. Also, assertiveness training may be an important treatment component, giving the firesetter "a voice" in his family or peer group.

For example, one program uses a seven-step problem-solving technique (Ritchey & Janekowski, 1989): (1) Define the problem, (2) brainstorm possible solutions or alternatives, (3) evaluate the solutions or alternatives, (4) select a solution, (5) plan the implementation, (6) try it, and (7) evaluate the effectiveness of the plan. Families are taught to follow each step and are provided practice in working out problems together. Other strategies that have been found to be of use with this group include traditional psychotherapy strategies, supportive and cognitive-behavioral methods, and role-playing techniques. In warranted cases, abuse or substance abuse treatment may be warranted. Marital and family therapy are almost always required if significant growth is to occur with these youth. The importance of interindividual systems in impacting the behaviors of developing individuals cannot be overestimated (Bronfenbrenner, 1977; Stewart & Culver, 1982; Winget & Whitnam, 1973). It is thought that counseling and psychoeducational interventions can help a family redefine the roles that lead to recidivism in firesetting youth (Jackson, Glass, & Hope, 1987; Kolko & Kazdin, 1992).

It should be noted that with the above non-pathological types, interviews should focus on education and brief interventions. Oftentimes, fire safety education, fire science, and family fire awareness can be provided in a cost-effective approach by fire service. Mental health professionals and school personnel can provide accountability awareness and a stronger understanding of thoughts, feelings, and actions. In cases that warrant it (such as with cry-for-help firesetters), basic educational components are connected with collaboration with mental health providers. Some social service coordination and support can be linked with intensive family services to ensure that individual needs and systemic issues are addressed.

The Delinquent/Antisocial Firesetter. Delinquent or antisocial firesetting is theorized to have a developmental trend. Delinquent tendencies are thought to begin during preadolescence and increase throughout adolescence. The delinquent type includes those that set fire for profit and those that set fire to cover another crime. This group tends to engage in vandalism and hate crimes. During preadolescence, delinquent firesetters show some empathy for others (Harris & Rice, 1996). Adolescent delinquent firesetters, however, show little empathy for others or little conscience for their behaviors. Though they have limited empathy for other members of their families/communities, adolescent delinquent types rarely attempt to harm others with fire. Significant property damage is common. As young adults, delinquent/antisocial firesetters may attempt to harm others.

Kolko and Kazdin (1991) found that higher rates of other deviant behaviors immediately preceded firesetting recidivism in firesetters when compared with other juveniles who had been psychiatric inpatients. As a group, delinquent firesetters show the greatest amount of deviancy and behavioral dysfunction. Firesetting behavior in this group is extinguished more easily than the other personality and behavior problems that accompany the firesetting (Showers & Pickrell, 1987).

A subgroup of the delinquent firesetter group are those older children or adolescents who are would-be heroes, setting fires so they may report them and/or put them out (Fineman, 1988). Occasionally, a youth engages in this behavior and wants to be caught, placing that behavior more in the "cry-for-help" category (Fineman, 1995). As with all forms of delinquent firesetters, significant individual and family intervention should occur. The delinquent type of firesetter requires behavior management and restitution for his or her actions. Community service has been found to be somewhat effective with mild cases, but professionals should be hesitant to use this approach with all delinquent firesetters. Because affective skills are often limited with this group, anger treatment, assertiveness training, and social skills training should be considered.

The Severely Disturbed Firesetter. Those few youthful firesetters who are diagnosed as severely disturbed firesetters are usually diagnosed with a wide variety of individual pathologies, such as PTSD, general anxiety disorder, conduct disorder, and oppositional defiant disorder (Jones

et al., 1994). Moore et al. (1996) found that compared with other inpatient adolescent boys without histories of firesetting, firesetters scored significantly higher on three clinical scales: mania, schizophrenia, and psychastenia.

Unlike the "cry-for-help" firesetter who tends to show similar symptomatology as a result of environmental circumstances, these severely disturbed children are likely to show early signs or symptoms as a result of individual psychopathology. Severely disturbed children are more likely than other types of firesetters to be found in inpatient populations and also show higher incidence of recidivism than outpatient populations (Kolko & Kazdin, 1988). Such diagnoses, however, have not been found to adequately characterize the conditions that surround these children and adolescents (Jones et al., 1994; Rice & Harris, 1996; Showers & Pickrell, 1987). While it is likely that other firesetting behaviors are the result of limited parenting, neglectful and abusive situations, and general environmental pathos, blame for severely disturbed firesetting is placed on the personality of the individual.

Also included in this category are paranoid and psychotic types, for whom the fixation on fire may be a major factor in the development of a mental disorder. The pyromaniac is a subtype of the severely disturbed category.

The primary diagnoses included with the severely disturbed type of firesetter include ADD/ADHD, major depression, conduct disorder, PTSD, and bipolar mood disorder. Behaviors associated with this group include impulsive acts without thinking, poor judgment with peers, restlessness, an inability to concentrate, limited communication skills, disobedience, and, oftentimes, aggression. This group is also plagued with significant stressors in the family: Parents may be found using alcohol and drugs; parents may be separated or divorced; youth may find themselves in new living arrangements with a family or held back in school, or they may be dealing with the death of a close friend or relative, an incarcerated parent, or a serious illness in the family.

More often than not, severely disturbed firesetters require a firesetting intervention triage. Such a system is critical in holding the intervention together, as well as defining what is required of interviews and professional interventions. At the beginning of an intervention, an initial interview should be scheduled to consider the following:

- *The identified fire incident:* Recognize that there is a behavioral concern, whether it be match play or firesetting.

- *Firesetting screening:* Potential assessment at the site of a fire or initial screening by task force professional.

- *Interim safety plan:* First make sure that the child is safe and unlikely to hurt self or others, whether with fire or otherwise.

- *Firesetting assessment:* Possible at this point—could use FEMA (Federal Emergency Management Agency) or task force forms (should check with local fire department for assistance).

- *Firesetting intervention group:* Critical with some kids to get the help they need.

- *Support services:* What other services are needed beyond psychoeducation and initial meeting with fire service and task force?

- *Intensive therapeutic intervention:* Some need prolonged service from mental health professional or educational professional (counseling office, social services, education).

As with all interventions, professionals need to be sure to be clear about what to expect from interviews and treatments. The goals of treatment should be specific and measurable outcomes. First and foremost, parties want to stop the firesetting behavior if they can. Further, professionals involved want to promote greater awareness of behavior, underscoring safe behavior and spelling out clear consequences for unsafe behavior. No intervention, however, is solely a success or failure. The interviewer needs to examine just what is needed with children—a failure at time 1 could become a success at time 2. Interventions will stumble and may fail, but professionals involved should be prepared for these eventualities. Sometimes when interventions fail, there is an opportunity hidden within the crisis—professionals need to be able to see that.

Because interventions with severely disturbed firesetters require involvement with so many different professionals, it is important for everyone on the treatment team to understand what goals are being reviewed. It is important that no one

expects a magic cure, as work with these juvenile firesetters is extreme and challenging. Knowing what to expect is part of their treatment readiness. When expectations are not met, it is important for everyone to understand why. Further, defining clear goals and benchmarks is a way to clarify what the expectations are and whether they are being met. Clear expectations for each professional participant should be understood. Depending on the firesetter, the following might be required (with related professionals):

- *Fire Service—Educational Group (cost-effective):* Fire safety education, fire science, general review linking thoughts, feelings, actions, accountability for fire and damage, and a review of family fire safety skills.

- *Educational Group and Mental Health and Social Services (somewhat more intensive):* Basic educational components, collaboration with mental health provider, social service coordination and support, and intensive family services.

- *Multisystemic Therapeutic Intervention (very expensive, very intensive):* Special therapeutic intervention, close collaboration with mental health and social services, close collaboration with family and all involved agencies.

For treatment to be effective, juveniles, caregivers, and the system must be prepared to perform the work required to make a significant impact. Professionals must be aware, however, that with other systemic issues, people may not be ready to focus on the issues: Educating the family about how important these issues are may be the first step in moving a unit closer to treatment readiness.

Also, the interviewer should be sure to identify the preparedness of the firesetter for treatment. The efficacy of interventions is likely only in the event that some appreciation for intervention is present. Some suggested areas for review include the following:

- *Is the child or adolescent ready?* Has the child or adolescent accepted responsibility for firesetting? Can the child or adolescent agree to all the terms of the treatment contract?

- *Is the caregiving system ready?* Do team members recognize the importance of the issue? Can they support the treatment contract? Can they support attending the groups as well as the assignments?

- *Is the systemic network ready?* Are the goals clearly defined and responsibilities identified? Is everyone ready to commit to sharing the work? Is everyone committed to communicating with each other?

The Cognitively Impaired Firesetter. Cognitively impaired firesetters typically include children or adolescents who hold diagnoses, such as severe ADD or ADHD, or are developmentally delayed. Also included are youth with neurological impairment and severe learning disabilities and those affected by fetal alcohol syndrome or by drugs taken by their mothers during pregnancy.

The view that most young firesetters are of low intelligence has been largely discounted in recent years by Showers and Pickrell (1987). Lower intelligence in juvenile firesetters may be better explained as a result of growing up under economic disadvantage and limited educational opportunities. Firesetters who are cognitively impaired tend to avoid intentional harm but lack acceptable judgment about match play and control of fire. Significant property damage is common with this group. Prognostically, they are acceptable candidates for therapy and educational intervention (Fineman, 1995).

In a study of mentally challenged arsonists, Barnett et al. (1997) found that unlike other types of firesetters, mentally challenged firesetters did not have histories of deviancy, legal offenses, or other forms of law breaking related to vandalism. The researchers did find, however, that mentally challenged firesetters had higher rates of recidivism than non-mentally challenged firesetters (Barnett et al., 1997). It has also been suggested that individuals with learning disabilities who set fires do so for the excitement of the destructiveness or the control they receive from fireplay (Murphy & Claire, 1996).

Treatment interventions need to focus on improved awareness of the implications of match play. One intervention modality that has proven very effective with this group is a psychoeducational approach. Mark Hanson, codirector of school-based services with Wediko Children's Services in Boston, developed a fire intervention program that included 10 weeks of intervention work. Wraparound services include the following:

- Fire intervention group coleaders: therapeutic group program, weekly team check-ins by phone or e-mail

- Mental health clinic team: weekly individual counseling, successful group attendance

- Family: family monitoring juvenile's safety, fire issue check-in during counseling

- Probation: weekly check-in with probation

- School liaison: weekly check-in, fire safety in the home and at school

Emphasis of programming includes clarification of all treatment goals in writing via written agreements. Also, everyone on the treatment team, including the juvenile and the family, signs the intervention contract. The contract is the roadmap to compliance and accountability for treatment, as well as a means of measuring progress.

The Sociocultural Firesetter. More often than not, sociocultural firesetters are young adult or adult arsonists who set fires primarily for the support they get for doing so by groups within their communities. Adolescents may copy their older role models. Sociocultural types who set fires typically are in the midst of civil unrest and either are enraged or enticed by the activity of others and follow suit or set fires with deliberation in order to call attention to the righteousness of their cause. These firesetters frequently lose control and harm others (Schwartzman et al., 1994).

Levin (1976) suggested that an analysis of firesetting behaviors needs to include whether the firesetter acted as an individual or within a group. He also suggested that the sociocultural type is most likely to utilize fire to embarrass or intimidate an opponent. This group is extremely resistant to treatment.

INTERVIEWING OBSTACLES AND SOLUTIONS

The chapter's emphasis on developmental factors that contribute to the initiation or continuation of juvenile firesetting has implications for the ways in which parents, educators, and counselors work with these youth and the responses of professionals who work with adult arsonists. Because firesetting occurs in tandem with other inappropriate and maladaptive behaviors, however, it often is difficult for mental health professionals to intervene appropriately. By acquiring information on firesetters from a variety of professional backgrounds and a variety of programming services, the author sought to acquire a more representative perspective of juvenile and adult firesetters. It is hoped that using information from many professionals will assist with the community's understanding of this problem, as well as improve the programming designed to intervene with firesetters of all ages.

One limitation of schemes that categorize firesetters or firesetting behavior is that they do not account for the diversity or heterogeneity of firesetters or the complex interaction of dispositional, situational, and environmental factors that might lead to an individual setting a fire. Further, these schemes give little by way of clinically relevant information to help with formulation or to guide treatment interventions. There cannot just be one measure to use when assessing a juvenile firesetter—there must be multiple tools to use in order to evaluate multiple factors.

Assessment goals must include an identification of individualized firesetting risks and some clinical indicators, a determination of targets for intervention, and provisions that include objective outcomes. Assessment domains should differ based on various factors, including both individual and environmental specifics (see beginning of chapter for review of factors).

INTERVIEWING PARENTS AND TEACHERS

To ensure that reliable information related to the firesetting is included in treatment, clinicians should meet with parents/guardians and staff from the firesetter's school or other significant social systems with which the youth interacts. Environmental characteristics are defined as supports, controls, models, and expectations of others that are thought to be meaningful phenomena to the juvenile (Jessor, 1987). When intraindividual factors are viewed in concert with a combination of environmental factors, such as interpersonal difficulties, the presence of abusive adults, and problems with home and school, the environment appears to be a better warning sign of youthful firesetting, adult violence, or criminality (Justice et al., 1974).

Family Problems

There are correlates between parental maladaptive behaviors and child maladaptive behaviors, especially as related to firesetting (Fineman, 1980; Kolko & Kazdin, 1988, 1991). Since a significant number of house fires were directly related to the activities of adults in the home, a review of adult actions with incendiary tools should be made. Poor supervision and a lax child care environment are better predictors of recidivism than are other (i.e., intraindividual) factors, so a discussion of supervision should occur. Moreover, a discussion of how adults keep track of incendiaries in the home should occur. For recidivism to be reduced, access to incendiaries, confirmation of adolescent remorse, and parental consequences for negative behavior should be discussed. As with all firesetters, the issues of involvement with children and parental support should be included in interview questions.

Other questions of interest during an interview would relate to experiences such as parental separation, violence within the home, parental alcohol and drug abuse, or some form of physical or sexual abuse. Emotional neglect and physical abuse should also be considered.

Economic Stressors

Stressful environmental circumstances, individual crises, and limited support at home are often the precursors to property damage through use of fire. Low socioeconomic stability has been identified as a prime stressor that can lead to firesetting, so economic stability should be reviewed. Lower levels of income are directly correlated with increased risk of residential fire.

School Problems

Many school-age juveniles who are drawn to using fire for whatever reason tend to use it in public places where it is likely to get noticed (as opposed to younger, preschool-age juveniles, who tend to use fire in private). School is a powerful place to communicate with fire, as it is likely to elicit much attention and receive negative retribution. Students who pull fire alarms are often found to defiantly act out with teachers and administrators, so firesetter behaviors at home and school should be considered. These youth bully other children and are likely to use fire to elicit responses from peers and adults. Youth grades, interactions with other peers, behaviors in the classroom, and support from school faculty should be considered as well.

Peer Problems

Juvenile firesetters are often found to have difficulty interacting with others, including family, peers, and teachers (Showers & Pickrell, 1987). A review with parents and teachers should include a review of the firesetter's friends. A baseline understanding of socialization skills and opportunities for communication and camaraderie would be core questions for an interview.

Case Illustration With Dialogue

Carl is 16 years old and lives with his mother and younger brother in a middle-class urban neighborhood. His mother and father divorced when he was 12, and his mother recently remarried. Carl's father has been absent for much of his life, and Carl's stepfather is presently out of work.

Carl's mother describes her son as "basically a good person" but wishes he had been more obedient and disciplined as a child. She says he is hard to talk to and rarely takes her seriously. Carl's aunt, who lives with the family, describes him as a charming young man who always seemed to get into trouble. Although Carl is very bright, he has been expelled several times throughout school due to his inability to follow rules. Schools characterize him as a bully and ringleader. He always seemed to be responsible for major class disruptions. Carl's grades were average and his conduct marginally acceptable.

Carl has a history of antisocial and delinquent behavior that began around the time of puberty. Shortly after his parents separated, he began missing several days of school for unexplained reasons. He would leave home early in the morning and return by dinner, offering no explanation of where he had been or what he had been doing. On several occasions, Carl's mother received late-night telephone calls from the local police reporting that they had caught her son and a few friends slashing car tires at a nearby shopping mall. Carl's mother was able to convince the police not to press charges. There have been four incidents of shoplifting, two convictions for possession of marijuana, and a conviction for arson at the age of 14 years.

Carl's firesetting behavior emerged at age 11 years, when he was caught setting trash can fires near his school. Both his parents and the school authorities admonished him. Shortly thereafter, Carl was asked to leave the school because of constant fighting with his peers. His most recent known fire (he has identified over 50 previously set fires) was of a more serious nature. Carl and several of his friends had been seen at a local park and recreation area. They thought it would be easy and fun to break into the building and steal the petty cash from the park director's desk. Once they had entered the building through an open window, they worked for several minutes to break into the desk. Unsuccessful and frustrated, they spotted a lighter on a nearby counter and ignited the papers in the trash can. They fled from the scene, but Carl stayed around the perimeter of the park to watch the excitement as the fire was discovered. He was picked up by the police immediately following the fire.

Reflection for Interviewers

Although a variety of questions and strategies for firesetters exist, a formal review of this case would include a discussion based on Carl's typology, which would likely be a delinquent firesetter. As such, the following questions might focus an initial interview of his case.

• *What purpose does fire serve to Carl?* Firesetting might have initially started as a curiosity for Carl but was likely used as a strategy to communicate individual concerns and environmental chaos as he entered early adolescence. As a late adolescent, firesetting does not provide any catharsis of emotions and no longer communicates his emotions to family and school personnel. If anything, firesetting at this age simply serves as a strategy to cover his crimes and for destructive purposes.

• *What reasons would you give for Carl using fire in the first place?* As with almost all firesetters, a history of firesetting took place throughout his childhood. Carl may have had access to incendiary tools from an early age due to the presence of smokers in his home and the prevalence of drugs, such as marijuana and crack, which would require such tools. The infrequency of attention, affection, and redirection in his home might also have complicated this behavior by leading Carl to use fire as a way of demonstrating his feelings (as well as providing evidence of limited communication skills).

• *What strategies would you suggest for dealing with Carl's arson?* As with any delinquent firesetter, professionals should recommend that he be prosecuted for his actions. To ensure that intervention services are mandated, involvement with the courts is warranted.

• *What strategies might assist Carl in stopping his firesetting?* As with all forms of delinquent firesetters, significant individual and family intervention should occur. Carl would require behavior management and should perform restitution for his actions. Community service is unlikely at this time to be effective with his case. Because affective skills are limited with this firesetter, anger treatment, assertiveness training, and social skills training should be considered.

Treatment Rationale

The approach to treatment draws on the "what works" literature in terms of the features of successful and effective interventions in the offender and delinquency fields (McGuire, 1995; Skett, 1995). This suggests that interventions should serve the following purposes:

• Are theoretically sound, cognitive-behavioral in nature, multifaceted in terms of the problem areas targeted, and oriented toward skills development

• Are responsive to the learning needs, styles, and preferences of both clients and therapists

• Focus on the criminogenic aspects of the clients presenting problems that are proximal rather than distal to offending behaviors

• Take into account the level of risk presented by clients by increasing the therapeutic "dosage" proportionately for those judged to be at higher risk for recidivism

• Attend to issues of program integrity by reducing or eliminating therapeutic drift, treatment gain reversal, and noncompliance with regard to the delivery of programs by therapists

• Be delivered by trained staff and evaluated independently

The treatment is a comprehensive and multifaceted program based on the approach outlined by Jackson, Glass, and Hope (1987); this approach is consistent with their "functional analysis paradigm" (p. 175) for recidivistic arson. Within a broad cognitive-behavioral framework, clients' offense cycles are analyzed with regard to (a) antecedent firesetting factors and triggers; (b) cognitions, emotions, and behavior they experienced at the time fires were started; and (c) positive and negative consequences of their firesetting behavior. Clients receive education concerning the dangers and costs associated with setting fires. The acquisition and rehearsal of skills to enhance future coping with emotional and interpersonal problems associated with previous firesetting behavior are emphasized. The development of personalized plans to prevent relapse is also an important aspect of the treatment package.

DIFFERENTIAL DIAGNOSIS AND BEHAVIORAL ASSESSMENT

In *DSM-IV* (APA, 1994) pyromania is classified as an impulse control disorder. Firesetting is not evidence for pyromania, however. Somewhat confusingly, the defining features of the disorder include deliberate and purposeful setting of fires involving "considerable advance preparation" (APA, 1994, p. 614). The definition also includes, as diagnostic criteria, fire fascination and pleasure and gratification associated with setting fires. These criteria make the definition very narrow and unlikely to apply to all but a very few arsonists. More pertinent, with regard to the population of interest in the context of this chapter, *DSM-IV* pyromania specifically excludes firesetters with mental retardation as a group whose firesetting is a result of impaired judgment.

Swaffer and Hollin (1995) made the distinction between arsonists, who have been apprehended, charged, and convicted of starting uncontrolled fires, and firesetters, who have committed acts of arson that may or may not have resulted in charges being brought or convictions. Health services and other human services that work with people with developmental disabilities and offending histories frequently deal with offenders who have committed acts of arson that have not been processed through the criminal justice system. Therefore, the term *firesetters* is the most appropriate to describe the population discussed in this chapter.

Jackson, Glass, and Hope (1987) distinguished between "pathological" and other types of firesetters. These are the five central criteria for pathological firesetting:

1. Recidivism

2. Setting fire to property, rather than against other people

3. Firesetting alone, or repetitively with a single identified accomplice

4. Evidence of personality, psychiatric, or emotional problems

5. Absence of financial or political gain as a motive for setting fires

Jackson and his colleagues consider this to be a more clinically relevant and useful concept that takes into account the evidence available concerning the prevalence and development of firesetting behavior.

SELECTION OF TREATMENT TARGETS AND REFERRAL

An examination of the juvenile-firesetting literature shows that a variety of variables define specific types of firesetters. It is critical that mental health professionals be clear, first, about the type of firesetter with whom they are working and, second, about the appropriate intervention strategy. Firesetting behaviors appear to differ as a result of both individual and environmental circumstances. Relevant literature suggests that an appropriate evaluation of a firesetter should include an examination of the offender's general personality and psychopathology, with a particular focus on the meaning of fire in the offender's life. Identification of the specifics of the index fire as well as the specifics of past fires are necessary.

Within the context of the early firesetting history are issues concerning early supervision for fire issues, fire safety training, and an analysis of fire fascination. Clinicians will be especially interested in acquiring information about the

cognitions and sensations that are relevant to the firesetting offense before, during, and after the index event. An analysis of general behavior relative to family, peers, school, and other maladaptive behaviors is required. Parent response to the index event as well as an analysis of the offender's reinforcement history for firesetting rounds out the evaluation (Fineman, 1995).

SUMMARY

Arson and firesetting are much more diverse and complex behaviors than many believe. Deviant fire behavior is sometimes used as a means of solving problems, both external and internal, by those who are unable to use more socially acceptable methods, owing to lack of opportunity, skill, or confidence. Thus, in addition to those who "solve" financial problems by intentionally setting fires to claim insurance payouts, there are those who use fire to express emotion (e.g., anger), attract attention, or gain satisfaction. These "pathological" types of arson require attention by mental health professionals as well as those in the criminal justice system.

The choice of firesetting as a means of solving problems has its roots in the individual's developmental history, often in events that occurred early in life. An interest in fire is normal for many youngsters, as it is for many adults, and clarification of developmental risk factors that predict firesetting is an important issue.

This chapter is intended to provide mental health professionals with a comprehensive review of the continuum of firesetting behaviors, a review of the literature, characteristics of firesetters, methods of identification and assessment, models for treatment of youthful and adult firesetters, a discussion of the interface between mental health and other agencies, prevention efforts, and implications for future research and treatment modalities.

REFERENCES

Achenbach, T. M. (1966). The classification of children's psychiatric symptoms: A factor analytic study. *Psychological Monographs, 80,* 615–632.

Adler, R. G., Nunn, R. J., Laverick, J., & Ross, R. (1988, October). *Royal Children's Hospital/Metropolitan Fire Brigade Juvenile Fire Awareness and Intervention Program: Research and intervention protocol.* Unpublished paper.

American Psychiatric Association. (1994). *Diagnostic and statistical manual of mental disorders* (4th ed.). Washington, DC: Author.

Bandura, A. (1977). *Social learning theory.* Englewood Cliffs, NJ: Prentice Hall.

Barnett, W., Richter, P., Sigmund, D., & Spitzer, M. (1997). Recidivism and concomitant criminality in pathological firesetters. *Journal of Forensic Sciences, 42,* 879–883.

Barnett, W., & Spitzer, M. (1994). Pathological firesetting 1951–1991: A review. *Medicine Science and the Law, 34,* 4–20.

Blumenberg, N. H. (1981). Arson update: A review of the literature on firesetting. *Bulletin of the American Academy of Psychiatry and the Law, 9,* 255–265.

Bronfenbrenner, U. (1977). Ecological systems theory. In R. Vasta (Ed.), *Annals of child development* (Vol. 6, pp. 1–67). Greenwich, CT: JAI Press.

Bumpass, E. R., Fagelman, F. D., & Brix, R. J. (1983). Intervention with children who set fires. *American Journal of Psychotherapy, 37,* 328–345.

Burgess, R., & Akers, R. (1966). A differential association reinforcement theory of criminal behavior. *Social Problems, 14,* 128–147.

Canter, D., & Frizon, K. (1998). Differentiating arsonists: A model of firesetting actions and characteristics. *Legal and Criminological Psychology, 3,* 73–96.

Carey, K. T. (1997). Preschool interventions. In A. P. Goldstein & J. C. Conoley (Eds.), *School violence intervention: A practical handbook* (pp. 93–106). New York: Guilford Press.

Carstens, C. (1982). Application of a work penalty threat in the treatment of and care of juvenile firesetting. *Journal of Behavior Therapy and Experimental Psychiatry, 13,* 159–161.

Cowell, P. (1985). Implosive therapy in the counselling of a pupil who sets fires. *British Journal of Guidance and Counselling, 13,* 157–165.

DeSalvatore, G., & Hornstein, R. (1991). Juvenile firesetting: Assessment and treatment in psychiatric hospitalization and residential placement. *Child and Youth Care Forum, 20,* 103–114.

Eisler, R. M. (1972). Crisis intervention in the family of a firesetter. *Psychotherapy: Theory, Research, and Practice, 9,* 76–79.

Federal Emergency Management Agency. (1995). *Socioeconomic factors and the incidence of fire.* Washington, DC: U.S. Fire Administration and National Fire Data Center.

Fineman, K. R. (1980). Firesetting in early childhood and adolescence. *Pediatric Clinics of North America, 3,* 483–500.

Fineman, K. R. (1988). Child, adolescent, and family interview forms. In J. Gaynor & C. Kartchmer (Eds.), *Adolescent firesetter handbook* (pp. 188–234). Washington, DC: Federal Emergency Management Agency.

Fineman, K. R. (1995). A model for the qualitative analysis of child and adult fire deviant behavior. *American Journal of Forensic Psychology, 13,* 31–60.

Fineman, K. R. (1997). Comprehensive fire risk assessment. In C. Poage, M. Doctor, J. Day, K. Rester, C. Velasquez, M. Moynihan, E. Flesher, P. Cooke & L. Marshburn (Eds.), *Juvenile Firesetter Prevention Program: Training Seminar* (Vol. I, pp. 1–25). Denver, CO: Colorado Division of Fire Safety.

Fineman, K. R., Day, J. B., Michaelis, L., Brudo, C., Brudo, E., & Morris, C. (1979). *Interviewing and counseling juvenile firesetters: The child under seven years of age* (Grant No. 77071). Washington, DC: Federal Emergency Management Agency.

Fineman, K. R., Day, J. B., Michaelis, L., Brudo, C., Brudo, E., & Morris, C. (1981). *Preadolescent Firesetter Handbook: Ages 0–7.* Washington, DC: Federal Emergency Management Agency.

Forehand, R., Wierson, M., Frame, C. L., Kemptom, T., & Armistead, L. (1991). Juvenile firesetting: A unique syndrome or an advanced level of antisocial behavior? *Behavior Research and Therapy, 29,* 125–128.

Gaynor, J. (2002). *Juvenile firesetter intervention handbook.* Washington, DC: U.S. Fire Administration and U.S. Government Printing Office.

Gaynor, J., & Hatcher, C. (1987). *The psychology of child firesetting: Detection and intervention.* New York: Brunner/Mazel.

Hall, J. (2003). *Children playing with fire.* Washington, DC: National Fire Protection Association.

Hanson, M., MacKay, S., Atkinson, L., Staley, S. (1994). Delinquent firesetters: A comparative study of delinquency and firesetting histories. *Canadian Journal of Psychiatry, 39,* 230–232.

Harris, G. T., & Rice, M. E. (1996). A typology of mentally disordered firesetters. *Journal of Interpersonal Violence, 11,* 351–363.

Heaven, P. C. L. (1994). Family of origin, personality, and self-reported delinquency. *Journal of Adolescence, 17,* 445–459.

Jackson, H. F., Glass, C., & Hope, S. (1987). A functional-analysis of recidivistic arson. *British Journal of Clinical Psychology, 26,* 175–185.

Jackson, H. F., Hope, S., & Glass, C. (1987). Why are arsonists not violent offenders? *International Journal of Offender Therapy and Comparative Criminology, 31,* 143–151.

Jessor, R. (1981). The perceived environment in psychological theory and research. In D. Magnusson (Ed.), *Toward a psychology of situations: An interactional perspective* (pp. 297–317). Mahwah, NJ: Lawrence Erlbaum.

Jessor, R. (1987). Problem-behavior theory, psychosocial development, and adolescent problem drinking. *British Journal of Addiction, 82,* 331–342.

Jessor, R., & Jessor, S. L. (1973). The perceived environment in behavioral science: Some conceptual issues and some illustrative data. *American Behavioral Scientist, 16,* 801–828.

Jones, R. T., Ribbe, D. P., & Cunningham, P. (1994). Psychosocial correlates of fire disaster among children and adolescents. *Journal of Traumatic Stress, 7,* 117–122.

Junger, M., & Wiegersma, A. (1995). The relations between accidents, deviance and leisure time. *Criminal Behavior and Mental Health, 53,* 144–174.

Justice, B., Justice, R., & Kraft, I.A. (1974). Early warning signs of violence: Is a triad enough? *American Journal of Psychiatry, 131,* 457–459.

Kazdin, A. E. (1990). Conduct disorder in early childhood. In M. Hersen & C. G. Last (Eds.), *Handbook of child and adult psychopathology: A longitudinal perspective* (pp. 89–121). New York: Pergamon Press.

Kolko, D. J. (1983). Multicomponent parental treatment of firesetting in a six-year old boy. *Journal of Behavioral Therapy and Experimental Psychiatry, 14,* 349–353.

Kolko, D. J. (1985). Juvenile firesetting: A review and methodological critique. *Clinical Psychology Review, 5,* 345–376.

Kolko, D. J., & Kazdin, A. E. (1986a). A conceptualization of firesetting in children and adolescents. *Journal of Abnormal Child Psychology, 14,* 49–61.

Kolko, D. J., & Kazdin, A. E. (1986b). Parent psychopathology and family functioning among early childhood firesetters. *Journal of Abnormal Child Psychology, 14,* 315–329.

Kolko, D. J., & Kazdin, A. E. (1988). Parent-child correspondence in identification of firesetting among child psychiatric patients. *Journal of Child Psychology and Psychiatry & Allied Disciplines, 29,* 175–184.

Kolko, D. J., & Kazdin, A. E. (1991). Motives of early childhood firesetters: Firesetting characteristics and psychological correlates. *Journal of Child Psychology and Psychiatry, 32,* 535–550.

Kolko, D. J., & Kazdin, A. E. (1992). The emergence and recurrence of child firesetting: A one-year prospective study. *Journal of Abnormal Child Psychology, 20,* 17–37.

Kolko, D. J., & Kazdin, A. E. (1994). Children's descriptions of their firesetting incidents: Characteristics and relationship to recidivism. *Journal of the American Academy of Child & Adolescent Psychiatry, 33,* 114–122.

Lee, M. I., & Miltenberger, R. G. (1996). School refusal behavior: Classification, assessment, and treatment issues. *Education and Treatment of Children, 19,* 474–486.

Levin, B. (1976). Psychological characteristics of firesetters. *Fire Journal, 70,* 36–41.

Loeber, R., DeLamatre, M. S., Keenan, K., & Zhang, Q. (1998). A prospective replication of developmental pathways in disruptive and delinquent behavior. In R. B. Cairns & L. R. Bergman (Eds.), *Methods and models for studying the individual* (pp. 185–218). Thousand Oaks, CA: Sage.

Loeber, R., & Stouthamer-Loeber, M. (1998). Development of juvenile aggression and violence: Some current misconceptions and controversies. *American Psychologist, 53,* 242–259.

Luby, J. L., Reich, W., & Earls, F. (1995). Failure to detect signs of psychological distress in the preschool children of alcoholic parents. *Journal of Child and Adolescent Substance Abuse, 4,* 77–89.

Macht, L. B., & Mack, J. E. (1968). The firesetter syndrome. *Psychiatry, 31,* 277–288.

McGrath, P., Marshall, P. G., & Prior, K. (1979). A comprehensive treatment program for a firesetting child. *Journal of Behavior Therapy and Experimental Psychiatry, 10,* 69–72.

McGuire, J. (1995). *What works: Reducing reoffending— Guidelines from research and practice.* Chichester, UK: John Wiley & Sons.

Moore, J. M., Thompson-Pope, S. K., & Whited, R.M. (1996). MMPI-A: Profiles of adolescent boys with a history of firesetting. *Journal of Personality Assessment, 67,* 116–126.

Murphy, G. H., & Claire, I. C. H. (1996). Analysis of motivation in people with mild learning disabilities (mental handicap) who set fires. *Psychology Crime and Law, 2,* 153–164.

National Fire Protection Association. (1999). *Statistics on the national fire problem.* Retrieved April 14, 2006, from http://www.fema.gov/nfpa/

Nielsen, G., Harrington, L., Sack, W. H., & Latham, S. (1985). A developmental study of aggression and self-destruction in adolescents who received residential treatment. *International Journal of Offender Therapy and Comparative Criminology, 29,* 211–226.

Patterson, G. (1982). *A social learning approach* (Vol. 1). Eugene, OR: Castilia.

Raines, J. C., & Foy, C. W. (1994). Extinguishing the fires within: Treating juvenile firesetters. *Families in Society: Journal of Contemporary Human Services, 75,* 595–607.

Rice, M. E., & Harris, G. T. (1996). Predicting the recidivism of mentally disordered firesetters. *Journal of Interpersonal Violence, 11,* 364–375.

Ritchey, K. M, & Jankowski, J. (1989). Problem-solving workshop for families. *Journal of Mental Health Counseling, 11,* 307–324.

Sakheim, G. A., & Osborn, E. (1999). Severe versus nonsevere firesetters revisited. *Child Welfare, 78,* 411–434.

Sakheim, G. A., Vidgor, M. C., Gordon, M., & Helprin, L. M. (1985). A psychological profile of juvenile firesetters in residential treatment. *Child Welfare, 64,* 453–476.

Saunders, E. B., & Awad, G. A. (1991). Adolescent female firesetters. Special issue: Child and adolescent psychiatry. *Canadian Journal of Psychiatry, 36,* 401–404.

Schaenman, P., Hall, Schainblatt, R., Swartz, A., & Karter, E. (1977). *Procedures for improving the measurement of local fire protection effectiveness.* Boston: National Fire Protection Association.

Schwartzman, P., Stambaugh, H., & Kimball, J. (1994). *Arson and juveniles: Responding to the violence. A review of teen firesetting and interventions.* Emmitsburg, MD: U.S. Fire Administration Federal Emergency Management Agency.

Showers, J., & Pickrell, E. (1987). Child firesetters: A study of three populations. *Hospital and Community Psychiatry, 38,* 495–501.

Skett, S. (1995). What works in the reduction of offending behavior? *Forensic Update, 42,* 20–27.

Slavkin, M. (2000). *Juvenile firesetting: An exploratory analysis.* For further information contact Michael Slavkin, Department of Teacher Education, University of Southern Indiana, 8600 University Boulevard, ED 3120, Evansville, IN 47712.

Squires, T., & Busuttil, A. (1995). Child fatalities in Scottish house fires: 1980–1990: A case of child neglect? *Child Abuse & Neglect, 19,* 865–873.

Stewart, M. A., & Culver, K. W. (1982). Children who start fires: The clinical picture and a follow-up. *British Journal of Psychiatry, 140,* 357–363.

Swaffer, T., & Hollin, C. R. (1995). Adolescent firesetting: Why do they say they do it? *Journal of Adolescence, 18,* 619–623.

Taylor, J. C., & Carr, E. G. (1994). Severe problem behaviors of children with developmental disabilities: Reciprocal social influences. In T. Thompson & D. Gray (Eds.), *Destructive behavior in developmental disabilities: Diagnosis and treatment* (pp. 274–289). Thousand Oaks, CA: Sage.

Thomas, A., & Grimes, J. (1994). *Children's needs: Psychological perspectives*. Silver Spring, MD: National Association of School Psychologists.

Vandersall, T. A., & Wiener, J. M. (1970). Children who set fires. *Archives of General Psychology, 22*, 63–71.

Williams, D. (1998). Delinquent and deliberate firesetters in the middle years of early childhood and adolescence. *Dissertational Abstracts, 1998*, 1–121.

Winget, C. N., & Whitnam, R. M. (1973). Coping with problems: Attitudes toward children who set fires. *American Journal of Psychiatry, 130*, 442–445.

Wolff, R. (1984). Satiation in the treatment of inappropriate firesetting. *Journal of Behavior Therapy and Experimental Psychiatry, 15*, 337–340.

Yalom, I. (1975). *The theory and practice of group psychotherapy* (2nd ed.). New York: Basic Books.

23

ENURESIS AND ENCOPRESIS

MICHAEL W. MELLON

Childhood incontinence becomes a disorder when it is developmentally inappropriate. The fact remains that all physiologically normal persons begin their lives unable to regulate urination and defecation in accordance to social expectations. Through physical maturation and the behavioral influences of caregivers, children learn the "when" and "where" of socially appropriate urination and defecation. Incontinence is influenced by many factors, including genetics, toilet training practices, diet, maturational delays in the nervous system, sleep differences, and other social influences that interfere with the learning processes of mastering continence. Oftentimes, the psychological literature regarding enuresis and encopresis combines these disorders in a common category. This chapter presents enuresis and encopresis separately because they are quite different in their etiologies and treatments. Much is known about enuresis and its treatment, so much so that the enuresis conditioning alarm is considered to be an "evidence-based" treatment. Less confident conclusions have been made regarding the effective treatment of encopresis. However, the optimal management of either disorder is affected by important physiological and social/behavioral factors that must be taken into account in order to allow for the most effective treatments to be delivered with fidelity. This chapter outlines the assessment process for

enuresis and encopresis in order to identify and manage those physiological and social/behavioral influences that would interfere with optimal treatment.

DESCRIPTION OF THE DISORDER

The accepted definition for *nocturnal enuresis* requires a child to pass urine into his or her clothing or bedding while asleep. The child must be over 5 years of age, have a frequency of at least two wetting accidents per week for 3 consecutive months (or causes sufficient emotional distress), and the urinary incontinence cannot be due to a medical problem or medication side effect (American Psychiatric Association [APA], 1994). The prevalence of bed-wetting is estimated to involve as many as 8% to 10% of the school-age population (Jarvelin, Vikevainen-Tervonen, Moilanen, & Huttunen, 1988). The spontaneous remission rate of enuresis is estimated to be 16% of those children ceasing to wet in any given year (Forsythe & Redmond, 1974). Daytime wetting (with or without nighttime wetting) is less common, with estimates ranging from 1% to 8% of school-age children (Bakker, van Sprundel, van der Auwera, van Gool, & Wyndaele, 2002). Nocturnal enuresis occurs twice as often in males than females up to the onset of puberty (De Jonge, 1973). In a survey of over 4,000 Belgian schoolchildren, however, daytime wetting (Bakker et al., 2002) occurred twice as often in girls. Of the 343 children in the sample who exhibited both day and night wetting, 54% were girls. Primary nocturnal enuresis accounts for approximately 80% of all children who wet the bed and describes the child who has been wetting continuously since birth and evidencing less than 6 consecutive months of dryness (Rawashde, Hvistendahl, Kamperis, & Djurhuus, 2002). In the United States alone, the reported prevalence rates suggest that as many as 4 million to 6 million children wet their beds nearly every night.

Perhaps due to the noticeable spontaneous remission for both diurnal and nocturnal enuresis, parents are often advised by health care providers to take a watchful-waiting approach to the problem to see whether the child will outgrow the wetting. The onset of diurnal enuresis, however, can be associated with potentially serious medical problems that can actually lead to permanent damage to the urinary tract if not immediately treated. Although serious medical problems are rare for children with monosymptomatic nocturnal enuresis (Jarvelin et al., 1991), given the availability of effective treatments for nocturnal enuresis, a watchful-waiting approach is no longer justified. The higher rate of medical problems preceding the diurnal enuresis makes it a very different problem than simple nocturnal enuresis. In either case, parents of children with diurnal or nocturnal enuresis should be advised to consult a health care provider for a medical examination prior to any treatment. The primary focus in this chapter is on nocturnal enuresis and factors related to its effective treatment.

Nocturnal enuresis is clearly influenced by genetic factors. For example, the likelihood that a child will wet the bed is 40% if one parent also happened to have wet the bed, and the likelihood increases to 70% if both parents had wet the bed (Norgaard, Djurhuus, Watanabe, Stenberg, & Lettgen, 1997). Furthermore, the best predictor of a child's spontaneous remission is the age at which his or her parent(s) stopped wetting the bed (Fergusson, Horwood, & Shannon, 1986). Finally, Eiberg, Berendt, and Mohr (1995) have demonstrated that the loci for nocturnal enuresis are on chromosomes 13q and 12q. Although genetic influences for nocturnal enuresis have been demonstrated, this information has not contributed to the development of more effective treatment.

The scientific investigation of psychosocial treatments for nocturnal enuresis has extended more than 50 years. These types of interventions have included hypnotism, psychoanalysis, play therapy, use of positive reinforcement for dry nights, punishment for wetting accidents, cognitive-behavioral therapy, classical and operant conditioning, and combinations of all of the above.

Several empirical reviews of the scientific literature (Glazener & Evans, 2003; Glazener, Evans, & Peto, 2005; Houts, Berman, & Abramson, & 1994; Kristensen & Jensen, 2003; Mellon & McGrath, 2000) have concluded that the enuresis conditioning alarm is an evidence-based treatment that leads to a cessation in wetting for 59% to 78% of enuretic children at the end of treatment and 34% to 43% of children at follow-up. Multicomponent treatments that utilize the enuresis conditioning alarm combined with other behavioral interventions have success rates as high as 64% to 86% of children stopping wetting at the end of treatment (Mellon & Houts, in press). These conclusions have been so consistent that Mellon and Houts have indicated that further research establishing the urine alarm as an effective treatment is unnecessary. Future studies should now focus on identifying empirically supported principles of behavior change that account for the success of this robust intervention. By systematically identifying moderators and mediators of treatment, future clinicians will be able to determine who will best benefit from the urine alarm and also to identify the processes through which the treatment works. At this point in time, the clinician will have to rely on what is currently known about moderators and mediators of effective urine alarm treatment through the process of a comprehensive assessment and interview prior to treatment.

INTERVIEWING STRATEGIES

The process of interviewing enuretic children and their parent(s) begins prior to the first contact. A variety of intake questionnaires regarding a child's development, psychosocial circumstances, demographic characteristics, health status, and behavioral functioning can be used to identify whether the patient is an appropriate candidate for enuresis conditioning treatment. The use of questionnaires represents the structured component of interviewing.

The clinician should attempt to strike a balance between obtaining necessary information and avoiding overwhelming the parents and child with too much paperwork. The author has developed a simple, topic-specific questionnaire for children referred to his enuresis clinic. The author's Enuresis Clinic Intake Questionnaire gathers demographic and patient contact information and identifies the child's primary care provider and current general health status. It asks the parents to describe pertinent toilet training history for bowel and bladder continence, age of attainment of daytime urinary and bowel continence, and methods used to attain these outcomes. Current habits of urinary and bowel activity are identified. Information regarding prior medical and psychosocial treatments is identified, in addition to strategies utilized by parents in their efforts to help the child overcome bed-wetting. Parents also report relevant family history of bed-wetting difficulties. The severity of the child's bed-wetting symptoms is described by the parents in terms of wet nights per week and how many wets occur each night. Information about responsibilities for managing the wet bed-clothes and sheets is collected. Parents are asked to describe any other behavioral difficulties exhibited by the child that may affect full participation in the treatment program by using a numerical rating (i.e., Likert scale) of how cooperative they believe the child to be.

Many reliable and valid parent report questionnaires are available to the clinician (e.g., Child Behavior Checklist, Behavioral Assessment System for Children [BASC]) to help identify patterns of behavior that have direct implications for the successful application of the urine alarm treatment. The author currently uses the BASC (Reynolds & Kamphaus, 1998), as it is a well-constructed and well-validated measure of behavioral functioning in children. Externalizing problems, including argumentativeness, oppositional behavior, aggression, impulsivity, and poor adaptability, are described in composite scores and in individual subscales. Internalizing behaviors, such as anxiety, depression, and withdrawn characteristics, are also described. Clinically significant elevations in these types of problems alert the clinician about potential problems in adherence to treatment and allow for a decision of whether the behavioral problems or bed-wetting should be a priority for treatment.

Parents are also asked to complete questionnaires regarding their own understanding of nocturnal enuresis, in terms of causes and how burdensome the problem is for themselves in their role as a parent. The Enuresis Tolerance Questionnaire (Butler, Brewin, & Forsythe, 1990; Morgan & Young, 1975) has been studied for decades and found to be helpful in predicting those children who will fail urine alarm treatment or terminate early. It is also helpful in identifying which children will relapse after successful treatment.

Finally, parents are asked to complete a baseline record of their child's bed-wetting for at least 2 weeks prior to the first interview. Information collected includes weekly number of wets, how large the wets were (if the child is not wearing a diaper), whether the child awakens after a wet or on his or her own to visit the toilet prior to a wet. The child's bedtime and time of morning awakening are also provided. This information is also collected throughout treatment to document the process of becoming dry and clearly indicates benchmarks for outcome, including whether the child has met the success criteria or failed treatment.

The unstructured component of the assessment is the verbal discussion between the clinician, parents, and enuretic child. The goals of the face-to-face discussion with the enuretic child and parents are to educate them regarding the epidemiology and etiology of enuresis in order to demystify the problem, to completely inform the parents of all available treatment options (medical and behavioral), and to assess the child's and parents' readiness and commitment to optimally implement the urine alarm treatment.

The author has developed a slide show that is presented on the first visit to help achieve these goals. The presentation describes how common the problem is in the school-age population, current information regarding causes of bed-wetting, and treatment options available for bed-wetting, with their known reported efficacy. The author explains that the vast majority of children who wet the bed are physiologically, behaviorally, and emotionally normal children who just happen to wet the bed. Finally, the author incorporates a behavioral contract between parents and child that outlines individual responsibilities for the urine alarm procedure and reasonable expectations during the course of treatment.

Although the presentation is didactic, the author frequently invites questions from the child and parents to engage them in the process of preparing for a decision regarding whether or not to pursue treatment. This informal or unstructured component of the assessment for enuresis treatment can be done individually or in a small group of four to six families. This flexibility is necessary for some older children or young teens who find the group format too intimidating or embarrassing. Many children find the group format reassuring to them, in that the presence of other children attests to how common enuresis is in the school-age population.

INTERVIEWING OBSTACLES AND SOLUTIONS

As previously mentioned, most enuretic children are considered to be physiologically and emotionally normal except for the fact that they happen to wet the bed. Therefore, very few children will be deemed poor candidates for enrollment into treatment with the urine alarm. However, common and uncommon obstacles to optimal participation in treatment can be identified during the interview process. Addressing these issues is essential to establish the right conditions for a satisfying outcome with the urine alarm or to suggest alternative treatment options to the child and parents.

It is unusual for children not to be troubled by their enuresis, especially after the age of approximately 6 or when they enter school. This is due to the common social experience of children being invited to a "sleepover" with friends and fearing that their bed-wetting problem will be discovered. Many enuretic children simply avoid these social experiences. Others may rely on disposable diapers that look like regular underwear in case they have a wetting accident. The author has heard many children report the significant embarrassment of other children teasing them for wearing diapers. This experience may produce enough motivation in the child and his parents to eventually seek out effective treatment.

The feeling of embarrassment can often be reduced through the process of demystifying the problem of enuresis by explaining how common it is among school-age children. The author has used the following method in this demystifying process. Based on the most current U.S. census data, the therapist obtains a rough estimate of all school-age children in his or her county (5–12 years old). Given that the average incidence of enuresis in this age rage is approximately 10%, multiply the number of school-age children by 10% to indicate the estimated number of bed-wetters in the county (in Rochester, Minnesota, that number comes to 1,880 bed-wetters). Most children and their parents are amazed at how many children there are, as evidenced by wide-open mouths and eyes.

When the child seems unaffected by the enuresis and is taken in for treatment by a parent who is frustrated with the extra laundry, more complicated issues must be addressed. Children that either are unbothered by the wetting or see some good reason to continue wetting the bed often have a worse outcome with the urine alarm treatment due to adherence problems (Butler, Redfern, & Forsythe, 1990). If a judgment can be made by the clinician that treatment is still warranted, establishing an incentive plan using a simple token economy to improve compliance with the urine alarm procedure can be helpful.

From the parents' perspective, feelings of frustration and intolerance for the child's bed-wetting can lead to premature withdrawal from treatment (Butler & Robinson, 2002; Morgan & Young, 1975). Simply explaining the etiology of enuresis and its common occurrence will be helpful in changing a parent's misperceptions of "why the child is doing this." Supporting the parents in implementing the token economy to focus both themselves and the child on the necessary work of treatment will be all that is necessary to ensure an optimal experience.

The way in which the family system functions has important implications for treatment. Any significant problems in the marital relationship, psychiatric problems in the primary caregiver, or drug or alcohol problems in the parents can interfere with the implementation of the urine alarm treatment. A mutual decision between the clinician and parents can often be made to defer the use of the urine alarm until family functioning that is conducive to completing the work of the urine alarm treatment can be obtained, with appropriate interventions to address those problems. Appropriate referrals for these treatments should be made by the therapist.

INTERVIEWING PARENTS AND TEACHERS

Simply due to the nature of nocturnal enuresis occurring at night, the need to involve teachers or other school staff is unnecessary. As previously mentioned, the interviews include the enuretic child and his or her parent(s). At times, it may be necessary to discuss with only the parents those sensitive issues that would be inappropriate in the presence of the child. These issues might include problems in the parents' marital relationship, personal problems that might cause the child to feel uncomfortable, or issues the parents have requested to be kept private from the child. The therapist will have to determine whether the private issues will interfere with the delivery of the treatment, as they may affect the cooperation needed between the parents and the child. Many parental and marital problems can be easily assessed in the intake process by using psychometrically sound questionnaires. The Symptom Checklist-90-R (Derogatis, 1983), the Beck Depression Inventory-II (Beck, Steer, & Brown, 1996), and the Locke-Wallace Marital Adjustment Scale (Locke & Wallace, 1959) are useful for this purpose and not burdensome for the parents to complete.

CASE ILLUSTRATION WITH DIALOGUE

Jimmy was 9 years old when he was referred by his primary care physician to the enuresis clinic. He had been wetting the bed regularly since infancy, with a wetting frequency of about 6 wet nights each week, with only one wet each night. He was living primarily with his mother (custodial parent) and a younger sister. His parents had divorced when he was 6 years old, and he had regular visitation with his father and stepmother. There were ongoing conflicts between his parents regarding child support and child-rearing practices. Jimmy and his mother attended the initial group session with this author. Jimmy was mostly quiet and reluctant to answer questions during the presentation; however, he did indicate his interest in overcoming the bed-wetting, as he wanted to accept invitations for sleepovers without having to worry about wearing a pull-up diaper. After the formal presentation, Jimmy's mother requested a private moment to discuss concerns. The discussion was as follows:

Mother:	I was wondering if Jimmy's anger problem would affect how well the urine alarm treatment would go.
Author:	Please tell me about the anger problem.
M:	Whenever I ask Jimmy to do something, he becomes resentful and argumentative. If something is not going right for Jimmy, he will become so angry, he demands immediate help, and if it is not given, he will say, "I wish I were dead!" This is what happened yesterday morning when he wanted me to cut his bagel. I was busy with something else and asked him to wait. He became enraged and threatened to stab himself. Luckily, I was able to get him to give me the knife, and he was sent to his room to calm down.
A:	Jimmy? Do little things get you angry?
J:	Yes.
A:	Did you think about doing something to hurt yourself?
J:	Yes. *[with tears in his eyes]*
A:	Would you like to talk with someone about why you so easily get angry? I can arrange for you to talk with a nice lady that can help you not feel so angry.
J:	Okay.
A:	After you and your mom feel as though you are doing a good job of controlling your feelings, we can get started on helping you with the bed-wetting. Does that sound like a good plan?
Jimmy and Mother:	Yes.

The author referred Jimmy and his mom immediately to a therapist, to address the family issues affecting Jimmy's frustration and to help Jimmy express his frustration and anger in less potentially destructive ways. Jimmy's mother was also interviewed separately regarding the level of potential harm in Jimmy's threats of self-destruction and was informed of access to the emergency room, if needed. Three brief sessions with the therapist to teach Jimmy's mother more effective parenting strategies and to teach Jimmy more appropriate anger expression with conflict resolution were all they needed. Jimmy's father and stepmother were also invited to a session to learn about the enuresis treatment and encourage their support of Jimmy in his effort to overcome the enuresis. This work also established the necessary level of parent-child cooperation to successfully implement the urine alarm treatment.

DIFFERENTIAL DIAGNOSIS AND BEHAVIORAL ASSESSMENT

The first step in the differential diagnosis begins with the primary care physician, with whom the therapist would have established a partnership in approaching nocturnal enuresis from a biobehavioral perspective. The medical assessment should identify any medical disorders that may be the cause of the nocturnal enuresis. A thorough medical history will help determine whether the onset of wetting may have been preceded by symptoms of urinary urgency, frequency, or burning. These symptoms may indicate an active urinary tract infection and can be assessed with a urinalysis and culturing the urine. Excessive urination may suggest nephritis or diabetes manifesting in polyuria. Less than 10% of children presenting with nocturnal enuresis evidence a medical history that would require these studies (Jarvelin et al., 1991). Another less common condition that can cause the onset of wetting symptoms is severe constipation (O'Regan, Yazbeck, Hamberger & Schick, 1986). All of these organic contributors to nocturnal enuresis should be addressed prior to initiating the urine alarm treatment.

The task of the therapist during a behavioral assessment is to identify whether the child evidences any clinically elevated problems that would interfere with the implementation of urine alarm treatment. Mellon and Houts (in press) reviewed the literature related to moderators of urine alarm treatment and listed factors such as behavior problems and the child's perception of wetting as an advantage as predictors of treatment failure and dropout. A parent's intolerance of the bed-wetting problem is also associated with premature withdrawal from treatment.

SELECTION OF TREATMENT TARGETS AND REFERRAL

During the course of treatment, the therapist will focus on pretreatment variables that may interfere with the child's success, as previously mentioned, as a minimal amount of professional supervision is necessary for a successful outcome in many cases. The therapist will also be aware of important process variables that may arise during as many as six visits spread over the course of 16 to 20 weeks of treatment. These include adherence issues, waking difficulties, and frustration by the child who requires a longer course of treatment. It cannot be stressed enough that objective evidence of treatment progression is essential. Recording bedtimes, times of each enuresis episode, size of the wet spot, any self-awakenings to visit the toilet, problems in completing the cleanup procedure after each wet, and the child's level of enthusiasm during treatment are all important potential targets of urine alarm treatment.

Treatment is not just the act of turning on the urine alarm each night. It also includes maintaining a positive attitude throughout treatment, with the encouragement of the parent. If resistance to full participation emerges, developing a simple reinforcement procedure may be required. If the child evidences difficulty in waking to the alarm, a waking procedure may need to be initiated to "resensitize" the child to this auditory stimulus. Finally, the important treatment component referred to as "overlearning" will be initiated after the child has achieved his first 14 consecutive dry nights with the urine alarm. Overlearning is a systematically increasing fluid load at bedtime that has been demonstrated to reduce the probability of relapse after successful treatment.

The therapist also provides support for the parents in terms of establishing appropriate expectations for treatment and preventing the child from dropping out before the full benefit of intervention can be realized, by providing consultation in problem solving over adherence issues. If this level of professional support is inadequate to enable a full trial of urine alarm treatment, the therapist may need to refer the child for alternative treatments.

Certainly, any indication that medical problems may have surfaced during treatment should immediately be addressed by referring the child back to the primary care physician. If behavioral and emotional problems become significant enough to interfere with the delivery of treatment, referring the child and parents for individual and family therapy should be pursued. In either case, once the issues have been resolved, the child can return to urine alarm treatment at a later date.

Description of the Disorder

Encopresis is the name given to a child's passing of fecal material into his or her clothing. The term applies when the child is over the age of 4 years, when the frequency of soiling accidents is at least once per month for at least 6 months, and when no organic cause can be found for the soiling (APA, 1994). It is reported that as many as 1.5% to 7.5% of school-age children meet the diagnostic criteria for encopresis (Bellman, 1966; Houts & Abramson, 1990). The problem of encopresis can unfold over a period of up to 5 years, including the constipation that leads to overflow soiling at the time the child presents for treatment (Partin, Hamill, Fischel, & Partin, 1992). Loening-Baucke (1993) has reported that as many as 68% to 86% of encopretic children experience years of painful defecation associated with severe stool withholding, and the condition is often referred to as *retentive encopresis*. Even after standard medical treatment for the encopresis, 36% to 42% of children will persist with constipation and soiling, attesting to the difficulty in effectively treating this common childhood disorder (Procter & Loader, 2003; Rockney, McQuade, Days, Linn, & Alario, 1996).

Most children undergo a developmental process that culminates in fecal continence 85% of the time by the age of 4 years (Bellman, 1966). Fecal continence is maintained as a dynamic balance between the involuntary and voluntary nervous systems of the lower gastrointestinal tract and the consistency of fecal material. The anal canal has a rich network of sensory nerve cells that allows the child to differentially recognize and respond to various physical qualities of the contents of the bowel. The sensitive tissue of the anal canal can thus discriminate between the physical states of rectal contents, such as solid, liquid, or gas, which enables the child to make socially appropriate decisions about how to respond in order to maintain continence (Bartolo & Macdonald, 2002).

If it is determined that a bowel movement is inappropriate, then the child voluntarily contracts the external anal sphincter, which pushes the contents back into the upper rectal area, reestablishing resting tone in the internal anal sphincter, and thus delaying a bowel movement. Fecal continence is maintained by having greater muscle tone in the external anal sphincter compared to pressures in the sigmoid rectum, with the anus acting essentially as the valve that selectively allows feces or flatus to pass. When defecation is deemed appropriate, assuming a squatting position on the toilet allows for more efficient passage of stool. Simultaneously executing a Valsalva contraction and relaxing the external anal sphincter allows for formed and soft stool to pass without discomfort.

Normal regularity ranges from a daily bowel movement to once every third day, with peristalsis being stimulated by the ingestion of a meal or vigorous physical activity (Quigley, 2002). This complex bodily function can be disrupted by a state of chronic constipation or severe fecal impaction in which the rectal tissue is abnormally stretched, leading to a loss of sensitivity, further stool withholding, and ultimately to incontinence. Mental health professionals will recognize the importance of reestablishing bowel regularity for normal functioning in the encopretic child and the need for a multidisciplinary approach to restore this functioning. Fecal incontinence in the absence of constipation and withholding behavior should be understood simply as failed toilet training and might suggest other psychosocial issues that could contribute to this failure, such as ineffective parenting or disruptions to normal family functioning (Taubman & Buzby, 1997).

Because encopresis is a problem that occurs almost exclusively during the daytime, there are often other types of behavioral problems that accompany the disorder. Psychological and behavioral factors are thought to have an effect not only on the evolution of fecal incontinence (e.g., coercive toilet training, birth of a sibling, start of school) but also on the maintenance of the problem (e.g., externalizing behavior and nonadherence, low self-esteem and hopelessness, family conflict, psychiatric problems in parents) (Cox et al., 2003). For example, children with encopresis demonstrate significantly more symptoms of anxiety or depression, less expressiveness and organization in the family environment, greater attention and social problems, more disruptive behaviors, and poorer school performance than asymptomatic children (Cox, Morris, Borowitz, & Sutphen, 2002). Furthermore, 20% more of the encopretic sample in a study (Cox et al., 2002) exceeded clinical thresholds in their behavioral symptoms compared with nonencopretic children. Additional evidence suggests lower levels of social competency in encopretic children versus nonclinical children (Young, Brennen, Baker & Baker, 1995). Thus, encopretic children appear to have demonstrable behavioral dysregulation.

The question of whether these behavioral differences precede or are the result of the stress incurred by having encopresis has yet to be answered. The behavioral-emotional difficulties observed in encopretic children, however, attest to the differences in the complexity of this problem compared with bed-wetting. This emotional–behavioral complexity, combined with the greater physiological complexity in the mastery of bowel continence, must be addressed in the design of effective treatments for childhood encopresis. In addition, the process of conducting an assessment with treatment utility becomes important in the goal of achieving a successful outcome. Although many components of the encopresis assessment are similar to that of enuresis, notable exceptions will be identified. In particular, the author has used components of "motivational interviewing" to establish rapport and negotiate readiness for treatment in both the encopretic child and his or her parents. Children who struggle with encopresis seem to exhibit greater levels of avoidance behavior that must be addressed as part of effective treatment. This pervasive avoidance that affects treatment has been described elsewhere (Mellon & Houts, in press).

INTERVIEWING STRATEGIES

Unlike the treatment for nocturnal enuresis, where the assessment process is designed to determine whether the child is a good candidate for pursuing conditioning treatment, it would be rare to assess a child with encopresis and not provide intervention. Given that encopresis occurs primarily during the daytime hours, the encopretic child is much more vulnerable to devastating psychosocial consequences as a result of being incontinent of bowel. Therefore, the assessment process for encopresis is designed to identify factors that would interfere with a successful outcome to treatment versus whether treatment should be pursued at all. Relevant information is obtained in a structured format utilizing objective behavior rating scales and in an unstructured manner in the verbal discussion between the therapist, child, and parents.

Often, encopretic children are referred for treatment by their primary care physicians or specialists, such as a pediatric gastroenterologist. Psychologists should view encopresis treatment as a collaborative effort with the referring physician. Researchers (Houts & Abramson, 1990; Mellon and Houts, in press) have described this collaboration as a "biobehavioral" approach that acknowledges the medical contributors to soiling and the behavioral methods that are essential for recovery. One-dimensional treatments that focus primarily on the constipation alone versus the reinforcement of appropriate use of the toilet or days without accidents will rarely be successful in helping an encopretic child to overcome years of chronic constipation, painful defecation, stool withholding, and avoidance of toileting and feelings of hopelessness.

Obtaining multiple sources of information is important in the interviewing process. The author utilizes informal paper-and-pencil demographic questionnaires, standardized behavioral measures, and face-to-face interviews of the child and parents. It is important to gather information regarding the child's developmental history, past and current medical problems related to toileting and bowel functioning, parents' efforts at toilet training, learning and behavioral problems, and the child's behavioral and social-adaptive functioning within the home and school environments. The developmental history questionnaire includes information regarding the pregnancy, labor and delivery, and postnatal period; when developmental milestones were met; medical history of significant illnesses or injuries; and particular emphasis on problems with the gastrointestinal tract. Information regarding toilet training methods and difficulties, feeding problems, and the parent-child relationship during the toilet training period is important for documenting a history that would account for the emergence of encopresis.

Formal questionnaires regarding a child's general behavioral functioning help identify potential problems in the child's willingness to adhere to treatment recommendations. Similar to nocturnal enuresis, the BASC, a parent report questionnaire, allows the clinician to survey externalizing and internalizing behavior problems and difficulties in adaptive functioning. Assessing self-esteem will often reveal whether the child has the necessary emotional resources to complete the work of treatment or how much avoidance behavior must be addressed that would interfere with cooperation in treatment. The Piers-Harris Self-Concept Scale (Piers, 1999) is used by the author. However, a disorder-specific measure of self-efficacy related to recovering from encopresis has been developed that appears to be promising in identifying who will recover from treatment and who will struggle (Cox et al., 2003).

Objective information regarding pretreatment and treatment process variables is essential. The author uses a record form to document the primary symptoms of fecal soiling, appropriate use of the toilet, and evidence that medications are being used as prescribed. This information is kept daily, with times of day that critical behaviors occur in order to target those times of day that are most problematic. The majority of encopretic children will typically have soiling accidents from the late afternoon through evening (Fishman, Rappaport, Schonwald, & Nurko, 2003). In addition, the author will have parents keep a diary of foods eaten to judge how much fiber is being ingested each day as part of the intervention. Similar to the assessment of nocturnal enuresis, a balance between obtaining treatment-relevant information and not overwhelming the child and parents with paperwork should be achieved. The author uses the same questionnaires to assess children with encopresis as those for nocturnal enuresis, due to their strong psychometric properties (i.e., BASC, SCL-90-R, Piers-Harris Self-Concept Scale, Locke-Wallace Marital Adjustment Scale).

The unstructured portion of the assessment process includes the interview of the child and parents and the initial educational components of the treatment. The author utilizes the concept of "motivational interviewing" (Rollnick, Mason, & Butler, 1999) in preparing both the child and parents for behavioral change and the self-efficacy to do so. The treatment for encopresis for the majority of patients is simple: Medically address the chronic constipation and fecal impaction,

reinforce the child's adherence to the medical components of treatment, reinforce the child's adherence with a toileting schedule, and assist the parents in taking on a supportive role in creating the conditions of effective treatment in the home. The parent's frustration with the child's soiling can be extreme, however, and coercive interactions between the child and parents are not uncommon. The child's avoidance of any aspect of defecation can also be entrenched with resistance to a parent's prompt to visit the toilet, cleanup after an accident, and adhering with medicines prescribed to treat the constipation and soiling. Therefore, the assessment should support the child and parents in deciding whether pursuing treatment is important to them, whether they have the confidence to change their patterns of behavior, and whether or not they are ready for these changes.

Once the parents are given information about the etiology of encopresis and informed about their role in assisting the child in recovering from the soiling, they are typically ready to change their own behavior through the collaboration with the therapist. In contrast, the child often needs a significant amount of support from the parents and therapist to engage in behaviors that are incompatible with avoidance and that will ultimately lead to recovery. It is helpful to conceptualize the treatment process as a partnership between parents and child, with guidance and support provided by the therapist.

INTERVIEWING OBSTACLES AND SOLUTIONS

By the time a child presents for treatment, there may have been years of suffering with painful defecation, abdominal discomfort, and multiple failed attempts at medically managing the soiling (Fishman et al., 2003). Oftentimes, parents have concluded that the child is purposefully soiling, which is a source of great frustration and establishes the conditions frequently leading to coercive parent-child interactions. These problems are initially addressed simply by educating the parents and child about the process of normal defecation, causes of constipation, and the disrupted dynamics of defecation that lead to persistence of constipation and soiling.

The author has developed a series of diagrams and drawings to use in the explanation portion of the interview. In addition, utilizing the child's very own abdominal flat-plate X-ray to show the extent of constipation is quite helpful. The educational process helps to demystify the problem for the child and parents and leads to an understanding by both that soiling is a "loss of control" and rarely is voluntary. The use of visual displays is quite engaging to children who are initially reluctant to talk about the soiling problem. Furthermore, the therapist speaking in a matter-of-fact and nonjudgmental tone, with appropriate use of humor, will function as a form of "exposure" to many of the emotionally painful experiences the child has previously avoided.

The therapist introduces the work to be done by the child and parents, which can be thought of as involving lifestyle changes. Remaining focused on the tasks of treatment, which both the parents and child have control over, as opposed to whether or not there is a "cure," will lead to a better outcome and greater satisfaction with treatment. The therapist emphasizes a long-term perspective for treatment versus a "quick fix," as the treatment can last as long as 6 to 9 months. These efforts by child and parents will allow both to immediately experience some level of success in order to persist in treatment.

INTERVIEWING PARENTS AND TEACHERS

The therapist should offer both the child and the parents an opportunity to be interviewed separately. The parents will typically want to do this in order to share information that may not be appropriate for the child to hear. This information may be related to embarrassing experiences that the child was unable to share with the therapist or may include issues in the marital relationship that could have an impact on successful implementation of treatment. Because the treatment is delivered in the home by the parents, the therapist must establish a working relationship with them. The parents should feel as though they have been heard and accepted by the therapist. Assisting the parents in preparing for behavioral change and enhancing their self-efficacy for change is needed prior to initiating the work of treatment.

Similar to that of the enuresis interview, assessing the marital relationship with the Locke-Wallace Marital Adjustment Scale (Locke & Wallace, 1959) will alert the therapist to any conflicts in the marriage that might undermine the efforts needed for successful treatment of the child's encopresis. Furthermore, inquiring about any mental health problems on the part of the parents will allow for assessing the need for additional psychological interventions for the parents separate from the work with the child's encopresis.

It is not uncommon for parents to inform the therapist that they are quite frustrated with the child's soiling and that they feel hopeless about having any impact on the problem. Parents will often announce to the therapist that they "have tried everything and nothing has worked." This resistance can be addressed through motivational-interviewing techniques that affirm that the parents have tried hard in the past and should be appreciated for those efforts. Eventually, with the therapist's explanation of the etiology of soiling, the parents begin to recognize how their efforts may not have been sustained long enough and in a coordinated fashion between the physician and psychologist to be effective in ameliorating the child's problem. By having the parents focus on the work of therapy, both managing the constipation and the behavioral resistance, they will begin to realize that they have control over the factors in the child's treatment that will lead to success. The focus on effective "treatment behavior" is incompatible with coercive interactions between the parents and child, including frequent parental prompts for the child to use the bathroom, the use of punishment for accidents, and an overgeneralized attitude of frustration and disgust.

When accidents are occurring in the school setting, gathering some information from the teacher may be needed. This can be simply done in a letter from the teacher to the therapist describing the problem or in a telephone call after appropriate releases of information have been obtained from the parents or guardian. The therapist should inquire about how the accidents are being managed, whether the child has access to a private bathroom, and whether there is any resistance from the child to cooperation with school staff. Typically, a written treatment plan for the school setting is all that is needed and would include record keeping of bowel activity, scheduled visits to the private bathroom, extra clothing after accidents occur, and a simple incentive plan for the child that shows any resistance to the plan. The author has found that the majority of school staff will appreciate any guidance in managing the soiling in the school setting. If more significant concerns are raised about behavior problems, additional structured assessment can be completed by using the teacher version of the Behavioral Assessment System for Children (Reynolds & Kamphaus, 1998).

CASE ILLUSTRATION WITH DIALOGUE

Anthony was a 7-year-old boy who presented with his mother due to fecal soiling primarily at home, but occasionally at school or on the bus ride home. Anthony was referred by his family medicine physician after unsuccessful efforts at treating his long-standing history of constipation and encopresis, beginning when he was 3 years old, at a well-child visit.

Anthony began to show less frequent stooling after his transition to regular food at 18 months. This became even more noticeable when toilet training was initiated at 30 months. Anthony reportedly resisted giving up his diaper and would actually ask for it on the rare occasion that he did need to have a bowel movement. Once his mother decided to no longer allow Anthony to use a diaper for bowel movements when he was 32 months old, he would reportedly sneak off to a private place in the home to have a bowel movement instead of using the toilet. Anthony would reluctantly comply with his mother's request to use the toilet, although it took much prompting and anger in her voice to gain his cooperation. By the time Anthony was evaluated by his primary care physician at 3 years, he was having about one bowel movement each week, which was described as "huge" and often clogged the toilet. Anthony was also having fecal accidents on a daily basis, ranging from small streaks in his underwear to larger amounts of solid stool that required his mother to soak clothing prior to putting them in the laundry.

Anthony's physician was able to palpate his abdomen and feel a large amount of stool in his descending colon and rectal area. A clean-out regimen consisting of one child-sized enema and a pamphlet regarding increased dietary fiber were given to the mother. At the 4-year-old checkup, however, Anthony's mother reported that he continued to have periodic large-diameter stools that caused great discomfort and he continued with daily accidents. Anthony's mother was becoming more frustrated with the problem, as Anthony would indicate he did not need to use the toilet after his mother's prompt, but would have a soiling accident while playing with his toys 30 minutes later. Once again, a clean-out regimen was initiated, with daily enemas for 3 days and the use of a stool softener. Although there was a reduction in accidents after the clean-out and increased toileting to two to three bowel movements per week, Anthony eventually regressed back to his baseline after about 3 months. Anthony continued with infrequent, large, and painful bowel movements in the toilet, and soiling accidents occurred on a daily basis.

This pattern continued until Anthony, at 7 years of age, was referred to the author's Encopresis Clinic. Anthony had also experienced a significant amount of verbal harassment from peers at school due to the soiling accidents in that environment and reportedly acquired the nickname of "dooky-boy." It was very difficult for Anthony even to admit that he had a soiling problem at the start of the interview. His mother was quite frustrated with him and was angry with her physician for referring to a psychologist, as she saw it as a waste of time because she had already "tried everything" and did not believe that the psychologist had anything to offer.

At this point in the interview, the author had completed the structured portion of the assessment and reviewed the questionnaires completed by Anthony and his mother. Anthony recently completed an abdominal flat-plate X-ray by his physician, which demonstrated significant amounts of stool throughout his colon, with the rectal area seriously impacted with stool. The author used diagrams and drawings that explained how normal digestion and defecation occurred. Anthony's X-ray was used to teach how chronic constipation causes the problem of fecal soiling after the child loses the ability to detect the presence of stool and how the years of painful defecation lead to stool withholding and inefficient defecation dynamics.

Author: Anthony, come close so you can look at your X-ray with me and your mom. You see these white things are your bones, as they are dense. The black spaces are air outside your body or in your small intestine. This grayish and speckled part is the outline of your large intestine. It is speckled like that because it is completely full of poop. *[It is okay to use the family's terminology for fecal material.]* This part down here in the middle of your pelvis is the rectum or the part that holds the poop before it comes out in a BM. You see that the rectum is 3 times the normal size. Once a person's bowel gets that stretched out with poop, it becomes hard to even know when you have to have a BM. When a child is exposed to the smell of stool constantly, he can become habituated to the smell. That means you stop smelling the poop. Oftentimes, children are not aware of an accident because of these effects of constipation.

Mother: I never realized how constipated he was and how uncomfortable that is for Anthony. I did not realize that he would lose the ability to feel the need to use the bathroom.

Anthony [looking curious about the X-ray]: So that is what my insides look like?

Au: Yes, that is the inside of your body.

A: I tried to tell my mom that it really hurts when I have to go poop and I get worried about her telling me to go do it.

M: I am sorry Anthony that I got so angry at you. I thought you were having accidents on purpose.

Au: Anthony, are you and your mom ready to do some work to stop having these accidents? Are you ready to feel like a big kid that doesn't have accidents any more?

A: What do I have to do?

Au: I want you and your mom to work as a team. Your job is to follow the treatment plan of taking medicine to make it easier to poop, practice sitting on the toilet to try and poop when your body might need to do so, and clean up after you have an accident. You'll also need to eat certain kinds of food to make your poop softer and make it easier to have a bowel movement. Your mom's job is to take care of the medicine for you, buy the foods that you like that have fiber in them, and keep records for me about how you are doing with the program. Anthony, because you are going to be doing work to get over your soiling accidents, I would like your mom to give you rewards for your work. Do you like that idea?

A: Yes, what kind of rewards?

M: Yes, what kind of rewards are you talking about?

Au: For each part of the treatment program you complete each day, including pooping in the toilet and having clean underwear, you will earn points. Your mom will keep track of your points. Anthony, your job is to write a list of 10 rewards you would like to use your points to buy. Make sure the rewards or prizes are things you like, but be reasonable about how much they cost. Your mom will let you know if the prize is inappropriate. Your mom will also let you know how many points it will take to earn that prize. I will ask your mom to make the number of points for each prize fair.

A: Hey, I like this idea.

Au: All I want you and your mom to do is your part in the plan. Mrs. L, I do not want Anthony to be punished for accidents. Help him stay enthusiastic about the work he has been assigned. Does this seem like a plan you both will be able to follow?

A and M: Yes. We can do this.

The author provided all the necessary record sheets for the parent and suggested a follow-up visit in approximately 2 to 3 weeks.

DIFFERENTIAL DIAGNOSIS AND BEHAVIORAL ASSESSMENT

Similar to that of enuresis, the differential diagnosis in the assessment of encopresis begins with the referring physician. Although rare, organic conditions that could cause the fecal soiling should be assessed and ruled out. Loening-Baucke (2002) reported that organic conditions associated with fecal soiling are anorectal malformations, such as rectal stenosis, anterior displacement of the anal opening, or postanal atresia repair. Malformations of the lower spine can include occult meningomyelocele, or tethered cord of the lower spinal cord. In addition, abnormalities of the colon include Hirschprung's disease. Fecal soiling can also present in children with mild cerebral palsy or generalized hypotonia. Other causes can include problems with endocrine, metabolic, and neuromuscular systems. Each of these organic causes must be ruled out by the physical examination and other appropriate tests, if called for. Fortunately, most children who present with fecal soiling meet the criteria for functional retentive encopresis.

The author has often been asked about encopresis as a symptom indicating the patient has been sexually abused. In fact, there is a small but often-cited literature that strongly suggests a connection between the trauma of sexual abuse and encopresis. Therefore, the author investigated further (Mellon, Whiteside, & Friedrich, 2006). It was determined that encopresis is not a sensitive predictor of abuse status when this symptom was assessed in three clearly distinct child populations: children with documented sexual abuse, children referred to a psychiatric outpatient clinic with abuse ruled out, and a group of children from a general pediatric population with abuse ruled out. The author demonstrated that "sexualized" behavior is a much better predictor of abuse status, and this behavior should be assessed when it is present.

The behavioral assessment of encopresis is more complicated than that of enuresis. The psychosocial implications of soiling can be devastating to the child and affect the parent-child relationship. Therefore, care in thoroughly assessing the child's behavioral functioning is essential. Mellon and Houts (in press) have proposed a model that accounts for the complexity of the factors involved in the etiology and maintenance of the soiling behavior. They emphasize the importance of directly addressing the avoidance of all aspects of the treatment, including the medical management of constipation and the child's adherence to the necessary behaviors needed to overcome the soiling behavior. If compliance issues are prominent in the parent-child relationship, this may well be the first intervention in order to set the stage for the necessary appropriate levels of cooperation.

The therapist will sometimes have to address the child's apparent indifference to the soiling problem, seemingly accepting his or her identity as a child who has accidents. This is clearly an example of the often entrenched hopelessness and avoidance of experiential pain associated with the psychosocial consequences of encopresis. The therapist will recognize this behavior and begin to lead the child to envisioning himself or herself as someone who no longer has accidents. The behavioral assessment of the parents will attempt to identify any marital or psychiatric issues that would prevent the parents from becoming the "cotherapists" necessary to the proper implementation of the treatment in the home.

SELECTION OF TREATMENT TARGETS AND REFERRAL

The assessment of encopresis begins with the questionnaires completed by the parent(s) and child prior to the interview. Given that most encopretic children experience years of constipation, painful defecation, abdominal discomfort, and significant frustration in the parent-child relationship in previously failed treatment efforts, most targets for treatment are evident. The child's avoidance of most aspects of normal defecation must be addressed in optimal application of medical treatments designed to overcome the constipation and help the child establish normal and nonpainful defecation. Any resistance by the child will be a target of behavioral interventions, including the use of a token economy or stimulus control techniques to help produce a bowel movement. The child's feelings of hopelessness can be treated with the educational process of demystifying the problem, the use of incentives designed to improve the child's adherence to the treatment program versus "trying to be immediately perfect and have no accidents," and developing a new identity as a child who no longer soils.

The targets of the intervention for the parents are to reduce any feelings of hostility or resentment toward the child that are contributing to coercive parent-child interactions. The educational process of demystifying the problem is immediately helpful in this regard. The therapist must also join with the parents in an effort to be "cotherapists" for the child. To prepare them for a good 6 to 9 months of treatment, the author has proposed using the strategy of "motivational interviewing" to assess both the child's and parents' readiness for change and their self-efficacy for change. The therapist must also be able to instruct the caregiver in the development of simple token economies in order to maintain the child's cooperation with all aspects of the treatment regimen and, when necessary, the appropriate use of negative consequences. Every effort to use positive means of changing the child's behavior is not only respectful and kind to the child but also prevents the development of more intense coercive interactions between the parents and child.

Finally, the frequency of follow-up visits with the therapist will be determined by the needs of the child and parents. The author will typically meet in 2- to 4-week intervals until the child is clearly making progress in more appropriate use of the toilet and reduction in accidents. The visits are then slowly faded out when the child and parents are confident they are successful and can manage on their own. Certainly, the child and parents are invited to return for further collaboration if necessary.

At times during treatment, the child may need to return to his or her primary care provider if it becomes clear that a fecal impaction has recurred. This will be evident from the parent's records and demonstrated by infrequent bowel movements in the toilet, large and painful passage of stool, and an increase in soiling frequency. In this case, the child will have to undergo another bowel cleanout regimen, followed by reinitiation of the behavioral part of treatment. The behavioral treatment must address the factors that allowed for the regression to occur.

SUMMARY

Enuresis and encopresis are two of the most common childhood disorders, and child psychologists will likely encounter these children and parents in their professional practices. Oftentimes, these children will be referred by their primary care providers. It is important to view enuresis and encopresis as biobehavioral problems that are best managed in a collaborative approach between physicians and psychologists. In the case of enuresis, frequently these children are physiologically and behaviorally normal. There is clear evidence that the use of the urine alarm (a nighttime behavioral conditioning device) will lead to a "cure" approximately 70% to 80% of the time, with minimal professional supervision (Mellon & McGrath, 2000).

The goal of an effective assessment is to determine whether the child and parents are ready to optimally participate in this treatment. The therapist will attempt to identify behavioral and emotional problems in the child and caregiver that may affect adherence to the urine alarm treatment. If these psychosocial issues are at a nonclinical level, additional behavior management strategies may be all that is needed. If the issues are significant and pervasive, delaying urine alarm treatment until the psychosocial issues have been resolved may be the most appropriate intervention with which to begin.

In the case of encopresis, the author has attempted to explain the greater complexity of the disorder in terms of physiological influences (i.e., constipation) and the frequent complication of avoidance and generalized behavioral problems. Frequently, the parent-child relationship can be quite strained and described as reciprocally "coercive." Great care is recommended in the assessment process to ensure that complete medical evaluation and treatment have been initiated prior to the psychological assessment. The goals of the psychological assessment are to identify behavioral problems in the child that would interfere with the delivery of treatment and to prepare the child and parents for a cooperative process in treatment.

Although much is known about treating both enuresis and encopresis and treatment manuals have been developed, the therapist should continue to appreciate the importance of an empirical approach to assessment of these disorders so that the treatment can be tailored to the individual needs of any given child and his or her family. The use of common parent and child report questionnaires with good psychometric properties is essential in this empirical approach. Further, directly recording treatment process variables, such as frequency of wetting and soiling and appropriate use of the toilet, is necessary for guiding the child and parents through treatment and knowing when the intervention has been successfully completed, or not. Without this evidence, the therapist would not know when and how to adjust the intervention to ultimately lead to a successful outcome.

REFERENCES

American Psychiatric Association. (1994). *Diagnostic and statistical manual of mental disorders* (4th ed.). Washington, DC: Author.

Bakker, E., van Sprundel, M., van der Auwera, J., van Gool, J., & Wyndaele, J. (2002). Voiding habits and wetting in a population of 4332 Belgian schoolchildren aged between 10 and 14 years. *Scandinavian Journal of Urology and Nephrology, 36,* 354–362.

Bartolo, D., & Macdonald, A. (2002). Fecal continence and defecation. In J. Pemberton, M. Swash, & M. Henry (Eds.), *The pelvic floor: Its function and disorders* (pp. 77–93). New York: W. B. Saunders.

Beck, A., Steer, R., & Brown, G. (1996). *Beck Depression Inventory-Second edition manual.* San Antonio, TX: The Psychological Corporation.

Bellman, M. (1966). Studies on encopresis. *Acta Paediatrica Scandinavica, 1*(Suppl. 170), 7–132.

Butler, R., Brewin, C., & Forsythe, I. (1990). Relapse in children treated for nocturnal enuresis: Prediction of response using pre-treatment variable. *Behavioural Psychotherapy, 18,* 65–72.

Butler, R., Redfern, E., & Forsythe, I. (1990). The child's construing of nocturnal enuresis: A method of inquiry and predication of outcome. *Journal of Child Psychology, 34,* 447–454.

Butler, R., & Robinson, J. (2002). Alarm treatment for childhood nocturnal enuresis: An investigation of within-treatment variables. *Scandinavian Journal of Urology and Nephrology, 36,* 268–272.

Cox, D., Morris, J., Borowitz, S., & Sutphen, J. (2002). Psychological differences between children with and without chronic encopresis. *Journal of Pediatric Psychology, 27,* 585–591.

Cox, D., Ritterband, L., Quillian, W., Kovatchev, B., Morris, J., Sutphen, J., et al. (2003). Assessment of behavioral mechanisms maintaining encopresis: Virginia Encopresis-Constipation Apperception Test. *Journal of Pediatric Psychology, 28,* 375–382.

De Jonge, G. (1973). Epidemiology of enuresis: A survey of the literature. In I. Kolvin, R. MacKeith, & S. Meadow (Eds.), *Bladder control and enuresis* (pp. 39–46). London: William Heinemann.

Derogatis, L. (1983). *SCL-90-R: Administration, scoring, and procedures manual II.* Towson, MD: Clinical Psychometric Research.

Eiberg, H., Berendt, I., & Mohr, J. (1995). Assignment of dominant inherited nocturnal enuresis (ENUR1) to chromosome 13q. *Nature Genetics, 10,* 354–356.

Fergusson, D., Horwood, I., & Shannon, F. (1986). Factors related to the age of attainment of nocturnal bladder control: An 8-year longitudinal study. *Pediatrics, 78,* 884–890.

Fishman, L., Rappaport, L., Schonwald, A., & Nurko, S. (2003). Trends in referral to a single encopresis clinic over 20 years. *Pediatrics, 111,* 604–607.

Forsythe, W., & Redmond, A. (1974). Enuresis and spontaneous cure rate: Study of 1129 enuretics. *Archives of Disease in Childhood, 49,* 259–263.

Glazener, C., & Evans, J. (2003). Simple behavioural and physical interventions for nocturnal enuresis in children. *Cochrane Database of Systematic Reviews, 1,* CD003637.

Glazener, C., Evans, J., & Peto, R (2005). Complex behavioural and educational interventions for nocturnal enuresis in children. *Cochrane Database of Systematic Reviews, 3,* CD004668.

Houts, A., & Abramson, H. (1990). Assessment and treatment for functional childhood enuresis and encopresis: Toward a partnership between health psychologists and physicians. In S. B. Morgan & T. M. Okwumabua (Eds.), *Child and adolescent disorders: Developmental and health psychology perspectives* (pp. 47–103). Hillsdale, NJ: Lawrence Erlbaum.

Houts, A., Berman, J., & Abramson, H. (1994). The effectiveness of psychological and pharmacological treatments for nocturnal enuresis. *Journal of Consulting and Clinical Psychology, 62,* 737–745.

Jarvelin, M., Moilanen, I., Kangas, P., Moring, K., Vikevainen-Tervonen, L., Moilanen, I., et al. (1991). Aetiological and precipitating factors for childhood enuresis. *Acta Pediatrica Scandinavia, 77,* 148–153.

Jarvelin, M., Vikevainen-Tervonen, L., Moilanen, I., & Huttunen, N. (1988). Enuresis in seven-year-old children. *Acta Paediatrica Scandinavica, 77,* 148–153.

Kristensen, G., & Jensen, I. (2003). Meta-analyses of results of alarm treatment for nocturnal enuresis. *Scandinavian Journal of Urology and Nephrology, 37,* 232–238.

Locke, H., & Wallace, K. (1959). Short marital adjustment and prediction test: Their reliability and validity. *Marriage and Family Living, 21,* 251–255.

Loening-Baucke, V. (1993). Constipation in early childhood: Patient characteristics, treatment, and long-term follow up. *Gut, 34,* 1400–1404.

Loening-Baucke, V. (2002). Encopresis. *Current Opinion in Pediatrics, 14,* 570–575.

Mellon, M., & Houts, A. (in press). Psychosocial treatments for enuresis and encopresis: Current knowledge and future directions. *Journal of Clinical Child and Adolescent Psychology.*

Mellon, M., & McGrath, M. (2000). Empirically supported treatments in pediatric psychology: Nocturnal enuresis. *Journal of Pediatric Psychology, 25,* 193–214.

Mellon, M., Whiteside, S., & Friedrich, W. (2006). The relevance of fecal soiling as an indicator of child sexual abuse: A preliminary analysis. *Journal of Developmental and Behavioral Pediatrics, 27,* 45–53.

Morgan, R., & Young, G. (1975). Parental attitudes and the conditioning treatment of childhood enuresis. *Behaviour Research & Therapy, 13,* 197–199.

Norgaard, J., Djurhuus, J., Watanabe, H., Stenberg, A., & Lettgen, B. (1997). Experience and current status of research into the pathophysiology of nocturnal enuresis. *British Journal of Urology, 79,* 825–835.

O'Regan, S., Yazbeck, S., Hamberger, B., & Schick, E. (1986). Constipation: A commonly unrecognized cause of enuresis. *American Journal of Diseases of Children, 140,* 260–261.

Partin, J., Hamill, S., Fischel, J., & Partin, J. (1992). Painful defecation and fecal soiling in children. *Pediatrics, 89,* 1007–1009.

Piers, E. (1999). *Piers-Harris Children's Self-Concept Scale: Revised manual 1984.* Los Angeles: Western Psychological Services.

Procter, E., & Loader, P. (2003). A 6-year follow-up study of chronic constipation and soiling in a specialist pediatric service. *Child: Care, Health, & Development, 29,* 103–109.

Quigley, E. (2002). Colonic motility and colonic function. In J. Pemberton, M. Swash, & M. Henry (Eds.), *The pelvic floor: Its function and disorders* (pp. 84–93). New York: W. B. Saunders.

Rawashde, Y., Hvistendahl, G., Kamperis, K., & Djurhuus, J. (2002). Demographics of enuresis patients attending a referral centre. *Scandinavian Journal of Urology & Nephrology, 36,* 348–353.

Reynolds, C., & Kamphaus, R. (1998). *Behavior assessment system for children: Manual.* Circle Pines, MN: American Guidance Services.

Rockney, R., McQuade, W., Days, A., Linn, H., & Alario, A. (1996). Encopresis treatment outcome: Long-term follow-up of 45 cases. *Journal of Developmental & Behavioral Pediatrics, 17,* 380–385.

Rollnick, S., Mason, P., & Butler, C. (1999). *Health behavior change: A guide for practitioners.* London: Churchill-Livingstone.

Taubman, B., & Buzby, M. (1997). Overflow encopresis and stool toileting refusal during toilet training: A prospective study on the effect of therapeutic efficacy. *Journal of Pediatrics, 131,* 768–771.

Young, M., Brennen, L., Baker, R., & Baker, S. (1995). Functional encopresis: Symptom reduction and behavioral improvement. *Developmental and Behavioral Pediatrics, 16,* 226–232.

24

SLEEP DISORDERS

BRETT R. KUHN

DESCRIPTION OF THE DISORDERS

The field of pediatric sleep medicine has witnessed a proliferation of recent activity, including the publication of professional review articles (Gordon & King, 2002; Kuhn & Elliott, 2003; Kuhn & Weidinger, 2000; Lewin, 2003; Mindell, 1999; Owens, France, & Wiggs, 1999; Owens & Witmans, 2004; Ramchandani, Wiggs, Webb, & Stores, 2000), clinical practice guidelines (Mindell, Kuhn, Lewin, Meltzer, & Sadeh, 2006; Mindell & Owens, 2003; Sheldon, Ferber, & Kryger, 2005; Stores, 2001), and self-help books (Friman, 2005; Mindell, 2005; Owens & Mindell, 2005; Sadeh, 2001). Studies consistently find that around 25% of children will display sleep problems (Armstrong, Quinn, & Dadds, 1994; Bixler, Kales, Scharf, Kales, & Leo, 1976; Kerr & Jowett, 1994; Lozoff, Wolf, & Davis, 1985; Mindell, Owens, & Carskadon, 1999; Owens, Spirito, McGuinn, & Nobile, 2000), and disturbed sleep is consistently identified among the most common concerns presented in clinical settings for children (Arndorfer, Allen, & Aljazireh, 1999; Keren, Feldman, & Tyano, 2001; Lavigne et al., 1999; Mesibov, Schroeder, & Wesson, 1977; Mindell, Moline, Zendell, Brown, & Fry, 1994). When sleep difficulties and crying endure, parents may become frustrated and fatigued, resulting in maternal malaise, negative parent-child interactions,

and impaired family satisfaction (Benoit, Zeanah, Boucher, & Minde, 1992; Kataria, Swanson, & Trevathan, 1987; Minde et al., 1993; Richman, 1981; Van Tassel, 1985).

Although certain pediatric sleep disorders clearly demand attention from a physician or sleep specialist (e.g., obstructive sleep apnea, narcolepsy), the majority require clinical assessment, analytical reasoning, and intervention skills that behavioral health specialists are ideally suited to provide. In addition, pediatric sleep experts from a variety of professional disciplines consider educational, psychological, and behavioral interventions as "first line" treatments for childhood sleep disturbance (Dahl, 1992; Kuhn & Weidinger, 2000; Mindell, Kuhn, et al., 2006; Morgenthaler et al., 2006; Younus & Labellarte, 2002).

The purpose of this chapter is to describe clinical interviewing strategies specific to the differential diagnosis and treatment of common pediatric sleep disorders. A functional framework of interviewing is introduced to directly inform a treatment plan, which can then be tailored to the unique clinical presentation, individual child characteristics, or family context. Readers interested in learning more about general skills, techniques, process, or content areas for interviewing children are directed elsewhere (Barker, 1990; Kanfer, Eyberg, & Krahn, 1992; Querido, Eyberg, Kanfer, & Krahn, 2001).

INTERVIEWING STRATEGIES

Mounting evidence indicates that disturbed and/or disordered sleep significantly impacts children's neurocognitive development, emotional regulation, attention, behavior, and academic performance (Beebe, 2005; Dahl, 1996, 1999; Fallone, Acebo, Seifer, & Carskadon, 2005; Fallone, Owens, & Deane, 2002; Lavigne et al., 1999; Owens, 2005; Sadeh, Gruber, & Raviv, 2002; Wolfson & Carskadon, 2003). Sleep problems are extremely common in children with developmental disabilities (Quine, 2001) and can be identified in nearly every psychiatric condition, including anxiety (Glod, Teicher, Hartman, & Harakal, 1997; Rapoport et al., 1981; Sadeh, 1996), depression (Gregory, Rijsdijk, Dahl, McGuffin, & Eley, 2006; Ivanenko, Crabtree, & Gozal, 2005), attention-deficit/hyperactivity disorder (ADHD) (Owens, 2005), and school refusal (Tomoda & Miike, 1996). The association is considered to be bidirectional; however, sleep disturbances at a young age have been found to predict subsequent emotional and behavioral problems during midadolescence (Gregory & O'Connor, 2002).

Given the relationship between sleep and children's emotional and behavioral regulation during the day, it is incumbent upon behavioral health clinicians to screen for pediatric sleep problems during the initial diagnostic evaluation. Children and their parents are often unaware of the connection between sleep, emotional regulation, and behavior problems and are unlikely to report sleep disturbances unless asked. At the very minimum, three screening questions should be incorporated into any initial diagnostic interview with the parent and/or the youth:

1. Do you have any concerns about your (or your child's) sleep?

2. How much sleep do you (or your child) usually get?

3. Has anyone told you that you snore? Does your child snore?

When concerns or potential sleep problems arise, a more detailed sleep history (sleep-specific clinical interview) is warranted. With slightly more time investment, behavioral health clinicians can get a more systematic sleep history by using the "BEARS" (Owens & Dalzell, 2001).

This pediatric sleep-screening tool is divided into five major sleep domains—Bedtime issues, Excessive daytime sleepiness, Awakening during the night, Regularity and duration of sleep, and Snoring—that affect children between 2 and 18 years of age.

Most pediatric sleep problems are behaviorally based, but children may present with multiple sleep disturbances. Behavioral health clinicians should be able to screen for primary sleep disorders (medically based) in order to remain within their scope of practice and to make appropriate referrals when indicated. Referral for an overnight sleep study, polysomnography (PSG), is indicated in cases involving suspected sleep-related breathing problems (sleep apnea) and cases of unexplained excessive daytime sleepiness (EDS). In contrast to subjective feelings of being tired, fatigued, or lacking energy, EDS refers to a child's propensity to fall asleep at inappropriate times during the day (Guilleminault & Brooks, 2001; Shen, Barbera, & Shapiro, 2006). PSG is also indicated in the evaluation and diagnosis of periodic limb movement disorder (PLMD) and for parasomnias that involve dangerous or violent behavior. Unless sleep-disordered breathing is suspected, PSG is not routinely indicated in the evaluation of insomnia or difficulty falling asleep, bedtime refusal or nighttime awakenings, circadian rhythm disorders, restless legs syndrome, or typical noninjurious parasomnias, such as bruxism, enuresis, sleepwalking, sleep terrors, or nightmares (ASDA, 1997; Kushida et al., 2005). An updated list of accredited sleep laboratories and sleep centers can be found on the American Academy of Sleep Medicine (AASM) Web site: http://www.aasmnet.org.

CLINICAL ASSESSMENT

Upon identifying that sleep is an area of concern during screening or the initial diagnostic evaluation, a more comprehensive and detailed sleep assessment is indicated. The clinical interview is often the richest source of information and remains the most universally used assessment procedure (Mash & Terdel, 1997). To increase confidence in predisposing (e.g., genetics), precipitating (e.g., acute stressors), and perpetuating factors (e.g., poor sleep habits) (Spielman, Conroy, & Glovinsky, 2003), clinicians are encouraged to obtain a multimethod, multi-informant clinical assessment (La Greca, Kuttler, & Stone, 2001). This may involve seeking information from others besides the parent and child, potentially including the child's siblings, day care providers, teachers, or grandparents. Relevant information can be obtained from a variety of procedures, including face-to-face or telephone interviews, standardized questionnaires, or direct observations of behavior, including nonverbal behavior and parent-child interactions. A few commonly used assessment measures are briefly described.

Broad-Band and Sleep-Specific Behavior Rating Scales

Standardized behavior rating scales allow time-efficient assessment of a broad range of behaviors from multiple informants (e.g., child, parents, teachers). Most scales require little time to administer, score, and interpret, and the results often aid the clinician in directing the clinical interview. Although numerous broad-band behavior scales are available, the Achenbach Child Behavior Checklist (CBCL) (Achenbach & Rescorla, 2000), Eyberg Child Behavior Inventory (ECBI) (Eyberg & Pincus, 1999), and Behavior Assessment System for Children-2 (BASC) (Reynolds & Kamphaus, 2005) serve dual purposes, because they also assess sleep-related behaviors. The CBCL Parent Report Form for 1½- to 5-year-olds includes a Sleep Problem subscale that has been found to be sensitive to treatment effects (Reid, Walter, & O'Leary, 1999). Although less widely published, a number of sleep-specific assessment tools have also been developed for children and adolescents, including the Sleep Disturbance Scale for Children (SDSC) (Bruni et al., 1996), Children's Sleep Habits Questionnaire (CSHSQ) (Owens, Spirito, & McGuinn, 2000), Pediatric Sleep Questionnaire (PSQ) (Chervin, Hedger, Dillon, & Pituch, 2000), Adolescent Sleep Hygiene Scale (ASHS) (LeBourgeois, Giannotti, Cortesi, Wolfson, & Harsh, 2005), and the Sleep Disorders Inventory for Students (SDIS) (Luginbuehl, 2004).

Sleep Diary

A typical sleep diary affords daily recording of sleep parameters, including bedtime, arising time, sleep-onset latency, number and duration of awakenings, naps, medication intake, and written notes detailing unusual events, such as illness or unique behaviors. Maintaining a daily sleep diary serves multiple purposes and has several advantages over relying solely on retrospective verbal report. For example, clients often recall nights when problems were at peak intensity (i.e., sleepless night) but fail to report nights when sleep or behavior was unremarkable. Systematic data collection allows the clinician to assess every night within a 2-week period, not just those that are problematic. The diary often provides critical information that may not otherwise be reported, such as when a child or adolescent makes up for "lost" sleep by sleeping late in the morning, taking a late afternoon nap, or sleeping excessively the following evening. A sleep diary also helps establish a baseline of the problem severity by which the clinician can monitor ongoing progress with treatment. Age-adjusted normative data are available for total sleep time, sleep-onset time, and napping (Weissbluth, 1995; Weissbluth et al., 1981).

Direct or Videotaped Observations

Verbal report, while easy to obtain, may correspond poorly with what actually occurs (Bernstein & Michael, 1990). Direct observation tends to be less subject to bias and distortion (Mash & Terdel, 1997) and to be more useful in obtaining a functional assessment of child behavior problems (McMahon & Estes, 1997). Clinicians must not overlook the utility of direct observations simply because the presenting problem occurs after dark. Observations in the clinic can be a rich source of information regarding child (or parent) skills deficits, behavioral excesses, and parent-child interactions that may directly contribute to sleep problems. The relationship between daytime behavior and disturbed sleep appears to be bidirectional; therefore, behavior problems (e.g., inattention, whining, temper tantrums, aggression) that contribute to the maintenance of sleep problems may also represent the consequent of disturbed sleep.

Directly observing a child's nighttime behaviors or sleep in the home is beyond practicality for most clinicians. This limitation can be overcome by asking parents to videotape at night. Videotapes can capture a wealth of information to aid, for example, in making the differential diagnosis of certain parasomnias or identifying parent-child interactions that maintain bedtime struggles. If a comprehensive clinical interview fails to identify child skill deficits, poor sleep habits, inappropriate schedules, or misplaced contingencies, additional information must be gathered to produce a clear clinical conceptualization of the problem. Ask parents to videotape (with the time stamp) a few nights, beginning with bedtime interactions through the morning awakening. Videotaping ensures that you obtained accurate information from parents, asked all the necessary questions, and did not lead the parent in responding.

Multi-Informant Report

Few clinicians have experienced a 4-year-old child entering the office saying, "Doc, you gotta help me. I just haven't been sleeping well lately." Until late childhood or adolescence, sleep-related complaints come from the parents rather than the child (Ferber, 1995b). Parents are usually the primary informants of their children's sleep habits and behaviors, and parents are the ones who typically make the final determination of what will be done, if anything, to address those habits and behaviors. Children are most often accompanied by their mothers to the initial clinic appointment; however, the father's presence is a critical component when completing the multi-informant interview, in order to clear up any discrepancies before providing feedback to both parents and agreeing on a treatment plan.

Children are the most accurate reporters of their own emotional states (Aronen & Soininen, 2000), but children below the age of 10 years tend to be unreliable in reporting their own symptoms (Edelbrock, Greenbaum, & Conover, 1985). Consequently, the amount of time invested in the individual child interview is often directly related to the child's age and cognitive abilities. Younger children rarely provide information critical to developing the treatment plan; however, the individual child interview can provide an estimate of the child's cognitive abilities and social skills, in addition to establishing rapport. The child interview can start simply: "Please tell me why you are here today." The child's response, followed by further questioning, will often give the clinician an idea of whether the identified sleep problem largely impacts the child or the parent(s). An adult with insomnia "can't sleep," but it is not uncommon for parents to drag a child into clinic because he or she "won't sleep." Research

continues to mount on the negative consequences of sleeplessness in children (Fallone et al., 2002; Wiggs & Stores, 2001); in addition, the impact of a sleepless child on family interactions and stress is finally being recognized. In fact, the new definition of *pediatric insomnia* now includes functional impact for the child *and* family (Mindell, Emslie, et al., 2006).

Behavioral Systems Framework

The goals, objectives, and specific techniques that make up the clinical interview typically reflect the theoretical model to which the practitioner subscribes. Accordingly, the semistructured clinical interview described in this chapter is based on a behavioral systems assessment-to-intervention framework (Mash & Terdel, 1997; Schroeder & Gordon, 2002) commonly practiced by professionals in clinical child and family behavior therapy, behavior modification, applied behavior analysis, and behavioral pediatrics. Consistent with the behavioral systems model of assessment, temporally remote factors such as demographics and historical information take a backseat to identifying current interactions and influences maintaining the presenting problem.

By tradition, a structural or descriptive assessment categorizes "symptoms" into diagnostic groups based on behavioral topography (what the behavior looks like or sounds like). This approach assumes homogeneity of the controlling and maintaining variables across children and families. For example, a busy clinician may diagnose a child who "doesn't sleep" with behavioral insomnia of childhood (AASM, 2005) and propose a one-size-fits-all recommendation such as, "She'll outgrow it," "Just let him cry it out," or "Let's try this medication to break the cycle."

In contrast to the structural approach, a functional approach to interviewing involves isolating factors influencing the problem, to allow the clinician to identify why a specific behavior occurs (Brown & Piazza, 1999). Functional interviewing moves beyond the overt topography of the behavior to identify antecedents and consequences that control behavior in natural environments (Vollmer & Smith, 1996). Most important, the functionally driven interview has greater potential to inform the treatment plan by more thoroughly identifying not only antecedent and consequent events but also skill repertoires, response interrelations, and support systems (Scotti, Morris, McNeil, & Hawkins, 1996). Identifying these factors during the sleep interview is critical, because skills, habits (i.e., sleep "hygiene"), and caregiving practices are the strongest predictors of which children will develop disturbed sleep (Adair, Bauchner, Philipp, Levenson, & Zuckerman, 1991; Anders, Halpern, & Hua, 1992; Fehlings, 2001; Touchette et al., 2005; Van Tassel, 1985).

To incorporate the advantages afforded by the functional approach, our pediatric sleep clinic transitioned from using a structural interview containing a sequential list of questions (see Kuhn, Mayfield, & Kuhn, 1999) to a conceptually driven interview that views sleep from a developmental, biobehavioral process that requires skill attainment (child and parent), setting events, and supporting contingencies. The following two interviews highlight the unique information that can be obtained, leading to two very different treatment plans for a 4-year-old girl with "insomnia."

Interview A:

Therapist: So, tell me the reason for your visit today.

Parent: Kristen absolutely cannot sleep.

T: Okay, specifically what do you mean by "She can't sleep." Exactly what is she doing?

P: I've tried everything, but she keeps coming out of her bedroom. First it's an extra hug, then she says she's hungry, next she'll ask me what we are doing tomorrow. I get so tired of taking her back to her room that I eventually just give up and let her stay with me to watch TV.

T: What is happening right before she comes out?

P: Nothing, really, her dad and I are usually watching TV.

T: Does she always approach you for these requests, or will she ask dad too?

P: No, dad's always nearby but she's a mommy's girl right now, so only my answers will do.

T: How does she respond when you talk to her or answer her questions?

P: She seems happy to just be there, but then she whines and cries when I tell her

to go back to bed. But then if I finally let her stay, she's all smiles and giggles.

T: Does she go?

P: Oh sure, but she comes right back out again 5 minutes later.

Interview B:

T: So, tell me the reason for your visit today.

P: Kristen absolutely cannot sleep.

T: Okay, specifically what do you mean by "She can't sleep." Exactly what is she doing?

P: I've tried everything, but she keeps coming out of her bedroom.

T: What is happening right before she comes out?

P: Well, I can't even get out of her bedroom. When I stand up to leave her bedroom she just panics, and she tries to follow me out into the living room.

T: Panics? What makes you think that she "panics"?

P: She starts screaming, "No mommy, don't leave," and she starts crying and trying to get out of the room with me. She fights me if I try to close the door. I usually just go back and lie next to her because I can't stand to see her so scared.

T: How does she respond when you return to lie next to her?

P: She seems very relieved. She usually calms right down and goes right to sleep, but then I'm stuck there all night. If I try to sneak out she wakes up.

T: How does she handle separation from you during the day?

P: Not good at all. In fact, we abandoned the idea of sending her to preschool this year after 4 straight days of crying when I tried to drop her off.

Given the results of these two contrasting interviews, recommending a one-size-fits-all (e.g., ignoring or door-closing) treatment plan would obviously be inappropriate. Although further information must be obtained, the first case will likely involve teaching the parent to use her attention as a tool to reinforce in-bedroom behavior, potentially recruiting the father to help manage out-of-bedroom behavior, and altering the child's sleep schedule if she is not sleepy at bedtime. The second presentation would likely dictate addressing the child's separation anxiety during the day before turning attention toward her bedtime problems.

The semistructured clinical interview presented in this section has been used in our pediatric sleep clinic for several years. It is not designed to be a "boilerplate," as we continue to update and refine it to meet our needs. Our clinicians do not conduct the interview in the same sequence or format with every family; rather, we attempt to remain flexible and follow the family's lead while jotting notes into the appropriate section of the page. Once the family is finished "telling their story," the clinician can ask additional questions to finish incomplete areas. The interview includes information about the presenting concern(s), treatment goals, previous treatment attempts, and five global domains (primary sleep disorders, sleep environment, sleep-wake schedule, parent-child bedtime interactions, daytime behavior and skills) that impact children's sleep. The precise wording and format of the interview are less important than the clinician's ability to interview in such a manner that isolates functional variables, leading to a behavioral formulation and integrated treatment plan.

The Presenting Concern(s)

The interview usually starts with a simple question such as "What brings you in to see us today?" Asking the older child the question before eliciting the parent's view frequently gives information on who is most concerned or experiencing the most distress. We try not to interrupt until the child and parent(s) have a chance to tell their whole stories, making sure to denote any key words or phrases ("She *never* sleeps") for later clarification.

Interview A:

T: Please tell me exactly what it is about Karlie's sleep pattern that concerns you.

P: Shortly after her second birthday, she started squirming and kicking whenever we try to put her to sleep.

T: Okay. Please describe what you mean by "put" her to sleep.

Interview B:

T: [addressing both parents] Who typically helps Mollie through her bedtime routine and gets her into bed?

Mom: [says nothing, points to dad]

Dad: Yes, Mollie insists that I do it.

T: What do you mean by she "insists"?

Dad: I don't know why, but she throws a fit if mom tries to put her to bed, so I just do it.

T: Hey Mollie, would you rather have mom or dad put you to bed tonight?

Mollie: Dad.

T: Why Dad?

M: He rubs my back, lets me read an extra book, and stays with me until I'm asleep.

Sometimes a child's request for a certain parent represents a preference for a routine to be completed in a specific manner or in a certain sequence. School-age children are often quite willing to help the clinician identify reinforcing interaction patterns that maintain the problem, and occasionally the clinician will find that these interactions are more readily available from one parent. In such cases, often a temporary switch to a different parent may be all that is needed to resolve the problem or may at least represent one component of the treatment plan.

Treatment Goals

"Begin with the end in mind" is not just a habit of effective people (Covey, 1990), it is routine clinical practice among successful behavioral health clinicians. Treatment goals help map the highway between pretreatment functioning and successful discharge. Goals are most effective when they are competency based, individualized, specific, objective, measurable, and in written format. Identified treatment goals do not necessarily need to remain child-centered, as many times a parent will exclaim, "I want to get my toddler to sleep so I can get some rest myself." Prepackaged goals that are "pasted" into a treatment plan fall short by failing to recognize the family's unique concerns, expectations, and cultural values. By taking time to establish agreed-upon outcome goals, the clinician ensures that the family's expectations are realistic, that the family and clinician are working on the same problems or goals, and that progress can be monitored by both parties.

In some cases, mental health practitioners will be faced with the task of educating the family or realigning expectations to be more reasonable and consistent with the course of normal child development. For example, we are frequently confronted with parents who want their children to sleep more hours than is developmentally appropriate or who want their infants to "sleep through the night without waking up." We help them establish treatment goals after showing them data on total sleep requirements across development or after informing them that children who are thought to "sleep through the night" actually awaken several times per night but have learned to quietly reinitiate sleep without their parents' awareness (Anders et al., 1992).

T: As you know from reading the brochure describing our service, this is a short-term, goal-oriented clinic designed to help parents resolve specific problems. Please think for a moment about the end of treatment. When will you know when you no longer need our services and will be finished here? In other words [sly smile], how will you know you've met your treatment goals and you're ready to fire me?

P: Oh, I guess I hadn't thought of it that way. I suppose when Byron can sleep all night long.

T: Okay. What does "all night" mean to you?

P: Well, when he sleeps all night long without hopping into our bed in the middle of the night.

T: Okay, so in other words you would like him to sleep all night in *his own* bed?

P: Absolutely. Well, except for when we travel to my mother's house because then we all have to sleep in the same bed.

T: Okay, so you would like him to sleep in his own bed every night that you are home?

P: Yes, every night.

T: Now, every family has their own preferred schedule. You would like Byron to sleep through the night, but what are you referring to in terms of a preferred bedtime and wake time in the morning?

P: My husband and I both agree that he does best when he's in bed by 9:00 p.m., and then he has to be awake by 7:00 a.m. to make it to school on time.

T: So, let me just summarize. If we could help you teach Byron to sleep in his own bed every night that you are home, from 9:00 p.m. to 7:00 a.m., without disturbing you two by hopping into your bed, we would be finished with treatment?

P: Yes!

T: Okay then, let's get to work.

Previous Treatment Attempts

Albert Einstein reportedly defined *insanity* as "doing the same thing over and over and expecting different results" (as cited in Moncur, n.d.). An essential component of the initial clinical interview is to determine what has already been done or attempted, so as not to repeat history. The clinician should carefully identify previous treatment attempts, who suggested them, their short-term and long-term effectiveness, whether they received a sufficient trial, and what factors may have accounted for their failure (e.g., side effects, lack of treatment effect, poor adherence) (Sateia, Doghramji, Hauri, & Morin, 2000). Clinicians should be confident they understand what caused past interventions to fail before attempting to make modifications or improvements or proposing a new treatment plan.

Common reasons for treatment failure with sleep-disturbed children include abandoning an intervention before it has an opportunity to take effect (frequently due to child protests or an extinction burst) and promising large rewards for demonstrating behaviors beyond reasonable expectation (i.e., setting the bar too high, based on the child's history). Parents also may have made changes that were not functionally related to the problem (e.g., purchasing a new bed, sheets, curtains, painting the bedroom) rather than addressing critical child skills deficits, inconsistent schedules, or sleep-impairing habits.

A child's response to past treatment attempts can also provide important functional clues regarding whether the problem represents a child skills deficit ("can't do") versus performance deficit ("won't do") (Duhon et al., 2004). Children with skills deficits are likely to show difficulty demonstrating the behavior even under optimal conditions (e.g., maximum opportunity for reinforcement or perfect sleep environment). We recently evaluated a young man whose parents promised him a trip to a national theme park if he could attain 2 consecutive weeks without wetting his bed. Never in his entire life had he accumulated more than 3 consecutive dry nights. All this "treatment program" did was keep him awake for several nights as he fervently attempted to remain dry at night; however, he eventually "crashed" and wet his bed. Child skills deficits usually call for a more gradual program involving direct teaching or shaping.

In contrast to skills deficits, a performance deficit indicates that the child has acquired the necessary behaviors or skills but doesn't perform them under the desired circumstances. This situation may occur if motivation is insufficient, the contingencies support other behaviors, or a child has difficulty discriminating when (or where) to exhibit the behavior. Past interventions that produced immediate, impressive, but short-term results followed by gradual decline (or immediate decline if the "program" is no longer in place) more likely represent a child with a performance deficit (assuming the environment has not changed). Depending on the nature of the performance deficit, creative use of reinforcement programs (e.g., *The Sleep Fairy*, Peterson & Peterson, 2003) can be highly successful toward increasing appropriate sleep-related behaviors (Burke, Kuhn, & Peterson, 2004; Robinson & Sheridan, 2000). Once the clinician gains a grasp of the treatment goals and past intervention attempts, the primary task for the remainder of the clinical interview is to identify the relevant and proximal factors that set the occasion for or maintain the child's sleep disturbance.

Primary Sleep Disorders and Intrinsic Factors

The clinical interview should never be a substitute for a thorough physical examination or overnight sleep study. Such testing, however, rarely produces unexpected findings in the absence of identified symptoms. Without expanding beyond their scope of practice, behavioral health clinicians can screen for symptoms of primary sleep disorders, such as obstructive sleep apnea, narcolepsy, periodic limb movement disorder (PLMD), and restless legs syndrome (RLS). Snoring is nearly a universal symptom in youngsters with significant obstructive sleep apnea syndrome (OSAS) (Hoban & Chervin, 2005); however, unlike adults, children with OSAS may present with inattention or irritable behavior rather than overt daytime sleepiness. Persistent loud snoring, mouth breathing, unusual sleeping postures, and morning headaches or vomiting should prompt the clinician to refer the child to a medical sleep professional (Whiteford, Fleming, & Henderson, 2004).

The most unique primary sleep disorder is narcolepsy, characterized by fragmented, unrefreshing sleep regardless of the amount of nocturnal sleep obtained. The primary symptoms of narcolepsy include overwhelming excessive daytime sleepiness (EDS), cataplexy (sudden complete or partial loss of muscle tone, usually in response to an emotional stimulus), sleep paralysis (temporary loss of voluntary muscle control at sleep onset or offset), and hypnagogic hallucinations (vivid, dreamlike experiences while falling asleep or dropping off). Only a minority of people with narcolepsy display all four symptoms. Older, more verbal children may be able to accurately report these experiences, while symptoms in younger children may have to be identified through repeated observations from caregivers (e.g., sleep attacks, drop attacks, or buckling knees, unusual behavior at sleep onset).

Periodic limb movement disorder (PLMD) involves periodic episodes of repetitive and highly stereotyped limb movements during sleep. The movements occur most frequently in the lower extremities, often with the child extending the big toe, flexing the ankle, knee, or hip. The repetitive episodes of muscle contraction last from one-half second to 5 seconds, with an interval of about 20 to 40 seconds. Children may report waking up feeling unrefreshed, but they are typically unaware of the involuntary movements. Therefore, questions during the clinical interview must be addressed to parents or caregivers who observe the child during sleep.

Restless legs syndrome (RLS) is a sensorimotor disorder characterized by unpleasant "creeping or crawling" sensations of the legs, sometimes experienced by children as "growing pains." Although RLS criteria for children are not as well validated, the clinical diagnosis for adults is based on the presence of the following symptoms: (a) an urge to move the limbs, with or without unpleasant sensations; (b) the urge/sensations worsen during periods of rest or inactivity; (c) symptoms improve with movement or activity; and (d) symptoms worsen or occur only in the evening or night. The following single-screening question has been shown to possess high sensitivity when screening for RLS (Ferri, Lanuzza, Cosentino, et al., 2006; Shapiro, Baughman, & Bourguet, 2006):

T: When you try to relax in the evening or sleep at night, do you ever have unpleasant, restless feelings that can be relieved by walking or movement?

Again, symptoms of RLS in younger or less verbal children, including those with developmental disabilities, must be confirmed through observation (e.g., "squirming" with impaired sleep onset) and supplemented by the family history. The diagnosis of RLS is based solely on the presence of clinical symptoms, while OSAS, narcolepsy, and PLMD require an overnight sleep study or multiple sleep latency test (MSLT).

Numerous "intrinsic" factors have the potential to impact sleep, including illness, pain, chronic medical conditions, and a child's inherent circadian preference ("owl" versus "lark"). Of course, certain substances such as caffeine, prescription medications, herbal preparations, drugs, and alcohol may have a significant impact on sleep (Pagel, 2005). Child temperament and personality characteristics also appear to play a role (Atkinson, Vetere, & Grayson, 1995; Bertelson & Monroe, 1979; Weissbluth, 1984). While some intrinsic factors can be easily altered, most cannot and therefore do not require a great deal of attention during the clinical interview. Chronic sleep disturbance is rarely the direct result of an isolated intrinsic factor. For this to be the case, sleep should wax and wane in direct relation to the child's medical condition or health status, unaltered by extrinsic influences. When the clinician can confirm that a child's sleep is normal in duration, timing, and quality under specific circumstances, it is unlikely that intrinsic factors, medical pathology, or primary sleep disorders are the culprits. The following interview question represents one therapist's attempt to isolate the controlling variables:

T: Has there been a time, place, or circumstance when Jackson had no problem falling to sleep or waking up in the morning?

P: Oh sure, during the summer when we allow him to go to bed later, around 1:00 a.m., he falls to sleep right away. He doesn't have to wake up for school so he sleeps a solid 10 hours and never falls asleep during the day. He's always so much happier and more like himself during the summertime.

Extrinsic Factors

Sleep Environment

A child's habitual sleep environment, including where and with whom the child sleeps, will vary greatly depending on family values, preferences, economic status, parenting style, and cultural beliefs (Jenni & O'Connor, 2005). Children all over the world readily adapt to falling asleep in a variety of settings, such as lying on a parent's chest, sleeping with the family on the floor in a single-room hut, or even slipping under 400-thread-count sheets in an extravagant Victorian canopy bed. Clinicians must be aware of their own cultural views and take special care not to impose these on others who may subscribe to different values (McKenna, 2000). Designing a culturally sensitive treatment plan is more easily accomplished when the family generates their own individualized treatment goals, as described earlier.

There are certainly individual differences in a person's ability to adapt to sleeping in different environments. Many well-intentioned parents, however, have purchased new beds and new bedding, bought silky pajamas, painted the bedroom walls, rearranged furniture, or added music from a specific genre, only to see their children continue to wake at night. Children do not need a bedroom that is ultraplush to sleep; they need simply to become accustomed to falling asleep in an environment that is sleep compatible. Experts in sleep ecology have long recognized that sleep quality and sleep duration are maximized in an environment that is dark, quiet, unstimulating, and perceived as safe (Siegel, 1995). The goal in assessing this area is simply to ensure the presence of a sleep-compatible environment and to confirm that the child is accustomed to falling asleep in such an environment.

The clinician should take the time to identify the location of the child's house and get an idea of the safety of the neighborhood. It is adaptive for sleep to be restricted in environments that are perceived to be unsafe (Dahl, 1996). The transition from wakefulness to sleep requires physical and mental relaxation and a reduction in vigilance (Lewin, 2003). Asking parents to briefly imagine themselves in their child's bed(room) at night will help them view the sleep environment from the child's perspective. Would they feel safe and secure? Parents (or the child) can be asked to describe the location of the child's bedroom within the house, the physical distance (e.g., different level) from the parent's bedroom, and where the parents spend their time when the child is in bed. The location of the child's bed in the room may also be important. For example, school-age children should not be able to look out the bedroom door into the living room to watch television. Again, expectations of both the parent and the child should be assessed. Is the child expected to sleep alone or to share a bedroom with a parent or sibling?

T: If you could magically create the perfect place or situation for you to sleep great, what would it look like?

Danny [age 9]:   I would move my bedroom down to the first floor of the house next to my parents' bedroom. Then, as long as the hall light was turned on, I think I could sleep fine.

The child and parents should be asked to briefly describe the physical characteristics of the bedroom or habitual sleep environment, including light, noise, temperature, and level of stimulation.

Light. Indeed, it seems basic, but we regularly encounter young children who have convinced their parents that they can sleep only in a room that is well lighted. Light is the strongest zeitgeber (time cue) entraining the sleep-wake cycle in human beings (Lewy, Emens, Sack, Hasler, & Bernert, 2003). Ordinary room light (100–200 lux) in the form of an overhead light, a bedside lamp, or a television may effectively suppress the pineal gland's secretion of melatonin (Lewy, Wehr, Goodwin, Newsome, & Markey, 1980), thereby delaying the sleep phase (Boivin & Czeisler, 1998; Waterhouse et al., 1998). While the amount of light output from a typical night-light

(about 1.5–7 watts) is unlikely to cause problems, the level of illumination from a nearby television or video display may interfere with sleep (Higuchi, Motohashi, Liu, Ahara, & Kaneko, 2003). Research indicates that sleep time increases when the duration of the dark period is lengthened, suggesting that children may be able to obtain more sleep if parents simply turn the lights off earlier.

Interview A:

T: Please tell me about the lighting in Jacob's bedroom while he is lying down to sleep.

P: Well, it seems pretty dark in there.

T: If you were lying down in his bed, could you see well enough to read a book?

P: Oh no, its much darker than that. All he has is a small night-light across the room.

T: Okay great, let's move on. . . .

Interview B:

T: Please tell me about the lighting in Jacob's bedroom while he is lying down to sleep.

P: I know this is bad, but he refuses to go to sleep with the lights off.

T: Which lights in or near his bedroom are turned on?

P: We have to keep his overhead light turned on or he will throw a fit, and then he takes forever to calm down and nobody sleeps. We just leave the light on until he's asleep and then my husband sneaks into his room to shut it off.

T: Do you know the wattage of the bulb in that overhead light?

P: I suppose it's around 60 watts.

Noise. Normal household noise in the form of an infant crying, a dog barking, or a dropped cooking pan can disturb sleep (Griefahn & Spreng, 2004). Intermittent noises tend to be particularly disruptive (Brackbill, 1970); therefore, living next to an airport or busy street may prolong sleep onset and produce more frequent awakenings (Jakovljevic, Belojevic, Paunovic, & Stojanov, 2006; Miedema & Vos, 2007; Ohrstrom, Hadzibajramovic, Holmes, & Svensson, 2006). Decreasing environmental noise can reduce infant crying and promote deeper sleep (Strauch,

Brandt, & Edwards Beckett, 1993). Alternatively, introducing continuous "white noise" (e.g., a fan, humidifier, commercial sound screen, air conditioner) can effectively mask intermittent environmental noise, increase the arousal threshold, and potentially improve sleep (Borkowski, Hunter, & Johnson, 2001; Forquer & Johnson, 2005; Spencer, Moran, Lee, & Talbert, 1990; Stanchina, Abu-Hijleh, Chaudhry, Carlisle, & Millman, 2005).

Temperature. Objective and subjective measures suggest that sleep is disturbed more by temperature than by noise (Libert et al., 1991). Although individual preferences vary, sleep environment outside of the range of 54°F to 75°F may impair sleep quality or reduce sleep time. The most appropriate air temperature for a covered sleeping adult is around 61°F (Muzet, Libert, & Candas, 1984). Slightly cooler sleep environments are more conducive to sleep. Well-intentioned parents of infants tend to overdress them for the environmental temperature (Tuohy & Tuohy, 1990), making them more likely to disturb their parents at night (Wailoo, Petersen, & Whitaker, 1990). Although it is rare for a parent to report that their child's bedroom is too warm or cold, children may occasionally speak up and say they would prefer the room to be a bit warmer or cooler. This would present a simple intervention that allows the child to take an active role in his or her treatment plan.

Stimulation. Sleep is incompatible with *vigilance,* as defined by awareness and responsiveness to the environment (Dahl, 1996). Factors such as family conflict may produce chronic hypervigilance and ensuing insomnia in children (Gregory, Caspi, Moffitt, & Poulton, 2006). A number of studies have documented the negative impact on children's sleep patterns of stimulation in the form of nighttime television (Johnson, Cohen, Kasen, First, & Brook, 2004; Owens et al., 1999; Paavonen, Pennonen, Roine, Valkonen, & Lahikainen, 2006; Thompson & Christakis, 2005; Van den Bulck, 2004). Even though the presence of a transitional object such as a blanket or stuffed animal can assist children in falling asleep (Wolf & Lozoff, 1989), children can get too much of a good thing. Children who use music, television, and computer games as sleep aids sleep fewer hours and are significantly more tired (Eggermont & Van den Bulck, 2006). Although the presence of numerous toys in the bed can result in a well-attended tea

party, it may also prevent much-needed sleep. Other forms of stimulation include excessive caffeine intake (Leibenluft, 1999), late-night exercise ("to wear him out"), or negative parent-child interactions at bedtime (e.g., scolding, yelling, spanking), which can backfire and further delay a child's transition to slumber.

Once the clinician is assured that the child's habitual sleep environment is safe, comfortable, and nonstimulating, it is time to move on to the next part of the interview.

T: Please describe Meghan's bedroom for me.

P: Well, she has her own bed, and we just bought her new sheets and a comforter. There are usually lots of clothes and toys strewn about on the floor because she never cleans her room.

T: Is it relatively dark? In other words, could you read a book if you were lying in her bed?

P: Oh no, the lights are turned off except for a small night-light.

T: And the temperature, is it comfortable during both the summer and winter months?

P: Oh yes, we have a large furnace and central air.

T: Okay, then we will move on because it sounds like Meghan's bedroom is a comfortable sleep environment.

P: Oh yes, it's very comfortable all right. I just wish we could get her to actually sleep there. You see, she falls asleep on the living room couch every night while she watches her favorite movie on TV.

T: Oops.

Indeed, the bedroom environment may be sufficiently dark, quiet, safe, and very comfortable. However, this means little if the child never sleeps there. It is important to identify whether or not a child is accustomed to falling asleep in the place he or she is expected to sleep all night. For this reason, we usually start this section by, first, determining whether the bedroom is a familiar setting and, then, identifying other locations where the infant or child falls asleep.

This is one situation where the manner in which you ask the question may produce different answers:

T: Do you *allow* him to fall asleep in your bed?

P: Of course not.

Alternatively:

T: I'd like to get a breakdown of Jonathon's [age 6] various sleep locations. During what occasions and under what conditions will Jonathon sleep somewhere other than his own bedroom?

P: He almost always sleeps in his own bedroom unless we travel away from home. However, I do remember a while back we found him in his older brother's bed the morning after a loud thunderstorm.

Clinicians may also gain more information by breaking habits or behaviors into frequencies and percentages rather than inquiring about the usual, typical, or average. Contrast the amount of information generated by following questions:

T: Where does he fall asleep at bedtime?

P: In his bedroom, of course.

The question above yields the most common scenario but provides no information regarding variability or situational factors.

T: Given your stated goal of having Jonathon sleep by himself in his own bed all night, I'd like you think back to his last 100 bedtimes. Try to help me generate a list of the various places that Jonathon fell asleep and their frequencies. I'd also like you to estimate the number of times he fell asleep with or without parental presence.

P: I would say he has fallen asleep in his own bedroom 95 times. We traveled on vacation last month so he fell asleep in our bed in the hotel room the other 5 times. However, when we are home, either his father or I lie next to him 100% of the time. I know it's a crutch, but he just won't fall asleep without one of us nearby.

Next, contrast the treatment implications from the response above to the following response from another parent:

P2:   Well, we've pretty much given up on getting him to sleep in his bed, so he usually just watches TV in the living room while we get things done in the kitchen.

T: Okay, so you would estimate that he has fallen asleep in the living room all of the last 100 bedtimes?

P2:   No, probably more like 60 of them. He fell asleep in our bed about 30 times, and I suppose he slept in his sister's bed the other 10.

When assessing the sleep environment, clinicians should be careful not to overlook sleep-onset associations. The sleep of infants and younger children will be more dependent on proximal stimuli in the environment, including the presence of specific music, TV, motion (rocking), skin-to-skin contact, sucking, a blanket, pacifier, or even their mothers' hair:

T: Is there anything your daughter *needs* to do, have done, or have nearby in order to fall asleep?

P: The only thing I can really think of is she absolutely has to have her teddy. Without her teddy right next to her in bed, she'd be up all night.

Infants and young children often initiate sleep quickly and easily as long they remain in contact with familiar sleep associations (e.g., being held, nursed, or rocked). The conditioned associations often promote sleep; therefore, parents rarely complain of problems at bedtime. Parents may not appreciate, however, having to wake up to re-create those conditions during the night. Children, like adults, awaken several times each night as they complete each phase of the normal sleep cycle. Most return to sleep quietly without parental assistance or awareness. Newborns and younger infants who have not mastered the skill of independent sleep initiation will require reunification with the person, object, or situation to reinitiate sleep following each awakening. With cognitive maturity and the development of motor skills, children begin to retrieve their own pacifiers or blankets and self-soothe themselves back to sleep. If parental presence or action is required to fall asleep, the infant contained in a crib will cry until the parent arrives. Once the child can crawl out of the crib, parents may expect many nighttime visits.

T: So, once he is asleep on the living room couch, does he stay there to sleep the remainder of the night?

P: No, once he is sound asleep, my husband carries him into his bedroom.

This child is falling asleep in one location and waking to find himself in a "foreign land," where he will likely have difficulty reinitiating sleep. In our experience, this pattern can produce a hypervigilant child who "fights" sleep and awakens frequently. The time to intervene in such cases is at bedtime, not during the middle of the night.

Sleep-Wake Schedule

Unlike adults, children typically do not decide when they go to bed and when they wake up. Consequently, some children may experience difficulty sleeping simply because there is a mismatch between their inherent circadian rhythms and the sleep-wake schedules imposed upon them. Theoretically, there is an "ideal" sleep-wake schedule for each individual child that would afford an appropriate sleep duration and timing.

During this portion of the interview, the clinician will assess whether the child is obtaining sufficient sleep to function optimally, ensure the presence of a reasonably consistent sleep-wake schedule across the week, and determine whether the timing of that schedule is in alignment with the child's inherent circadian rhythm. Optimally, the interview occurs as the clinician is looking at the completed pretreatment sleep diary to be able to ask questions or clarify ambiguities, such as unscheduled naps, unusual sleep and wake times, or to obtain a description of the child's behavior during specific awakenings. This section of the interview aids the clinician in making diagnostic decisions for presentations involving insomnia, circadian rhythm disorders, and EDS. Obtaining the child's sleep-wake schedule may provide clinicians with the opportunity to educate parents regarding normal sleep development and appropriate sleep expectations. It also helps parents and clinicians monitor the effectiveness (or ineffectiveness) of treatment and to enhance the effectiveness of behavioral treatments by aligning or stabilizing the schedule. Finally, clinicians will be in a better position to recognize subtle changes in

sleep patterns (i.e., "loopholes") that can sabotage a treatment plan, such as when a child attempts to "make up" for lost sleep following a difficult night during the initial phases of treatment. Although a sleep diary is the preferred method for assessing the child's sleep schedule, the clinical interview can be used to derive a general impression fairly quickly.

T: She is usually in bed by . . . ?

P: Most nights by 8:30 p.m.

T: Okay, and she is usually asleep by . . . ?

P: Oh, it's different every night, but usually by 9:00.

T: Okay, good. And, what time does she typically awaken in the morning?

P: She has to be up by 7:00 a.m. every day for school.

T: Does she typically wake up on her own, or do you usually awaken her?

P: No, I always have to get her up. It's a struggle some days.

T: Does she ever take a nap or sleep during the day? This could include falling asleep in school, during car rides, or while watching TV.

P: She almost always falls to sleep in the car on our way home from school.

To determine what is "abnormal," clinicians must have a general knowledge and understanding about what constitutes "normal" child sleep. Readers are encouraged to familiarize themselves, at a minimum, with total sleep time requirements and napping patterns across childhood (Anders, Sadeh, & Appareddy, 1995; Davis, Parker, & Montgomery, 2004; Weissbluth, 1981, 1995). Clinicians can prepare themselves to make "on-the-spot" comparisons by keeping a few normative sleep duration "guideposts" in mind: about 16 hours for newborn infants, 12½ hours for 2-year-olds, 10 hours at 10 years, and 9 hours for adolescents.

In pure form, problems related to inappropriate sleep schedules come in four "flavors," representing two deviations from each of the two factors (homeostatic drive and circadian timing), described in the two-process model of sleep (Borbely, 1982). Put simply, a child's sleep duration is either sufficient or insufficient, and the sleep schedule is either appropriate or inappropriate. Four deviations in the sleep schedule are described below, along with common clinical manifestations that clinicians can inquire about during the interview. Treatments for children with "mismatched" schedules generally fall into two areas: (1) adapting the sleep schedule or environment to more closely accommodate the child or (2) modifying a child's sleep schedule to correspond more closely with family expectations or societal convention. In some cases, compensatory measures may be taken during the day.

TST>TIB. The child's individual total sleep time (TST) requirement exceeds the duration of time spent in bed (TIB). For example, Kelsi is a 13-year-old female who requires, on average, 9 hours sleep per night to wake up feeling alert and well rested. Due to sports practice before school, dance lessons after school, and a heavy homework load, she sleeps from approximately 11:00 p.m. to 6:30 a.m. (TST = 7.5 hours) on school nights. By Friday of each school week, Kelsi is carrying a 7.5-hour sleep debt (1.5 × 5). Clinical manifestations of insufficient sleep include daytime sleepiness and all its secondary effects, including short-term, but reversible, impairments in behavior, mood, and academic performance (Fallone et al., 2001; Fallone et al., 2005; Fallone et al., 2002; Randazzo, Muehlbach, Schweitzer, & Walsh, 1998). Interviewing clinicians can look for a child who falls asleep quickly (often under 10 minutes), remains asleep throughout the night, and has difficulty waking up in the morning due to sleep debt. Although there are certainly more serious causes of daytime sleepiness (e.g., narcolepsy, sleep apnea), "behaviorally induced insufficient sleep syndrome" (AASM, 2005) is by far the most common, to the point that it is becoming a public health issue in many Westernized societies (Colten & Altevogt, 2006).

In concept, the treatment of TST>TIB is simple. Because one's inherent sleep need cannot be reduced, the child must spend more time in bed (referred to as "sleep extension") to afford more sleep. Efforts to modify the child's sleep schedule or the environment could include making bedtime earlier, making morning wake time later, or adding a nap. Attempting to modify a child's schedule usually requires the clinician to expand the interview to consider family activity patterns for the entire 24-hour day, because spending more time in bed requires less time allocated to other activities. A family's timing of activities and their hours of light exposure heavily influence when and how much a child sleeps throughout development (Herman, 2005).

At the societal level, a few public school systems have taken strides to delay the school start times in an attempt to allow students more time to sleep, in hopes that they will arrive to school better rested and more alert (Wahlstrom, Wrobel, & Kubow, 1998). In some cases, attempts to increase a child's time spent in bed will require parents to address child factors such as managing an infant's independent sleep skills, addressing a preschool child's bedtime refusal, or eliminating an adolescent's access to late-night electronics. Occasionally, efforts require targeting not just the child's skills but also the parents,' such as in the case of a chaotic lifestyle or ineffective limit setting. Finally, when interventions fail to increase a child's time in bed and erase chronic sleep debt, it is not unusual to observe efforts to increase the child's ability to remain alert through self-administered stimulants (e.g., caffeinated beverages), prescribed psychostimulants (methylphenidate, modafinil), or psychoactive agents to treat daytime behaviors (e.g., irritability, aggression, agitation) that are often the byproduct of chronic sleep deprivation.

TIB >TST. The time spent in bed (TIB) exceeds the child's inherent total sleep time (TST) requirement (Galofre, Santacana, & Ferber, 1992). Simply stated, a child cannot be "made" to sleep more hours than his or her natural sleep requirement (short of heavy sedation) (Ferber, 1995a). Of the four presentations, this one is the easiest to assess and treat; however, it also the least recognized, leading to improper management.

C. J. is a 10-year-old with cerebral palsy who has been experiencing awakenings at 2:00 a.m., lasting nearly an hour every night. The following interview represents the therapist's attempt to gain information to isolate the problem:

T: By what time is C. J. usually in bed?

P: 8:30 every night. We are very consistent with his bedtime. We've been lucky in that he's never been one to fight bedtime.

T: And, he's usually asleep by . . . ?

P: Usually within 15 minutes. It's just his waking up that worries me.

T: And then what time does he wake in the morning?

P: He usually wakes up on his own around 7:30 to get dressed for school.

T: Does that change on weekends?

P: No, he wakes up at about the same time every morning, even Saturday and Sunday.

T: So C. J., is there anything that you need to have with you to fall asleep easily at bedtime?

C. J.: Not really, just my pillow.

P: Okay then. When you wake up in the night, is there anything different or missing that makes it hard for you to go back to sleep?

C. J.: No, there's nothing wrong. I just can't seem to fall back to sleep.

T: Then, what do you do while you're awake?

C. J.: Nothing much. I just lie in bed thinking about school or my friends. Sometime I'll get really bored so I'll go find my dog, Gunnar, and play with him in my bedroom.

T: Mom, how do you know he's awake at night?

P: Well, for a long time I didn't know. He just recently told me that he's been waking up and having trouble falling back to sleep. I may hear him going into the bathroom, but I had no idea he was staying awake for so long.

T: Hey C. J., do you ever take a nap during the day, fall asleep in school, or drop off accidentally?

C. J.: Nope, never.

T: Mom, have you noticed that C. J. makes up for that hour of lost sleep by sleeping more the next day? And does he show signs of being more irritable or sleepy?

P: No, that's what amazes me. It doesn't seem to bother him at all.

T: Mom, how many hours of sleep would you guess most 10-year-olds need?

P: Um . . . I guess I'm not really sure.

In less than 3 minutes, the therapist in the preceding interview assessed the child's total sleep time requirement (roughly 10 hours) and

concluded that it was within developmental expectations for a 10-year-old. The therapist assessed the child's time spent in bed (11 hours) and ruled out missing sleep associations or behavior problems that might interfere with sleep initiation at bedtime or following awakenings. A consistent sleep schedule was confirmed, and it was noted that the child woke up in the morning on his own, without difficulty. Finally, and perhaps most important, the therapist established that the child was well rested and showed no signs of daytime sleepiness.

A child with a 10-hour nightly sleep requirement who spends 11 hours in bed will experience 1 hour of wakefulness each night. Older, well-behaved children may remain in bed or play quietly by themselves, but they typically do not persistently seek out anything (e.g., parent, familiar item) to help them reinitiate sleep. Younger children may play alone or decide to explore the house. This form of sleep schedule problem may present in one of three ways. The child may present with bedtime "insomnia" and bedtime struggles. The child may awaken earlier in the morning than desired, fully alert and ready to start the day. Finally, younger children may display extended middle-of-the-night awakenings during which they are alert, happy, and ready to play. In the latter case, the child's total sleep time is normal but divided into a biphasic pattern. This sleep schedule "mismatch" may result from parents overestimating the child's sleep requirement. In some cases, the child's time in bed is based on convenience rather than the child's total sleep requirement.

Intervention attempts to modify the child (e.g., behavior extinction, sedative medications) usually fail. The most appropriate intervention in this case is to simply reduce the time in bed to more closely match the child's total sleep requirement, often referred to as *sleep restriction* therapy or *bedtime curtailment*. Parents may decide to either delay the child's bedtime or advance the morning awakening time. Clinicians may want to help caregivers plan for the extra time in which the child will be awake, which may be more challenging for parents of busy toddlers and children with developmental disabilities or medically handicapping conditions.

DSPS. The third type of sleep schedule problem is *delayed sleep phase syndrome* (DSPS), in which the major sleep episode is delayed significantly, such that falling asleep at bedtime and waking in the morning become major struggles. Tami, for example, is a 16-year-old Junior in high school whose inherent circadian rhythm makes it nearly impossible for her to fall asleep before 11 p.m. or wake up before 8 a.m. On school days, Tami's mother struggles greatly to awaken her by 6:30 a.m. and get her to school. When Tami does make it to school on time, she "zones out" and has trouble focusing during her first two class periods. Despite getting good grades, Tami faces the possibility of having to take summer classes because of missed school days and frequent tardiness.

Interview findings consistent with DSPS may include a positive genetic history, such as a parent who works the night shift or is a self-described "night owl"; delayed mealtimes and activity patterns (no appetite upon early awakening, hungry late in evening); or increased activity at a late hour (often after the child's official bedtime). Students may display inattention, academic struggles, and behavior problems or fall asleep during morning classes. Unlike children with "insomnia," children with DSPS typically have normal sleep onset and sleep duration when they are allowed to follow their desired schedules. During the school year, however, they may carry a heavy sleep debt due to being awakened early for school. They frequently make up for their sleep debt by sleeping much later on weekends, creating further delay in their circadian physiology. Clinicians will want to inquire about discrepant sleep patterns across the school week, weekends, and vacations. Although a rating scale is available to help clinicians assess a person's circadian preference (Horne & Ostberg, 1976), a reasonable estimate can be obtained with the following question:

T: Pretend you are on vacation, with no school to attend, no responsibilities, and no particular reason to go to bed or wake up at a specific time. What time would you choose to go to bed and wake up in the morning?

Interventions designed to modify the environment may include delaying the bedtime to more closely match the child's natural sleep initiation time, shortening the morning routine to allow for a later wake time, or, in some cases, making special allowances for later school attendance. On a larger scale, some school systems have delayed school start time to accommodate the biological drift in circadian timing that appears to be triggered by puberty (Carskadon, Vieira, & Acebo, 1993; Wolfson & Carskadon, 1996). Young adults who struggle with DSPS in high school may experience fewer problems once they enroll in college and can adapt their academic schedules to suit their desired circadian preferences. Interventions targeting the child generally aim to shift the child's sleep phase toward a more socially conventional clock time. This shift can be accomplished through phase delay "chronotherapy" (Czeisler et al., 1981), carefully controlled light therapy (Rosenthal et al., 1990), or administration of exogenous melatonin (Nagtegaal, Kerkhof, Smits, Swart, & Van Der Meer, 1998). The clinician's biggest challenge is to help the child and family address factors that produced the delayed phase in the first place, such as failure to maintain a reasonably consistent sleep schedule in the face of academic demands and social pressure (Kuhn et al., 1999). Finally, the clinical interview for presentations involving DSPS would not be complete without considering functional variables. Sleeping late in the morning may serve an escape/avoidance mechanism for children with anxiety, learning problems, or social difficulties, sometimes described as "motivated sleep phase delay" or "school refusal" (Ferber, 1983; Kearney & Albano, 2000).

ASPS. Advanced sleep phase syndrome (ASPS) is characterized by a major sleep episode that is significantly advanced, resulting in earlier than desired sleep onset and early-morning awakening. ASPS is rare (Schrader, Bovim, & Sand, 1993); therefore, it is covered briefly. People with ASPS likely have an inherent "lark" circadian clock (Horne & Ostberg, 1977), although the prevalence clearly increases with age, because the sleep-wake cycles of the elderly tend to be advanced (Baker & Zee, 2000). Infants and toddlers may display an early sleep phase, tending to fall asleep early in the evening whether placed in bed or not (Ferber, 1995a). Parents usually don't mind when the infant falls asleep early; however, they may not appreciate waking early. Parents usually try to adapt to their "early bird" by returning home early from late-night socialization and trading morning responsibilities. Interventions targeting the child include delaying nap and mealtime schedules, incorporating high-activity games in the evening, and gradually delaying the child's bedtime. Evening bright light can be used along with keeping the bedroom dark in the morning.

Before settling on a diagnosis of ASPS, clinicians should first rule out other reasons for early-morning awakenings. The child with ASPS falls asleep early and then wakes early in the morning after obtaining a full night's sleep. Some early-morning "risers," however, fall asleep at a normal clock hour but still wake early, regardless of the time they went to sleep. This awakening may be triggered by the signal of light entering their bedroom. These children often display reduced nocturnal sleep time and sleepiness later in the day. Clinicians should inquire about access to reinforcers (TV movie, parents' bed) immediately upon awakening, as this pattern may reflect a child who simply chooses to start the day rather than returning to sleep to complete the final sleep cycle.

Parent-Child Bedtime Interactions

Parent-child interactions can either facilitate or impair a child's transition to sleep. Bidirectional parent-child interactions are especially important to evaluate when the presenting problem involves dawdling during the prebedtime routine, coming out of the bedroom, calling out or crying during the bedtime routine, and nighttime or early-morning awakenings. Because a bedroom environment should be sleep compatible, it needs to be relatively devoid of stimulation. Unfortunately, this type of environment closely approximates time-out for children. Consequently, bedtime or the bedroom environment itself can trigger child misbehavior, much like a long, boring car ride or when a parent becomes preoccupied talking on the phone. Children quickly figure out that lying quietly in bed is not an effective strategy to recruit attention or parental presence. Therefore, they may leave the bedroom numerous times to access more interesting environments or engage in behaviors to draw a parent into the bedroom. These "devious" child behaviors are referred to as "curtain calls," in which the child requests extra hugs, kisses, or suddenly becomes interested in discovering why the sky is blue. Most parents, by the time they deliver the 16th glass of water in a single night, figure out that it is not thirst that the child is trying to quench.

The clinician's goal when interviewing parents is to evaluate whether they possess the necessary contingency management skills to get the child into bed, keep the child in bed, and limit the access to alternative activities other than sleep.

It is human nature to hide one's own mistakes, shortcomings, and poor habits. Parents are no different, but the skilled interviewer can get parents to open up and divulge accurate information to fuel a stronger treatment plan. The interviewer must not come across as blaming or judgmental; in fact, it may be helpful to initially assume the worst. Pejorative words should be avoided, such as "cave in," "give in," or "allow," even if the parent used them first. For example, instead of asking, "Do you allow her to sleep in your bed?" the interviewer could simply ask, "Does she ever sleep with you in your bed and, if so, under what conditions?"

The interviewer might even preface a line of sensitive questioning with "teamwork pep talk":

T: Okay, we all know we are here for a common purpose, which is to help Hannah sleep better and in turn help you get some sleep. I'm not interested in assigning blame, so I'm going to encourage you to be brutally honest in your responses to my questions. It's very important for me to identify exactly what you've been doing so I can evaluate your child's learning history and help you come up with a treatment plan that will work.

Listed below are a few factors for clinicians to inquire about during this section of the interview.

Getting the Child Into Bed. What is the final task of the prebedtime routine? Is it positive, and does it occur in the child's bedroom? It is easier to entice children than push them. If enticing hasn't been successful, then further questioning should try to identify precisely what the child may be avoiding and why (e.g., separation, darkness). Is the bedtime struggle simply representative of generalized noncompliance that occurs throughout the day, not just at bedtime?

Keeping the Child in Bed: What is the relative availability of reinforcement available to the child inside the bedroom versus outside the bedroom? Does the child remain quietly in bed for even a short time, and, if so, are these behaviors attended to and reinforced? Are behaviors interfering with sleep, such as leaving the bedroom, reinforced more saliently or at a higher rate? Below are a few sample questions that represent this line of thinking:

T: During that 45 minutes that it takes Jimmy to fall asleep, how many times will he typically come out of his bedroom?

T: On average, how long does he remain out of his bedroom each time?

T: What is the shortest and longest time he may remain out of his bedroom?

T: What does he typically do or say when he comes out of the room, and how do you typically respond?

T: Please help me out here by just being honest. Out of 10 times he comes out of his room, how many times does he sit beside you, watch a little more TV, grab an extra snack, or get a few extra hugs and kisses?

T: Put yourself in Jimmy's shoes, or bed, for a minute. On a typical night, how many times might he expect you to enter his bedroom to initiate positive interactions if he remains in bed quietly?

Middle-of-the-Night Waking. The clinician will want to inquire about the three most common reasons children wake at night. First, determine that the child has the skill to initiate sleep independently in the habitual sleep environment. Children who are accustomed to falling asleep under certain conditions (e.g., living room couch) but awaken to find different conditions (bedroom) often display extended night-time awakenings or "sleepwalking" events as they attempt to return to their original, familiar sleep location. Next, identify potential reinforcers that a child might seek rather than simply returning to sleep. The key question is "What does the child usually do once awake?" Some children find that they can "fly under the radar" at night and gain access to forbidden candy, snacks, or television. Others may get undivided one-on-one parental attention that is unavailable when siblings are awake during the day, while other children simply prefer the parental bed to their own. Finally, if the child has the necessary skills to initiate sleep but takes a long time to reinitiate sleep even in a desired sleep environment, the clinician must

consider the appropriateness of the sleep schedule. A slight change in sleep schedule may be indicated to increase the child's sleep pressure, such as reducing overall time in bed (see *TIB>TST*). Contrast the implications for treatment planning based on responses to the following interviews.

T: It is my understanding that you are here to address Jonathon's nighttime awakenings and that you would like him to sleep in his own bedroom at night. For a moment, though, I'd like you to think back 3 months or so. For how many of the past 100 bedtimes did Jonathon fall asleep independently, in his own bedroom, without parental presence or assistance?

P: Probably none.

T: Okay, that's fine. However, I suspect it will be easier for Jonathon and the entire family if we first focus on teaching Jonathon to fall asleep independently at bedtime for a couple weeks before turning our attention to those nighttime awakenings.

Alternatively:

T: For how many of the past 100 bedtimes did Jonathon fall asleep independently, in his own bedroom, without parental presence or assistance?

P: Oh, I would say 98% of the time. He has no difficulty falling asleep on his own at bedtime.

T: Okay, good. Now, I need you to be straight with me on this one. What percentage of the time when he wakes up do you just tell yourself, "To heck with it, I'm too exhausted to fight this" and bring Sammy into your bed at night?

P: I really do try to return him to bed, but to be honest, he ends up sleeping with us the rest of the night about half the time.

Clinicians should be aware that a family's decision to practice solitary sleeping or cosleeping is a highly personal choice, often dictated by personal preferences, family values, and cultural practices (Jenni & O'Connor, 2005). The literature suggests that cosleeping is not a unitary construct (Ramos, 2003). Some families purposefully choose to sleep with their young children (intentional cosleepers), often every night, all night. Reactive cosleepers instead use cosleeping in response to children's sleep problems (e.g., bringing them to the parental bed when they wake), which tends to maintain long-term sleep problems and impair family satisfaction (Madansky & Edelbrock, 1990). Clinicians must be careful to not impose their own values regarding sleep practices or cosleeping. This is more easily accomplished when the clinician prompts the family to identify their own individualized treatment goals early in the clinical interview.

Daytime Behaviors and Skills

Even when sleep disturbance is the presenting concern, the astute clinician will not ignore behaviors, skill repertoires, and interpersonal interactions that occur during the day. While sleep disturbances occur in the context of psychiatric disorders (Dahl & Puig-Antich, 1990; Ivanenko, Crabtree, & Gozal, 2004), the most common culprits involve incomplete skill attainment or poor habits that, when targeted for intervention during the day, can generalize to successful bedtimes and undisturbed sleep. Skill attainment should be viewed within a transactional developmental perspective. Newborns have few skills and rely largely on the parent for feeding, soothing, and helping them sleep. Throughout the unfolding of development, however, children learn new skills and become more flexible and independent as parents fade their assistance and gradually turn over responsibility.

This section of the clinical interview is intended to further isolate functional variables impairing a child's sleep. By inquiring about a child's daytime skills and behaviors, the clinician can gain a better idea of whether the child's sleep disturbance may be related to a child's (or parent's) skills deficit or performance deficit. For example, if a child can easily separate from a parent to attend day care, then problems separating at bedtime more likely reflect a failure to perform under bedtime conditions than a more global skills deficit. Parents are often more willing to set limits or remain consistent with recommendations at night when clinicians help them recognize that the child is perfectly capable of displaying a behavior, based on his or her daytime performance. On the other hand, if a child displays difficulties during the day (e.g., excessive fear in dark rooms), it would be more reasonable to address these issues during the day, when the child and parents are not fatigued or under time constraints

at the end of the day. To help guide this section of the interview, several daytime problems that directly relate to child sleep are discussed briefly.

Parental Limit Setting and Child Compliance. The move from an enclosed crib to a freestanding toddler bed places increased responsibility on parents to keep the child calm, quiet, and in bed. The words "It's time for bed" prompts many young children to engage in a stream of behavior that may include requests for more stories, drinks of water, adjustments in lighting or environment, and extended hugs or kisses. Parents unable or unwilling to set and enforce limits will quickly find themselves engulfed in increasingly longer and more complex bedtime routines, floating bedtimes, and delayed sleep onset. By the time the family reaches the clinic, a parent may sheepishly admit to hand delivering the child crushed ice (shaken, not stirred) in her third drink of bottled water. The clinician might recognize other signs of poor limit setting, such as when the child consistently falls asleep in the living room in front of a video game or television or is allowed to stay "just a bit longer" after leaving the bedroom. Clinicians may listen for clues in the child's or parents' choice of words that suggest ineffective limit setting or coercive interactions.

Parent of a 3-year-old: He won't let us. . . . He *insists* that we . . .

12-year-old: My parents won't make me do that because they know I'd make their life miserable.

Ineffective parental limit setting is more likely a primary factor when the child goes to bed and falls asleep more quickly for other caregivers. Clinicians will often be able to identify evidence of overly permissive parenting during the day. Sometimes, the sleep environment itself contributes to parental-limit-setting problems, such as when child protests (e.g., loud screaming, crying) interfere with the sleep of others sharing a bedroom (siblings), house (grandparents), or apartment complex (neighbors). Unfortunately, there are few treatment outcome studies to guide clinicians treating school-age children with bedtime struggles and parental-limit-setting sleep problems (Kuhn & Elliott, 2003).

Even with effective parental limit setting, some children turn nearly every routine into a power struggle. Many children dawdle, stall, or resist parental influence when it comes time for bed. Children with oppositional defiant disorder, attention-deficit/hyperactivity disorder, or conduct disorder, however, display disruptive and argumentative behavior not just during bedtime, but in response to parental requests during the morning routine, mealtimes, chore completion, and public outings (e.g., stores). Evidenced-based treatment for noncompliant, disruptive, and aggressive children consists of behaviorally oriented family-based therapy (Brinkmeyer & Eyberg, 2003; McMahon & Forehand, 2003; Patterson, 1976; Webster-Stratton, 1992).

Child Self-Calming Skills. With maturity and experience, infants begin to acquire self-soothing and self-entertainment skills as they naturally become less reliant on others to entertain or calm them when they get upset. For infants and toddlers, these skills may involve playing with their own fingers, batting at a mobile, retrieving a pacifier, or sucking a thumb. Delays in the development of self-entertaining or self-quieting skills can result in a child who becomes overreliant on caregivers to entertain them or initiate soothing strategies. Attempting an extinction-based intervention for children with poor self-calming skills may result in vomiting during the initial stages of treatment and prompt parents to quickly abandon the intervention. Intervening during the day would allow gradual skill attainment at a time when the child and parents are less subject to frustration and reduced willpower (Teitelbaum, 1977). Guidelines for shaping age-appropriate self-quieting skills and increasing independent play skills have been published (Christophersen, 1994). Time-lapse video confirms that parents can influence sleep onset by teaching children self-quieting skills during the day, referred to as "day correction" of bedtime problems (Christophersen & Mortweet, 2001; Edwards, 1993).

Parents differ greatly in their tolerance for child distress (i.e., crying). For some, a few minutes of listening to an infant crying seems like hours, while other parents expertly ignore a toddler temper tantrum for 30 minutes. Parental tolerance for child misbehavior also plays a role at bedtime, as parents who are quick to anger may need to learn to calmly and quietly return a child to the bedroom to avoid increasing physiological arousal. Clinicians can ask parents to provide an honest rating (informal 1–10 point scale) of the degree of distress they experience when their children scream or cry out. In some cases, prescribing the child a sedating medication is clearly inappropriate when the problem can be resolved by teaching parents self-regulation skills to become less hyperreactive to mild forms of child distress (Tyson, 1996).

Feeding Habits and Schedule. Clinicians assessing infants and toddlers with nocturnal awakenings will want to inquire about feeding habits, both during the day and night. Some children display frequent awakenings, with considerable difficulty returning to sleep without feeding or drinking. Most experts agree that by the time an infant is 4 to 6 months old, there is rarely a nutritional basis to middle-of-the-night feedings (Douglas & Richman, 1985; Ferber, 1995b). This pattern of frequent waking, followed by quick sleep onset upon feeding may be more common in infants who are nursed frequently during the day or given a bottle in response to minor signs of distress (Kuhn & Weidinger, 2000). Intervention involves gradually lengthening feeding intervals during the day before phasing out the nighttime feedings (Ferber & Boyle, 1983; Mindell, 1990).

Anxiety. Children who are fearful or anxious tend to experience more trouble sleeping (Johnson, Chilcoat, & Breslau, 2000). One study found that fearful children took 54 minutes longer than nonfearful children to fall asleep (Mooney, 1985). Nighttime fears are especially common in preschool and school-age children (Muris, Merckelbach, Ollendick, King, & Bogie, 2001). These fears are heterogeneous and may be related to personal safety, fear of separation, worry about loss of loved ones, fear of imaginary creatures, fear of frightening dreams, and fear of the dark (Mooney, Graziano, & Katz, 1985).

Separation anxiety involves developmentally inappropriate and excessive anxiety upon separation or anticipated separation from major attachment figures. Because bedtime typically involves separation from familiar people, objects, and activities (Freud, 1965), going to bed can induce considerable anxiety in predisposed children. In fact, refusal to sleep alone is the top reason for referral in specialty clinics for separation anxiety disorder (Eisen & Schaefer, 2005).

Another common nighttime problem is fear of the dark. Ollendick (1979) indicated that darkness is the 4-year-old child's single most predominant fear. As with most anxiety disorders, the critical treatment component is exposure

(Sheslow, Bondy, & Nelson, 1982), which can be accomplished gradually by reinforcing children for tolerating increasingly darker environments for longer stretches of time. Success can also be obtained by systematically reducing ambient bedroom light by 20 watts every third or fourth night. Friedman (1992) provided functionally based, semistructured parent and child interviews for children presenting with nocturnal fears or fear of the dark (Friedman & Campbell, 1992).

The following interview with a 9-year-old, Kyle, is based on Eisen's (Eisen & Schaefer, 2005) model of negotiating with children to gradually approach and master their fears.

T: You say you get really scared when your parents turn off the lights in your bedroom. How fearful would you become if the lights were turned off, but a parent stayed with you?

K: Only a little.

T: How fearful would you become if you slept in your parents' bedroom with the lights off?

K: Not that scared.

T: How scared would you become of the dark if your older brother slept in a bed next to you?

K: I'd be a little scared, but I'd probably try not to show it.

T: Okay, last one. How scared would you be in your dark bedroom if, say, on a weekend, you went to bed 2 hours later than your normal bedtime?

K: I'd be pretty scared, but I'd probably be so sleepy that I'd go to sleep fast anyway.

T: I notice that your answers suggest that the amount of fear you feel changes depending on the situation. Can you think of any other ways that we might make it easier for you stay in your own darkened bedroom at night?

K: Well, maybe I could do it if I started on a weekend so I could make sure I'm really tired. Maybe my dad could leave the closet light on.

T: Good, now we're getting somewhere. Can you think of anything else?

K: Maybe listening to radio would keep me from being so afraid.

T: Great! Keep going.

K: Well, I know my parents won't stay with me the whole time, but maybe I could ask them to come in to check on me every so often.

T: I like your plan.

Parasomnias

The main task in interviewing parents about their children's parasomnia activities is to obtain a clear picture of the events to make an accurate clinical diagnosis. Effective treatments are available, but the nature of treatment is highly dependent on the type of parasomnia displayed (Kuhn & Elliott, 2003). Partial-arousal parasomnias, in the form of sleep terrors or sleepwalking, are common in young children. Primary considerations in the differential diagnosis of partial-arousal disorders include nightmares and sleep-related epileptic seizures.

Clinicians can usually help parents distinguish between sleep terrors and nightmares through information derived from the clinical interview. Sleep terrors often occur "like clockwork" during the first 2 or 3 hours of sleep, as the child completes the first sleep cycle. Nightmares occur primarily during REM sleep, which predominates later in the sleep cycle toward the morning hours. The behavioral manifestations of a sleep terror usually reflect a severe "panic" state. The child may act disoriented and confused and reject parental attempts to soothe. Children awakening after nightmares may show visible signs of distress, but they will be awake and interactive. Verbal children may relate the dream content. Children typically do not remember sleep terrors, but they may remember nightmares for days or weeks.

Referral for medical evaluation is indicated for children who display unusual or frequent nocturnal behaviors that lack a family history for partial arousals (a) when onset occurs in late childhood, (b) when event timing is variable across the night, (c) when stereotypic motor behavior is observed, or (d) when daytime sleepiness ensues, as these symptoms may reflect nocturnal seizure activity.

SELECTION OF TREATMENT TARGETS

Although the purpose of this chapter is to describe clinical interview strategies for children with sleep disorders, there would be no reason to interview if it were not for the purpose of constructing an effective treatment plan. Consequently, we use the case of Jamie to show how the information obtained in the clinical interview can be directly integrated into an individualized treatment plan.

The following information was gleaned from the semistructured interview described in this chapter. Jamie, age 4 years, goes to bed around 8:30 p.m. with no problem. He immediately tantrums when his mother walks out of room. He comes out of his bedroom numerous times each night. After an hour of screaming, multiple trips into the bedroom to quiet him, and returning him to his bedroom eight times, Jamie is finally taken to the parental bedroom, where his favorite movie is played on TV to keep him in bed and quiet. He finally falls asleep around 10:00 p.m. Jamie's parents note that this is not an uncommon scenario, as they estimate that he falls asleep in his own bed "about 2 times in 100." Once Jamie is asleep, dad transfers him to his own bed. Because Jamie complains that he is afraid of the dark, the bedroom lights are always left on. Jamie awakens on his own between 8:00 a.m. and 9:30 a.m. He does not nap during the day. Mother reports that Jamie has great difficulty separating from her during the day; therefore, she rarely leaves him with other caregivers. She added that she tries not to upset Jamie too much because he once cried so hard that he vomited.

It should now be readily apparent that the clinical interview has great potential to identify a number of factors influencing a child's sleep. When results of the interview identify that multiple interventions may be needed to address a complex problem, the clinician must carefully construct a treatment plan that is manageable for the family. One way to accomplish this task is to gradually add components as the child or family attains mastery. In the case of teaching sleep skills, a family might first ensure that the child falls asleep in a sleep-compatible environment, gradually moving to more difficult tasks, such as modifying parent-child interactions during bedtime. Based on this philosophy, a sample multicomponent treatment plan for the case presentation of Jamie is presented.

Week 1: Dad temporarily lies in bed next to Jamie, but Jamie is now required to fall asleep in his own bed every time. Bells are hung on the parents' bedroom door to signal Jamie's midnight entry into their room. If he enters, they immediately return him to his own bedroom and (for now) lie next to him until he falls asleep. The bedroom light is faded by systematically reducing the bulb to 7 watts. Jamie's favorite movie is replaced with a less interesting TV channel and eventually eliminated altogether.

Week 2: Self-calming skills are targeted during the day by implementing time-out for misbehavior. Jamie's release from time-out is made contingent upon self-calming (3–5 seconds of sitting quietly).

Week 3: Graduated-exposure therapy is initiated to give Jamie planned opportunities to experience enjoyable separations from his mother during the day.

Week 4: In preparation for a more difficult change, Jamie's bedtime is temporarily delayed to 10:00 p.m. to ensure that Jamie is sleepy when placed in bed. The bedtime is faded 15 minutes earlier the following night if he falls asleep within 15 minutes (Piazza & Fisher, 1991). The morning wake time is held constant to prevent Jamie from oversleeping if he has a poor night's sleep. Now that Jamie is accustomed and comfortable falling asleep in his own bedroom and can tolerate separating from his mother, parental presence is faded from the bedroom to allow Jamie to initiate sleep independently. Tangible reinforcers (see *The Sleep Fairy,* Burke et al., 2004) are put in place for Jamie as he begins to demonstrate appropriate bedtime skills and sleeps through the night. These reinforcers are faded and are replaced by social praise and recognition.

Summary

The semistructured interview presented in this chapter was constructed to help clinicians isolate variables that influence children's sleep. Identifying these variables, in turn, should allow clinicians to construct an individualized treatment plan based on a functional conceptualization of the presenting problem. The accumulation of clinically rich information obtained from skilled interviewing with cases like Jamie will, ideally, catapult pediatric professionals beyond using inappropriate, one-size-fits-all approaches (e.g., "Just let him cry it out" or "Let's try a sedative medication to break the cycle") and finally help children, parents, and their therapists gain some much-deserved sleep.

REFERENCES

Achenbach, T. M., & Rescorla, L. A. (2000). *Manual for the ASEBA preschool forms & profiles*. Burlington: University of Vermont, Department of Psychiatry.

Adair, R., Bauchner, H., Philipp, B., Levenson, S., & Zuckerman, B. (1991). Night waking during infancy: Role of parental presence at bedtime. *Pediatrics, 87*, 500–504.

American Academy of Sleep Medicine. (2005). *International classification of sleep disorders: Diagnostic and coding manual* (2nd ed.). Westchester, IL: Author.

American Sleep Disorders Association. (1997). Practice parameters for the indications for polysomnography and related procedures. *Sleep, 20*, 406–422.

Anders, T. F., Halpern, L. F., & Hua, J. (1992). Sleeping through the night: A developmental perspective. *Pediatrics, 9*, 554–560.

Anders, T. F., Sadeh, A., & Appareddy, V. (1995). Normal sleep in neonates and children. In R. Ferber & M. Kryger (Eds.), *Principles and practice of sleep medicine in the child* (pp. 7–18). Philadelphia: Saunders.

Armstrong, K. L., Quinn, R. A., & Dadds, M. R. (1994). The sleep patterns of normal children. *Medical Journal of Australia, 161*, 202–206.

Arndorfer, R. E., Allen, K. D., & Aljazireh, L. (1999). Behavioral health needs in pediatric medicine and the acceptability of behavioral solutions: Implications for behavioral psychologists. *Behavior Therapy, 30*, 137–148.

Aronen, E. T., & Soininen, M. (2000). Childhood depressive symptoms predict psychiatric problems in young adults. *Canadian Journal of Psychiatry, 45*, 465–470.

Atkinson, E., Vetere, A., & Grayson, K. (1995). Sleep disruption in young children: The influence of temperament on the sleep patterns of pre-school children. *Child: Care, Health, & Development, 21*, 233–246.

Baker, S. K., & Zee, P. C. (2000). Circadian disorders of the sleep-wake cycle. In M. H. Kryger, T. Roth, & W. C. Dement (Eds.), *Principles and practices of sleep medicine* (3rd ed., pp. 606–614). New York: Saunders.

Barker, P. (1990). *Clinical interviews with children and adolescents*. New York: Norton.

Beebe, D. W. (2005). Neurobehavioral effects of obstructive sleep apnea: An overview and heuristic model. *Current Opinion in Pulmonary Medicine, 11*, 494–500.

Benoit, D., Zeanah, C. H., Boucher, C., & Minde, K. K. (1992). Sleep disorders in early childhood: Association with insecure maternal attachment. *Journal of the American Academy of Child & Adolescent Psychiatry, 31*, 86–93.

Bernstein, D. J., & Michael, R. L. (1990). The utility of verbal and behavioral assessments of value. Special Issue: The experimental analysis of human behavior. *Journal of the Experimental Analysis of Behavior, 54*, 173–184.

Bertelson, A. D., & Monroe, L. J. (1979). Personality patterns of adolescent poor and good sleepers. *Journal of Abnormal Child Psychology, 7*, 191–197.

Bixler, E. O., Kales, J. D., Scharf, M. B., Kales, A., & Leo, L. A. (1976). Incidence of sleep disorders in medical practice: A physician survey. *Sleep Research, 5*, 62.

Boivin, D. B., & Czeisler, C. A. (1998). Resetting of circadian melatonin and cortisol rhythms in humans by ordinary room light. *Neuroreport, 9*, 779–782.

Borbely, A. A. (1982). A two process model of sleep regulation. *Human Neurobiology, 1*, 195–204.

Borkowski, M. M., Hunter, K. E., & Johnson, C. E. (2001). White noise and scheduled bedtime routines to reduce infant and childhood sleep disturbances. *Behavior Therapist, 24*, 29–37, 46–47.

Brackbill, Y. (1970). Acoustic variation and arousal level in infants. *Psychophysiology, 6*, 517–526.

Brinkmeyer, M. Y., & Eyberg, S. M. (2003). Parent-child interaction therapy for oppositional children. In A. E. Kazdin & J. R. Weisz (Eds.), *Evidence-based psychotherapies for children and adolescents* (pp. 204–223). New York: Guilford Press.

Brown, K. A., & Piazza, C. C. (1999). Commentary: Enhancing the effectiveness of sleep treatments: Developing a functional approach. *Journal of Pediatric Psychology, 24*, 487–489.

Bruni, O., Ottaviano, S., Guidetti, V., Romoli, M., Innocenzi, M., Cortesi, F., et al. (1996). The Sleep Disturbance Scale for Children (SDSC). Construction and validation of an instrument to evaluate sleep disturbances in childhood and adolescence. *Journal of Sleep Research, 5*, 251–261.

Burke, R. V., Kuhn, B. R., & Peterson, J. L. (2004). Brief report: A "storybook" ending to children's bedtime problems—The use of a rewarding social story to reduce bedtime resistance and frequent night waking. *Journal of Pediatric Psychology, 29*, 389–396.

Carskadon, M. A., Vieira, C., & Acebo, C. (1993). Association between puberty and delayed phase preference. *Sleep, 16*, 258–262.

Chervin, R. D., Hedger, K., Dillon, J. E., & Pituch, K. J. (2000). Pediatric sleep questionnaire (PSQ): Validity and reliability of scales for sleep-disordered breathing, snoring, sleepiness, and behavioral problems. *Sleep Medicine, 1*, 21–32.

Christophersen, E. R. (1994). *Pediatric compliance: A guide for the primary care physician*. New York: Plenum Press.

Christophersen, E. R., & Mortweet, S. L. (2001). *Treatments that work with children: Empirically supported strategies for managing childhood problems*. Washington, DC: American Psychological Association.

Colten, H. R., & Altevogt, B. M. (2006). *Sleep disorders and sleep deprivation: An unmet public health problem*. Washington, DC: National Academies Press.

Covey, S. R. (1990). *The 7 habits of highly effective people*. New York: Simon & Schuster.

Czeisler, C. A., Richardson, G. S., Coleman, R. M., Zimmerman, J. C., Moore-Ede, M. C., Dement, W. C., et al. (1981). Chronotherapy: Resetting the circadian clocks of patients with delayed sleep phase insomnia. *Sleep, 4*, 1–21.

Dahl, R. E. (1992). The pharmacologic treatment of sleep disorders. *Psychiatric Clinics of North America, 15*, 161–178.

Dahl, R. E. (1996). The impact of inadequate sleep on children's daytime cognitive function. *Seminars in Pediatric Neurology, 3*, 44–50.

Dahl, R. E. (1996). The regulation of sleep and arousal: Development and psychopathology. *Development and Psychopathology, 8,* 3–27.

Dahl, R. E. (1999, January). The consequences of insufficient sleep for adolescents: Links between sleep and emotional regulation. *Phi Delta Kappan,* pp. 354–358.

Dahl, R. E., & Puig-Antich, J. (1990). Sleep disturbances in child and adolescent psychiatric disorders. *Pediatrician, 17,* 32–37.

Davis, K. F., Parker, K. P., & Montgomery, G. L. (2004). Sleep in infants and young children. Part 1: Normal sleep. *Journal of Pediatric Health Care, 18,* 65–71.

Douglas, J., & Richman, N. (1985). *Sleep management manual.* London: London Institute of Child Health, Hospital for Sick Children, Gt. Ormond Street.

Duhon, G. J., Noell, G. H., Witt, J. C., Freeland, J. T., Dufrene, B. A., & Gilbertson, D. N. (2004). Identifying academic skill and performance deficits: The experimental analysis of brief assessments of academic skills. *School Psychology Review, 33,* 429–443.

Edelbrock, C., Greenbaum, R., & Conover, N. C. (1985). Reliability and concurrent relations between the teacher version of the Child Behavior Profile and the Conners' Revised Teacher Rating Scale. *Journal of Abnormal Child Psychology, 13,* 295–303.

Edwards, K. J. (1993). Automated data acquisition through time-lapse videotape recording. *Journal of Behavior Analysis, 26,* 503–504.

Eggermont, S., & Van den Bulck, J. (2006). Nodding off or switching off? The use of popular media as a sleep aid in secondary-school children. *Journal of Pediatrics and Child Health, 42,* 428–433.

Eisen, A. R., & Schaefer, C. E. (2005). *Separation anxiety in children and adolescents.* New York: Guilford Press.

Eyberg, S. M., & Pincus, D. (1999). *The Eyberg Child Behavior Inventory and Sutter-Eyberg Student Behavior Inventory: Professional manual.* Lutz, FL: Psychological Assessment Resources.

Fallone, G., Acebo, C., Arnedt, J. T., Seifer, R., & Carskadon, M. A. (2001). Effects of acute sleep restriction on behavior, sustained attention, and response inhibition in children. *Perceptual and Motor Skills, 93,* 213–229.

Fallone, G., Acebo, C., Seifer, R., & Carskadon, M. A. (2005). Experimental restriction of sleep opportunity in children: Effects on teacher ratings. *Sleep, 28,* 1561–1567.

Fallone, G., Owens, J. A., & Deane, J. (2002). Sleepiness in children and adolescents: Clinical implications. *Sleep Medicine Reviews, 6,* 287–306.

Fehlings, D. (2001). Frequent night awakenings in infants and preschool children referred to a sleep disorders clinic: The role of non-adaptive sleep associations. *Children's Health Care, 30,* 43–55.

Ferber, R. (1995a). Circadian rhythm sleep disorders in childhood. In R. Ferber & M. Kryger (Eds.), *Principles and practice of sleep medicine in the child* (pp. 91–98). Philadelphia: Saunders.

Ferber, R. (1995b). Sleeplessness in children. In R. Ferber & M. Kryger (Eds.), *Principles and practice of sleep medicine in the child* (pp. 79–89). Philadelphia: Saunders.

Ferber, R., & Boyle, M. P. (1983). Nocturnal fluid intake: A cause of, not treatment for, sleep disruption in infants and toddlers. *Sleep Research, 12,* 243.

Ferber, R. A. (1983). Delayed sleep phase syndrome versus motivated sleep phase delay in adolescents. *Sleep Research, 12,* 239.

Ferri, R., Lanuzza, B., Cosentino, F. I., et al. (2006, June). *A single question for the rapid screening of restless legs syndrome in the neurological clinical practice.* Program and abstracts of 20th Meeting of the Associated Professional Sleep Societies, Salt Lake City, UT. (Abstract 0820)

Forquer, L. M., & Johnson, C. M. (2005). Continuous white noise to reduce resistance going to sleep and night wakings in toddlers. *Child & Family Behavior Therapy, 27*(2), 1–10.

Freud, A. (1965). *Normality and pathology in childhood.* New York: International University Press.

Friedman, A. G., & Campbell, T. A. (1992). Children's nighttime fears: A behavioral approach to assessment and treatment. In L. VandeCreek, S. Knapp, & T. L. Jackson (Eds.), *Innovations in clinical practice: A source book* (Vol. 11, pp. 139–155). Sarasota, FL: Professional Resource Press/ Professional.

Friman, P. C. (2005). *Good night, sweet dreams, I love you: Now get into bed and go to sleep!* Boys Town, NE: Boys Town Press.

Galofre, I., Santacana, P., & Ferber, R. A. (1992). The "TIB>TST"syndrome. A cause of wakefulness in children. *Sleep Research, 21,* 199.

Glod, C. A., Teicher, M. H., Hartman, C. R., & Harakal, T. (1997). Increased nocturnal activity and impaired sleep maintenance in abused children. *Journal of the American Academy of Child & Adolescent Psychiatry, 36,* 1236–1243.

Gordon, J., & King, N. (2002). Children's night-time fears: An overview. *Counselling Psychology Quarterly, 15,* 121–132.

Gregory, A. M., Caspi, A., Moffitt, T. E., & Poulton, R. (2006). Family conflict in childhood: A predictor of later insomnia. *Sleep, 29,* 1063–1067.

Gregory, A. M., & O'Connor, T. G. (2002). Sleep problems in childhood: a longitudinal study of developmental change and association with behavioral problems. *Journal of the American Academy of Child & Adolescent Psychiatry, 41,* 964–971.

Gregory, A. M., Rijsdijk, F. V., Dahl, R. E., McGuffin, P., & Eley, T. C. (2006). Associations between sleep problems, anxiety, and depression in twins at 8 years of age. *Pediatrics, 118,* 1124–1132.

Griefahn, B., & Spreng, M. (2004). Disturbed sleep patterns and limitation of noise. *Noise & Health, 6,* 27–33.

Guilleminault, C., & Brooks, S. N. (2001). Excessive daytime sleepiness: A challenge for the practising neurologist. *Brain, 124,* 1482–1491.

Herman, J. H. (2005). Chronobiology of sleep in children. In S. H. Sheldon, R. Ferber, & M. H. Kryger (Eds.), *Principles and practice of pediatric sleep medicine* (pp. 85–99). New York: Elsevier Saunders.

Higuchi, S., Motohashi, Y., Liu, Y., Ahara, M., & Kaneko, Y. (2003). Effects of VDT tasks with a bright display at night on melatonin, core temperature, heart rate, and

sleepiness. *Journal of Applied Physiology,*
94, 1773–1776.

Hoban, T. F., & Chervin, R. D. (2005). Pediatric sleep-related breathing disorders and restless legs syndrome: How children are different. *Neurologist,* *11,* 325–337.

Horne, J. A., & Ostberg, O. (1976). A self-assessment questionnaire to determine morningness-eveningness in human circadian rhythms. *International Journal of Chronobiology, 4,* 97–110.

Horne, J. A., & Ostberg, O. (1977). Individual differences in human circadian rhythms. *Biological Psychology,* *5,* 179–190.

Ivanenko, A., Crabtree, V. M., & Gozal, D. (2004). Sleep in children with psychiatric disorders. *Pediatric Clinics of North America, 51*(1), 51–68.

Ivanenko, A., Crabtree, V. M., & Gozal, D. (2005). Sleep and depression in children and adolescents. *Sleep Medicine Reviews, 9,* 115–129.

Jakovljevic, B., Belojevic, G., Paunovic, K., & Stojanov, V. (2006). Road traffic noise and sleep disturbances in an urban population: Cross-sectional study. *Croatian Medical Journal, 47,* 125–133.

Jenni, O. G., & O'Connor, B. B. (2005). Children's sleep: An interplay between culture and biology. *Pediatrics,* *115,* 204–216.

Johnson, E. O., Chilcoat, H. D., & Breslau, N. (2000). Trouble sleeping and anxiety/depression in childhood. *Psychiatry Research, 94,* 93–102.

Johnson, J. G., Cohen, P., Kasen, S., First, M. B., & Brook, J. S. (2004). Association between television viewing and sleep problems during adolescence and early adulthood. *Archives of Pediatric and Adolescent Medicine, 158,* 562–568.

Kanfer, R., Eyberg, S. M., & Krahn, G. L. (1992). Interviewing strategies in child assessment. In C. E. Walker & M. C. Roberts (Eds.), *Handbook of clinical child psychology* (2nd ed., pp. 49–62). New York: Wiley.

Kataria, S., Swanson, M. S., & Trevathan, G. E. (1987). Persistence of sleep disturbances in preschool children. *Journal of Pediatrics, 110,* 642–646.

Kearney, C. A., & Albano, A. M. (2000). *When children refuse school: A cognitive-behavioral therapy approach/Parent workbook.* San Antonio, TX: The Psychological Corporation/Oxford University Press.

Keren, M., Feldman, R., & Tyano, S. (2001). Diagnoses and interactive patterns of infants referred to a community-based infant mental health clinic. *Journal of the American Academy of Child & Adolescent Psychiatry, 40,* 27–35.

Kerr, S., & Jowett, S. (1994). Sleep problems in pre-school children: A review of the literature. *Child: Care, Health, & Development, 20,* 379–391.

Kuhn, B. R., & Elliott, A. J. (2003). Treatment efficacy in behavioral pediatric sleep medicine. *Journal of Psychosomatic Research, 54,* 587–597.

Kuhn, B. R., Mayfield, J. W., & Kuhn, R. H. (1999). Clinical assessment of child and adolescent sleep disturbance. *Journal of Counseling & Development, 77,* 359–368.

Kuhn, B. R., & Weidinger, D. (2000). Interventions for infant and toddler sleep disturbance: A review. *Child & Family Behavior Therapy, 22*(2), 33–50.

Kushida, C. A., Littner, M. R., Morgenthaler, T., Alessi, C. A., Bailey, D., Coleman, J., Jr., et al. (2005). Practice parameters for the indications for polysomnography and related procedures: An update for 2005. *Sleep,* *28,* 499–521.

La Greca, A. M., Kuttler, A. F., & Stone, W. L. (2001). Assessing children through interviews and behavioral observations. In C. E. Walker & M. C. Roberts (Eds.), *Handbook of clinical child psychology* (3rd ed., pp. 90–110). New York: Wiley.

Lavigne, J. V., Arend, R., Rosenbaum, D., Smith, A., Weissbluth, M., Binns, H. J., et al. (1999). Sleep and behavior problems among preschoolers. *Journal of Developmental and Behavioral Pediatrics, 20,* 164–169.

LeBourgeois, M. K., Giannotti, F., Cortesi, F., Wolfson, A. R., & Harsh, J. (2005). The relationship between reported sleep quality and sleep hygiene in Italian and American adolescents. *Pediatrics, 115*(Suppl. 1), 257–265.

Leibenluft, J. (1999). The effects of caffeine on the sleep-wake cycles of children and adults. *Sleep Research Society Bulletin, 5,* 50–51.

Lewin, D. S. (2003). Behavioral insomnias of childhood-limit setting and sleep onset association disorder: Diagnostic issues, behavioral treatment, and future directions. In M. L. Perlis & K. L. Lichstein (Eds.), *Treating sleep disorders: Principles and practice of behavioral sleep medicine* (pp. 365–392). Hoboken, NJ: Wiley.

Lewy, A. J., Emens, J., Sack, R. L., Hasler, B. P., & Bernert, R. A. (2003). Zeitgeber hierarchy in humans: Resetting the circadian phase positions of blind people using melatonin. *International Journal of Chronobiology,* *20,* 837–852.

Lewy, A. J., Wehr, T. A., Goodwin, F. K., Newsome, D. A., & Markey, S. P. (1980). Light suppresses melatonin secretion in humans. *Science, 210,* 1267–1269.

Libert, J. P., Bach, V., Johnson, L. C., Ehrhart, J., Wittersheim, G., & Keller, D. (1991). Relative and combined effects of heat and noise exposure on sleep in humans. *Sleep, 14,* 24–31.

Lozoff, B., Wolf, A. W., & Davis, N. S. (1985). Sleep problems seen in pediatric practice. *Pediatrics,* *75,* 477–483.

Luginbuehl, M. (2004). *Manual for the sleep disorders inventory for students.* Clearwater, FL: Child Uplift.

Madansky, D., & Edelbrock, C. (1990). Cosleeping in a community sample of 2- and 3-year-old children [published erratum appears in *Pediatrics, 86,* 702, 1990]. *Pediatrics, 86,* 197–203.

Mash, E. J., & Terdel, L. G. (1997). Assessment of child and family disturbance: A behavioral-systems approach. In E. J. Mash & L. G. Terdel (Eds.), *Assessment of childhood disorders* (3rd ed., pp. 3–68). New York: Guilford Press.

McKenna, J. J. (2000). Cultural influences on infant and childhood sleep biology, and the science that studies it: Toward a more inclusive paradigm. In G. M. Loughlin, J. C. Carroll, & C. L. Marcus (Eds.), *Sleep and breathing in children: A developmental approach* (pp. 199–230). New York: Marcell Dekker.

McMahon, R. J., & Estes, A. M. (1997). Conduct problems. In E. J. Mash & L. G. Terdel (Eds.), *Assessment of childhood disorders* (3rd ed., pp. 130–193). New York: Guilford Press.

McMahon, R. J., & Forehand, R. L. (2003). *Helping the noncompliant child: Family-based treatment for oppositional behavior* (2nd ed.). New York: Guilford Press.

Mesibov, G. B., Schroeder, C. S., & Wesson, L. (1977). Parental concerns about their children. In M. C. Roberts, G. P. Koocher, D. K. Routh, & D. J. Willis (Eds.), *Readings in pediatric psychology* (pp. 307–316). New York: Plenum Press.

Miedema, H. M. E., & Vos, H. (2007). Associations between self-reported sleep disturbance and environmental noise based on reanalyses of pooled data from 24 Studies. *Behavioral Sleep Medicine, 5,* 1–20.

Minde, K., Popiel, K., Leos, N., Falkner, S., Parker, K., & Handley-Derry, M. (1993). The evaluation and treatment of sleep disturbances in young children. *Journal of Child Psychology and Psychiatry, 34,* 521–533.

Mindell, J. A. (1990). Treatment of night wakings in early childhood through generalization effects. *Sleep Research, 19,* 121.

Mindell, J. A. (1999). Empirically supported treatments in pediatric psychology: Bedtime refusal and night wakings in young children. *Journal of Pediacric Psychology, 24,* 465–481.

Mindell, J. A. (2005). *Sleeping through the night: How infants, toddlers, and their parents can get a good night's sleep* (Rev. ed.). New York: HarperCollins.

Mindell, J. A., Emslie, G., Blumer, J., Genel, M., Glaze, D., Ivanenko, A., et al. (2006). Pharmacologic management of insomnia in children and adolescents: Consensus statement. *Pediatrics, 117,* e1223–1232.

Mindell, J. A., Kuhn, B., Lewin, D. S., Meltzer, L. J., & Sadeh, A. (2006). Behavioral treatment of bedtime problems and night wakings in infants and young children. *Sleep, 29,* 1263–1276.

Mindell, J. A., Moline, M. L., Zendell, S. M., Brown, L. W., & Fry, J. M. (1994). Pediatricians and sleep disorders: Training and practice. *Pediatrics, 94,* 194–200.

Mindell, J. A., & Owens, J. A. (2003). *A clinical guide to pediatric sleep: diagnosis and management of sleep problems.* Philadelphia: Lippincott Williams & Wilkins.

Mindell, J. A., Owens, J. A., & Carskadon, M. A. (1999). Developmental features of sleep. *Child and Adolescent Psychiatric Clinics of North America, 8,* 695–725.

Moncur, M. (n.d.). *Michael Moncur's (cynical) quotations.* Retrieved September 19, 2006, from http://www.quotationspage.com/quote/26032.html

Mooney, K. C. (1985). Children's nighttime fears: Ratings of content and coping behaviors. *Cognitive Therapy and Research, 9,* 309–319.

Mooney, K. C., Graziano, A. M., & Katz, J. N. (1985). A factor analytic investigation of children's nighttime fear and coping responses. *Journal of Genetic Psychology, 146,* 205–215.

Morgenthaler, T. I., Owens, J., Alessi, C., Boehlecke, B., Brown, T. M., Coleman, J., Jr., et al. (2006). Practice parameters for behavioral treatment of bedtime problems and night wakings in infants and young children. *Sleep, 29,* 1277–1281.

Muris, P., Merckelbach, H., Ollendick, T. H., King, N. J., & Bogie, N. (2001). Children's nighttime fears: Parent-child ratings of frequency, content, origins, coping behaviors and severity. *Behaviour Research & Therapy, 39,* 13–28.

Muzet, A., Libert, J. P., & Candas, V. (1984). Ambient temperature and human sleep. *Experientia, 40,* 425–429.

Nagtegaal, J. E., Kerkhof, G. A., Smits, M. G., Swart, A. C., & Van Der Meer, Y. G. (1998). Delayed sleep phase syndrome: A placebo-controlled cross-over study on the effects of melatonin administered five hours before the individual dim light melatonin onset. *Sleep Research, 7,* 135–143.

Ohrstrom, E., Hadzibajramovic, E., Holmes, M., & Svensson, H. (2006). Effects of road traffic noise on sleep: Studies on children and adults. *Journal of Environmental Psychology, 26,* 116–126.

Ollendick, T. H. (1979). Fear reduction techniques in children. In M. Hersen, R. M. Eisler, & P. M. Miller (Eds.), *Progress in behavior modification* (Vol. 8, pp. 127–168). New York: Academic Press.

Owens, J., Maxim, R., McGuinn, M., Nobile, C., Msall, M., & Alario, A. (1999). Television-viewing habits and sleep disturbance in school children. *Pediatrics, 104,* e27.

Owens, J. A. (2005). The ADHD and sleep conundrum: A review. *Journal of Developmental and Behavioral Pediatrics, 26,* 312–322.

Owens, J. A., & Dalzell, V. P. (2001). The "BEARS": Screening for pediatric sleep problems in the primary care setting. *Sleep, 24*(Suppl.), A216.

Owens, J. A., & Mindell, J. A. (2005). *Take charge of your child's sleep: The all-in-one resource for solving sleep problems in kids and teens.* New York: Marlowe.

Owens, J. A., Spirito, A., & McGuinn, M. (2000). The Children's Sleep Habits Questionnaire (CSHQ): Psychometric properties of a survey instrument for school-aged children. *Sleep, 23,* 1043–1051.

Owens, J. A., Spirito, A., McGuinn, M., & Nobile, C. (2000). Sleep habits and sleep disturbance in elementary school-aged children. *Journal of Developmental and Behavioral Pediatrics, 21,* 27–36.

Owens, J. A., & Witmans, M. (2004). Sleep problems. *Current Problems in Pediatric and Adolescent Health Care, 34,* 154–179.

Owens, J. L., France, K. G., & Wiggs, L. (1999). Behavioral and cognitive-behavioral interventions for sleep disorders in infants and children: A review. *Sleep Medicine Reviews, 3,* 281–302.

Paavonen, E. J., Pennonen, M., Roine, M., Valkonen, S., & Lahikainen, A. R. (2006). TV exposure associated with sleep disturbances in 5- to 6-year-old children. *Sleep Research, 15,* 154–161.

Pagel, J. F. (2005). Medications and their effects on sleep. *Primary Care, 32,* 491–509.

Patterson, G. R. (1976). *Living with children: New methods for parents and teachers* (Rev. ed.). Champaign, IL: Research Press.

Peterson, J. L., & Peterson, M. (2003). *The sleep fairy.* Omaha, NE: Behave'n Kids Press.

Piazza, C. C., & Fisher, W. W. (1991). Bedtime fading in the treatment of pediatric insomnia. *Journal of Behavioral Therapy and Experimental Psychiatry, 22,* 53–56.

Querido, J. G., Eyberg, S. M., Kanfer, R., & Krahn, G. L. (2001). The process of the clinical child assessment interview. In C. E. Walker & M. C. Roberts (Eds.), *Handbook of clinical child psychology* (3rd ed., pp. 75–89). New York: Wiley.

Quine, L. (2001). Sleep problems in primary school children: comparison between mainstream and special school children. *Child: Care, Health, & Development, 27,* 201–221.

Ramchandani, P., Wiggs, L., Webb, V., & Stores, G. (2000). A systematic review of treatments for settling problems and night waking in young children. *British Medical Journal, 320,* 209–213.

Ramos, K. D. (2003). Intentional versus reactive cosleeping. *Sleep Research Online, 5,* 141–147.

Randazzo, A. C., Muehlbach, M. J., Schweitzer, P. K., & Walsh, J. K. (1998). Cognitive function following acute sleep restriction in children ages 10–14. *Sleep, 21,* 861–868.

Rapoport, J., Elkins, R., Langer, D. H., Sceery, W., Buchsbaum, M. S., Gillin, J. C., et al. (1981). Childhood obsessive-compulsive disorder. *American Journal of Psychiatry, 138,* 1545–1554.

Reid, M. J., Walter, A. L., & O'Leary, S. G. (1999). Treatment of young children's bedtime refusal and nighttime wakings: A comparison of "standard" and graduated ignoring procedures. *Journal of Abnormal Child Psychology, 27,* 5–16.

Reynolds, C. R., & Kamphaus, R. W. (2005). *The Behavior Assessment System for Children-Second edition* (BASC-2). Circle Pines, MN: AGS.

Richman, N. (1981). A community survey of characteristics of one- to two- year-olds with sleep disruptions. *Journal of American Academy of Child Psychiatry, 20,* 281–291.

Robinson, K. E., & Sheridan, S. M. (2000). Using the Mystery Motivator to improve child bedtime compliance. *Child & Family Behavior Therapy, 22*(1), 29–49.

Rosenthal, N. E., Joseph-Vanderpool, J. R., Levendosky, A. A., Johnston, S. H., Allen, R., Kelly, K. A., et al. (1990). Phase-shifting effects of bright morning light as treatment for delayed sleep phase syndrome. *Sleep, 13,* 354–361.

Sadeh, A. (1996). Stress, trauma, and sleep in children. *Child and Adolescent Psychiatric Clinics of North America, 5,* 685–700.

Sadeh, A. (2001). *Sleeping like a baby: A sensitive and sensible approach to solving your child's sleep problems.* London: Yale University Press.

Sadeh, A., Gruber, R., & Raviv, A. (2002). Sleep, neurobehavioral functioning, and behavior problems in school-age children. *Child Development, 73,* 405–417.

Sateia, M. J., Doghramji, K., Hauri, P. J., & Morin, C. M. (2000). Evaluation of chronic insomnia: An American Academy of Sleep Medicine review. *Sleep, 23,* 243–308.

Schrader, H., Bovim, G., & Sand, T. (1993). The prevalence of delayed and advanced sleep phase syndromes. *Sleep Research, 2,* 51–55.

Schroeder, C. S., & Gordon, B. N. (2002). Assessment to intervention. In *Assessment and treatment of childhood problems: A clinician's guide* (2nd ed., pp. 40–78). New York: Guilford Press.

Scotti, J. R., Morris, T. L., McNeil, C. B., & Hawkins, R. P. (1996). *DSM-IV* and disorders of childhood and adolescence: Can structural criteria be functional? *Journal of Consulting and Clinical Psychology, 64,* 1177–1191.

Shapiro, H., Baughman, K. R., & Bourguet, C. (2006, June). *Accuracy of the single item screening question for restless legs syndrome within a community hospital sleep center.* Program and abstracts of the 20th Meeting of the Associated Professional Sleep Societies, Salt Lake City, UT. (Abstract 0836)

Sheldon, S. H., Ferber, R., & Kryger, M. (Eds.). (2005). *Principles and practice of pediatric sleep medicine.* Philadelphia: Elsevier.

Shen, J., Barbera, J., & Shapiro, C. M. (2006). Distinguishing sleepiness and fatigue: Focus on definition and measurement. *Sleep Medicine Reviews, 10,* 63–76.

Sheslow, D. V., Bondy, A. S., & Nelson, R. O. (1982). A comparison of graduated exposure, verbal coping skills, and their combination in the treatment of children's fear of the dark. *Child & Family Behavior Therapy, 4*(2/3), 33–45.

Siegel, J. M. (1995). Phylogeny and the function of REM sleep. *Behavioural Brain Research, 69,* 29–34.

Spencer, J. A., Moran, D. J., Lee, A., & Talbert, D. (1990). White noise and sleep induction. *Archives of Disease in Childhood, 65,* 135–137.

Spielman, A. J., Conroy, D., & Glovinsky, P. B. (2003). Evaluation of insomnia. In M. L. Perlis & K. L. Lichstein (Eds.), *Treating sleep disorders: Principles and practice of behavioral sleep medicine* (pp. 190–213). Hoboken, NJ: Wiley.

Stanchina, M. L., Abu-Hijleh, M., Chaudhry, B. K., Carlisle, C. C., & Millman, R. P. (2005). The influence of white noise on sleep in subjects exposed to ICU noise. *Sleep Medicine, 6,* 423–428.

Stores, G. (2001). *A clinical guide to sleep disorders in children and adolescents.* Cambridge, UK: Cambridge University Press.

Strauch, C., Brandt, S., & Edwards Beckett, J. (1993). Implementation of a quiet hour: effect on noise levels and infant sleep states. *Neonatal Network: Journal of Neonatal Nursing, 12,* 31–35.

Teitelbaum, P. (1977). Levels of integration of the operant. In W. K. Honig & J. E. R. Staddon (Eds.), *Handbook of operant behavior* (pp. 7–27). Upper Saddle River, NJ: Prentice Hall.

Thompson, D. A., & Christakis, D. A. (2005). The association between television viewing and irregular sleep schedules among children less than 3 years of age. *Pediatrics, 116,* 851–856.

Tomoda, A., & Miike, T. (1996). Disturbed circadian core body temperature rhythm and sleep disturbance in school refusal children and adolescents. *International Journal of Psychology, 31,* 54162–54162.

Touchette, E., Petit, D., Paquet, J., Boivin, M., Japel, C., Tremblay, R. E., et al. (2005). Factors associated with fragmented sleep at night across early childhood. *Archives of Pediatric and Adolescent Medicine, 159,* 242–249.

Tuohy, P. G., & Tuohy, R. J. (1990). The overnight thermal environment of infants. *New Zealand Medical Journal, 103,* 36–38.

Tyson, P. D. (1996). Biodesensitization: Biofeedback-controlled systematic desensitization of the stress response to infant crying. *Biofeedback and Self Regulation, 21,* 273–290.

Van den Bulck, J. (2004). Television viewing, computer game playing, and Internet use and self-reported time to bed and time out of bed in secondary-school children. *Sleep, 27,* 101–104.

Van Tassel, E. B. (1985). The relative influence of child and environmental characteristics on sleep disturbances in the first and second years of life. *Journal of Developmental and Behavioral Pediatrics, 6,* 81–85.

Vollmer, T. R., & Smith, R. G. (1996). Some current themes in functional analysis research. *Research in Developmental Disabilities, 17,* 229–249.

Wahlstrom, K., Wrobel, G., & Kubow, P. (1998). *Minneapolis Public Schools start time study: Executive summary.* Minneapolis, MN: Center for Applied Research and Educational Improvement.

Wailoo, M. P., Petersen, S. A., & Whitaker, H. (1990). Disturbed nights and 3–4 month old infants: The effects of feeding and thermal environment. *Archives of Disease in Childhood, 65,* 499–501.

Waterhouse, J., Minors, D., Folkard, S., Owens, D., Atkinson, G., Macdonald, I., et al. (1998). Light of domestic intensity produces phase shifts of the circadian oscillator in humans. *Neuroscience Letters, 245,* 97–100.

Webster-Stratton, C. (1992). *The incredible years: A troubleshooting guide for parents of children ages 3–8 years.* Toronto, Canada: Umbrella Press.

Weissbluth, M. (1981). Sleep duration and infant temperament. *Journal of Pediatrics, 99,* 817–819.

Weissbluth, M. (1984). Sleep duration, temperament, and Conners' ratings of three-year-old children. *Journal of Developmental and Behavioral Pediatrics, 5,* 120–123.

Weissbluth, M. (1995). Naps in children: 6 months–7 years. *Sleep, 18,* 82–87.

Weissbluth, M., Poncher, I., Given, G., Schwab, J., Mervis, R., & Rosenberg, M. (1981). Sleep duration and television viewing. *Journal of Pediatrics, 99,* 486–488.

Whiteford, L., Fleming, P., & Henderson, A. J. (2004). Who should have a sleep study for sleep-related breathing disorders? *Archives of Disease in Childhood, 89,* 851–855.

Wiggs, L., & Stores, G. (2001). Behavioural treatment for sleep problems in children with severe intellectual disabilities and daytime challenging behaviour: Effect on mothers and fathers. *British Journal of Health Psychology, 6,* 257–269.

Wolf, A. W., & Lozoff, B. (1989). Object attachment, thumbsucking, and the passage to sleep. *Journal of the American Academy of Child & Adolescent Psychiatry, 28,* 287–292.

Wolfson, A. R., & Carskadon, M. A. (1996). Early school start times affect sleep and daytime functioning in adolescents. *Sleep Research, 25,* 117.

Wolfson, A. R., & Carskadon, M. A. (2003). Understanding adolescents' sleep patterns and school performance: a critical appraisal. *Sleep Medicine Reviews, 7,* 491–506.

Younus, M., & Labellarte, M. J. (2002). Insomnia in children: When are hypnotics indicated? *Pediatric Drugs, 4,* 391–403.

AUTHOR INDEX

SUBJECT INDEX

ABOUT THE EDITORS

Michel Hersen, PhD (SUNY–Buffalo, 1966), is Professor and Dean of the School of Professional Psychology at Pacific University and a Clinical Professor in the Department of Psychiatry at the Oregon Health Sciences University. His research interests include assessment and treatment of older adults, behavioral assessment and treatment of children, single-case research, and administration. He is a fellow of Division 12 (Clinical Psychology) of the American Psychological Association and the American Board of Medical Psychotherapists and Psychodiagnosticians, which awarded him their Lifetime Achievement Award, and is a past president of the Association for Advancement of Behavior Therapy. He has held editorships with nine journals, including *Clinical Case Studies, Behavior Modification, Clinical Psychology Review,* and the *Journal of Anxiety Disorders.* He has edited or authored 223 papers and 128 books, including many classic reference volumes.

Jay C. Thomas, PhD (University of Akron, 1981), American Board of Professional Psychology, is Professor and Program Director of Counseling Psychology in the School of Professional Psychology at Pacific University. His research interests include applied research methodology, psychometrics, career and life development, and behavioral change. He is a member of the American Psychological Association, American Psychological Society, and the American Statistical Association. He has authored numerous research papers and book chapters and has edited several books, including *Understanding Research in Clinical and Counseling Psychology* and the *Comprehensive Handbook of Personality and Psychopathology.*

ABOUT THE CONTRIBUTORS

Amanda C. Adcock, MS, is a graduate student in the Clinical Psychology Program at the University of North Texas. Her professional interests are in the assessment of experiential avoidance, valuing, and mindfulness, as well as behavioral and values-oriented treatment approaches.

Maureen A. Allwood, PhD (University of Missouri–Columbia, 2005), is a Postdoctoral Research Fellow at Brown Medical School and Rhode Island Hospital. Her graduate school research focused on child and adolescent post-traumatic stress disorder (PTSD) and other responses to violent trauma exposure, including externalizing behaviors. She has coauthored scientific journal articles on the topics of children's response to violent trauma, the relations between PTSD symptoms and attention problems in children, as well as the integration of science and practice in clinical training.

Debora J. Bell, PhD (West Virginia University, 1989), completed her clinical internship at Western Psychiatric Institute and Clinic and is currently Associate Professor, Department of Psychological Sciences, University of Missouri–Columbia. She serves as Director of Clinical Training and Associate Chair of Clinical Science at MU and directs the MU Psychological Services Clinic. Her primary research interests focus on social-cognitive and socioaffective aspects of child anxiety and depression. She has authored numerous conference presentations, book chapters, and scientific journal articles on child anxiety, depression, and trauma.

Scott Bethay is a graduate student in clinical psychology at the University of Mississippi. His research interests include child psychopathology and applied behavior analysis.

Jessica Bolton is a student in the Clinical Psychology Doctoral Program at Pacific University School of Professional Psychology. Her primary focus is child clinical psychology. Past experiences with children include working in educational settings, inpatient settings, and various volunteer positions as a camp counselor and group facilitator. Current interests include school-based mental health needs assessment and program development.

Alison Brodhagen is a doctoral student in clinical psychology in the School of Professional Psychology at Pacific University. She is currently completing her predoctoral internship in New Haven, Connecticut, at the Clifford Beers Clinic and the Posttraumatic Stress Center, both of which specialize in treating individuals and families who have been exposed to traumatic events. Her research interests include resilience following trauma, with a particular focus on dispositional optimism.

Lisa Roberts Christiansen, PsyD, is an Assistant Professor at Pacific University School of Professional Psychology. Her primary focus is assessment. She is a licensed psychologist in the state of Oregon and has evaluated children and adolescents in outpatient and inpatient settings.

Lara Delmolino, PhD, is a Research Assistant Professor at the Graduate School of Applied and Professional Psychology and also serves as the Assistant Director for the Douglass Developmental Disabilities Center, both at Rutgers, the State University of New Jersey. She participates in clinical work and applied research in the field of autism and teaches graduate courses in applied behavior analysis. Her interests include diagnosis, treatment outcome, and best practices in intervention for individuals with autism.

Stephanie A. Devore is an undergraduate psychology major at the University of Nevada, Las Vegas. She is also a research assistant in a federal grant funded by the National Institute on Drug Abuse to develop and formally evaluate treatments for substance-abusing mothers who have been founded for child maltreatment.

Sean Dodge is a doctoral student at the School of Professional Psychology at Pacific University in Hillsboro, Oregon. He earned his bachelor's degree from Westminster College in Salt Lake City, Utah. He has clinical experience working with adolescents and their families in residential settings. His primary areas of interest include individual therapy and assessment with adolescents.

Brad C. Donohue, PhD, is an Associate Professor at the University of Nevada, Las Vegas (UNLV). He is the director of the Achievement Center at UNLV. His primary research interests include the development and evaluation of cognitive-behavioral treatment programs targeting substance abuse, child maltreatment, and conduct disorders. He has directed projects funded by NIDA, NIMH, and SAMHSA. He is currently involved in three projects: a clinical outcome study involving concurrent HIV prevention and treatment for child-neglecting and drug-abusing mothers and their families, a clinical trial involving violence prevention within school context, and determining best practices relevant to teaching community counselors to utilize evidence-based adolescent drug abuse treatments.

Melissa Fiorito is a doctoral candidate at Seton Hall University in South Orange, New Jersey. She received her Educational Specialist degree in Mental Health Counseling from Seton Hall University and a bachelor's degree from the University of Delaware. Her research and career interests have predominantly focused on pediatric neuropsychology. She has presented at several local and national conferences and has been an active member of a research project investigating the relationship between fatigue and learning processes in children and adults. She recently completed an international practicum in Trinidad, working with developmentally delayed children and adults. She had training in neuropsychological assessment at New York University Epilepsy Center and is currently completing a practicum placement at Hackensack University Medical Center, working with children and families, and Bellevue Hospital Center Traumatic Brain Injury Unit.

Kate E. Fiske is an advanced doctoral candidate in Clinical Psychology at Rutgers, the State University of New Jersey. She has served as both a teacher and a behavior consultant for children with autism over the past 8 years and currently works as the Research Coordinator at the Douglass Developmental Disabilities Center at Rutgers. Her research interests include the development of pretense in children with autism as well as the unique experiences of parents and siblings of individuals with autism.

Christopher A. Flessner is a doctoral student in Clinical Psychology at the University of Wisconsin–Milwaukee. He received his master's degree in Clinical Psychology at North Dakota State University. His primary areas of research interest are in the study of tic disorders, trichotillomania, and other obsessive-compulsive spectrum disorders in both children and adults. His current research focuses on the examination of possible subtypes of hair pulling in individuals with trichotillomania and phenomenological similarities between various obsessive-compulsive spectrum disorders.

Elizabeth Rehberg Gaebler is a graduate student in the School Psychology Program at the University of Wisconsin–Madison.

Alan M. Gross is a professor of psychology and director of clinical training at the University of Mississippi. His research interests focus on dating violence and behavior disorders in children.

Michael L. Handwerk, PhD, is the Director of Clinical Services, Research, & Internship Training at Girls and Boys Town, a large child care organization. He received his PhD from the University of Texas at Austin. Dr. Handwerk oversees the APA-approved internship program, the pediatric outpatient clinic, an assessment center, and the substance abuse program. He has published over 25 articles and chapters on the assessment and treatment of child and adolescents. Currently, he is conducting research on the utilization of psychotropic medication in residential care, the potential iatrogenic effects of group intervention, the relationship between therapeutic alliance and outcomes for children in residential care, and the effectiveness of clinical interventions for externalizing problems.

Sandra L. Harris, PhD, is a Board of Governors Distinguished Service Professor at Rutgers, the State University of New Jersey. She is the Executive Director and founder of the Douglass Developmental Disabilities Center at Rutgers and in that role has been involved in a range of research and other scholarly projects, as well as writing a series of books for parents and teachers on the fundamentals of applied behavior analysis (ABA) and on the experiences of siblings of children who have a brother or sister on the autism spectrum. She gives talks nationally and internationally to promote the use of ABA in educating children, adolescents, and adults with autism.

Heather H. Hill is a graduate student in the University of Nevada, Las Vegas Clinical Psychology PhD program. She is currently Program Coordinator for an R01 NIDA-funded controlled clinical trial involving concurrent drug abuse treatment and HIV prevention in child-neglecting mothers. In addition, she has several publications in the areas of child maltreatment and drug abuse.

Elizabeth B. Holmberg is a James B. Duke Scholar in the Clinical Psychology Doctoral program at Duke University. She received her BA (2003) from Duke, where she examined emotional responses to aesthetic works. Her research currently assesses racial and gender differences in the trajectory of substance use across the life course and its implications for academic achievement and occupational prestige.

Jason T. Hurwitz, MS, is a dissertator in the APA- and NASP-accredited School Psychology Program at the University of Wisconsin–Madison, where he received his master's degree. His research interests include prevention, problem-solving consultation, and program evaluation. Jason is also a project assistant on a U.S. Department of Education research grant. He recently completed his predoctoral internship at the Waisman Center, where he assisted in the interdisciplinary assessment of young children with developmental disabilities, and at Rogers Memorial Hospital, where he helped treat adolescents with obsessive-compulsive disorder. He also taught for 3 years in Grades K–12 at public schools in California and Japan.

Christy Jayne is a graduate student in clinical psychology at the University of Mississippi. Her research interests focus on nutrition and physical activity in children.

Danielle T. Knatz is a doctoral candidate in clinical psychology at the University of Nevada, Las Vegas. She received her master's degree in psychology from New York University. Her research and clinical interests focus on neuropsychological functioning in adults and children, and specifically the functional consequences of neurocognitive deficits.

Thomas R. Kratochwill, PhD, is Sears-Bascom Professor at the University of Wisconsin–Madison and Director of the School Psychology Program. He is also Director of the Educational and Psychological Training Center, an interdisciplinary unit for clinical and applied training, and Codirector of the Child and Adolescent Mental Health and Education Resource Center. He is the author of over 200 journal articles and book chapters, has written or edited over 30 books, and has made over 300 professional presentations. He was selected as the founding editor of the APA Division 16 journal *School Psychology Quarterly*, serving from 1984 to 1992. He is past President of the Society for the Study of School Psychology and Cochair of the Task Force on Evidence-Based Interventions in School Psychology.

Brett R. Kuhn, PhD, CBSM, earned his doctorate in clinical psychology from Oklahoma State University before completing a clinical internship at the Medical University of South Carolina. He is a licensed psychologist and Associate Professor of Pediatrics at the University of Nebraska Medical Center (UNMC). He is certified in behavioral sleep medicine by the American Academy of Sleep Medicine, directed the Pediatric Sleep Clinic at UNMC for 12 years, and recently joined the Pediatric Sleep Medicine Clinic at Children's Hospital in Omaha. He has served on the editorial board for *Behavioral Sleep Medicine* since its inception. He has published over 30 professional journal articles and book chapters on children's behavioral health issues, including sleep problems, elimination disorders, and disruptive behavior.

Robert H. LaRue is an Assistant Research Professor at the Graduate School of Applied and Professional Psychology at Rutgers University. He is the Assistant Director of Research & Training at the Douglass Developmental Disabilities Center. He earned a dual doctorate in biological and school psychology from Louisiana State University. He completed his predoctoral internship with the Kennedy Krieger Institute at Johns Hopkins University and a postdoctoral fellowship with the Marcus Institute at Emory University. He has coauthored published articles in peer-reviewed journals and presented at national and international conferences. His interests include the assessment and treatment of maladaptive behavior, staff and teacher training, and behavioral pharmacology.

Susan Tinsley Li, PhD, is an associate professor in the School of Professional Psychology at Pacific University, where she teaches in the clinical psychology doctoral program and the counseling psychology master's program. Dr. Li obtained her degree in clinical psychology from Arizona State University in 1997, with emphases in child/adolescent psychology and minority mental health. She completed an APA-approved internship at the University of Miami School of Medicine/Jackson Memorial Hospital and a postdoctoral fellowship at Barrow Neurological Institute. Prior to her work at Pacific, Dr. Li was a faculty member at Loyola University Chicago.

Rachel L. Loewy, PhD, received an MA in psychology from the University of Pennsylvania and a PhD in clinical psychology from the University of California, Los Angeles. Her research focuses on assessment and intervention with adolescents and young adults in the early phase of psychotic disorders. She has extensive experience in psychodiagnostic interviewing with adolescents suffering from psychotic spectrum disorders. She is currently an Adjunct Assistant Professor in the Department of Psychiatry at the University of California, San Francisco.

Michelle Heffner Macera completed a PhD in clinical psychology from West Virginia University. She is first author of *The Anorexia Workbook* and has published several case studies, empirical research, and book chapters on eating disorder assessment and treatment. She is employed at the Center for Hope of the Sierras, an eating disorder residential treatment center in Reno, Nevada.

Jennifer Magneson, MA (Pacific University, 2004), is a graduate student at Pacific University, School of Professional Psychology, in Portland, Oregon. She is currently employed as a school psychologist with the Northwest Regional Education Service District in Hillsboro, Oregon, and is completing her practicum requirements at the Clark County Juvenile Court in Vancouver, Washington. Her main interests include assessment and treatment of severely emotionally disturbed children.

Megan Martins is a doctoral student in clinical psychology at Rutgers, The State University of New Jersey. She is presently completing her internship in the developmental disabilities track at the Semel Institute for Neuroscience and Human Behavior at UCLA. Her research interests include evaluating treatment outcome and social skills interventions for children with autism and developing supports for families of individuals with developmental disabilities.

Brian P. Marx, PhD, is a staff psychologist at the National Center for Posttraumatic Stress Disorder (PTSD) at the VA Boston Healthcare System. Prior to joining the National Center for PTSD, he was Associate Professor of Psychology at Temple University. He received his PhD from the University of Mississippi in 1996 and completed his internship at the University of Mississippi Medical Center/Jackson VAMC Consortium. He has published one book and over 50 articles and book chapters, primarily on sexual assault, psychological trauma, and PTSD.

Michael W. Mellon, PhD, is a consultant and pediatric psychologist in the Department of Psychiatry and Psychology at the Mayo Clinic. He earned his PhD from the University of Memphis and completed an internship at the University of Mississippi Medical Center. He is the codirector of the Mayo Clinic-Dana Child Development and Learning Disorders Program, and Director of the Enuresis and Encopresis Clinic. He has published and presented papers at national conferences in the areas of behavioral treatments for enuresis and encopresis. Recent research activities include a current status assessment of adults previously identified as learning disabled and/or ADHD, psychosocial characteristics of ADHD children undergoing social skills training, and predictors of outcome in conditioning treatment of primary nocturnal enuresis.

Bethany Michel received a bachelor's degree in psychology from Stanford University and is currently a graduate student in the Experimental Psychopathology and Clinical Psychology Program in the Department of Psychology at Harvard University.

Catherine Miller, PhD, received her doctoral degree from West Virginia University in Morgantown, West Virginia, in 1993. She has worked at a state hospital, a community mental health center, a court clinic, and in private practice and has been licensed in four states. She currently is an Associate Professor and the Director of Academic Issues at the School of Professional Psychology at Pacific University in Forest Grove, Oregon, where she has been working since 1999. She teaches courses in ethics, juvenile forensics, and child treatment, and she supervises graduate students at the school's in-house training clinic.

J. Scott Mizes, PhD, is a Professor of Behavioral Medicine and Psychiatry, West Virginia University School of Medicine, and Director of the Eating, Body Image, and Weight Disorders Clinic. He is a Diplomate in Clinical Psychology, American Board of Professional Psychology; Fellow of the Academy of Eating Disorders; and Fellow of the American Psychological Association (Divisions of Clinical Psychology and of Health Psychology). For many years, he was a member of the Eating Disorders Research Society. He is the author and developer of the Mizes Anorectic Cognitions questionnaire and coedited a book on the treatment of eating disorders: K. J. Miller & J. S. Mizes (Eds.), *Comparative Treatments of Eating Disorders*. New York: Springer, 2000.

Matthew K. Nock, PhD, is Assistant Professor of Psychology and Director of the Laboratory for Clinical and Developmental Research in the Department of Psychology at Harvard University, where he also teaches courses on statistics, research methodology, and self-injurious behaviors. He received his MS (2000), M.Phil. (2001), and PhD (2003) in psychology from Yale University and completed his clinical internship at the NYU Child Study Center–Bellevue Hospital

Center. His research focuses primarily on the etiology, assessment, and treatment of self-injurious and aggressive behaviors.

William H. O'Brien is an Associate Professor in the Clinical Psychology Training Program at Bowling Green State University. He is board certified in Behavioral Psychology by the American Board of Professional Psychology and is a Fellow in the American Academy of Behavioral Psychology. His research and clinical interests center on cognitive-behavioral assessment and clinical psychophysiology. He has published a number of articles and chapters on behavioral assessment, functional analysis, clinical decision making, and the assessment and treatment of psychophysiological disorders.

Laura Palmer, PhD, a licensed psychologist, is a tenured Associate Professor and Chair of the Professional Psychology and Family Therapy Department and Director of Training for the PhD Program in Counseling Psychology at Seton Hall University, S. Orange, New Jersey. She is President-Elect of the New Jersey Psychological Association and a past chair of the Council of Counseling Psychology Training Programs. She has worked in the field of pediatric mental health services since 1980. Her research activities include the investigation of emotional and neurocognitive sequelae of trauma, the neuropsychology of learning disabilities, and the role of fatigue and stress in learning processes in learning-disabled children and college students. She also maintains a private practice in Madison, New Jersey.

Valerie I. Photos, MA, is a doctoral student in clinical psychology at Harvard University. She received her BA (2003) in human development and psychology from The University of Chicago. Her research interests include the study of risk factors (e.g., cognitive, affective, and social deficits) among young adults who engage in aggressive, self-injurious, or suicidal behaviors. She is also interested in the evaluation and implementation of policy related to the treatment of severe mental illness and the prevention of self-injury and violence.

David Reitman, PhD, is an Associate Professor at the Nova Southeastern University (NSU) Center for Psychological Studies. He received his doctoral degree from the University of Mississippi in 1995 and served as an Assistant Professor of Psychology at Louisiana State University before coming to NSU in 2001. Dr. Reitman is the author of over 30 scholarly publications concerned with child and adolescent behavior problems, parenting, and behavioral assessment and therapy. He serves on the editorial boards of several journals and recently coedited the book *Practitioner's Guide to Empirically Based Measures of School Behavior.* He has served as a consultant to numerous and diverse agencies concerned with the welfare of children. He is presently the director of the ADHD Assessment, Consultation, and Treatment program (AACT) at the NSU Center for Psychological Studies.

Yasmin Rey, MS, is a doctoral student in Life Span Developmental Science at Florida International University, in Miami, Florida. She is presently involved in research at the Child Anxiety and Phobia Program at Florida International University. She is working toward a career in academia in which she can continue her research on Latino youth and families, focusing on internalizing problems in this population. She also serves as student representative of APA Division 53 (Society of Clinical Child and Adolescent Psychology).

Benson Schaeffer, PhD, received his doctorate from UCLA; taught in the Psychology Department, University of Oregon, Eugene, from September 1966 to June 1980; and was a Research Psychologist for 2 years in the Cognitive Neuropsychology Laboratory at Good Samaritan Hospital, Portland, Oregon. He was licensed in 1975 and has been in private practice in Portland since March 1982. He has published research and chapters about language instruction for children with autism, counseling families with children with seizure disorders, attention deficits and learning disabilities in the workplace, concept and number development in children, and adult semantic memory. He specializes in child clinical neuropsychology, consults to treatment programs and school districts, and teaches assessment and supervises research at the School of Professional Psychology, Pacific University.

Wendy K. Silverman, PhD, American Board of Professional Psychology, is Professor of Psychology at Florida International University in Miami. She is the recipient of several grants from the National Institute of Mental Health aimed at developing and evaluating psychosocial treatments for anxiety disorders in children. She has published four books on the topic of children and anxiety disorders and more than 150 scientific articles and book chapters. She is the former editor of the *Journal of Clinical Child and Adolescent Psychology,* current associate editor of the *Journal of Consulting and Clinical Psychology,* and president of the American Psychological Association Division 53, Society of Clinical Child and Adolescent Psychology. She also serves on the child intervention NIMH review panel.

Rachel E. Simmons is currently a graduate student in the Clinical Psychology Doctoral program at the University of Nevada, Las Vegas (UNLV), where she earned a bachelor of arts degree in psychology. Her current research interests include investigating multicultural issues inherent in resistance to therapy and designing culturally competent interventions. While still an undergraduate, she was employed by a research facility, where she worked on numerous pharmaceutical studies of ADHD as a research assistant, behavioral rater, and study coordinator. Key among these studies were a Phase 2, randomized crossover study of adults with ADHD and several analog classroom design studies for children with the disorder.

Michael Slavkin, PhD, was the founder and first President of the Vanderburgh County Juvenile Firesetter Task Force in Vanderburgh County, Indiana. He has worked with over 1,000 firesetters and their families during the past 15 years. He received his PhD in educational psychology, with an emphasis in development and learning, cognition, and instruction, from Indiana University–Bloomington. His is the father of two beautiful children and husband to a patient high school special education teacher!

Jose M. Soler-Baillo is a graduate student in clinical psychology at Temple University. He earned his BS from the University of Florida and worked for 2 years at the Center for the Study of Emotion and Attention, where he developed interests in psychophysiological processes and anxiety. He earned a Minority Fellowship Award from the APA and has coauthored papers on risk assessment and psychophysiological reactivity among survivors of sexual assault. He is also interested in the impact of personal choice, responsibility, and decision making in psychotherapy.

Tracy Tabaczynski is a doctoral student at Bowling Green State University in cognitive psychology, with an emphasis on psycholinguistics. She received a degree in semiotics from Brown University. Her research interests include children's language development and cognitive processes in psychopathology. She has published and presented papers in the areas of information processing and the derivation of meaning from written works and the media. She has also worked in clinical contexts as an interviewer and psychological assessor of preschool children in the Head Start Program.

Laura J. Tagliareni is a doctoral student in the Counseling Psychology PhD program in the Professional Psychology and Family Therapy Department at Seton Hall University. She received her undergraduate degree from Pennsylvania State University and her master's degree from Seton Hall. Her focus in pediatric neuropsychology has led to clinical experiences, including neuropsychological assessment of oncology and hematology patients, sexually and physically abused children, and autistic children. She has also had international clinical experience with severely disabled children and adolescents. Her research interests include executive functioning in cancer survivors, emotional and cognitive functioning in learning-disabled students, neurocognitive deficits in sickle cell anemia patients, and current trends in feminism.

Manuela Villa, MS, is a doctoral candidate at Nova Southeastern University's (NSU) Center for Psychological Studies. Her interests are in child and adolescent behavior problems and the influence of culture on perceptions of psychopathology.

Christina L. Wilder received her bachelor's degree in psychology from Virginia Commonwealth University in 2000. She moved to Portland, Oregon, to attend graduate school in 2002. She received a master's degree in Clinical Psychology in 2004, and she is in the process of completing a doctorate degree from Pacific University. Her primary research interest is factors, such as abuse, which may contribute to the development and the perpetuation of severe behavior problems among children and adolescents.

Deborah Wise, PhD, received her doctorate in clinical psychology from the University of Missouri–St. Louis. She completed her predoctoral internship at the Boston Consortium, where she worked at the National Center for Posttraumatic Stress Disorder with male and female veterans, and at the Boston Medical Center, where she worked with children and adolescents with histories of traumatic events. She previously worked at the Children's Advocacy Service of Greater St. Louis, where she engaged in research and clinical work with sexually abused children and adolescents. She is currently an Assistant Professor at the Pacific University School of Professional Psychology and works in private practice. Her clinical interests include cognitive behavioral therapies for children, adolescents, and adults who have experienced traumatic events. Her recent research has been on posttraumatic stress disorder among children who have been abused and vicarious traumatization among therapists and caseworkers who work with sexually abused children.

Doug Woods received his PhD in Clinical Psychology from Western Michigan University in 1999. He is an expert in the assessment and treatment of tic disorders and trichotillomania and is currently an Associate Professor and Director of Clinical Training at the University of Wisconsin–Milwaukee. He has authored or coauthored over 90 papers and chapters and has edited two books describing behavioral interventions for tic disorders, trichotillomania, and other repetitive behavior problems. He has presented his work nationally and internationally with over 100 conference presentations and numerous invited talks. He is a member of the Tourette Syndrome Association Medical Advisory Board and serves on the Scientific Advisory Board of the Trichotillomania Learning Center.

Cindy M. Yee-Bradbury, PhD, received her doctorate in clinical psychology from the University of Illinois at Urbana–Champaign. She is an Associate Professor in the Department of Psychology and in the Department of Psychiatry and Biobehavioral Sciences at the University of California, Los Angeles. Her research interests include schizophrenia, ranging from the prodromal and first episode to chronic phases of the illness; neurocognitive and emotional abnormalities; stress; attention; and clinical neuroscience.